New Science of Learning

Myint Swe Khine · Issa M. Saleh
Editors

New Science of Learning

Cognition, Computers and Collaboration in Education

Springer

Editors
Myint Swe Khine
Emirates College for
Advanced Education
United Arab Emirates
mskhine@ecae.ac.ae

Issa M. Saleh
Emirates College for
Advanced Education
United Arab Emirates
isaleh@ecae.ac.ae

ISBN 978-1-4419-5715-3 e-ISBN 978-1-4419-5716-0
DOI 10.1007/978-1-4419-5716-0
Springer New York Dordrecht Heidelberg London

Library of Congress Control Number: 2010921497

Printed on acid-free paper

Springer is part of Springer Science+Business Media (www.springer.com)

Foreword

In *The Naked Sun*, by Isaac Asimov (1957), detective Elijah Bailey, assisted by his robot assistant Daneel Olivaw, is confronted by what appears to be an impossible crime. A man has been murdered for the first time in the history of the planet Solaria. The murder seems to be an impossible one, however. People on Solaria have virtually no contact with each other at all. Rather, they live on vast estates, surrounded only by robots. They have contact with each other through computers and even generation of holographic images, but that is all. Sex is carefully controlled and looked at as a disgusting necessity to maintain the small population of the planet. So who could have been the murderer, when there is no record of any human entry? The only possibilities are the robots, who are programmed absolutely not to kill, and the man's wife, who had no known contact with him?

In those days of my early teenage, I was an avid science fiction reader. When I first read Asimov's book, I found the utterly dystopic futuristic society of Solaria fascinating. What an imagination Asimov had to create such a world! In contrast, when I read the science fiction series of Tom Swift—not Tom Swift, Jr., but rather the original Tom Swift, with his "aerial warship" and his "giant telescope" and his "motor-boat," I found the books boring, because all of those things were common in the world in which I lived. These books, produced between 1910 and 1941, were worse than out of date because what had seemed like fantastic inventions and life experiences had all become mundane.

What I did not realize in the early 1960s, any more than did the youth of a generation before, was that the science fiction of my generation would become the reality of the next. Solaria does not exist, or at least, has not yet been discovered; but the world it depicts is becoming closer and closer to reality.

The editors of *The New Science of Learning: Cognition, Computers, and Collaboration in Education* have recruited much of the top talent in the field of learning to write about the latest developments in the science of learning. But to me, the most interesting feature of this title is not the first part, but rather, the part after the colon. Just what are the relationships between cognition, computers, and collaboration?

In today's world, there are different models for this relationship.

One model is the Solarian model, described above, of people in isolation with little but virtual contact. I have already described that model, so will say no more.

A second model is of children working together in a computer laboratory reading lessons presented in a fascinating way via computer. This model would appear to be very different from the Solarian model, but is it? When I have walked into computer labs, often there are many individuals situated in the room, but they are oblivious to each other. They might just as well be in separate estates surrounded by robots. Their cognition interacts with the computer in the presence of others, but not with their active collaboration.

A third model is that of distance learning. Like many others, I have myself been involved in such learning. One even can do group projects with others, completing the projects without seeing any of the others in the group or having the foggiest idea of what they look like. In extreme cases, one could be involved in an elaborate Turing test, interacting with a computer while one thought one is interacting with others, without even realizing that the others are simulacra. Here, cognition interacts actively with others through the computer, but in the absence of the face-to-face contact that still is important in much of life. Many of the cues we use to read others' intentions are nonverbal, and those cues do not come across through the computer. This third model may seem to be similar to the Solarian model, but it differs in one key respect, at least, so far. It is typically seen as a second choice. That is, distance learning is used when face-to-face learning is not feasible. But the distinction is getting blurred. I was recently on a large state-university campus where distance learning was being used so that students could take courses via computer rather than through personal interaction—from their dormitory rooms!

A fourth model is group-interactive projects that use the computer but take place in classrooms or laboratories or libraries with humans in face-to-face interactions. More and more libraries across the world are creating what are sometimes called "learning commons," which are spaces for precisely such interaction to occur. For many purposes, this is perhaps the best of the three models, because it uses computers to enhance interactions among the cognitions (and emotions) of human beings in proximity to each other.

But is the fourth model the one that is coming to dominate education, or the world? Perhaps not. Social-networking sites such as Facebook.com and Myspace.com increasingly are coming to dominate the worlds of young people as bases for interpersonal exchange. These sites seem more to approximate the Solarian model and one could even imagine virtual beings exchanging social information, with the human beings none the wiser after the Turing test has come to be seen as a mere curiosity and it becomes well nigh impossible to distinguish humans from computers. The question then is whether such a Solarian model is something we should worry about, or perhaps welcome. Is my resistance merely due to the fact that I am of a previous generation, one that finds a world dominated by social-network sites a bit uncomfortable, but one that soon will die off (well, hopefully, not too soon)?

The Solarian model, or at least approximations to it, has advantages.

First, there are now possibilities for interactions among people that, in the past, we could only dream of. For example, young and old people alike can network with people from other cities, other states, and even other countries and cultures with the same or even greater ease as has been possible in the past for next-door neighbors. We can learn about people who before were at best inaccessible, and at worst, unavailable to us.

Second, through our interactions with the computer, we can enhance our knowledge base in truly dramatic ways. When I was young, we bought the *Encyclopedia Britannica.* Part of what sold my family on the encyclopedia was the annual yearbooks, which updated the encyclopedia, and also a feature whereby we could get several free research reports from the company on topics of our choosing (early shades of the current services which have expanded such service into the writing of term papers!). Today, we do not need yearbooks and probably not the research-report service either. Information on the Internet is constantly being updated so that I, for example, can consult the Internet several times a day for the latest news and the latest information on my friends and acquaintances. If astronomers decide that Pluto is no longer a planet, this decision need not await the textbooks of several years hence to be incorporated into astronomy learning materials. Online learning materials can incorporate the change instantly.

Third, as the chapters in this volume make clear, the computer enables us to provide exciting interactive vehicles for learning that were never possible before. In the early days of computer, computer learning often consisted of little more than textbook-like material being presented in virtual format with little more than a book on a screen. Today's good software, however, is far more interactive and motivating and enables students to learn interactively and dynamically in a way that is much more absorbing than interactions with a static vehicle such as a book.

Fourth, it is possible to interact simultaneously with many other minds on the computer, as was true on Solaria, but with minds far away from one's physical location. One can have a meeting of minds of people who are, say, simultaneously in Bangor, Bangkok, Bangalore, Bristol, and Brazzaville. We can learn about how other people think and react in ways that were not possible before.

Fifth, this Internet communication is low cost or, in many cases, free. It used to be that if you wanted to have a conversation between Bangor and Bangalore, you would have to travel on a very expensive boat trip or, later, plane trip; or you could talk by phone, but that was tremendously expensive as well, and the connection probably not very good. Today you can have the conversation for free, and you even can read virtual editions of newspapers, magazines, and other media for free. This development, of course, has created havoc with the traditional business model of the media, and it is not clear yet what viable business model will replace the old one. Even books can be had on the Internet either for free or at very low cost, as through electronic book readers.

Sixth, the range of content available through computer and on the Internet is staggering compared with what was available in the past. One might have gone to a small-town library in the past and found only a relatively narrow range of content. Today, the content on the Internet exceeds that of the world's largest libraries of bound books and journals. This means it is possible to access material that in the past would have been available, at best, only to those with a library card to one of the world's greatest libraries. You no longer have to live in New York or London to have access to the stunning range of material available.

Seventh, it is now possible to multitask in a way that was never possible before. At the same time, one can have multiple windows onto the world open on a single computer. One can be writing an e-mail, reading about polar bears, reading the latest news about a friend on a social-networking site, and learning about Alpha Centauri, all through multiple windows simultaneously open on a single computer.

Finally, language, although still a barrier, is no longer the barrier it once was. The Internet has made it possible and economically feasible for much information to be available in a variety of languages. It might not have been feasible for a media company to publish separate print journals in each of a number of languages. It is more feasible when they only have to deal with content available on the Web.

With all these advantages for interactive cognitive systems through collaborations made possible by computers, why would anyone hesitate, or even invoke the dystopian world of Solaria in speaking of the new modes of communication available? What are the disadvantages?

First, interaction is becoming more, well, Solarian. People more and more are communicating via computer rather than individually. These communications have endearing features of their own, but what they lack is the face-to-face contact and the intricacies of voice cues, visual cues, bodily cues, and other cues that have in the past always been an important part of communication. The information one receives in impoverished as a result of the absence of such cues.

Second, people's communication styles are different on the Internet. Perhaps this is nowhere more evident than on Twitter, where messages are limited to 140 characters. When the site was introduced, who would have expected it to have the success it has had, at least at the time I am writing this foreword? Are we becoming a world that is so simplified that 140 characters can say what we wish to say? Or was all the rest beyond those 140 characters always excess verbiage anyway? People also often are more aggressive in their Internet communications because they do not have to face the person with whom they are communicating, or hear the pain in their voice upon receiving an aggressive message.

Third, research is beginning to suggest that multitasking is not all it is cracked up to be. A recent study shows that texting while driving increases the risk of a crash by a huge margin. Drivers were 23 times more likely to have a crash if texting while driving (Richtel, 2009). And almost all of us have had the experience of talking to someone on the phone who seems to be not quite there, because that someone is doing his or her e-mail or doing something else while talking to us. Communication is not enriched, but impoverished by the multitasking.

Fourth, at least so far, students are proving themselves to be less than stellar at distinguishing good from bad information the Internet. Some of them seem to believe that, if something is on the Internet, it must be true. In the past, quality control was exercised, at least to some extent, through libraries. One had to go through a quality-control process to get something published, and then through another quality-control process to get that something into a library (or bookstore).

Information can get onto the Internet, however, with no quality-control process whatsoever. People are not always sufficiently critical of the information the read, believing what they are told by whomever they are told it.

Fifth, some psychologists, including myself, are concerned that our virtual world is creating societies of individuals with induced attention-deficit disorder. People used to be able to sit down and concentrate on a single task for an extended period of time—or at least some people with some tasks. But the roaming possible through the computer and the Internet may induce a mindset whereby people have trouble concentrating on any one thing for any period of time. In my later middle age, I find myself having more trouble concentrating on a single task for a long period of time. Maybe it is age, but I suspect it is a habit I have picked up from Internet usage.

Sixth, the huge range of content available to us is not necessarily all for the good. Schwartz (2005) has suggested that when it comes to choice, more can be less. His book summarizes a number of studies suggesting that when people are confronted with too many choices, they can go into a state of information overload, and actually make worse choices than when they have less information.

Seventh, people may actually come to view virtual communication as equal to, or better than, face-to-face communication, as was the case on Solaria. One is spared so many inconveniences online—having to go to and from seeing someone, having to deal directly with their emotions, having even to look presentable. We risk becoming more and more like the Solarians, whose world was restricted by choice and then by design.

So is the new world we are creating better or worse? This brief analysis suggests it is some of both. In some ways it is better, and in other ways, worse. The challenge of today's educators is how to create a world, through education, that capitalizes on the strengths of, and compensates for the weaknesses of, the interfaces between cognition, computers, and collaboration in the contemporary world. How can one accomplish such a difficult task? One has no better way of finding out than to keep turning the pages of this book and moving on to read it!

Robert J. Sternberg

Tufts University, Medford, MA, USA

References

Asimov, I. (1957). *The naked sun*. New York: Doubleday.

Richtel, M. (2009, July 27). In study, texting while driving lifts crash risk by large margin. Retrieved August 8, 2009, from http://www.nytimes.com/2009/07/28/technology/28texting.html?_r=1&scp=3&sq=texting%20while%20driving&st=cse.

Schwartz, B. (2005). *The paradox of choice: Why more is less*. New York: Harper Perennial.

Contents

Contributors

Roger Azevedo Cognition and Technology Research Lab, Department of Psychology, Institute for Intelligent Systems, University of Memphis, Memphis, TN, USA

Megan Bang TERC and American Indian Center of Chicago, Cambridge, MA, USA

Laura Beals Developmental Technologies Research Group, Eliot Pearson Department of Child Development, Tufts University, Medford, MA, USA

Aaron S. Benjamin University of Illinois at Urbana-Champaign, Champaign, IL, USA

John B. Black Teachers College, Columbia University, New York, NY 10027, USA

Shel Bockman California State University, San Bernardino, CA, USA

Candice Burkett Cognition and Technology Research Lab, Department of Psychology, Institute for Intelligent Systems, University of Memphis, Memphis, TN, USA

Shannon Chapman Menominee Tribal School, Neopit, WI, USA

Clement Chau Developmental Technologies Research Group, Eliot Pearson Department of Child Development, Tufts University, Medford, MA, USA

Amber Chauncey Cognition and Technology Research Lab, Department of Psychology, Institute for Intelligent Systems, University of Memphis, Memphis, TN, USA

Roby Coles Department of Psychology, The University of Memphis, Memphis, TN 38152, USA

Scotty D. Craig Department of Psychology, The University of Memphis, Memphis, TN 38152, USA

Theo Dawson Developmental Testing Service, LCC, Northampton, MA, USA

Kyle B. Dempsey University of Memphis, Memphis, TN, USA

Pierre Dillenbourg Swiss Federal Institute of Technology Lausanne (EPFL), Lausanne, Switzerland

Paul Eggen University of North Florida, Jacksonville, FL, USA

Jason R. Finley University of Illinois at Urbana-Champaign, Champaign, IL, USA

Kurt W. Fischer Harvard University Graduate School of Education, Cambridge, MA, USA

Howard Gardner The Developing Minds and Digital Media Project, Harvard University, Project Zero, Cambridge, MA 02138, USA

Barry Gholson Department of Psychology, The University of Memphis, Memphis, TN 38152, USA

Chris Greenhalgh Learning Sciences Research Institute, University of Nottingham, Nottingham, England

Noelle Griffin UCLA, Los Angeles, CA, USA

Hope J. Hartman School of Education, The City College of New York, New York, USA; Educational Psychology Program, City University of New York Graduate Center, New York, USA

Friedrich W. Hesse Knowledge Media Research Center, Konrad-Adenauer-Strasse 40, D-72072 Tuebingen, Germany

Cindy E. Hmelo-Silver Rutgers, the State University of New Jersey, New Brunswick, NJ, USA

Theresa Horstman University of Washington, Seattle, WA, USA

Kedmon Hungwe Michigan Technological University, Houghton, MI, USA

G. Tanner Jackson University of Memphis, Memphis, TN, USA

Patrick Jermann Swiss Federal Institute of Technology Lausanne (EPFL), Lausanne, Switzerland

Amy Johnson Cognition and Technology Research Lab, Department of Psychology, Institute for Intelligent Systems, University of Memphis, Memphis, TN, USA

Heather Kanuka University of Alberta, Edmonton, Alberta, Canada

Stephen Kerr University of Washington, Seattle, WA, USA

Nauman Khan Developmental Technologies Research Group, Eliot Pearson Department of Child Development, Tufts University, Medford, MA, USA

Myint Swe Khine Emirates College for Advanced Education, Abu Dhabi, UAE

Karsten Krauskopf Knowledge Media Research Center, Konrad-Adenauer-Strasse 40, D-72072 Tuebingen, Germany

Thérèse Laferrière Laval University, Quebec, Canada

Ming Lai Division of Information and Technology studies, Faculty of Education, The University of Hong Kong, Pokfulam Road, Pokfulam, Hong Kong

Mary Lamon Lamon Consulting, Toronto, Canada

Nancy Law Division of Information and Technology studies, Faculty of Education, The University of Hong Kong, Pokfulam Road, Pokfulam, Hong Kong

Heather Leary Department of Instructional Technology and Learning Sciences, Utah State University, Logan, UT, 84322-2830, USA

Hyo Jin Lim University of Southern California, Los Angeles, CA, USA

Lei Liu University of Pennsylvania, Philadelphia, PA, USA

Jingyan Lu Division of Information and Technology studies, Faculty of Education, The University of Hong Kong, Pokfulam Road, Pokfulam, Hong Kong

Nasser Mansour Graduate School of Education, The University of Exeter, Exeter, UK

Lina Markauskaite Faculty of Education and Social Work, The University of Sydney, Sydney, Australia

Robin Mason Open University, Milton Keynes, UK

Helle Mathiasen Department of Information and Media Studies, Aarhus University, Aarhus, Denmark

Danielle S. McNamara University of Memphis, Memphis, TN, USA

Douglas Medin Northwestern University, Evanston, IL, USA

Jitti Niramitranon Learning Sciences Research Institute, University of Nottingham, Nottingham, England

Harold F. O'Neil University of Southern California, Los Angeles, CA, USA

Roy Pea Stanford Center for Innovations in Learning, 450 Serra Mall, Wallenberg Hall, Stanford CA 94305 USA

Mimi Recker Department of Instructional Technology and Learning Sciences, Utah State University, Logan, UT, 84322-2830, USA

Peter Reimann Faculty of Education and Social Work, The University of Sydney, Sydney, Australia

Frank Rennie Lews Castle College, University of the Highlands and Islands Millennium Institute, Stornoway, Isle of Lewis, Scotland

M. Brooke Robertshaw Department of Instructional Technology and Learning Sciences, Utah State University, Logan, UT, 84322-2830, USA

Robert Rueda University of Southern California, Los Angeles, CA, USA

Issa M. Saleh Emirates College for Advanced Education, Abu Dhabi, UAE

Keiko Satoh Developmental Technologies Research Group, Eliot Pearson Department of Child Development, Tufts University, Medford, MA, USA

Suzanne Schellenberg University of North Florida, Jacksonville, FL, USA

Lynne Schrum College of Education and Human Development, George Mason University, Fairfax, VA, USA

Linda Sellers Department of Instructional Technology and Learning Sciences, Utah State University, Logan, UT, 84322-2830, USA

Mike Sharples Learning Sciences Research Institute, University of Nottingham, Nottingham, England

Barbara Sirotnik California State University, San Bernardino, CA, USA

Gerry Stahl College of Information Science & Technology, Drexel University, Philadelphia, PA 19104, USA

Zachary Stein Developmental Testing Service, LCC, Northampton, MA, USA; Harvard University Graduate School of Education, Cambridge, MA, USA

Celka Straughn Spencer Museum of Art, University of Kansas, 1301 Mississippi St, Lawrence, KS 66045

Keith S. Taber Faculty of Education, University of Cambridge, Cambridge, UK

Jonathan G. Tullis University of Illinois at Urbana-Champaign, Champaign, IL, USA

Marina Umaschi Bers Developmental Technologies Research Group, Eliot Pearson Department of Child Development, Tufts University, Medford, MA, USA

Andrew Walker Department of Instructional Technology and Learning Sciences, Utah State University, Logan, UT, 84322-2830, USA

Karen Washinawatok Menominee Language and Culture Commission, Keshena, WI, USA

Rupert Wegerif Graduate School of Education, The University of Exeter, Exeter, UK

Margaret Weigel The Developing Minds and Digital Media Project, Harvard University, Project Zero, Cambridge, MA 02138, USA

Carmen Zahn Knowledge Media Research Center, Konrad-Adenauer-Strasse 40, D-72072 Tuebingen, Germany

About the Contributors

Roger Azevedo is an associate professor in the Department of Psychology at the University of Memphis (http://azevedolab.autotutor.org/). He is also affiliated with the Institute of Intelligent Systems. His research interests include self-regulated learning, metacognition, temporal analyses of self-regulatory processes during complex learning, and the use of advanced learning technologies to enhance students' understanding of scientific phenomena.

Megan Bang is a senior researcher at TERC and the Director of Education at the American Indian Center (AIC). Dr. Bang received her BA from Williams College and Ph.D. from Northwestern University. Her research interests are focused on understanding culture and cognition and more specifically the design of more effective learning environments. Current research projects include student and teacher learning in science, positive adolescent identity development in urban Indian youth, and early childhood education and development. Dr. Bang manages professional development programs, after-school programs, and early childhood programming at the AIC. She is a former teacher and youth worker.

Laura Beals is a doctoral student at Turfs University, USA working in Professor Marina Ber's Developmental Technologies research group.

Aaron S. Benjamin is Associate Professor of Psychology at the University of Illinois at Urbana-Champaign and Associate Editor of the *Journal of Experimental Psychology: Learning, Memory, and Cognition*. His research uses empirical and computational techniques to understand memory, metamemory, and decision-making in younger and older adults.

Marina Bers is an assistant professor at the Eliot-Pearson Department of Child Development and an adjunct professor in the Computer Science Department at Tufts University. She is also a scientific research associate at Boston Children's Hospital. Her research involves the design and study of innovative learning technologies to promote children's positive development. At Tufts, Professor Bers heads the interdisciplinary Developmental Technologies research group. Dr. Bers is from Argentina, where she did her undergraduate studies in Social Communication at Buenos Aires University. In 1994 she came to the USA where she received a master's degree in Educational Media and Technology from Boston University and a master of science and Ph.D. from the MIT Media Laboratory.

John B. Black is a professor of Telecommunications and Education, Chair Department of Human Development, Director Institute for Learning Technologies at Teachers College at Colombia University. He has a Ph.D. in Cognitive Psychology, Stanford University. Basic research in cognition, especially grounded/embodied approaches to cognition, and its application to improving learning, memory, understanding, problem solving, and motivation. Especially interested in using technologies like multiuser virtual environments, video games, TV/videos, intelligent tutoring systems, and robots to improve learning, memory, understanding, problem solving, and motivation.

Shel Bockman, Ph.D., is a professor of management at California State University, San Bernardino, and IAR codirector. Dr. Bockman's Ph.D. is in sociology from Indiana University. Formerly he taught in the departments of sociology at Purdue University and University of California, Riverside. His areas of expertise include research methods, demographic analysis, and organizational design. Dr. Bockman has been the recipient of a Ford Foundation Urban Crisis Grant and a National Science Foundation grant. He also has published and presented various papers in his areas of expertise.

Candice Burkett is a senior undergraduate honors student majoring in Psychology at the University of Memphis. Upon graduation she is planning to enter a Psychology graduate program with a concentration in Cognitive Psychology. Her current interests include self-regulated learning, metacognitive processes, learning about complex science topics, and error detection processes.

Shannon Chapman is Assistant Principal at the Menominee Tribal School in Neopit, Wisconsin. She earned her bachelor's degree at St. Norbert College and her master's degree at Marian College. Her background includes teaching, tutoring as well as working with at-risk students. She has also worked as a logging contractor with Menominee Tribal Enterprises.

Clement Chau is a doctoral student at Turfs University, USA working in Professor Marina Ber's Developmental Technologies research group.

Amber Chauncey is currently a doctoral student in Experimental Psychology, cognitive track, at the University of Memphis and working as a graduate assistant in the Cognition and Technology Lab under the mentorship of Dr. Roger Azevedo. Her thesis focuses on the role of emotion, metacognitive judgments, and complex multimedia learning.

Robert M. Coles was a graduate student at the University of Memphis, Department of Psychology. He received his master's degree in Psychology in 2008. Some parts of this book chapter grew out of milestones for the fulfillment of his degree requirements.

Scotty D. Craig is a research scientist at the University of Memphis with the IIS/Department of Psychology. His past work includes areas such as emotion and learning, discourse processing, intelligent tutoring systems, multimedia learning, and vicarious learning environments in both laboratory and applied classroom settings. His current contributions to the field consist of 16 journal articles, two book chapters, 26 published conference proceedings, 27 unpublished conference presentations, and two edited newsletters. Dr. Craig has served as ad hoc reviewer for many academic journals and conferences. He is currently on the editorial board for the *International Journal of Learning Technology*.

Theo Linda Dawson is the owner of the Developmental Testing Service, LLC, and the founder of DiscoTest, an organization that delivers free stand-alone online cognitive developmental assessments. In 1998, she received her Ph.D. from UC Berkeley. In 1999, she received dissertation awards from both UC Berkeley and the APA. From 1998 to 2002, she received funding from the Spencer Foundation to develop a computerized approach to developmental scoring. During this time, she also developed the Lectical Assessment System and a methodology called Developmental Maieutics. She has taught at UC Berkeley, Harvard, and Hampshire College and has authored numerous refereed articles.

Kyle Dempsey is a Ph.D. student at the Institute for Intelligent Systems and the University of Memphis. He is working toward a degree in Experimental Psychology with a concentration in Cognitive Science. His research interests are in the areas of instructional manipulations of reading purpose, human–computer interactions, and educational game design. He has served as a research assistant on multiple projects including iSTART, Coh-Metrix, and W-Pal. He is currently working on projects that will combine positive aspects of intelligent tutoring systems with social aspects of learning.

Pierre Dillenbourg is Professor of Pedagogy and Learning Technologies in the School of Computer and Communication Sciences at the Swiss Federal Institute of Technology in Lausanne (EPFL). A former teacher in elementary school, Pierre Dillenbourg graduated in educational science (University of Mons, Belgium). He started his research on learning technologies in 1984. He obtained a Ph.D. in computer science from the University of Lancaster (UK), in the domain of artificial intelligence applications for educational software. He has been working for 12 years University of Geneva. He joined EPFL in 2002 as associate professor and became full professor in 2008. His curriculum vitae includes more than 80 publications and 120 conferences worldwide. His two main papers received more than 600 citations each. His research concerns computer-supported collaborative learning (CSCL): More precisely his team conducts research on scripts that enhance collaborative learning, on interactive furniture that scaffold productive dialogue, on the use of dual eye-tracking methods and on the role of technologies in vocational training. Most of his research projects combine the design of new collaborative environments with empirical studies. Both the technology and the experiments are elaborated to address basic research questions on the mechanisms that turn collaborative problem solving into learning experiences. Pierre Dillenbourg has been president of the International Society for the Learning Sciences. He is the leader of DUAL-T, the leading house on technologies for vocational training. He is also the director of CRAFT, the pedagogical unit at EPFL.

Paul Eggan is a professor of education at the University of North Florida. He is the author of several prominent textbooks in the areas of educational psychology and teacher development. Dr. Eggen is an international consultant who has worked with teachers in more than 30 countries in Europe, Asia, Africa, and South America. The recipient of several awards for his teaching and writing, he lives in Jacksonville, Florida with his wife, Judy, who has taught in public schools for 35 years.

Jason R. Finley is a graduate student in the Department of Psychology at the University of Illinois at Urbana-Champaign. His research interests concern compensating for systematic limitations of human cognition by improving metacognition or by offloading cognition onto the environment (particularly, using emerging technology).

Kurt Fischer is Director of the Mind, Brain, and Education Program and Charles Bigelow Professor at the Harvard Graduate School of Education. In his research, he analyzes cognition, emotion, and learning and their relation to biological development and educational assessment. He has discovered a scale that assesses learning and development in any domain. Leading an international movement to connect biology and cognitive science to education, he is founding editor of the journal *Mind, Brain, and Education* (Blackwell), which received the award for Best New Journal by the Association of American Publishers. His most recent books include *The Educated Brain* (Cambridge University Press, 2008).

Howard Gardner is Hobbs Professor of Cognition and Education at the Harvard Graduate School of Education. He is a leading thinker about education and human development; he has studied and written extensively about intelligence, creativity, leadership, and professional ethics. Gardner's most recent books include *Good Work: When Excellence and Ethics Meet*, *Five Minds for the Future*, and *The Development and Education of the Mind*, a collection of his writings in education. He has been honored with the MacArthur "Genius" award, the University of Louisville Grawemeyer Award, and 25 honorary doctorates. He lives in Cambridge, Massachusetts.

Barry Gholson is presently a full professor in the Department of Psychology and a member of the interdisciplinary Institute for Intelligent Systems. Dr. Gholson's expertise is in cognitive psychology, cognitive development, cognitive science, and the learning sciences. He has 30 years of experience as a specialist in cognitive development research. His current specific interests are in question asking, human/computer interaction, vicarious learning, and multimedia learning. He was the PI of the IDRIVE grant (R305H050169) that implemented Vicarious learning environments into the classroom.

Chris Greenhalgh is a professor of Computer Science at the University of Nottingham, and a principal investigator in the Mixed Reality Laboratory. His interests center on distributed system support for multiuser interactive applications. He has been the primary architect of the EQUATOR Integrated Platform (EQUIP), an adaptive software architecture for ubiquitous computing and mobile applications, the Digital Replay System (DRS), a desktop e-social science tool for analyzing video, transcripts, and system log files, and three generations of the MASSIVE Collaborative Virtual Environment system. Together these have underpinned numerous public performances, experiences, and trials across many research projects.

Noelle Griffin is Assistant Director for research and evaluation at the National Center for Research on Evaluation, Standards, and Student Testing (CRESST) at UCLA. Through her work at CRESST she has led program evaluations in a variety of educational settings, including evaluations of professional development, science instruction, math instruction, and social services programs. Dr. Griffin has particularly focused on the evaluation of arts-based education and its integration into the K-12 curriculum and, in addition to her work with the Webplay program, she also led the national evaluation of the Leonard Bernstein Center Artful Learning Model. Prior to returning to CRESST in 2006, she served as director of assessment for Loyola Marymount University and has a continued interest in assessment and evaluation issues at the higher education level.

Hope J. Hartman is Professor of Psychological Foundations in the School of Education at The City College of the City University of New York (CCNY) and Professor of Educational Psychology at the City University of New York Graduate and University Center. She was Director of the City College of New York Center for Excellence in Teaching and Learning from 2006 to 2008. Her Ph.D. is in cognitive psychology, from Rutgers University. At CCNY she has served as Chair of the Department of Secondary Education, Director of the City College Tutoring and Cooperative Learning Program, and Program Head of Social and Psychological Foundations. Her areas of specialization are instructional technology, instructional techniques that emphasize active learning, and improving thinking and learning skills In addition to peer-reviewed articles, she has authored the following books: *Tips for the Mathematics Teacher: Research-Based Strategies to Help Students Learn*, 1998 with Alfred Posamentier and Constanze Kaiser published by Corwin Press (Hartman is second author); *Tips for the Science Teacher: Research-Based Strategies to Help Students Learn* 2002 (Hartman is the first author, it is coauthored with Neal Glasgow) published by Corwin Press; and *Metacognition in Learning and Instruction: Theory, Research and Practice.* 2001, Vol. 19 *Neuropsychology and Cognition*, published by Springer. (Hartman is the editor and author of three chapters). Her book, *A Guide to Reflective Practice for New and Experienced Teachers* was published by McGraw-Hill in February, 2009.

Friedrich W. Hesse is Executive Director of the Knowledge Media Research Center (KMRC) at Tuebingen, Germany. He studied psychology at the University of Marburg and the University of Duesseldorf, received his Ph.D. in 1979 from the University of Aachen, and qualified as professor for psychology (1989) at the University of Goettingen. Since 1990 up to the present he has been professor for psychology in Tuebingen—from 1993 until 2000 as Head of the Department of Applied Cognitive Science at the German Institute of Research for Distance Education (DIFF). Since 2000 he has been holding his current chair. His main research interests include learning with new media, net-based knowledge communication, Computer-supported collaborative learning (CSCL), Web 2.0, and Social Software.

Cindy E. Hmelo-Silver is an associate professor of Educational Psychology at Rutgers, the State University of New Jersey in the USA. She received her Ph.D. from Vanderbilt University in 1994. She served postdoctoral fellowships at the Georgia Institute of Technology and University of Pittsburgh's Learning Research and Development Center. Her research interests focus on how people learn about complex phenomena and how technology can help support that learning. As part of this work, she studies problem-based learning, collaborative knowledge construction, and computer-supported collaborative learning. Professor Hmelo-Silver has published numerous journal articles, book chapters, and edited two books in these areas, and is coeditor in chief of *Journal of the Learning Sciences*.

Theresa Horstman is a doctoral student in Learning Sciences at the University of Washington, USA. She received her BA with a focus in philosophy from The Evergreen State College and her M.Ed. from the University of Washington. Her interests include comparative analysis of video game and e-learning design methodologies and the correlation between the metaphoric process and creative process in designing instruction for virtual environments.

Kedmon Hungwe is an associate professor of Teacher Education at Michigan Technological University. His current research interests are adult and adolescent development, teacher professional development, and the development of spatial intelligence in middle grade and high school students. He has published in the *Journal of Adult Development* (forthcoming), *Engineering Design Graphics Journal*, *Journal of Curriculum Studies*, *International Journal of Learning, and Media, Culture and Society*, among other places.

G. Tanner Jackson is a postdoctoral research fellow at the Institute for Intelligent Systems at the University of Memphis. He received his PhD in 2007 at the University of Memphis in Experimental Psychology with a concentration of training in the field of cognitive science. His primary research interests and pursuits are in the areas of human–computer interaction, intelligent feedback mechanisms, tutorial dialogue, and learning environments. He has served as a key researcher in a variety of projects to develop and test intelligent tutoring systems such as AutoTutor, iSTART, W-Pal, and HURAA. He is currently working on projects geared toward developing educational games to enhance motivational aspects of intelligent tutoring systems. He has also conducted research and development in the area of interface design for agencies such as Sandia National Laboratories.

Patrick Jermann obtained a degree in psychology from the University of Geneva followed by a master's degree in educational technologies in 1996. While at TECFA (University of Geneva), Patrick Jermann and Pierre Dillenbourg developed a virtual campus in which they invented innovative CSCL scripts. Following that time at TECFA, he worked for 3 years as a Research Associate at the University of Pittsburgh in the learning Research and Development Center (LDRC). There he designed and developed environments dedicated to online lesson planning for the Institute for Learning. In 2003, Patrick Jermann joined the CRAFT team where he is responsible for the coordination of eLearning projects at EPFL (Swiss Institute of Technology, Lausanne). He is leading projects on tangible environments for vocational training and on the use of dual eye-tracking methods for understanding collaborative processes. He is responsible for the e-learning project at EPFL.

Amy Johnson is a doctoral student in cognitive psychology in the Department of Psychology at the University of Memphis. She holds a bachelor's degree and a master's degree in Psychology. She is also affiliated with the Institute of Intelligent Systems. Her research interests include the role of multiple representations in multimedia and hypermedia learning, analyses of the cognitive and metacognitive self-regulated processes, and the use of learning technologies to foster learning.

Heather Kanuka is Academic Director and Associate Professor at the University of Alberta, Canada. Prior to her recent appointment to the University of Alberta, Dr. Kanuka was a Canada Research Chair in e-Learning. Dr. Kanuka's research on e-learning has focused the need for Canadian administrators and policy makers to monitor closely transformations resulting from advances in Internet technologies in order to better understand the technological drivers of change and possible ensuing consequences on the learning process, with a particular focus on issues relating to the reshaping of institutional barriers, learner support, and transformations of teaching practices within the Canadian context. Higher education in Canada is moving into a third decade of profound changes in how courses and programs are designed and delivered resulting from the increased integration of Internet communication technologies into the learning process. Many new possibilities have become apparent, but also many new challenges. Dr. Kanuka's research has revealed that existing and emerging Internet technologies are having intense, immediate, and disruptive transformations on Canadian higher education institutions—and nowhere is the impact felt more than on the academic staff who teach with Internet communication technologies.

Stephen T. Kerr is Professor of Education in the College of Education at the University of Washington. His research on educational technology has included studies of e-learning design and development, teachers' acceptance and use of technology in classroom settings, studies of roles and role changes in education as influenced by technology, and way finding in complex information systems. He has also examined how information technology has encouraged educational reform in the schools of Russia and the former Soviet Union. He is currently studying how social networking tools can extend teachers skills and contribute to a new language of professional practice. He received a Ph.D. in Education from the University of Washington, an MA in Sociology from Columbia University, and a BA in Slavic Languages from Princeton University.

Nauman Khan is a doctoral student at Turfs University, USA working in Professor Marina Ber's Developmental Technologies research group.

Myint Swe Khine is Associate Professor at the Emirates College for Advanced Education in the United Arab Emirates. He received his master's degrees from the University of Southern California, Los Angeles, USA and University of Surrey, Guildford, UK; and Doctor of Education from Curtin University of Technology, Australia. He worked in Nanyang Technology University, Singapore and Murdoch University, Australia before taking up the position in the United Arab Emirates. He has published widely and he is the Series Editor of *Contemporary Approaches to Research in Learning Innovations*, published by the Sense Publishers, Rotterdam, the Netherlands.

Karsten Krauskopf is a researcher and Ph.D. student at the Knowledge Media Research Center (KMRC) at Tuebingen, Germany. He studied psychology and Japanese Studies at the Humboldt University of Berlin and graduated in 2008 in pedagogical psychology (master's thesis: "Surface and Deeper Level Characteristics of Instruction" in cooperation with the Max Planck Institute for Human Development, Berlin). His dissertation project is concerned with the mental models of digital video technologies of teachers as a cognitive factor for the integration of new developments in digital media in teaching–learning processes in the classroom.

Thérèse Laferrière is a full professor of pedagogy at Laval University, Quebec City, Canada. Her research activities focus on networked learning environments (learning communities, communities or practice, and knowledge-building communities) and especially teacher–student(s) interactions and peer interactions as electronically linked classrooms become reality in elementary and secondary schools as well as in faculties of education and postsecondary education in general. In 2007, she published with Paul Resta an article entitled Technology in support of collaborative learning in the *Educational Psychological Review*.

Ming Lai is a Ph.D. candidate in education at the University of Hong Kong. His current research examines the relationship between argumentation and knowledge building in a CSCL context.

Mary Lamon is Director of Lamon Consulting, an education technology support and advisory company. She received a BA degree from the University of Toronto in psychology, an MA degree from the University of Toronto in cognitive psychology, and a Ph.D. degree from the University of Toronto in cognitive psychology. She is also a Senior Research Scientist at the Institute for Knowledge Innovation and Technology at the Ontario Institute for Studies in Education and the University of Toronto.

Nancy Law is a director of the Centre for Information Technology in Education (CITE) and Professor & Head of Division of Information and Technology Studies of the Faculty of Education in the University of Hong Kong. Educated initially in Hong Kong, she graduated with a Ph.D. from the Institute of Education at the University of London in 1990. Since joining the University of Hong Kong in 1986 she has been contributing to education in various capacities within the university, including headship of the Department of Curriculum Studies in 1996–1997. She has also served on a variety of policy advisory committees in education in Hong Kong, including the Steering Committee on Strategic Development of Information Technology in Education of the Education & Manpower Bureau of the HKSAR government.

Heather Leary is a doctoral student at Utah State University and a member of the Department of Instructional Technology and Learning Sciences, Utah State University, USA.

Hyo Jin Lim is a recipient of the USC Dissertation Completion Fellowship, and received a BA in Education and MA in Counseling Psychology at Seoul National University, South Korea. Before coming to Rossier School of Education (RSOE), she was also a student in the master's program of Graduate School of Education and Information Studies at UCLA. She is working with Dr. Robert Rueda on the School Readiness Initiative project for evaluating programs. Her research interests include development of optimal and rational assessment and screening for English language learners.

Lei Liu is a postdoctoral fellow in the Graduate School of Education at the University of Pennsylvania, Philadelphia, Pennsylvania, USA. She received her Ph.D. in 2008 from Rutgers, the State University of New Jersey. She is the project director of an NSF-funded ITEST project at Penn's Graduate School of Education. Her research is focused on investigating the affordances of technology in science learning and learning about complex systems. Her dissertation developed a new framework—the collaborative scientific conceptual change framework, to study trajectories of conceptual change in CSCL learning environments through the lens of collaborative discourse, epistemic practices, and cognitive development. She has also experiences in designing technology-rich learning environment to facilitate middle and high school science learning and teaching and applying complex systems approaches in both constructing curricula for students and teacher professional development programs. She has been actively involved in research communities such as CSCL, ICLS, NARST, EARLI, and AERA.

Jingyan Lu is a research assistant professor in Division of Information and Technology Studies, The University of Hong Kong. She received her Ph.D. from Department of Educational and Counselling Psychology, McGill University, Canada. The focus of her Ph.D. study was designing cognitive tools to support collaborative medical problem solving. She joined the University of Hong Kong in 2007 and since then she worked collaboratively with the research team led by Professor Nancy Law on designing, implementing, and assessing teaching and learning with Web 2.0 technology. She is also collaborating with medical and speech and hearing faculty members to advance the teaching and learning in problem-based learning.

Nasser Mansour is a research fellow at the School of Education and Lifelong Learning at Exeter University. He is an experienced science educator and teacher trainer. His recent Ph.D. was on the interaction between Culture and the teaching of Science and has led to several papers published in prestigious science education journals as well as a best paper award at the European Educational Research Association conference. He now conducts research on Computer-Supported Collaborative Learning tools, Argunaut, and InterLoc, seeing these as a means of providing dialogue across difference and of supporting reflective communities of practice.

Lina Markauskaite is a senior lecturer in eResearch in the Faculty of Education and Social Work at the University of Sydney. Over the last 12 years her research included studies in the areas of information and communication technology literacy; cognitive and social engagement with online learning; advanced educational research methods, and application of ICT in educational research. Her present research focus is epistemic fluency in interdisciplinary knowledge work; e-Research in education and broader implications of e-Research on scientific research practices. Her main teaching areas include educational research methodologies and the learning sciences.

Robin Mason was a professor of research and practice of online teaching and learning at the Open University UK. She was one of the early pioneers in developing the medium of computer conferencing for distance education, and completed her Ph.D. on this—one of the very first on the subject—in 1989. Since then she has published prolifically on the web, in journal articles, and in seven books. She has worked with many course teams across the Open University in the design, tutoring, and evaluation of online courses. She worked extensively on the Open University's Master's Programme in Online and Distance Education, as course developer, tutor, and as Director of the Programme. In 2000, she conceived of the idea of a Virtual Graduation for the first cohort of master's students and developed the concept with the Open University's Knowledge Media Institute. She was the production Chair of the course called Learning in the Connected Economy which was written entirely in "learning object" format. The latest course for which she authored sections is called the E-learning Professional and centers on the use of e-portfolios. Her research interests focused on e-learning: course design, assessment, re-usability, and e-portfolios. She recently coauthored a *Key Concepts* book for the Routledge series which contains an overview of e-learning as well as extensive glossary items.

Helle Mathiasen is a professor and director of Center for Research in IT & Learning in Department of Information and Media Studies, Faculty of Humanities at Aarhus University. Her research and teaching embraces the educational system with specific focus on the use of digital media and net-mediated communication forums. She has edited books concerning the relationship between technology, learning, and teaching and written numerous articles with a focal point in the pedagogical perspectives using IT in the educational system. Helle is currently member of the editor-team of the *Journal of Danish University Pedagogy.*

Danielle S. McNamara is a professor in the psychology department and Director of the Institute for Intelligent Systems. Her academic background includes a Linguistics BA (1982), a Clinical Psychology MS (1989), and a PhD in Cognitive Psychology (1992; UC-Boulder). Her research involves the theoretical study of cognitive processes as well as the application of cognitive principles in educational practice. The overarching theme of her research is to better understand cognitive processes involved in memory, knowledge acquisition, reading, and writing and to apply that understanding to educational practice by creating and testing educational technologies (e.g., Coh-Metrix, the iSTART Reading Strategy tutor, Writing Pal the writing strategy tutor). She has served on the editorial boards of *Discourse Processes, Memory & Cognition,* and *JEP:LMC* and currently serves as Associate Editor for three journals, *topiCS,* the *Cognitive Science Journal,* and the *Journal of Educational Psychology.* She serves on standing review panels for the Institute of Education Sciences (IES) and National Institute of Health (NIH) and has served on numerous review panels for IES, the National Science Foundation (NSF), and the National Institute of Child Health and Human Development (NICHD). She is on the Governing Boards for the Society for Text and Discourse and the Cognitive Science Society.

Douglas Medin is Louis L. Menk Professor of Psychology and a Professor in Education and Social Policy at Northwestern University. Best known for his research on concepts and categorization, his recent interests have extended to cross-cultural studies of biological categorization and reasoning, cultural and cognitive dimensions of moral reasoning and decision making, and culturally and community-based science education. He recently served on the NRC committee on Informal Science Learning, is a recipient of the APA Distinguished Scientific Contribution Award, and is a member of the American Academy of Arts and Sciences and the National Academy of Sciences.

Jitti Niramitranon is a Ph.D. student at the Learning Sciences Research Institute, University of Nottingham. His research interests include technology enhanced learning, and learning design for a one-to-one technology-enabled classroom. He proposed and developed a system to orchestrate teaching and learning in the classroom, comprising a scenarios designer (SceDer), an interchange language (COML), and an interpreter and management tool for delivering the teaching. His project has been tested with the Group Scribbles software, to form a novel interactive learning environment for math and science teaching classroom in the UK. He has been refining the system to improve its performance, based on the findings from a classroom evaluation.

Harold F. O'Neil is a professor of Educational Psychology and Technology at the University of Southern California's Rossier School of Education and a project director at the UCLA National Center for Research on Evaluation, Standards, and Student Testing (CRESST). His research interests include the computer-based assessment of workforce readiness, particularly problem-solving and collaboration skills, the teaching and measurement of self-regulation skills, the role of motivation in testing, and the training effectiveness of games. Dr. O'Neil has conducted cross-cultural research in Japan on the role of test anxiety and performance, and in Taiwan and Korea on the role of self-regulation and achievement. In all of these research areas, he is interested in technology applications. He has published extensively. He is a Fellow of the American Psychological Association, a Fellow of the American Educational Research Association, and a Certified Performance Technologist. He teaches courses in accountability and learning. A prolific writer, Dr. O'Neil has recently coedited four books—*What Works in Distance Learning: Guidelines* (2005), *Web-Based Learning: Theory, Research and Practice* (2006), *Assessment of Problem Solving Using Simulations* (2008), and *Computer Games and Team and Adult Learning* (2008).

Roy Pea is Professor of Education and the Learning Sciences at Stanford University, Co-PI of the LIFE Center, and Co-Director of the Human Sciences and Technologies Advanced Research (H-STAR) Institute. He has published widely on learning and education fostered by advanced technologies including scientific visualization, online communities, digital video collaboratories, and wireless handheld computers (http://www.stanford.edu/~roypea). His current work is developing the DIVER paradigm for everyday networked video interactions for learning and communications, and examining how informal and formal learning can be better understood and connected, as Co-PI of the LIFE Center funded by the NSF. He was coeditor of the 2007 volume *Video Research in the Learning Sciences*, and coauthor of the 2000 National Academy volume *How People Learn*. He is a Fellow of the National Academy of Education, Association for Psychological Science, The Center for Advanced Study in the Behavioral Sciences, and the American Educational Research Association.

Mimi Recker is Professor and Department Head at Utah State University. She has a Ph.D. from University of California, Berkeley, CA. Research interests include design and evaluation of interactive learning environments; educational uses of new media, information, and communication technologies; human–computer interaction; models of multimedia information access; and social context of dynamic information ecologies.

Peter Reimann is Professor for Education in the Faculty of Education and Social Work at the University of Sydney and codirector of the Faculty's Centre for Research on Computer-Supported Learning and Cognition. He has a background in cognitive psychology and educational computing and has been conducting research in multimedia-based and knowledge-based learning environments. Recent projects include work on computer-based support for net-based teams and informal learning supported by mobile technology.

Frank Rennie is Professor of Sustainable Rural Development at the UHI Millennium Institute in the Highlands and Islands of Scotland and is the Head of Research and Post Graduate Development at Lews Castle College, UHI. He is the Course Leader for the M.Sc. in Managing Sustainable Rural Development at the UHI, and tutors mainly postgraduate students. His research interests lie in the general areas of rural and community development, especially in community-based approaches to integrated sustainable development. Recent work has been on new approaches to online education and distributed learning with rural communities and individuals, particularly Open Access and Open Content resources. He has been an advisor to several government committees and is a Fellow of a number of learned societies. Frank has been involved in developing and delivering various combinations of distributed learning solutions (with a particular emphasis on networked solutions for rural areas) with colleges and university partners in Europe, Asia, Amazonia, Africa, and New Zealand. He has published a wide range of resources related to rural issues, including over 25 books, most recently *E-learning: the Key Concepts* and *E-learning and Social Networking Handbook*. For further details see URL: http://www.lews.uhi.ac.uk/frennie

M. Brooke Robertshaw is a doctoral student at Utah State University and a member of the Department of Instructional Technology and Learning Sciences, Utah State University, USA.

Robert Rueda is a professor in the area of Psychology in Education at the Rossier School of Education at the University of Southern California. He completed his doctoral work at the University of California at Los Angeles in Educational Psychology and completed a postdoctoral fellowship at the Laboratory of Comparative Human Cognition at the University of California, San Diego. His research has centered on the sociocultural basis of motivation, learning, and instruction, with a focus reading and literacy in English learners, and students in at-risk conditions, and he teaches courses in learning and motivation. He recently served as a panel member on the National Academy of Science Report on the Overrepresentation of Minority Students in Special Education, and also served as a member of the National Literacy Panel (SRI International and Center for Applied Linguistics) looking at issues in early reading with English language learners. He is a fellow of the American Psychological Association and of the American Educational Research Association, and recently served as the associate editor of the *American Educational Research Journal*. He serves on the editorial boards of several educational journals, and is a member of the International Reading Association and the National Reading Conference.

Issa M. Saleh is an assistant professor at the Emirates College for Advanced Education (ECAE), United Arab Emirates. He received his bachelor's degree, master's degree, and Doctorate in Education from the University of North Florida, Jacksonville, USA. He has taught at A. Phillip Randolph Academy of Technology (APR) for several years and also taught at University of North Florida and Florida Community College in Jacksonville, Florida. Dr. Saleh was the science department head and principal investigator in understanding of science teaching and learning at APR for in-service science teachers for several years. He has participated in systemic initiatives to reform science classrooms in Duval Public Schools. He was the Dean of Students Services and Curriculum Instruction for the Health Science Academy before he joined ECAE.

Keiko Satoh is a doctoral student at Turfs University, USA working in Professor Marina Ber's Developmental Technologies research group.

Lynne Schrum is a professor and director of Teacher Education in the College of Education and Human Development at George Mason University. Previously, she served as Chair of the Department of Teaching and Learning at the University of Utah. Her research and teaching focus on appropriate uses of information technology, online and distance learning, and preparing future teachers for the twenty-first century. She has written four books and numerous articles on these subjects; the most recent is *New Tools, New Schools: Getting Started with Web 2.0*. Lynne is the current president of the AERA Special Interest Group: Technology as an Agent of Change in Teaching and Learning (TACTL), past president of the International Society for Technology in Education (ISTE), and currently is the editor of the *Journal of Research on Technology in Education (JRTE)* (2002–2011). More information can be found at http://mason.gmu.edu/~lschrum.

Linda Sellers is a master's student and a member of the Department of Instructional Technology and Learning Sciences, Utah State University, USA.

Mike Sharples is Professor of Learning Sciences and Director of the Learning Sciences Research Institute at the University of Nottingham. He has an international reputation for research in mobile learning and the design of learning technologies. He inaugurated the mLearn conference series and is President of the International Association for Mobile Learning. His current projects include PI: Personal Inquiry, a collaboration with the Open University, UK to develop twenty-first century science learning between formal and informal settings, a national survey of social networked learning at home and school, and research on curriculum and pedagogy to inform the UK Government's Harnessing Technology Strategy. He is author of 160 publications in the areas of interactive systems design, artificial intelligence, and educational technology.

Barbara W. Sirotnik, Ph.D., is a professor of statistics and supply chain management at California State University, San Bernardino, and IAR codirector. Dr. Sirotnik's Ph.D. is in statistics, and her additional areas of expertise include operations management, information management, computer programming, and research methods. She has authored and coauthored theoretical articles in the areas of paired comparisons and contingency table analysis, and has published applied research in factor analysis. She has extensive consulting experience for agencies such as the Bureau of Land Management, the Riverside County Health Department, various colleges and universities, the city of San Bernardino Redevelopment Agency, and San Bernardino Department of Public Social Services.

Gerry Stahl teaches, publishes, and conducts research in human–computer interaction (HCI) and computer-supported collaborative learning (CSCL). His 2006 book, *Group Cognition: Computer Support for Building Collaborative Knowledge* is published by MIT Press. He is founding Executive Editor of the *International Journal* *of Computer-Supported Collaborative Learning* (ijCSCL). He is the Principal Investigator of the Virtual Math Teams Project, a 7-year research effort in collaboration with the Math Forum@Drexel. He served as Program Chair for the international CSCL '02 conference and Workshops Chair for CSCL '03, '05, '07, and '09. He teaches undergraduate, master's, and Ph.D. courses in HCI, CSCW, and CSCL at the College of Information Science and Technology of Drexel.

Zachary Stein received a BA in philosophy from Hampshire College and an Ed.M. in Mind, Brain, and Education from the Harvard University Graduate School of Education. He is currently a student of philosophy and cognitive development pursing a doctorate at Harvard. He is also the Senior Analyst for the Developmental Testing Service where has worked for years employing cognitive developmental models and metrics in a variety real-world contexts. While at Harvard he has received many awards including an Intellectual Contribution Award and a Faculty Tribute Fellowship. He has published in a variety of outlets on issues ranging from cognitive development and pedagogy to philosophy of education and interdisciplinarity.

Celka Straughn is a research assistant at Harvard Project Zero working on the Developing Minds and Digital Media project, examining the intersection of new digital media and cognitive development. Previously, she worked as a Senior Research Assistant on Learning in and From Museum Study Centers, a collaborative research project with the Harvard Art Museum and Project Zero. Celka has also held various curatorial and museum education positions. She recently received her Ph.D. in art history from the University of Chicago.

Keith S. Taber is a senior lecturer in science education in the Faculty of Education at the University of Cambridge, United Kingdom. He was previously a science teacher in the secondary and further education sectors. His research interests are focused upon aspects of learning about science, including the nature of students' thinking, conceptual development, conceptual integration, and the nature of high ability in science. He is the author of *Chemical Misconceptions: Prevention, Diagnosis and Cure* (2002: Royal Society of Chemistry); *Science: Teaching School Subjects 11–19* (with Vanessa Kind, 2005: Routledge), *Enriching School Science for the Gifted Learner* (2007: Gatsby Science Enhancement Programme), and editor of *Science Education for Gifted Learners* (2007: Routledge).

Jonathan G. Tullis is a graduate student in the Department of Psychology at the University of Illinois at Urbana-Champaign. He investigates educational and instructional techniques that rely on the innate strengths of memory and cognition to maximize learning.

Andrew Walker is an assistant professor at Utah State University and has also taught at Lehigh University. He is currently a member of the Department of Instructional Technology and Learning Sciences, Utah State University, USA.

Karen Washinawatok is currently Director of the Menominee Language and Culture Commission. She earned her bachelor's degree at NAES college and has a master's degree in Language, Reading, and Culture from the University of Arizona. She has served as Campus Dean and Campus Director for NAES College and East-West University, Keshena campus. She has also served on the Menominee Tribal Legislature and as Tribal Chair. Her teaching experience includes working as a Language Instructor at St. Norbert's College. She has also served on the National Indian School Board.

Rupert Wegerif of Exeter University has researched and published widely in the fields of educational theory, education with new technology, and teaching thinking. His recent book: *Dialogic Education and Technology: Expanding the Space of Learning* (2007 Springer) develops a dialogic theory of the connection between educational technology and teaching thinking for the needs of the emerging global network society. He advises the UK government on the future of education, is coeditor of the journal *Thinking Skills and Creativity* and President of the 2011 European Association of Research on Learning and Instruction (EARLI) Conference to be held at Exeter.

Margaret Weigel joins Project Zero (PZ) as a researcher specializing in media forms and practices working primarily on the GoodPlay project and on a evolving project examining the intersection of new digital media and cognitive development. Prior to PZ, Margaret was the Research Manager for MIT's New Media Literacies project, led by Henry Jenkins, a designer of historically themed ubiquitous games for a local start-up company, and a writer on media, art, and culture for WBUR.com, one of Boston's NPR affiliates. She earned her BA in Sociology at Brandeis and holds advanced degrees in American history and comparative media studies.

Carmen Zahn is Postdoctoral Researcher at the Knowledge Media Research Center (KMRC) at Tuebingen, Germany. She studied psychology and media science at the University of Tuebingen and received her Ph.D. in 2003 in cognitive psychology (Dissertation: "Knowledge Communication by Hypervideo" funded by the German Science Foundation, DFG). She has published on (audio) visual knowledge communication, interactive video and CSCL in formal and informal educational settings. Since 2007 she has been the leader of a DFG-funded project on "Fostering deep understanding and skills acquisition by means of digital video in the classroom" and coleader of the project "Learning in Museums—the role of digital media" (funded by the German Leibniz Association).

Part I
Cognition and New Science of Learning

Chapter 1
New Digital Media and Their Potential Cognitive Impact on Youth Learning

Margaret Weigel[1], Celka Straughn[2], and Howard Gardner[1]

[1] The Developing Minds and Digital Media Project, Harvard University, Project Zero, Cambridge, MA 02138, USA, e-mail: margaret_weigel@pz.harvard.edu; hgasst@pz.harvard.edu
[2]Spencer Museum of Art, University of Kansas, 1301 Mississippi St, Lawrence, KS 66045, e-mail: straughn@ku.edu

Introduction

In his 2009 book *Grown up Digital*, Don Tapscott presents a very positive view of the new digital media (NDM). "The early evidence suggests that the digital immersion [for youth] has a tangible, positive impact. Not only do video game players notice more, but they have more highly developed partial skills. . . the Net Gen mind seems to be incredibly flexible, adaptable and multimedia savvy" (Tapscott, 2008, p. 98). In this new order, others praise the transformational power of social networks which can topple (or at least circumvent) existing hierarchical structures (Benkler, 2007; Shirkey, 2009; Surowiecki, 2004) and potentially reinvent civic engagement (Pettingill, 2008).

Tapscott and his like-mined peers do not represent a consensus. A collection of scholars, educators, and concerned citizens counter it. Rather than ushering in a utopian era of self-directed youth learning across time and space, NDM are in fact making us "dumber" (Bauerlein, 2008) and actually harming our brains (Healy, 1999). While Tapscott and others salute the democratizing power of information on the Internet, Jean Twenge expresses concern: "Suddenly, you don't have to write a textbook or have a column in a major newspaper for thousands of people to read your words. . . In this environment, there is no authority: information is free, diffuse, and comes from everyone. (Whether it is correct is another matter)" (Twenge, 2006, p. 30).

Of course, it is possible that each of these sides has some truth to it; it is also possible that the NDM will not exert much of an effect. In education, for example,

M. Weigel (✉)
The Developing Minds and Digital Media Project, Harvard University, Project Zero, Cambridge, MA 02138, USA
e-mail: margaret_weigel@pz.harvard.edu

M.S. Khine, I.M. Saleh (eds.), *New Science of Learning*,
DOI 10.1007/978-1-4419-5716-0_1, © Springer Science+Business Media, LLC 2010

despite all of the predictions—positive and negative—about radio, television, slide projector, and so on, the most likely generalization is that not much has happened in education as a direct result of the introduction of earlier instantiations of new media.

One reason for the enormous range of opinion about the NDM is that it is extremely difficult to secure significant data on these issues. The ideal experiments—in which one would divide a polity in half, at random, expose one half to the full range of the NDM, and make it impossible for the other half to have any exposure whatsoever—cannot be conducted. The best hope is to triangulate from a number of sources and see what picture(s) gradually emerge. Studies addressing youth engagements online have leaned toward the social at the expense of considering cognitive or developmental implications (i.e., Blais, Craig, Pepler, & Connolly, 2008; Gee, 2004; Jenkins, Purushotma, Clinton, Weigel, & Robison, 2006; Ito et al., 2008). Those who do address developmental issues (Greenfield, 2004; Schouten, Valkenburg, & Peter, 2007; Subrahmanyama, Greenfield, Kraut, & Gross, 2001; Valkenburg & Peter, 2007) are largely descriptive and do not consider ethical issues.

In our own research for The Developing Minds and Digital Media (DM2) project[1] (a component of the GoodWork Project[2] at Harvard Project Zero), we wanted to secure a more holistic record of change related to NDM. Our research was driven by the basic question of whether NDM may, or may not, be impacting the way youth think and behave. We focus in particular on changes to students' "habits of mind," the mental models which underlie and direct how they engage with the world.[3]

Methods

A fundamental challenge for this effort was how to determine what actually constitutes a change. In order to assess gradations of difference over time, it was necessary to capture data on two fronts: youth's habits in the past and youth's habits

[1]The first phase of the Developing Minds and Digital Media (DM2) study was funded by a generous grant from Judy Dimon. The study investigated possible links between cognitive changes over time and new digital media as manifested in a high school aged population. Literature reviews, qualitative research, and data analyses were completed between June 1, 2007, and May 31, 2009. We thank our colleagues at the GoodWork project, in particular Katie Davis, Wendy Fischman, Andrea Flores, John Francis, Sam Gilbert, Jen Ryan and Margaret Rundle, with special thanks to GoodWork Research Director Carrie James.

[2]The GoodWork Project is a long-term, multi-site investigation examining the intersection of excellence, engagement, and ethics at work.

[3]Portions of this chapter are based on GoodWork unpublished works (Weigel, Davis, James, & Gardner, 2009a; 2009b).

today. We asked which individual(s) or groups are in a favorable position to have observed cohorts of youth over an extensive period of time. Many groups might have something to say, but it seemed to us that classroom teachers of long standing experience might have especially keen insights to share. We sought to obtain a longitudinal view of the problem space by talking to 40 experienced educators who have observed changes in students and education over time. We sought out educators with a minimum of 15 years of school-based experience in order to capture data relating to students before the widespread public adoption of a graphical browser web interface in 1992/1993. This 15-year time frame allowed us to focus on changes in youth habits and behaviors related to NDM while limiting other variables to the greatest extent possible. Educators were identified via peer and professional recommendations.

The educators we spoke with are from 18 different schools, largely within the Greater Boston area, and represented a broad range of disciplines across the arts and humanities, the social, physical and biological sciences, and athletics. Our research controlled for socioeconomic factors, with nearly 75% of the youth at the schools from households earning an average annual income of more than $100 k, with close to 50% in the $150 K–$300 k range. In narrowing our focus, we helped to ensure that the students we examine were not barred from participating in NDM activities for economic reasons.

It should be noted that our educator participants are not typical classroom practitioners; they have at least a decade and a half of experience in the classroom and were recommended by peers and administrators as remarkably observant, thoughtful, and reflective with respect to their students. They also teach in schools where there is considerable freedom in the curriculum. As noted, they also represent a specific demography—central New England.

Interviews were conducted between May 2008 and February 2009. Two interviewers conducted a qualitative interview with each educator for approximately 90–120 min. The interviewers paid special attention to cited changes in cognition, social cognition, and moral and ethical priorities as they relate to NDM engagement. It should be noted, however, that we explicitly omitted direct references to NDM in the first half of the interview, allowing the topic to rise spontaneously (which it usually did). Almost every interview was audio recorded, and each interviewer took detailed notes. A multiple choice questionnaire designed to capture important facts relating to rates of NDM adoption, usage, and demographic information was also administered. As a whole the interviews offer a unique vantage point into areas of change among youth both more generally as well as in relation to NDM.

Post-interview, the two sets of notes were distilled into a single master account and a briefer overview focused on key points. After 20 interviews, work began on identifying emerging themes; these themes formed the basis of a detailed project matrix. As the interview progressed, the matrix was modified as needed to summarize a more nuanced portrait of significant themes.

Findings and Discussion

The Changing Youth Environment

NDM—their production, popularity and obsolescence—are linked to multiple social, economic, cultural, and intellectual phenomena. Before turning specifically to NDM, one needs to take into account other factors that might contribute to observed changes; in the course of our interviews, broader cultural changes that may impact youth practices frequently emerged. We identify two important external factors that are likely influencing youth's appropriations and uses of NDM: demographic trends and the rise in extracurricular commitments. These factors should be given due consideration when examining evidence of youth behaviors overall.

Demographic Trends

Demographic trends appear to have a significant impact on subsequent observed changes over time in youth. The annual number of high school graduates in the United States has been steadily increasing over the past 15 years and is expected to peak at about 2009 to 2.9 million as the children of the baby boomer generation reach adolescence (Finder, 2008).

While matriculating at a top college or university has always been a challenge, the sheer volume of qualified applicants has increased the competition for coveted spots. It is unclear to what extent this rise in applicants has in fact resulted in increased competition. However, the educators with whom we spoke report that both students and parents alike are extremely concerned about students gaining admission to their preferred college, or sometimes any college at all; this situation has resulted in part in a more anxious student population unwilling to deviate from prescribed markers of academic success for fear of jeopardizing their chances of earning a spot at their top college.

The Rise in Extracurricular Commitments

Another major change in the contemporary student's environment is an increase in the type and intensity of activities he engages in. Students are committed to more homework requirements and school-sponsored and external extracurricular pursuits, which combine to consume nearly all of a student's time out of school. In a recently published essay, a college junior readily admits that he spends more time and energy with extracurricular newspaper work than on his academic assignments, eking by academically on hastily written term papers and cramming for exams (Flow, 2009).

Youth athletics have become a sophisticated system consisting of high school athletes who specialize in a single sport and are expected to participate in non-school athletic leagues and sport-specific training throughout the year. Similarly, students in the performing arts are asked to commit to extended rehearsals, touring, and hours of nightly practice. While the odds that these students will be able to convert their passion into professional careers are slim, students and parents alike often view excellence in an extracurricular activity as another chit in the well-rounded college application.

A compelling experience with service learning or volunteer work, a requirement at every school we spoke with, is considered another valuable asset. Such service can encompass a variety of experiences ranging from the mundane to the transformational, with the latter seen as potentially meaningful and also appealing on a college application. Whether service learning is considered a rewarding experience, a ticket to the Ivy League, or simply a requirement for graduation, it consumes another block of time out of the busy student's day.

According to the educators we spoke with, after-hours homework assignments may consume up to 5 h a night of a student's non-school time. The amount of homework varies depending on the teacher and the class requirements; some do not assign any homework out of concern that students are sacrificing sleep in order to fulfill their daily time commitments.

NDM's Impact on Youth Learning

Our findings indicate despite changes in certain behaviors over time, the motivations driving their students remain unchanged. A physics teacher is fairly representative of many of our participants, gently insisting that there had been no change in how students learn or spend their time, what excites and interests them, and how they make (often poor, but sometimes insightful) decisions. School remains the primary pathway for cultivating mastery and competence in a variety of domains. An adolescent's sense of self is still determined by his/her experiences, achievements and failures; peer relationships and the onset of romantic liaisons consume their energies. As one educator puts it, "students want to be smart, popular, accepted, and know what makes them special."

While our study does not include an analysis of what specific NDM content youth engage in or what youth text or talk about, we were able to capture a broad picture of NDM usage across a variety of contexts. In some ways, NDM have been integrated into the social fabric similar to earlier technologies such as the widespread adoption of the telephone in the early twentieth century. Computers, for instance, are no longer considered extraordinary; close to 60% of the schools we spoke with had integrated computers for teaching by 1999 (the figures would likely be lower in a less privileged educational environment).

Given that computers have been incorporated into contemporary homes, workspaces, and classrooms, it is easy to forget that they have in certain ways revolutionized youth learning and educational practices. The task of writing a term paper, for instance, will never be the same. With their limitless capacity for revising, reverting back to an earlier version, spell checking, grammar checking, and word counting, word processing programs allow for a process of writing unimaginable with pen and paper, or even a typewriter. With the ability to access information via the Internet, students hardly need to visit the library anymore. With the capacity to chat with friends and strangers about one's task, it may not necessarily take a village to write a paper but it may well be the work of many hands. Sometimes, it can be someone else's work altogether as reports of school plagiarism, both unintentional and deliberate, rises in the digital age (Josephson Institute of Ethics, 2006; Williams, 2007).

Similarly important to youth learning and educational practices is the proliferation of portable, affordable, and personal digital devices. While schools have a large measure of control over the computers they provide, virtually every student owns at minimum a cellphone with texting capabilities. Students can be seen accessing their mobile devices before the school day begins, during classes and study halls, in the few minutes between classes, during lunch, and immediately after school.[4] Most of these students are conversing with friends or parents.

In the subsequent sections, we analyze the cognitive and socially based changes in the youth of 2008 and 2009 as compared to the youth of 1992 or earlier as discussed with us by our 40 educator participants.

Changes in Student Attention

A large number of our educator participants mention that their students' capacity for attention is on the decline when compared to the earlier, pre-NDM generation of students. In particular, they cite a rapid change shift to shorter attention spans and greater distractibility over a relatively short period of time.[5] Many of the educators we spoke with also find that their current students experience difficulty sitting and listening for extended periods of time.

Part of this reported change reflects more awareness and diagnoses of attention-related illnesses such as attention deficit disorder (ADD), shifts in pedagogical approaches and understanding, and a rise in distractions overall. Several educators also attribute students' shorter periods of focused attention in part to the rapid flow of information and communication with NDM. A few further cite a greater impatience and frustration with delayed gratification, suggesting that these may be a response to the sense of immediacy with which students have become accustomed to using new technologies. Moreover, students appear more "distracted by technology," observes a biology educator, with email, iTunes, cell phones, IM, television, and video games.

As one history teacher puts it, students today "multitask like crazy," and quite a few educators also associate the decline in student attention with the practice of multitasking with various media (digital and electronic) such as cell phones,

---

[4]The more specific characteristics of this type of engagement depend to a large extent on school access to the necessary networks and policies on the use of such devices during the school day.

[5]One subject did specifically remark that students have long attention spans and are noticeable for *not* having changed. This may be due in part to that particular school's environment of self-selected, independent students, although many educators at the private schools in particular note an increase of stronger students.

the Internet, and television. Our educator participants often reference the typical student practice of partially listening to the educator's talk while engaging with multiple programs open on the computer and texting. According to one visual arts educator, this situation characterizes their work environment and now is what students need to—or feel that they need to—have access to before they can concentrate.

For many of our educator participants, multitasking seems to indicate a decrease in focused time spent on specific tasks. Several educators link multitasking with distractions; they claim that such distractions contribute to a change in students' ability to compartmentalize and to stay on task. Additionally, according to several educator participants, students today appear to have more difficulty attaining and sustaining concentration on a particular task. There is also research supporting the claim that multitasking comes at a cost to depth and attention (Fried, 2008; Hembrooke & Gay, 2003).

The educators we interviewed differ in their views of the effectiveness and impact of multitasking on student learning. Some students reportedly can balance all of their multiple activities with little difficulty. More typical, however, is the student who believes he is capable of adeptly balancing the influx of information but in fact struggles and does not succeed. Other educator participants suggest that multitasking potentially impacts both the quantity and the quality of student work. One physics educator attributes students' tendency to process "snippets," or "little pieces of information"—something many educators mention—to the culture of multitasking, with the implication that students may lack the training to focus singly and sharply over significant periods of time.

Another potential casualty of multitasking and fractured attention is a lack of depth and facility for synthesizing information. Calling his students' approach to information "surfacey," a chemistry educator notices a recent decline in their capacities to get a little frustrated and dig deeper. His students' ability to grasp, wrestle with, and apply chemical concepts has not changed, but how they get there has. He finds that they now look quickly at and analyze material less thoroughly. Similarly, a theater educator claims that students can quickly process a lot of information that exists on the surface, but the implications of that information may elude the student.

A biology educator observes that her students increasingly do not want to take the time to process, and instead, they look to her for more direct guidance. Going a little further, a history educator proposes that a big change with the current generation is that students today have more difficulty feeling comfortable with an interpretative stance of their own. Their ability to synthesize and think independently is accordingly hindered.

In part as a way to address attention issues, most of our educator participants integrate a variety of teaching styles, adopt more student-centered activities, incorporate images as attention "hooks," and/or insert more "commercial breaks," in the words of one chemistry teacher. One English teacher we spoke with suggests that students develop better executive-level skills to counteract all the distractions, yet she also acknowledges that focused attention remains a struggle for some, particularly boys. Students still manage to complete tasks, though for many it seems to take longer, and, as we heard from a few educators, students are simply more exhausted.

Changes in Information Preferences

Shifts Toward the Visual. Students today are increasingly "keyed to the visual", declares one English teacher, characterizing a widespread observation among those interviewed. We heard recurrent accounts of students increasingly attuned to images and non-text visuals, as well as time-based media such as animation, film, and multimedia. Students' preference for classroom material that resembles contemporary entertainment activities is not new; an earlier generation of students, for instance, was delighted when the TV cart was wheeled into the classroom. Students today, a science educator suggests, are more visually stimulated because they are "out there" online, and educators seek to provide corresponding teaching and learning opportunities.

The proliferation of visual and multimedia materials online also provides educators access to a wide array of affordable materials that they can—and do—incorporate into their classrooms. Many of the educators we interviewed describe using images from the Internet, incorporated into a PowerPoint presentation, as a way to capture student attention. A musical theater educator explains that since students today have difficulty listening without additional stimulation, integrating more visual materials helps keep them more engaged. Identifying the interactive nature of teaching and learning through technology as a "revolution," a music educator believes that the primary challenge for teachers today is how best to exploit the resources and structure of the Internet.

We also heard from a few educators about different uses and expectations for the enhanced visual offerings of NDM, beyond serving as means to enliven classroom practices for their students. One educator, for instance, proposes a potential shift in the support of logic-based arguments, with future students able to rely less on written evidence and more on audio-visual forms to build support for one's position.

Shifts in Text-Based Practices. The rise in visual and multimediated learning suggests a corresponding decline in text-based learning strategies. Whether related in some ways to NDM or not, several educator participants more generally observe a "gap in writing skills," with these gaps encompassing both structural and compositional problems, as well as greater difficulties with syntax, grammar, and expressing complex ideas on paper. The reasons for this gap are not entirely clear and may be due to factors besides NDM engagement, such as an emphasis on cultivating STEM (science, technology, engineering, and mathematics) skill sets.

Many educators note that reading printed material, even texts assigned in school, has declined. An athletics educator suggests that students no longer read fully, but rather read just enough to find the answer they need. However, it appears that students still read or at least sample a great deal of material, although it is material that they find online. It may well be that for most youth, the practice of reading is becoming less about digesting substantial content and more about sampling a variety of textual tidbits. A primary difference between book-based and NDM-based reading is the content, with students less likely to maintain sustained focus with online material (Weigel & Gardner, 2009). One history teacher proposes that reading in chunks online makes students less comfortable reading long texts. Another important difference lies in the more dynamic, interactive and multimodal forms reading online assumes. A student, for instance, can find a complete edition of Toqueville's two-volume *Democracy in America* online, follow links embedded in the text to related content sites, view a video on the topic, and then discuss what he discovered with his friends.

With respect to pleasure reading, most youth are reading information online in various formats. Rather than books, explains a theater educator, students today prefer multiple modalities and media. Another possibility for the decline, proposed by a veteran English teacher, is that there are so many other activities for a student to pursue in his free time.

With respect to academic reading, it may well be that students in the past were not thrilled with their assignments, either, but felt obliged to complete the reading. Students in the last 50 years, however, have had access to study guides such as the Cliff Notes brand, which provides quick, abbreviated overviews of popular school texts such as *Romeo and Juliet*, *Moby-Dick*, or *Beowulf*, as well as many contemporary titles. Today, an online search using any of the popular search engines will not only provide the student with materials related to his/her topic but also provide ready-made copy that can be easily cut and pasted into a written homework assignment.

Perhaps the biggest change in using a word processing program on the computer is the ability to revise easily; as mentioned earlier, this innovation has liberated the practice of paper writing from its ink-smeared drafts, scribbles, and illegible handwritten past. Interestingly, a history teacher says that students now want to edit perpetually and have difficulty determining when a paper is sufficiently complete.[6] Another unexpected ramification of computer-based writing, according to several other educators we interviewed, is that students do not proof or edit as much as before. Reasons for this range from students considering proofreading an "arduous task," suffering from too many responsibilities to fulfill or are lazy, or presenting papers which look "polished" thanks to clean computer printouts.

With respect to students' paper content and organization, we heard mixed opinions. One educator of almost 50 years claims that student writing done on a computer is not as organized and coherent as those written by hand. A number of NDM-related causes are directly attributable to demonstrable declines in the quality of student writing. A few educators remark that they can tell when student work is written while students are multitasking, particularly when interrupted while instant

[6]Reasons for this desire to edit continually are unclear, though from the interview they appear to stem in part from changing standards, (perceived) higher expectations, less risk-taking, and a focus on grades.

messaging (IMing); such papers jump all over, lack transitions, express incomplete thoughts, and are unedited. One social science educator further comments that she notices the effects of texting and IMing on language: sentences tend to be incomplete, devoid of color, and lacking in embellishment.

Others that we spoke with, however, find that academic writing has improved. This reported trend may have to do more with particular schools and with these students' prior academic backgrounds which, as a history educator surmises, trains them to be more linear thinkers, "at home with the printed page. . .and written word." He explains that he is more likely to flag imprecise word choices today than structural problems.

Nearly all the educators who reference changes in writing habits mention a reduction in student vocabulary. They also often comment that students who read more have more robust vocabularies upon which to draw. Comparing the writing skills of non-readers and readers, one art and media specialist explains that non-readers would rather ingest a story via media (e.g. television, movies) than via text, frequently employ colloquialisms and slang, and consider writing more difficult than do their peers who read more.

Changes in Student Research Practices

The proliferation of NDM has overhauled traditional, research practices; virtually all changes relating to older iterations of research relate in some capacity to how these new technologies have transformed access to information. In the words of one history educator, students still write "old-fashioned" research papers but rely on "new-fangled" Internet sources, including blogs and wikis; in addition they also have greater access to primary materials such as historical documents or original recordings. Our educator participants characterize this new means of acquiring information as a mixed blessing.

The speed and facility of the Internet are a big attraction for youth. One educator describes students as generally resistant to doing something the "slow way," such as a trip to the library or other institution; instead, today's pupils look for quicker ways to research papers and to accrue information in general. Some educators report requiring that their students find, read, and cite a minimum number of offline sources such as books or periodicals. One educator reports that when she asked her students to look at some paintings for a class assignment, most of them elected to complete the assignment by locating an online museum site versus viewing the actual works of art in the physical museum space.

This relative speed of information retrieval may both facilitate task completion and unintentionally conflict with the acquisition of a more impactful understanding of the material; students, able to obtain material quickly, tend to move on to the next task with limited reflection. Several educators attribute changes in information processing in part to the increased pace of information and the increased pressures of student time. "It's a radical thing to have them slow down and just absorb things," claims a visual arts educator. In the final analysis, many of our educator participants find that their students may be easily and quickly obtain various sources, but they can equally easily get lost in cyberspace and waste lots of time, making one wonder just how much time and effort is saved by locating information online.

Once online, students today "do a lot more searching and a lot less digging," comments an athletics educator. Greater breadth and less depth of information with student research surfaces as the general consensus from our interviews. Students can now more easily and independently "plumb the depths" of a particular subject. But educator participants explain that with the greater breadth of material students encounter on the Internet, they correspondingly require better "filtering" mechanisms. As a physics educator recounts, it was more self-limiting when teachers directed students to specific books; today students need to learn how to find—and process—information, a responsibility for which he/she is not sure that teachers are adequately prepared to teach. The Internet now constitutes students' primary research tool, largely replacing books and visits to the library.

Although excited by the wealth of information available to their students online, the educators we spoke with also caution against information overload. As one history educator puts it, research "used to be a hunt, now you're swimming in it." A visual arts teacher suggests students are cowed by how much they feel they should know and that makes it more difficult for them to make and reflect upon connections.[7] According to a theater educator, students also tend to assume information online is correct unless they happen to encounter a contradictory point of view. In the past, a publisher's profit depended in part on the credibility of its materials, and publications were vetted through an independent editor. Conversely, published voices tended to reflect only a limited spectrum of voices. The Internet, on the other hand, allows one to self-publish free from profit concerns or censorship. It can also easily bypass the standard third-party editorial oversight process. One English teacher says that the main challenge facing students conducting research today is how to determine what constitutes reliable information.

Plagiarism. While students may use NDM to cheat in a variety of ways, we focus here on the growing problem of plagiarism. Our educator participants tell us that incidences of academic cheating have risen in recent years. Plagiarism has been in the rise since the 1960s, with a sharp rise in the Internet age. In a 2006 report, 35% of high-school students report inappropriately borrowing text or other information from the Internet; the percentage rises to 40% for undergraduate behaviors (Josephson, 2006). The current phenomenon of cheating is a "perfect storm" of environmental pressures, shifting ethical norms, and the complications around negotiating proper engagement with NDM-based information.

It is true that some students have always cheated but educators describe students today as taking greater risks, adopting a dogged "get by at all costs" attitude, and demonstrating a greater acceptance of those who do cheat. Researchers Stephens and Nicholson (2008) propose four contemporary models of cheating: (1) unable (students who try to complete assignments and fail), (2) under-interested (those not

[7] The significance of the ability to synthesize information is examined in detail in *Five Minds for the Future* (Gardner, 2007).

trying and failing), (3) under pressure (those who cannot find the time due to competing commitments), and (4) the unrepentant (those who do not care). Our findings suggest that most students fall either into the first and third categories. Most educators feel that plagiarism is not an indicator of a broader moral decline in their students' ethics; instead, they interpret this behavior as the inevitable outcome of the intense pressure to succeed academically. The student most likely to cheat this way, according to our educators, is one who is struggling. He will likely resort to this tactic toward the end of the academic term, when opportunities to raise his grade by legitimate means diminish.

Other educators understand the rise in plagiarism as indicative of a broader social shift in what in fact constitutes plagiarism. One educator identifies an increase in the "grey and greyer area" of distinction between the inadvertent appropriation of someone else's work due to improper, absent citations, or a misunderstanding around ownership issues, and outright plagiarism. A "little" plagiarism is seen as acceptable by his students, or not even identified as such. Similarly, students who "snatch a line or two" from someone else's work, or download music without paying for it shrug it off and dismiss charges of stealing or plagiarism. "Students aren't sure what crosses the line between cheating and plagiarism," says the director of a science department.

Part of the student confusion around plagiarism from online sources, according to our educators, stems from the ease of accessing information. Students in the past were not able to access other people's term papers or free copies of music with the click of a mouse; before the advent of word processing, the practice of cutting and pasting text into a document did not exist. The Internet and NDM allow users to access an enormous array of information, including articles, blog posts, and informal writing on virtually every subject, and that the computer functions as both a portal to the Internet and the platform for paper composition makes copying and pasting information from online sources into one's assignment extremely simple. It can be difficult for a young person to understand that just because an article, for instance, may not cite an author or require a fee to access does not mean that it is "there for the taking," with no responsibilities or strings attached. "It's so easy to do, just copy and paste," a college-level piano instructor reports.

While the Internet provides students easy access to relevant course materials ripe for appropriation, it provides comprehensive access to their teachers as well. Many of the educators we spoke with report that their institutions utilize sophisticated software such as Turnitin.com for detecting whether a suspect passage has an antecedent online. One educator says that his school encourages students to check their own papers for improper citations using Turnitin, allowing students to learn in advance of turning in an assignment how their teacher will interpret the submission.

Schools try to stem the tide of plagiarism through outreach and education, including group discussions around copyright issues, workshops on definitions of plagiarism, tutoring on how to vet and credit Internet sources appropriately, and conveying general expectations with respect to honesty and ethical behavior. Yet, some educators sense an uphill battle against a culture that encourages and implicitly supports plagiarist practices. "In the dorms, at the beginning of the school year, we have a discussion around trust, responsibility and good behaviors," reports a former boarding school housemaster. "But now, there's a difficult culture where it's 'cooler' to do as little as possible and get away with it."

Changes in the Student–Educator Relationship

The student–educator relationship plays a significant role in the student's social and academic development; NDM appear to impact the student–educator relationship on both a personal and a professional level. Many of the social changes discussed by our educator participants relate to altered modes of communication and shifts in power and agency from educators to students. While some of these changes stem from deliberate pedagogical choices, others appear to be the unintended consequences of technology.

Overall, teachers are pleased by this loosening of hierarchical strictures, which they feel have led to better communication and better educational practices. There is also evidence suggesting the sharp boundaries between disciplines such as art, science, literature, and performance are more open to negotiation in general; it should be noted that this type of progressive, interdisciplinary pedagogy is the exception and not the norm in most American high schools. In one biology classroom, for instance, students can pick a research topic and determine the form the final product will assume—a conventional research paper, a video, a sculptural model, or another form of their own choosing. Several educators remark how the ready availability of visual and multimedia elements online have positively impacted their pedagogies and have been received enthusiastically by their students.

Most of today's students rely on the Internet for companionship, entertainment, and information; the technically inclined can find communities of like-minded peers (Gee, 2004), the socially adept can keep tabs on myriads of friends, and the bored can find a game to play, an intriguing news item, or a humorous video to watch (Ito et al., 2008). In contrast, most of the educators we spoke with spent more of their time offline, leading toward a correlation between one's length of classroom experience and one's discomfort with new media. Educators coexist in the same cultural mix as their students, but they may have the additional challenge of having to 'unlearn' certain assumptions as well as face steep learning curves as technologies grow more diverse and, all too often, more complicated. The net result is a youth population more familiar with online tools and practices. This generational difference in experiences was expressed by the educators.

Interpersonal Changes. Informal face-to-face engagements between educators and students have declined for any number of reasons, some of which include NDM's speed, efficiency, convenience, and ability to negotiate thornier issues from a safer, rehearsed position. It is easier, say educators, for students to email difficult conversations versus conducting them face to face, when emotions potentially come into play.

Our participant educators describe a high level of communication between themselves and their students today, as compared to pre-NDM levels before the widespread availability of email. Students appear to make deliberate decisions regarding what type of NDM communication to use with their teachers: rather than sending an instant message to the teacher, they instead choose to email questions when they arise. Educators on the whole appreciate the freedom and time flexibility associated with the exchange of asynchronous messages with their students.

Despite the asynchronous nature of most student–educator online communications, expectations relating to response times differ significantly. Students often spend their evenings online listening to music, live chatting with friends, watching videos, playing games, and other related activities, and they tend to expect that their teachers will also be online to answer their queries very quickly. Educators, on the other hand, report markedly different practices relating to evening engagement. While some participate in online practices similar to their students, the majority report less engagement online in the evenings and spend more time offline. Educators report receiving student emails about the following day's assignment late the prior evening. One science teachers at a boarding school had to instruct his students to not email him after 8 pm and not to expect an immediate response.

Despite its convenience, email and similar online communications can often prove problematic. The absence of social cues and misinterpretations of language can easily lead to misunderstandings between parties. In this context, too, expectations differ between educators and students. About a quarter of our educators claim that students do not acknowledge the need to use a different voice when corresponding with them, and that in general, students "don't think about tone" and "need to distinguish [tones] for different recipients." Some educators enjoy the more casual nature of more informal email correspondences versus previous, more formal exchanges with students. Others, however, interpret overly casual emails from students as showing a disregard for the educator's professional role.

Changes Outside of the Classroom. The standard definition of the term "homework" conjures up a lone individual attempting to master a set of assigned tasks. He/She is likely supported by some external supports such as paper and pencil, books, perhaps a calculator, or a typewriter. In this conception of homework, third-party support from a parent or tutor is considered acceptable, but allowing others to complete one's assignments is considered a form of cheating.

This traditional definition of homework, however, is challenged by the introduction of the networked computer in the workspace. Our educator participants report that a majority of their students are online while they work at home to complete school assignments, either finding information on the web or collaborating with peers. In response, many educators have attempted to design homework assignments less amenable to collaboration. Others have dispensed with homework altogether. Students not collaborating on homework assignments with peers may be chatting online instead, or simultaneously engaging in homework and socializing.

Changes in Classroom Participation: In the past, a teacher might have struggled with a slide carousel, the VHS player, or the overhead projector, and either asked for assistance or accepted an offer of help from a student. Today's digital tools, however, are increasingly present, more complex, and often used by students in their free time. In nearly all the interviews we conducted, educators describe their students as "technically savvy": most students are capable of remedying problem technologies ranging from classroom tools to broader institutional infrastructure planning. Students are on the whole more comfortable with technology than their teachers.

Before the advent of networked devices, students had little recourse but to accept the content of a classroom lecture; NDM, however, provide students with tools with which to challenge what the teacher says and does in real time. Cellphones and networked computers in the classroom afford students a powerful portal to a growing compendium of knowledge relating to classroom curricula as well as NDM themselves. Educators may find their knowledge challenged by students surfing the web.

At times such challenges may be interpreted as a contestation of the authority of the educator. Student investigations conducted outside of the classroom and then shared with the educator for possible curriculum inclusion, however, are generally better received; they are considered as an indicator of authentic learning. One physics educator with whom we spoke incorporated an online video a student found into his lesson on electricity and conductivity; another educator relies on her web-savvy students to update her on the latest Broadway theater news. While students have long shared their informal learning with their teachers, NDM allow students to find and share material more quickly and easily.

The affordances of network access in the classroom are often used by students less to satisfy academic curiosity and more to socialize with peers. Before the proliferation of networked devices, student sociality was very limited. Now networked devices can also provide adolescents with a means to communicate with remote parties—both locally situated and very distant—while ostensibly sitting in class. Adolescents often engage in hypersocial behavior as they attempt to define who they are; networked devices such as the Internet, cellphones with texting and IM capacity allow students to continue interacting with friends regardless of context. The pervasive use of these tools can distract students from tasks at hand; if unmonitored, assignments can turn into a collaborative effort with classmates, friends, or random associates in an online chatroom.

Educators in our study report that girls engage in "persistent socializing" via NDM and are subjected to increased social pressures in part because of the potential to stay in contact with peers digitally at any time. A drama teacher at a boarding school finds that because of NDM, there are no longer any boundaries between "home" and "school." "Social networking feeds into social pressures," he says. "You can communicate anytime...if you make a social mistake you can make it better with more social work 24/7." Others mention that the typical student receives social communications via NDM across multiple contexts, including at school. One educator calls the ubiquitous interruptions a "method of peer-driven social control."

Changes in the Student–Student Relationship

While the student–educator relationship suggests a shift in power in student's favor, one facilitated in part by NDM affordances, the student–student relationship has no such firmly set hierarchical structure. Adolescence is generally a period of engaging and experimenting with complex social realities such as status, popularity, and success, with social behaviors taking center stage. Moreover, sorting out changes in the contemporary student–student relationship brought about by engagement with NDM tools poses a unique challenge, as NDM use is so ubiquitous it has become a standard point for social contact.

Most of the educators we spoke with insist that the basic desires of teens have remained essentially unchanged: they make friends and enemies, flirt, engage in romantic liaisons, and painful breakups. However, adolescents have less time to devote to peer relationships and casual recreational activities. In the past, says a foreign language teacher, there was much more unstructured time available to students. NDM appear to help bridge the gap by allowing teens to converse throughout the school day despite prohibitions to the contrary.

Managing Offline Relationships: Whether interacting with peers or teachers, students use the same strategies of removal and elective distance. A student wearing headphones or texting someone sends a signal to others that he is otherwise occupied. An art teacher at an elite private school reports, "There used to be a boom box in the print room. Now it's an individual environment. Most people listen to their iPods, and there's less of a sense that 'we're all doing this together.'"

A few educators in our study note an increase in the number of students who appear to have fewer or no discernible social connections with their classmates or who shy away from face-to-face interactions with others altogether. While there may be many reasons for this development, a significant change facilitated by NDM is how a student can retreat to his room alone but continue to engage with peers through online media. Given the nature of our study, however, we cannot determine with what frequency this happens (cf. Ito et al., 2008).

Managing Online Relationships: Educator participants note that their students often use NDM as a way to manage social contact, as one educator puts it, their "socialization is mediated by electronic devices." Students in our study rely heavily upon sites such as MySpace and Facebook to communicate with their friends and to keep tabs on associates. In the past, there was no Facebook or MySpace, no "online" space for adolescents to meet, no texting; given the relative newness of the technology, it is stunning how fully integrated into teen life these tools have become.

Online socializing may transpire in chatrooms, SNS sites, or (again primarily relevant for young men) video games that are played together online. Online social engagements are particularly popular for both youth residing in boarding schools and commuter students living at home and likely at some distance from their classmates. Online socializing is also attractive to students who are less socially adept, with the media inserting a measure of distance between the parties and lessening the problematic intensity engendered by face-to-face social interactions.

A number of teachers mention that the typical student needs to be online constantly, even during school hours, both to observe social interactions between other people and to monitor one's own reputation from slanderous attacks. Cyberbullying, in particular, is a widespread problem related specifically to the ease of posting anonymous, slanderous attacks on others, allowing around the clock contact, and enabling the participation of many colleagues with the click of a button. Bullying behavior appears to reach its apex at some point during junior high and declines thereafter; it still remains a part of high-school social life (Swearer, Espelage, & Napolitano, 2009; "When and Where does Bullying Occur?").

In the past, bullying may have occurred at school, but the student enjoyed a reprieve when removed from that specific context. NDM, however, make it possible for a bully (or group of bullies) to access or "haunt" his/her target constantly. Similarly, most past instances of bullying were not anonymous and were in fact a way to assert one's status, but NDM allow anyone to hide behind a pseudonym, harass the target, and evade responsibility. Finally, bullying, which may have been limited to a small cadre of perpetrators and victims, can now spread more quickly and easily to a larger population. Many of our educators shared stories of such hostile peer-to-peer behavior.

One interesting aspect of NDM-facilitated cyberbullying is that it may include participants of significantly different age groups. In our study group, one public school music educator recounts how a student in her school posted a photo and derogatory comments about a science teacher on MySpace. The student's identity was revealed, and she maintained her right to "free speech"; the science teacher resigned at the end of the school year.

Conclusion

NDM, according to our educator participants, can engage their students and provide unprecedented tools for expanding intellectual and social opportunities. They can also bestow upon their adolescent users enhanced authority, considerable freedom, and a high level of engagement via the relatively safe parameters of a screen interface. Conversely, NDM have been associated with fracturing attention spans and inadvertently encouraging less meaningful and more distant interactions with both people and information.

Whether NDM are seen as the problem (a la Bauerlein) or the solution (Tapscott) to current educational challenges remains to be determined. In the testimony of our 40 knowledgeable teachers, one can find both utopian and dystopic themes and trends. Adolescents will continue to engage with NDM; the question for educators is how to utilize the best of what these tools have to offer while mitigating the less desirable habits of mind they can cultivate. Our educator participants were relatively aligned with respect to how youth engage with digital media, and the ways in which this engagement can be improved:

- Most educators agree that successful online engagement requires the cultivation of higher-order meta-cognitive skills. Such skills are required to help students better assess the legitimacy of online information and to stay focused in the face of multiple digital enticements which can easily lead surfers astray. Most educators

are more comfortable imparting information related to specific topics, but in the culture increasingly saturated with NDM, there is a growing need for students to be able to critique the media they find online and circulate to peers. Students, for instance, would benefit from being able to determine and discuss the motivation behind the animation "Al Gore's Penguin Army," which at first blush appears to be an individual's humorous critique of the movie *An Inconvenient Truth* but was actually the product of a corporate "astroturf" PR group.
- Most educators express delight over the wealth of information easily available to students online but are somewhat unclear how to engage with this type of informal learning outside of the classroom. While the form and content of what interests youth—athletes, starlets, the latest rap hit—can feel alien to some educators, informal learning online can be a valuable key to engaging youth in more pedagogically appropriate subject matter. For instance, it was recently revealed that a simple web search for celebrity wallpaper, ringtones, and the like could expose the user to a number of computer viruses, embedded in celebrity sites by malicious hackers (Goldsmith, 2009). While celebrities Jessica Biel and Ashley Tinsdale may not appear to inspire teachable moments at first blush, this story provides an opportunity to get students thinking about who might be interested in what they download and why.
- Our informants return repeatedly to the decline in downtime for youth. In the past, youth had more opportunities to goof around, blow off steam, and play without the pressure of their free time needing to be spent in meaningful, productive pursuits. NDM have a way of sneaking into the crevices of one's free time. While such media can eliminate boredom, they also regard boredom as the problem and not a symptom of what might be a broader issue, such as a lack of alignment between an individual, his cognitive capacities, and his environmental conditions (Craighead & Nemeroff, 2004).
- Finally, we heard from educators that NDM can easily trigger ethical conflicts that students (and perhaps their elders) may not be equipped to handle responsibly. The temptation to plagiarize material from the web, even if it was written by a friend or colleague, may be irresistible (Stephenson & Nicholson, 2008). The GoodPlay project, also based at Harvard's Project Zero, found a host of emergent ethical issues related to young people and ethical engagement online (Gardner and James 2008).

Our study provides a detailed picture of today's digital youth, as gleaned from the testimony of experienced teachers in elite institutions. We cannot determine the extent to which this picture would be obtained with respect to other, less advantaged youth populations, though many of the themes we encountered have been reported elsewhere in the journalistic and research literature. Focused interviews of other adult groups, such as camp counselors to therapists, who have had sustained interactions with youth could also be informative. To determine more "in-depth" changes in the era of digital youth, ranging from nature of emotional reactions to the capacity for imaginative leaps, will require both devising of new methods of investigation as well as strategic triangulation of findings from various types of studies.

References

Al Gore's Penguin Army (2006). Posted by toutsmith. Youtube.com, May 26, 2006. http://www.youtube.com/watch?v=IZSqXUSwHRI

Bauerlein, M. (2008). *The dumbest generation: How the digital age stupefies young Americans and jeopardizes our future (or, don't trust anyone under 30)* (272 pp.). New York: Tarcher.

Benkler, Y. (2007). *The wealth of networks: How social production transforms markets and freedom*. New Haven, CT: Yale University Press.

Blais, J. J., Craig, W. M., Pepler, D., & Connolly, J. (2008). Adolescents online: The importance of internet activity choices to salient relationships. *Journal of Youth Adolescence, 37*, 522–536.

Craighead, W. E., & Nemeroff, C. B. (2004). Boredom and Boredom Proness. *The concise Corsini encyclopedia of psychology and behavioral science* (pp. 133–135). Hoboken, NJ: Wiley.

Finder, A. (2008). Demographic dip may cool college-admission race. *New York Times*. Accessed March 9, 2008 at http://www.dispatch.com/live/content/national_world/stories/2008/03/09/college_admissions_0309.ART_ART_03-09-08_A8_PQ9JA82.html?sid=101.

Flow, C. (2009, September/October). Why Harvard needs to get harder. Harvard magazine. Accessed August 24, 2009 at http://harvardmagazine.com/2009/09/harvard-needs-to-get-harder

Fried, C. B. (2008, April). In-class laptop use and its effects on student learning. *Computers & Education, 50*(3), 906–914.

Gardner, H. (2007). *Five Minds for the Future*. Boston: Harvard Business School Press.

Gardner, H., James, C., (2008). *Individualism, morality and ethics online: Finding among digital youth*. Unpublished working paper. Harvard Graduate School of Education.

Gee, J. P. (2004). Affinity spaces. *Situated language and learning: A critique of traditional schooling*. London: Routledge.

Goldsmith, B. (2009). "Jessica Biel Tops Brad Pitt as internet's Most Dangerous Search". Wired.com, first published August 25, 2009. Accessed August 25, 2009 at http://www.wired.com/epicenter/2009/08/jessica-biel-tops-brad-pitt-as-internets-most-dangerous-search/

Greenfield, P. M. (2004). Developmental consideration for determining appropriate internet use guidelines for children and adolescents. *Journal of Applied Developmental Psychology, 25*, 751–762.

Healy, J. (1999). *Failure to connect: What the internet does to our children's minds – and what we can do about it* (352 pp.). New York: Simon and Schuster.

Hembrooke, H., & Gay, G. (2003, Fall). The laptop and the lecture: The effects of multitasking in learning environments. *Journal of Computing in Higher Education, 15*(1), 46–64.

Ito, M., Horst, H. A., Bittanti, M., boyd, d., Herr-Stephenson, B., Lange, P. G., et al. (2008, November). *Living and learning with new media: Summary of findings from the digital youth project*. The John D. and Catherine T. MacArthur Foundation Reports on Digital Media and Learning.

Jenkins, H., Purushotma, R., Clinton, K., Weigel, M., & Robison, A. (2006, September). Confronting the challenges of participatory culture: Media education for the 21st century. White paper for the MacArthur Foundation.

Josephson Institute of Ethics (2006). 2006 Josephson Institute report card on the ethics of the American Youth: Part One, Integrity. Accessed August 24, 2009 at http://www.josephsoninstitute.org/pdf/ReportCard_press-release_2006-1013.pdf

Pettingill, L. (2008, April 03). *Engagement 2.0? How the new digital media can invigorate civic engagement*. Paper presented at the annual meeting of the MPSA Annual National Conference, Palmer House Hotel, Hilton, Chicago, IL. Accessed August 25, 2008 at http://www.allacademic.com/meta/p266567_index.html

Schouten, A. P., Valkenburg, P. M., & Peter, J. (2007). Precursors and underlying processes of adolescents' online self-disclosure: Developing and testing an 'internet-attribute-perception' model. *Media Psychology, 10*(2), 292–315.

Shirkey, C. (2009). *Here comes everybody: The power of organizing without organizations* (352 pp.). New York: Penguin Two.
Stephens, J. M., & Nicholson, H. (2008, October). Cases of incongruity: Exploring the divide between adolescents' beliefs and behavior related to academic dishonesty. *Educational Studies, 34*(4), 361–376.
Subrahmanyama, K., Greenfield, P., Kraut, R., & Gross, E. (2001). The impact of computer use on children's and adolescents' development. *Journal of Applied Developmental Psychology, 22*(1), 7–30.
Surowiecki, J. (2004). *The wisdom of crowds: Why the many are smarter than the few and how collective wisdom shapes business, economies, societies and nations* (320 pp.). New York: Doubleday.
Swearer, S., Espelage, D. L., & Napolitano, S. A. (2009). *Bullying prevention and intervention: Realistic strategies for schools. The Guilford practical intervention in the schools series.* Paperback. New York: Guilford Publications.
Tapscott, D. (2008). *Grown up digital: How the net generation is changing your world.* New York: McGraw Hill.
Twenge, J. M. (2006). *Generation me: Why today's young Americans are more confident, assertive, entitled and more miserable than ever before.* New York: Free Press.
Valkenburg, P. M., & Peter, J. (2007). Preadolescents' and adolescents' online communication and their closeness to friends. *Developmental Psychology, 43*(2), 267–277.
Weigel, M., Davis, K., James, C., & Gardner, H. (2009a). *New digital media, social institutions and the changing roles of youth.* Unpublished working paper, the Developing Minds and Digital Media Project. http://www.pzpublications.com/411.html
Weigel, M., & Gardner, H. (2009). The best of both literacies. *Educational Leadership, 66*(6), 38–41.
Weigel, M., Straughn, C., Gardner, H., & James, C. (2009b). *Multiple worlds: Adolescents, new digital media, and shifts in habits of mind.* Final report, the Developing Minds and Digital Media Project (in process).
Williams, B. T. (2007). Literacy & identity trust, betrayal, and authorship: Plagiarism and how we perceive students. *Journal of Adolescent & Adult Literacy, 51*(4), 350–354.
"When and where does bullying occur?" web page. (2009). U.S. Department of Education. First accessed August 31, 2009 at http://www.ed.gov/admins/lead/safety/training/bullying/bullying_pg3.html#where

Chapter 2
Group Cognition as a Foundation for the New Science of Learning

Gerry Stahl

College of Information Science & Technology, Drexel University, Philadelphia, PA 19104, USA,
e-mail: gerry@gerrystahl.net

"It takes a village to raise a child." This ancient African proverb reflects the direct bearing of social relations on learning. In pre-industrial society, the individual, family-of-origin, extended family, clan, tribe, village and culture blended into one another almost seamlessly. With the rise of capitalism, the individual was uprooted from its social ground and celebrated as a free spirit—in order to compete unencumbered on the labor market (Marx, 1867/1976). With globalization, the forces of production require information-processing tasks that exceed the capabilities of individual minds, necessitating the formation of well-coordinated knowledge-building teams. Thus, Hillary Clinton's use of the proverb (Clinton, 1996) not only looks back nostalgically to a romanticized past of homogeneous villages and neighborly towns but also reflects the realities of our increasingly interconnected global village.

The nature of learning is transformed—along with other aspects of human social existence—by societal upheavals. But our thinking about learning lags behind these changes. Furthermore, the evolution of social institutions is uneven, and past forms linger on in confusing mixtures. So our theories of learning, founded upon popular conceptions or "folk theories" (Bereiter, 2002), confuse individual, group and community characteristics, while still exalting the individual learner.

It is time for a new science of learning because, as Bob Dylan already announced to the youth social movement of the 1960s, "the times they are a-changin'." Foremost in our reconceptualization of learning must be a recognition not only of the role of the (post-modern) village, but also of the often ephemeral small groups that mediate between the tangible individual learner and the insubstantial communities within which the learner comes to participate. Imagine the gatherings of friends who listened to Dylan's lyrics together, forming cadre of the new age awakening around the world a half century ago. The interactions in these peer groups contributed to the new identities of the individuals involved as well as of their generation. Creative ways of thinking, making meaning and viewing the world emerged.

G. Stahl (✉)
College of Information Science & Technology, Drexel University, Philadelphia, PA 19104, USA
e-mail: gerry@gerrystahl.net

M.S. Khine, I.M. Saleh (eds.), *New Science of Learning*,
DOI 10.1007/978-1-4419-5716-0_2,

The scientific disciplines with their traditional methods are not equipped to analyze the interpenetration of such learning processes at the individual, small-group and community levels.

The Need for a New Science of Group Cognition

The idea of a science of group cognition was originally motivated by issues of software design for collaborative learning. The design of software to support group work, knowledge building and problem solving should be built on the foundation of an understanding of the nature of group interaction and group meaning making. However, previous research in computer-supported collaborative learning (CSCL) is mostly based on an ad hoc collection of incommensurable theories, which are not grounded in an explicit investigation of group interaction. What is needed is a science of group interaction focused on the group level of description to complement psychological theories of individuals and social theories of communities.

CSCL is fundamentally different from other domains of study in the learning sciences (Stahl, 2002). It takes as its subject matter *collaborative* learning, that is, what takes place when small groups of workers or students engage together in cognitive activities like problem solving or knowledge building (Koschmann, 1996; Stahl, 2006, chap. 11). On a theoretical level, CSCL is strongly oriented toward Vygotsky (1930/1978), who stressed that learning and other higher psychological processes originally take place socially, intersubjectively. Piaget (1985), too, pointed to intersubject processes like conflicting perspectives as a fundamental driver for creativity and cognitive development. Despite this powerful insight, even Vygotsky, Piaget and their followers generally maintain a psychological focus on the individual mind in their empirical studies and do not systematically investigate the intersubjective phenomena of small-group interaction.

A science of group interaction would aim to unpack what happens at the small-group unit of analysis (Stahl, 2004b). Thus, it would be particularly relevant for CSCL, but may not be as directly applicable to other forms of learning, where the individual or the community level predominates. As a science of the group, it would complement existing theories of acting, learning and cognition, to the extent that they focus either on the individual or the community or that they reduce group phenomena to these other levels of description.

In the chapters of *Studying Virtual Math Teams* (VMT) (Stahl, 2009) and of *Group Cognition* (Stahl, 2006), my colleagues and I have reviewed some of the research literature on small-group learning, on small-group processes and on collaborative mathematics. We have noticed that small-group studies generally look for quantitative correlations among variables—such as the effect of group size on measures of participation—rather than trying to observe group knowledge-building processes. Studies of small-group processes from psychology, sociology and other social sciences also tend to focus on non-cognitive aspects of group process or else attribute all cognition to the individual minds rather than to group processes. This was true of writings on cooperative learning in the 1970s and 1980s as well, e.g., Johnson and Johnson (1989).

There are some notable exceptions; in particular, we viewed Barron (2000, 2003), Cohen, Lotan, Abram, Scarloss, & Schultz (2002), Sawyer (2003), Schwartz (1995) as important preliminary studies of group cognition within the learning sciences. However, even theories in cognate fields that seem quite relevant to our concerns, like distributed cognition (Hutchins, 1996), actor-network theory (Latour, 2007), situated cognition (Lave & Wenger, 1991), ethnomethodology (Garfinkel, 1967) and activity theory (Engeström, 1987) adopt a different focus, generally on interaction of individuals with artifacts rather than among people, indicating an orientation to the larger community scale of social sciences.

Recent commentaries on situated cognition (Robbins & Aydede, 2009) and distributed cognition (Adams & Aizawa, 2008) frame the issues at the individual level, even reducing all cognitive phenomena to neural phenomena. At the other extreme, social theories focus on community phenomena like division of labor, apprenticeship training, linguistic structure and laboratory organization. For all its insight into small-group interaction and its analysis, even ethnomethodology maintains a sociological perspective, concerned with linguistic communities. Similarly, even when activity theory addresses the study of teams—in the most detail in Chapter 6 of Engeström (2008)—it is mostly concerned with the group's situation in the larger industrial and historical context; rather than analyzing how groups interactionally build knowledge, it paraphrases how they deal politically with organizational management issues. These theories provide valuable insights into group interaction, but none of them thematizes the small-group level as a domain of scientific study. As sciences, these are sciences of the individual or of the society, not of the collaborative group.

Each of the three levels of description is populated with a different set of phenomena and processes. For instance, *individuals* in a chat or threaded discussion interpret recent postings and design new postings in response; the *group* constructs, maintains and repairs a joint problem space and the *community* evolves its practices and institutions of social organization. The description of the individual level is the province of psychology; that of the community is the realm of sociology or anthropology; *the small-group level has no corresponding science.*

A science of group interaction would take its irreducible position between the psychological sciences of the individual and the social sciences of the community—much as biology analyzes phenomena that are influenced by both chemicals and organisms without being reducible to either. The science of group interaction would fill a lacuna in the multi-disciplinary work of the human sciences—including the learning sciences. This science would not be primarily oriented toward the "low level" processes of groups, such as mechanical or rote behaviors, but would be concerned with the accomplishment of creative intellectual tasks. Intellectual teamwork, knowledge work and knowledge-building activities would be prototypical objects of study. The focus would be on group cognition.

The bifurcation of the human sciences into individual and societal creates an irreconcilable opposition between individual creative freedom and restrictive social institutions. A science of group cognition would flesh out the concept of structuration, demonstrating with detailed analyses of empirical data how group interactions can mediate between individual behavior and social practices (Stahl, 2009, chap. 11).

The Construct of Group Cognition

The term *group cognition* does not signify an object or phenomenon to analyze like brain functions or social institutions (Stahl, 2004a). It is a proposal for a new science or focus within the human sciences. It hypothesizes

> When small groups engage in cooperative problem solving or collaborative knowledge building, there are distinctive processes of interest at the individual, small-group and community levels of analysis, which interact strongly with each other. The science of group cognition is the study of the processes at the small-group level.

The science of group cognition is a human science, not a predictive science like chemistry nor a predominantly quantitative one like physics. It deals with human meanings in unique situations, necessarily relying upon interpretive case studies and descriptions of inter-personal processes.

Processes at the small-group level are not necessarily reducible to processes of individual minds nor do they imply the existence of some sort of group mind. Rather, they may take place through the weaving of semantic and indexical references within a group discourse. The indexical field (Hanks, 1992) or joint problem space (Teasley & Roschelle, 1993) co-constructed through the sequential interaction of a group (Çakır, Zemel & Stahl, 2009) has the requisite complexity to constitute an irreducible cognitive act in its own right. Cognitive science broadened the definition of "cognition" beyond an activity of human minds in order to include artificial intelligence of computers. What counts as cognitive is now a matter of computational complexity. Anything that can compute well enough to play chess or prove theorems can be a cognitive agent—whether they are a person, computer or collaborative small group (Stahl, 2005).

Largely because of its linguistic form, the phrase "group cognition" is often taken to refer to some kind of physical or mental object. But it is a theoretical construct, not an object, as indicated by the hypothesis stated above. Commonsensical folk theories assume that we generally talk about physical objects. However, if one looks closely, most sciences deal with hypothesized entities, not physical objects; mental representations are a prime example at the individual level and cultural norms or social rules at the community level.

The group that engages in group cognition is not necessarily a set of physical people who interact together in the present moment. For example, group processes of problem solving, meaning making and knowledge building can be found in computer logs of chat or threaded discussion, where the people who contributed are now long gone. The interaction is captured and remains in the log. The interaction is not like physical interaction but can bring together references from the distant past or into the future. The interaction itself constitutes the discourse as a group interaction, by, for instance, addressing proposals to the group as a whole.

The Group Unit of Description

The theory of group cognition stakes out a new domain for exploration: the domain of group meaning-making processes. Importantly, it distinguishes this domain from the traditional domains of sciences of individual learning and of the development of social practices in communities. Virtually all discussions in the learning sciences have been ambiguous in their terminology when it comes to distinguishing the individual, group and cultural levels of description. My own writings have used the relevant terminology in a loose way. Therefore, it may be helpful to try to codify a set of terms for speaking at the three different levels (see Table 2.1).

Of course, some of this classification of terms is arbitrary and inconsistent with prior usage. In particular, the terms related to groups and cultures have not been

Table 2.1 Terminology distinguishing the three levels of description

Level of description	Individual	Group	Culture
Role	Person/student	Group participant	Community member
Adjective	Personal	Collaborative	Social
Object of analysis	Mind	Discourse	Culture
Unit of analysis	Mental representation	Utterance response pair	Mediating artifact
Form of knowledge	Subjective	Intersubjective	Cultural
Form of meaning	Interpretation	Shared understanding, joint meaning making, common ground	Domain vocabulary, artifacts, institutions, norms, rules
Learning activity	Learn	Build knowledge	Science
Way to accomplish cognitive tasks	Skill	Group method	Member method/social practice
Communication	Thought	Interaction	Membership
Mode of construction	Constructed	Co-constructed	Socially constructed
Context of cognitive task	Personal problem	Joint problem space	Problem domain
Context of activity	Embodiment	Situation	World
Referential system	Associations	Indexical field	Cultural world
Form of existence	Being there	Being with	Folk
Temporal structure	Subjective experiential internal time	Co-constructed shared temporality	Measurable objective time
Theory of cognition	Constructivist	Post-cognitive	Socio-cultural
Science	Cognitive and educational psychology	Group cognition	Sociology, anthropology, linguistics

kept distinct. Even Vygotsky, who pioneered in distinguishing the social from the individual, would use terms like "social" and "intersubjective" to apply to anything from a dyad to all of society. Within the learning sciences, "knowledge building" has been used at every level, resulting in confusion about whether classrooms are communities-of-practice, for instance. The characteristics of scientific research communities were projected onto classrooms, project groups and individuals without carefully distinguishing their different ways of building knowledge.

Such ambiguity of terminological usage even led to pseudo-problems, which can now be resolved by the theory of group cognition, showing how small groups mediate between the individual and the social phenomena. To take one example, the seeming irreconcilability of subjective and objective time can be bridged by considering how small groups co-construct their shared temporal reference system. Significantly, the co-construction can be observed in logs of interaction and analyzed in detail—which cannot be done for either the subjective sense of internal time (Husserl, 1917/1991) or the abstract dimension of scientifically measured time (Heidegger, 1927/1996).

The move from the individual to the group level of description entails an important philosophical step: from cognitivism to post-cognitivism. This step has its basis in philosophy (Hegel, 1807/1967; Heidegger, 1927/1996; Marx, 1867/1976; Merleau-Ponty, 1945/2002; Wittgenstein, 1953), in social science (Bourdieu, 1972/1995; Geertz, 1973; Giddens, 1984a) and in analytic methods of ethnomethodology and conversation analysis (Garfinkel, 1967; Livingston, 1987; Sacks, 1962/1995; Schegloff, 2007). Post-cognitive theories influential in CSCL and the learning sciences include the following: the critique of cognitivism (Dreyfus, 1972; Polanyi, 1962; Schön, 1983; Winograd & Flores, 1986), situated action (Suchman, 1987), situated learning (Lave & Wenger, 1991), activity theory (Engeström, 1987), distributed cognition (Hutchins, 1996), actor-network theory (Latour, 2007) and knowledge building (Scardamalia & Bereiter, 1996).

In two seminal statements of post-cognitivist theory, Hutchins has explicitly pointed to group cognitive phenomena: *Cognitive processes may be distributed across the members of a social group* (Hollan, Hutchins & Kirsh, 2000, p. 176). *The cognitive properties of groups are produced by interaction between structures internal to individuals and structures external to individuals* (Hutchins, 1996, p. 262). *The group performing the cognitive task may have cognitive properties that differ from the cognitive properties of any individual* (Hutchins, 1996, p. 176). However, rather than focusing on these group phenomena in detail, he analyzes socio-technical systems and the cognitive role of highly developed artifacts (airplane cockpits, ship navigation tools). Certainly, these artifacts have encapsulated past cultural knowledge (community cognition), and Hutchins' discussions of this are important. But in focusing on what is really the cultural level—characteristically for a cultural anthropologist—he does not analyze the cognitive meaning making of the group itself.

In general, the related literature on small groups and on post-cognitivist phenomena provide some nice studies of the pivotal role of small groups but do not account for this level of description theoretically. They are almost always in the final analysis based on either a psychological view of individuals or a sociological view of rules, etc. at the community level. None of them have a foundational conception of small groups as a distinct level. They confuse talk at the group level and at the social level, and they lack a developed account of the relationships between individual, group and community.

If we take group phenomena seriously as "first-class objects" of our theory, then we can study: interpersonal trains of thought, shared understandings of diagrams, joint problem conceptualizations, common references, coordination of problem-solving efforts, planning, deducing, designing, describing, problem solving, explaining, defining, generalizing, representing, remembering and reflecting as a group. In our studies, we will see that the group-cognitive accomplishments emerge from the network of meaningful references built up by, for instance, textual postings in online chat. We will see how the group and its cognitive accomplishments are enacted in situated interaction.

A Model of the New Science

Having motivated the development of a science of group cognition as future work, let us see how the VMT Project (Stahl, 2009) may have begun to prepare the way. Preparing for a new science requires three major undertakings:

(a) The domain of the science must not only be defined, it must be explored and captured in the form of a data corpus.
(b) Methods for analyzing the data must be selected, adapted, refined and mastered.
(c) Analytic findings must be organized in terms of a framework of theoretical conceptualizations.

The VMT Project at Drexel University has approached these tasks by

(a) creating a synchronous online service in which small groups of students engaged in problem-solving work in mathematics;
(b) conducting chat interaction analysis of a number of case studies from the data recorded in that service and
(c) conceptualizing some of the features of the small-group interactions that were observed.

The first step in the VMT design-based research process was to start simply and see what issues came up. We had seen in face-to-face case studies that there were problems with (i) recording and transcribing the verbal interaction, (ii) capturing the visual interaction and (iii) knowing about all the influences on the interaction. We decided to form groups of students who did not know each other and who only interacted through text chat. Students were recruited through the Math Forum at Drexel University, an established online resource center. We used AIM, AOL's

Instant Messaging system, which was freely available and was already familiar to many students. We included a researcher in the chat room with each small group of students. The facilitator told the students their math task, dealt with any technical difficulties, posted drawings from the students on a web page where they could be seen by all the students, notified the group when the session was over and saved an automatically generated log of the chat. In this way, we obtained a complete and objective log of the interaction, captured everything that the students shared on their computers and excluded any unknown influences from affecting the interaction.

The issue of including everything affecting the interaction is a subtle issue. Of course, the interaction is influenced by the life histories, personalities, previous knowledge and physical environment of each student. A student may have windows other than AIM open on the computer, including Internet browsers with math resources. A student may be working out math problems on a piece of paper next to the computer. Also, a student may leave the computer for some time to eat, listen to music, talk on the phone and so on without telling anyone in the chat. In such ways, we do not have information about everything involved in a particular student's online experience. We do not even know the student's gender or age. We do not know whether the student is shy or attractive, speaks with an accent or stutters. We do not know if the student usually gets good grades or likes math. We do not know what the student is thinking or feeling. We only know that the students are in an approximate age group and academic level—because we recruited them through teachers. However, the VMT Project is only concerned with analyzing the interaction at the *group unit of analysis*. Notice that the things that are unknown to us as researchers are also unknown to the student group as a whole. The students do not know specifics about each other's background or activities—except to the extent that these specifics are brought into the chat. If they are mentioned or referenced in the chat, then we can be aware of them to the same extent as are the other students.

The desire to generate a complete record for analysis of everything that was involved in a team's interaction often conflicted with the exploration of technology and service design options. For instance, we avoided speech-based interaction (VOIP, Skype, WIMBA) and support for individual work (e.g. whiteboards for individual students to sketch ideas privately), because these would complicate our review of the interactions. We tried to form teams that did not include people who knew each other or who could interact outside of the VMT environment.

In addition to personal influences, the chat is responsive to linguistic and cultural matters. Of course, both students and researchers must know English to understand the chats. In particular, forms of English that have evolved with text chat and cell-phone texting have introduced abbreviations, symbols and emoticons into the online language. The linguistic subculture of teenagers also shows up in the VMT chats. An interdisciplinary team of researchers comes in handy for interpreting the chats. In our case, the research team brought in experience with online youth lingo based on their backgrounds as Math Forum staff, teachers or parents.

The early AIM chats used simple math problems, taken from standardized math tests and Math Forum Problems-of-the-Week. One experiment to compare individual and group work used problems from a standardized multiple-choice college-admissions test. These problems had unique correct answers. While these provided a good starting point for our research, they were not well suited for collaborative knowledge building. Discourse around them was often confined to seeing who thought they knew the answer and then checking for correctness. For the VMT Spring Fests in 2005, 2006 and 2007, we moved to more involved math topics that could inspire several hours of joint inquiry.

Even with straightforward geometry problems, it became clear that students needed the ability to create, share and modify drawings within the VMT environment. We determined that we needed an object-oriented draw program, where geometric objects could be manipulated (unlike a pixel-based paint program). We contracted with the developers of ConcertChat to use and extend their text chat and shared whiteboard system, which is now available in Open Source. This system included a graphical referencing tool as well as social awareness and history features (Mühlpfordt & Stahl, 2007). In order to help students find desirable chat rooms and to preserve team findings for all to see, we developed the VMT Lobby and integrated a Wiki with the Lobby and chat rooms (Stahl, 2008). Gradually, the technology and the math topics became much more complicated in response to the needs that were revealed when we analyzed the trials of the earlier versions of the VMT service. As the system matured, other research groups began to use it for their own trials, with their own math topics, procedures, analytic methods or even new technical features. These groups included researchers from Singapore, Rutgers, Hawai'i, Romania and Carnegie-Mellon (Stahl, 2009).

The Nature of the New Science

The approach to chat interaction analysis that emerged in the VMT Project will now be discussed in terms of a number of issues (which correspond to general issues of most research methodologies, as indicated in parentheses):

Group Cognition in a Virtual Math Team (Research Question)

Learning—whether in a classroom, a workplace or a research lab—is not a simplistic memorization or storage of facts or propositions, as traditional folk theories had it. The term *learning* is a gloss for a broad range of phenomena, including the development of tacit skills, the ability to see things differently, access to resources for problem solving, the discursive facility to articulate in a new vocabulary, the power to explain, being able to produce arguments or the making of new connections among prior understandings (Stahl & Herrmann, 1999). We can distinguish these phenomena as taking place within individual minds, small-group interactions or communities of practice. The analysis of learning phenomena at these various levels of analysis requires different research methodologies, appropriate to corresponding research questions. The VMT Project was intended to explore the phenomena of group cognition and accordingly pursued the research question:

> How does learning take place in small groups, specifically in small groups of students discussing math in a text-based online environment? What are the distinctive mechanisms or processes that take place at the small-group level of description when the group is engaged in problem-solving or knowledge-building tasks?

While learning phenomena at the other levels of analysis are important and interact strongly with the group level, we have tried to isolate and make visible the small-group phenomena and to generate a corpus of data for which the analysis of the group-level interactions can be distinguished from the effects of the individual and community levels.

The methods used to gather and analyze one's data should be appropriate to one's research question. To support such research, one must generate and collect data that are adequate for the selected kinds of analysis. Because we were interested in the group processes that take place in VMT, we had to form teams that could meet together online. In the Spring Fests, students had to be able to come back together in the same teams on several subsequent occasions. The VMT environment had to be instrumented to record all messages and activities that were visible to the whole team in a way that could be played back by the analysts. The math problems and the feedback to the teams had to be designed to encourage the kinds of math discussions that would demonstrate processes of group cognition, such as formulating questions and proposals, coordinating drawings and textual narratives, checking proposed symbolic solutions, reviewing the team's work and so on. A sense of these desirable group activities and the skill of designing problems to encourage them had to develop gradually through the design-based research iterations.

Non-laboratory Experimental Design (Validity)

Of course, to isolate the small-group phenomena we do not literally isolate our subject groups from individuals and communities. The groups consist of students, who are individuals and who make individual contributions to the group discourse based on their individual readings of the discourse. In addition, the groups exist and operate within community and social contexts, drawing upon the language and practices of their math courses and of their teen and online subcultures. These are essential features of a real-world context and we would not wish to exclude them even to the extent possible by confining the interaction to a controlled laboratory setting. We want the students to feel that they are in a natural setting, interacting with peers. We do not try to restrict their use of language in any way (e.g., by providing standardized prompts for chat postings or scripting their interactions with each other).

We are designing a service that can be used by students and others under a broad array of scenarios: integrated with school class work, as extra-curricular activities, as social experiences for home-schooled students, as cross-national team adventures or simply as opportunities (in a largely math-phobic world) to discuss mathematics.

To get a sense of how such activities might work, we have to explore interactions in naturalistic settings, where the students feel like they are engaged in such activities rather than being laboratory subjects.

Data Collection at the Group Level of Description (Unit of Analysis)

Take the network of references in a chat-threading diagram (see Fig. 2.1) as an image of meaning making at the group level (Stahl, 2007). One could almost say that the figure consists entirely of contributions from individuals (the chat postings and whiteboard drawings) and resources from the math community, that everything exists on either the individual or community level, not on the group level. Yet, what is important in the figure is the network of densely interwoven references, more than the objects that are connected by them. This network exists at the group level. It mediates the individual and the community by forming the joint problem space (Sarmiento, 2007; Teasley & Roschelle, 1993), indexical ground (Hanks, 1992), referential network (Heidegger, 1927/1996) or situation (Suchman, 2007) within which meanings, significant objects and temporal relations are intersubjectively co-constructed (Dourish, 2001). On the individual level, these shared group meanings

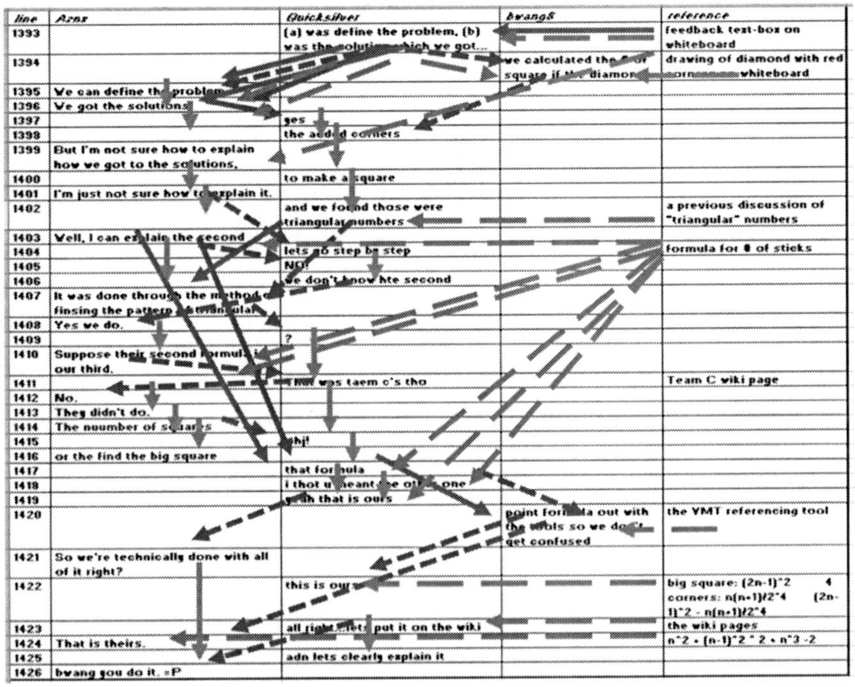

Fig. 2.1 The network of references in a chat log excerpt

are interpreted and influence the articulation of subsequent postings and actions. On the community level, the meanings may contribute to a continually evolving culture through structuration processes (Giddens, 1984b). The VMT Project is oriented toward the processes at the group unit of analysis, which build upon, connect and mediate the individual and community phenomena.

Elements from the individual and community levels only affect the group level if they are referenced in the team's interaction. Therefore, we do not need to gather data about the students or their communities other than what appears in the interaction record. We do not engage in surveys or interviews of the students or their teachers. For one thing, the design of the VMT Project prohibits access to these sources of data, because the students are only available during the chat sessions. External sources of data would be of great interest for other research questions having to do with individual learning or cultural changes, but for our research question, they are unnecessary and might even form a distraction or skew our analysis because it would cause our readings of the postings to be influenced by information that the group had not had.

By moving to the disembodied online realm of group cognition in VMT, it is easier for us to abandon the positivist metaphors of the mechanistic worldview. Not only is it clear that the virtual group does not exist in the form of a physical object with a persistent memory akin to a computer storage unit, but even the individual participants lack physical presence. All that exists when we observe the replayed chats are the traces of a discourse that took place years ago. Metaphors that might come naturally to an observer of live teamwork in a workplace or classroom—personalities, the group, learning, etc.—no longer seem fundamental. What exist immediately are the textual, graphical and symbolic inscriptions. These are significant fragments, whose meaning derives from the multi-layered references to each other and to the events, artifacts and agents of concern in the group discourse. This meaning is as fresh now as when the discourse originated and can still be read off the traces by an analyst, much as by the original participants. This shows that the meanings shared by the groups are not dependent upon mental states of the individual students—although the students may have had interpretations of those meanings in mind, external to the shared experience. The form of our data reinforces our focus on the level of the shared-group-meaning making as an interactional phenomenon rather than a psychological one.

Instrumentation and Data Formats (Objectivity)

It was noted above that when one videotapes small-group interactions a number of practical problems arise. Data on face-to-face classroom collaboration runs into issues of (i) recording and transcribing the verbal interaction, (ii) capturing the visual interaction and (iii) knowing about all the influences on the interaction. The data are in effect already partially interpreted by selective placement of the microphone and camera. It is further interpreted by transcription of the talk and is restricted by limited access to facial expressions and bodily gestures. Much happens in a classroom influencing the student teams that is not recorded.

The online setting of the VMT sessions eliminates many of these problems. As already described, the automatic computer log of the session captures everything that influences the group as a whole. This includes all the postings and whiteboard activity, along with their precise timing. They are captured at the same granularity as they are presented to the students. Chat postings appear as complete messages, defined by the author pressing the Enter button. Whiteboard textboxes appear as complete when the author clicks outside of the textbox. Whiteboard graphics appear gradually, as each graphical element is positioned by the author. Computer-generated social-awareness messages (when people enter or exit the chat room, begin or end typing, move a graphical object, etc.) are also accurately recorded. The precision of the log recording is assured because it consists of the original actions (as implemented by the computer software) with their timestamps. The original display to the students is generated from the server using the same log data that are used by the VMT Replayer. There is no selectivity or interpretation imposed by the analysts in the preparation of the full session record.

For our analysis of chats, we use a VMT Replayer. The Replayer is simply an extended version of the Java applet that serves as the chat/whiteboard room in the

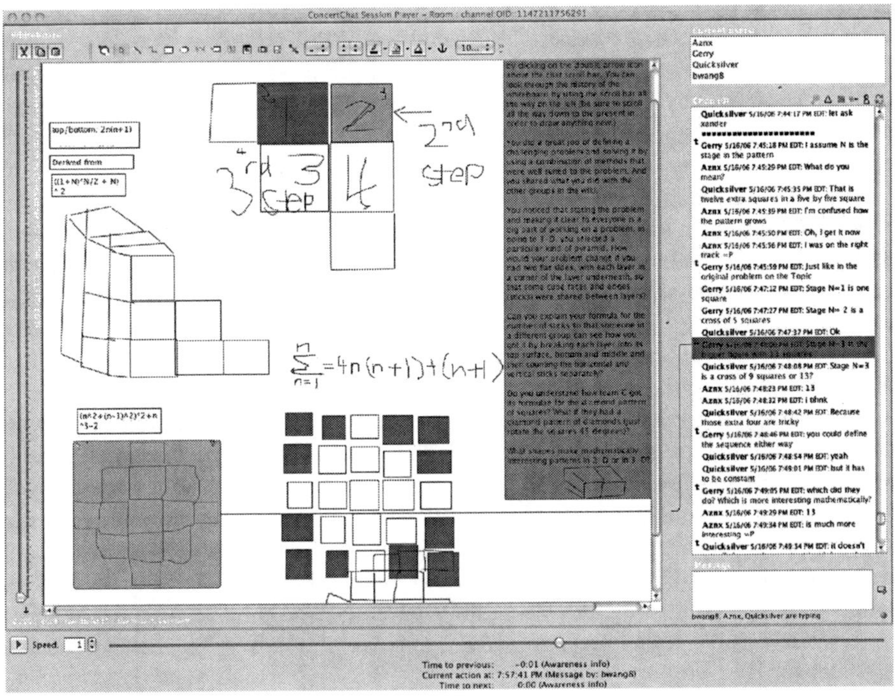

Fig. 2.2 The VMT Replayer

VMT environment. The reproduced chat room is separated by a thin line at the bottom from a VCR-like interface for replaying the session (see Fig. 2.2). The session can be replayed in real time or at any integral multiple of this speed. It can be started and stopped at any point. An analyst can drag the pointer along the timeline to scroll both the whiteboard history and the chat history in coordination. One can also step through the recorded actions, including all the awareness messages. In addition, spreadsheet logs can be automatically generated in various useful formats.

The data analyzed in the VMT Project is recorded with complete objectivity. There is no selectivity involved in the data generation, recording or collecting process. Furthermore, the complete recording can be made available to other researchers as a basis for their reviews of our analyses or the conducting of their own analyses. For instance, there have been multiple published analyses of the VMT data by other research groups following somewhat different research questions, theories and methods (Koschmann & Stahl, 2009; Stahl, 2009). While collaborative sessions are each unique and in principle impossible to reproduce, it is quite possible to reproduce the unfolding of a given session from the persistent, comprehensive and replayable record.

Collaborative Data Sessions (Reliability)

Interpretation of data in the VMT Project first begins with an attempt to describe what is happening in a chat session. We usually start this process with a data session (Jordan & Henderson, 1995) involving six to twelve researchers. A typical data session is initiated by a researcher who is interested in having a particular segment of a session log discussed by the group. Generally, the segment seems to be both confusing and interesting in terms of a particular research question.

For our data sessions, we sit around a circle of tables and project an image of the VMT Replayer onto a screen visible to everyone. Most of us have laptop computers displaying the same Replayer, so that we can scan back and forth in the segment privately to explore details of the interaction that we may want to bring to the attention of the group. The group might start by playing the segment once or twice in real time to get a feel for how it unfolds. Then we typically go back to the beginning and discuss each line of the chat sequentially in some detail.

The interpretation of a given chat line becomes a deeply collaborative process. Generally, one person will make a first stab at proposing a hypothesis about the interactional work that line is doing in the logged discourse. Others will respond with suggested refinements or alternatives to the proposal. The group may then engage in exploration of the timing of chat posts, references back to previous postings or events, etc. Eventually the data analysis will move on to consider how the student group took up the posting. An interesting interpretation may require the analysts to return to earlier ground and revise their tentative previous understandings (Stahl, 2009, chap. 10).

The boundaries of a segment must be considered as an important part of the analysis. When does the interaction of interest really get started and when is it resolved?

Often, increasingly deep analysis drives the starting point back as we realize that earlier occurrences were relevant.

It is usually first necessary to clarify the referential structure of the chat postings and how they relate to events in the whiteboard or to the comings and goings of participants. The threading of the chat postings provides the primary structure of the online, text-based discourse in much the same way that turn taking provides the core structure of spoken informal conversation. Because of the overlap in the typing of chat postings, it is sometimes tricky to figure out who is responding to what. Looking at the timestamps of posts and even at the timestamps of awareness messages about who is typing can provide evidence about what was visible when a posting was being typed. This can often suggest that a given post could or could not have been responding to a specific other post, although this is sometimes impossible to determine. When it is hard for the analyst to know the threading, it may have also been hard for most of the chat participants (other than the typist) to know; this may result in signs of trouble or misunderstandings in the subsequent chat.

The test of *correctness* of chat interaction analysis is not a matter of what was in individuals' minds but of how postings function in the interaction. Most of the multi-layered referencing takes place without conscious awareness by the participants, who are experts at semantic, syntactic and pragmatic referencing and can design utterances in response to local resources without formulating explicit plans (Suchman, 2007). Thus, inspection of participants' memories would not reveal causes. Of course, participants could retroactively tell stories about why they posted what they did, but these stories would be based upon their current (not original) interpretations using their linguistic competence and upon their response to their current (not original) situation, including their sense of what the person interviewing them wants to hear. Thus, interpretations by the participants are not in principle privileged over those of the analyst and others with the relevant interpretive competence (Gadamer, 1960/1988). The conscious memories that a participant may have of the interaction are, according to Vygotsky's theory, just more interaction—but this time sub-vocal self-talk; if they were brought into the analysis, they would be in need of interpretation just as much as the original discourse.

Since our research question involves the group as the unit of analysis, we do not raise questions in the data session about what one student or another may have been doing, thinking or feeling as an individual. Rather, we ask what a given posting is doing interactionally within the group process, how it responds to and takes up other posts and what opportunities it opens for future posts. We look at how a post is situated in the sequential structure of the group discourse, in the evolving social order and in the team's meaning making. What is this posting doing here and now in the referential network? Why is it "designed to be read" (Livingston, 1995) in just this way? How else could it have been phrased and why would that not have achieved the same effect in the group discourse?

We also look at how a given posting *positions* (Harré & Moghaddam, 2003) both the author and the readers in certain ways. We do not attribute constant personalities or fixed roles to the individuals, but rather look at how the group is organized through the details of the discourse. Perhaps directing a question toward another student will temporarily bestow upon him/her a form of *situated expertise* (Zhou, Zemel, & Stahl, 2008) such that he/she is expected to provide an extended sequence of *expository* postings (Mercer & Wegerif, 1999).

The discussion during a data session can be quite unorderly. Different people see different possible understandings of the log and propose alternative analyses. Generally, discussion of a particular posting continues until a consensus is tentatively established or someone agrees to look into the matter further and come back next week with an analysis. Notes are often taken on the data session's findings, but the productive result of the discussion most often occurs when one researcher is inspired to write about it in a conference paper or dissertation section. When ideas are taken up this way, the author will usually bring the more developed analysis back for a subsequent data session and circulate the paper.

In coding analysis, it is conventional to train two people to code some of the same log units and to compare their results to produce an inter-rater reliability measure (Strijbos & Stahl, 2007). In our chat interaction analysis, we do not pretend that the log can be unproblematically partitioned into distinct units, which can be uniquely assigned to a small number of unambiguous codes. Rather, most interesting group discourse segments have a complex network of interwoven references. The analysis of such log segments requires a sophisticated human understanding of semantics, interpersonal dynamics, mathematics, argumentation and so on. Much is ultimately ambiguous and can be comprehended in multiple ways—sometimes the chat participants were intentionally ambiguous. At the same time, it is quite possible for analysts to make mistakes and to propose analyses that can be shown to be in error. To attain a reasonable level of reliability of our analyses, we make heavy use of data sessions. This ensures that a number of experienced researchers agree on the analyses that emerge from the data sessions. In addition, we try to provide logs—or even the entire session data with the Replayer—in our papers so that readers of our analyses can judge for themselves the interpretations that are necessarily part of chat analysis.

Describing Group Practices (Generalizability)

The research question that drives the VMT Project is: What are the distinctive mechanisms or processes that take place at the small-group level of description when the group is engaged in problem-solving or knowledge-building tasks? Therefore, we are interested in describing the inter-personal practices of the groups that interact in the VMT environment. There are, of course, many models and theories in the learning sciences describing the psychological practices of *individuals* involved in learning. At the opposite extreme, Lave and Wenger's (1991) theory of situated learning describes social practices of *communities* of practice, whereby a community renews itself by moving newcomers into increasingly central forms of legitimate peripheral participation. However, there are few descriptions specifically of how *small groups* engage in learning practices.

Vygotsky (1930/1978) argued that learning takes place inter-subjectively (in dyads or groups) before it takes place intra-subjectively (by individuals). For instance, in his analysis of the infant and mother (p. 56), he outlines the process through which an infant's unsuccessful grasping at some object becomes established by the mother–child dyad as a pointing at the object. This shared practice of pointing subsequently becomes ritualized by the dyad (LeBaron & Streeck, 2000) and then mediated and "internalized" by the infant as a pointing gesture. The pointing gesture—as a foundational form of deictic reference—is a skill of the young child, which he can use for selecting objects in his world and learning about them. The gesture is understood by his mother because it was intersubjectively established with her. In this prototypical example, Vygotsky describes learning as an inter-subjective or small-group practice of a dyad.

While we can imagine that Vygotsky's description is based on a concrete interaction of a specific infant and mother in a particular time and place, the pointing gesture that he analyzed is ubiquitous in human culture. In this sense, the analysis of a unique interaction can provide a generalizable finding. The science of ethnomethodology (the study of the methods used by people) (Garfinkel, 1967) is based on the fact that people in a given culture or linguistic community share a vast repertoire of social practices for accomplishing their mundane tasks. It is only because we share and understand this stock of practices that we can so quickly interpret each other's verbal and gestural actions, even in novel variations under unfamiliar circumstances. The analysis of unique case studies can result in the description of social practices that are generalizable (Maxwell, 2004). The methods developed in specific situated encounters are likely to be typical of a broad range of cases under similar conditions.

In our data sessions, we find the same kinds of moves occurring in case after case that we analyze. On the one hand, group methods are extremely sensitive to changes in the environment, such as differences in features and affordances of the communication media. On the other hand, groups of people tend to adapt widespread methods of interaction to changing circumstances in similar ways—to support general human and social needs. Group methods are not arbitrary but draw on rich cultural stocks of shared behavior and adapt the outward appearances in order to maintain the underlying structure under different conditions.

By describing the structure of group methods in detailed case studies, we can characterize general methods of group behavior, group learning or group cognition. Findings from analyses of case studies can lead to the proposal of theoretical categories, conceptualizations, structures or principles—in short, to a science of group interaction.

The Foundational Role of Group Cognition

As discussed above, students in VMT are active as individuals, as group participants and as community members. They each engage in their own, private *individual* activities, such as reading, interpreting, reflecting upon and typing chat messages.

Their typed messages also function as *group* actions, contributing to the on-going problem solving of the team. Viewed as *community* events, the chats participate in the socialization process of the society, through which the students become increasingly skilled members of the community of mathematically literate citizens.

A thesis of the theory of group cognition is "Small groups are the engines of knowledge building. The knowing that groups build up in manifold forms is what becomes internalized by their members as individual learning and externalized in their communities as certifiable knowledge" (Stahl, 2006, p. 16). Despite their centrality, small groups have not been theorized or studied extensively.

Some small-group literature has been produced from either the methodological perspective of psychology or that of sociology, primarily since World War II. Traumatized by the mass-culture horrors of fascism and by extreme forms of mentalist pseudo-science, these predominantly behaviorist studies focused on the negative aspects of "group think" and caricatured the notion of "group mind"—which had a well-respected history before the rise of positivism (Wegner, 1986). These studies miss the pivotal role of small groups in processes of learning.

More recent theories like distributed cognition, situated action or activity theory actually conduct case studies of small-group interaction, but they do not theorize the small group as their unit of analysis and therefore they do not produce descriptions of small-group methods as such. Even Hutchins (1996), in studying distributed cognition in the wild, does not thematize the interpersonal interactions but focuses on the cognitive unit of analysis, simply broadening it to include the external computational and physical representational artifacts that an individual worker uses. Furthermore, the cognitive accomplishments he studies are fundamentally routine, well scripted procedures that do not involve creative solutions to ill-structured problems; the coordination of the navigational team is fixed by naval protocol, not co-constructed through the interaction, although it must still be enacted in concrete situations.

The VMT studies provide a model for describing the small-group methods as distinct from individual behaviors and community practices. They look at rich interactions in groups larger than dyads, where individual identities play a smaller role. They analyze group efforts in high-order cognition such as mathematical problem solving and reflection on the group problem-solving trajectory. They investigate groups that meet exclusively online, where the familiar visual, physical and aural modes of communication are unavailable and where communication is mediated by designed technological environments.

Understanding how a collaborative group as a whole constructs knowledge through joint activity in a CSCL setting is what sets the science of group cognition apart from other approaches to the study of learning. Successful collaboration involves not only the incorporation of contributions of individuals into the group discourse but also the effort to make sure that participating individuals understand what is taking place at the group level. The contributions of individuals to the group and of understandings from the group to the individuals cannot be studied by analyses at the individual unit of analysis but only by studying the interactions at the group level. The group knowledge-construction process synthesizes innumerable resources from language, culture, the group's own history, individual backgrounds, relevant contexts and the sequential unfolding of the group discourse in which the individuals participate. Although the group process is dependent upon contributions and understanding of individuals, their individual cognition is essentially situated in the group process. Group cognition is the science of cognitive processes at the group unit of analysis. These group processes—such as the sequential flow of proposals, questioning, building common ground, maintaining a joint problem space, establishing intersubjective meanings, positioning actors in evolving roles, building knowledge collaboratively and solving problems together—are not analyzable as individual behaviors.

There is a scientific lacuna within the learning sciences between sciences of the individual and sciences of communities. There are important cognitive achievements at the small-group level of description, which should be studied by a science of groups. Online small groups are becoming increasingly possible and important in the global networked world, and a post-cognitive science of virtual groups could help the design of collaborative software for working and learning. It could provide an effective foundation for the new science of learning.

References

Adams, F., & Aizawa, K. (2008). *The bounds of cognition*. Malden, MA: Blackwell.

Barron, B. (2000). Achieving coordination in collaborative problem-solving groups. *Journal of the Learning Sciences*, *9*(4), 403–436.

Barron, B. (2003). When smart groups fail. *The Journal of the Learning Sciences*, *12*(3), 307–359.

Bereiter, C. (2002). *Education and mind in the knowledge age*. Hillsdale, NJ: Lawrence Erlbaum Associates.

Bourdieu, P. (1972/1995). *Outline of a theory of practice* (R. Nice, Trans.). Cambridge, UK: Cambridge University Press.

Çakır, M. P., Zemel, A., & Stahl, G. (2009). The joint organization of interaction within a multimodal CSCL medium. *International Journal of Computer-Supported Collaborative Learning*, *4*(2), 115–149. Available at http://dx.doi.org/10.1007/s11412-009-9061-0

Clinton, H. (1996). *It takes a village: And other lessons children teach us*. New York: Simon & Shuster.

Cohen, E. G., Lotan, R. A., Abram, P. L., Scarloss, B. A., & Schultz, S. E. (2002). Can groups learn? *Teachers College Record*, *104*(6), 1045–1068.

Dourish, P. (2001). *Where the action is: The foundations of embodied interaction*. Cambridge, MA: MIT Press.

Dreyfus, H. (1972). *What computers cannot do*. New York: Harper and Row.

Engeström, Y. (1987). *Learning by expanding: An activity-theoretical approach to developmental research*. Helsinki, Finland: Orienta-Kosultit Oy.

Engeström, Y. (2008). *From teams to knots*. Cambridge, UK: Cambridge University Press.

Gadamer, H.-G. (1960/1988). *Truth and method*. New York: Crossroads.

Garfinkel, H. (1967). *Studies in ethnomethodology*. Englewood Cliffs, NJ: Prentice-Hall.

Geertz, C. (1973). *The interpretation of cultures*. New York: Basic Books.

Giddens, A. (1984a). Elements of the theory of structuration. *The constitution of society* (pp. 1–40). Berkeley, CA: University of California Press.

Giddens, A. (1984b). *The constitution of society. Outline of the theory of structuration*. Berkeley, CA: University of California Press.

Hanks, W. (1992). The indexical ground of deictic reference. In C. Goodwin & A. Duranti (Eds.), *Rethinking context: Language as an interactive phenomenon*. Cambridge, UK: Cambridge University Press.

Harré, R., & Moghaddam, F. (2003). Introduction: The self and others in traditional psychology and in positioning theory. In R. Harré & F. Moghaddam (Eds.), *The self and others* (pp. 1–11). Westport, CT: Praeger.

Hegel, G. W. F. (1807/1967). *Phenomenology of spirit* (J. B. Baillie, Trans.). New York: Harper & Row.

Heidegger, M. (1927/1996). *Being and time: A translation of Sein und Zeit* (J. Stambaugh, Trans.). Albany, NY: SUNY Press.

Hollan, J., Hutchins, E., & Kirsh, D. (2000). Distributed cognition: Toward a new foundation of human-computer interaction research. *ACM Transactions on Computer-Human Interaction, 7*(2), 174–196.

Husserl, E. (1917/1991). *On the phenomenology of internal time (1893–1917)* (J. Brough, Trans.). Dodrecht, the Netherlands: Kluwer.

Hutchins, E. (1996). *Cognition in the wild*. Cambridge, MA: MIT Press.

Johnson, D. W., & Johnson, R. T. (1989). *Cooperation and competition: Theory and research*. Edina, MN: Interaction Book Company.

Jordan, B., & Henderson, A. (1995). Interaction analysis: Foundations and practice. *Journal of the Learning Sciences, 4*(1), 39–103. Available at http://lrs.ed.uiuc.edu/students/c-merkel/document4.HTM

Koschmann, T. (1996). Paradigm shifts and instructional technology. In T. Koschmann (Ed.), *CSCL: Theory and practice of an emerging paradigm* (pp. 1–23). Mahwah, NJ: Lawrence Erlbaum.

Koschmann, T., & Stahl, G. (2009 of Conference). *Symposium: Examining practices of computer-mediated learning*. Paper presented at the international conference on Computer Support for Collaborative Learning (CSCL 2009), Rhodes, Greece. Available at http://GerryStahl.net/pub/cscl2009koschmann.pdf

Latour, B. (2007). *Reassembling the social: An introduction to actor-network-theory*. Cambridge, UK: Cambridge University Press.

Lave, J., & Wenger, E. (1991). *Situated learning: Legitimate peripheral participation*. Cambridge, UK: Cambridge University Press.

LeBaron, C., & Streeck, J. (2000). Gesture, knowledge and the world. In D. McNeill (Ed.), *Language and gesture* (pp. 118–138). Cambridge, UK: Cambridge University Press.

Livingston, E. (1987). *Making sense of ethnomethodology*. London, UK: Routledge & Kegan Paul.

Livingston, E. (1995). *An anthropology of reading*. Bloomington: IN: Indiana University Press.

Marx, K. (1867/1976). *Capital* (B. Fowkes, Trans. Vol. I). New York: Vintage.

Maxwell, J. (2004). Causal explanation, qualitative research, and scientific inquiry in education. *Educational Researcher, 33*(2), 3–11. Available at http://www.aera.net/pubs/er/pdf/vol33_02/2026-02_pp03-11.pdf

Mercer, N., & Wegerif, R. (1999). Is "Exploratory talk" Productive talk? In K. Littleton & P. Light (Eds.), *Learning with computers: Analyzing productive interaction* (pp. 79–101). New York: Routledge.

Merleau-Ponty, M. (1945/2002). *The phenomenology of perception* (C. Smith, Trans. 2 ed.). New York: Routledge.

Mühlpfordt, M., & Stahl, G. (2007). The integration of synchronous communication across dual interaction spaces. In C. Chinn, G. Erkens & S. Puntambekar (Eds.), *The proceedings of CSCL 2007: Of mice, minds, and society (CSCL 2007)*. New Brunswick, NJ. Available at http://GerryStahl.net/vmtwiki/martin.pdf

Piaget, J. (1985). *The equilibrium of cognitive structures: The central problem of intellectual development*. Chicago, IL: Chicago University Press.

Polanyi, M. (1962). *Personal knowledge*. London, UK: Routledge & Kegan Paul.

Robbins, P., & Aydede, M. (Eds.). (2009). *The Cambridge handbook of situated cognition*. Cambridge, UK: Cambridge University Press.

Sacks, H. (1962/1995). *Lectures on conversation*. Oxford, UK: Blackwell.

Sarmiento, J. (2007). *Bridging: Interactional mechanisms used by online groups to sustain knowledge building over time*. Paper presented at the international conference on Computer-Supported Collaborative Learning (CSCL '07), New Brunswick, NJ. Available at http://GerryStahl.net/vmtwiki/johann.pdf

Sawyer, R. K. (2003). *Group creativity: Music, theater, collaboration*. Mahwah, NJ: Lawrence Erlbaum.

Scardamalia, M., & Bereiter, C. (1996). Computer support for knowledge-building communities. In T. Koschmann (Ed.), *CSCL: Theory and practice of an emerging paradigm* (pp. 249–268). Hillsdale, NJ: Lawrence Erlbaum Associates.

Schegloff, E. A. (2007). *Sequence organization in interaction: A primer in conversation analysis*. Cambridge, UK: Cambridge University Press.

Schwartz, D. (1995). The emergence of abstract representations in dyad problem solving. *Journal of the Learning Sciences*, *4*(3), 321–354.

Schön, D. A. (1983). *The reflective practitioner: How professionals think in action*. New York: Basic Books.

Stahl, G. (2002). Rediscovering CSCL. In T. Koschmann, R. Hall & N. Miyake (Eds.), *CSCL 2: Carrying forward the conversation* (pp. 169–181). Hillsdale, NJ: Lawrence Erlbaum Associates. Available at http://GerryStahl.net/cscl/papers/ch01.pdf

Stahl, G. (2004a). Mediation of group cognition. *SigGroup Bulletin*, *24*(4), 13–17. Available at http://GerryStahl.net/publications/journals/Mediation%20of%20Group%20Cognition.pdf

Stahl, G. (2004b). *Thinking at the group unit of analysis*. Paper presented at the CSCL SIG Symposium of the European Union Kaleidoscope Network of Excellence (KAL '04), Lausanne, Switzerland. Available at http://GerryStahl.net/pub/kal2004.pdf & http://GerryStahl.net/pub/kal2004ppt.pdf

Stahl, G. (2005). *Group cognition: The collaborative locus of agency in CSCL*. Paper presented at the international conference on Computer Support for Collaborative Learning (CSCL '05), Taipei, Taiwan. Proceedings, pp. 632–640. Lawrence Erlbaum Associates. Available at http://GerryStahl.net/pub/cscl2005.pdf & http://GerryStahl.net/pub/cscl2005ppt.pdf

Stahl, G. (2006). *Group cognition: Computer support for building collaborative knowledge*. Cambridge, MA: MIT Press. Available at http://GerryStahl.net/mit/

Stahl, G. (2007). *Meaning making in CSCL: Conditions and preconditions for cognitive processes by groups*. Paper presented at the international conference on Computer-Supported Collaborative Learning (CSCL '07), New Brunswick, NJ: ISLS. Available at http://GerryStahl.net/pub/cscl07.pdf

Stahl, G. (2008). *Integrating a wiki into support for group cognition*. Paper presented at the International Conference of the Learning Sciences (ICLS 2008), Utrecht, the Netherlands. Available at http://GerryStahl.net/pub/icls2008wiki.pdf

Stahl, G. (2009). *Studying virtual math teams*. New York: Springer. Available at http://GerryStahl.net/vmt/book

Stahl, G., & Herrmann, T. (1999). *Intertwining perspectives and negotiation*. Paper presented at the ACM SIGGROUP Conference on Supporting Group Work (Group '99), Phoenix, AZ. Proceedings pp. 316–324. Available at http://GerryStahl.net/cscl/papers/ch07.pdf

Strijbos, J. W., & Stahl, G. (2007). Methodological issues in developing a multi-dimensional coding procedure for small group chat communication. *Learning & Instruction. Special Issue on Measurement Challenges in Collaborative Learning Research*, *17*(4), 394–404. Available at http://GerryStahl.net/vmtwiki/jw.pdf

Suchman, L. (1987). *Plans and situated actions: The problem of human-machine communication*. Cambridge, UK: Cambridge University Press.

Suchman, L. A. (2007). *Human-machine reconfigurations: Plans and situated actions* (2nd ed.). Cambridge, UK: Cambridge University Press.

Teasley, S. D., & Roschelle, J. (1993). Constructing a joint problem space: The computer as a tool for sharing knowledge. In S. P. Lajoie & S. J. Derry (Eds.), *Computers as cognitive tools* (pp. 229–258). Mahwah, NJ: Lawrence Erlbaum Associates, Inc.

Vygotsky, L. (1930/1978). *Mind in society*. Cambridge, MA: Harvard University Press.

Wegner, D. (1986). Transactive memory: A contemporary analysis of the group mind. In B. Mullen & G. R. Goethals (Eds.), *Theories of group behavior* (pp. 185–208). New York: Springer Verlag.

Winograd, T., & Flores, F. (1986). *Understanding computers and cognition: A new foundation of design*. Reading, MA: Addison-Wesley.

Wittgenstein, L. (1953). *Philosophical investigations*. New York: Macmillan.

Zhou, N., Zemel, A., & Stahl, G. (2008). *Questioning and responding in online small groups engaged in collaborative math problem solving*. Paper presented at the International Conference of the Learning Sciences (ICLS 2008), Utrecht, Netherlands. Available at http://GerryStahl.net/pub/icls2008nan.pdf

Chapter 3
An Embodied/Grounded Cognition Perspective on Educational Technology

John B. Black

Teachers College, Columbia University, New York, NY 10027, USA

Students typically learn in school in ways that are disconnected to their own experience, and so they learn to know about subject areas rather than have a feel for them. Thus, what they learn in school becomes stored in memory as abstract symbolic knowledge that is not connected to their experience in the world, so they do not think to apply it in their everyday life (or other contexts) when it might be appropriate. For example, students learn physics formulas in school that they practice applying to problems in their physics courses, but they do not understand the implications of these formulas for how they reason about the physical dynamics of the real world. Similarly they learn formulas for solving statistics problems in school but that does not affect the way they reason about uncertain or statistical phenomenon that they encounter in other contexts. The problem is that the students do not have a body of perceptual experiences that they draw upon when learning this new subject matter for they only learn about the subject matter rather than also develop a feel so it. Recent basic cognitive research in perceptually grounded or embodied cognition provides a framework for understanding this distinction and for designing educational environments that foster this deeper level of understanding.

Grounded/Embodied Cognition

Perceptually grounded or embodied cognition is an increasingly prominent area of basic cognitive research (Barsalou, 2008). This perspective says that a full understanding of something involves being able to create a mental perceptual simulation of it when retrieving the information or reasoning about it. Both behavior and neuroimaging experiments have shown that many phenomena that were thought to be purely symbolic actually show perceptual effects. For example, property verification (e.g., retrieving the fact that a horse has a mane) was thought to involve a search from a concept node (horse) to a property node (mane) in a symbolic propositional network and thus the time to answer and errors were determined by how many

J.B. Black (✉)
Teachers College, Columbia University, New York, NY 10027, USA
e-mail: black@tc.edu

M.S. Khine, I.M. Saleh (eds.), *New Science of Learning*,
DOI 10.1007/978-1-4419-5716-0_3,

network links needed to be searched and how many other distracting links were present. However, grounded cognition research has shown that perceptual variables like size (e.g., the bigger the property to be retrieved the faster) affect verification times and errors (Solomon & Barsalou, 2004). Also, neuroimaging results (e.g., fMRI) show that perceptual areas of the brain (involving shape, color, size, sound and touch) also become active during this task, not just the symbolic areas (e.g., Martin, 2007). Thus, if one is familiar with horses and manes then doing even this simple property verification involves a perceptual simulation.

Even text comprehension shows spatial (perceptual) effects. For example a switch in point of view in a narrative creates longer reading times and more memory errors because the reader has to switch the spatial perspective from which they are viewing the narrative scene in their imagination. For example

> John was working in the front yard then he went inside

is read faster than with a one word change that switches the point of view (Bower, Black, & Turner, 1979):

> John was working in the front yard then he came inside.

Thus, when reading even this brief sentence the reader is forming a simple spatial layout of the scene being described and imaging an actor moving around it—i.e., this is a simple perceptual simulation.

Glenberg, Gutierrez, Levin, Japuntich and Kaschak (2004) have shown how to teach reading comprehension using a grounded cognition approach. Specifically, these studies found that having 2nd grade students act out stories about farms using farmers, workers, animals and objects increased their understanding and memory of the stories they read. Further, if they also imagined these actions for another related story after acting it out with toys, they seemed to acquire the skill of forming the imaginary world of the story (Black, 2007) when reading other stories, and this increased their understanding and memory of these stories. Thus, this grounded cognition approach increased the students' reading comprehension. These studies also seem to indicate that there are three steps involved in a grounded cognition approach to learning something:

1. Have a perceptually grounded experience
2. Learn to imagine the perceptually grounded experience
3. Imagine the experience when learning from symbolic materials

Gaining Embodied/Grounded Experiences from Video Games

Hammer and Black (2009) showed that video games can serve to create perceptually grounded experiences that can serve to increase later symbolic learning and understanding. Specifically, they found that expert players of the *Civilization* historical simulation game did not show any superior knowledge of the history covered in the game compared to expert players of another academically oriented game (*Sim City*), so they did not seem to learn much about history directly from playing the game.

However, when given a college textbook chapter about a related historical topic that was not covered in the game they were able to learn much more from that chapter than the expert players of the comparison game—and they were able to learn facts, images, procedures and systems knowledge better. Thus, the grounding experiences of grappling with historical issues in the Civilization historical simulation game prepared the expert players for future learning from the formal symbolic task of reading a college history textbook chapter (Bransford & Schwartz, 2001). This result also fits with Dewey's (1938) stress on the importance of having related experiences when trying to learn something new; these experiences provide the needed perceptual grounding need for the symbolic learning to make sense.

Similarly, Ahn (2007) found that college business school students' experiences in playing an entrepreneurship business game yielded the best learning and understanding when combined with a more formal symbolic learning experience that involved contemplating the strategies used in the game and relating those strategies to background readings in the course. Here again, the experiences provided from playing the entrepreneurship business game (several times in this case) provided the grounding needed to learn more from the college course readings.

Learning from Graphical Computer Simulations with Movement and Animation

In learning a mental model for a system, students need to learn and understand the component functional relations that each describe now as a system entity changes as a function of changes in another system entity. Chan and Black (2006) found that graphic computer simulations involving movement and animation were a good way to learn these functional relations between system entities. For example, the roller coaster graphical computer simulation shown in Fig. 3.1 allows students to learn the functional relation between the height of the roller coaster cars in the gravity field and the kinetic and potential energy by having students move the slider at the bottom of the screen to move the roller coaster cars along the peaks and valleys of the track and simultaneously see the resulting changes in kinetic and potential energy shown in the animation of the bar graph changes. Thus one variable (the height in the gravity field) is directly manipulated by movement (of the student's hand and mouse) and the other two variables (kinetic and potential energy) are shown by animated changes in the bar graph.

The direct manipulation animation version of the simulation was compared to other versions involving just text, text and pictures (screen shots of the simulation), and a "slide show" showing screen shots, and the more grounded/embodied direct manipulation animation version yielded the best memory, problem solving and transfer problem solving to another context. Further research has shown that for simple systems (e.g., a swing instead of a roller coaster), text and text-plus-diagrams are sufficient for 6th grade students to master the system, but 5th grade students do better with the direct manipulation animation. For more complex systems (e.g., a pole vault instead of a roller coaster) both 5th and 6th grade students needed a direct

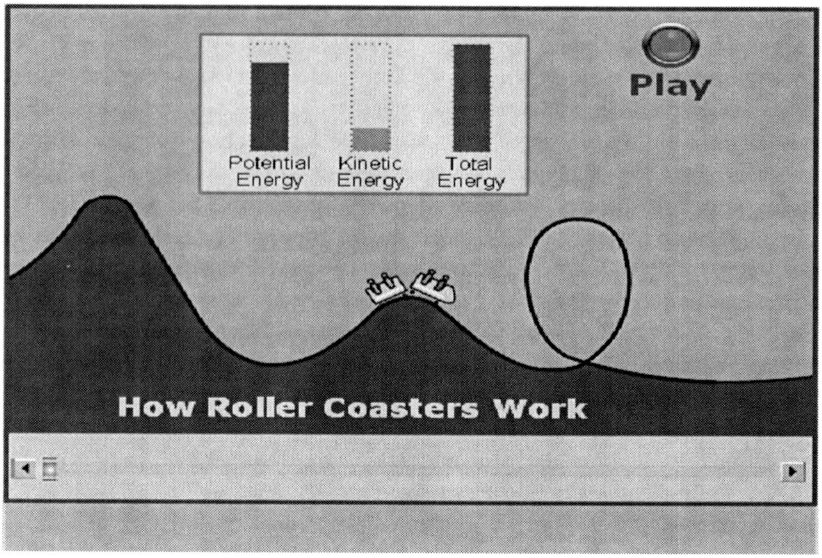

Fig. 3.1 Roller coaster graphic simulation with movement (mouse and slider) and animation

manipulation animation for best memory, problem solving and transfer. It seems likely that the students are learning to imagine perceptual simulations in all cases (although one would need a neuroimaging study to know for sure, and such studies are planned) but that the learning materials needed to enable this imagined simulation vary depending on the complexity of the system and the cognitive development (grade level in this case) of the students.

Han and her colleagues (Han, Black, Paley, & Hallman, 2009; Hallman, Paley, Han, & Black, 2009) have enhanced the movement part of these interactive graphical simulations by adding force feedback to the movement using simulations such as that shown in Fig. 3.2. Here the student moves the gears shown in the middle by moving the joy stick shown in the lower left, and the bar graphs show the input and output force levels for the two gears; here again allowing the student to directly manipulate the gears enhances the students' memory and problem solving, and enriching the movement experience by adding force feedback increases the students' performance even more. Thus the richer the perceptual experience, and therefore the mental perceptual simulation acquired, the better the student learning and understanding.

McVeigh, Black, and Flimlin (2008) showed that even when the learning experience is fully embodied using hands-on activities adding these kinds of interactive graphic simulations can enhance student learning and understanding. Here the students learn about water chemistry and fish and plant biological systems by having a small fish tank in their classrooms while also observing a larger fish tank (using a video link over the internet) in a large remote greenhouse located at a local university. Thus the students can directly alter the water chemistry in the classroom fish

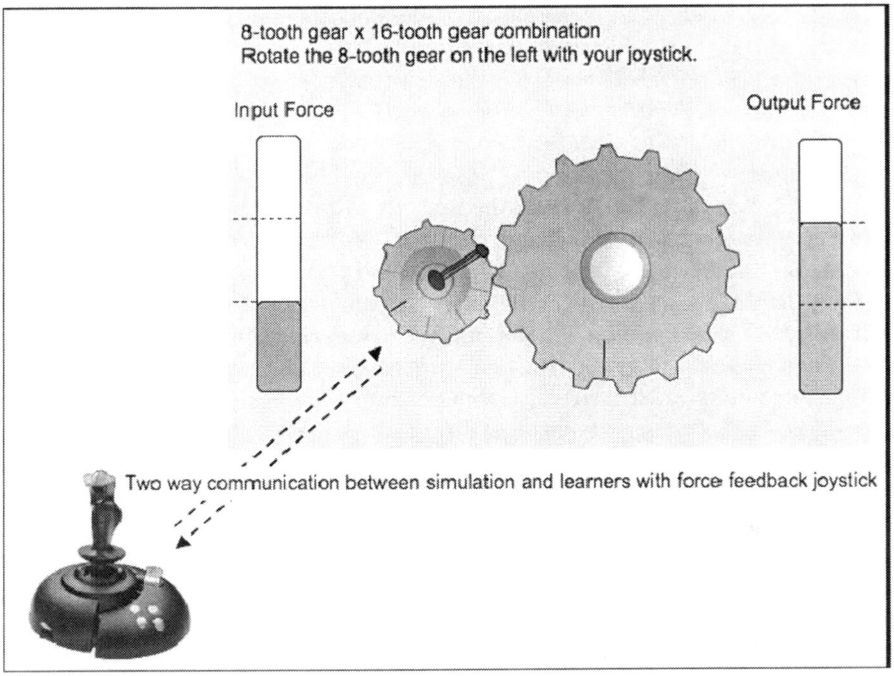

Fig. 3.2 Gear graphic simulation with movement (joystick and gears) and animation with force feedback (joystick)

tank and also in the large remote one by a controlling robot arm. Thus, this situation provides considerable embodiment, but student learning and understanding was increased when a graphic computer simulation was added for the fish tank where the student could directly manipulate the variables involved (e.g., the temperature of the water) and observe animations of the results on other components of the fish tank ecology. The interpretation of these results is that the graphical computer simulation involving movement and animation helped the students form the mental grounded perceptual simulations that they need for better learning and understanding.

Creating Video Games to Embody Understanding

In the Teachable Agent (TA) project (Schwartz, Blair, Biswas, Leelalong, & Davis, 2007) and the Reflective Agent Learning (REAL) environment project (Bai & Black, 2010) students learn by specifying what their agents know in a video-game-like virtual world, then get feedback by how well their agents do in the virtual world with the knowledge the students have given them. In the TA project, agent Betty is given knowledge about something like river ecology by the students studying that topic and then drawing a concept map that gives both propositional relations (e.g., fish have gills) and system functional relations (e.g., increasing the number of plants increases the amount of oxygen). Based on this concept map, Betty can then answer questions or fail to be able to answer them, and she can be compared with other agents who were provided knowledge through concept maps by other students using a TV quiz-show-like virtual world. The research with TAs shows that students learn more this way than with other instructional methods—including just doing concept maps without the agent cover story. There is even a "protégé effect" (Chase, Chin, Oppezzo, & Schwartz, 2009) where the students will work harder to try to give their agent good concept map knowledge than they will to prepare themselves for the quiz show (i.e., they want their agent "protégé" to perform well).

In the REAL Business project (there are different versions of REAL for different content areas) shown in Fig. 3.3, the students learn some simple statistics by using procedural networks to specify what an agent running an ice cream shop knows that will enable him to order the right amount of each ice cream flavor based on prior experiences with customer agents that flow through the ice cream shop (doing well involves knowing about statistical sampling). REAL Planet is another version of REAL that involves ecological knowledge similar to the TA project, although in the REAL case the agents move through the virtual world and interact with it. REAL does not yet have any research results on student learning and understanding, but its research results seem likely to be similar to the TA results. In both the TA and REAL projects, student learning and understanding is increased by being able to embody their understanding in animated agents (their "protégés") in virtual worlds and then try out and revise their knowledge based on their agents' performances in the virtual world.

Recently Fadjo and colleagues (Fadjo, Hallman, Harris, & Black, 2009) have been exploring using the simpler *Scratch* programming language from the MIT

Fig. 3.3 REAL (reflective agent learning environment) business involving specifying decision procedures for Manager Agent to order ice cream for customer agents

Media Lab to have students in elementary and middle school program simple video games to embody their understanding of something in the agents in those video games. Scratch is a computer programming language that tries to teach programming through video game construction. Initial results indicate that having students act out agent actions using their own bodies (a real embodied experience) then programming the virtual agents to do the same thing (a virtual embodied experience) is a particularly effective learning approach. Other recent work is trying to do the same thing by programming robots to move around in and interacting with the real world (instead of a virtual world) to embody and test the student understanding (Li, Kang, Lu, Han, & Black, 2009).

Conclusions

Recent basic cognitive research and theory in perceptually grounded or embodied cognition provides a framework for considering how we can deepen and increase student learning and understanding by having them develop a "feel" for what they are learning in addition to knowing about it. Used in ways guided by this theoretical framework, video game playing together with more formal learning, interactive graphic computer simulations involving movement and animation (and force feedback), video game programming and robot programming can be used to increase student learning and understanding.

References

Ahn, J. (2007). Application of experiential learning cycle in learning from a business simulation game. Doctoral Dissertation, New York: Teachers College, Columbia University.

Bai, X., & Black, J. B. (2010). Enhancing intelligent tutoring systems with the agent paradigm. In S. Stankov, M. Rosov, and V. Glavinic (Eds.), *Intelligent tutoring systems in eLearning environments: Design, implementation and evaluation* (pp. 195–218). Hershey, PA: IGI Global Publishing.

Barsalou, L. W. (2008). Grounded cognition. *Annual Review of Psychology, 59*, 617–645.

Black, J. B. (2007) Imaginary worlds. In M. A. Gluck, J. R. Anderson, & S. M. Kosslyn (Eds.), *Memory and mind*. Mahwah, NJ: Lawrence Erlbaum Associates.

Black, J. B., Turner, T. J., & Bower, G. H. (1979). Point of view in narrative comprehension, memory and production. *Journal of Verbal Learning and Verbal Behavior, 18*, 187–198.

Bransford, J., & Schwartz, D. (2001). Rethinking transfer: A simple proposal with multiple implications. In A. Iran-Nejad & P. D. Pearson (Eds.), *Review of research in education* (Vol. 24, pp. 61–100). Washington, DC: American Educational Research Association.

Chan, M. S., & Black, J. B. (2006). *Direct-manipulation animation: Incorporating the haptic channel in the learning process to support middle school students in science learning and mental model acquisition*. Proceedings of the International Conference of the Learning Sciences. Mahwah, NJ: LEA.

Chase, C., Chin, D. B., Oppezzo, M., & Schwartz, D. (2009). *Journal of Science Education and Technology*.

Dewey, J. (1938). *Experience and education*. New York: Touchstone.

Fadjo, C., Hallman, G. Jr., Harris, R., & Black, J. (2009). *Surrogate embodiment, mathematics instruction and video game programming*. In Proceedings of world conference on educational multimedia, hypermedia and telecommunications 2009 (pp. 2787–2792). Chesapeake, VA: AACE.

Glenberg, A. M., Gutierrez, T., Levin, J. R., Japuntich, S., & Kaschak, M. P. (2004). Activity and imagined activity can enhance young children's reading comprehension. *Journal of Educational Psychology*, *96*, 424–436.

Hallman, G., Paley, I., Han, I., & Black, J. (2009). *Possibilities of haptic feedback simulation for physics learning*. In Proceedings of world conference on educational multimedia, hypermedia and telecommunications 2009 (pp. 3597–3602). Chesapeake, VA: AACE.

Hammer, J., & Black, J. (2009). Games and (preparation for future) learning. *Educational Technology*, *49*, 29–34.

Han, I., Black, J., Paley, I., & Hallman, G. (2009). Feel, imagine and learn: Learning from visual and haptic simulations. *Subway Summit 2009*. New York: Fordham University.

Li, D., Kang, S., Lu, C., Han, I., & Black, J. (2009). *Case studies of developing programming skills via embodied experiences in an after-school LEGO Robotics Program for elementary school students*. In Proceedings of world conference on educational multimedia, hypermedia and telecommunications 2009 (pp. 2209–2216). Chesapeake, VA.

Martin, A. (2007). The representation of object concepts in the brain. *Annual Review of Psychology*, *58*, 25–45.

McVeigh, D., Black, J., & Flimlin, G. (2008). How system simulations improve student learning by assisting in the creation of clear mental models. In K. McFerrin et al. (Eds.), *Proceedings of society for information technology and teacher education international conference 2008* (pp. 1767–1773). Chesapeake, VA: AACE.

Schwartz, D., Blair, K., Biswas, G., Leelawong, K., & Davis, J. (2007). Animations of thought: Interactivity in the teachable agents paradigm. In R. Lowe & W. Schnotz (Eds.), *Learning with animation: Research and implications for design*. UK: Cambridge University Press.

Solomon, K., & Barsalou, L. (2004). Perceptual simulation in property verification. *Memory and Cognition*, *32*, 244–259.

Chapter 4
Features of Computerized Multimedia Environments that Support Vicarious Learning Processes

Barry Gholson, Roby Coles, and Scotty D. Craig

Department of Psychology, The University of Memphis, Memphis, TN 38152, USA

The broad aim of this chapter is to explore how cognitive activities may be facilitated when the goal is to construct new knowledge in computerized environments designed to support vicarious learning (Cox, McKendree, Tobin, Lee, & Mayes, 1999; Craig, Gholson, & Driscoll, 2002; Gholson & Craig, 2006; McKendree, Good, & Lee, 2001; McNamara, Levinstein, & Boonthum, 2004; Scardamelia et al., 1992). As used here, *vicarious learning* takes place in environments in which learners have no opportunity to control any aspect of the source or content of materials they attempt to master. For example, in these environments vicarious learners are *not* required to engage in collaborative activities (Butcher, 2006; Chi, Roy, & Hausmann, 2008; Hausmann & Chi, 2002; Mayer, 1997, 2001; Rummel & Spada, 2005), to control the flow of input information (Chi, Bassok, Lewis, Reimann & Glaser, 1989; Mayer & Chandler, 2001; Mayer, 2001), or to answer questions (Ge & Land, 2003; Graesser & Person, 1994). Although learners may voluntarily choose to engage in overt activities, no attempt is made to control, monitor, or record them. Thus, as used here, vicarious learning involves *only* covert activities and, of course, any unspecified overt activities in which learners may spontaneously engage while looking and listening. Our discussion will highlight how specific features of computer-presented course content that support vicarious learning may be readily implemented in multimedia environments.

We will only briefly mention vicarious learning research presented prior to the last couple of decades (e.g., Bandura, Ross, & Ross, 1963; Rosenthal & Zimmerman, 1978). It mostly involved modeling and imitation, only tangentially addressed issues of concern in this selected review, and was usually conducted in a behaviorist context. Bandura's classic studies (1962; Bandura, Ross, & Ross, 1961; Bandura et al., 1963) in which children imitated physical and verbal aggression modeled by adults assaulting Bobo dolls are, of course, familiar to anyone who has read an introductory psychology textbook in the past few decades. His work brought one kind of vicarious learning (imitation) into the mainstream of academia and the broader social milieu. It fueled an enormous amount of research during

---

B. Gholson (✉)
Department of Psychology, The University of Memphis, Memphis, TN 38152, USA
e-mail: barry-gholson@mail.psyc.memphis.edu

M.S. Khine, I.M. Saleh (eds.), *New Science of Learning*,
DOI 10.1007/978-1-4419-5716-0_4, © Springer Science+Business Media, LLC 2010

the following decades. The research was presented under a variety of labels such as observational learning, social learning, as well as modeling and imitation (for reviews, see Bandura, 1977; Rosenthal & Bandura, 1978; Rosenthal & Zimmerman, 1978). Earlier work and controversies were largely overlooked (see Rosenthal & Zimmerman, 1978). Although some early proponents of experimental psychology emphasized vicarious learning as an important contributor to both human learning and development (Baldwin, 1906; Humphrey, 1921; James, 1890; McDougall, 1926), others strongly opposed the notion that any new knowledge could be acquired vicariously (Smith & Guthrie, 1921; Thorndike, 1911; Watson, 1914). Thus, vicarious learning (mostly imitation) received some attention during the first half of the twentieth century (e.g., Hull, 1920; Miller & Dollard, 1941), but it remained outside the mainstream prior to the 1960s. Although Bandura's (1963) work brought vicarious learning into the mainstream of experimental psychology, work in the following couple of decades did not address issues of current concern, so our selected review will focus on more recent research.

This recent research was fueled by cognitive theory and emphasized more complex learning processes (Bandura, 1977). Our survey will begin with research that focused exclusively on specific features of vicarious learning environments that have been show to promote comprehension and learning. In a later section we will illustrate related work in which researchers added the requirement that learners engage in various overt activities designed to supplement vicarious learning processes (Chi et al., 2008; Ge & Land, 2003; Hausmann & VanLehn, 2007; Mayer & Chandler, 2001; Rummel & Spada, 2005). Examples of these overt activities include engaging in scripted collaboration (Rummel & Spada, 2005), asking or answering questions (Ge & Land, 2003), and controlling the flow of input information (Mayer & Chandler, 2001; Rummel & Spada, 2005). Some (combinations) of overt activities in these environments clearly enhanced learning outcomes. Few attempts were made, however, to specify which specific overt activities were actually responsible for the improved performances, and even fewer attempts were made to implement vicarious analogs of the activities. In our selective review of this research we will attempt to identify specific overt activities that supported learning outcomes and highlight how these overt activities may be readily implemented in multimedia environments suitable for applications of the kinds considered here.

Environmental Features Supporting Vicarious Comprehension and Learning

Focus on Comprehension

Comprehension and understanding are, of course, fundamentally involved in all aspects of learning, so when we attempt to construct new knowledge from an input stream any factors that affect our comprehension of that stream are fundamental.

Thus, in this subsection we focus on research that explored aspects of the input stream that have been shown to affect comprehension. While this research relied on a variety of tasks and assessment measures, ranging from referential communication measures to knowledge applications, each study attempted to improve comprehension while varying facets of the input stream by manipulating such variables as number of perspectives and voice style. Research that focused on learning *per se* will be considered in the next subsection.

Schober and Clark (1989) reported research in which participants either participated in referential communication dialog or overheard audio recordings of that dialog. In one condition, a conversational participant, called a *matcher*, attempted to place randomly arranged sets of abstract shapes, called tangrams, into an order that was described by a second conversational participant, called a *director*. The dialogs between the matchers and directors were audio recorded and presented to participants, called *overhearers*, in a second condition. The overhearers, who listened to dialogs, attempted to place the tangrams in the orders described in the audiotape. The matchers who participated in the dialogs by conversing with directors, while placing the tangrams in order, significantly outperformed the matchers who simply overheard the tapes. Much of the same results were obtained in a second study in which vicarious matchers directly overheard dialogs between directors and matchers. Schober and Clark (1989, p. 211) suggested that the matchers who participated in the dialogs outperformed overhearers because "the very process of understanding is different for addressees and overhearers."

Fox Tree (1999) used a similar referential communication task to explore the roles of overhearing dialog and monolog in facilitating vicarious comprehension. In order to obtain audio tapes for use in the vicarious comprehension experiment, pairs of college students were divided into directors and matchers, as in the Schober and Clark studies (1989). Directors in the dialog condition conversed freely with matchers, but in the monolog condition directors only gave instructions while matchers listened and attempted to place the tangrams in the correct order. All sessions were audio recorded. Eight audio tapes of monologs and eight tapes of dialogs (of about the same length), in which matchers flawlessly placed the tangrams (Fox Tree, 1999, p. 43) in the correct order, were selected for use in the main vicarious comprehension experiment.

Results revealed that vicarious comprehenders who overheard dialogs evidenced superior performance, in that they made significantly fewer errors in placing the tangrams in the correct order when compared with those in the vicarious monolog condition. In more recent research, Fox Tree and Mayer (2008) reported two experiments contrasting single versus multiple perspectives overheard in either monolog or dialog discourse. Several other variables, including discourse markers, were explored in correlational analyses. Participants listened to auditory descriptions of tangrams (Fox Tree, 1999; Schober & Clark, 1989) and attempted to identify specific exemplars from an array of tangrams located on a monitor.

In both studies, those who overheard discourse that included multiple *perspectives* correctly identified significantly more tangrams than those who overheard only one perspective in the discourse. Whether the discourse was presented as monolog or dialog had no significant effects. This finding indicates that Fox Tree's (1999) earlier evidence of better comprehension in her dialog condition was probably because multiple perspectives are more likely to be presented in natural dialog than monolog. It should be noted, though, that Schober and Clark (1989) obtained superior performance among those who participated in dialog than those who only overheard the dialog, a discrepancy that remains to be resolved. Fox Tree and Mayer (2008) also explored whether accuracy correlated with seven stimulus variables. Three correlation coefficients were significant (pp. 172–173). Accuracy was positively correlated with the liveliness of the description, but there were two significant negative correlations, one between accuracy and number of discourse markers (cf. Fox Tree, 1999) and another between accuracy and the number of disfluencies. It seems quite possible that the enhanced comprehension that resulted from multiple perspectives was due to an increased likelihood that listeners overheard a perspective that (partially) mapped onto an existing mental model (or schema) and allowed deeper processing (Chi, 2000; Chandler & Sweller, 1992).

McKendree et al. (2001) explored the role of questions in another referential communication task, one involving the use of the Map Task Corpus (see Map Task Corpus, URL, in references; also Brown, Anderson, Shillcock, & Yule, 1984). In the Map Task each of the two participants received schematic maps that were not totally consistent, in that some landmarks were represented differently. An instruction *giver's* map contained a route drawn from a start point to an end point. The giver's task was to describe the route on the map to an instruction *follower*, whose task was to draw in the route.

McKendree et al. (2001) noted that when Anderson (1995; Anderson, Clark, & Mullin, 1994) examined a large corpus of Map Task data she found that comprehension was enhanced when new map features were introduced into the dialog by interrogatives rather than declaratives. Inspired by these findings, McKendree et al. (2001) selected two audiotapes of dialogs between givers and followers from the original Map Task Corpus. Followers in the McKendree et al. (2001) study attempted to draw routes on maps identical to those used to collect data in the original Map Task Corpus. In one taped dialog 12 new map features were introduced using questions (High-Intro), while in the other only five new map features were introduced using questions (Low-Intro). Listeners heard either the tape of the High-Intro or Low-Intro dialog. Those in the Low-Intro condition made deviation errors nearly three times as large as those in the High-Intro condition. McKendree et al. pointed out that comprehension of their overhearers in the High-Intro group was also slightly superior to the total group of active participants (the followers conversing with the givers) in the original Map Task research (Brown et al., 1984), who used the same map and route but were not selected on the basis of the number of questions included in the dialog. It seems reasonable to conclude that a second feature of discourse that facilitates comprehension, in addition to overhearing multiple perspectives (Fox Tree & Mayer, 2008), is increasing the number of embedded questions used to introduce new information (Anderson, 1995; Mckendree et al., 2001).

A variable that has been show to have a considerable effect on a reader's comprehension is the *coherence* (or cohesion) of written text (Britton & Gulgoz, 1991; McNamara & Kintsch, 1996; Vidale-Abarca, Martinez, Gilbert, 2000). McNamara (2001) defines coherence as the extent to which ideas in the text are made explicit. Two types of text coherence are specified (Ainsworth & Burcham, 2007): global and local. *Global* coherence involves using (a) topic headings that summarize the block of text that follows and (b) macro-propositions that link consecutive paragraphs to each other and to the topic. *Local* coherence is achieved by (a) replacing pronouns with nouns when the referent is potentially ambiguous, (b) linking unfamiliar concepts to familiar concepts or to previous information presented in the text, and (c) using connectives that specify relations between consecutive sentences (Ainsworth & Burcham, 2007). A variety of dependent measures have been reported (McNamara, Kintsch, Butler Songer, & Kintsch, 1996; McKowen, Beck, Sanatra, & Loxterman, 1992), ranging from shallow definitions and explicit knowledge taken directly from the text to implicit questions and inference questions that involved deeper knowledge and required integration of textual information and the use of prior knowledge (Kintsch, 1998). While increased coherence has little effect on surface knowledge of the text, like definitions, deeper knowledge reflected in implicit questions and inferences increases significantly. Coherent text apparently helps learners compare an existing mental model with a model presented in the text, while detecting any flaws or knowledge gaps, and repairing them to bring that model in line with the one presented in the text. As indicated directly above, methods for improving text coherence are straightforward and readily implemented (Ainsworth & Burcham, 2007, p. 291).

Two features of the speaker's voice, the *style* (formal, personal) and the *quality* (accented, non-accented, synthesized) have been shown to affect comprehension (and learning) in monolog presentations. Mayer, Fennell, Farmer, and Campbell (2004) explored voice style in three experiments by presenting an animation depicting (a) how air is inhaled into the lungs, (b) how carbon dioxide and oxygen are exchanged, and (c) how air is exhaled (p. 390). The animation was accompanied by a 100-word narration in either formal or personalized style. Both narrations were spoken by a male with a standard unaccented American voice (p. 391). In the formal style the narrator said, for example, "the diaphragm moves. . .," "for the lungs. . .," and "through the throat. . .." In the personalized style the word "the" was replaced 12 times in the passage by "your." Thus these participants heard "your diaphragm moves. . .," etc. In each of the three studies comprehension was significantly enhanced by narration presented in personalized style, in that scores were significantly higher on transfer tasks involving applications of the content. These and earlier findings (Moreno & Mayer, 2000) were taken to indicate that personalized narratives containing self-referential language promote better comprehension through deeper processing of the content (Rogers, Kuiper, & Kirker, 1977; Symons & Johnson, 1997).

Mayer, Sobko, and Mautone (2003) investigated the role of the voice quality in two experiments in which participants heard monolog presentations of 16 steps describing how lightning is formed while they simultaneously watched a 2-min animation showing how the steps were implemented. In Exp. 1 each step in the animation was described by a male with a standard unaccented American voice or it was spoken by a similar voice with a Russian accent. Participants presented with the unaccented narrative showed significantly better comprehension and learning than did those presented with the accented voice through performance on a task that tapped deep understanding. Those hearing the unaccented voice also rated the speaker more positively than those presented the accented voice. In a second study, Mayer et al. (2003, Exp. 2) reported that those listening to the unaccented voice also outperformed a machine-synthesized voice on ratings of learning difficulty and voice quality.

Atkinson, Mayer, and Merrill (2005) extended work on the role of voice quality during comprehension in two experiments involving 40-min instruction periods (as opposed to 2 min in Mayer et al., 2003) on four worked-out examples of math problems. Narratives were spoken by animated agents with English-accented female voices, either a human voice or a machine-synthesized voice. The narrations were presented in a multimedia display that involved verbal descriptions of each problem's solution steps along with visual displays of those steps. In Exp. 1, college students in laboratory settings showed significantly better comprehension through performance on versions of the four practice problems, near transfer problems, far transfer problems, and in ratings of the on-screen agent. Experiment 2 was conducted in a high-school computer lab with entire classes of college preparatory students present. Results completely replicated the laboratory findings obtained in Exp. 1. The authors concluded that their findings were consistent with social agency theory, which posits that appropriate social cues support comprehension in multimedia presentations by encouraging listeners to engage in human–computer interactions in ways similar to human–human interactions (Beck, McKeown, Sandora, Kucan, & Worthy, 1996; Grice, 1975; Reeves & Nass, 1996).

It seems reasonable to conclude that several readily implemented variables of the input stream improve comprehension of course content. First, they provide multiple perspectives of the conceptual content. It appears that, when multiple perspectives are included, whether the content is presented in dialog or monolog format is no consequence (Fox Tree & Mayer, 2008). Second, the McKendree et al. (2001) research indicates that introducing new content with questions promotes comprehension when contrasted with using simple declaratives (see below, Craig, Sullins, Witherspoon, & Gholson, 2006; Gholson & Craig, 2006). The McKendree et al. (2001) data suggest that overhearing content introduced by questions may be at least as effective as participating in dialog. Third, the coherence of written text plays an important role in readers' comprehension. So, making ideas in the text explicit by avoiding potentially ambiguous pronouns, linking concepts together, along with tying paragraphs to each other, and the topic headings with macro-propositions improves comprehension of written text. It seems reasonable to assume that these features would play similar roles when text is spoken. Finally, a personalized voice style produces better comprehension than a formal style when presenting course content, and voice quality plays a role in that an unaccented human voice produces better comprehension than either accented or synthesized voices.

Focus on Learning

Cox et al. (1999) studied college students as they learned syntax through vicarious exposure to demonstrations of sentence parsing and the construction of syntactic tree diagrams. Learning was assessed in a pretest-to-posttest design that evaluated three types of knowledge: identifying syntactic categories, recalling category labels, and constructing syntactic tree diagrams of new sentences not used in training. Four intervention groups and a no-intervention control condition were included. In a *dialog* condition vicarious learners observed video of a student who engaged in tutorial dialog with a teacher who simultaneously constructed tree diagrams of four sentences. The tutorial dialog was printed on the screen in a text window to the right of a video of the tree diagrams as they were dynamically constructed. In a *discourse* condition learners viewed a teacher constructing diagrams on screen, while the teacher's monolog instructions were presented in the text window. In a *diagram-only* condition, only the dynamic tree diagram constructions from the discourse condition were presented, with no on-screen text. In a fourth condition, called *text-only*, only the printed monolog instructions were presented, with no tree diagrams. In the *no-intervention* control condition only the pretests and posttests were administered. There was no audio in any of the conditions.

Results revealed that all four intervention groups showed significant learning gains from pretest to posttest when contrasted with the no-intervention control condition. The difference between the combined dialog and discourse groups approached significance when contrasted with the combined diagram-only and text-only conditions. The authors concluded that, when viewing dynamically constructed syntactic tree diagrams, vicarious learners' exposure to tutorial dialog was as effective at producing deep learning as was exposure to carefully crafted monolog instructions that were combined with those diagrams. It seems clear, then, that combining either printed tutorial dialog or printed instructional text along with dynamic animations facilitates vicarious learning relative to presenting only written instructions or only animations, results also reported in related research reported earlier (Mayer, 2001; Sweller, 1994, 1999). The diagram-only condition also showed (marginally) improved performance when compared with the text-only condition but only on test items requiring construction of new tree diagrams. Thus, despite some evidence to the contrary (Schnotz, Boeckheler & Grozondziel, 1997; Stasko, Badre, & Lewis, 1993), the authors tentatively concluded that presenting animations displaying the dynamic processes involved in constructing diagrams, even in the absence of textual descriptions of those processes, may be effective in promoting deep learning.

Evidence for the role of vicarious dialog in acquiring the cognitive skill of asking deep-level reasoning questions (henceforth, deep questions) was presented by Craig, Gholson, Ventura, Graesser, and TRG (2000). *Asking* deep questions facilitates cognitive activities (e.g., Graesser & Person, 1994; Rosenshine, Meister, & Chapman, 1996) that support comprehension, problem solving, and knowledge construction among both adults and children (Craig et al., 2000; Davey & McBride, 1986; Gavelek & Raphael, 1985; Graesser, Baggett, & Williams, 1996; King, 1989,

1994; King, Staffieri, & Adelgais, 1998; Palincsar & Brown, 1984). Students rarely ask questions of any kind in the classroom, however, and those they do ask usually involve only shallow reasoning (e.g., Dillon, 1988; Graesser & Person, 1994; Van der Meij, 1988). Deep questions usually require logical reasoning, causal reasoning, or goal-orientation reasoning (Bloom, 1956; Flavell, 1963; Graesser & Person, 1994; Piaget, 1952, 1968). These involve such question stems as "What happens when...?", "How does the...?", and "Why was the...?" Deep questions may be contrasted with shallow questions (Bloom, 1956; Gholson & Craig, 2006; Graesser & Person, 1994). The latter usually require one-word answers. They include stems such as "Is it true that...?", "Did X or Y occur?", and "What's the membrane between...?"

Craig et al. (2000) explored the use of vicarious dialog designed to induce college students to ask deep questions (Kintsch, 1998; Palinscar & Brown, 1984). A computer-controlled virtual tutor and a virtual tutee, located on opposite sides of a monitor, discussed a series of eight computer-literacy topics. Pictures relevant to each topic under discussion were also sequentially presented, located between the two virtual agents.

During acquisition vicarious learners either *overheard* the virtual tutor carry on a scripted dialog with the virtual tutee on the course content of each topic (*dialog* condition) or they overheard the tutor present a monolog-like discourse (*monolog* condition) concerning the same content. At the outset of each topic the virtual tutor presented a brief information delivery. Then, in the monolog condition, the virtual tutee asked one broad question that provided a context for what followed. The virtual tutor then answered in a monolog discourse that presented all the information on that topic. In the dialog condition, each brief information delivery was followed by a lively series of conversational exchanges. The virtual tutee asked a series of deep questions, a total of 66 across the course content presented on the eight topics (Bloom, 1956; Gholson & Craig, 2006; Graesser & Person, 1994), which the virtual tutor immediately answered. The exact words spoken by the virtual tutor were identical in both conditions. At the conclusion of acquisition, free-recall questions on the discourse content were administered prior to a transfer task.

In transfer the learners were presented with a series of eight new computer-literacy topics and were given the opportunity to ask questions on each. At the outset of each topic the virtual tutor presented a brief information delivery and immediately told the learner to direct queries to any information that would help them understand the topic. The experimenter immediately answered each. Learners continued their queries until they said they were finished with the topic. This was followed by a brief information delivery by the virtual tutor on the next topic, etc. Free-recall questions on the discourse content were administered after the last transfer topic was finished.

In the transfer task learners in the dialog condition took significantly more conversational turns, generated significantly more queries, and exhibited a significantly greater proportion of deep questions than those in the monolog condition. On the free-recall questions following transfer, students in the dialog condition also wrote significantly more content than those in the monolog condition. Clearly vicarious learners who overheard dialog that included deep questions in the original task employed the cognitive skills that supported asking deep questions in the transfer task, and they also learned more.

An unexpected finding was that following acquisition those who overheard deep questions also outperformed those in the monolog condition on free-recall questions. The difference was only marginally significant, but the effect size (Cohen's *d*) was 0.44. This suggested that overhearing deep questions embedded in course content may lead vicarious learners to not only generate more deep questions and learn more in a transfer task but they might also learn more of the content presented directly in the context of those deep questions. Thus, an issue that remained to be determined was: do students not only learn to ask deep questions (Graesser & Person, 1994), but also comprehend and learn more course content when they overhear that content presented in the context of discourse containing deep questions than they learn when they overhear the exact same content presented in question-free monolog?

Driscoll et al. (2003) explored whether, given more precise measures, the trend in favor of the dialog condition obtained by Craig et al. (2000) following acquisition would prove more robust. Because the between-subject variability was extreme in the Craig et al. study, an attempt was made to increase precision by making discourse type (dialog vs. monolog) a within-subject variable in the Driscoll et al. (2003) experiments. In Exp. 1 and the one that followed, two computer-controlled male-animated agents, a virtual tutor and virtual tutee, engaged in both dialog and monolog discourse. Each vicarious learner overheard four computer literacy topics discussed in dialog format and four in monolog format. As in Craig et al. (2000) the virtual tutee asked one broad question at the outset of each of the four topics presented as monolog, but in the dialog condition he asked a deep question before each content sentence presented on each topic. Results revealed that learning was significantly greater on topics overheard in dialog format than in monolog format.

As part of a larger study, Driscoll et al. (2003) designed Exp. 2 to explore several features of dialog that might have been responsible for the effects that were obtained in Exp. 1. The study included three dialog conditions with discourse type (dialog vs. monolog) as a within-subject manipulation in each. The monolog condition was identical in each dialog condition. Four topics were presented in dialog format and four in monolog.

In Exp. 2, the virtual tutee's contributions in one condition were deep questions (e.g., "How does the CPU use RAM when you run applications?"), and in a second condition they were transformed into shallow (one-word answers) questions (e.g., "Does the CPU use RAM when you run an application?"). In the third condition, they were converted into simple assertions (e.g., "The CPU uses RAM when you run an application.") spoken by the virtual tutee. It was suggested that if the deep questions used by Craig et al. (2000) and by Driscoll et al. in Exp. 1 functioned as advance organizers (Lorch & Lorch, 1995), then shallow questions and assertions should produce the same increments in learning as deep questions when the dialog conditions were contrasted with the monolog condition. If questions *per se* were critical, then those in the deep and shallow question conditions should both outperform those in the assertion condition. After acquisition, free-recall questions on topics presented in dialog and monolog formats were administered.

Results yielded a significant difference in favor of the dialog condition as compared to the monolog only among learners in the deep questions condition. Differences between dialog and monolog were small in the other conditions, slightly favoring topics in the dialog format in one condition and the monolog in the other. Clearly then, deep questions included in the dialog, rather than questions *per se* or simply presenting dialog, accounted for the difference in favor of the dialog condition in Exp. 1 and in Craig et al. (2000). Presenting deep questions prior to each content statement is, of course, easily implemented in computerized multimedia environments.

Findings lending indirect support for the conclusions of Driscoll et al. (2003) were obtained by Lin et al. (2005). They presented three groups of college students with an animation depicting the parts, locations, and functions of the human heart. Learners in one group were presented with written *descriptive* advance organizers along with static pictures prior to dynamic animations. Those in a second condition received written shallow *question* organizers, along with the static pictures, prior to the animations, and in a control group learners only viewed the animations. The descriptive organizers specified parts and functions of the heart. The question organizers asked shallow questions such as "What is the heart muscle that controls...?" (see Lin et al. 2005, Fig 4.2). As would be predicted by the Driscoll et al. (2003, Exp. 2) findings, there were no differences between the three groups on any of four tests used to assess learning. As Lin et al. (2005) pointed out, "The advance organizers cued the learner to critical information but did not create the necessary environment for students to expend the effort needed to rehearse, internalize, and synthesize information in meaningful ways necessary for higher-order learning to occur." In terms of the Driscoll et al. (2003) conclusions, neither the descriptive organizers nor the shallow question organizers supported deep-level learning processes.

Craig et al. (2006) conducted related research on deep questions. Learning gains from several vicarious learning conditions were contrasted with those obtained by learners in interactive tutoring sessions with an intelligent tutoring system, called AutoTutor. AutoTutor yields learning gains of about 1.0–2.1 standard deviation units when compared to various controls (Graesser et al., 2004; VanLehn et al., 2007). AutoTutor helps students learn by holding a conversation in natural language. Each topic begins with an *information delivery*, followed by a question presented to the learner. An *ideal answer* to the question is decomposed into a set of key concepts (sentences), called *expectations*. Latent semantic analysis (e.g., Graesser, Person, & Harter, 2001; Landauer & Dumais, 1997) assesses the learner's progress by comparing their contributions to the content of each expectation. After all expectations for the topic are covered, a *brief summary* is presented before AutoTutor moves on to the next topic.

In the Craig et al. (2006) interactive tutoring condition there was interactive tutorial dialog between the learners and AutoTutor for 35–40 min on 12 topics concerned with computer literacy. The video and audio from each learner in this *interactive* condition were recorded and presented to a participant in a *yoked-vicarious* condition. In a second vicarious condition a virtual tutor presented a *monolog* on each of the 12 topics that contained all (102) content statements in the ideal answer and expectations from AutoTutor's script. In a *half questions* vicarious condition, half (51) of the sentence in the ideal answers and expectations were each preceded by a deep question spoken by a second voice engine, with the remainder presented as monolog. In a *full-questions* vicarious condition each sentence in both the ideal answers and the expectations was preceded by a deep question (total = 102 questions). Total time in the latter three conditions was about 30 min.

Results yielded a significant effect of instruction condition. Learners in the full-questions vicarious condition significantly outperformed those in each of the other four conditions. The pretest-to-posttest learning gains for the other four conditions were reasonably comparable (see Craig et al., 2006, Table 1). A major finding of the study, of course, was that learners in the full-questions vicarious condition outperformed those who were engaged in the interactive tutorial dialog. This finding highlights the impact on vicarious learning of embedding deep questions into educational content as part of dialog when presenting course content. It should be pointed out, though, that the 51 deep questions presented in the half questions condition were not sufficient to significantly enhance learning compared to tutoring in the interactive condition, the yoked vicarious, or the monolog condition. Because the impact of embedding deep questions in educational content may have important implications for curriculum design in distance learning and in computerized learning environments in general, it was deemed necessary to replicate the finding, first among college students (Craig et al., 2006) and then among younger students (Gholson et al., 2009).

In Exp. 2., Craig et al. (2006) included four instruction conditions: interactive tutoring by AutoTutor, yoked-vicarious, full-questions vicarious with (102) deep questions and content statements presented as dialog, and full-questions vicarious with deep questions presented as part of monolog. In the full-questions monolog condition, the same agent and voice engine used in the interactive tutoring and the yoked-vicarious conditions spoke both the deep questions and the content statements. In the full-questions dialog condition, the questions were asked by a second, distinct voice engine.

Analyses revealed that the two deep questions conditions significantly outperformed both the interactive and the yoked-vicarious conditions. Neither the two former nor the two latter conditions differed from each other. The Craig et al. (2006) research, then, replicated the facilitating effects of deep questions as a feature of discourse among college students during vicarious learning, even when compared to interactive tutoring (Craig et al., 2000; Gholson & Craig, 2006; Graesser et al., 1996, 2004; King, 1989, 1994; Kintsch, Welsch, Schmalhofer, & Zimny, 1990; Otero & Kintsch, 1992; Rosenshine et al., 1996). Moreover, what appears to be important is the number of deep questions that are presented as part of the discourse, not whether the questions are embedded as part of dialog or as part of monolog.

The next study Gholson et al. (in press) in the series explored the generality of the deep questions effect in research with younger students and included a new curriculum domain. It contrasted 8th, 9th, 10th, and 11th grade students presented with interactive (AutoTutor) tutoring sessions with similar students presented vicarious learning conditions involving either computer literacy or Newtonian physics. The 8th and 10th graders were asked to learn computer literacy, while the 9th and 11th graders were presented with Newtonian physics. Three conditions at each grade level included interactive sessions with AutoTutor, monolog presentations of sentences in the ideal answers and expectations, and dialog with deep questions preceding each sentence in the ideal answers and expectations, as described in Craig et al., 2006; Gholson & Craig, 2006).

The analysis of most interest revealed significant differences between the experimental conditions. Those in the dialog (with deep questions) condition showed pretest to posttest learning gains nearly twice as large as those in the interactive and monolog conditions. The interactive and monolog conditions did not differ from each other. These data provide support for the "deep questions effect" (Craig et al., 2006; Gholson & Craig, 2006) among 8th to 11th graders in the domains of computer literacy and Newtonian physics. As noted earlier, the effect had previously been shown only among college students in the domain of computer literacy (see Craig et al., 2006; Driscoll et al., 2003; Gholson & Craig, 2006).

Next we consider the potential role of presenting vicarious explanations of course content during learning. During the past two decades, researchers have shown that when learners overtly explain aloud each concept or solution step as it is presented to them, those *self-explanations* produce very large learning gains when compared to various controls (Ainsworth & Burcham, 2007; Chi, 2000; Chi et al., 1989; Chi, Leew, Chia, & LaVancher, 1994; Chi, Siler, Jeong, Yamauchi, & Hausmann, 2001; Rummel & Spada, 2005). Self-explanations tie new content to previously presented materials and/or embed into a rich web of prior knowledge. Chi (2000; Chi et al., 2001) suggested that self-explanations increase knowledge acquisition by encouraging cognitive activities that fill knowledge gaps, modify existing schemas, and link new content to related material (Chi et al., 1989; McNamara et al., 2004).

This research led to the following question: What learning gains might be achieved by vicarious learners under conditions in which they overhear a virtual agent provide scripted "self-explanations" of course content? Would overhearing dialog that included virtual agents presenting scripted self-explanations of course content facilitate learning gains? Thus, as part of preliminary investigations Craig, Brittingham, Williams, Cheney, & Gholson (2009) included conditions in which vicarious statements analogous to a self-explanations (e.g., Chi et al., 2001) were presented to each student by a virtual tutee. Following each statement containing course content, spoken by a virtual tutor, the virtual tutee provided an explanation that was analogous to the self-explanations provided by learners in earlier research (e.g., Chi, 2000; Chi et al., 1989).

The first study was conducted in the laboratory and included only college students as participants. Students with high or low knowledge (based on pretest scores) concerning Newton's three laws of motion were randomly assigned to one of four experimental conditions: In a vicarious *question + explanation* condition, the presentation of each concept involved a three-event sequence. First the virtual tutee asked a deep question about the concept, second the virtual tutor presented a content statement that elaborated the meaning and use of the concept, and third the virtual tutee provided a "self-explanation" of the concept. The three-event sequence involving the next concept was then presented. A total of 50 of these three event-sequences was presented. In an *explanation* condition the first event was omitted from each sequence. In a *question* condition the third event was omitted from each sequence. Finally, in a *monolog* condition both the first and third events in the sequence were omitted. That is, only the virtual tutor's content statements containing the concepts were presented in this latter condition. The two agents were located on each student's monitor throughout in all four conditions, and a series of images appropriate to the content were located between the two agents.

Analyses of the pretest scores yielded no differences among the four experimental conditions at either the high or low knowledge level. Analysis of pretest-to-posttest change scores yielded a significant interaction between knowledge level and experimental condition. In the question + explanation condition the low-knowledge learners (31% gain) significantly outperformed those in the high-knowledge condition 7% gain). The low-knowledge learners in the question + explanation condition outperformed those with low knowledge in the question condition (21% gain), and the difference approached significance when they were contrasted with the monolog condition (23% gain). It seems, consistent with some previous findings (McNamara & Kintsch, 1996; McNamara & Shapiro, 2005), that more knowledgeable learners were unable to take advantage of that knowledge in a condition (i.e., question + explanation) that enabled greater learning gains among those with lower knowledge. Among those with high knowledge, the question condition (21% gain) significantly outperformed the question + explanation condition, and performance in the latter condition was also exceeded by the two remaining conditions (i.e., monolog = 19%, explanation = 14%), but the difference was not significant.

A second preliminary study of the vicarious explanation effect was conducted in high-school physics classes. Three conditions were used: question + explanation, question, and monolog. A total of 50 three event, two event, and single event sequences were used in the respective conditions. These were presented via laptops during the first part (about 18 min) of each of seven consecutive daily physics classes. The vicarious presentations were intended to provide conceptual understanding of the content presented by the regular classroom physics teacher during the remainder of each session. The classroom teacher provided equations and applications that gave quantitative expression to the conceptual content presented earlier in each daily computerized presentation.

Results revealed that learners in the question + explanation condition significantly outperformed those in both the monolog and question conditions, which did not differ from each other. Learners in the question condition did not outperform those in the monolog condition, which failed to support some earlier findings (Craig et al., 2000, 2006; Driscoll et al. 2003; Gholson & Craig, 2006). It should be pointed out, though, that more than 50 questions were generally presented in each session when the deep-questions effect was obtained. For example, Craig et al.

(2006, see above) used 102 deep questions in their full-questions vicarious condition that outperformed the half-questions condition, which included 51 questions.

Findings in the question + explanation conditions in the two preliminary studies are very encouraging. As noted above, Chi et al. (2001), Chi (2000), King (1994), and King et al. (1998) have shown that overt self-explanations encourage learners to engage in the kinds of deep reasoning activities that fill knowledge gaps and relate current content to a rich network of related material. Future research will determine the relationship between deep questions and explanations in promoting vicarious learning, but it does seem clear that vicarious explanatory statements relating the current content to earlier information show considerable promise.

Several readily implemented features of computerized multimedia environments, then, have been shown to support vicarious learning processes. Combining either written tutorial dialog or carefully crafted instructions with dynamic diagrams produces significant increments when contrasted with either dynamic diagrams or written text alone (Mayer, 2001; Sweller, 1999). Deep-level reasoning questions that precede statements containing course content presented by voice engines were shown to produce consistent learning gains that significantly exceed those produced by several other conditions, including presenting the course content alone, combining it with surface-level questions, or combining it with declaratives (Craig et al., 2000; Driscoll et al., 2003). Deep question conditions were also shown to produce greater learning gains than an intelligent tutoring system (AutoTutor) that produces learning gains of 1.0–2.1 standard deviation units (Craig et al., 2006; Gholson et al., 2009). Finally, preliminary research indicates that providing vicarious explanations, analogous to "self-explanations," that link current content to previously presented materials shows some promise of supporting learning gains similar to those produced by deep questions.

Overt Activities Designed to Support Vicarious Learning Processes

In this subsection we illustrate selected research in which learners engaged in various overt activities designed to enhance the cognitive activities that support vicarious learning in multimedia environments. Rummel and Spada (2005) investigated the acquisition of collaborative problem solving skills using a video conferencing system. Dyads of students, one psychology student and one medical student, collaborated on diagnosis and treatment plans for cases involving psychological disorders that coincided with physical illnesses. Case 1, panic disorder combined with cardiac dysrhythmia, was used in the learning phase of the study. Case 2, depression plus multiple sclerosis, was used in the application phase. Because both medical and psychological aspects of each case had to be considered, both psychological and medical knowledge were needed for effective diagnosis and treatment.

Four conditions were used in the study. In a *model* condition, vicarious learners heard an audio presentation of two model collaborators using dialog to arrive at a diagnosis and a therapy plan for Case1 in the learning phase. These learners were also presented animated slide clips displaying the development of the joint solution by the model collaborators as they clarified questions about the case. As learners viewed the animation clips, they were prompted by the experimenter (a) to *self-explain* activities of the model collaborators and (b) to *collaborate* as the models clarified questions about the case. In a *script* condition vicarious learners received precise written instructions (O'Donnell, 1999) telling them how to interact. This script specified the exact collaborative steps that were required to accomplish the diagnosis and treatment plans for evaluating each part of Case 1. After learners read the scripted instructions written on paper, the experimenter told them they had 7 min to ask each other questions and were prompted to "Make use of each other's knowledge to clarify information given to you about the patient in the case description before turning to the diagnosis" (p. 220). In an *unscripted* condition the learners engaged in collaborative problem solving for Case 1 without any instructional guidance whatsoever. In a *control* condition, only the application phase (Case 2) was included. In the application phase learners in all four conditions used the video-conferencing system while formulating a diagnosis and treatment plan for Case 2. Following the application phase, a posttest with subscales assessing knowledge of good collaboration, diagnosis, and treatment plans was administered.

Several measures of performance were obtained during the application phase. These included patterns of activity as recorded in log files, characteristics of the dialog, and the quality of both the diagnosis and treatment plans. Performances on posttest scales were also reported. The model and script conditions significantly outperformed the unscripted and control conditions on all measures. On the posttest scales there were also some small differences between the model and script conditions and between the unscripted and control conditions. Rummel and Spada (2005) concluded that the quality of the performances exhibited by learners in both the model and script conditions was improved by the instructional guidance they received during the learning phase: the learners acquired considerable skill in collaborating and were able to share their knowledge to arrive at good diagnosis and treatment plans, as evidenced during the application phase; both groups also acquired explicit knowledge about effective diagnosis and treatment, as evidenced by the posttest scales.

Clearly, vicarious learners, who overheard model collaborators discussing Case 1, while viewing corresponding animation clips and being prompted to discuss features of the solution, achieved substantial learning gains. Similarly, learners who read precise instructions on the collaborative steps needed to evaluate Case 1 and were instructed to ask each other questions in order to share knowledge, also achieved real gains. Both groups acquired the knowledge needed to collaborate effectively, share knowledge, and use their knowledge to successfully diagnose and treat a clinical case. These findings of Rummel and Spada (2005) are important and will no doubt inspire other research and applications.

The various manipulations used in the model and script conditions were not consistent, however, and their exact contributions could not be specified. In the model condition, for example, learners (a) overheard model collaboration, (b) viewed animation clips, and were prompted by the experimenter (c) to self-explain, and (d) to ask questions. In the script condition learners (a) were given precise written instructions that explained how to successfully collaborate in carrying out each step in the learning phase and (b) were prompted to both ask each other questions to share their knowledge. Thus, we cannot presently determine how much each of these specific manipulations contributed to the learning gains. It is clear, however, that vicarious analogs of the prompting and guidance provided by the experimenter at specific junctures in both the model and script conditions could be readily implemented in computer-based vicarious environments. A final note on Rummel and Spada (2005) is that those in the unscripted condition, who received no guidance, failed to outperform the non-intervention condition. This suggests, consistent with some earlier findings (Craig, Driscoll, & Gholson, 2004; but see Chi et al., 2008, below), that collaboration *per se*, without any further guidance, may be of limited value. Research relating to the roles of prompting and collaborative viewing has been reported and will be considered in that order.

Hausmann and Chi (2002, Exp. 2) contrasted the role of *prompts* to self-explain presented by a human tutor, who was sensitive to the learner's current knowledge state, with automated prompts presented at arbitrary locations by computer in a vicarious learning environment. As indicated above, research has established that self-explanations lead to learning gains, that prompting promotes these explanations (Chi et al., 1989, 1994), and that vicarious self-explanations may also lead to learning gains, at least when combined with deep questions (Craig, Brittingham, et al., 2009). In a preliminary study, Hausmann and Chi (2002, Exp. 1) presented two groups of learners with 62 computer-generated statements describing how the human circulatory system works. Vicarious learners were instructed at the outset either (a) to generate and type their self-explanations for each of the 62 statements using a keyboard or (b) to simply listen to each statement, with no keyboard provided. No further instructions or prompts were provided to either group. Few self-explanations were exhibited. Learners in the group instructed to self-explain at the outset of the session averaged about one each and the two groups did not differ on any measure. It seems, then, that simply instructing students to generate self-explanations at the outset of a learning session without training or practice (cf. Ainsworth & Burcham, 2007, on effective training procedures) is ineffective, at least when they are required to type them.

In their main study, Hausmann and Chi (2002, Exp. 2) contrasted human prompting with automated prompting by computer as learners observed the same 62 statements on the circulatory system that were presented in Exp. 1. Participants who received human prompting had two options following presentation of each statement presented on the monitor: they could either type a self-explanation or they could type "ok," signaling they had nothing to say. What was typed immediately appeared on the prompter's monitor, and (only) if it was deemed appropriate the human prompter requested a self-explanation prior to presentation of the next statement. Each learner in the automated prompting condition was yoked to one in the human prompting condition. For example, if the learner in the human prompting condition typed a self-explanation on statement 12 (whether prompted or not), the computer prompted the yoked learner to self-explain on that statement. On average vicarious learners in both groups generated 16 self-explanations and each averaged seven *integrative* self-explanations (Chi, 2000; Chi et al., 1994; previous subsection also). Both groups exhibited significant learning gains and did not differ from each other. When Hausmann and Chi combined the two groups and divided learners on the basis of the number of integrative self-explanations (Chi et al., 1994, 2001) into high and low, the high self-explainers showed learning gains about twice as large as the low self-explainers. It seems clear, then, that prompting students to self-explain promotes learning gains. Furthermore, as Housmann and Chi demonstrated, automated prompting is readily implemented, and giving them at arbitrary locations during a learning session are just as effective as prompts presented by humans who attempt to be sensitive to the learner's current knowledge state. Hausmann and Chi (2002) and Chi (2000) clearly showed that prompting to self-explain leads to learning gains. As noted above, though, in the Rummel and Spada (2005) report we cannot determine how the prompting for each of the various activities may have contributed to learning the collaboration skills or the knowledge about diagnosis and treatment skills that were obtained.

Ge and Land (2003) reported support for the role of automated *question* prompts in research on problem solving in an ill-structured task. College students in classroom settings either (a) received the problem materials along with 10 major question prompts probing a total of four knowledge categories or (b) they received only the problem materials, with no question prompts. The knowledge categories prompted by questions were as follows: (a) problem representation, (b) solution, (c) justification, and (d) monitoring and evaluation. Each of these category also included some sub-question prompts. For example, after being asked to define (represent) the problem, students were then asked to specify individual parts of the problem (Ge & Land, 2003, Appendix A). They also manipulated peer interaction: each student either worked in a group with three other collaborators or they worked alone.

The learners were asked to find an information technology-based solution for placing items in a supermarket that would maximize how quickly customers could locate them. While considering the problem individually or in groups, with or without question prompts available, the learners wrote a two- to three-page report that was used as a criterion task. Results revealed that learners who had the question prompts available exhibited significantly more knowledge in each of the four prompted categories: their problem representations, the solutions they generated, the justifications they provided, and their monitoring and evaluation activities, whether they worked with peers or alone. Ge, Chen, and Davis (2005) have more recently suggested the possibility that specific kinds of question prompts may play different roles in improving knowledge in the four categories they investigated. While having question prompts available while problem solving increase knowledge construction, direct comparisons with earlier research on questions that used very different methodologies appear premature (Craig et al., 2000; Gholson & Craig,

2006; Rummel & Spada, 2005), because Ge and Land made all their question prompts available while the criterion report was produced.

Chi and colleagues have studied the role of vicarious learning by collaboratively observing expert human tutors in the domain of quantitative kinematics in applications of Newton's three laws of motion. This method has been shown to be effective in both laboratory (Chi et al., 2008) and classroom settings (Craig, Chi, & VanLehn, 2009). After studying a text and meeting a knowledge criterion involving physics problems, college students were administered a pretest, followed by an intervention and a posttest. In one intervention condition individual learners were tutored (interactive *tutoring*) by an experienced expert tutor who was a physics professor while solving three problems. In a second condition, pairs of learners collaborated with each other while viewing a videotape (*collaborative observing*) of a session taken from the tutoring condition while solving the same problems. In a third condition, pairs of learners simply collaborated (*collaboration alone*) while solving the three problems. In a fourth, individual students observed a videotape (*individual observing*) taken from the tutoring condition while solving the three problems. In a fifth (*solo solving*) condition individual learners simply attempted to solve the three problems, using their textbook as a resource. Learners in both collaborative conditions (collaborative observing, collaboration alone) were encouraged to discuss their understanding and those in the collaborative observing condition were also encouraged to discuss events observed on the tape. Those in the two observing conditions (collaborative observing and individual observing) also self-paced the video tape, by stopping it, starting, and rewinding it at any time.

Only some of the results reported by Chi et al. (2008) will be summarized here. This is because they reported multiple detailed descriptions of their findings, even dividing learners in the various conditions in terms of pretest scores on some measures for detailed analyses. Their major findings were that those in the collaborative observing condition achieved learning gains equivalent to those in the interactive tutoring condition. This finding is important, because being tutored by an experienced expert (Bloom, 1984) is generally taken as the gold standard (Bloom, 1984; Cohen, Kulik, & Kulik, 1982; Graesser & Person, 1994) when various learning environments, including standard classroom instruction, are contrasted. Learners in the collaboration-alone condition, who were not presented with the recorded tutoring session, also exhibited significant gains on some measures, when contrasted with the individual observing and the solo solving conditions. Collaboration alone, however, failed to produce the same level of performance as the collaborative observing or tutoring conditions. This result from the collaboration-alone condition is somewhat inconsistent with earlier findings (Craig et al., 2004), including those of Rummel and Spada (2005), who failed to find any difference between their unscripted collaboration-alone condition and controls who received no intervention at all prior to the criterion task.

It should be pointed out that being able to control the pace of the videotape might have played some role in the collaborative observing and individual observing conditions. Chi et al. (2008) did not, however, report the amount of self-pacing in the two conditions, so what role it might have played is unknown. However, Chi et al.

(2008) did report that active lone observers who significantly outperformed non-active learners also manipulated the tutoring tape more often with a $M = 29.75$ and $M = 19.33$, respectively. Mayer and Chandler (2001) reported that, when compared to a conditions in which the presentation rate was uninterrupted, superior performance resulted when learners self-paced (stopped, started, rewound) the presentation rate of 16 segments in a multimedia explanation of lightning formation (see also, Dillon & Gabbard, 1998; Lepper, 1985; Williams, 1996).

In this section, we described a few selected studies that requested learners to engage in overt activities designed to support vicarious learning processes. Both Rummel and Spada (2005) and Chi et al. (2008) showed the important role played by observing model collaborations, whether observing two learners solving problems together or a tutor working with a learner. The learning gains were comparable to those obtained by learners working with experienced tutors. Rummel and Spada, however, prompted learners in their model condition to self-explain and to collaborate with each other, while Chi et al. (2008) encouraged those in the collaborative observing condition to discuss the tutoring session, and the learners also self-paced the videotape. While the roles played by these overt activities in supporting vicarious learning currently cannot be specified (cf. Mayer & Chandler, 2001), learner control of the input flow and vicarious analogs of instructions to collaborate may be readily implemented. Taken together, research described in this section provides further evidence supporting the roles of (a) viewing successful collaborative activities, (b) prompting learners to discuss, self-explain, and/or to ask or answer questions, and (c) letting learners self-pace the flow of input information in supporting learning processes. All of these features may be readily implemented in computerized multimedia environments.

Summary and Conclusions

This report explored how cognitive activities involved in vicarious comprehension and learning are supported by identifiable features of multimedia educational environments. Comprehension is, of course, integrally involved in deep learning and the latter would rarely be expected in the absence of comprehension, but the two were considered separately for purposes of this report. Several readily implemented manipulations of the input improve comprehension. First, they provide multiple perspectives of the conceptual content, and whether they are presented in dialog or monolog format is of no consequence (Fox Tree & Mayer, 2008; cf. Schober & Clark, 1989). Second, research indicates that introducing new content with questions promotes comprehension when contrasted with using simple declaratives (McKendree et al., 2001), and it may be as effective as participating in goal-directed dialog. Third, the coherence of written text plays an important role in comprehension: make ideas in the text explicit by avoiding ambiguous pronouns, linking concepts together by using macro-propositions that tie paragraphs to each other and to topic headings (Ainsworth & Burcham, 2007). It seems reasonable to assume that these features would play similar roles when text is spoken, although no direct comparisons were located. Furthermore, a personalized voice style produces better comprehension than a formal style (Mayer et al., 2004) and voice quality plays a role in that an unaccented human voice produces better comprehension than either accented or synthesized voices (Atkinson et al., 2005).

In focusing on specific manipulations in vicarious multimedia environments that support learning processes, we first considered research that isolated specific features and then considered related research that required learners to engage in a variety of overt activities that support those processes. Cox et al. (1999) reported that observing either written tutorial dialog or written instructions that are combined with dynamically constructed diagrams increased learning gains when contrasted with viewing written discourse alone or just watching diagrams being constructed (see also, Mayer, 2001; Sweller, 1999).

Deep (reasoning) questions (Graesser & Person, 1994) that precede statements containing course content presented by voice engines were shown to produce learning gains that significantly exceeded those produced by several other conditions (Craig et al., 2000). These include combining course content with surface-level questions, combining it with declaratives or presenting the course content alone (Driscoll et al., 2003). Deep questions conditions were also shown, surprisingly, to produce greater learning gains than an intelligent tutoring system (AutoTutor) that produces consistent learning gains of 1.0–2.1 standard deviation units (Craig et al., 2006; Gholson & Craig, 2006; Gholson et al., 2009). Finally, recent preliminary research indicates that providing vicarious explanations, analogous to "self-explanations," that link current content to previously presented materials shows some promise of supporting learning gains similar to those produced by deep questions (Craig, Brittingham et al., 2009).

Several overt activities have been shown to support vicarious learning processes: these include responding to prompts to self-explain, collaborate, and/or to ask or answer questions (Chi et al., 2008; Rummel & Spada 2005), as well as permitting learners to self-pace the flow of input information (Mayer & Chandler, 2001). Both Rummel and Spada (2005) and Chi et al. (2008) provided support for an important role played by prompting while observing. Rummel and Spada prompted learners to self-explain and to collaborate with each other while observing models solving problems. Chi et al. (2008) prompted learners who observed video tapes of tutoring sessions to discuss the session and also to self-pace the tapes. The roles played by some of these overt activities in supporting vicarious learning cannot presently be specified (cf. Mayer & Chandler, 2001), but vicarious analogs of them may be readily implemented in multimedia environments.

It does seem clear, though, that both directly incorporated cognitive activities and overt activities have considerable promise for improving vicarious learning processes. These vicarious learning processes are fairly easily implemented into computerized multimedia environments with current off the shelf technology. This makes these environments easily incorporated into web-based distance learning environments and blended classroom environments to provide efficient, cost-effective, and highly reusable learning alternatives.

Acknowledgment The research reported here was supported by the Institute of Education Sciences, U.S. Department of Education, through Grant # R305H0R0169 to The University of Memphis. The opinions expressed are those of the authors and do not represent views of the Institute or the U.S. Department of Education.

References

Ainsworth, S., & Burcham, S. (2007). The impact of text coherence on learning by self-explanation. *Learning and Instruction, 17*, 286–303.

Anderson, A. (1995). Negotiating coherence in dialogue. In M. A. Gernsbacher & T. Givon (Eds.), *Coherence in spontaneous text* (pp. 1–40). Philadelphia: John Benjamins Publishing.

Anderson, A. H., Clark, A., & Mullin, J. (1994). Interactive skills in children. *Journal of Child Language, 21*, 1–25.

Atkinson, R. K., Mayer, R. E., & Merrill, M. M. (2005). Fostering social agency in multimedia learning: Examining the impact of an animated agent's voice. *Contemporary Educational Psychology, 30*(1), 117–139.

Baldwin, J. M. (1906). *Mental development in the child and the race* (3rd rev. ed.). New York: Macmillan.

Bandura, A. (1962). Social learning through imitation. In M. R. Jones (Ed.), *Nebraska symposium of motivation* (pp. 211–269). Lincoln, NB: University of Nebraska Press.

Bandura, A. (1977). *Social learning theory*. Englewood Cliffs, NJ: Prentice Hall.

Bandura, A., Ross, D., & Ross, S. (1961). Transmission of aggression through imitation of aggressive models. *Journal of Abnormal and Social Psychology, 63*, 575–582.

Bandura, A., Ross, D., & Ross, S. (1963). Vicarious reinforcement and initiative learning. *Journal of Abnormal and Social Psychology, 67*, 601–607.

Beck, L., McKeown, M. G., Sandora, C., Kucan, L., & Worthy, J. (1996). Questioning the author: A yearlong classroom implementation to engage students in text. *Elementary School Journal, 96*, 385–414.

Bloom, B. S. (1956). *Taxonomy of educational objectives: The classification of educational goals. Handbook 1. Cognitive Domain*. New York: McKay.

Bloom, B. S. (1964). The 2-Sigma problem: The search for methods of group instruction as effective as one-to-one tutoring. *Educational Research, 13*, 4–16.

Bloom, B. S. (1984). The 2-sigma problem: The search for methods of group instruction as effective as one-to-one tutoring. *Educational Research, 13*, 4–16.

Britton, B. K., & Gulgoz, S. (1991). Using Kintsch's computational model to improve instructional text: Effects of repairing inference calls on recall and cognitive structures. *Journal of Educational Psychology, 83*, 329–345.

Brown, G., Anderson, A. H., Shillcock, R., & Yule, G. (1984). *Teaching talk*. Cambridge: Cambridge University Press.

Butcher, K. R. (2006). Learning from text with diagrams: promoting mental model development and inference generation. *Journal of Educational Psychology, 98*, 182–197.

Chandler, P., & Sweller, J. (1992). The split-attention effect as a factor in the design of instruction. *British Journal of Educational Psychology, 62*, 233–246.

Chi, M. T. H. (2000). Self-explaining expository texts: The dual processes of generating inferences and repairing mental models. In Glaser, R. (Ed.), *Advances in instructional psychology* (pp. 161–238). Hillsdale, NJ: Erlbaum.

Chi, M. T. H., Bassok, M., Lewis, M. W., Reimann, P., & Glaser, R. (1989). Self-explanations: How students study and use examples in learning to solve problems. *Cognitive Science, 13*, 145–182.

Chi, M. T. H., Roy, M., & Hausmann, R. G. M. (2008). Observing tutorial dialogues collaboratively: Insights about human tutoring effectiveness from vicarious learning. *Cognitive Science, 32*, 301–341.

Chi, M. T. H., Siler, S. A., Jeong, H., Yamauchi, T., & Hausmann, R. G. (2001). Learning from human tutoring. *Cognitive Science, 25*, 471–533.

Chi, M. T. H., de Leew, N., Chiu, M., & LaVancher, C. (1994). Eliciting self explanations improves understanding. *Cognitive Science, 18*, 439–477.

Cohen, P. A., Kulik, J. A., & Kulik, C. C. (1982). Educational outcomes of tutoring: A meta-analysis of findings. *American Educational Research Journal, 19*, 237–248.

Cox, R., McKendree, J., Tobin, R., Lee, J., & Mayes, T. (1999). Vicarious learning from dialogue and discourse. *Instructional Science, 27*, 431–458.

Craig, S. D., Brittingham, J., Williams, J., Cheney, K. R., & Gholson, B. (2009). Incorporating vicarious learning environments with discourse scaffolds into physics classrooms. In V. Dimitrova, R. Mizoguchi, B. du Boulay, & A. C. Graesser (Eds.), *Artificial Intelligence in Education, Building learning systems that care: From Knowledge representation to affective modeling* (680–682). Washington, DC: IOS Press.

Craig, S. D., Chi, M. T. H., & VanLehn, K. (2009). Improving classroom learning by collaboratively observing human tutoring videos while problem solving. *Journal of Educational Psychology 101,* 779–789.

Craig, S. D., Driscoll, D., & Gholson, B. (2004). Constructing knowledge from dialogue in an intelligent tutoring system: Interactive learning, vicarious learning, and pedagogical agents. *Journal of Educational Multimedia and Hypermedia, 13*, 163–183.

Craig, S. D., Gholson, B., & Driscoll, D. (2002). Animated pedagogical agents in multimedia educational environments: Effects of agent properties, picture features, and redundancy. *Journal of Educational Psychology, 94*, 428–434.

Craig, S. D., Gholson, B., Ventura, M., Graesser, A. C., & The Tutoring Research Group. (2000). Overhearing dialogues and monologues in virtual tutoring sessions: Effects on questioning and vicarious learning. *International Journal of Artificial Intelligence in Education, 11*, 242–253.

Craig, S. D., Sullins, J., Witherspoon, A., & Gholson, B. (2006). The deep-level- reasoning-question effect: The role of dialogue and deep-level reasoning questions during vicarious learning. *Cognition and Instruction, 24*(4), 565–591.

Davey, B., & McBride, S. (1986). Effects of question generating training on reading comprehension. *Journal of Educational Psychology, 78*, 256–262.

Dillon, J. T. (1988). *Questioning and teaching: A manual of practice*. New York: Teachers College Press.

Dillon, A., & Gabbard, R. (1998). Hypermedia as an educational technology: A review of the quantitative research literature on leaning comprehension, control, and style. *Review of Educational Research, 68*, 322–349.

Driscoll, D., Craig, S. D., Gholson, B., Ventura, M., Hu, X., & Graesser, A. (2003). Vicarious learning: Effects of overhearing dialogue and monologue-like discourse in a virtual tutoring session. *Journal of Educational Computing Research, 29*, 431–450.

Flavell, J. H. (1963). *The developmental psychology of Jean Piaget*. New York: Van Nostrand Reinhold.

Fox Tree, J. E. (1999). Listening in on monologues and dialogues. *Discourse Processes, 27*, 35–53.

Fox Tree, J. E., & Mayer, S. A. (2008). Overhearing single and multiple perspectives. *Discourse Processes, 45*, 160–179.

Gavelek, J., & Raphael, T. (1985). Metacognition, instruction, and the role of questioning activities. In D. Forrest-Pressley, G. MacKinnon, & T. Waller (Eds.), *Metacognition, cognition, and human performance*. New York: Academic Press.

Ge, X., Chen, C.-H., & Davis, K. K. (2005). Scaffolding novice instructional designers: Problem-solving processes using question prompts in a web-based learning environment. *Journal of Educational Computing Research, 33*, 219–248.

Ge, X., & Land, S. M. (2003). Scaffolding students' problem-solving processes in an ill-structured task using question prompts and peer interactions. *Educational Technology Research and Development, 51*(1), 21–38.

Gholson, B., & Craig, S. D. (2006). Promoting constructive activities that support learning during computer-based instruction. *Educational Psychology Review*, *18*, 119–139.
Gholson, B., Witherspoon, A., Morgan, B., Brittingham, J., Coles, R., Graesser, A. C., Sullins, J., & Craig, S. D. (2009). Exploring the deep-level reasoning questions effect during vicarious learning among eighth to eleventh graders in the domains of computer literacy and Newtonian physics. *Instructional Science*, *37*, 487–493.
Graesser, A. C., Baggett, W., & Williams, K. (1996). Question-driven explanatory reasoning. *Applied Cognitive Psychology*, *10*, S17–S32.
Graesser, A. C., Lu, S., Jackson, G. T., Mitchell, H., Ventura, M., Olney, A., & Louwerse, M. M. (2004). AutoTutor: A tutor with dialogue in natural language behavior research methods. *Instruments & Computers*, *36*, 180–193.
Graesser, A. C., & Person, N. (1994). Question asking during tutoring. *American Educational Research Journal*, *31*, 104–137.
Graesser, A. C., Person, N., Harter, D., & The Tutoring Research Group (2001). Teaching tactics and dialog in auto tutor. *International Journal of Artificial Intelligence in Education*, *12*, 257–279.
Grice, H. P. (1975). Logic and conversation. In P. Cole & J. Morgan (Eds.), *Syntax and semantics* (Vol. 3, pp. 41–58). New York: Academic Press.
Hausmann, R. G. M., & Chi, M. T. H. (2002). Can a computer interface support self- explaining? *Cognitive Technology*, *7*, 4–14.
Hausmann, R. G. M., & VanLehn, K. (2007). *Explaining self-explaining: A contrast between content and generation*. Paper presented at the 13th International Conference on Artificial Intelligence in Education, Marina Del Rey, CA.
Hull, C. L. (1920). Quantitative aspects of the evolution of concepts, an experimental study. *Psychological Monographs*, *28*, (1, Whole No. 123).
Humphrey, G. (1921). Imitation and the conditioned reflex. *Pedagogical Seminary*, *28*, 1–21.
James, W. (1890). *The principles of psychology*. New York: Holt.
King, A. (1989). Effects of self-questioning training on college students' comprehension of lectures. *Contemporary Educational Psychology*, *14*, 366–381.
King, A. (1994). Guiding knowledge construction in the classroom: Effect of teaching children how to question and explain. *American Educational Research Journal*, *31*, 338–368.
King, A., Staffieri, A., & Adelgais, A. (1998). Mutual peer tutoring: Effects of structuring tutorial interaction to scaffold peer learning. *Journal of Educational Psychology*, *90*, 134–152.
Kintsch, W. (1998). *Comprehension: A paradigm for cognition*. Cambridge, UK: Cambridge University Press.
Kintsch, W., Welsch, D. M., Schmalhofer, F., & Zimny, S. (1990). Sentence memory: Aetical analysis. *Journal of Memory and Language*, *29*, 133–159.
Landauer, T. K., & Dumais, S. T. (1997). A solution to Plato's problem: The latent semantic analysis theory of acquisition, induction, and representation of knowledge. *Psychological Review*, *104*, 211–240.
Lepper, M. R. (1985). Microcomputers in education: Motivational and social issues. *American Psychologist*, *40*, 1–18.
Lin, H., Kidwai, K., Munyofu, M., Swain, J., Ausman, B., & Dwyer, F. (2005). The effect of verbal advance organizers in complementing animated instruction. *Journal of Visual Literacy*, *25*, 237–248.
Lorch, R. F. Jr., & Lorch, E. P. (1995). Effects of organizational signals on text processing strategies. *Journal of Educational Psychology*, *87*, 537–544.
Map Task Corpus: http://www.hcrc.ed.ac.uk/maptask/ (accessed: October 12, 2008).
Mayer, R. E. (1997). Multimedia learning: Are we asking the right questions? *Educational Psychologist*, *32*, 1–19.
Mayer, R. E. (2001). *Multimedia learning*. New York: Cambridge University Press.
Mayer, R. E., & Chandler, P. (2001). When learning is just a click away: Does simple user interaction foster deeper understanding of multimedia messages? *Journal of Educational Psychology*, *93*, 390–397.

Mayer, R.E., Fennell, S., Farmer, L., & Campbell, J. (2004). Personalization effect in multimedia learning: Students learn better when words are in conversational style rather than formal style. *Journal of Educational Psychology, 96*(2), 389–395.

Mayer, R. E., & Moreno, R. (1998). A split-attention effect in multimedia learning: Evidence for dual processing systems in working memory. *Journal of Educational Psychology, 90*, 312–320.

Mayer, R. E., Sobko, K., & Mautone, P. D. (2003). Social cues in multimedia learning: Role of speaker's voice. *Journal of Educational Psychology, 95*(2), 419–425.

McDougall, W. (1926). *An introduction to social psychology* (Rev. ed.). Boston: John W. Luce.

McKendree, J., Good, J., & Lee, J. (2001, June). *Effects of dialogue characteristics on performance of overhearers*. Presented at the International Conference on Communication, Problem-solving, and Learning. Strathclyde, Scotland.

McKowen, M. G., Beck, I. L., Sanatra, G. M., & Loxterman, J. A. (1992). The contribution of prior knowledge and coherent text to comprehension. *Reading research Quarterly, 27*, 78–93.

McNamara, D. S. (2001). Reading both high coherence and effects of text sequence and prior knowledge. *Canadian Journal of Experimental Psychology-Revue Canadienne De Psychologie Experimentale, 55*, 51–62.

McNamara, D. S., & Kintsch, W (1996). Learning from text: Effects of prior knowledge and coherence. *Discourse Processes, 22*, 247–288.

McNamara, D. S., Kintsch, E., Butler Songer, N., & Kintsch, W. (1996). Are good tests always better? Interaction of text coherence, background knowledge, and levels of understanding in learning from text. *Cognition and Instruction, 14*, 1–43.

McNamara, D. S., Levinstein, I. B., & Boonthum, C. (2004). iStart: Interactive strategy training for active reading and thinking. *Behavior Research Methods, Instruments, & Computers, 36*, 222–233.

McNamara, D. S., & Shapiro, A. M. (2005). Multimedia and hypermedia solutions for promoting metacognitive engagement, coherence, and learning. *Educational Computing Research, 33*, 1–29.

Miller, N. E., & Dollard, J. (1941). *Social learning and imitation*. New Haven, CT: Yale University Press.

Moreno, R., & Mayer, R. E. (2000). A coherence effect in multimedia learning: The case for minimizing irrelevant sounds in the design of multimedia instructional messages. *Journal of Educational Psychology, 92*, 117–125.

Otero, J., & Kintsch, W. (1992). Failures to detect contradictions in text: What readers believe vs. what they read. *Psychological Science, 3*, 229–234.

O'Donnell, A. M. (1999). Structuring dyadic interaction through scripted cooperation. In O'Donnell, A. M. & King, A. (Eds.), *Cognitive perspectives on peer learning* (pp. 179–196). Mahwah, NJ: Lawrence Erlbaum Associates.

Palincsar, A. S., & Brown, A. L. (1984). Reciprocal teaching of comprehension fostering and comprehension monitoring activities. *Cognition and Instruction, 1*, 117–175.

Piaget, J. (1952). *The origins of intelligence*. Madison, CT: International University Press.

Piaget, J. (1968). The mental development of the child. In D. Elkind (Ed.), *Six psychological studies* (pp. 3–73). New York: Vintage Books.

Reeves, B., & Nass, C. (1996). *The media equation*. New York: Cambridge University Press.

Rogers, T. B., Kuiper, N. A., & Kirker, W. S. (1977). Self reference and the encoding of personal information. *Journal of Personality and Social Psychology, 35*, 677–688.

Rosenshine, B., Meister, C., & Chapman, S. (1996). Teaching students to ask questions: A review of intervention studies. *Review of Educational Research, 66*, 181–221.

Rosenthal, T. L., & Bandura, A. (1978). Psychological modeling: Theory and practice. In S. L. Garfield & A. E. Bergin (Eds.), *Handbook of psychotherapy and behavior change: An empirical analysis*. (2nd ed., pp. 621–658). New York: Wiley.

Rosenthal, R. L., & Zimmerman, B. J. (1978). *Social learning and cognition*. New York: Academic Press.

Roy, M., & Chi, M. T. H. (2005). The self-explanation principle in multimedia learning. In R. E. Mayer (Ed.), *The Cambridge handbook of multimedia learning* (pp. 271–286). Cambridge: Cambridge University Press.

Rummel, N., & Spada, H. (2005). Learning to collaborate: An instructional approach to promoting problem-solving in computer-mediated settings. *The Journal of the Learning Sciences*, *14*(2), 201–241.

Scardamelia, M., Bereiter, C., Brett, C., Burtis, P. J., Calhoun, C., & Smith Lea, N. (1992). Educational applications of a networked communal database. *Interactive Learning Environments*, *2*(1), 45–71.

Schnotz, W., Boeckheler, J., & Grozondziel, H. (1997). *Individual and co-operative acquisition of knowledge with static and animated pictures in computer-based learning environments*. Proceedings of the European Association for Research on Learning and Instruction (EARLI) (pp. 182–183). Gutenberg University Publications.

Schober, M. F., & Clark, H. H. (1989). Understanding by addressees and overhearers. *Cognitive Psychology*, *21*, 211–232.

Smith, S., & Guthrie, E. R. (1921). *General psychology in terms of behavior*. New York: Appleton.

Stasko, J., Badre, A., & Lewis, C. (1993). *Do algorithm animations assist learning? An empirical study and analysis*. Proceedings of the INTERCHI '93 conference of human factors in computing systems (pp. 61–66). The Netherlands: Amsterdam.

Sweller, J. (1988). Cognitive load during problem solving: Effects on learning, *Cognitive Science*, *12*(2), 257–285.

Sweller, J. (1994). Cognitive load theory, learning difficulty, and instructional design. *Learning and Instruction*, *4*, 295–312.

Sweller, J. (1999). *Instructional design in technical areas*. Melbourne: Australian Council for Educational Research.

Symons, C. S., & Johnson, B. T. (1997). The self-reliance effect in memory: A meta-analysis. *Psychological Bulletin*, *121*, 371–394.

Thorndike, E. L. (1911). *Animal intelligence: Experimental studies*. New York: MacMillan.

Van der Meij, H. (1988). Constraints on question asking in classrooms. *Journal of Educational Psychology*, *80*, 401–405.

VanLehn, K., Graesser, A. C., Jackson, G. T., Jordan, P., Olney, A., & Rose, C. P. (2007). Natural language tutoring: A comparison of human tutors, computer tutors and text. *Cognitive Science*, *31*, 3–52.

Vidale-Abarca, E., Martinez, G., & Gilbert, R. (2000). Two procedures to improve instructional text: Effects on memory and learning. *Journal of Educational Psychology*, *92*, 107–116.

Watson, J. B. (1914). *Behavior: An introduction to comparative psychology*. New York: Holt, Rinehart & Winston.

Williams, M. D. (1996). Learner-control and instructional technologies. In D. H. Jonassen (Ed.), *Handbook of research for educational communications and technology* (pp. 957–983). New York: Macmillan.

Chapter 5
Human Memory and the New Science of Learning

Paul Eggen and Suzanne Schellenberg

University of North Florida, Jacksonville, FL, USA

Introduction

People throughout history have been fascinated by memory. We lament our forgetfulness, and comments such as "Oh yes, I remember" or "It's on the tip of my tongue, but I just can't quite remember" are common. We rack our brains to remember isolated facts, such as William Faulkner's most famous novel (perhaps *The Sound and the Fury*), the general in charge of the Vietnam War (Westmoreland), or the capital of Columbia (Bogota). We also solve problems and identify relationships. All of these factors are related to human memory, the topic of this chapter.

To begin, please do the following simple experiments. Study the following list of words for 20 s, then cover them up and write down as many as you can remember in any order that you choose. Here they are.

Broom	Else	Evening
Sooner	Salary	Destroy
Jug	Jaw	Group
Planet	Friend	Smirk
Work	Salmon	Goose
Plug	Some	Large
President	Fastener	

Now, try it once more. The following is a second list, also of 20 words. Again, look at the list for 20 s and then write down as many as you can recall in any order you choose.

P. Eggen (✉)
University of North Florida, Jacksonville, FL, USA
e-mail: peggen@unf.edu

M.S. Khine, I.M. Saleh (eds.), *New Science of Learning*,
DOI 10.1007/978-1-4419-5716-0_5, © Springer Science+Business Media, LLC 2010

North	Judy	Dime
Celery	Red	Cucumber
Karen	South	Purple
Blue	Carrot	Donna
Quarter	Nickel	Tomato
West	Brown	Betty
Penny	East	

Almost certainly you were able to recall more of the second than of the first list. In this chapter we analyze the characteristics of human memory that help us understand why this is the case and also examine the implications of memory for learning and teaching.

Cognitive Perspectives on Learning

Until about the middle of the twentieth century, behaviorism was the dominant view of learning. Behaviorism explains learning in terms of observable changes in behavior that occur as a result of experience with the environment. For example, many of us (guys) tend to leave our dirty socks on the floor of the bedroom, which results in mild to harsh reprimands from our wives or significant others. As a result, we are more likely to pick them up, and because our behavior has changed from not picking up our socks to picking them up, behaviorists would say that learning has occurred. The environmental experience is the reprimand from our significant other.

Behaviorism is able to explain simple behaviors, such as picking up dirty socks, driving slower after being picked up for speeding, or children's attempts to answer teachers' questions because they are being praised for their efforts. However, behaviorism is not able to explain the development of complex skills, such as problem solving, insights and novel ideas, or the acquisition of language (Chomsky, 1959). Factors such as these, combined with the development of computers, all led to a search for different explanations for people's behaviors. The result was the "cognitive revolution," which marked a shift toward *cognitive learning theories*, theories that explain learning in terms of changes in the mental structures and processes involved in acquiring, organizing, and using knowledge (Royer, 2005; Sawyer, 2006). They help us explain tasks as simple as remembering a phone number. They also explain the ability to solve ill-defined problems and understand complex relationships, such as the influence Marco Polo's visit to the Far East and the Portuguese explorers had on Columbus's discovery of the Americas, or how the vast difference in the temperature on the side of Mercury facing the sun compared to the side facing away from the sun is related to its period of rotation.

The cognitive revolution occurred between the mid-1950s and early 1970s, and its influence on our understanding of learning and its implications for teaching have steadily increased since that time (Berliner, 2006).

Principles of Cognitive Learning Theory

Cognitive learning theories are grounded in the following principles:

- Learning and development depend on learners' experiences.
- Learners are mentally active in their attempts to make sense of those experiences.
- Learners construct—they do not record—knowledge in the process of developing an understanding of their experiences.
- Knowledge that is constructed depends on knowledge that learners already possess.
- Learning is enhanced in a social environment.
- Learning requires practice and feedback.

Learning and Development Depend on Learners' Experiences

To see how experience influences learning and development, think about learning to drive a car. Most cars now have automatic transmissions, so most likely you originally learned to drive a car that had an automatic. However, suppose you have a friend who asks you to help him move, but he has a pickup truck with a stick shift. You struggle, but after several jerks, your friend's worry about tearing out the rear end of his pickup, and killing the motor a few times, you get the hang of it. In fact, you now are able to drive vehicles with stick shifts without difficulty. Because of your experience you have now learned to drive vehicles with stick shifts, and your driving skills are more fully developed than they would have been if you had not acquired the experience. The famous developmental psychologists Jean Piaget (1952, 1959) and Lev Vygotsky (1978, 1986) both emphasized the importance of experience in promoting development, and it is illustrated in you learning to drive vehicles with stick shifts.

One of essential roles of education is to provide students with the experiences that become the raw material for their development.

Learners Are Mentally Active in Their Attempts to Make Sense of Their Experiences

Cognitive learning theorists view students as "goal-directed agents who actively seek information" (Bransford, Brown, & Cocking, 2000, p. 10). For example, think about the number of times you have said to yourself or to someone else, "That makes sense," "That doesn't make any sense," or "That sounds sensible." These simple statements reflect people's innate desire to understand their experiences, and it is arguably the most fundamental cognitive principle that exists. It explains why we are uncomfortable when faced with new situations that we do not understand and why we derive satisfaction from solving a unique problem or gaining a new insight.

This principle also helps us understand aspects of motivation. We want our experiences to make sense to us, and when they do not, we are motivated to understand why. This explains why small children will repeat the same task over and over. When the results of the task are the same each time, a form of cognitive equilibrium exists, and developmental theory suggests that the drive for equilibrium is fundamental in humans (Piaget, 1970, 1980). This principle also helps us understand why we are bothered by inconsistency and why we are motivated to resolve the inconsistency if possible.

Learners Construct Knowledge

In attempts to understand their experiences, people—instead of recording information in their memories in the exact form in which it is presented—construct knowledge that makes sense to them (Greeno, Collins, & Resnick, 1996; Mayer, 2002). As a result, individuals are likely to construct different meaning from the same experiences, and individual students will differ in the way they understand the ideas they are being taught based on what makes sense to them.

Knowledge that Is Constructed Depends on Learners' Prior Knowledge

People do not construct knowledge in a vacuum; their knowledge constructions depend on what they already know. For example, a child who has traveled with his/her parents is more likely to find geography meaningful than is someone who has not traveled, since she will have more experiences to which new knowledge can be related.

Prior knowledge can also lead to misconceptions. For instance, some children mistakenly believe that a fraction with a larger denominator, such as 1/5, is greater than one with a smaller denominator, like 1/3. Knowing that 5 is greater than 3, they conclude that 1/5 should be greater than 1/3. Other examples exist in most content areas. For example, people often conclude that adverbs are words that end in *ly*, but many adverbs do not end in *ly*. People make this conclusion because many of the adverbs people encounter do indeed end in *ly*. Also, most people believe that the force on an object moving at constant speed, such as an automobile, is greater in the direction the object is moving than it is in the opposite direction. In fact the forces are equal. People construct these misconceptions because the misconceptions make sense to them, and the people have prior experiences that support the misconceptions.

Learning Is Enhanced in a Social Environment

Vygotsky's work (1978, 1986) and increased attention from researchers (e.g., Moll & Whitmore, 1993; Rogoff, 1998) have helped educators understand that the process of knowledge construction is enhanced by social interaction. For example, think about some of your experiences in working with another person. It is likely that you were able to solve problems or figure out ideas together that you were not able to figure out on your own.

Learning Requires Practice and Feedback

People learn to do well only what they practice doing (Schunk, 2004; Willingham, 2009). This principle is also self-evident and is supported by neurological studies (Craig, 2003). To shoot baskets accurately we practice shooting; to become skilled writers we practice writing; to solve problems effectively we solve many problems. The same is true for all learning. Discussing ideas is a form of practice, and the more people discuss and work with information, the deeper their understanding becomes.

Feedback is information about existing understanding used to increase future understanding. As learners construct understanding they use additional information to determine the extent to which their understanding is valid. For instance, if a child's understanding of dogs is based on experience with his/her family's gentle, lovable pooch, he/she is likely to conclude that all dogs are friendly. When he encounters one that growls and nips his hand, he will revise his understanding and conclude that some dogs are friendly but others are not. The growl and nip are feedback the child uses to revise his understanding.

As with practice, this is true for all learning. One of teachers' most important roles is to provide students with feedback that can help them arrive at more sophisticated understanding. In this regard, feedback is an additional experience that learners use to enhance their learning.

These learning principles provide a foundation for helping us understand how learning occurs, but they also raise additional questions. For example, how do people acquire the experiences they use to construct their knowledge and how is prior knowledge combined with new experiences? Where is the knowledge that is constructed and stored, and in what form is it stored? The answers to these and other questions are the focus of the rest of this chapter.

A Model of Human Memory

While cognitive learning theorists do not totally agree on the structure of human memory, most use a model similar to what you see in Fig. 5.1, which was initially proposed by Atkinson and Shiffrin (1968) and is often described in the framework of *information processing theory*. Since it was originally proposed, this theory has generated a great deal of research and has undergone considerable refinement. We discuss this model and modifications made to it as the rest of the chapter unfolds.

The model has three major components:

- Memory stores
- Cognitive processes
- Metacognition

We examine these components in the following sections.

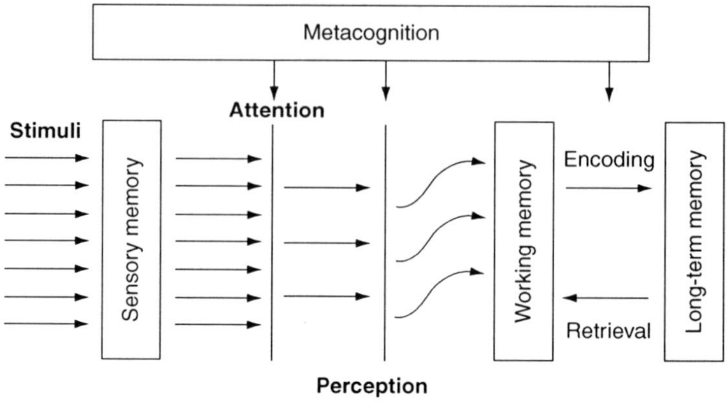

Fig. 5.1 A model of human memory

Memory Stores

Memory stores are repositories that hold information, in some cases in a raw state and in others in organized, meaningful form. They are *sensory memory*, *working memory*, and *long-term memory*.

Sensory Memory

Hold your finger in front of you and rapidly wiggle it. Do you see a faint "shadow" that trails behind your finger as it moves. This shadow is the image of your finger that has been briefly stored in your visual sensory memory. Likewise, when someone says, "That's an oxymoron," you retain "Ox see moron" in your auditory sensory memory, even if it has no meaning for you.

Sensory memory is the store that briefly holds incoming stimuli from the environment until they can be processed (Neisser, 1967). Sensory memory is nearly unlimited in capacity, but if processing does not begin almost immediately, the memory trace quickly fades away. Sensory memory is estimated to retain information for about 1 s for vision and 2–4 s for hearing (Pashler & Carrier, 1996).

Sensory memory is the beginning point for further processing. In reading, for example, it would be impossible to get meaning from a sentence if the words at the beginning were lost from your visual sensory memory before you got to the end. It holds the information until you attach meaning to it and transfer it to working memory, the next store.

Working Memory

Working memory is the store that holds information as you process and try to make sense of it. It is the workbench of our minds where "conscious" thinking occurs (Paas, Renkl, & Sweller, 2004), and it is where we construct our knowledge. We are not aware of the contents of either sensory memory or long-term memory until they are pulled into working memory for processing.

A Model of Working Memory

Figure 5.1 represents working memory as a single unit, and this is how it was initially described by researchers (Atkinson & Shiffrin, 1968). However, current views of working memory suggest that it is composed of three components that work together to process information (Baddeley, 1986, 2001). This model is outlined in Fig. 5.2.

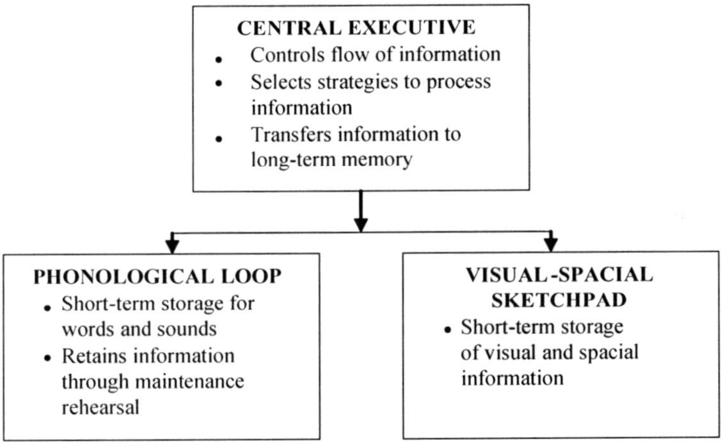

Fig. 5.2 A model of working memory

To illustrate these components find the area of the figure you see here.

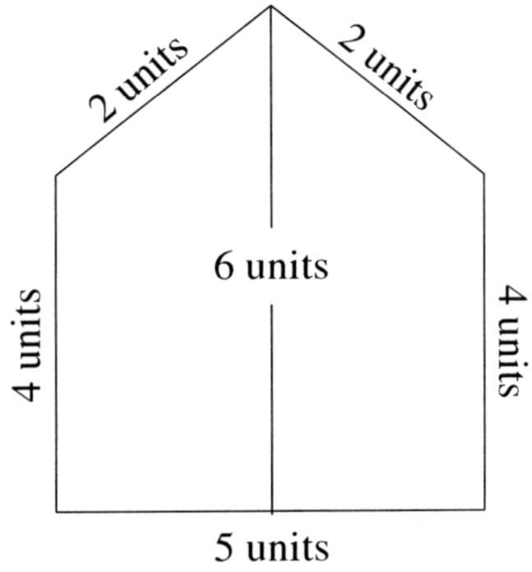

Fig. 5.3 Irregular pentagon

To solve the problem you probably subtracted the 4 from the 6 to determine that the height of the triangular portion of the figure was 2 units. You recalled that the formulas for the areas of a triangle and a rectangle are ½ (b)(h) and (l)(w), respectively, and you calculated the areas to be (½)(5)(2) = 5 units^2 and (5)(4) = 20 units^2. Adding the two, you found the total area to be 25 units^2.

Components of the Model. Let us see how the components of working memory executed the task. The *central executive*, a supervisory system, controls the flow of information to and from the other components. For instance, the decision to break the figure into a triangle and rectangle, find the area of each, and add the two was a function of the central executive.

The *phonological loop*, a short-term storage system for words and sounds, temporarily held the formulas and the dimensions of the figure until the calculations could be made. Information can be kept in the phonological loop indefinitely through *maintenance rehearsal*, the process of repeating information over and over, either out loud or silently, without altering its form (Atkinson & Shiffrin, 1968). For example, you look up a phone number, repeat it to yourself until you dial it, and then it is quickly lost. (We examine rehearsal in more detail later in the chapter.)

The *visual–spatial sketchpad*, a short-term storage system for visual and spatial information, allows you to picture the figure and see that it could be broken into a rectangle and triangle. The visual–spatial sketchpad and the phonological loop are independent, so each can perform mental work without taxing the resources of the other (Baddeley, 1986, 2001). They serve the functions that historically were attributed to *short-term memory*. "Short-term memory loss" is the phrase often used to describe someone who has difficulty remembering specific events or people's names. This loss actually reflects impairment in the phonological loop or, less commonly, in the visual–spatial sketchpad.

Baddeley (1986, 2001) suggests that the phonological loop can hold about as much information as we can say to ourselves in 1.5–2 s, and the visual–spatial sketchpad is also limited. We examine these limitations in the next section.

A considerable amount of research has examined the working memory model and how it impacts learning. For instance, researchers have found that learners with attention-deficit/hyperactivity disorder (ADHD) rehearse verbal and spatial information as effectively as healthy children, but their central executive is impaired (Karateken, 2004), whereas learners with reading disabilities have impaired functioning of the phonological loop (Kibby, Marks, & Morgan, 2004). Students with ADHD have trouble controlling their attention and selecting effective learning strategies, and students with reading difficulties have trouble processing verbal information.

Limitations of Working Memory

The most striking feature of working memory is its inability to hold large amounts of information for extended periods (Sweller, van Merrienboer & Paas, 1998).

Early experiments suggested that it can hold about seven items of information at a time (Miller, 1956), particularly when new information is being received, and it can hold the information only briefly—about 10–20 s for adults. Selecting and organizing information also use working memory space, so we "are probably only able to deal with two or three items of information simultaneously when required to process rather than merely hold information" (Sweller et al., 1998, p. 252). These limitations are important because working memory is where we make conscious decisions about how to link new information from the environment to our existing knowledge (Clark & Mayer, 2003). If you have ever said, "I'm suffering from mental overload," you were referring to your working memory.

The limited capacity of working memory has important implications for learning and teaching. Consider the following research results:

- Students' writing often improves more rapidly if they are initially allowed to ignore grammar, punctuation, and spelling (McCutchen, 2000).
- Despite research about its ineffectiveness and staff-development efforts to promote more sophisticated forms of instruction, lecturing persists as the most common teaching strategy (Cuban, 1993).
- Students write better essays using word processors if their word processing skills are well developed. If not, handwritten essays are superior (Roblyer, 2006).

The limitations of working memory relate to these findings through the concept of *cognitive load*, which is the amount of mental activity imposed on the working memory. The number of elements that you must attend to is one factor that contributes to cognitive load (Paas et al., 2004). For instance, remembering sequences of digits like 7, 9, 5, 3 and 3, 9, 2, 4, 6, 7 can be thought of as having cognitive loads of 4 and 6, respectively.

A second factor influencing cognitive load is the extent to which the elements interact with one another (Paas et al., 2004). For example, attempting to create a well-organized essay, while at the same time using correct grammar, punctuation, and spelling, imposes a heavy cognitive load on the writer, and using sophisticated teaching strategies, such as guiding students with questioning, imposes a heavy cognitive load on teachers. If students' computer skills are not well developed, executing the mechanics of the word processing program, combined with attempts to construct a quality essay, imposes a cognitive load so heavy that developing writers compose better handwritten essays. The cognitive load on students is also reduced if they are allowed to ignore grammar, punctuation, and spelling, and teachers reduce it by lecturing, a less cognitively demanding instructional strategy.

Reducing cognitive load in these ways is undesirable, however, because students must ultimately use correct grammar, spelling, and punctuation in their writing, and teachers are encouraged to interact with their students. We address these issues in the next section.

Reducing Cognitive Load: Accommodating the Limitations of Working Memory

We can accommodate the limitations of working memory by reducing cognitive load in three primary ways:

- Chunking
- Automaticity
- Distributed processing

Chunking. Chunking is the process of mentally combining separate items into larger, more meaningful units (Miller, 1956). For example, the sequence 9, 0, 4, 6, 2, 0, 1, 7, 5, 2 is the phone number for one of your authors, but it is not written as phone numbers appear. Now, as normally written, 904-620-1752, it has been "chunked" into three larger units, which reduces cognitive load. Interestingly, working memory is sensitive only to the number of chunks and not their size. "Although the number of elements is limited, the size, complexity and sophistication of elements [are] not" (Sweller et al., 1998, p. 256).

Developing Automaticity. If you have an electric garage door opener, it is likely that you sometimes cannot remember if you have put the garage door down when you left home, so you drive back to check, and you see that you have indeed closed it. *Automaticity*, which is the ability to perform mental operations with little awareness or conscious effort (Feldon, 2007; Schneider & Shiffrin, 1977), can explain your actions. You put the garage door down without thinking about it.

Automaticity is a second way of reducing cognitive load, and computer keyboarding skill is an example of its power and efficiency. Once our word processing capabilities become automatic, we can devote our working memory space to the composition of our writing. Until then, we must devote working memory to placing our hands on the keys, and the cognitive load becomes too great to compose quality products. This explains why students compose better essays on word processors but only if they are skilled at word processing. Also, students' grammar, punctuation, and spelling must eventually become automatic if they are to be good writers, and essential teaching skills, such as questioning, are automatic for expert teachers.

Using Distributed Processing. Earlier we saw that the visual–spatial sketchpad and the phonological loop are independent, so each can perform mental work without taxing the resources of the other (Baddeley, 1986, 2001). This suggests that learning is made easier if verbal explanations are combined with visual representations (Clark & Mayer, 2003; Moreno & Duran, 2004). For example, suppose you buy a new end table. You are in the process of assembling it, so you attempt to follow the directions. Completing the assembly job is much easier if you have both the diagrams and the words as guides. The visual processor supplements the verbal processor and vice versa. When teaching, "The integration of words and pictures is made easier by lessons that present the verbal and visual information together rather than separated" (Clark & Mayer, 2003, p. 38).

Teachers at the junior high, high school, and university levels often use words, alone, to present information, which reduces learning by wasting some of working memory's processing capability and often imposing a cognitive load greater than working memory's capacity.

Long-Term Memory

Long-term memory is our permanent information store. It is like a library with millions of entries and a network that allows them to be retrieved for reference and use (Schacter, 2001; Sweller, 2003). Long-term memory's capacity is vast and durable; some experts suggest that information in it remains for a lifetime.

Long-term memory contains three kinds of knowledge: *declarative knowledge*, *procedural knowledge*, and *conditional knowledge*. *Declarative knowledge* is knowledge of facts, concepts, procedures, and rules, and within this category, some researchers (e.g., Tulving, 2002) have distinguished between *semantic memory*, which is memory for concepts, principles, and the relationships among them, and *episodic memory*, which is memory for personal experiences.

The lines between episodic and semantic memory are often blurred, but one factor is significant. When people have strong emotional reactions to an event, episodic memories are more enduring. For example, you probably remember exactly where you were and what you were doing when you received word of the terrorist attacks of 9/11. Similarly, you likely recall the events surrounding your first date or kiss. These events are stored in your episodic memory. Teachers can capitalize on episodic memory by personalizing content or teaching it in such a way that it also has an emotional impact on our students.

Procedural knowledge is knowledge of how to perform tasks, and *conditional knowledge* is knowledge of where and when to use declarative and procedural knowledge (Anderson, 2005; Hergenhahn & Olson, 2001). For example, consider the following problems:

$$2/7 + 4/7 =$$

$$1/4 + 2/3 =$$

You know that to add fractions you first must have like denominators. This is a form of declarative knowledge. Recognizing that you must find a common denominator in the second problem but not in the first is a form of conditional knowledge, and actually finding that the answer to the first problem is 6/7 and the answer to the second is 11/12 requires procedural knowledge.

Declarative knowledge can be determined from a person's comments, and most declarative knowledge is *explicit*, meaning once we recall it, we are aware of what we know. On the other hand procedural and conditional knowledge are inferred from a person's performance, and this knowledge is often *implicit*, meaning we cannot recall or explain it. For instance, when working at a computer, you cannot recall the knowledge you use as you move your fingers over the keyboard, and you are unable to explain exactly what you are doing. The relationships among these different forms of knowledge are outlined in Fig. 5.4.

Now, let us look at how these different forms of knowledge are stored in long-term memory.

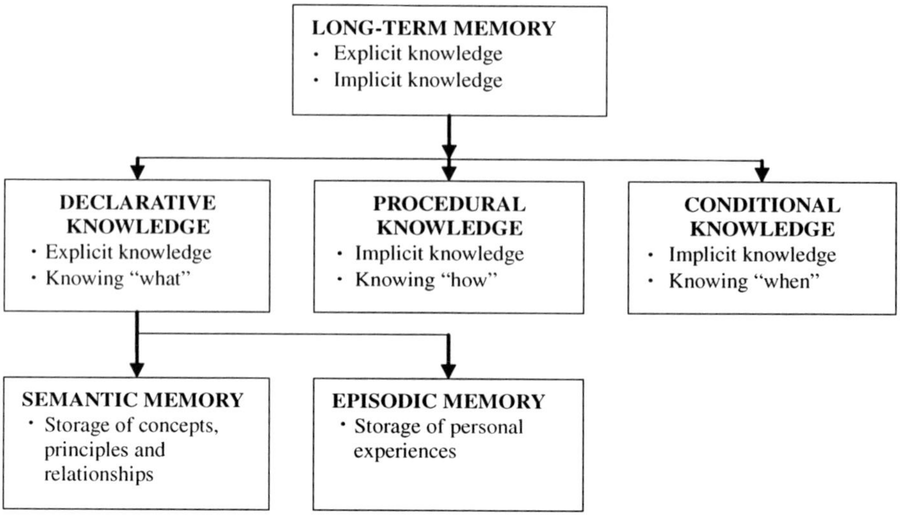

Fig. 5.4 Knowledge in long-term memory

Representing Declarative Knowledge in Long-Term Memory

Acquiring declarative knowledge involves integrating new information with existing knowledge. So, people learn more effectively when they have well-developed knowledge to which new information can be related. This knowledge is organized in the form of *schemas* (also called schemata), and though theorists do not totally agree on a definition, they can be viewed as cognitive constructs that organize information into *meaningful systems* in long-term memory (Anderson, 2005; Willingham, 2004).

Meaningful Learning. To begin this section, think back to the two experiments you did in the introduction to this chapter. It is likely that you remembered more of the items in the second list, because they can be classified into meaningful groups. The categories are outlined below.

Directions	Tomato	Brown
North	*Women's Names*	Purple
West	Judy	*Coins*
South	Karen	Dime
East	Donna	Quarter
Vegetables	Betty	Penny
Celery	*Colors*	Nickel
Cucumber	Red	
Carrot	Blue	

Five categories exist with four related items in each category, but no such relationships exist in the first list at the beginning of the chapter. As a result the second list is more *meaningful*. *Meaningfulness* describes the extent to which individual elements of a schema are interconnected in long-term memory (Gagne, Yekovich, & Yekovich, 1997). As another example, we commented at the beginning of the chapter about Marco Polo, the Portuguese explorers, and Columbus's visit to the new world. In our history courses we learned that Marco Polo visited the Far East in the 1200's and wrote a best selling book about his travels. We also learned about Portuguese explorers, such as Bartolomeu Dias, the first European known to have sailed around the tip of Africa. And, of course we know about Columbus's discovery of the new world. We most likely learned them as isolated items of information, but they would have made more sense, and we would have remembered the individual items more easily if we had understood the relationship among them. For instance, interest in the Far East and the trade routes that followed were influenced by Marco Polo's book, and they inspired both the Portuguese explorer's and Columbu's interest in finding a water route as an alternative to the lengthy land travels. And, Columbus was motivated to sail west because of the Moorish dominance of the Indian Ocean. Understanding the relationships among these items of information would have made the information more *meaningful*.

A long history of research indicates that meaningful learning is more effective than *rote learning* or learning that involves acquiring information in isolated pieces, most commonly through memorization (Lin, 2007; Mayer, 2002). We can illustrate these ideas with the information about Maro Polo, the Portuguese explorers, and Columbus as outlined in Fig. 5.5 below.

Fig. 5.5 A meaningful schema

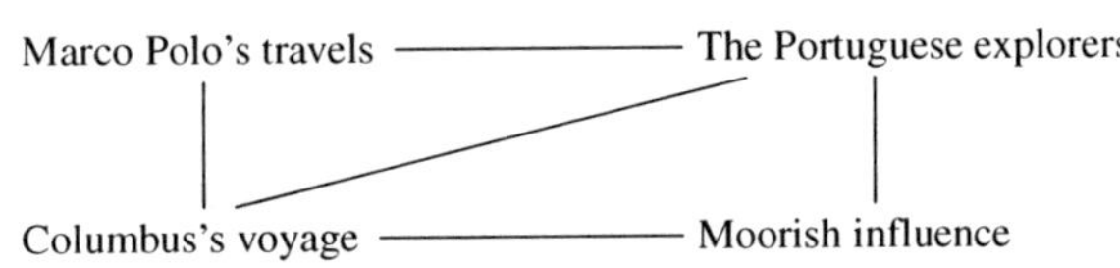

You saw earlier that the number of chunks working memory can hold is limited, but the size and complexity of the chunks are not (Sweller et al., 1998). If we understand the connections among the items of information as illustrated in Fig. 5.5, the schema behaves like one chunk (Bransford et al., 2000), so it takes up only one slot when we retrieve it from long-term memory back into working memory. Because the individual items are less connected, they take up more slots in working memory, the cognitive load is greater, and we are more likely to forget the information. Because a considerable amount of learning that occurs in schools is not meaningful, students forget a great deal of what they "learned." Some authors believe that the lack of meaningful learning explains why many students do not like school (Willingham, 2009).

Meaningful Learning: Implications for Learners and Teachers. To promote meaningful learning, *information should be taught as interconnected ideas rather than isolated pieces*. Isolated information imposes a heavy load on student's working memories, which helps explain why they seem to retain so little of what they are taught. Connecting ideas reduces the load, makes the information more meaningful, and increases learning by providing more places to attach new information.

Meaningfulness also has implications for learners. When we study, we should look for relationships in the content instead of studying ideas in isolation. This explains why memorizing definitions and other individual items of information is an ineffective study strategy.

Schemas as Scripts. In addition to organizing information, schemas can also guide our actions. For example, when we first enter a college class, we often ask questions such as the following:

- What are the instructor's expectations?
- How should I prepare for quizzes and other assessments?
- How will I interact with my peers?

Answers to these questions come from scripts, which can be thought of as schemas for events, developed over years of experience (Nuthall, 2000; Schank & Abelson, 1977). For example, you have a script that guides your behavior as you anticipate attending a party. You know that you must talk to the other partygoers, avoid drinking too much, pay attention to your spouse or date, and thank your host when you leave. In this regard, scripts also contain procedural knowledge, which we consider next.

Representing Procedural Knowledge in Long-Term Memory

The effectiveness of procedural knowledge depends on both declarative and conditional knowledge (Anderson, 2005; Star, 2004). For example, think back to the problems with fractions. Your ability to add them depended on your declarative knowledge of the rules for adding fractions and your conditional knowledge, so you knew when finding a common denominator was necessary and when it was not.

Developing Procedural Knowledge: Implications for Learning. The goal in developing procedural knowledge is to reach automaticity, which requires a great deal of time and effort (Star, 2005; Taraban, Anderson, & DeFinis, 2007). This suggests that we need to spend a great deal of time practicing the skill we are trying to develop.

Also, the way procedural knowledge is developed helps us understand why context is so important (Star, 2004). For example, students should practice their grammar, spelling, and punctuation in the context of their writing instead of practicing on isolated sentences. And, math students should develop their skills in the context of word problems that require a variety of operations, so students learn to identify different conditions and apply the appropriate actions (Bransford et al., 2000).

The development of procedural knowledge also has implications for teachers' growth. Skills, such as questioning, will improve even after years of teaching, and with experience they learn to recognize different learning conditions that require different strategies.

As a review of this section, look at Table 5.1 which outlines the characteristics of the memory stores.

Table 5.1 Characteristics of the Memory Stores

Store	Characteristics
Sensory memory	• Virtually unlimited capacity • Holds information in unorganized form • Information is quickly lost if it is not further processed
Working memory	• Limited capacity • Conscious component of the memory stores • The workbench where thinking and problem solving occur • A processing bottleneck • Contains a verbal and visual processor that work independently
Long-term memory	• Virtually unlimited capacity • Permanent information store • Stores information in the form of schemas and images, encoded from working memory

Cognitive Processes

We examined the characteristics of the memory stores, but how does information move from one memory store to another? And, how do we store information most efficiently? To answer these questions, let us look again at the model of human memory first presented in Fig. 5.1, focusing now on the processes—*attention, perception, encoding,* and *retrieval*—that move information from one store to another. They are highlighted in Fig. 5.6 and discussed in the sections that follow.

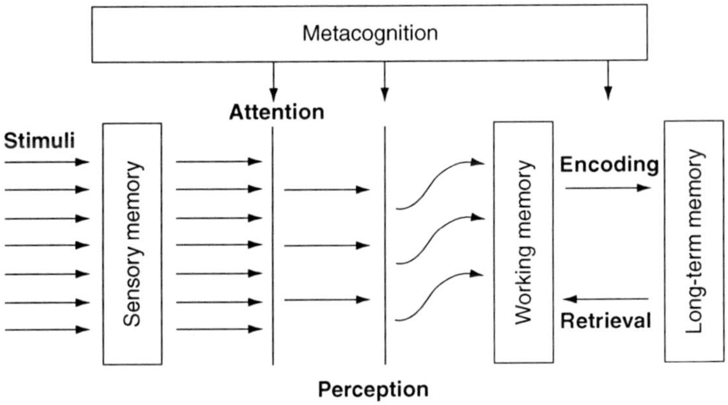

Fig. 5.6 Cognitive processes

Attention

Early in the chapter you saw that learning and development depend on learners' experiences. They are gathered through everything we see, hear, touch, taste, or smell. This process is represented in Fig. 5.6 as stimuli entering our sensory memories. However, we remain unaware of the stimuli until we consciously *attend* to them. For instance, we likely do not "pay attention" to the whisper of an air conditioner until we are made aware of the fact that it is running. This is illustrated in the model by fewer arrows coming out of "attention" than enter it. Our attention acts as a screen, allowing us to filter out unimportant information.

Two characteristics of attention are important. First, while individual differences in people exist, everyone's attention is limited, both in capacity and in duration (Curtindale, Laurie-Rose, & Bennett-Murphy, 2007; Zhou, Hofer, & Eisenberg, 2007). So, for example, students are likely to pay attention to parts of teachers' explanations but miss others.

Second, our attention easily shifts from one stimulus to another; people in general are easily distracted (Zhou et al., 2007). This helps us understand why students seem to derive less from teachers' explanations that they should. A myriad of distractions exist in classrooms—students whispering, noises outside the room, and people in the hallway, among others. Any one or more of these can cause students to miss parts of teachers' explanations.

Attracting and Maintaining Attention

Because attention is where learning begins, maintaining attention is essential when we are attempting to learn new material and attracting and maintaining attention are essential when teaching (Curtindale et al., 2007; Valenzeno, Alibali, & Klatzky, 2003). We are more likely to pay attention when we are actively involved in an learning experience, and technology is often effective because of its ability to hold our attention. Effective teachers plan their lessons so students attend to what is being taught and ignore irrelevant stimuli. On the other hand, listening passively to a lecture often results in lack of attention, which helps us understand why lecture is a generally ineffective teaching strategy (Dolezal, Welsh, Pressley, & Vincent, 2003; Taylor, Pearson, Peterson, & Rodriguez, 2003).

Perception

We often think of *perception* as the way we interpret objects and events. This is the way it is commonly used in our everyday life, and it depends on factors such as learners' dispositions and expectations (Huan, Yeo, & Ang, 2006; Way, Reddy, & Rhodes, 2007). For example, consider the following:

> "How was your interview?" Lenore, a job applicant asked her friend, Kelly, who was also applying for a job at the same school.

"Terrible," Kelly responded. "He grilled me, asking me specifically how I would teach a certain topic, and what I would do in the case of two students disrupting my class. He treated me like I didn't know anything. Brenna, a friend of mine who teaches there, told me about him... How was yours?"

"Gosh, I thought mine was good. He asked me the same questions, but I thought he was just trying to find out how we would think about teaching if he hired us."

Kelly and Lenore interpreted their interviews very differently, Kelly viewing it as being "grilled" but Lenore feeling as if the interviewer only wanted to examine her thinking. Kelly's interpretation was influenced by her friend, Brenna, whose description created a set of expectations in her.

People's perceptions are constructed, and because they are constructed they differ among students. The arrows to the right of *perception* in Fig. 5.6 are curved to remind you that peoples' perceptions will vary. And, since the knowledge people construct depends on what they already know, perceptions also depend on prior knowledge. This helps us understand why two people who have the same experience or witness the same event may interpret it very differently.

Accurate perceptions are essential for learning, because our perceptions of what we see, hear, touch, taste, or smell are what enter working memory, and if these perceptions are not accurate, the information that is ultimately stored in long-term memory will also be inaccurate.

The only way we can determine whether we are accurately perceiving what others mean is to ask them. This is the source of activities in human relations workshops where people are taught *perception checking* in the form of questions, such as, "What I hear you saying is ... Is that correct?" While the question does indeed seem sort of artificial, it is a mechanism for increasing the accuracy of perceptions.

Encoding

After people attend to and perceive information and organize it in working memory it is ready for *encoding*, which is the process of representing information in long-term memory (Anderson, 2007). This information can be represented either visually or verbally, when people construct schemas that relate ideas to each other.

Earlier in the chapter we described *maintenance rehearsal*, which was defined as the process of retaining information in working memory until it is used or forgotten. However, if rehearsed enough, this information can be transferred to long-term memory, and this is the strategy learners often use to remember factual information, such as specific dates and math facts like $6 \times 9 = 54$. Teachers commonly use rehearsal, such as practicing with flash cards, to help their students learn math facts. Rehearsal is an inefficient encoding strategy, however, because the information in long-term memory exists in isolation. This was described earlier in the chapter as *rote learning*.

In contrast with rote learning, we want the information to be encoded meaningfully; we want it to be connected to other information, such as the illustration with

Marco Polo, the Portuguese explorers, and Columbus. Several strategies exist that promote meaningful encoding, and we examine four of them in this section. They are

- imagery
- organization
- schema activation
- elaboration

The strategies are outlined in Fig. 5.7 and discussed in the sections that follow.

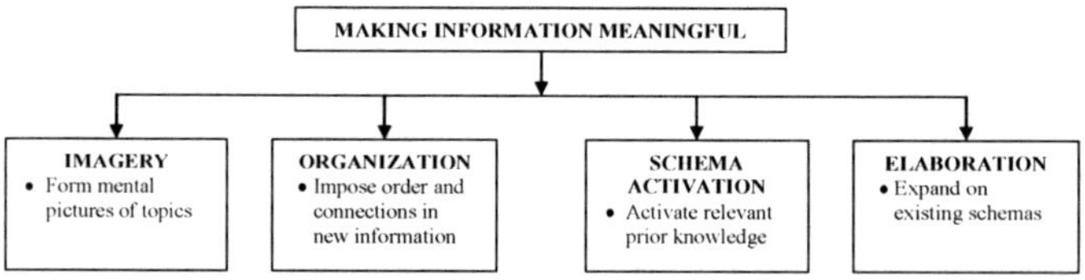

Fig. 5.7 Strategies for promoting meaningful encoding

Imagery

Imagery is the process of forming mental pictures of an idea (Schwartz & Heiser, 2006), and its value as an encoding strategy is supported by *dual-coding theory*, which suggests that long-term memory contains two distinct memory systems: one for verbal information and one for images (Paivio 1991; Sadoski & Paivio, 2001). According to dual-coding theory, ideas that can be represented both visually and verbally, such as *ball*, *house*, or *dog*, are easier to remember than ideas that are more difficult to visualize, such as *value*, *truth*, and *ability* (Paivio, 1986).

As we study human memory, for example, the fact that we can both visualize the models in Figs. 5.1 and 5.6 and read about the information in them helps us capitalize on the dual-coding capability of long-term memory. Information in the model becomes more meaningfully encoded than it would be if we had only described it verbally (Clark & Paivio, 1991; Willoughby, Porter, Belsito, & Yearsley, 1999). Dual-coding theory again reminds us of the importance of supplementing verbal information with visual representations (Igo, Kiewra, & Bruning, 2004). This capitalizes on both distributed processing in working memory and the dual-coding capability of long-term memory.

Imagery can be particularly helpful in problem solving (Kozhevnikov, Hegarty, & Mayer, 1999). It would have been harder for you to solve the area-of-the-pentagon problem, for example, if you had not been given the drawing as an aid.

Organization

Organization is an encoding strategy that involves the clustering of related items of content into categories that illustrate relationships. Because well-organized content illustrates connections among its elements, cognitive load is decreased, and encoding (and subsequent retrieval) is more effective (Mayer, 2008). Research in reading, memory, and classroom instruction confirms the value of organization in promoting learning (Mayer, 2008; Nuthall, 1999b). Research indicates that experts learn more efficiently than novices because their knowledge in long-term memory is better organized, allowing them to access it and connect it to new information (Bransford et al., 2000; Simon, 2001).

We can organize information in several ways:

- *Charts and matrices:* Useful for organizing large amounts of information into categories.
- *Hierarchies:* Effective when new information can be subsumed under existing ideas.
- *Models:* Helpful for representing relationships that cannot be observed directly. The model of human memory in this chapter is an example.
- *Outlines:* Useful for representing the organizational structure in a body of written materials.

Other types of organization include graphs, tables, flowcharts, and maps (Merkley & Jefferies, 2001). Learners can also use these organizers as personal study aids in their attempts to make the information they are studying meaningful.

A word of caution: As you saw in the list of learning principles at the beginning of the chapter, people construct knowledge that makes sense to them, so if the organizational structure offered by a writer or teacher does not make sense to readers or learners, they will (mentally) reorganize it in a way that does, whether or not it is correct. When the way content is organized is unclear, people often memorize snippets of it, resulting in rote learning, or they ignore it altogether.

Discussion is essential to making the organization of new material meaningful to learners. This is the reason people join book clubs, for example. As they discuss the book, its organization and the author's intent become clearer to the participants.

Schema Activation

Think back to some of your most effective teachers. In most cases it is likely that they began their classes with a review of the previous class, and a long history of research supports the effectiveness of well-structured reviews in promoting student achievement (Berliner, 1986; Rutter, Maughan, Mortimore, Ousten, & Smith, 1979; Shuell, 1996).

Reviews capitalize on *schema activation*, which is an encoding strategy that involves activating relevant prior knowledge so that new knowledge can be connected to it (Mayer & Wittrock, 2006). Schema activation is illustrated in Jeopardy, the popular game show syndicated on American television. With the topic being "State capitals" the following was the final Jeopardy answer in one episode:

This state capital was a compromise between the North Platters and the South Platters.

To respond correctly you had to activate a schema about geography and state capitals. For example, you needed to infer that "Platter" related to the Platte River. And, you needed to know that the Platte River runs through Nebraska and that Lincoln is Nebraska's capital. Indeed, "What is Lincoln?" is the correct question. Any time we form conceptual bridges between what we already know and what we are to learn is a form of schema activation.

Elaboration

You are at a noisy party. When you miss some of the conversation, you fill in details, trying to make sense of an incomplete message. You do the same when you read a text or listen to a lecture. You expand on (and sometimes distort) information to make it fit your expectations and current understanding. In each case, you are *elaborating* on either the message or what you already know.

Elaboration is an encoding strategy that increases the meaningfulness of new information by connecting it to existing knowledge (Terry, 2006). For example, a student who remembers the location of the Atlantic ocean on the globe because it starts with an "a" and the Americas and Africa also begin with "a," or a student who remembers $6 \times 9 = 54$ because the sum of the digits in the product of a number times 9 always equals 9 ($5 + 4 = 9$) is capitalizing on elaboration as an encoding strategy. When elaboration is used to remember factual information such as the location of the Atlantic Ocean or $6 \times 9 = 54$, it is often called *elaborative rehearsal*. Research confirms the superiority of elaborative rehearsal for long-term retention of information (Craik, 1979; King-Friedrichs & Browne, 2001).

In addition to elaborative rehearsal, two additional elaboration strategies can be effective. They are (1) the use of examples and analogies and (2) mnemonics.

Examples and Analogies. One of the most effective ways of promoting elaboration is through examples and other representations that illustrate the topic being taught. Working with examples—constructing, finding, or analyzing them—is arguably the most powerful elaboration strategy that exists because it also capitalizes on schema activation (Cassady, 1999). When people create or identify a new example of an idea, they activate their prior knowledge and then elaborate on their understanding of that idea. The attempt to illustrate the content of this chapter is our attempt to capitalize on elaboration as an encoding strategy. Teachers who use examples extensively also capitalize on elaboration as an encoding strategy. Examples also help accommodate lack of prior knowledge related to the topic.

When examples are not available, using *analogies*, descriptions of relationships that are similar in some but not all respects, can be an effective elaboration strategy

(Bulgren, Deshler, Schumaker, & Lentz, 2000). As an example, consider the following analogy from science: *Our circulatory system is like a pumping system that carries the blood around our bodies. The veins and arteries are the pipes, and the heart is the pump.*

The veins and arteries are similar, but not identical, to pipes, and the heart is a type of pump. The analogy is an effective form of elaboration because it links new information to a pumping station, an idea learners already understand.

Good fiction also makes extensive use of analogies in the form of similes and metaphors, and authors are encouraged to use them in their writing. For example, "He approached the door with the silent footsteps of a jungle cat" makes the story both more meaningful and more interesting.

Mnemonic devices are memory strategies that create associations that do not exist naturally in the content (Terry, 2006). Mnemonics link knowledge to be learned to familiar information, and they have been proven effective in a variety of content areas (Bloom & Lamkin, 2006; Uygur & Ozdas, 2007) with learners ranging from children to older adults (Brehmer & Li, 2007).

Mnemonics can take several forms. We can use acronyms, for example, such as HOMES to remember the names of the Great Lakes (Huron, Ontario, Michigan, Erie, and Superior) and phrases, such as "Every good boy does fine," to remember the names of the notes in the treble clef (E, G, B, D, and F). When learners think of the mnemonic, they link it to the information it represents, which aids the recall of information.

Mnemonics are used to help remember vocabulary, names, rules, lists, and other kinds of factual knowledge. Table 5.2 provides some additional examples.

The Importance of Cognitive Activity

Regardless of the encoding strategy being employed, it is essential that we are cognitively active when we attempt to use the strategy. For example, suppose you and a friend are studying for a math exam and have practice problems with worked solutions available. You read and attempt to solve the problems and then study the worked solutions. Your friend simply reads each problem and then studies the solution. Your approach is more effective because *you've placed yourself in a more cognitively active role than has your friend.* Thinking about and attempting to write a solution is active, and it capitalizes on both schema activation and elaboration. You attempt to activate a relevant schema by searching long-term memory for information related to the problems, and you then use elaboration when you answer them. Merely reading the solutions is passive, resulting in fewer connections to information in long-term memory and less meaningful learning. Similarly, when teachers ask students to provide additional examples, they place the students in cognitively active roles; a teacher providing the example does not encourage as much active processing (Bransford et al., 2000).

Table 5.2 Types and examples of mnemonic devices

Mnemonic	Description	Example
Method of loci	Learner combines imagery with specific locations in a familiar environment, such as the chair, sofa, lamp, end table, and footstool, in a living room	Student wanting to remember the first five elements of the periodic table visualizes hydrogen at the chair, helium at the sofa, lithium at the lamp, and so on
Peg-word method	Learner memorizes a series of "pegs"—such as "one is bun" and "two is shoe"—on which to-be-remembered information is hung	A person wanting to get pickles and carrots at the grocery store visualizes a pickle in a bun and a carrot stuck in a shoe
Link method	Individual visually links items to be remembered	A student visualizes *homework* stuck in a *notebook*, which is bound to his/her *textbook*, *pencil*, and *pen* with a rubber band to remember to take the (italicized) items to class
Key-word method	Learner uses imagery and rhyming words to remember unfamiliar words	A learner remembers that *trigo,* which rhymes with tree, is the Spanish word for wheat by visualizing a sheaf of wheat sticking out of a tree
First-letter method	An individual creates a word out of the first letters of the items to be remembered	A student creates the word *Wajmma* to remember the first six presidents in order: Washington, Adams, Jefferson, Madison, Monroe, and Adams

Forgetting

Forgetting is the loss of, or inability to retrieve, information from long-term memory, and it is both a real part of people's everyday lives and an important factor in learning.

Look again at the model first presented in Fig. 5.1. There we see that information lost from both sensory memory and working memory is unrecoverable. However, information in long-term memory has been encoded. Why can't we find it?

Forgetting as Interference

Some experts explain forgetting with the concept *interference*, the loss of information because something learned either before or after detracts from understanding (Howe, 2004). For example, students learn that the rule for forming singular possessives states that an apostrophe *s* is added to the singular noun. If their understanding of the rule for forming singular possessives later interferes with learning the rules for forming plural possessives and contractions, *proactive interference*, prior learning interfering with new understanding, has occurred. On the other hand, if the rules for forming plural possessives confuses their prior understanding, *retroactive interference* has occurred. Students' understanding of plural possessives and contractions can interfere with their understanding of singular possessives and vice versa.

Studying closely related ideas—such as communism and fascism, longitude and latitude, and adding fractions with similar and different denominators—together is perhaps the most effective strategy that exists for reducing interference (Hamilton, 1997). In doing so, we recognize similarities and differences and identify areas that are easily confused.

We can also reduce interference by reviewing previously studied material before we move to a new topic, which activates prior knowledge and provides a bridge to the new topic.

Forgetting as Retrieval Failure

Retrieval is the process of pulling information from long-term memory back into working memory, and many researchers believe that "forgetting" is actually the inability to retrieve information from long-term memory (Williams & Zacks, 2001). We have all had the experience of realizing that we know a name, fact, or some other information, but we simply cannot pull it up.

Retrieval depends on context and the way information is encoded (Williams & Zacks, 2001). For instance, you know a person at school, but you cannot remember his name when you see him at a party; his name was encoded in the school context, and you are trying to retrieve it in the context of the party.

Meaningfulness is the key to retrieval. The more detailed and interconnected knowledge is in long-term memory, the easier it is to retrieve (Nuthall, 1999a). Practice to the point of automaticity also facilitates retrieval (Chaffen & Imreh, 2002). When students know their math facts to the point of automaticity, for example, they can easily retrieve them for use in problem solving, leaving more working memory space to focus on solutions.

Metacognition: Knowledge and Control of Cognitive Processes

Have you ever said to yourself, "I'm going to sit near the front of the class so I won't fall asleep," or "I'm beat today. I'd better drink a cup of coffee before I go to class." If you have, you were being metacognitive. *Metacognition*, commonly described as "knowing about knowing," is our awareness of and control over our cognitive processes, and *meta-attention*, knowledge of and control over our ability to pay attention, is one type of metacognition (Meltzer, Pollica, & Barzillai, 2007; Pressley & Hilden, 2006). You were aware of the fact that your drowsiness might affect your ability to attend, and you exercised control over it by sitting near the front of the class or drinking a cup of coffee. Metacognition also explains why we make lists. We realize that we may forget to pick up some items at the store, and we exercise control by writing the items on a list.

Students who are aware of the way they study and learn achieve more than those less so (Kuhn & Dean, 2004). In other words, students who are metacognitive learn more than those who are not (Anderson & Nashon, 2007; Smith, Rook, & Smith, 2007), and at least four reasons exist for these differences.

First, students who are aware of the importance of attention are more likely to create effective personal learning environments, which can be as simple as moving to the front of the class or turning off a radio while studying. Second, learners who are aware of the possibility of misperceptions attempt to find corroborating information or ask if their understanding is accurate.

Third, metacognition helps regulate the flow of information through working memory. When you say to yourself, "I'd better write this down or I'll never remember it," you are exercising *metamemory*—knowledge and control of memory strategies. The ability to monitor the processing of information in working memory is essential because of its limited capacity.

Finally, metacognition influences the meaningfulness of encoding. For example, students who are metacognitive about their encoding consciously look for relationships in the topics they study. This influences their study strategies and ultimately how much they learn.

Putting the Memory Model into Perspective

The human memory model made an important contribution to increasing our understanding of the way we gather and organize information and store it for further use. However, the model, as initially presented in Fig. 5.1 oversimplifies the nature of human memory. For example, the model presents attention as a filter between sensory memory and working memory, but some evidence indicates that the central executive in working memory governs what we pay attention to and how we perceive that information. So, attending to incoming stimuli and attaching meaning to them are not as simple as the one-way flow of information that is suggested by the model (Demetriou, Christou, Spanoudis, & Platsidou, 2002). In addition, some researchers question whether or not working memory and long-term memory are as distinct as the model suggests (Baddeley, 2001; Wolz, 2003).

The memory model has also been criticized for failing to adequately consider the social context in which learning occurs (Greeno & van de Sande, 2007), as well as cultural and personal factors that influence learning, such as students' emotions (Nasir, Rosebery, Warren, & Lee, 2006). Critics also argue that it does not adequately account for the extent to which learners construct their own knowledge, one of the principles of cognitive learning theory presented at the beginning of the chapter (Kafai, 2006).

However, despite these criticisms, virtually all cognitive descriptions of learning, including those endorsing the principle that learners construct knowledge, accept the basic structure of the human memory model, including a limited-capacity working memory, a long-term memory that stores information in organized form, cognitive processes that move the information from one store to another, and the regulatory mechanisms of metacognition (Bransford et al., 2000; Sweller et al., 1998). These components help us explain learning events that behavioral views of learning cannot explain.

Summary

Principles of cognitive learning theory suggest the following: (a) learning and development depend on learners' experiences, (b) learners are mentally active in their attempts to make sense of those experiences, (c) learners construct knowledge, (d) prior knowledge influences knowledge construction, (e) learning is enhanced in a social environment, and (f) learning requires practice and feedback.

The human memory model is the cognitive architecture that can be used to describe how people gather, organize, and store their experiences. It is where knowledge is constructed and where prior knowledge is stored until needed for new knowledge construction.

Human memory is considered to consist of memory stores that hold information together with cognitive processes that move information from one store to another and organize the information so that it makes sense to the individual.

The memory stores consist of sensory memory, working memory, and long-term memory. Sensory memory is the store that briefly holds stimuli from the environment until they can be processed. Working memory is the conscious part of our information processing system. It is where knowledge is constructed and it is where deliberate thinking takes place. Its most significant feature is its limited capacity. Long-term memory is our permanent information store, and it is where declarative, procedural, and conditional knowledge are stored. When students struggle with complex tasks, such as writing or solving problems, lack of prior knowledge stored in long-term memory or skills that have not been developed to automaticity is often the cause.

The cognitive processes consist of attention, perception, rehearsal, encoding, and retrieval. Attention and perception move information from sensory memory to working memory. Attention is the process of consciously focusing on a stimulus, and perception is the meaning we attach to the stimulus. Learners use rehearsal to retain information in the phonological loop of working memory, and intensive rehearsal can move information into long-term memory. Encoding represents information in long-term memory. Learners encode information more effectively if it is represented both visually and verbally than if it is represented in only one way. Retrieval is the process of pulling information from long-term memory back into working memory for problem solving or further processing.

Metacognition is defined as individual's knowledge of, and control over, their cognitive processes. Metacognition influences learning by making learners aware of the way they study and learn and by providing strategies to increase learning. Metacognition is developmental, with young children being less aware of their study strategies than their older counterparts.

Acknowledgments We thank the major contributions that Don Kauchak, a respected colleague and friend, has made to the original work that provided the framework for this chapter. Without his contribution, preparing this chapter would have been extremely difficult. We want to use this opportunity to express our sincere gratitude.

References

Anderson, J. R. (2005). *Cognitive psychology and its implications* (6th ed.). New York: Worth.

Anderson, J. R. (2007). Information-processing modules and their relative modality specificity. *Cognitive Psychology, 54*(3), 185–217.

Anderson, D., & Nashon, S. (2007). Predators of knowledge construction: interpreting students' metacognition in an amusement park physics program. *Science Education, 91*, 298–320.

Atkinson, R., & Shiffrin, R. (1968). Human memory: A proposed system and its control processes. In K. Spence & J. Spence (Eds.), *The psychology of learning and motivation: Advances in research and theory* (Vol. 2). San Diego, CA: Academic Press.

Baddeley, A. D. (1986). *Working memory: Theory and practice.* London: Oxford University Press.

Baddeley, A. (2001). Is working memory still working? *American Psychologist, 56*, 851–864.

Berliner, D. C. (1986). In pursuit of the expert pedagogue. *Educational Researcher, 15*, 5–13.

Berliner, D. C. (2006). Educational psychology: Searching for essence throughout a century of influence. In P. A. Alexander & P. H. Winne (Eds.), *Handbook of educational psychology* (2nd ed., pp. 3–42). Mahwah, NJ: Erlbaum.

Bloom, C. M., & Lamkin, D. M. (2006). The olympian struggle to remember the cranial nerves: Mnemonics and student success. *Teaching of Psychology, 33*, 128–129.

Bransford, J., Brown, A., & Cocking, R. (Eds.). (2000). *How people learn: Brain, mind, experience, and school.* Washington, DC: National Academy Press.

Brehmer, Y., & Li, S. -C. (2007). Memory plasticity across the life span: Uncovering children's latent potential. *Developmental Psychology, 43*, 465–478.

Bulgren, J., Deshler, D., Schumaker, J., & Lenz, B. K. (2000). The use and effectiveness of analogical instruction in diverse secondary content classrooms. *Journal of Educational Psychology, 92*(3), 426–441.

Cassady, J. (1999, April). *The effects of examples as elaboration in text on memory and learning.* Paper presented at the annual meeting of the American Educational Research Association, Montreal, Canada.

Chaffen, R., & Imreh, G. (2002). Practicing perfection: Piano performance and expert memory. *Psychological Science, 13*, 342–349.

Chomsky, N. (1959). A review of Skinner's verbal behavior. *Language, 35*, 25–58.

Clark, R. C., & Mayer, R. E. (2003). *e-Learning and the science of instruction: Proven guidelines for consumers and designers of multimedia learning.* San Francisco: Pfeiffer/Wiley.

Clark, J., & Paivio, A. (1991). Dual coding theory and education. *Educational Psychology Review, 3*, 149–210.

Craig, D. (2003). Brain-compatible learning: Principles and applications in athletic training. *Journal of Athletic Training, 38*(4), 342–350.

Craik, F. I. M. (1979). Human memory. *Annual Review of Psychology, 30*, 63–102.

Cuban, L. (1993). *How teachers taught: Constancy and change in American classrooms: 1890–1990* (2nd ed.). New York: Teachers College Press.

Curtindale, L., Laurie-Rose, C., & Bennett-Murphy., L. (2007). Sensory modality, temperament, and the development of sustained attention: A vigilance study in children and adults. *Developmental Psychology, 43*(3), 576–589.

Demetriou, A., Christou, C., Spanoudis, G., & Platsidou, M. (2002). The development of mental processing: Efficiency, working memory, and thinking. *Monographs of the society for research in child development* (Serial No. 268, Vol. 67, No. 1). Boston, MA: Blackwell Publishing.

Dolezal, S., Welsh, L., Pressley, M., & Vincent, M. (2003). How nine third-grade teachers motivate student academic engagement. *Elementary School Journal, 103*, 239–268.

Feldon, D. F. (2007). The implications of research on expertise for curriculum and pedagogy. *Educational Psychology Review, 19*(2), 91–110.

Gagne, E. D., Yekovich, F. R., & Yekovich, C. W. (1997). *The cognitive psychology of school learning* (2nd ed.). Boston, MA: Allyn & Bacon.

Greeno, J., & van de Sande, C. (2007). Perspectival understanding of conceptions and conceptual growth in interaction. *Educational Psychologist, 42*(1), 9–24.

Greeno, J., Collins, A., & Resnick, L. (1996). Cognition and learning. In D. Berliner & R. Calfee (Eds.), *Handbook of educational psychology* (pp. 15–46). New York: Macmillan.

Hamilton, R. (1997). Effects of three types of elaboration on learning concepts from text. *Contemporary Education Psychology, 22*, 299–318.

Hergenhahn, B. R., & Olson, M. H. (2001). *An introduction to theories of learning* (6th ed.). Upper Saddle River, NJ: Merrill/Prentice Hall.

Howe, M. L. (2004). The role of conceptual recoding in reducing children's retroactive interference. *Developmental Psychology, 40*, 131–139.

Huan, V. S., Yeo, L. S., & Ang, R. P. (2006). The influence of dispositional optimism and gender on adolescents' perception of academic stress. *Adolescence, 41*, 533–546.

Igo, L. B., Kiewra, K., & Bruning, R. (2004). Removing the snare from the pair: Using pictures to learn confusing word pairs. *Journal of Experimental Education, 72*(3), 165–178.

Kafai, Y. (2006). Constructionism. In R. K. Sawyer (Ed.), *The Cambridge handbook of the learning sciences* (pp. 35–46). New York: Cambridge University Press.

Karateken, C. (2004). A test of the integrity of the components of Baddeley's model of working memory in attention-deficit/hyperactivity disorder (ADHD). *The Journal of Child Psychology and Psychiatry and Allied Disciplines, 45*(5), 912–926.

Kibby, M. Y., Marks, W., & Morgan, S. (2004). Specific impairment in developmental reading disabilities: A working memory approach. *Journal of Learning Disabilities, 37*(4), 349–363.

King-Friedrichs, J., & Browne, D. (2001). Learning to remember. *The Science Teacher, 68*, 44–46.

Kozhevnikov, M., Hegarty, M., & Mayer, R. (1999, April). *Students' use of imagery in solving qualitative problems in kinematics*. Paper presented at the annual meeting of the American Educational Research Association, Montreal, Canada.

Kuhn, D., & Dean, D., Jr. (2004). Metacognition: A bridge between cognitive psychology and educational practice. *Theory into Practice, 43*(4), 268–273.

Lin, J. -R. (2007). Responses to anomalous data obtained from repeatable experiments in the laboratory. *Journal of Research in Science Teaching, 44*(3), 506–528.

Mayer, R. (2002). *The promise of educational psychology: Volume II. Teaching for meaningful learning*. Upper Saddle River, NJ: Merrilll/ Prentice Hall.

Mayer, R. (2008). *Learning and instruction*. Upper Saddle River, NJ: Pearson.

Mayer, R. E., & Wittrock, M. C. (2006). Problem solving. In P. A. Alexander & P. H. Winne (Eds.), *Handbook of educational psychology* (2, pp. 287–303). Mahwah, NJ: Erlbaum.

McCutchen, D. (2000). Knowledge, processing, and working memory: Implications for a theory of writing. *Educational Psychologist, 35*(1), 13–23.

Merkley, D., & Jefferies, D. (2001). Guidelines for implementing a graphic organizer. *Reading Teacher, 54*(4), 350–357.

Miller, G. (1956). The magical number seven, plus or minus two: Some limits on our capacity for processing information. *Psychological Review, 63*, 81–97.

Moll, L. C., & Whitmore, K. (1993). Vygotsky in classroom practice: Moving from individual transmission to social transaction. In E. Forman, N. Minick, & C. Stone (Eds.), *Contexts for learning* (pp. 19–42). New York: Oxford University Press.

Moreno, R., & Duran, R. (2004). Do multiple representations need explanations: The role of verbal guidance and individual differences in multimedia mathematics learning. *Journal of Educational Psychology, 96*, 492–503.

Nasir, N., Rosebery, A., Warren, B., & Lee, C. (2006). Learning as a cultural process: Achieving equity through diversity. In R. K. Sawyer (Ed.), *The Cambridge handbook of the learning sciences* (pp. 489–504). New York: Cambridge University Press.
Neisser, U. (1967). *Cognitive psychology*. New York: Appleton-Century-Crofts.
Nuthall, G. (1999a). Learning how to learn: The evolution of students' minds through the social processes and culture of the classroom. *International Journal of Educational Research, 31*(3), 141–256.
Nuthall, G. (1999b). The way students learn: Acquiring knowledge from an integrated science and social studies unit. *Elementary School Journal, 99*(4), 303–342.
Nuthall, G. A. (2000). The role of memory in the acquisition and retention of knowledge in science and social studies units. *Cognition and Instruction, 18*(1), 83–139.
Paas, F., Renkl, A., & Sweller, J. (2004). Cognitive load theory: Instructional implications of the interaction between information structures and cognitive architecture. *Instructional Science, 32*(1), 1–8.
Paivio, A. (1986). *Mental representations: A dual-coding approach*. New York: Oxford University.
Paivio, A. (1991). Dual coding theory: Retrospect and current status. *Canadian Journal of Psychology, 45*, 255–287.
Pashler, H., & Carrier, M. (1996). Structures, processes, and the flow of information. In E. Bjork & R. Bjork (Eds.), *Memory* (pp. 3–29). San Diego, CA: Academic Press.
Piaget, J. (1952). *Origins of intelligence in children*. New York: International Universities Press.
Piaget, J. (1959). *Language and thought of the child* (M. Grabain, Trans.). New York: Humanities Press.
Piaget, J. (1970). *The science of education and the psychology of the child*. New York: Orion Press.
Piaget, J. (1980). *Adaptation and intelligence: Organic selection and phenocopy* (S. Eames, Trans.). Chicago, IL: University of Chicago Press.
Pressley, M., & Hilden, K. (2006). Cognitive strategies. In D. Kuhn, & R. Siegler (Eds.), *Handbook of child psychology* (6th ed., Vol. 2, pp. 511–556). Hoboken, NJ: John Wiley & Sons, Inc.
Roblyer, M. (2006). *Integrating educational technology into teaching* (4th ed.). Upper Saddle River, NJ: Merrill/Prentice Hall.
Rogoff, B. (1998). Cognition as a collaborative process. (In W. Damon (Series Ed.), D. Kuhn, & R. S. Siegler (Vol. Eds.)), *Handbook of child psychology: Vol. 2* (5th ed., pp. 679–744). New York: Wiley.
Royer, J. (Ed.). (2005). *The cognitive revolution in educational psychology*. Greenwich, CT: Information Age Publishing.
Rutter, M., Maughan, B., Mortimore, P., Ousten, J., & Smith, A. (1979). *Fifteen thousand hours. Secondary schools and their effects on children*. Cambridge, MA: Harvard University Press.
Sadoski, M., & Paivio, A. (2001). *Imagery and text: A dual coding theory of reading and writing*. Mahwah, NJ: Erlbaum.
Sawyer, R. K. (2006). Introduction: The new science of learning. In R. K. Sawyer (Ed.), *The Cambridge handbook of the learning sciences* (pp. 1–18). New York: Cambridge University Press.
Schacter, D. (2001). *The seven deadly sins of memory*. Boston: Houghton Mifflin.
Schank, R. C., & Abelson, R. (1977). *Scripts, plans, goals, and understanding*. Mahwah, NJ: Erlbaum.
Schneider, W., & Shiffrin, R. (1977). Controlled and automatic human information processing: Detection, search, and attention. *Psychological Review 84*, 1–66.
Schunk, D. (2004). *Learning theories: An educational perspective* (4th ed.). Upper Saddle River, NJ: Merrill/Pearson.
Schwartz, D., & Heiser, J. (2006). Spatial representations and imagery in learning. In R. K. Sawyer (Ed.), *The Cambridge handbook of the learning sciences* (pp. 283–298). New York: Cambridge University Press.
Shuell, T. (1996). Teaching and learning in a classroom context. In D. Berliner & R. Calfee (Eds.), *Handbook of educational psychology* (pp. 726–764). New York: Macmillan.

Simon, H. (2001). Learning to research about learning. In S. M. Carver & D. Klake (Eds.), *Cognition and instruction*. Mahwah, NJ: Erlbaum.
Smith, K. S., Rook, J. E., & Smith, T. W. (2007). Increasing student engagement using effective and metacognitive writing strategies in content areas. *Preventing School Failure, 51*, 43–48.
Star, J. (2004, April). *The development of flexible procedural knowledge in equation solving*. Paper presented at the annual meeting of the American Educational Research Association, San Diego.
Star., J. R. (2005). Reconceptualizing procedural knowledge. *Journal for Research in Mathematics Education, 36*(5), 404–411.
Sweller, J. (2003). Evolution of human cognitive architecture. *The Psychology of Learning and Motivation, 43*, 215–266.
Sweller, J., van Merrienboer, J., & Paas, F. (1998). Cognitive architecture and instructional design. *Educational Psychology Review, 10*, 251–296.
Taraban, R., Anderson, E. E., & DeFinis, A. (2007). First steps in understanding engineering students' growth of conceptual and procedural knowledge in an interactive learning context. *Journal of Engineering Education, 96*, 57–68.
Taylor, B., Pearson, P. D., Peterson, D., & Rodriguez, M. (2003). Reading growth in high-poverty classrooms: The influence of teacher practices that encourage cognitive engagement in literacy learning. *Elementary School Journal, 104*(1), 3–28.
Terry, S. (2006). *Learning and memory: Basic principles, process, and procedures* (3rd ed.). Boston, MA: Allyn & Bacon.
Tulving, E. (2002). Episodic memory: From mind to brain. *Annual review of psychology, 53*, 1–25.
Uygur, T., & Ozdas, A. (2007). The effect of arrow diagrams on achievement in applying the chain rule. *Primus, 17*, 131–147.
Valenzeno, L., Alibali, M., & Klatsky, R. (2003). Teachers' gestures facilitate students' learning: A lesson in symmetry. *Contemporary Educational Psychology, 28*, 187–204.
Vygotsky, L. (1978). *Mind in society: The development of higher psychological processes* (M. Cole, V. John-Steiner, S. Scribner, & E. Souberman, Eds. & Trans.). Cambridge, MA: Harvard University Press.
Vygotsky, L. (1986). *Thought and language*. Cambridge, MA: MIT Press.
Way, N., Reddy, R., & Rhodes, J. (2007). Students' perceptions of school climate during the middle school years: Associations with trajectories of psychological and behavioral adjustment. *American Journal of Community Psychology, 40*, 194–213.
Williams, C., & Zacks, R. (2001). Is retrieval-induced forgetting an inhibitory process? *American Journal of Psychology, 114*, 329–354.
Willingham, D. T. (2004). *Cognition: The thinking animal* (2nd ed.). Upper Saddle River, NJ: Merrill/Prentice Hall.
Willingham, D. T. (2009). *Why don't students like school?* San Francisco: Jossey-Bass.
Willingham, D. T. (2009). *Why don't students like school? A cognitive scientist answers questions about how the mind words and what it means for your classroom*. San Francisco: Jossey-Bass.
Willoughby, T., Porter, L., Belsito, L., & Yearsley, T. (1999). Use of elaboration strategies by students in grades two, four, and six. *Elementary School Journal, 99*(3), 221–232.
Wolz, D. J. (2003). Implicit cognitive processes as aptitudes for learning. *Educational Psychologist, 38*, 95–104.
Zhou, Q., Hofer, C., & Eisenberg, N. (2007). The developmental trajectories of attention focusing, attentional and behavioral persistence, and externalizing problems during school-age years. *Developmental Psychology, 43*, 369–385.

Chapter 6
Metacognitive Control of Learning and Remembering

Jason R. Finley, Jonathan G. Tullis, and Aaron S. Benjamin

University of Illinois at Urbana-Champaign, Champaign, IL, USA

Introduction

The study of learning and memory has a long and veritable history in psychological research. One recent and important development is the growth of research in *metamemory*—the study of what people understand about their memory and how they use that knowledge to direct their own learning experiences in service of their goals. Metamemory research has been guided in part by the framework proposed by Nelson and Narens (1994), which differentiates between *metacognitive monitoring* of one's states of learning and *metacognitive control* over the processes by which one achieves desired levels of skill and memory. These processes are guided by learners' knowledge and beliefs about how memory works, about what aspects of performance are reliable indicators of durable learning, and about what actions are effective for advancing learning (cf. Dunlosky & Hertzog, 2000; Hertzog, Dunlosky, & Robinson, 2007).

This chapter will discuss the role of metacognition in the learning of simple verbal materials, with a particular emphasis on metacognitive control. Learners can regulate their study experience to enhance learning in a myriad of ways (cf. Benjamin, 2008; Dunlosky, Serra, & Baker, 2007; Serra & Metcalfe, 2009). Here we consider forms of control that have been studied in simple laboratory tasks and that generalize in a straightforward way to options available to students studying for tests: self-pacing study effectively, devising efficient study schedules, judiciously selecting items for study and re-study, strategically making use of self-testing strategies, accommodating study to anticipated test conditions, and using successful retrieval strategies. We will review research that reveals how learners use these strategies in simple laboratory tasks and that suggests how such metacognitive skills can be improved through instruction or experience. We will end by addressing the supportive role that information technology can play in the processes by which metacognition influences learning and memory.

J.R. Finley (✉)
University of Illinois at Urbana-Champaign, Champaign, IL, USA
e-mail: jrfinley@uiuc.edu

M.S. Khine, I.M. Saleh (eds.), *New Science of Learning*,
DOI 10.1007/978-1-4419-5716-0_6, © Springer Science+Business Media, LLC 2010

Interplay Between Metacognitive Monitoring and Control

In this section, we review evidence on the relationship between monitoring and control. The effective control of learning behavior requires accurate assessments of current states of knowledge (Benjamin, Bjork, & Schwartz, 1998; Benjamin, 2005; Konopka & Benjamin, 2009), the current rate of learning (Metcalfe & Kornell, 2005), the effects of various stimulus factors on learning (Benjamin, 2003), the effectiveness of competing strategies in promoting additional learning (Benjamin & Bird, 2006; Son, 2004), the nature and payoff structure of the upcoming test (Benjamin, 2003; Dunlosky & Thiede, 1998), and the exact form of the learning function for the particular study material (Son & Sethi, 2006).

Metacognitive monitoring is theorized to directly impact control of learning behavior. According to the "monitoring affects control" hypothesis (Nelson & Leonesio, 1988), objective item difficulty influences a person's beliefs about item difficulty, which in turn influence control processes such as study time allocation, item selection, retrieval strategies, and output decisions.

Monitoring of Ongoing Learning

The most prominent example of monitoring affecting control comes from research on self-pacing (i.e., allocation of study time). The *discrepancy reduction* model of self-pacing (Thiede & Dunlosky, 1999) suggests that learners set a desired state of learning, continuously monitor their current state of learning while studying, and only stop studying when their current state meets or exceeds the desired state. As this model predicts, learners usually do allocate more study time to material judged as more difficult, across a wide range of circumstances—from children to older adults (Dufresne & Kobasigawa, 1988, 1989; Kobasigawa & Metcalf-Haggert, 1993), from recognition to free recall tasks (Belmont & Butterfield, 1971; Le Ny, Denheire, & Taillanter, 1972; Zacks, 1969), and from simple to complex study materials (Baker & Anderson, 1982; Maki & Serra, 1992; Son & Metcalfe, 2000).

Another position on how learners choose to self-pace learning of differentially challenging materials is the *region of proximal learning* hypothesis, which posits that learners preferentially allocate study time not to items that are furthest from their current grasp (as specified by the discrepancy reduction model) but rather to items that are just slightly beyond their current grasp. According to this hypothesis, learners monitor their current *rate* of learning and continue to study items until that rate drops below a pre-determined threshold. This contrasts with the discrepancy reduction model, in which learners study until the item reaches a predetermined *level* of learning. Research on the influence of domain expertise and on the influence of learning goals supports aspects of the region of proximal learning hypothesis: experts allocate their study time to more difficult items than do novices, and conditions inducing low performance goals (e.g., time pressure or penalties for remembering too many items) lead learners to spend more time on easy items, abandoning the more difficult items (Thiede & Dunlosky, 1999; Son & Metcalfe, 2000).

For the purposes of this chapter, the critical aspect of both theories is that they incorporate a predominant role for the monitoring of ongoing learning in determining what to study and how to distribute study time across materials.

Judgments of Learning as an Index of Current Learning

One difficulty in evaluating how learners operate upon materials of varying difficulty is the presence of idiosyncratic differences in knowledge and intellectual skills. What is difficult for one learner may be easy for another, for a variety of reasons relating to their constitution and experience. In research on metacognition, this problem is often addressed by asking learners to make explicit assessments of their level of learning; such *judgments of learning* (JOLs) are reflective of normative difficulty (e.g., Dunlosky & Matvey, 2001) and show reasonable correlations with learners' later test performance (e.g., Arbuckle & Cuddy, 1969; Dunlosky & Nelson, 1992, 1994; Lovelace, 1984). Although there are numerous cases in which JOLs are dissociable from actual learning (e.g., Benjamin, 2003, 2005; Benjamin & Bjork, 1996; Benjamin et al., 1998; Finn & Metcalfe, 2008; Schwartz & Metcalfe, 1994; Metcalfe, Schwartz, & Joaquim, 1993), subjective JOLs are likely to be a reasonable proxy variable for a learner's objective current learning state under most conditions.

In a meta-analysis of published research examining the relationship between JOLs and study time allocation, Son and Metcalfe (2000) found that 35 out of 46 published papers revealed a negative correlation: learners devote more time to items they have rated as the least well learned. In addition, choice of items for re-study is related to learners' JOLs: when given the option of re-studying a portion of previously studied materials, learners typically choose to re-study those items to which they gave the lowest JOLs (Nelson, Dunlosky, Graf, & Narens, 1994). Even in situations where JOLs are unrelated to final recall performance, learners choose to re-study items based on their JOLs and not on their ultimate recall performance (Finn & Metcalfe, 2008). Such evidence suggests that learners control their studying based on the results of their monitoring, generally choosing to re-study and spend more time on items they have judged most difficult to remember.

Monitoring of Retrieval Processes and Control of Output

Monitoring has also been found to influence control at the time of retrieval. For example, when learners give high *feelings of knowing* to unrecalled answers—that is, high judgments of knowing the answer even though they cannot currently recall it—they are willing to search memory for a longer period of time (Costermans, Lories, & Ansay, 1992; Nelson & Narens, 1990). A similar process appears to underlie how learners respond to general information questions. An initial, rapid feeling of knowing guides a strategic choice: if they think they have enough relevant knowledge, learners will try to directly retrieve the answer from memory, but if they do not think they have enough relevant knowledge, they will instead try to compute a plausible answer from a set of related facts stored in memory (Reder, 1987).

After learners find an answer in their memory or derive a plausible one from relevant knowledge, they control whether to withhold or report the answer. This decision is greatly influenced by another form of monitoring: their *confidence* in the answer. A strong correlation has been found between subjective confidence in the correctness of an answer and the willingness to report that answer (Koriat & Goldsmith, 1996). When forced to provide a response for every general knowledge question posed, learners report more answers but have lower overall accuracy compared to learners who are allowed to respond with "I don't know." This shows that under "free report" circumstances, learners selectively withhold low confidence answers in order to boost their overall accuracy. Furthermore, learners shift their confidence criteria for reporting answers in response to external reward structures, suggesting that learners have great control over which answers they report. Learners are willing to report lower confidence answers when external incentives reward quantity over accuracy but withhold these lower confidence answers when the external incentives reward overall accuracy instead of quantity.

The Study of Metacognitive Control

In laboratory experiments, the relative effectiveness of metacognitive control is evaluated by comparing memory performance following learner-based versus experimenter-based control of some aspect of study. The implicit assumption in such a comparison is that learners seek primarily to maximize performance. It is worth noting, however, that students and other learners outside the laboratory may have more complex goals. Such learners have constraints on the time they have to spend (Son & Metcalfe, 2000) and the effort they are willing to expend and may be seeking to satisfice rather than optimize (Simon, 1957).

Given this complex interplay of goals and abilities, as well as the high demand for effective metacognitive monitoring, it is all the more impressive that there is a wealth of results indicating that metacognitive control is widely used and often quite effective. The next portion of this chapter will focus on examples of such metacognitive control.

Effectiveness of Metacognitive Control

Self-Pacing of Study

One way of assessing the value of metacognitive control is to evaluate the efficacy of self-paced study (or study-time allocation). As discussed earlier, learners usually devote more time to the items which they judge to be most difficult; however, spending additional time studying difficult material sometimes results in no benefit for memory of those items (labeled the "labor in vain" effect, cf. Nelson & Leonesio, 1988). It is not obvious that allowing learners to self-pace can improve their performance compared to controls who do not self-pace. In a study by Koriat, Ma'ayan, and Nussinson (2006), learners either self-paced their study of a word list or spent the same amount of time studying the words but were forced to view words for uniform amounts of time across items. Self-pacing did not lead to any significant improvement in performance on a cued recall task. However, using a recognition task (a more sensitive measure of memory), Tullis and Benjamin (2009) found that learners who were allowed to allocate their own study time performed significantly better than did learners forced to spend uniform amounts of time across items. Interestingly, the improvement in memory performance was found only for learners who allocated more time to the normatively difficult items at the expense of the easy items. This result demonstrates that the net effect of self-control over the pace of study can benefit performance, but only for learners who engage in an effective allocation strategy.

There is also evidence that the effectiveness of study time allocation increases with age and expertise. Liu and Fang (2005) found that older grade school students were more selective about which items they spent more time studying and that free recall performance correspondingly increased with age. Liu and Fang (2006) found that older students spent less time on easy items and more time on difficult items as compared to younger students. Metcalfe (2002) found a difference in the way novices versus experts allocated study time across English–Spanish word pairs of varying difficulty. Both groups appear to selectively allocate time to unlearned items that were closest to being learned. For the experts (self-identified Spanish speakers), those were the most difficult items; for the novices, those were items that were somewhat easier.

Devising Study Schedules

Although strategically scheduling one's own study is a common activity, few experiments have investigated how learners do so in laboratory tasks. One important aspect of scheduling that has received some attention is the temporal distribution of multiple study trials for the same item. It is well established that spacing out such trials, rather than massing them together, results in superior memory performance at a delay (cf. Cepeda, Pashler, Vul, Wixted, & Rohrer, 2006). Son (2004) investigated learners' tendency to effectively employ spacing. Learners were presented with synonym word pairs (e.g., "hirsute—hairy") for 1 s each. After each presentation, learners made a JOL, then chose whether to re-study the pair immediately, at a delay, or not at all. Finally, learners were given a cued recall test after a 15-min delay. Results showed that learners scheduled re-study based on their metacognitive monitoring, tending to space items they judged as harder and mass items they judged as easier. Thus, in contrast to findings on self-pacing that support the discrepancy reduction model, learners used the more effective scheduling strategy (spacing) on less difficult items. However, Benjamin and Bird (2006) found the opposite effect when they increased initial presentation time to 5 s and added the constraints that all pairs be restudied, half massed and half spaced. Toppino, Cohen, Davis, and Moors (2009) sought to elucidate these discrepant findings by manipulating initial presentation time (1 vs. 5 s). They found that learners tended to space harder pairs when given more time and vice versa when given less time. The preference for massed re-study in the 1 s condition appeared to arise from inadequate time to fully perceive the pair, which happened more often for pairs consisting of longer and lower-frequency words (i.e., the harder pairs). When given enough time for initial encoding, learners indeed employ effective scheduling for more difficult material.

Selection of Items for Study and Re-study

Learners make sensible decisions about which items they should re-study (or drop from studying), but are overly optimistic about their final level of memory performance. Kornell and Metcalfe (2006) gave learners a list of general knowledge facts to study once. Learners then decided which half of the items they needed to re-study, and these decisions were either honored (learners restudied the items they selected) or dishonored (learners studied the items they did not choose). Honoring learners' choices about which items to re-study led to greater final test performance than did dishonoring those choices. This demonstrates that learners can make reasonable choices about which items to re-study and that giving learners control over their own study can improve memory performance.

However, giving learners more control over item selection does not always lead to better performance. Kornell and Bjork (2008) and Atkinson (1972) showed that learners with less control over which items they re-studied outperformed those with more control. In the study by Kornell and Bjork, some learners were allowed to drop English–Swahili word pairs from their study routine, while others had no choice but to re-study the entire list of pairs. Allowing learners to drop items from their study routine generally hurt performance (compared to making the learners re-study the entire list of items) on a final cued recall test, both immediately and at 1 week delay, even when the groups were given the same overall amount of study time. In combination with the Kornell and Metcalfe study (2006), this shows that learners are effective at choosing which items they need to re-study, but overly optimistic about their ability to recall information later. Atkinson evaluated memory performance under conditions in which item selection was controlled by learners, determined randomly, or determined by an experimenter-designed adaptive algorithm. He found that performance by the self-controlled group was higher than the random group, but lower than the algorithm group. Thus, learners choose items for re-study effectively to some extent but less than optimally.

Strategic Use of Self-Testing

Kornell and Son (2009) investigated the extent to which learners would employ self-testing when studying word pairs using a flashcard-like paradigm. After an initial presentation, learners could chose to either re-study all items or receive a practice test on all items. They more often chose to self-test, which produced greater final test performance than did re-study. Curiously, however, learners rated re-study as more effective. This, along with survey data (cf. Kornell & Bjork, 2007) suggests that learners may choose self-testing not out of a belief that it will directly enhance memory but rather as a useful tool for self-assessment.

Accommodating Study to Anticipated Test Conditions

Learners' expectations about the format of an upcoming test influence the way they study (a.k.a. encoding strategy) and their ultimate performance. For example, learners expecting a recall test have been found to outperform learners expecting a recognition test on a final test of either format (cf. Neely & Balota, 1981). Kang (2009) investigated learners' tendencies to choose different forms of self-testing as a form of practice and whether that tendency could be improved. Learners studied Malay–English word pairs, and when explicitly presented with study options that included practice cued recall or practice multiple choice, learners more frequently chose the study option that matched the test format they were induced to expect. On a final cued recall test after a 2 day delay, learners who had chosen practice cued recall outperformed those who had chosen practice multiple choice, demonstrating the effectiveness of their self-testing choice.

Although learners do appear to tailor their encoding strategies toward the expected demands of an upcoming test, they do not always do so effectively. In a study by Finley and Benjamin (2009) learners studied word pairs across multiple study-test cycles. One group received free recall tests for only the target (right-hand) words. Even after an initial study-test cycle, these learners still employed unhelpful strategies, such as attending to the relationship between the left- and right-hand words. However, as we will detail later, their use of an appropriate encoding strategy did improve with further experience.

Retrieval Strategies

Metacognitive control may be exercised during retrieval as well as encoding. For example, in a typical laboratory free recall test, learners may output items in any order, thus allowing them to implement whatever retrieval strategy they wish. In a serial recall test, learners are instead forced to output items in a specific order (typically the same order in which items were presented), reducing the amount of control they can exercise over their retrieval processes. Several studies have found that total recall is lower for immediate serial recall tests than for immediate free recall tests (Bhatarah, Ward, & Tan, 2008; Earhard, 1967; Klein, Addis, & Kahana, 2005; Waugh, 1961). This result demonstrates that, left to their druthers, people choose an output strategy that increases performance relative to having no control over output order.

Taken together, the results in this section speak both to the basic effectiveness of learners' metacognitive control and to implications for improving control. That is, learners are generally effective at controlling study, but there is room for improvement.

Improving Metacognitive Control

Improving Monitoring

To improve memory performance, one can focus on metacognitive monitoring or control. Superior evaluation of what is likely to be difficult and what is likely to be easy can enable more effective allocation of one's time and resources, even as one's control policy remains consistent.

One way of increasing the accuracy of metacognitive monitoring is to delay judgments until some time after study, rather than making them immediately following study (Nelson & Dunlosky, 1991), and furthermore to make judgments without looking at the complete answer, thus encouraging active retrieval of relevant information from memory (Dunlosky & Nelson, 1992). Thiede, Anderson, and Therriault (2003) extended these results to a more complex task. They found that generating keywords after reading a text passage led to more accurate self-ratings of text comprehension compared to no keyword generation, and this advantage was even greater when keyword generation was done at a delay. Furthermore, the more accurate monitoring was followed by more strategic choices of which texts to re-study and higher scores on a final test. Thus, a condition which improved metacognitive monitoring also promoted more effective study choices. Dunlosky, Hertzog, Kennedy, and Thiede (2005) reviewed other data showing enhanced performance resulting from improvements in metacognitive monitoring.

Improved metacognitive monitoring may enable more effective implementations of control processes. But a focus on directly improving metacognitive control may also be an effective way to improve learning.

Improving Control at Encoding Via Direct Instruction

It is well known that learners can follow instructions (a.k.a. "orienting tasks") to encode or retrieve material differently, resulting in changes in performance. For example, Craik and Lockhart (1972) demonstrated that semantic ("deep") encoding of words, such as deciding whether each word would fit into a category or not, led to superior subsequent memory performance versus more "shallow" encoding, such as making judgments about a word's font.

Another relevant principle in human learning and memory is that of *transfer-appropriate processing*: memory performance is enhanced to the extent that mental processes at encoding and retrieval are similar. This principle suggests that effective encoding strategies are those that employ processes most closely matching those that will be used at the time of retrieval. This is borne out in a study by Morris, Bransford, and Franks (1977). In that study, learners were presented with single words that were each preceded by an orienting sentence that either induced semantic processing (e.g., "The—had a silver engine." ... "TRAIN") or phonetic processing (e.g., "– rhymes with legal." ... "EAGLE"). Learners responded "yes" or "no" to each item, either judging whether the word was appropriate in the sentence or judging whether the word indeed rhymed. Learners were then given either a standard recognition test for the originally presented words or a recognition test for words that rhymed with the original words. For the standard recognition test (which presumably induces more emphasis on the meaning of words), performance was highest for items that had undergone semantic processing at encoding. However, for the rhyming recognition test, performance was highest for items that had undergone phonetic processing at encoding. Thus, performance on each test type was superior for items that had been processed in a transfer-appropriate way at encoding.

Learners can also be instructed to use various *mnemonic* strategies to enhance learning (Bellezza, 1996). For example, Roediger (1980) instructed learners to study word lists using elaborative rehearsal (repeating each word and its meaning to themselves multiple times), visual imagery for each word, visual imagery that linked words, the loci method (imagining each word in a familiar sequential location), or the peg method (associating each word with a pre-learned sequence of "peg" words, such as "gun" for position one). On immediate and 24-h delayed tests, learners were instructed to try to recall words in the same order that they had been studied. The linked imagery, loci, and peg mnemonics led to greater performance than elaborative rehearsal and individual imagery, in terms of total number of words recalled, and especially words recalled in their correct order. This demonstrates that learners can capably employ metacognitive control processes from direct instruction and that these acts can enhance learning, particularly when such processes are well-suited for the retrieval task (although the costs of such strategies may be worth considering as well; e.g., Benjamin & Bjork, 2000).

Improving Control at Encoding via Experience

To what extent can metacognitive control be improved via experience rather than instructions? Relevant research here has chiefly used multiple study-test cycles to investigate changes in metacognitive control. Repeated exposure to the conditions of study and test can lead learners to adopt more effective control strategies, particularly when they are also assisted in assessing their own performance as a function of the control processes they implement.

Postman (1964) found that learning improved across a series of unrelated word lists as learners acclimated to the task, a phenomenon he dubbed “learning to learn.” It is also clear from studies of intentional versus incidental learning that knowledge at all of an upcoming test can change the way learners encode information, though specific knowledge about the test format may do so more potently (McDaniel, Blischak, & Challis, 1994). What changes in metacognitive control of study may give rise to such effects?

Learners have been shown to adjust their amount of study after experience with the nature of the material and the demands of the test. For example, d’Ydewalle, Swerts, and De Corte (1983, Experiment 2) had learners study a passage of text for as long as they wanted, followed by either a fill-in-the-blank test or a multiple choice test. Learners were led to expect that they would receive the same test format for a second study-test cycle (using a new text passage of the same length). Learners spent more time studying the passage in the second cycle than they had during the first cycle. Furthermore, they spent more time if they expected a fill-in-the-blank test versus a multiple choice test. These changes in study duration were appropriate considering that performance on the first test was rarely perfect and that the fill-in-the-blank test was more difficult than the multiple choice test.

Finley and Benjamin (2009) evaluated learners’ abilities to adaptively modify their encoding strategies to better reflect the demands of upcoming tests as they gained more experience with the tests. Across four study-test cycles, learners were induced to expect either cued or free recall tests by studying lists of word pairs and receiving the same test format for each list. Tests required recall of the target (right-hand) words either in the presence (cued recall) or in the absence (free recall) of the cue (left-hand) words. A fifth and final cycle included either the expected or the alternate, unexpected test format. On both cued and free recall final tests, learners who had expected that format outperformed those who had not expected it, as shown in Fig. 6.1. Furthermore, on subsequent tests of recognition, cued-expecting learners showed superior recognition of cue words and superior associative recognition of intact word pairs, with such recognition decreasing across lists for free-expecting learners. These results demonstrate that learners were not merely modulating study *effort* based on anticipated test difficulty but were adopting qualitatively different encoding strategies that were appropriate to the demands of the expected test. Specifically, free-expecting learners learned to attend predominantly to the target words, abandoning the cue-target associative strategy with which they had begun.

In another experiment, Finley and Benjamin (2009) investigated adaptive changes in control of self-paced study. Learners were allowed to control study time across three cued recall and three free recall study-test cycles. They were instructed as to the nature of each upcoming test before they began the study. Importantly, each cycle included word pairs of both high and low associative strength, a variable that affected performance for cued recall (higher recall for high associative strength pairs) but not free recall. Learners began the task by allocating more study time to pairs with low associative strength when expecting either test format. As shown in Fig. 6.2, learners continued this pattern of allocation across cued-recall study-test

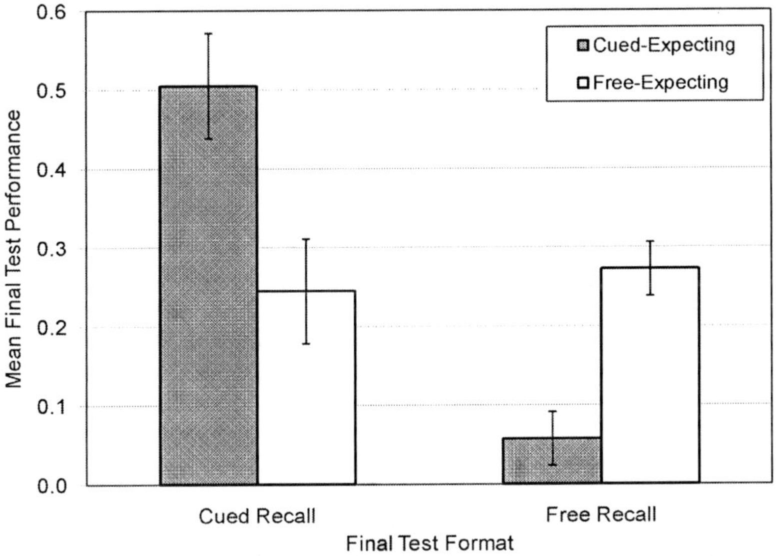

Fig. 6.1 Mean final recall performance as a function of actual final test format (cued vs. free recall) and expected test format (cued vs. free recall). Error bars represent standard error pooled within final test format

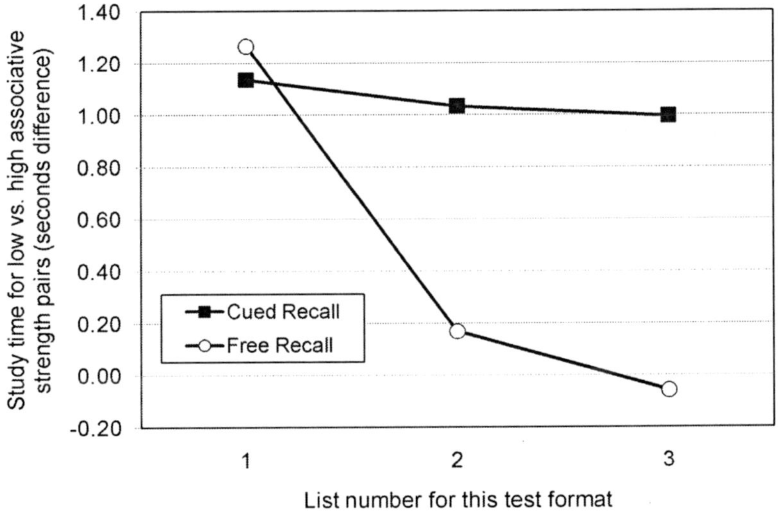

Fig. 6.2 Mean study time allocation (seconds) for low versus high associative strength word pairs (difference in learner medians) as a function of expected test format (cued vs. free recall) across three study-test cycles

cycles but decreasingly differentiated between high and low associative strength pairs across free recall study-test cycles. Thus, experience with the nature of a specific test format and the effectiveness of their metacognitive control led learners to increasingly adopt more effective encoding strategies and study-time allocation strategies.

Another demonstration of improved metacognitive control via experience is provided by deWinstanley and Bjork (2004). They investigated the possibility of enhancing learners' sensitivity to the advantages of generating versus reading to-be-learned words. The generation effect (Slamecka & Graf, 1978) is the well established finding that information generated by a learner tends to be better remembered than information merely read by the learner. In the experiments by deWinstanley and Bjork, learners completed two study-test cycles. Materials were sentences from an introductory psychology textbook in which critical words were either printed in red in their entirety (read condition) or printed in red with several letters missing (generate condition). Tests were fill-in-the blank recall that used previously studied phrases from which critical words had been removed and did not provide feedback. Results of the first experiment indicated that when learners were given a chance to experience the differential performance benefits (on the first test) for generated versus read items, they improved their subsequent performance (on the second test) for read items to the level of the generated items; this suggests that learners spontaneously, and adaptively, changed the way they processed the read items. This result was not obtained when learners were not given the critical experience, such as when reading versus generating was manipulated across the two study-test cycles or across learners.

In addition to finding that learners preferred to self-test over re-study as described earlier, Kornell and Son (2009) found that across experience with multiple study-test cycles, learners learned to self-test themselves more and did so at a faster rate when there was feedback on the tests at the end of each cycle. Because self-testing indeed produced higher performance, this study showed that learners' metacognitive control became more effective with experience.

Kang (2009) also investigated whether learners would tend to self-test more with experience. In this follow-up to the experiment described earlier, learners completed two study-test cycles. In the first cycle, following an initial presentation, items were either represented, practiced via cued recall, or neither. Learners were either given a cued recall test at a 2-day delay or given no test for this cycle. In the second study-test cycle, following initial presentation, learners were allowed to choose how to practice each item: representation, cued recall, or no practice. Learners who had received the cued recall test following the first list chose the recall practice option more frequently than did learners who did not receive that test. Furthermore, Kang found that learners who had experienced a large advantage for recalled over represented items on that test chose cued recall practice more frequently in the second cycle, revealing that the experience at test of the downstream benefits of self-testing practice was the central factor promoting later choice of that strategy.

Improving Control at Retrieval Via Direct Instruction

Although research on improving self-directed learning has largely emphasized processes at encoding, there is also potential for making improvements at retrieval (cf. Adams, 1985).

In recognition memory tasks, learners study a list of items and are later given a test containing some studied items and some unstudied items. Their task is to identify the studied items as "old" and the unstudied items as "new." Each individual's performance consist of two components: the sensitivity of his or her memory to this distinction and his or her response bias (a.k.a. criterion): a tendency to say "old" more often than "new" or vice versa (for further discussion see Rotello and Macmillan, 2008). Postma (1999) found that response bias can be manipulated via instructions to respond liberally (to say "old" if "they had even only a weak notion that they had studied it previously") or conservatively (to say "old" only to items for "which they were very certain").

Reder (1987) presents evidence that learners can make use of different strategies in answering questions about material they have learned. Specifically, they may use a strategy of directly retrieving specific information from memory to answer the question or a strategy of inferring an answer based on the gist of the material or on related retrieved information. In one experiment, learners read short stories (e.g., about a village in Burma that hires a hunter to kill a man-eating tiger) and were then given sentences that had either been presented in the story or not and that varied in their plausibility in the overall context of the story (e.g., "The villagers were afraid of the tiger" [plausible] and "The villagers make their living primarily by hunting" [implausible]). The task for each sentence was to judge whether it was plausible or implausible. Each sentence was also preceded by advice on which strategy to use: either to "try to retrieve a specific fact to use in judgment" or to "try to infer the answer." Advice was manipulated within-subjects on an item-by-item basis. Results showed that advice to infer led to greater sensitivity (as measured by response time) to the plausibility of the sentence than did advice to retrieve, while advice to retrieve led to greater sensitivity to whether the sentence was presented or not than did advice to infer. Furthermore, performance was enhanced when the advice given was appropriate (retrieve advice for items actually presented and infer advice for items not presented). These results demonstrate that learners can indeed use their memories differently in response to instructions, and this can influence their performance.

Williams and Hollan (1981) described numerous retrieval strategies spontaneously used as learners tried to recall as many names as possible of classmates from high school. A number of these strategies have been experimentally demonstrated to be effective in improving the amount of accurate recall. One such strategy is the adoption of more than one perspective at retrieval. In a study by Anderson and Pichert (1978), learners read a brief story about a house after first being instructed to adopt the perspective (a.k.a. schema) of a burglar, or of a homebuyer. After a 12-min delay, learners were given a first free recall test, on which they were instructed to write down as much of the story as they could remember. After another delay of 5 min, learners were given a second free recall test, on which they were either reminded of the perspective they had been given at reading or instructed to adopt the alternative perspective. Learners who were instructed to switch perspective for the second test recalled more information important to the new perspective than did learners who were instructed to keep the same perspective (see also Surber, 1983).

Reinstating the context of learning is another strategy that can enhance retrieval. In a study by Smith (1979), learners studied a word list in one room and were later tested either in the same room or a different one. Being tested in the original room yielded higher free recall performance than did being tested in the different one, demonstrating the effect of environmental context (Bjork & Richardson-Klavehn, 1989). Interestingly, Smith also found that instructing learners to mentally reinstate the original room enhanced performance to the same extent as actually testing them in the original room.

In addition to reinstatement of context, retrieval can also be improved by reinstatement of processing. Recall the principle of transfer-appropriate processing, reviewed earlier. Just as performance is enhanced when learners employ an encoding strategy appropriate for a particular test, performance should also be enhanced when learners employ retrieval strategies consistent with the way information was encoded. This is borne out in a study by Fisher and Craik (1977). Learners were presented with single words that were each preceded by one of three orienting questions: whether the target word rhymed with a particular other word, whether the target word fit into a particular category, or whether the target word fit into a particular sentence. Learners were then given a cued recall test in which each target word was cued by either the same type of question used for that word at encoding or one of the two alternative question types. For each of the three encoding conditions, performance was highest when the retrieval cue was of the same type as that used at encoding. These results, considered alongside those from Morris et al. (1977), demonstrate that instructing subjects on compatible means by which to encode and retrieve studied information can have a big effect on performance, suggesting that choosing a learning strategy to match the upcoming task, or a retrieval strategy that matches the prior learning, is an effective means of enhancing performance. It remains to be seen whether learners can do so effectively in the absence of direct instruction.

Finally, we consider an applied example of improving metacognitive control at retrieval via direct instruction. The cognitive interview (Fisher & Geiselman, 1992) is a technique for questioning eyewitnesses to crimes that has been found effective in increasing the amount and accuracy of recalled information (Geiselman et al., 1984). It incorporates a number of effective retrieval strategies, including reinstating physical and mental context, minimizing distractions, encouraging multiple and extensive retrieval attempts, and requesting retrieval in multiple temporal orders and from multiple perspectives.

Improving Control at Retrieval Via Experience

Just as learners can be induced via instructions to shift their response bias in a recognition task, they have also been shown—in some circumstances—to adaptively adjust their bias across experience with a task. For example, Benjamin (2001; see also Benjamin & Bawa, 2004) found that presenting a word list three times, rather than only once, led young adult learners to adopt a more conservative response bias and thus to less frequently falsely endorse unstudied items that were highly related to studied items. Han and Dobbins (2009) found that learners shifted their bias in response to experience with misleading feedback. Learners who were told that they were correct when they replied "new" to a studied item adopted a more conservative bias (increasing misses), while learners who were told that they were correct when they replied "old" to an unstudied item adopted a more liberal bias (increasing false alarms). However, whether a learner engages in a response bias shift and whether that shift increases accuracy depends on a host of as-yet unidentified factors, and there are numerous cases in which such strategic shifts are not obtained (Healy & Kubovy, 1977; Stretch & Wixted, 1998).

In free recall tests, learners tend to output the most recently studied items first (Deese & Kaufman, 1957). Furthermore, learners increasingly adopt this retrieval strategy across experience with multiple study-test cycles (Huang, 1986; Huang, Tomasini, & Nikl, 1977). This effect can be seen as learners learning to take advantage of the fact that not only are the most recently studied items better recalled than older items on an immediate test (Murdock, 1962), but this recency effect quickly evaporates (Jahnke, 1968). This would be consistent with the findings of Castel (2008): learners' JOLs reflected an improved appreciation for serial position effects (the benefits of primacy and recency) when learners were given experience across multiple study-test cycles and when serial position was made salient by either collecting JOLs prior to presenting each item or by explicitly presenting each item's serial position during study.

When a subset of studied material is again presented at a free recall test, ostensibly to help the learner remember the rest of the material, these cues can actually impair that performance. This is known as the part-list cuing or part-set cuing effect (e.g., Nickerson, 1984). Liu, Finley, and Benjamin (2009) investigated whether learners would come to appreciate the potentially deleterious effects of part-list cues across five study-test cycles in which learners were allowed to choose how many cues they would receive on the test. In each cycle, learners first studied a list of 30 words presented one at a time. At the end of this presentation, learners chose how many of the words (from 0 to 15) they wanted to be given as cues on the test to help them remember the rest of the words. Finally, learners were given a free recall test that represented the number of cues they had requested and instructed learners to recall the non-cue words. Learners indeed chose fewer cues across cycles, demonstrating a strategic improvement in their choices of testing condition. This is consistent with work by Rhodes and Castel (2008) which showed that learners' predictions of their own memory performance (JOLs) were only sensitive to the detriments of part-list cuing after experience with the task.

Role of Information Technology

Implementing Metacognitive Control

Actually executing what is good for learning can be onerous. Thus, information technology can be used to implement effective metacognitive control on behalf of the learner. A cornucopia of software programs, sometimes termed "computer-based learning environments," have been developed with the aim of assisting learning by, among other strategies, automating metacognitive control processes (Clark & Mayer, 2008; Lajoie, 2000; Linn, Davis, & Bell, 2004). We summarize here two examples that have been inspired by research in cognitive psychology.

SuperMemo (http://www.supermemo.com) is a program that automates scheduling of review for pieces of information (e.g., foreign language vocabulary) that the learner wants to remember indefinitely (cf. Wolf, 2008). The review trials administered by the program are similar to flashcards: cued recall followed by feedback plus the learner's self-assessment of his or her answer. SuperMemo leverages the benefits of spaced rehearsal to not only enhance learning but also to make it more efficient. It implements a schedule of expanding retrieval practice (Landauer & Bjork, 1978; cf. Balota, Duchek, & Logan, 2007) by which review is scheduled at short intervals soon after an item is first encoded and successively longer intervals as the item becomes better learned. By adaptively adjusting intervals based on a learner's performance, the program seeks to help learners retrieve information just before it is forgotten, when such retrieval should afford the most benefit (Bjork & Bjork, 1992; Wozniak & Gorzelańczyk, 1994). Managing, let alone optimizing, such a complex schedule of study without the aid of a computer would be daunting if not impossible.

A second example of efforts to offload metacognitive control onto software is the Cognitive Tutor program (http://www.carnegielearning.com). This program is one of a class of "intelligent tutoring systems" (for another such example, ALEKS, see Falmagne, Cosyn, Doignon, & Thiéry, 2003). The Cognitive Tutor maintains a cognitive model of the learner's present knowledge and skills, rooted in the ACT-R theory of how knowledge is represented and acquired (Anderson et al., 2004), and updates the state of the model based on the learner's interactions with the program. The program then tailors instruction to move the learner from his or her current state toward a goal state, which is defined by the curriculum designers for a particular domain (e.g., algebra). Among other pedagogical design features, the Cognitive Tutor selects material for display and problems for practice that are most appropriate based on its model of the learners' current understanding. It focuses the instruction on the learner's least developed skills, moving on to new material only when all skills in a section are mastered to a criterion. Thus it takes on the burden of judicious item selection and self-testing, which learners may not optimize on their own. Classroom experiments have found evidence that Cognitive Tutor enhances student learning compared to traditional teaching and study methods (Ritter, Anderson, Koedinger, & Corbett, 2007).

Training Metacognitive Control

A potential consequence of the approaches outlined above is to promote learning at the cost of developing improved metacognitive control skills. Such skills can be crucial for self-regulated lifelong learning beyond the structured learning environment. Note, however, that whether control skills really do need to be learned depends on one's goals and contexts; some control tasks may be best relinquished to the environment. Nevertheless, another approach is for information technology to guide learners toward improved metacognitive control: that is, to help learners learn how to learn.

The Cognitive Tutor program has been adapted to model, and thus also to tutor, certain metacognitive control behaviors (Koedinger, Aleven, Roll, & Baker, 2009). For example, Roll, Aleven, McLaren, and Koedinger (2007) sought to improve strategic help-seeking behavior of learners when using the built-in help functions of the Geometry Cognitive Tutor. Learners using this program had been observed to engage in maladaptive behaviors such as not seeking help at all (even after making multiple errors on the same type of problem) or quickly using the help functions to retrieve a complete answer to the current problem rather than only seeking help when they made errors or got stuck. A cognitive model of help-seeking was built, which encompassed both maladaptive and adaptive behaviors, and this was used to give learners immediate feedback when they used the help functions in suboptimal ways. There was some improvement in help-seeking under such tutelage; however, it is unclear whether learners truly developed improved skills or were merely complying with the metacognitive advice provided.

Winne and Nesbit (2009) outline important characteristics of software-enabled attempts to scaffold improved metacognition. They point out that, in addition to suggesting normatively optimal learning behaviors, educational software that logs learners' interactions (e.g., their program, gStudy) can be adapted to also present graphical representations of the strategies that learners have used and how those strategies have influenced performance. This would enable, and perhaps even motivate, learners to assess for themselves the effectiveness of their control processes—an important step in improving metacognitive control, as suggested by the data from deWinstanley and Bjork (2004).

Development of software to foster improved metacognitive control still has a long way to go (cf. Azevedo, 2007). But given that so much learning takes place outside of structured learning environments, there is much to be gained from leveraging technology to increase our self-regulated learning skills.

Summary

In this chapter, we have reviewed cognitive psychological research on self-directed learning in simple laboratory tasks. As learners monitor their own learning, they can also enhance it by exercising various forms of metacognitive control. In many cases learners do so effectively, but there is certainly room for improvement. We reviewed research suggesting a number of ways in which control can potentially be improved, at the time of encoding or retrieval, and via direct instruction or experience. Finally, we reviewed the promising role that information technology can play in implementing and training improved metacognitive control, with the ultimate goal of enhancing learning. One important lesson of research on metacognition in general is that learning can effectively be enhanced by improving our understanding of, and control over, our limited cognitive capacities.

References

Adams, L. T. (1985). Improving memory: Can retrieval strategies help? *Human Learning, 4*, 281–297.

Anderson, J. R., Bothell, D., Byrne, M. D., Douglass, S., Lebiere, C., & Qin, Y. (2004). An integrated theory of the mind. *Psychological Review, 111*(4), 1036–1060.

Anderson, R. C., & Pichert, J. W. (1978). Recall of previously unrecallable information following a shift in perspective. *Journal of Verbal Learning & Verbal Behavior, 17*(1), 1–12.

Arbuckle, T. Y., & Cuddy, L. L. (1969). Discrimination of item strength at time of presentation. *Journal of Experimental Psychology, 81*(1), 126–131.

Atkinson, R. C. (1972). Optimizing the learning of a second-language vocabulary. *Journal of Experimental Psychology, 96*, 124–129.

Azevedo, R. (2007). Understanding the complex nature of self-regulatory processes in learning with computer-based learning environments: An introduction. *Metacognition and Learning, 2*(2–3), 57–65.

Baker, L., & Anderson, R. I. (1982). Effects of inconsistent information on text processing: Evidence for comprehension monitoring. *Reading Research Quarterly, 17*, 281–294.

Balota, D. A., Duchek, J. M., & Logan, J. M. (2007). Is expanded retrieval practice a superior form of spaced retrieval? A critical review of the extant literature. In J. S. Nairne (Ed.), *The foundations of remembering: Essays in honor of Henry L. Roediger, III* (pp. 83–105). New York: Psychology Press.

Bellezza, F. S. (1996). Mnemonic methods for storage and retrieval. In E. L. Bjork & R. A. Bjork (Eds.), *Memory* (pp. 345–380). San Diego, CA: Academic Press.

Belmont, J. M., & Butterfield, E. C. (1971). Learning strategies as determinants of memory deficiencies. *Cognitive Psychology, 2*, 411–420.

Benjamin, A. S. (2001). On the dual effects of repetition on false recognition. *Journal of Experimental Psychology: Learning, Memory, and Cognition, 27*, 941–947.

Benjamin, A. S. (2003). Predicting and postdicting the effects of word frequency on memory. *Memory & Cognition, 31*, 297–305.

Benjamin, A. S. (2005). Response speeding mediates the contribution of cue familiarity and target retrievability to metamnemonic judgments. *Psychonomic Bulletin & Review, 12*, 874–879.

Benjamin, A. S. (2008). Memory is more than just remembering: Strategic control of encoding, accessing memory, and making decisions. In A. S. Benjamin & B. H. Ross (Eds.), *The Psychology of Learning and Motivation: Skill and Strategy in Memory Use* (Vol. 48, pp. 175–223). London: Academic Press.

Benjamin, A. S., & Bawa, S. (2004). Distractor plausibility and criterion placement in recognition. *Journal of Memory & Language, 51*, 159–172.

Benjamin, A. S., & Bird, R. D. (2006). Metacognitive control of the spacing of study repetitions. *Journal of Memory and Language, 55*, 126–137.

Benjamin, A. S., Bjork, R. A., & Schwartz, B. L. (1998). The mismeasure of memory: When retrieval fluency is misleading as a metamnemonic index. *Journal of Experimental Psychology: General, 127*, 55–68.

Benjamin, A. S., & Bjork, R. A. (1996). Retrieval fluency as a metacognitive index. In L. Reder (Ed.), *Implicit Memory and Metacognition*. Mahwah, NJ: Erlbaum.

Benjamin, A. S., & Bjork, R. A. (2000). On the relationship between recognition speed and accuracy for words rehearsed via rote versus elaborative rehearsal. *Journal of Experimental Psychology: Learning, Memory, and Cognition, 26*, 638–648.

Bhatarah, P., Ward, G., & Tan, L. (2008). Examining the relationship between free recall and immediate serial recall: the serial nature of recall and the effect of test expectancy. *Memory & Cognition, 36*(1), 20–34.

Bjork, R. A., & Bjork, E. L. (1992). A new theory of disuse and an old theory of stimulus fluctuation. In A. Healy, S. Kosslyn, & R. Shiffrin (Eds.), *From learning processes to cognitive processes: Essays in honor of William K. Estes* (Vol. 2, pp. 35–67). Hillsdale, NJ: Erlbaum.

Bjork, R. A., & Richardson-Klavehn, A. (1989). On the puzzling relationship between environmental context and human memory. In C. Izawa (Ed.), *Current issues in cognitive processes: The Tulane Flowerree Symposium on Cognition* (pp. 313–344). Hillsdale, NJ: Erlbaum.

Castel, A. D. (2008). Metacognition and learning about primacy and recency effects in free recall: The utilization of intrinsic and extrinsic cues when making judgments of learning. *Memory & Cognition, 36*, 429–437.

Cepeda, N. J., Pashler, H., Vul, E., Wixted, J. T., & Rohrer, D. (2006). Distributed practice in verbal recall tasks: A review and quantitative synthesis. *Psychological Bulletin, 132*, 354–380.

Clark, R., & Mayer, R. E. (2008). E-learning and the science of instruction (2nd ed). San Francisco, CA: Jossey-Bass.

Costermans, J., Lories, G., & Ansay, C. (1992). Confidence level and feeling of knowing in question answering: The weight of inferential processes. *Journal of Experimental Psychology: Learning, Memory, and Cognition, 18*, 142–150.

Craik, F. I. M., & Lockhart, R. S. (1972). Levels of processing: A framework for memory research. *Journal of Verbal Learning & Verbal Behavior, 11*(6), 671–684.

Deese, J., & Kaufman, R. A. (1957). Serial effects in recall of unorganized and sequentially organized verbal material. *Journal of Experimental Psychology, 54*(3), 180–187.

deWinstanley, P. A., & Bjork, E. L. (2004). Processing strategies and the generation effect: Implications for making a better reader. *Memory & Cognition, 32*(6), 945–955.

Dufresne, A., & Kobasigawa, A. (1988). Developmental differences in children's allocation of study time. *The Journal of Genetic Psychology, 149*, 87–92.

Dufresne, A., & Kobasigawa, A. (1989). Children's spontaneous allocation of study time: Differential and sufficient aspects. *Journal of Experimental Child Psychology, 47*, 274–296.

Dunlosky, J., & Hertzog, C. (2000). Updating knowledge about strategy effectiveness: A componential analysis of learning about strategy effectiveness from task experience. *Psychology & Aging, 15*, 462–474.

Dunlosky, J., Hertzog, C., Kennedy, M., & Thiede, K. (2005). The self-monitoring approach for effective learning. *Cognitive Technology, 10*, 4–11.

Dunlosky, J., & Matvey, G. (2001). Empirical analysis of the intrinsic-extrinsic distinction of judgments of learning (JOLs): Effects of relatedness and serial position on JOLs. *Journal of Experimental Psychology: Learning, Memory, and Cognition, 27*, 1180–1191.

Dunlosky, J., & Nelson, T. O. (1992). Importance of the kind of cue for judgments of learning (JOL) and the delayed-JOL effect. *Memory & Cognition. Special Issue: Memory and Cognition Applied, 20*(4), 374–380.

Dunlosky, J., & Nelson, T. O. (1994). Does the sensitivity of judgments of learning (JOLs) to the effects of various study activities depend on when the JOLs occur? *Journal of Memory and Language, 33*(4), 545–565.

Dunlosky, J., & Thiede, K. W. (1998). What makes people study more? An evaluation of factors that affect people's self-paced study and yield "labor-and-gain" effects. *Acta Psychologica, 98*, 37–56.

Dunlosky, J., Serra, M., & Baker, J. M. C. (2007). Metamemory. In F. Durso, R. Nickerson, S. Dumais, S. Lewandowsky, & T. Perfect (Eds.), *Handbook of Applied Cognition* (2nd ed., pp. 137–159). New York, NY: Wiley.

d'Ydewalle, G., Swerts, A., & De Corte, E. (1983). Study time and test performance as a function of test expectations. *Contemporary Educational Psychology, 8*(1), 55–67.

Earhard, M. (1967). Subjective organization and list organization as determinants of free-recall and serial-recall memorization. *Journal of Verbal Learning & Verbal Behavior, 6*, 501–507.

Falmagne, J., Cosyn, E., Doignon, J., & Thiéry, N. (2003). The assessment of knowledge, in theory and practice. Retrieved June 14, 2009, from http://www.aleks.com/about_aleks/Science_Behind_ALEKS.pdf

Finley, J. R., & Benjamin, A. S., (2009). Adaptive changes in encoding strategy with experience: evidence from the test expectancy paradigm. Manuscript in preparation.

Finn, B., & Metcalfe, J. (2008). Judgments of learning are influenced by memory for past test. *Journal of Memory and Language, 58*(1), 19–34.

Fisher, R. P., & Craik, F. I. (1977). Interaction between encoding and retrieval operations in cued recall. *Journal of Experimental Psychology: Human Learning and Memory, 3*(6), 701–711.

Fisher, R. P., & Geiselman, R. E. (1992). *Memory-enhancing techniques in investigative interviewing: The cognitive interview*. Springfield, IL: C. C. Thomas.

Geiselman, R. E., Fisher, R. P., Firstenberg, I., Hutton, L. A., Sullivan, S. J., Avetisssian, I. V., et al. (1984). Enhancement of eyewitness memory: An empirical evaluation of the cognitive interview. *Journal of Police Science and Administration, 12*(1), 74–80.

Han, S., & Dobbins, I. G. (2009). Regulating recognition decisions through incremental reinforcement learning. *Psychonomic Bulletin & Review, 16*(3), 469–474.

Healy, A. F., & Kubovy, M. (1977). A comparison of recognition memory to numerical decision: How prior probabilities affect cutoff location. *Memory & Cognition, 5*(1), 3–9.

Hertzog, C., Dunlosky, J., & Robinson, A. E. (2007). Intellectual abilities and metacognitive beliefs influence spontaneous use of effective encoding strategies. Retrieved June 4, 2009, from Georgia Institute of Technology web site: http://www.psychology.gatech.edu/chertzog/papers/esm-15.pdf

Huang, I. (1986). Transitory Changes of Primacy and Recency in Successive Single-Trial Free Recall. *Journal of General Psychology, 113*(1), 5–21.

Huang, I., Tomasini, J., & Nikl, L. (1977). The primacy and recency effects in successive single-trial immediate free recall. *Journal of General Psychology, 97*(2), 157–165.

Jahnke, J. C. (1968). Delayed recall and the serial-position effect of short-term memory. *Journal of Experimental Psychology, 76*(4, Pt. 1), 618–622.

Kang, S. H. K. (2009). The Influence of Test Expectancy, Test Format, and Test Experience on Study Strategy Selection and Long-term Retention. Unpublished doctoral dissertation, Washington University at St. Louis.

Klein, K. A., Addis, K. M., & Kahana, M. J. (2005). A comparative analysis of serial and free recall. *Memory & Cognition, 33*(5), 833–839.

Kobasigawa, A., & Metcalf-Haggert, A. (1993). Spontaneous allocation of study-time by first- and third- grade children on a simple memory task. *The Journal of Genetic Psychology, 154*, 223–235.

Koedinger, K. R., Aleven, V., Roll, I., & Baker, R. S. Jd. (2009). In vivo experiments on whether supporting metacognition in intelligent tutoring systems yields robust learning.In D. J. Hacker, J. Dunlosky & A. C. Graesser (Eds.), *Handbook of metacognition in education*. London: Routledge.

Konopka, A. E., & Benjamin, A. S. (2009). Schematic knowledge changes what judgments of learning predict in a source memory task. *Memory & Cognition*, *37*(1), 42–51.
Koriat, A., & Goldsmith, M. (1996). Monitoring and control processes in the strategic regulation of memory accuracy. *Psychological Review*, *103*, 490–517.
Koriat, A., Ma'ayan, H., & Nussinson, R. (2006). The intricate relationships between monitoring and control in metacogntion: Lessons for the cause-and-effect relation between subjective experience and behavior. *Journal of Experimental Psychology: General*, *135*(1), 36–69.
Kornell, N., & Bjork, R. A. (2007). The promise and perils of self-regulated study. *Psychonomic Bulletin & Review*, *14*, 219–224.
Kornell, N., & Bjork, R. A. (2008). Optimizing self-regulated study: The benefits-and costs-of dropping flashcards. *Memory*, *16*, 125–136.
Kornell, N., & Metcalfe, J. (2006). Study efficacy and the region of proximal learning framework. *Journal of Experimental Psychology: Learning, Memory, & Cognition*, *32*, 609–622.
Kornell, N., & Son, L. K. (2009). Learners' choices and beliefs about self-testing. *Memory*, *17*(5), 493–501.
Lajoie, S. P. (Ed.). (2000). Computers as cognitive tools (vol. 2): No more walls. Mahwah, NJ: Erlbaum.
Landauer, T. K., & Bjork, R. A. (1978). Optimum rehearsal patterns and name learning. In M. M. Gruneberg, P. E. Morris, & R. N. Sykes (Eds.), *Practical aspects of memory* (pp. 625–632). London: Academic Press.
Le Ny, J. F., Denheire, G., & Taillanter, D. (1972). Regulation of study-time and interstimulus similarity in self-paced learning conditions. *Acta Psychologica*, *36*, 280–289.
Linn, M. C., Davis, E. A., & Bell, P. (Eds.). (2004). Internet Environments for Science Education. Mahwah, NJ: Lawrence Erlbaum Associates.
Liu, X., Finley, J. R., & Benjamin, A. S. (2009). Learning to avoid part-list cues. Manuscript in preparation.
Liu, X., & Fang, G. (2005). Development of children's strategy on allocation of study time. *Acta Psychologica Sinica*, *37*(5), 623–631.
Liu, X., & Fang, G. (2006). Development of elementary school students on allocation of study time under different time limit. *Acta Psychologica Sinica*, *38*(3), 365–374.
Lovelace, E. A. (1984). Metamemory: Monitoring future recallability during study. *Journal of Experimental Psychology: Learning, Memory, and Cognition*, *10*(4), 756–766.
Maki, R. H., & Serra, M. (1992). The basis of test predictions for text material. *The Journal of Experimental Psychology: Learning, Memory, and Cognition*, *18*, 116–126.
McDaniel, M. A., Blischak, D. M., & Challis, B. (1994). The effects of test expectancy on processing and memory of prose. *Contemporary Educational Psychology*, *19*(2), 230–248.
Metcalfe, J. (2002). Is study time allocated selectively to a region of proximal learning? *Journal of Experimental Psychology: General*, *131*, 349–363.
Metcalfe, J., & Kornell, N. (2005). A region of proximal learning model of study time allocation. *Journal of Memory and Language*, *52*, 463–477.
Metcalfe, J., Schwartz, B. L., & Joaquim, S. G. (1993). The cue familiarity heuristic in metacognition. *Journal of Experimental Psychology: Learning, Memory, and Cognition*, *19*, 851–861.
Morris, C. D., Bransford, J. D., & Franks, J. J. (1977). Levels of processing versus transfer appropriate processing. *Journal of Verbal Learning & Verbal Behavior*, *16*(5), 519–533.
Murdock, B. B. (1962). The serial position effect of free recall. *Journal of Experimental Psychology*, *64*, 482–488.
Neely, J. H., & Balota, D. A. (1981). Test-expectancy and semantic-organization effects in recall and recognition. *Memory & cognition*, *9*(3), 283–300.
Nelson, T. O., & Dunlosky, J. (1991). When people's judgments of learning (JOLs) are extremely accurate at predicting subsequent recall: The "delayed-JOL effect". *Psychological Science*, *2*(4), 267–270.

Nelson, T. O., Dunlosky, J., Graf, A., & Narens, L. (1994). Utilization of metacognitive judgments in the allocation of study during multitrial learning. *Psychological Science, 5*, 207–213.

Nelson, T. O., & Leonesio, R. J. (1988). Allocation of self-paced study time and the "labor-in-vain effect". *Journal of Experimental Psychology: Learning, Memory, and Cognition, 14*, 676–686.

Nelson, T. O., & Narens, L. (1990). Metamemory: A theoretical framework and new findings. In G. H. Bower (Ed.), *The psychology of learning and motivation* (Vol. 26, pp. 125–141). New York: Academic Press.

Nelson, T. O., & Narens, L. (1994). Why investigate metacognition? In J. Metcalfe, & A. P. Shimamura (Eds.), *Metacognition: Knowing about knowing* (pp. 1–25). Cambridge, MA: The MIT Press.

Nickerson, R. S. (1984). Retrieval inhibition from part-set cuing: A persisting enigma in memory research. *Memory & cognition, 12*(6), 531–552.

Postma, A. (1999). The influence of decision criteria upon remembering and knowing in recognition memory. *Acta Psychologica, 103*(1–2), 65–76.

Postman, L. (1964). Studies of learning to learn: II. Changes in transfer as a function of practice. *Journal of Verbal Learning & Verbal Behavior, 3*(5), 437–447.

Reder, L. M. (1987). Strategy selection in question answering. *Cognitive Psychology, 19*, 90–138.

Rhodes, M. G., & Castel, A. D. (2008). Metacognition and part-set cuing: Can interference be predicted at retrieval? *Memory & Cognition, 36*, 1429–1438.

Ritter, S., Anderson, J. R., Koedinger, K. R., & Corbett, A. (2007). Cognitive tutor: Applied research in mathematics education. *Psychonomic Bulletin & Review, 14*(2), 249–255.

Roediger, H. L., III. (1980). The effectiveness of four mnemonics in ordering recall. *Journal of Experimental Psychology: Human Learning & Memory, 6*(5), 558–567.

Roll, I., Aleven, V., McLaren, B. M., & Koedinger, K. R. (2007). Can help seeking be tutored? Searching for the secret sauce of metacognitive tutoring. In R. Luckin, K. Koedinger, & J. Greer (Eds.), *Proceedings of the 13th International Conference on Artificial Intelligence in Education, AIED 2007* (pp. 203–210). Amsterdam, the Netherlands: IOS Press.

Rotello, C. M., & Macmillan, N. A. (2008). Response bias in recognition memory. In A. S. Benjamin & B. H. Ross (Eds.), *The Psychology of Learning and Motivation: Skill and Strategy in Memory Use* (Vol. 48, pp. 61–94). London: Academic Press.

Schwartz, B. L., & Metcalfe, J. (1994). Methodological problems and pitfalls in the study of human metacognition. In J. Metcalfe & A. Shimamura (Eds.), *Metacognition: Knowing about knowing* (pp. 93–114). Cambridge, MA: MIT Press.

Serra, M. J., & Metcalfe, J. (2009). Effective implementation of metacognition. In D. Hacker, J. Dunlosky, & A. Graesser (Eds.), *Handbook of Metacognition and Education* (pp. 278-298). New York, NY: Routledge.

Simon, H. A. (1957). *Models of man: Social and rational*. New York: Wiley.

Slamecka, N. J., & Graf, P. (1978). The generation effect: Delineation of a phenomenon. *Journal of Experimental Psychology: Human Learning & Memory, 4*, 592–604.

Smith, S. M. (1979). Remembering in and out of context. *Journal of Experimental Psychology: Human Learning and Memory, 5*(5), 460–471.

Son, L. K. (2004). Spacing one's study: Evidence for a metacognitive control strategy. *Journal of Experimental Psychology: Learning, Memory, and Cognition, 30*, 601–604.

Son, L. K., & Metcalfe, J. (2000). Metacognitive and control strategies in study-time allocation. *Journal of Experimental Psychology: Learning, Memory, and Cognition, 26*, 204–221.

Son, L. K., & Sethi, R. (2006). Metacognitive control and optimal learning. *Cognitive Science, 30*, 759–774.

Stretch, V., & Wixted, J. T. (1998). On the difference between strength-based and frequency-based mirror effects in recognition memory. *Journal of Experimental Psychology: Learning, Memory, and Cognition, 24*, 1379–1396.

Surber, J. R. (1983). The influence of decision factors on what is reported in free recall of a brief narrative. *Contemporary Educational Psychology, 8*(2), 119–126.

Thiede, K. W., Anderson, M. C. M., & Therriault, D. (2003). Accuracy of metacognitive monitoring affects learning of texts. *Journal of Educational Psychology, 95*(1), 66–73.
Thiede, K. W., & Dunlosky, J. (1999). Toward a general model of self-regulated study: Analysis of selection of items for study and self-paced study time. *Journal of Experimental Psychology: Learning, Memory, & Cognition, 4*, 1024–1037.
Toppino, T. C., Cohen, M. S., Davis, M. L., & Moors, A. C. (2009). Metacognitive control over the distribution of practice: When is spacing preferred? *Journal of Experimental Psychology: Learning, Memory, and Cognition, 35*(5), 1352–1358.
Tullis, J. G., & Benjamin, A. S. (2009). The effectiveness of self-paced study. Manuscript submitted for publication.
Waugh, N. C. (1961). Free versus serial recall. *Journal of Experimental Psychology, 62*(5), 496–502.
Williams, M. D., & Hollan, J. D. (1981). The process of retrieval from very long term memory. *Cognitive Science, 5*(2), 87–119.
Winne, P. H., & Nesbit, J. C. (2009). Supporting self-regulated learning with cognitive tools. In D. J. Hacker, J. Dunlosky & A. C. Graesser (Eds.), *Handbook of metacognition in education*. London: Routledge.
Wolf, G. (2008, May). Want to remember everything you'll ever learn? Surrender to this algorithm. *Wired, 16*.
Wozniak, P. A., & Gorzelañczyk, E. J. (1994). Optimization of repetition spacing in the practice of learning. *Acta Neurobiologiae Experimentalis, 54*, 59–62.
Zacks, R. T. (1969). Invariance of total learning time under different conditions of practice. *Journal of Experimental Psychology, 32*, 441–447.

Chapter 7
Ethnic Differences on Students' Approaches to Learning: Self-Regulatory Cognitive and Motivational Predictors of Academic Achievement for Latino/a and White College Students

Robert Rueda[1], Hyo Jin Lim[1], Harold F. O'Neil[1], Noelle Griffin[2], Shel Bockman[3], and Barbara Sirotnik[3]

[1] University of Southern California, Los Angeles, CA, USA
[2] UCLA, Los Angeles, CA, USA
[3] California State University, San Bernardino, CA, USA

The national move toward accountability, primarily focused on K-12 schools, has begun to focus on postsecondary education as well. Accountability demands for student academic performance and persistence rates are growing (Carey, 2004, 2005; Hearn & Holdsworth, 2002). In addition, postsecondary education is widely seen as only a minimum goal in education, as a high-school diploma is no longer seen as sufficient preparation for contemporary workforce demands. However, there are wide disparities in the success rates among groups in the country. In 2007–2008, for example, there were 2,757 4-year postsecondary institutions in the United States, and one third of these (33.1%) were public institutions. Within these institutions, 67% of the degrees conferred were awarded to White, non-Hispanic students. In contrast, 8.5 and 7.1% of the degrees were awarded to Black, non-Hispanic and Hispanic students, respectively (Knapp, Kelly-Reid, & Ginder, 2008). These data belie significant differences in other college-related outcomes between Latino and other students in the United States.

Latinos have been found to lag every other population group in attaining college degrees, especially bachelor's degrees. To better understand that problem and help identify policy responses, the Pew Hispanic Center conducted a new analysis of the educational performance of Latino high-school graduates. This analysis is based on Current Population Survey data collected by the US Census Bureau from 1997 to 2000. The data were combined and averaged to create a solid statistical basis for assessing different forms of college attendance for Latinos as compared with other groups and for making important distinctions among sub-groups of the Latino

H.F. O'Neil (✉)
University of Southern California, Los Angeles, CA, USA
e-mail: honeil@usc.edu

M.S. Khine, I.M. Saleh (eds.), *New Science of Learning*,
DOI 10.1007/978-1-4419-5716-0_7,

population. The report (Fry, 2002) revealed that there is a substantial enrollment gap between Latinos and all other groups among 18- to 24-year-olds. For example, only 35% of Latino high-school graduates in that age group are enrolled in college compared to 46% of Whites. Also, Latinos are far more likely to be enrolled in 2-year colleges than any other group (about 40% of Latinos in the 18- to 24-year-old range, compared to about 25% of White and Black students in that age group). Furthermore, Latinos are more likely to be part time students (about 85% of Whites are enrolled full time compared to about 75% of Latinos).

There are within-group differences that have been reported as well. For example, first-generation students (those whose parents did not attend college and who are most often African American or Latino) also have a lower rate of postsecondary attainment than White students. Based on the National Education Longitudinal Study of 1988 (National Center for Education Statistics [NCES], 2005), 43% of the first-generation students who enrolled in postsecondary education between 1992 and 2000 "left without a degree" and 25% had attained an undergraduate degree by 2000. In contrast, 20% of the students whose parents had a bachelor's degree or higher "left without a degree" from a postsecondary institution, while almost 70% attained an undergraduate degree by 2000.

These inequities in outcomes are troubling for a number of reasons; yet they only document the current situation rather than suggesting a solution. Attempts to examine the underlying causes of these achievement differences have focused on a number of areas including correlates resulting in hypothesized or possible causes of the achievement patterns noted above. These are described below.

Achievement Differences Among Subgroups in Higher Education: Social and Cultural Factors

College enrollment has been found to be influenced by a variety of academic, personal, social, and economic factors. Cultural and family-related values play an integral role in modeling student perceptions and motivation as well, especially in populations of students from minority backgrounds (Alfaro, Umana-Taylor, & Bamaca, 2006; Esparza & Sanchez, 2008; Fuligni, Tseng, & Lam, 1999; Plunkett & Bamaca-Gomez, 2003; Plunkett, Henry, Houltberg, Sands, & Abarca-Mortensen, 2008). For instance, Eccles, Vida, and Barber (2004) found that high-school achievement, family expectations, mother's education level and family income were predictors of college enrollment. Abrego (2006) took a qualitative approach to examining the problem of undocumented youth in high school, and her findings revealed how these students faced the difficult and often impossible task of entering college or finding a job due to their undocumented status, thus resulting in decreased motivation and increased tendency to drop out.

In regards to families, Goldenberg, Gallimore, Reese, and Garnier (2001) looked at how the aspirations and expectations of immigrant Latino families impact student performance. This study found that low performing students do not come from families with low expectations. In fact, the contrary was found, in that immigrant families hold high expectations and aspirations for their children's current and future performance in school. Additionally, these beliefs are influenced by their children's performance in school, rather than the beliefs influencing performance (Goldenberg et al., 2001), and these beliefs later affect students' enrollment in college (Davis-Kean, Vida, & Eccles, 2001).

Other commonly examined sociocultural factors include gender, ethnic/racial background, and socioeconomic status (SES). Those variables have been found to either predict or moderate the prediction of college retention and grade point average (GPA) (Nettles, Thoeny, & Gosman, 1986; Nguyen, Allen, & Fraccastoro, 2005; Robbins, Allen, Casillas, Peterson, & Le, 2006; Robbins et al., 2004). We consider each of these in the following paragraphs.

Gender. There is a significant amount of work on the issue of gender differences in academic achievement in general, and math achievement specifically, spanning several decades (Caplan & Caplan, 1999; Chipman, 1996; Favreau, 1997). Historically, males generally outperformed girls on measures of math and science achievement, with the gap increasing in middle and high school (Byrnes, 2001, 2005; Halpern, 2000). Although some more recent large-scale studies have documented girls performing lower on math and science assessments than their math peers (Braswell et al., 2001; NCES, 2005; OECD, 2000), other researchers have found this trend diminished or even reversed (see Baker, Griffin, & Choi, 2008 for a review).

Women in particular tend to outperform men in terms of many post-secondary outcomes, with differences particularly evident for African-American and Hispanic students (Freeman, 2004). For example, females currently have greater success than males in attaining post-secondary education, have higher aspirations than males while in high school, are more likely to enroll in college immediately after graduating from high school, and persist and complete degrees at higher rates than males. Measures of post-secondary academic achievement (e.g., GPA) also tend to be higher for women than men. More than half of all bachelor's and master's degrees are awarded to females. Nevertheless, gender differences in majors still exist, with female bachelor's degree recipients much less likely than their male peers to major in computer science, engineering, and physical sciences.

One important line of investigation in this area has targeted metacognitive and motivational variables as contributors to differences in outcomes. For example, as part of the large-scale PISA (Program in International Student Assessment) study, Marsh, Hau, Artelt, Baumert, and Peschar (2006) found gender differences in math-related metacognitive, motivational, and affective factors. Hong, O'Neil, and Feldon (2005) found no significant gender effects on math achievement; however, they did identify gender differences in state-based anxiety and self-regulation, which themselves predicted math outcomes. Given this background, it is clear that gender is an important variable in examining group differences in achievement, and it was included in this study.

Ethnicity. Almost all discussions about the achievement gap in US education include ethnic, racial, and cultural aspects. As noted earlier, achievement based on ethnic and cultural differences are prominent features of the educational system. Surveys conducted by the NCES indicated that, on average, minority students (primarily Latino and African American) lagged behind their White peers in terms of academic achievement (US Department of Education, 2000). While early work tended to focus on presumed cultural deficits as a primary cause of ethnic/racial/cultural achievement gaps, this view has been widely discredited (Graham & Hudley, 2005; Gutierrez & Rogoff, 2003). More recently, other factors have been suggested, including the effects of living in low-income households or in single-parent families, low parental education levels, and schools with lower resources. All of these factors are components of SES and linked to academic achievement (National Commission on Children, 1991). We consider some of these factors below.

Socioeconomic status. SES is one of the most widely used contextual variables in education research and is often looked at in relation to academic achievement (Bornstein & Bradley, 2003; Brooks-Gunn & Duncan, 1997; Coleman, 1988). There seems to be relatively widespread agreement that SES is comprised of three components: parental income, parental education, and parental occupation (Gottfried, 1985; Hauser, 1994). While these variables are often moderately correlated, there is evidence that the components are unique and that each one measures a substantially different aspect of SES that should be considered to be separate from the others (Bollen, Glanville, & Stecklov, 2001; Hauser & Huang, 1997). In this study, we used a combination of mother's education and parental income.

An early, comprehensive meta-analysis of SES and academic achievement (White, 1982) showed that the relation varies significantly with a number of factors such as the types of SES and academic achievement measures, and later studies have reported inconsistent findings. Correlations have ranged from strong (e.g., Lamdin, 1996; Sutton & Soderstrom, 1999) to no significant correlation at all (e.g., Ripple & Luthar, 2000; Seyfried, 1998). A more recent analysis (Sirin, 2005) examined journal articles published between 1990 and 2000 and included 101,157 students, 6,871 schools, and 128 school districts gathered from 74 independent samples. The results showed a medium to strong SES–achievement relation. However, the relation was moderated by the unit (e.g., the individual student vs. an aggregated unit), the source (e.g., secondary sources vs. self-report), the range of SES variable, and the type of SES–achievement measure. The relation was also contingent upon school level, minority status, and school location. In terms of grade level, the mean effect size (ES) was 0.19 for the kindergarten students, 0.27 for the elementary school students, 0.31 for middle-school students, and 0.26 for high-school students. In addition, the mean ES for White student samples (0.27) was significantly larger than the mean ES for minority student samples (0.17). Unfortunately, the review did not consider information on college-level effects.

Overall, the average correlation in Sirin's (2005) review was 0.30, as compared with White's (1982) average correlation of 0.34. In sum, the best evidence indicates that using Cohen's (1977) ES guidelines, the overall ES of Sirin's analysis suggests a medium level of association between SES and academic achievement at the student level and a larger degree of association at the school level. Importantly, the review also suggests that parents' location in the overall SES hierarchy has a strong impact on students' academic achievement. As Coleman (1988) has suggested, family SES sets the stage for students' academic performance both by directly providing resources at home and by indirectly providing the social capital that is necessary to succeed in school. This same factor also helps to determine the kind of school and classroom environment to which the student has access (Reynolds & Walberg, 1991). These indirect influences of SES are often subsumed under the conceptually larger label of opportunity to learn (OTL), which is considered next.

Secondary Effects: Opportunity to Learn and Prior Knowledge

OTL is a way of measuring and reporting whether students have access to the different ingredients that make up quality schools, for example, access to challenging curriculum and to qualified teachers. The more OTL ingredients that are present in individual students' educational history, the more opportunities students have to benefit from a high-quality education. OTL standards provide a benchmark against which the opportunities that a school provides can be measured. The notion of OTL is important since it opens the possibility that student outcomes are not solely a function of inherent student or family characteristics.

Examples of OTL indicators include students' access to qualified teachers, clean and safe facilities, up-to-date books and quality learning materials, high-quality coursework, and related school conditions that provide students a fair and equal opportunity to learn and achieve knowledge and skills. For example, taking a high-level math course is the one consistent course predictor of college preparedness. Adelman (1999) found that the single greatest predictor of successful college completion was the taking of high-level mathematics courses during high school. If students do not successfully complete algebra, they are unlikely to succeed in institutions of postsecondary education (Checkley, 2001). Thus, if students find themselves in a school that does not offer high-level courses or teachers qualified to teach such content, a negative relationship to academic outcomes would be expected.

Cognitive and Motivational Factors in Learning and Achievement

It is clear that social and cultural factors are critical in considering achievement differences in college and other academic settings. In addition, cognitive and motivational factors have been shown to be related to a wide variety of academic outcomes, and here we describe some of the relationships that have been found in the literature. We consider two of the motivational variables that have been heavily studied and that have been shown to be important influences on learning, self-efficacy, and goal orientation.

Self-efficacy. Self-efficacy is defined as "[P]eople's judgments of their capabilities to organize and execute courses of action required to attain designated types of performances" (Bandura, 1986, p. 391). Although there are many motivational constructs, self-efficacy is central to promoting students' engagement and learning. These context-specific and domain-specific beliefs affect behavior by influencing the choices that people make and the courses of action they follow (Linnenbrink & Pintrich, 2004).

One reason that self-efficacy is important is that it has been associated with a variety of other motivational and learning-related variables. For example, Ross, Shannon, Salisbury-Glennon, and Guarino (2002) point out that a large number of studies have demonstrated a positive relationship between mastery goal orientation and self-efficacy. There is also evidence that when students feel confident they can learn, they tend to use more self-regulatory strategies (Pintrich & De Groot, 1990; Zimmerman, 2000b).

Although much of the work on self-efficacy has been carried out with young students, one important study with college-age students was reported by Chemers, Hu, and Garcia (2001). The study involved the entire freshman class at a major university in California. Academic self-efficacy was measured along with high-school GPA and first year college GPA. While high-school grades were significantly related to college grades, self-efficacy at the time of college entrance was related to grades at the end of the first year of college, even when prior GPA was controlled. Other recent studies (Pietsch, Walker, & Chapman, 2003; Pintrich, 2003) as well as a recent review of self-efficacy studies (Valentine, DuBois, & Cooper, 2004) have confirmed these patterns. Consistent with this body of research, it was expected that self-efficacy would be related to learning strategies and achievement.

Goal orientation. Students' perceptions about achievement behaviors and the meanings they assign to such behaviors is the root of goal orientation theory. The classroom environment influences the goals students adopt. Mastery and performance goals are two major constructs of goal orientation. Students with a mastery goal orientation have the desire to learn for understanding, knowledge or insight, whereas students with a performance goal orientation want to be perceived as competent in comparison to their peers and may seek to outperform their classmates (Ames, 1992; Dweck, 1986; Dweck & Leggett, 1988; Elliot, 1999). Goal theorists have made an important distinction between those achievement goals that are performance-approach in which students want to look good in comparison to their peers and those that are performance-avoidance in which students want to not look bad in comparison to their peers. In general, the research suggests that mastery and performance-approach goals tend to be positively related to academic achievement, and performance-avoidance goals sometimes related negatively to academic achievement (Harackiewicz, Barron, Pintrich, Elliot, & Thrash, 2002).

One consistent finding in the achievement goal literature is that students who support mastery goals are more likely to use deep-level strategies such as elaboration and organization than students who support performance goals (Fredricks, Blumenfeld, & Paris, 2004; Ross et al., 2002; Wolters, Yu, & Pintrich, 1996). A great deal of research, as Patrick, Kaplan, and Ryan (2007) point out, has documented that mastery goals are connected with students' use of cognitive and self-regulatory strategies and interacting with others about their ideas and understanding. Multiple studies found that performance goals, especially performance avoidance, were positively correlated with low levels of cognitive engagement (Patrick et al., 2007). Mastery goals are usually associated with many positive cognitive, motivational, and behavioral outcomes (Pintrich, 2003). Improvements in student achievement are found when students go beyond the classroom requirements and do more work than is required (Fredricks et al., 2004). Given the preceding research, it was expected that mastery goals would be positively related to the use of learning strategies and negatively related to maladaptive help-seeking and worry.

Learning strategies and self-regulated learning. Research has suggested that self-regulated learning incorporates cognitive, motivational, and metacognitive dimensions (Zimmerman & Schunk, 2001) and suggests the importance of self-regulatory skills in academic achievement (Zimmerman, 1990; Zimmerman & Martinez-Pons, 1990). Research also indicates that students who self-monitor their learning progress and engagement with tasks generate internal feedback. This internal feedback works to assess possible gaps in performance, and the result may lead to improved learning outcomes (Azevedo & Cromley, 2004; Butler & Winne, 1995; Ley & Young, 2001). Students who are capable of effective learning tend to choose appropriate learning goals, and use adaptive knowledge and skills to direct their learning. These students are also able to select effective learning strategies appropriate to the task at hand. In other words, they are able to regulate their learning and take responsibility for the acquisition and maintenance of new skills.

One of the central aspects of self-regulated learning is students' ability to select, combine, and coordinate learning activities (Zimmerman & Martinez-Pons, 1990). The cognitive aspects of effective self-regulated learning are elaboration (e.g., exploring how the information might be useful in the real world) and control strategies. Additionally, effective learning requires adaptive motivational beliefs related to factors such as self-efficacy, interest, goal orientation, attributions, and other variables which in turn affect effort and persistence in learning. There is a significant body of research findings that support the connection between motivational variables, learning strategies, self-regulatory behavior, and academic achievement (Bandura, 1997; Deci & Ryan, 1985; Zimmerman, 1990, 2000a).

With respect to performance goals in particular, some work has found that they are negatively related to self-regulation of learning, decreasing the use of deep cognitive processing strategies that lead to better understanding (Graham & Golan, 1991; Meece, Blumenfeld, & Hoyle, 1988; Nolen, 1988). In contrast, mastery goal orientations held by individuals have been found to influence self-regulatory strategies (e.g., surface processing, deep processing, and help-seeking behaviors) and academic achievement (e.g., Elliot, McGregor, & Gable, 1999; Middleton & Midgley, 1997). However, other research has found no relation between classroom performance goals and self-regulated learning (Ames & Archer, 1988), and one study (Ryan & Pintrich, 1997) found no relation between performance goals and adaptive help-seeking, one form of self-regulated learning. In line with this research, it was expected that students' self-regulatory and learning strategies would be related to achievement because of the centrality of these factors to a wide range of variables associated with improved academic outcomes.

In terms of group differences in learning strategies, there are important studies that examine different approaches used by different groups. For instance, Garcia, Yu, and Coppola's (1993) study unpacked gender and ethnic differences in science achievement. The design was a pre-post test at two different times to examine changes in patterns of motivation and learning strategies. Latino and African-American students' success was correlated with motivation and prior achievement and not with learning strategies. Also, minority students (African American, Latino and Asian) reported a higher extrinsic motivation orientation over their White counterparts. These strategies included metacognitive awareness (e.g., planning, monitoring, regulating) and effort management. The authors conclude that gender and ethnicity do not affect achievement outcomes, but preparedness, motivation, and use of learning strategies do.

In one of the first studies to look at cross-cultural differences in self-regulated learning and learning strategies, Purdie, Hattie, and Douglas (1996) looked at conceptions of learning and use of strategies, suggesting that conceptions inform strategies used. They found that Japanese students use strategies of rote memorization and textbooks, and do not seek help from others. Both groups used learning strategies (e.g., "environmental structuring," "self-evaluating") at similar frequencies and the only difference in strategies was which ones were used more by both groups ("reviewing previous work" was the least used strategy of both groups). In other words, there was no between-group difference in types of strategies used.

Help-seeking. Adaptive help-seeking has been described as asking for help needed in order to learn independently, not simply to obtain the correct answer. It is manifested when students monitor their academic performance, show awareness of difficulty they cannot overcome on their own, and exhibit the wherewithal and self-determination to remedy that difficulty by requesting assistance from a more knowledgeable individual, they are exhibiting mature, strategic behavior (Newman, 2002, p. 132).

Research indicates that students who tend to seek more help are also more likely to seek instrumental help (Karabenick, 2003; Tobias, 2006). Research further indicates that students who engage in instrumental help-seeking become more competent and independent learners, and they are more self-regulated and metacognitively aware, which influences their awareness of a need for help (Tobias, 2006; Karabenick, 2003). Karabenick (2003) found that mastery-oriented students not only tend to seek more help but also perform better. In contrast, performance-oriented students tend to have lower achievement due to their threat of help-seeking and resistance to obtaining the help they need, thereby decreasing their chances of success (Karabenick, 2003). Studies have also shown that help-seeking behaviors can lead to increased academic achievement (Karabenick, 2003; Wigfield & Eccles, 2002). Help-seeking is related to motivational variables as well. For example, students who have higher efficacy are more likely to seek help (Ryan, Gheen, & Midgley, 1998). Students may modify their engagement by adjusting or setting new goals. They may further reexamine their learning tactics and strategies and select more productive approaches, adapt available skills, or even generate new learning or monitoring procedures (Butler & Winne, 1995).

Unfortunately, students who need help the most are often those least likely to seek it out (e.g. Ryan & Pintrich, 1997; 1998). In addition, while help-seeking can be an important self-regulatory strategy, it is not necessarily always positive. Students who are motivated by work-avoidance goals are reluctant to seek help or seek help for the wrong reasons. Students may ask for assistance when it is not necessary, for example, or when they have not attempted the work on their own. They may also be motivated to seek help in order to complete a task and move on to other activities, or they may seek help for social rather than academic reasons.

Test anxiety and worry. There is a significant amount of work in the area of motivation that has examined the role of affect or emotion on academic performance (Hembree, 1988; Zeidner & Matthews, 2005). One important emotion is test anxiety because of the obvious connections to achievement. Test anxiety is often seen as a specific form of generalized anxiety, in reference to test or evaluative situations. It is recognized as having phenomenological, physiological, and behavioral responses that occur in conjunction with concern about possible negative consequences of low performance (Zeidner, 1998). In addition, researchers often distinguish trait anxiety, which is more stable and enduring, from state anxiety, which is more context-specific (Covington, 1992; Spielberger, 1972). Test anxiety is also commonly seen as having a cognitive component (worry) and an emotional component (emotionality such as fear and uneasiness) (Zeidner & Matthews, 2005).

There are two general patterns in this literature. First, the negative effects of test anxiety on performance are strong and consistent (Hembree, 1988; Hill & Wigfield, 1984). Hembree (1988) found an effect size of −0.33 in his meta-analysis between test anxiety and achievement. Second, the worry component of test anxiety is more closely linked to performance and achievement than the emotionality component (Covington, 1992). The effects on performance have been suggested as resulting from various sources including interference with attentional processes and thus increased cognitive load, as well as to a more generalized lack of access to efficient learning strategies which impacts encoding and retrieval (Schutz & Davis, 2000; Zeidner, 1998). Given these findings, it was hypothesized that worry would be negatively related to achievement.

Summary and Purpose of the Study

There is some evidence from large-scale research studies that there is invariance among a broad range of cultural groups on self-regulatory, motivational, and learning strategy constructs (Marsh et al., 2006). However, there is also some evidence for cultural specificity in these domains (McInerney & Van Etten, 2001; Urdan, 2004; Urdan & Giancarlo, 2001; Watkins, McInerney, Akande, & Lee, 2003; Rueda & Chen, 2005; Vansteenviste, Zhou, Lens, & Soenens, 2005). While the learning and motivation literature has increasingly recognized sociocultural factors as important, there is only limited work exploring the robustness of the relationships among these factors for students from different ethnic, linguistic, and cultural groups, especially in the US context with specific groups such as the increasingly large Latino population.

To address this gap, this study included constructs tapping students' approaches to learning, motivation related factors (e.g., academic efficacy and goal orientation), OTL (e.g., advanced level of math and science education in high school), and demographic/background variables (e.g., gender, ethnicity, SES and prior knowledge). The first specific purpose of this study was to examine cross-ethnic invariance across White and Latino students in terms of self-regulatory beliefs, learning strategies, and motivational constructs in a 4-year college setting. In addition, a second purpose of the study was to develop and test a structural model of relationships between student background characteristics, OTL, learning strategies, motivational variables, and academic achievement.

Method

Research Context

The study examined the relationship between learning strategies and academic achievement and the differences between Hispanic[1] and non-Hispanic students' use of strategies, educational attitudes, and motivation to learn in a 4-year state college setting in the Southwest. This college selects from among the top 30% of high-school students in California. At the time of the study, the college had a total of 16,479 enrolled students. The majority of students attending were of Mexican American, Hispanic descent. The breakdown for the campus by ethnicity was 36.9% Hispanic, 13.0% African American, 0.9% Native American, 6.3% Asians, 0.5% Pacific Islander, 36.4% White, 3.0% Filipino, and 3.1% other ethnicities. The percentage of new freshmen was 30.41% and 44.2% of the new transfers attended local community colleges.

Subjects

There were two components to the data collection: a *phone* survey and an *online* survey. The final number of students contacted for the *phone* survey was 2,232 non-Hispanics (63.4% of the total sample) of which the majority were White (1,402, 39.8%) and the remainder of the sample were Hispanic/Latino (1,295, 38.7%). The final number of students responding to the *online* survey was 2,012 (1,307 65% non-Hispanics and 705 35% Hispanics).

[1]There are a variety of terms found in the literature including the generic terms Latino and Hispanic as well as more population-specific terms such as Mexican-American or Cuban. There is no widespread agreement about the use of a single term, and arguments for different choices based on political and other considerations are numerous. In this chapter we use the term Hispanic and Latino interchangeably.

Measures

The measures included questions about students' demographic characteristics, educational attitudes and beliefs, academic efficacy, and learning strategies such as elaboration and control.

Background variables. For the students' background variables, SES was measured by using a combination of mother's highest degree of education (1 = *didn't finish high school*, 4 = *graduated from college*) and income (1 = *less than \$25,000*, 4 = *more than \$75,000*). Two questions assessed students' *prior achievement level (prior knowledge)* including high-school GPA ($M = 3.13$, $SD = 0.47$), SAT1 verbal score ($M = 455.33$, $SD = 91.27$), and SAT1 math score ($M = 462.18$, $SD = 86.93$).

Opportunity to learn. This construct measured whether students had received different educational or instructional ingredients that make up quality school experience. Our questions included "how many semesters of advanced placement (AP) math did you take in high school?" and "how many semesters of AP science did you take in high school?" The questions ranged from 1 to 8.

Motivation and attitudes. The questions about educational attitudes and motivation were revised from Marsh et al.'s (2006) student approaches to learning (SAL) instrument. *Academic efficacy* consisted of four items asking students' beliefs in their capabilities to master the skills being taught and to overcome barriers through their own efforts. The *Worry* scale was adopted from Spielberger's (1980) test anxiety inventory ($\alpha = 0.92$) and is conceptualized as cognitive concern over failure. Eight items were used to indicate how they felt while taking the exam and how they felt anxiety on failing the exam. Students were instructed to select a number ranging from 1 (*almost never*) to 4 (*almost always*) for each item of these scales.

Personal motivational beliefs. The items from this scale were from Anderman, Urdan, and Roeser's (2003) Patterns of Adaptive Learning Scale. Three personal goal orientations were assessed. *Mastery goal orientation* included five items reflecting students' emphasis on learning and their concern with understanding, developing competence, and improvement. ($\alpha = 0.85$). *Performance approach goal orientation* consisted of five items that tapped into students' desire to demonstrate competence, for example; by outperforming others in their class work ($\alpha = 0.89$). Four items assessed *performance avoidance goal orientation*, reflecting students' concern with not appearing incompetent or less competent than others in their class work ($\alpha = 0.74$). Students indicated their response to each item on a five-point scale (1 = *not at all true*, 5 = *very much true*).

Learning strategies. Students' use of different learning strategies was assessed with items derived from Marsh et al.'s (2006) SAL instrument. *Elaboration* consisted of four items measuring how often students engage in construction, integration, and transfer strategies when completing class work. *Control* included five items and measured the extent to which students adopt a self-regulating perspective during the learning process. This scale asked questions about whether students engage in activities such as checking that they remember what they have already learned or what they do not yet understand ($\alpha = 0.83$). *Effort* included four items tapping into students' levels of effort expended, as well as their willingness to continue to try even when presented with difficult material. Students responded on a 1 (*almost never*) to 4 (*almost always*) in those scales.

Finally, six questions were adapted from Meuschke, Dembo, and Gribbons's (2006) Adaptive Help-Seeking Scale to assess students' use of *maladaptive help-seeking* strategies (e.g., guessing, simply avoiding the work, or giving up the task without asking for help). The items were scored on a five-point scale ranging from 1 (*not at all true*) to 5 (*very much true*) ($\alpha = 0.72$). Each of the scales above was averaged to form nine distinct constructs (*Elaboration, Control, Maladaptive help-seeking, Effort, Worry, Academic efficacy, Mastery goal orientation, Performance approach goal orientation,* and *Performance avoidance goal orientation*).

Academic achievement. The outcome variable of this study was measured by students' total GPA ($M = 2.92$, $SD = 0.52$).

Procedure

Data were obtained from the Office of Institutional Research in the form of a list of all 16,488 students registered at the college for the 2006 Fall quarter. Graduate students were deleted from the list, as were students who were not American citizens. Further, students with no contact information were deleted. The final sampling frame contained contact information for 11,569 undergraduate students. Our data were collected in the fall of 2006 using two methods of data collection—a phone survey that included 3,523 students (2,232 non-Hispanics and 1,295 Hispanics) and an online survey that included 2,012 students (1,306 non-Hispanics and 705 Hispanics).

Telephone interview. Students were initially contacted by phone in order to explain the purpose of the research. Interviewers asked the student respondents a few questions to elicit some basic demographic data as well as some initial questions regarding their learning strategies. In addition, interviewers confirmed the student's e-mail address so that a link to a web survey could be sent. The link to the web survey was then sent to each student, with at least two follow-up reminders sent to all non-respondents. In addition, a lottery system was used by which students could win money/coupons to be used to purchase items at the University's bookstore.

In the telephone survey part of the data collection, telephone surveys on demographics and students' background were conducted by trained staff from a research institute of the college, using computer-assisted telephone interviewing (CATI) equipment and software. In an effort to ensure the quality and reliability of the interviews, institute research staff supervised all interviews conducted. To further ensure quality control, supervisory personnel randomly selected completed interviews (at least one completion per interviewer) and made call-backs for verification. A pairwise method was used for missing data.

Online survey. For the second part of the data collection, on-line surveys related to academic motivation and the use of learning strategies were completed from the students' own computer or in computer labs in the college.

Data Analysis

The first part of the analysis focused on evaluating the psychometric characteristics of the measures. We examined internal consistency of scales by calculating Cronbach's alpha coefficients. Also, in order to evaluate responses to the same instrument by different groups (in this case Latino and White students) separately, the second part of analysis examines whether the constructs were the same across White and Latino/a groups. Therefore, multiple group confirmatory factor analysis (MG-CFA) was employed to test factorial invariance between those groups. MG-CFA test traditionally posits a series of nested models in which the end point is the least restrictive model with no invariance constraints and the most restrictive (total invariance) model with all parameters constrained to be equal across all groups. Thus, we first examined the extent to which the theoretical structure of the instrument was invariant to ensure the structural equivalence of underlying constructs between White and Latino/a groups. We also investigated the extent to which the factor patterns and weighing of loadings were invariant, in order to ensure the equivalent interpretation of item content across two different groups. Finally, we aimed to determine how demographic and background information related to motivation/learning strategies and academic achievement for White and Latino/a college students. We initially developed a model for the entire sample ($n = 3{,}257$) to test the theoretical SEM and then we estimated two single-group SEMs using White students and Latino students to compare the significant path coefficients between two groups.

Results

Reliabilities, Descriptive Statistics, and Intercorrelations

Reliabilities. Cronbach's alpha reliability coefficients were computed for nine scales on motivation/learning strategies items. Scale reliabilities for all scales were generally satisfactory (see Table 7.1). For the total sample of 3,527 participants, reliability coefficients varied from 0.71 to 0.93 ($M = 0.84$). This average reliability and the reliabilities of each of the nine scales are higher than at least 0.70, suggesting that the measures used in this study appear to meet basic psychometric criteria. Descriptive analyses were conducted to provide overall information of the study variables. Table 7.2 presents means and standard deviations of primary variables.

Table 7.1 Reliability coefficients

	N of items	All (*n* = 3,527)	Latino/a (*n* = 1,125)			White (*n* = 1,156)		
		A	α	Mean	*SD*	α	Mean	*SD*
Elaboration	4	0.82	0.80	2.81	0.65	0.83	2.90	0.66
Control	5	0.71	0.71	3.07	0.53	0.72	3.06	0.54
Maladaptive help-seeking	6	0.86	0.86	2.25	0.83	0.87	2.05	0.77
Academic efficacy	4	0.82	0.81	2.72	0.62	0.83	2.84	0.64
Effort	4	0.80	0.81	3.05	0.62	0.82	3.06	0.62
Worry	8	0.89	0.88	2.09	0.70	0.90	1.83	0.67
Mastery goal orientation	5	0.87	0.85	4.08	0.73	0.88	3.90	0.76
Performance approach	5	0.93	0.91	1.98	0.96	0.93	2.17	1.00
Performance avoidance	4	0.86	0.85	2.26	0.99	0.87	2.41	0.99
All	45	0.84	0.86	2.65	0.35	0.84	2.61	0.32

Table 7.2 Descriptive statistics for study variables ($N = 3,527$)

Variable	*M*	*SD*	Observed range
High school GPA	3.10	0.47	1.1–4.3
SAT1 verbal	455.6	90.7	200–730
SAT1 math	462.4	86.3	200–790
Elaboration	2.88	0.66	1–4
Control	3.08	0.54	1–4
Maladaptive help-seeking	2.12	0.79	1–5
Academic efficacy	2.78	0.64	1–4
Effort	3.05	0.62	1–4
Worry	1.96	0.69	1–4
Mastery goal orientation	3.99	0.77	1–5
Performance approach	2.12	0.99	1–5
Performance avoidance	2.32	0.99	1–5
Total GPA	2.84	.53	0.67–4.25

Intercorrelations among key variables. The relationships among scales revealed that all of the correlations (see Table 7.3 for the entire sample) among the adaptive learning strategies (elaboration, control, and effort) measures were positive and statistically significant ($r = 0.38$ to 0.59, $p < 0.01$). Elaboration, control, and effort scales were positively correlated with the efficacy scale ($r = 0.40, 0.39, 0.39$, respectively, $p < 0.01$) but negatively correlated with worry ($r = -0.07, -0.09, -0.07, p < 0.01$). Maladaptive help-seeking had a negative correlation with efficacy ($r = -0.33$, $p < 0.01$), but it was positively correlated with worry ($r = 0.38$, $p < 0.01$). With regard to personal motivational beliefs, two of the performance goal

Table 7.3 Bivariate correlations among primary indicators of motivation and learning strategies (White and Latino students N=2,281)

	1	2	3	4	5	6	7	8	9	10	11	12	13	14	15	16	17
1. Gender (female = 0)	–																
2. Ethnicity (White = 0)	0.06**	–															
3. AP math	0.01	.03	–														
4. AP science	0.01	.00	.61**	–													
5. High-school GPA	−0.12**	0.12**	0.09**	0.05	–												
6. SAT1 verbal	0.09**	0.27**	0.10**	0.16**	0.25**	–											
7. SAT1 math	0.20**	0.29**	0.16**	0.16**	0.30**	0.62**	–										
8. Efficacy	0.18**	0.09**	0.10**	0.11**	0.11**	0.25**	0.17**	–									
9. Worry	−0.12**	−0.19**	−0.07*	−0.04	−0.19**	−0.34**	−0.34**	−0.38**	–								
10. Elaboration	0.05	0.07*	0.05	0.06*	0.07	0.14**	0.11**	0.40**	−0.07**	–							
11. Control	−0.07*	−0.01	0.05	0.03	0.12**	0.02	−0.02	0.39**	−0.09**	0.45**	–						
12. Effort	−0.12**	0.03	0.05	0.01	0.05	−0.11**	−0.11**	0.39**	−0.07**	0.38**	0.59**	–					
13. Mastery goal	0.00	−0.12**	0.05	0.05	−0.01	−0.07	−0.12**	0.35**	−0.03	0.39**	0.48**	0.54**	–				
14. Performance approach	0.04	0.10**	0.05	0.07*	0.05	0.04	0.04	0.03	0.13**	0.07**	−0.03	−0.09**	−0.02	–			
15. Performance avoidance	0.01	0.08**	0.02	0.02	0.08	0.06	0.07	−0.03	0.18**	0.03	−0.01	−0.09**	−0.02	0.74**	–		
16. Maladaptive helpseek	0.03	−0.13**	−0.05	−0.01	−0.09*	−0.05	0.00	−0.33**	0.38**	−0.25**	−0.33**	−0.42**	−0.28**	0.22**	0.30**	–	
17. Total GPA	−0.03	0.25**	0.01	0.01	0.38**	0.39**	0.32**	0.24**	−0.34**	0.12**	0.17**	0.20**	0.05	0.04	0.02	−0.26**	–

* $p < .05$; ** $p < .01$.

orientation scales (performance approach and performance avoidance) were found to be highly correlated with each other ($r = 0.74, p < 0.01$). However, those performance goal-orientation scales showed no statistically significant correlations with mastery goal orientation. Mastery goal orientation scale was positively correlated with all of the learning strategies (elaboration: $r = 0.39$, $p < 0.01$; control: $r = 0.48, p < 0.01$; effort: $r = 0.54, p < 0.01$). Both of the performance goal orientation scales were correlated only with elaboration ($r = 0.07$ to $0.03, p < 0.01$) and effort ($r = -0.09, p < 0.01$). Finally, performance goal orientation scales showed positive correlations with worry ($r = 0.13$ to $0.18, p < 0.01$) whereas mastery goal orientation showed no statistically significant correlation with worry.

With regard to personal motivational beliefs, two of the performance goal orientation scales (performance approach and performance avoidance) were found to be highly correlated with each other ($r = 0.74, p < 0.01$). However, those performance goal orientation scales showed no statistically significant correlations with mastery goal orientation. Mastery goal orientation scale was positively correlated with all of the learning strategies (elaboration: $r = 0.39, p < 0.01$; control: $r = 0.48, p < 0.01$; effort: $r = 0.54$, $p < 0.01$). Both of the performance goal orientation scales were correlated only with elaboration ($r = 0.07$ to $0.03, p < 0.01$) and effort ($r = -0.09$, $p < 0.01$). Finally, performance goal orientation scales showed positive correlations with worry ($r = 0.13$ to 0.18, $p < 0.01$) whereas mastery goal orientation showed no statistically significant correlation with worry.

Correlations between learning strategies and achievement. Consistent with the findings from prior research, learning strategies were positively correlated with the achievement variable (elaboration: $r = 0.12$, $p < 0.01$; control: $r = 0.17$, $p < 0.01$; effort: $r = 0.20$, $p < 0.01$). However, maladaptive help-seeking had a negative correlation with achievement ($r = -0.26$, $p < 0.01$). Academic efficacy was also positively correlated with achievement ($r = 0.24, p < 0.01$), whereas worry was negatively correlated ($r = -0.34$, $p < 0.01$). Research on worry supports the negative effects of worry and academic outcome (Elliot & McGregor, 1999; Vagg & Papsdorf, 1995).

Multi-Group Confirmatory Factor Analysis

Preliminary CFA for overall model. Preliminary confirmatory factor analyses were conducted with M plus 3.13 (Muthén & Muthén, 2004) using maximum likelihood estimation. We hypothesized a nine-factor model in which the items for each factor load on their respective latent variable. The results supported the hypothesized theoretical model, indicating that all the factor loadings were significant and our nine-factor solution had a good fit to the data with regard to acceptable levels of fit (Comparative Fit Index [CFA] = 0.96; Tucker-Lewis Index [TLI] = 0.96; root-mean-square error of approximation [RMSEA] = 0.03), although the chi-square value was statistically significant (χ^2= 2,429.14, df = 878, p = 0.000). It should be noted that chi-square is sensitive to sample size, and the larger the sample size, the more likely the rejection of the model and the more likely a Type II error. Thus, as the case here, with large samples, even small differences between the observed model and the perfect-fit model may be found significant. One fit index that is less sensitive to sample size is the chi-square/*df* statistic (Bryant & Yarnold, 2001). In the factor analysis reported above, the value of χ^2/df was 2.77, within acceptable limits.

Multiple-group CFA. For this aspect of the analysis, we selected the two ethnic groups focused on in the study, including White (n = 1,156, 32.8%) and Latino (n = 1,125, 31.9%). Our confirmatory factor analysis next dealt with the question of whether the nine measures were equivalent across the White and Latino/a subgroups. The assumption of structural equivalence was tested using a multi-group CFA that allows factorial invariance across groups. Testing for factorial invariance involves comparing a set of models in which factor structure and factor loadings are held equal across groups and assessing fit indices when elements of these structures are constrained (Marsh et al., 2006). Thus, we developed an initial baseline model (Model 1), which is totally non-invariant in that there were no assumptions being made about group invariance across groups. Then we imposed invariance constraints for factor loadings and factor means (Model 2), and factor variances (Model 3).

Model 1 examined whether the items in each of the nine factors were grouped in accordance with theoretical expectations (χ^2 = 3,199.21, df = 1,792, p = 0.000, χ^2/df = 2.14, CFI = 0.95, TLI = 0.95, RMSEA = 0.04). Model 2 tested whether factor loadings and factor means were the same across groups. This model is important because a minimal criterion for structural equivalence is that the factor loadings relating each indicator to its hypothesized factor are the same across all groups. (χ^2 = 3,360.47, df = 1,837, p = 0.000, χ^2/df = 1.83, CFI = 0.947, TLI = 0.943, RMSEA = 0.039). The difference in chi-square between the constrained and unconstrained models was significant ($\Delta\chi^2$ = 161.26, Δdf = 45, $p < 0.000$); however, the differences in RMSEA and other fit indices were very small.

We then tested the assumption that factor variances as well as factor loadings and factor means were equal across groups (Model 3). The most restrictive model provided a good fit to the data (χ^2 = 3,397.08, df = 1,855, p = 0.000, χ^2/df = 1.83, CFI = 0.946, TLI = 0.943, RMSEA = 0.039), and the Bayesian Information Criteria (BIC) showed that this model best fit to the data. Although all three models showed good fit, Model 3 is most parsimonious in terms of number of parameters to be estimated. In summary, there was good support for the invariance of factor loadings, factor means, and factor variances across White and Latino/a groups.

Structural Equation Model Analysis

SEM MIMIC model for Latino and White students. An approach based on a multiple-indicator-multiple-indicator cause model (MIMIC; Kaplan, 2000, Jöreskog & Sörbom, 1993) was used for evaluating relations between motivational and learning strategy factors and background variables. This extended SEM MIMIC model was seen as appropriate here given that it is based on latent constructs having measurement error and that it allows for a test of the underlying structural model (Marsh et al., 2006). We hypothesized a structural model among cognitive and motivational factors and other criterion variables (see Figs. 7.1 and 7.2).

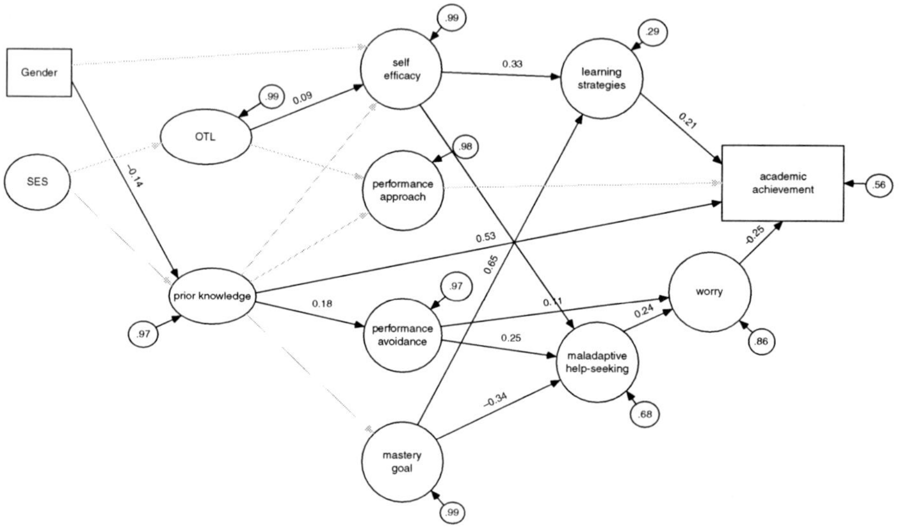

Fig. 7.1 Estimation of cognitive and motivational factors of academic achievement for White students ($N = 1{,}156$)

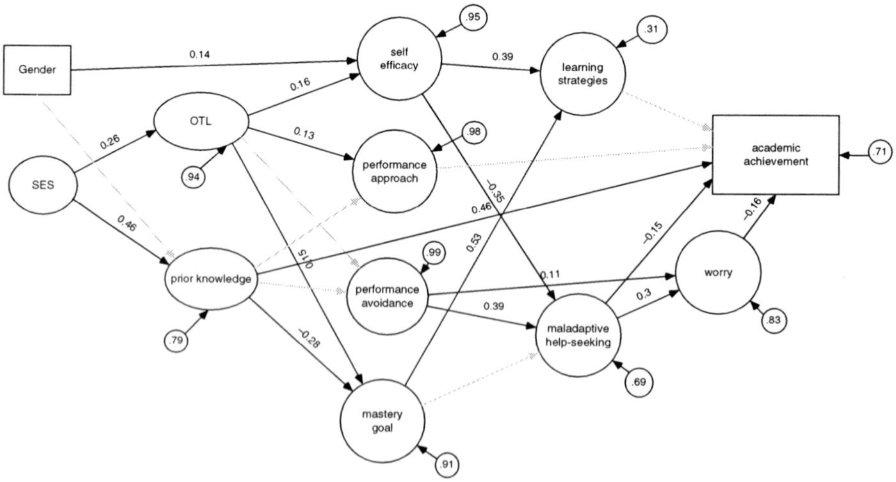

Fig. 7.2 Estimation of cognitive and motivational factors of academic achievement for Latino students ($N = 1{,}125$)

The SEM results produced good fits to data (Latino/a group—χ^2 = 2,498.05, df = 1,322, p = 0.000, χ^2/df = 1.90, CFI = 0.92, TLI = 0.92, RMSEA = 0.03; White—χ^2 = 2,540.59, df = 1,322, p = 0.000, χ^2/df = 1.92, CFI = 0.94, TLI = 0.93, RMSEA = 0.03).

For Latino/a students, the overall relationships among opportunities to learn, prior level of achievement, and motivation factors were similar to those of all students (e.g., positive effects of motivation factors—efficacy, mastery goal—on learning strategies). However, unlike the overall SEM, the Latino subgroup did not show any significant effect of prior knowledge on performance avoidance, although they showed a positive effect of OTL on performance approach ($\beta = 0.12$, $p < 0.001$). We also found that male Latino students reported more academic efficacy than female Latino students ($\beta = 0.14$, $p < 0.001$), as expected in findings from the studies on gender and self-efficacy. Efficacy and mastery influenced learning strategies positively ($\beta = 0.39$ and $\beta = 0.53$, respectively, $p < 0.001$) but efficacy had negatively influenced help-seeking ($\beta = -0.34$, $p = 0.001$). Maladaptive help-seeking strategies were positively associated with worry ($\beta = 0.30$, $p < 0.001$). The pattern of effects on GPA (positive effects of prior knowledge, negative effects of worry, and help-seeking) was similar to those of the overall model.

For White students, the results showed different patterns in relations of SES to prior knowledge and OTL. White female students achieved more in high school than their male peers ($\beta = -0.14$, $p < 0.001$) and students who had more OTL reported higher self-efficacy ($\beta = 0.09$, $p < 0.001$). Also, there was no effect of OTL on mastery goal orientation, whereas there was a positive effect of prior knowledge on performance avoidance ($\beta = 0.19$, $p < 0.001$). Self-efficacy and mastery goal orientation positively affected learning strategies ($\beta = 0.33$ and $\beta = 0.65$, respectively, $p < 0.001$). Like Latino students, both maladaptive help-seeking and performance avoidance positively affected worry ($\beta = 0.24$ and $\beta = 0.11$, respectively, $p < 0.001$) and worry had a negative effect on achievement ($\beta = -0.25$, $p < 0.001$). Prior knowledge and learning strategies were found to be two prominent predictors of academic achievement ($\beta = 0.53$ and $\beta = 0.21$, respectively, $p < 0.001$).

Multiple-group SEM: White and Latino groups. Finally, we analyzed a multi-group SEM for White and Latino groups to examine the extent to which parameter estimates in our theoretical model differ between White and Latino groups (See Fig. 7.3). We first estimated the constrained model, which fixed all common parameters between groups. Our constrained model resulted in a CFI of 0.91 and TLI of 0.90 with χ^2 = 6,083.70 (df = 2,773, χ^2/df = 2.19, $p < 0.000$). We then performed chi-square difference tests several times, in order to identify which pairs of path coefficients were significantly different in multiple groups. For example, we freed the parameter of the path from gender to prior knowledge to test whether there was a significant chi-square decrease. The model improved significantly ($\Delta\chi^2 = 82.11$, $\Delta df = 1, p < 0.001$) which means that there was a significant difference in parameter estimates between two groups.

In other words, although both of the standardized path coefficients were negative, the effect of gender on prior knowledge was slightly greater for Latino students

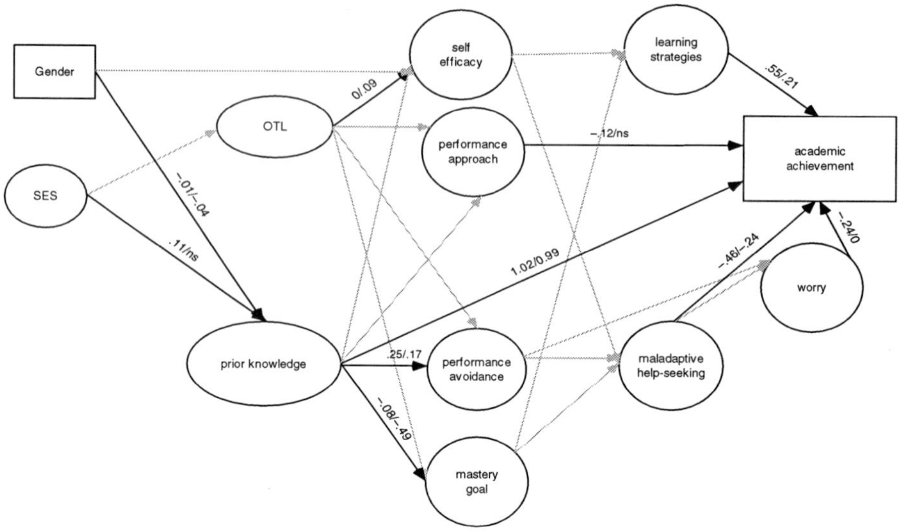

Fig. 7.3 Multiple-group (White/Latino) estimation of cognitive and motivational factors of academic achievement (White = 1,156, Latino = 1,125)

($\beta = -0.04, p < 0.001$) than for White students ($\beta = -0.01, p < 0.001$). Figure 7.3 shows different effects for White and Latino students for our theoretical model.[2]

Latino students had a positive effect of OTL on self-efficacy ($\beta = 0.09$, $p < 0.001$) but White students showed no effect of OTL. Prior knowledge had a negative effect on mastery goal orientation but had a stronger relation for Latino students ($\beta = -0.08$ for White and $\beta = -0.49$ for Latino, $p < 0.001$). Prior knowledge was also one of the strong predictor of academic achievement ($\beta = 1.02$ for White and $\beta = 0.99$ for Latino, $p < 0.001$). Interestingly, it revealed that there was a weaker effect of prior knowledge on performance avoidance for Latino students ($\beta = 0.17, p < 0.001$) than for White students ($\beta = 0.25, p < 0.001$). Performance approach goal orientation showed a different pattern of relationship between groups. It had a negative impact on GPA for White students ($\beta = -0.12, p < 0.001$) but no effect for Latinos.

The effects of adaptive/maladaptive learning strategies also showed some interesting differences in White and Latino groups. First, while both groups had positive relations of learning strategies to GPA, the latent factor had a greater impact on GPA among White ($\beta = 0.55, p < 0.001$) than Latino ($\beta = 0.21, p < 0.001$) students. Second, maladaptive help-seeking had negative effects for both White and Latino groups, but the relation was stronger for White ($\beta = -0.46, p < 0.001$) than

[2]All of the unconstrained model results in this section produced good fit indices (CFI and TLIs = 0.90–0.91 and RMSEAs < 0.04). All of the chi-square difference tests reported in this section showed significant model improvement, indicated by significant chi-square decrease.

for Latino ($\beta = -0.24$, $p < 0.001$) students. Lastly, worry had a negative effect on achievement for White students ($\beta = -0.24$, $p < 0.001$) but no effect for Latinos.

Summary Findings

Scale reliabilities were generally satisfactory: For the total sample of 3,527 participants, reliability estimates of the measures ranged from 0.71 to 0.93. Confirmatory factor analysis results for the total combined sample showed that the cognitive and motivational factors of effective learning strategies were well defined in a nine-factor solution and the results of the multiple-group CFA indicated that there was good support for a totally invariant model with a nine-factor solution across White and Latino groups. In terms of ethnic differences between groups, gender was related negatively to prior knowledge for both groups, but Latino groups had slightly greater relations among those. SES was positively related to prior knowledge for White students but not Latino students. For White students, having a family with higher income and more educated mothers significantly affected students' prior levels of achievement, but this relation was not statistically significant for Latino students. Latino students showed a stronger association between OTL and academic efficacy than White students. For White students, the effect of prior knowledge on the achievement was greater than for Latino students. The White group also appeared to be more influenced by maladaptive help-seeking and worry compared to the Latino group. Although both groups had positive effects of learning strategies on GPA, the relation of White students was greater than that of Latino students.

Discussion and Conclusion

The results of this study provide support for factors that previous literature and theory have shown to be important for self-regulated learning and the relationships to motivational and learning strategy use. From an educational perspective, this is encouraging news, since the motivational and learning strategies of the type examined in this investigation are amenable to instruction and modifiable. This is important because of a tendency of postsecondary institutions, as well as the field of education in general, to consider low achievement a function of unmodifiable student or family deficits (Bensimon, 2005, Valencia, 1997). While there is some concern in psychological research about the tendency to focus on a limited range of sociocultural contexts and populations (Arnett, 2008), there is good evidence that there are similarities across sociocultural groups with respect to the motivational and learning-related constructs examined here, as evidenced by the PISA international data (Marsh et al., 2006). This is consistent with the significant body of research findings that support the connection between motivational variables, learning strategies, self-regulatory behavior, and academic achievement (Bandura, 1997; Deci & Ryan, 1985; Zimmerman, 1990, 2000a). This does not negate the importance of sociocultural factors, however.

In spite of the invariance of the constructs investigated, there were some differences between the two groups examined. Latinos were somewhat lower on elaboration, academic efficacy, performance approach, and performance avoidance for example, and somewhat higher on maladaptive help-seeking, worry, and mastery goal orientation. There is no simple explanation for these differences, as the literature focusing on comparisons between the two groups in this study is too small. One factor that may be important is the select nature of the Latino students in this sample. Given that they were in a 4-year college, they may not be comparable to the general population of Latino students. While their prior grades and SAT scores were lower than those of White students, the fact that they were admitted to a relatively selective institution may have been a factor in higher mastery goal orientation, and lower levels of prior knowledge (high school GPA and SAT verbal and math) may have been related to lower efficacy and increased maladaptive help-seeking. The findings here were somewhat consistent with Garcia et al.'s (1993) study with Latino and African American students who found that success was correlated with motivation and prior achievement, and not with learning strategies. Given the extensive literature that suggests the impact of learning strategies on academic outcomes (Azevedo & Cromley, 2004; Butler & Winne, 1995; Ley & Young, 2001; Zimmerman, 1990; Zimmerman & Martinez-Pons, 1990: Zimmerman & Schunk, 2001), this deserves more exploration.

In addition, SES was related to OTL and prior knowledge for Latino but not for White students. This may be a function of other prior work on differences in OTL between low-SES schools and higher-SES schools. As noted earlier, differences have been found in instructional arrangements, materials, teacher experience, and teacher–student ratio (Wenglinsky, 1998). Interestingly, while OTL was not found to have significant direct effects on achievement, it was related to other motivational variables such as self-efficacy, performance approach, and mastery goal orientation in the study relative to White students (academic self-efficacy only).

One of the most interesting findings was the very strong effect of prior knowledge on GPA in comparison to the relatively smaller effects of background variables (and other variables as well) such as OTL and SES compared to what we expected. For example, prior knowledge was found to be strongly and positively related to achievement for both White and Latino students. This is a different pattern than what other studies have found, in particular the relatively stronger impact of self-efficacy compared to prior knowledge. Chemers et al. (2001), for example, found that while high-school grades were significantly related to college grades, self-efficacy at the time of college entrance was related to grades at the end of the first year of college, even when prior GPA was controlled. Other recent studies (Pietsch et al., 2003; Pintrich, 2003) as well as a recent review of self-efficacy studies (Valentine et al., 2004) have confirmed these patterns. Because the focus of this study was on math in particular, this may have had an impact on the present findings.

An additional interesting finding was the lack of direct effects of the motivational variables on achievement. As the previous literature has suggested, arguments have been made for a multiple-goal approach in which mastery and performance approach goals play a positive role in academic performance (Pintrich, 2003). Previous studies have found, similar to the present results (Harackiewicz, Barron, Tauer, & Elliot, 2002: Harackiewicz, Barron, Tauer, Carter, & Elliot, 2000), that in studies with college students, mastery goals did not predict course grades, but rather predicted increased interest, enjoyment, and course-taking (in psychology courses). While these variables were not measured in this study, future studies should consider adding them as important mediators.

This study was also consistent with findings in the achievement goal literature that students who support mastery goals are more likely to use deep-level strategies such as elaboration and organization than students who support performance goals (Fredricks et al., 2004; Patrick et al., 2007; Ross et al., 2002; Wolters et al., 1996). A great deal of research, as Patrick et al. (2007) point out, has documented that mastery goals are connected with students' use of cognitive and self-regulatory strategies. Yet it is puzzling why these factors did not exhibit stronger effects on achievement for either group. A more significant and stronger (negative) relationship to achievement was found for worry, the cognitive component of stress and anxiety, consistent with the work in this area (Zeidner & Matthews, 2005).

This study is one of the few studies which have investigated sociocultural-, learning-, and motivation-related factors with college-aged Latino students. Because relatively little work has been done with ethnic differences among college-level students' approach to learning, this study contributes to the knowledge that aims to describe the relationships among those aspects of learning students have already obtained in a given domain, those aspects that are still being developed, and those where students need further support. Rather than exclusively focusing on programs which rely on social and academic integration or financial aid, colleges should continue investigating the sociocultural, motivational, and learning aspects of academic achievement, addressing issues of students' different approaches to learning and how these can be bolstered both prior to and after students arrive on campus. Few faculty members in college teaching positions receive educational experiences which provide the knowledge to consider these factors in their classroom instruction. This is increasingly important, however, as college campuses experience both increasing diversity as well as continued pressure for accountability and student learning outcomes. Drawing upon studies such as this, institutions of higher education should be able to establish professional development programs in order to train faculty at all levels in motivational principles and learning strategies methods which are appropriate to the needs of at-risk students, informed by possible between-group as well as individual differences.

Acknowledgments The work reported herein was supported under US Department of Education Award Number R305C80015. The work was also supported by the Office of Naval Research under Award Number N000140810126. The findings and opinions expressed in this report do not necessarily reflect the positions or policies of the US Department of Education or the Office of Naval Research.

References

Abrego, L. J. (2006). "I can't go to college because I don't have papers": Incorporation patterns of Latino undocumented youth. *Latino Studies*, *4*(3), 212–231.

Adelman, C. (1999). *Answers in the tool box: Academic intensity, attendance patterns, and bachelor's degree attainment*. Washington, DC: U.S. Department of Education, Office of Educational Research and Improvement.

Alfaro, E. C., Umana-Taylor, A. J., & Bamaca, M. Y. (2006). The influence of academic support on Latino adolescents' academic motivation. *Family Relations*, *55*(3), 279–291.

Ames, C. (1992). Achievement goals and the classroom motivational climate. In J. Meece & D. Schunk (Eds.), *Student perceptions in the classroom* (pp. 327–348). Hillsdale, NJ: Erlbaum.

Ames, C., & Archer, J. (1988). Achievement goals in the classroom: Students' learning strategies and motivation processes. *Journal of Educational Psychology*, *80*, 260–267.

Anderman, E. M., Urdan, T. U., & Roeser, R. (2003, March). The patterns of adaptive learning survey: History, development, and psychometric properties. Paper prepared for the *Indicators of Positive Development Conference,* Washington, DC.

Arnett, J. J. (2008). The neglected 95%: Why American psychology needs to become less American. *American Psychologist*, *63*(7), 602–614.

Azevedo, R., & Cromley, J. G. (2004). Does training on self regulated learning facilitate students' learning with hypermedia? *Journal of Educational Psychology*, *96*(3), 523–535.

Baker, E. L., Griffin, N. C., & Choi, K. (2008). *The achievement gap in California: Context, status, and approaches for improvement.* Davis, CA: University of California, Davis School of Education Center for Applied Policy in Education.

Bandura, A. (1986). *Social foundations of thought and action: A social cognitive theory.* Englewood Cliffs, NJ: Prentice Hall.

Bandura, A. (1997). *Self-efficacy: The exercise of control.* New York: Freeman.

Bensimon, E. M. (2005). Closing the achievement gap in higher education: An organizational learning perspective. In A.Kezar (Ed.), *Organizational learning in higher education. New directions for higher education* (pp. 131, 99–111). San Francisco: Jossey-Bass.

Bollen, K., Glanville, J. A., & Stecklov, G. (2001). Socioeconomic status and class in studies of fertility and health in developing countries. *Annual Review of Sociology*, *27*, 153–185.

Bornstein, M. C., & Bradley, R. H. (Eds.). (2003). *Socioeconmic status, parenting, and child development*. Mahwah, NJ: Lawrence Erlbaum.

Braswell, J. S., Lutkus, A. D., Grigg, W. S., Santapau, S. L., Tay-Lim, B., & Johnson, M. (2001). *The Nation's Report Card: Mathematics 2000, NCES 2001–517.* Washington, DC: U.S. Department of Education. Office of Educational Research and Improvement. National Center for Education Statistics.

Brooks-Gunn, J., & Duncan, G. J. (1997). The effects of poverty on children. *The future of children*, *7*(2), 55–71.

Bryant, F. B., & Yarnold, P. R. (2001). Principal component analysis and exploratory and confirmatory factor analysis. In L. G. Grimm & P. R. Yarnold (Eds.), *Reading and understanding multivariate statistics* (pp. 99–136). Washington, DC: American Psychological Association.

Butler, D., & Winne, P. H. (1995). Feedback and self-regulated learning: A theoretical synthesis. *Review of Educational Research*, *65*(3), 245–281.

Byrnes, J. P. (2001). *Cognitive development and learning in instructional contexts* (2). Needham Heights, MA: Allyn & Bacon.

Byrnes, J. P. (2005). Gender differences in math: Cognitive processes in an expanded framework. In A. M. Gallagher & J. C. Kaufman (Eds.), *Gender differences in mathematics: An integrative psychological approach* (pp. 73–98). Cambridge: Cambridge University Press.

Caplan, P. J., & Caplan, J. B. (1999). *Thinking critically about research on sex and gender* (2). New York: Addison-Wesley Longman Inc.

Carey, K. (2004). *A matter of degrees: Improving graduation rates in four-year colleges and universities*. Washington, DC: The Education Trust.

Carey, K. (2005). *One step from the finish line: Higher college graduation rates are within our reach*. Washington, DC: The Education Trust.
Checkley, K. (2001). Algebra and activism: Removing the shackles of low expectations: A conversation with Robert P. Moses. *Educational Leadership, 59*, 6–11.
Chemers, M. M., Hu, L., & Garcia, B. F. (2001). Academic self-efficacy and first-year college student performance and adjustment. *Journal of Educational Psychology, 93*, 55–64.
Chipman, S. F. (1996). Female participation in the study of mathematics: The U.S. situation. In G. Hanna (Ed.), *Towards gender equity in mathematics education* (pp. 285–296). Boston: Kluwer Academic.
Cohen, J. (1977). *Statistical power analysis for the behavioral sciences*. New York: Academic Press.
Coleman, J. S. (1988). Social capital in the creation of human capital. *American Journal of Sociology, 94*, S95–S120.
Covington, M. V. (1992). *Making the grade: a self-worth perspective on motivation and school reform*. New York: Cambridge University Press.
Davis-Kean, P. E., Vida, M., & Eccles, J. (2001). *Influences on parental expectations for post-high school transitions*. Paper presented at the Society for Research on Child Development Biennial Conference.
Deci, E. L., & Ryan, R. M. (1985). *Intrinsic motivation and self-determination in human behavior*. New York: Plenum Press.
Dweck, C. S. (1986). Motivational processes affecting learning. *American Psychologist, 41*, 1040–1048.
Dweck, C. S., & Leggett, E. S. (1988). A social-cognitive approach to motivation and personality. *Psychological Review, 95*, 256–273.
Eccles, J. S., Vida, M. N., & Barber, B. (2004). The relation of early adolescents' college plans and both academic ability and task-value beliefs to subsequent college enrollment. *Journal of Early Adolescence, 24*(1), 63–77.
Elliot, A. J. (1999). Approach and avoidance motivation and achievement goals. *Educational Psychologist, 34*, 169–190.
Elliot, A. J., & McGregor, H. A. (1999). Test anxiety and the hierarchical model of approach and avoidance achievement motivation. *Journal of Personality and Social Psychology, 76*, 628–644.
Elliot, A. J., McGregor, H. A., & Gable, S. (1999). Achievement goals, study strategies, and exam performance: A mediational analysis. *Journal of Educational Psychology, 91*(3), 549–563.
Esparza, P., & Sanchez, B. (2008). The role of attitudinal familism in academic outcomes: a study of urban, Latino high school seniors. *Cultural Diversity and Ethnic Minority Psychology, 14*(3), 193–200.
Favreau, O. E. (1997). Sex and gender comparisons: Does null hypothesis testing create a false dichotomy? *Feminism & Psychology, 7*(1), 63–81.
Fredricks, J. A., Blumenfeld, P. C., & Paris, A. H. (2004). School engagement: Potential of the concept, state of the evidence. *Review of Educational Research, 74*(1), 59–109.
Freeman, C. E. (2004). *Trends in Educational Equity of Girls & Women: 2004*. (NCES 2005–016). U.S. Department of Education, National Center for Education Statistics. Washington, DC: U.S. Government Printing Office.
Fry, R. (2002). *Latinos in higher education: Many enroll, too few graduate*. Washington, DC: The Pew Hispanic Center.
Fuligni, A. J., Tseng, V., & Lam, M. (1999). Attitudes toward family obligations among American adolescents from Asian, Latin American, and European backgrounds. *Child Development, 70*, 1030–1044.
Garcia, T., Yu, S. L., & Coppola, B. P. (1993). *Women and minorities in science: Motivational and cognitive correlates of achievement*. Paper presented at the Annual Meeting of the American Educational Research Association

Goldenberg, C., Gallimore, R., Reese, L., & Garnier, H. (2001). Cause or effect? A longitudinal study of immigrant Latino parents' aspirations and expectations, and their children's school performance. *American Educational Research Journal, 38*(3), 547–582.

Gottfried, A. (1985). Measures of socioeconomic status in child development research: Data and recommendations. *Merrill-Palmer Quarterly, 31*(1), 85–92.

Graham, S., & Golan, S. (1991). Motivational influences on cognition: Task involvement, ego involvement, and depth of information processing. *Journal of Educational Psychology, 83*, 187–194.

Graham, S., & Hudley, C. (2005). Race and ethnicity in the study of motivation and competence. In A. J. Elliot and C. S. Dweck (Eds.), *Handbook of competence and motivation* (pp. 392–413). New York: Guilford Press.

Gutierrez, K. D., & Rogoff, B. (2003). Cultural ways of learning: Individual traits or repertoires of practice. *Educational Researcher, 32*(5), 19–25.

Halpern, D. F. (2000). *Sex differences in cognitive abilities* (3rd ed.). Mahwah, NJ: Lawrence Erlbaum Associates.

Harackiewicz, J. M., Barron, K. E., Pintrich, P. R., Elliot, A. J., & Thrash, T. M. (2002). Revsion of achievement goal theory: Necessary and illuminating. *Journal of Educational Psychology, 94*(3), 638–645.

Harackiewicz, J. M., Barron, K. E., Tauer, J. M., Carter, S. M., & Elliot, A. J. (2000). Short term and long-term consequences of achievement goals: Predicting interest and performance over time. *Journal of Educational Psychology, 92*, 316–330.

Harackiewicz, J. M., Barron, K. E., Tauer, J. M., & Elliot, A. J. (2002). Predicting success in college: A longitudinal study of achievement goals and abilitymeasures as predictors of interest and performance from freshman year through graduation. *Journal of Educational Psychology, 94*, 562–575.

Hauser, R. M. (1994). Measuring socioeconomic status in studies of child development. *Child Development, 65*(6), 1541–1545.

Hauser, R. M., & Huang, M. H. (1997). Verbal ability and socioeconomic success: A trend analysis. *Social Science Research, 26*, 331–376.

Hearn, J. C., & Holdsworth, J. M. (2002). Influences of state-level policies and practices on college students' learning. *Peabody Journal of Education, 77*, 6–39.

Hembree, R. (1988). Correlates, causes, effects, and treatment of test anxiety. *Review of Educational Research, 58*, 47–77.

Hill, K. T., & Wigfield, A. (1984). Test anxiety: A major educational problem and what can be done about it. *Elementary School Journal, 85*, 105–126.

Hong, E., O'Neil, H. F., & Feldon, D. (2005). Gender effects on mathematics achievement. In Gallagher, A. M. & Kaufman, J. C. (Eds.), *Gender differences in mathematics: An integrative psychological approach* (pp. 264–293). Cambridge: Cambridge University Press.

Jöreskog, K. G., & Sörbom, D. (1993). *LISREL 8: Structual equating modeling with the SIMPLIS command language*. Chicago IL: Scientific Software International.

Kaplan, D. (2000). *Structural Equation Modeling: Foundations and extensions*. Newbury Park, CA: Sage.

Karabenick, S. A. (2003). Seeking help in large college classes: A person centered approach. *Contemporary Educational Psychology, 28*, 37–58.

Knapp, L. G., Kelly-Reid, J. E., & Ginder, S. A. (2008). *Postsecondary Institutions in the United States: Fall 2007, Degrees and Other Awards Conferred: 2006–07 , and 12-Month Enrollment: 2006–07* (NCES 2008-159). National Center for Education Statistics, Institute of Education Sciences, U.S. Department of Education. Washington, DC. Retrieved October 1, 2008 from http://nces.ed.gov/pubsearch

Lamdin, D. J. (1996). Evidence of student attendance as an independent variable in education production functions. *Journal of Educational Research, 89*(3), 155–162.

Ley, K., & Young, D. B. (2001). Instructional principles for self regulation. *Educational Technology, Research and Development, 49*(2), 93–103.

Linnenbrink, E. A., & Pintrich, P. R. (2004). Role of affect in cognitive processing in academic contexts. In D. Y. Dai & R. J. Sternberg (Eds.), *Motivation, emotion, and cognition: Integrative perpectives on intellectual functioning and development* (pp. 57–87). Mahwah, NJ: Erlbaum.
Marsh, H. W., Hau, K., Artelt, C., Baumert, J., & Peschar, J. L. (2006). OECD's brief self-report measure of educational psychology's most useful affective constructs: Cross-cultural, psychometric comparisons across 25 countries. *International Journal of Testing*, *6*(4), 311–360.
McInerney, D., & Van Etten, S. (2001). *Research on sociocultural influences on motivation and learning*. Greenwich, CN: Information Age Publishers.
Meece, J. L., Blumenfeld, P. C., & Hoyle, R. H. (1988). Students' goal orientations and cognitive engagement in classroom activities. *Journal of Educational Psychology*, *80*, 514–523.
Meuschke, D. M., Dembo, M. H., & Gribbons, B. C. (2006, April). *The relationship between goal-orientation, help-seeking, math self-efficacy, and mathematics achievement in a community college*. Paper presented at the annual meeting of the American Educational Research Association, San Francisco, CA.
Middleton, M. J., & Midgley, C. (1997). Avoiding the demonstration of lack of ability: An underexplored aspect of goal theory. *Journal of Educational Psychology*, *89*(4), 710–718.
Muthén, L., & Muthén, B. O. (2004). *Mplus Version 4.1*. http://www.statmodel.com
National Center for Education Statistics. (2005). *First-generation students in postsecondary education: A look at their college transcripts*. NCES 2005-171, by X. Chen. Project Officer. C. Dennis Carroll. Washington, DC: U.S. Department of Education.
National Commission on Children (U.S.). (1991). *Beyond rhetoric: A new American agenda for children and families*. Washington, DC: National Commission on Children.
Nettles, M. T., Thoeny, A. R., & Gosman, E. J. (1986). Comparative and predictive analyses of black and white students' college achievement and experiences. *Journal of Higher Education*, *37*, 289–318.
Newman, R. S. (2002). How self-regulated learners cope with academic difficulty: The role of adaptive help seeking. *Theory into Practice*, *41*(2), 132–138.
Nguyen, N. T., Allen, L. C., & Fraccastoro, K. (2005). Personality predicts academic performance: Exploring the moderating role of gender. *Journal of Higher Education Policy and Management*, *27*, 105–116.
Nolen, S. B. (1988). Reasons for studying: Motivational orientations and study strategies. *Cognition and Instruction*, *5*, 269–287.
Organization for Economic Cooperation and Development (OECD). (2000). *Knowledge and skills for life: First results from PISA 2000*. Paris: Author.
Patrick, H., Kaplan, A., & Ryan, A. (2007). Early adolescents' perceptions of the classroom social environment, motivational beliefs, and engagement. *Journal of Educational Psychology*, *99*(1), 83–98.
Pietsch, J., Walker, R., & Chapman, E. (2003). The relationship among self-concept, self-efficacy, and performance in mathematics during secondary school. *Journal of Educational Psychology*, *95*, 589–603.
Pintrich, P. R. (2003). A motivational science perspective on the role of student motivation in learning and teaching contexts. *Journal of Educational Psychology*, *95*(4), 667–686.
Pintrich, P. R., & De Groot, R. V. (1990). Motivational and self-regulated learning components of classroom academic performance. *Journal of Educational Psychology*, *82*, 33–40.
Plunkett, S. W., & Bamaca-Gomez, M. Y. (2003). The relationship between parenting, acculturation, and adolescent academics in Mexican-origin immigrant families in Los Angeles. *Hispanic Journal of Behavioral Sciences*, *25*(2), 222–239.
Plunkett, S. W., Henry, C. S., Houltberg, B. J., Sands, T., & Abarca-Mortensen, S. (2008). Academic support by significant others and educational resilience in Mexican-origin ninth grade students from intact families. *Journal of Early Adolescence*, *28*(3), 333–355.
Purdie, N., Hattie, J., & Douglas, G. (1996). Student conceptions of learning and their use of self-regulated learning strategies: A cross-cultural comparison. *Journal of Educational Psychology*, *88*(1), 87–100.

Reynolds, A. H., & Walberg, H. J. (1991). A structural model of science achievement. *Journal of Educational Psychology, 83*(1), 97–107.
Ripple, C. H., & Luthar, S. S. (2000). Academic risk among inner-city adolescents: The role of personal attributes. *Journal of School Psychology, 38*(3), 277–298.
Robbins, S. B., Allen, J., Casillas, A., Peterson, C., & Le, H. (2006). Unraveling the differential effects of motivational and skills, social, and self-management measures from traditional predictors of college outcomes. *Journal of Educational Pschology, 98*(3), 598–616.
Robbins, S. B., Lauver, K., Le, H., Davis, D., Langley, R., & Carlstrom, A. (2004). Do psychosocial and study skill factors predict college outcomes? A meta-analysis. *Psychological Bulletin, 130*, 261–288.
Ross, M. E., Shannon, D. M., Salisbury-Glennon, J. D., & Guarino, A. (2002). The patterns of adaptive learning survey: A comparison across grade levels. *Educational and Psychological Measurement, 62*(3), 483–497.
Rueda, R., & Chen, C. (2005). Assessing motivational factors in foreign language learning: Cultural variation in key constructs. *Educational Assessment, 10*(3), 209–229.
Ryan, A. M., Gheen, M. H., & Midgley, C. (1998). Why do some students avoid seeking help? An examination of the interplay among students' academic efficacy, teachers' social-emotional role, and the classroom goal structure. *Journal of Educational Psychology, 90*(3), 528–535.
Ryan, A. M., & Pintrich, P. R. (1997). Should I ask for help? The role of motivation and attitudes in adolescents' help seeking in math class. *Journal of Educational Psychology, 89*, 329–341.
Ryan, A. M., & Pintrich, P. R. (1998). Achievement and social motivational influences on help seeking in the classroom. In S. A. Karabenick (Ed.), *Strategic help seeking: Implications for learning and teaching* (pp. 117–139). Mahwah, NJ: Erlbaum.
Schutz, P., & Davis, H. (2000). Emotions and self-regulation during test-taking. *Educational Psychologist, 35*, 243–256.
Seyfried, S. F. (1998). Academic achievement of African American preadolescents: The influence of teacher perceptions. *American Journal of Community Psychology, 26*(3), 381–402.
Sirin, S. R. (2005). Socioeconomic status and academic achievement: A meta-analytic review of research. *Review of Educational Research, 75*(3), 417–453.
Spielberger, C. D. (1972). Anxiety as an emotional state. In C. D. Spielberger (Ed.), *Anxiety: Current trends in theory and research* (pp. 23–49). New York: Academic Press.
Spielberger, C. D. (1980). Test Anxiety Inventory. Preliminary professional manual. Palo Alto, CA: Consulting Psychologists Press.
Sutton, A., & Soderstrom, I. (1999). Predicting elementary and secondary school achievement with school-related and demographic factors. *Journal of Educational Research, 92*, 330–338.
Tobias, S. (2006). The importance of motivation, metacognition, and help seeking in web-based learning. In H. F. O'Neil & R. S. Perez (Eds.), *Web-based learning: Theory, research, and practice* (pp. 203–220). Mahwah, NJ: Lawrence Erlbaum Associates.
U.S. Department of Education, National Center for Education Statistics. (2000). *The Condition of Education 2000* (NCES 2000-602). Washington, DC: Government Printing Office.
Urdan, T. (2004). Predictors of academic self-handicapping and achievement: Examining achievement goals, classroom goal structures, and culture. *Journal of Educational Psychology, 96*(2), 251–264.
Urdan, T., & Giancarlo, C. (2001). A comparison of motivational and critical thinking orientations across ethnic groups. In D. M. McInerney and S. V. Etten (Eds.), *Research on sociocultural influences on motivation and learning* (vol. 1, pp. 37–60). Greenwich, CT: Information Age Publishing.
Vagg, P. R., & Papsdorf, J. D. (1995). Cognitive therapy, study skills training, and biofeedback the treatment of test anxiety. In C. D. Spielberger and P. R. Vagg (Eds.), *Test anxiety: Theory, assessment, and treatment* (pp. 183–194). Washington, DC: Taylor & Francis.
Valencia, R. R. (1997). *The evolution of deficit thinking: Educational thought and practice*. Bristol, PA: Falmer Press, Taylor & Francis, Inc.

Valentine, J. C., DuBois, D. L., & Cooper, H. (2004). The relation between self-beliefs and academic achievement: A meta-analytic review. *Educational Psychologist, 39*, 111–133.

Vansteenviste, M., Zhou, M., Lens, W., & Soenens, B. (2005). Experiences of autonomy and control among Chinese learners: Vitalizing or immobilizing? *Journal of Educational Psychology, 97*(3), 468–483.

Watkins, D., McInerney, D. M., Akande, A., & Lee, C. (2003). An investigation of ethnic differences in the motivation strategies for learning of students in desegregated South African schools. *Journal of Cross-Cultural Psychology, 34*, 189–194.

Wenglinsky, H. (1998). Finance equalization and within-school equity: The relationship between education spending and the social distribution of achievement. *Educational Evaluation and Policy Analysis, 20*(4), 269–283.

White, K. (1982). The relation between socioeconomic status and academic achievement. *Psychological Bulletin, 91*, 461–481.

Wigfield, A., & Eccles, J. S. (Eds.). (2002). *Development of achievement motivation*. San Diego, CA: Academic Press.

Wolters, C., Yu, S., & Pintrich, P. R. (1996). The relation between goal orientation and students' motivational beliefs and self-regulated learning. *Learning and Individual Differences, 8*, 211–238.

Zeidner, M. (1998). *Test anxiety: The state of the art*. New York: Plenum.

Zeidner, M., & Matthews, G. (2005). Evaluation anxiety: Current theory and research. In A. J. Elliot & C. S. Dweck (Eds.), *Handbook of competence and motivation* (pp. 141–163). New York: Guilford Press.

Zimmerman, B. J. (1990). Student differences in self-regulated learning: Relating grade, sex, and giftedness to self-efficacy and strategy use. *Journal of Educational Psychology, 80*, 284–290.

Zimmerman, B. J. (2000a). Attaining self-regulation: A social-cognitive perspective. In M. Boekaerts, P. R. Pintrich, & M. Zeidner (Eds.), *Handbook of self-regulation* (pp. 13–39). San Diego, CA: Academic Press.

Zimmerman, B. J. (2000b). Self-efficacy: An essential motive to learn. *Contemporary Educational Psychology, 25*, 82–91.

Zimmerman, B. J., & Martinez-Pons, M. (1990). Student differences in self-regulated learning: Relating grade, sex, and giftedness to self-efficacy and strategy use. *Journal of Educational Psychology, 82*, 51–59.

Zimmerman, B. J., & Schunk, D. H. (Eds.). (2001). *Self-regulated learning and academic achievement: Theory, research and practice*. New York: Springer-Verlag.

Chapter 8
Intuitions, Conceptions and Frameworks: Modelling Student Cognition in Science Learning

Keith S. Taber

Faculty of Education, University of Cambridge, Cambridge, UK

Modelling Student Cognition in Relation to Academic Learning

This chapter is about how researchers (and teachers) can model student cognition to make sense of the learning and understanding of school and college subjects. The premise of the chapter is that educational research into student learning has produced a great deal of descriptive material about student ideas: but has been hampered by a lack of understanding of the nature of what is studied. Familiar, but central, terms—such as "knowledge", "thinking", "ideas"—tend to be poorly defined, and the relationships between data elicited in studies and the entities posited by researchers—such as "alternative conceptual frameworks" and "intuitive theories"—have not always been convincing. However, it is argued here, that the cognitive sciences (Gardner, 1977) increasingly offer useful conceptual tools to better inform such research. Indeed, progress is leading to strong integration between neuroscience and traditional work in experimental psychology (Goswami, 2008; Pretz & Sternberg, 2005), such that knowledge of brain function and structure may soon significantly inform educational practice (Goswami, 2006).

The context of much of the work discussed here is the learning of science subjects, as there is an immense research base into student thinking and developing understanding of science concepts (Duit, 2007). It seems highly likely, however, that much of what has been found in this area is—at least generally—applicable across other areas of "academic" learning. Indeed it is worth noting that whilst science education has become established as something of a discrete field within education (Fensham, 2004), the content of science learning is diverse—so that understanding Hooke's law (based on a mathematical relationship), is rather different from understanding the nature of acidity or oxidation (historically shifting concepts that are contingent upon chemists selecting to pay attention to particular patterns in material behaviour which offer particular utility value), and different

K.S. Taber (✉)
Faculty of Education, University of Cambridge, Cambridge, UK
e-mail: kst24@cam.ac.uk

M.S. Khine, I.M. Saleh (eds.), *New Science of Learning*,
DOI 10.1007/978-1-4419-5716-0_8,

again from understanding the most widely accepted theories of evolution (a complex argument coordinating a wide range of considerations which together offer a viable explanatory account of the diversity of life on Earth) or appreciating the ethical issues involved in pre-natal testing for genetic disease (considering how people with diverse value systems may make different judgements about the social implications of science). Certainly, concepts taught in the humanities and social sciences have much in common with at least *some* of what is studied in many natural science classes.

Student Learning Difficulties in Science Subjects

There has been a substantial research effort to explore student thinking about topics taught in the sciences (Taber, 2006, 2009). The motivation for this work may be seen as the need to respond to students' difficulties in learning science that have commonly been found.

Science concepts tend to be considered hierarchical in the sense that it is usually possible to identify clear prerequisite knowledge needed for making sense of any new ideas introduced. This offered a basis for considering students' problems in learning science—clearly it was important for learning to be "programmed" in the sense of making sure students met concepts in a logical order, so that they were not expected to understand the more advanced concepts before those on which such concepts were built (Herron, Cantu, Ward, & Srinivasan, 1977). So if a perfectly elastic collision is one where kinetic energy is conserved, there is little point attempting to teach the concept of an elastic collision before the students have been introduced to the concept of kinetic energy.

Unfortunately, clear and careful concept analysis designed to avoid such problems was found to be insufficient to avoid many of the learning difficulties common among learners. It became clear that understanding the structure of the subject matter was not enough to design effective teaching, and that it was necessary to also understand more about the learning process.

Jean Piaget's (1972) work suggested that abstract concepts could only be effectively learnt once students' brains had matured sufficiently to attain a level of cognitive development that was not found until at least adolescence. Certainly this approach brought useful insights (Shayer & Adey, 1981). However this again did not seem to be the whole story. For one thing, it was found that advanced concepts *did* seem to be within the grasp of younger learners if teaching took into account the need to present the ideas in sufficiently concrete ways (Bruner, 1960). Conversely, older students who had clearly demonstrated the higher levels of cognition, still commonly had difficulties attaining some of the scientific concepts commonly taught in school and college. Levels of cognitive development might be important, but could not explain why so often students failed to learn the concepts they met in science as taught.

The focus in science education shifted to exploring the nature of the ideas students did have. It was soon recognised both that (a) often in science lessons students came to class with existing alternative notions of the topics to be studied and (b) that often students who failed to acquire target knowledge did learn from their science classes, but developed understanding inconsistent with what the teacher was attempting to teach (Driver & Erickson, 1983; Gilbert & Watts, 1983). A very active research programme developed which explored the nature of the students' ideas presented before, during and after teaching, and which was concerned with how conceptual change occurred and what kind of teaching best facilitated the desired shifts in student thinking (Taber, 2009).

Examples of Students' Ideas

The literature describing learners' ideas in science (reported as "misconceptions", "naive physics", "intuitive theories", "alternative conceptions", "alternative frameworks", etc.) is vast, so for readers not familiar with this research I offer a few examples of the kinds of ideas that have been found to be common among learners.

One of the most well-established examples that has been widely reported concerns how people (not just children) understand the relationship of force and motion. According to physics, an object will remain in its state of motion unless acted upon by a force. So an object moving in a straight line continues to do so at the same velocity unless subjected to a force. Although this idea is well established in science (since Newton) it is at odds with what most people expect. Students are commonly found to consider that an object will only remain moving if a force is continuously applied in the direction of motion (Taber, 2009, pp. 223–224).

Another example concerns the growth of plants. It is commonly considered that the material in a plant, for example a tree, is incorporated into the tissues after being extracted from the soil through the roots. Whilst this is not entirely contrary to scientific thinking—minerals are accessed in this way, and are incorporated into tissue—it is inconsistent with the scientific model, where photosynthesis allows the plant to acquire carbon that forms the basis of new tissue from the carbon dioxide in the air (Taber, 2009, pp. 224–225).

Chemistry also offers many examples. So learners commonly consider *neutralisation* (the type of reaction that occurs between an acid and a base) to be a process that necessarily leads to *neutral* products (Schmidt, 1991). However, this is only the case when the acid and base are of similar strength. If the weak acid ethanoic acid reacts with the strong base sodium hydroxide, then the product, sodium ethanoate, is not neutral but basic.

Learners also commonly suggest that the reason chemical reactions occur is because the atoms in the chemicals "need" to obtain full electron shells, which they do by interacting with other atoms to donate, share or acquire electrons (Taber, 1998). This notion is widespread despite most commonly studied reactions in school science occurring between reactants where the atoms already "have" full electron shells. The scientific explanations concern how the reactions involve interactions between the charged particles in reactant molecules (or ions) that lead to new configurations that are more stable. Forces act between the charges to bring about lower energy arrangements.

Alternative ideas have been reported across the sciences, so student understanding of the solar system may fare no better than their understanding of the atom. As one example, it is common for youngsters to associate summer and winter with the Earth being at its closest and furthest positions from the Sun in its orbit (Hsu, Wu, & Hwang, 2008). If this were the case, both hemispheres should experience seasons in phase. The scientific model is related to the Earth's angle of tilt compared to the plane of its orbit around the Sun. When the Southern hemisphere is leaning towards the Sun it undergoes summer, but it is simultaneously winter in the Northern hemisphere that is leaning away. This offers the possibility of celebrating Christmas with snow in the North and beach barbeques in Australia.

The Uncertain Nature of Students' Alternative Ideas

Initially, the research programme into learners' ideas in science proved very fruitful, as researchers around the world started cataloguing common ideas elicited from students of different ages about various science topics. However the research effort was somewhat undermined by confused notions of what these ideas represented, and how best to describe and label them. References to the objects of enquiry being found in students' conceptual or cognitive structures (White, 1985) offered an impression of a clear ontological basis for the research, but often studies were undertaken with limited thought to the exact nature of what was being elicited.

So some researchers reported intuitive theories that were largely tacit, and only made explicit when students were asked to verbalise their thinking. Other researchers reported alternative conceptions that took the form of explicit propositional knowledge. Some researchers claimed that such alternative conceptions were tenacious and highly resistant to being changed by instruction; where others saw misconceptions that could be readily corrected once identified. Some researchers referred to mini-theories that had very restricted ranges of application; whilst others reported alternative conceptual frameworks that were widely applied. Some researchers saw student thinking as reflecting life-world norms, being more concerned with maintaining social cohesion than reflecting rigorous analysis; where others claimed student thinking was consistent and coherent and deserved to be called theoretical. Such differences had the potential to undermine the research programme, offering very different interpretations of both the significance of learners' ideas for teaching, and of the kinds of pedagogy that might be appropriate (Taber, 2009, pp. 199–200).

Some of the differences reported could be explained—to a certain extent—by the paradigmatic commitments and methodological choices of different researchers: workers took different fundamental assumptions into their studies about what they were enquiring into, and selected different approaches to their research depending upon the type of knowledge they thought would be possible and useful. So for example, common approaches based on idiographic assumptions (about the uniqueness of individuals) and informed by phenomenology and ethnography found a diversity of student ideas, whereas approaches that were informed by more normative assumptions tended to characterise responses into modest typologies (Taber, 2007, pp. 47–51). However, research in any field tends to have an iterative nature, so that even if different camps begin with very different assumptions about a phenomenon and plan their initial enquiries accordingly, over time we might expect a gradual convergence as researchers take on board the "feedback" provided by their data.

This did not happen in science education, suggesting that here the phenomenon was complex and multifaceted, allowing different researchers to find evidence to support very different characterisations of student thinking about science (Taber, 2009, pp. 226–256). So science teachers work with students who come to class with ideas which are at variance with the target knowledge in the curriculum to different degrees: and which may sometimes be labile, but sometimes inert; sometimes fragmentary and sometimes coherent; sometimes similar to those of many other students, but sometimes idiosyncratic; sometimes a useful intermediate conception that can lead to target knowledge; and sometimes a substantial impediment to the desired learning. This makes life more interesting for researchers and teachers, but clearly such a complex picture is not helpful in informing pedagogy.

Without understanding the origins of this variety found within learners' ideas about science, there is no reason not to suspect that much the same pattern (or perhaps lack of apparent pattern) could be found when students are taught new concepts in other academic areas such as history, economics, literary criticism or theory of music.

This fascinating but challenging variety in the apparent nature of conceptions students bring to class confuses attempts to use research into learners' ideas to inform teaching—which is after all a key rationale for educational research. Advising teachers how to respond to students' ideas depends upon being able to systematise the research findings, so as to start to know how and when learners' ideas have certain characteristics, and so when it might be best to ignore, mould or discredit their ideas.

Whereas eliciting and characterising students' ideas can be undertaken from "within" education, the programme to build a systematic and inclusive model from the disparate research findings needs to draw upon ideas from the cognitive sciences. In particular, science educators (and their colleagues exploring teaching and learning in other subject disciplines) need to understand better the nature of the objects of research (learners' ideas), and especially the origins and development of students' thinking. This is not a new idea. Researchers in the field have for example recommended drawing upon information processing models, either instead of focussing on students' ideas (Johnstone, 1991), or as a means for understanding their origins and development (Osborne & Wittrock, 1983). Despite this, much research has reported findings in what are largely phenomenological terms, without seeking to interpret what is reported in terms of a cognitive science framework.

Considering Cognitive Development and Conceptual Learning

The Soviet psychologist Lev Vygotsky (1934/1986) drew the distinction between two types of concepts—those that an individual develops spontaneously without formal instruction, and those that are acquired only through formal teaching of some kind. Whilst something of a simplification, this proves to be a useful distinction when thinking about student learning. Vygotsky's class of taught concepts may be labelled as "academic", although interestingly the common translation is "scientific".

Whereas "spontaneous" concepts are considered to derive from the individual's inherent "sense-making" of the environment, Vygotsky's "scientific" or "academic" concepts are considered to be part of the cultural capital of the society in which an individual is raised, and to be culturally "transmitted"—often intergenerationally. This may of course be seen as one function of formal educational institutions (schools, colleges, universities): that is to impart that knowledge valued by a society and considered suitable and appropriate to pass on to the young.

Spontaneous Learning

Before considering some issues surrounding the learning of academic or scientific concepts, it is useful to consider how concepts may be learnt spontaneously. This discussion will be largely framed in terms of the learning of individuals, an important point to which I will return.

The learning of "spontaneous" concepts can be understood in terms of the principles discussed by such thinkers as Piaget and Dewey. John Dewey had a notion of people as learning through experience in terms of how their expectations were or were not met in particular interactions with the world (Biesta & Burbules, 2003). In effect, people are naive scientists who form models of the world that allow them to act intelligently by predicting the effect of various behaviours. When expectations are not met, that experience leads us to modify the models that we hold and apply. That is, we act as scientists with an instrumentalist epistemology: our knowledge of the world is tentative, acts as the best currently available basis for action, and (in principle at least) is always open to revision when new evidence suggests this is indicated (Glasersfeld, 1988). In practice, of course, people are well known to often fail to shift their thinking even when acknowledging the lack of match between predictions based upon their existing models of the world and new experiences. Indeed this issue is at the basis of personal construct theory, an approach to therapy developed by George Kelly (1963) to help clients "shift" ways of construing the world that were considered to be counterproductive and acting as barriers to personal happiness and growth.

A clear problem for Dewey's approach (which was primarily philosophical) is the issue of a starting point: how do we get to the point where we make sense of the world enough to form those initial models that can guide our actions? To borrow William James's phrase—how do we get past the point where our perception of the world is just a "blooming, buzzing confusion"?

Piaget (1979) had a scientific background and considered cognition accordingly. Humans have evolved over a very long period, and natural selection has equipped modern humans with apparatus to allow intelligent behaviour in the world, that is to modify behaviour patterns in the light of experience as Dewey had noted. A human being does not enter the world ex nihilo but as the outcome of a long-term selection process that provides genetic instructions that offer the organism some compatibility with the environment. Those genetic instructions support the development of a brain that has structures similar to those that have allowed previous generations to survive and procreate in the world: we might say our brains are structured to "fit" the world. This is especially so for humans who despite lacking any exceptional qualities in terms of strength or speed or visual acuity or sense of smell or tolerance of hot and arid or cold conditions, etc., are however endowed with facilities to make enough sense of the world to have a good chance of surviving in it. One aspect of this is that the newly born infant's brain is "programmed" to learn (as this is something that has been selected for): to learn new behaviours, and—in particular—to learn to "re-programme" itself to some extent.

It was in this context that Piaget developed his highly influential model of cognitive development (Bliss, 1995). The newly born baby is equipped to interact with the environment, and to modify its actions on that environment through feedback. This pre-supposes the existence of mental structures, schema, that have plasticity. These schema are sensori-motor: according to Piaget, "thinking" at this stage is through moving, pushing, touching, sucking, etc. However, Piaget's argument was that the developing apparatus could not only refine its sensori-motor schema through feedback processes, but that the ongoing maturation of the brain allowed this level of cognition to provide the foundations for the development of qualitatively different new structures which supported a more abstract form of cognition (Sugarman, 1987). In Piaget's model there were four main "stages" of cognitive development that occurred through this interaction of brain development (maturation) with feedback from experience—learning. The most advanced of the stages in Piaget's system is formal operations, which supports the use of logical operations in such areas as science and mathematics.

Many of the details of Piaget's scheme have come under criticism, but some of the key elements remain highly pertinent. Piaget offered us the modern view of the brain as an organ which has evolved to *both* develop according to a common general pattern through childhood and adolescence, and to retain plasticity throughout the lifespan.

The Cognitive and the Conceptual

Here then we have the basis of another example of a very useful if over-simplistic distinction. All human brains tend to have strong similarities in terms of the basic cognitive apparatus and how this develops as we mature. Yet each brain is unique, not only because of the specific generic instructions in a person's genome, but also because unique experience of the world leads to unique learning.

It is useful to consider the development of *cognitive* abilities as largely under genetic control, if conditional upon suitable triggers from experience. Here we might consider that life experience has some effect on the rate of development, and the degree to which potential is met.

However, the specific "conceptual" knowledge an individual develops is primarily the result of particular learning experiences, *albeit* noting that those experiences are filtered and channelled by the available cognitive apparatus. A new born baby will not develop abstract knowledge regardless of the richness of the learning environment, because it has not yet developed the apparatus to do so.

The nature of concepts is—like so many constructs in education and the cognitive sciences—not universally agreed (Gilbert & Watts, 1983). However, here I would adopt a common notion that an individual "has" conceptual knowledge[1] if they are able to make discriminations on the basis of that knowledge. So a young child who is able to reliably distinguish between cats and dogs, or between the cat that lives next door, and a stray, is demonstrating conceptual knowledge: that is previously experienced patterns in the perceptual field have somehow been modelled and then represented in the brain in a form that guides the individual in responding to current patterns in the perceptual field that are judged as related.

Of course such a description becomes problematic in practice. In everyday life we seldom have sufficient data to be quite sure whether others are making reliable discriminations—and even in clinical studies such judgements rely on agreed protocols that at best offer statistical likelihood. The absence of such behaviour does not *imply* absence of the conceptual knowledge that could *potentially* enable the behaviour. Moreover, evidence of a desired discrimination offers no assurance that the conceptual knowledge being applied matches anyone else's version of the concept. These are not merely inconveniences in research, but fundamental issues that teachers have to work with in their professional lives.

So, just to offer one example, consider a learner in an elementary class learning about the concept "animal". Imagine that the learner was able to classify living things as animals or not animals as below:

Animal	Not animal
Cow	Moss
Dog	Maple tree
Hamster	Rose
Horse	Mushroom
Dolphin	Grass

[1] The term "knowledge" is not here used in the sense of certain, justified belief (the meaning of the term preferred by some philosophers) but rather in the sense of what we think we know about the world. The latter sense better described how the term is widely used in cognitive science and in education.

The teacher might feel that the learner had grasped what scientists mean by the concept label animal. However given a different set of examples, the same learner may well have excluded from the category "animals": humans (considered people not animals); whale (considered a big fish—which it is not of course—not an animal); a butterfly (considered an insect, or in the USA a "bug", not an animal); pigeon (considered a bird not an animal) and so forth. In this particular case it is well established that the common taxonomic class of animal applied by most people in everyday life does not fit with the scientific version. A teacher who was aware of this would chose their examples accordingly, but no matter how many examples we might use to test out a learners' application of a general concept, and no matter how good the match between their discriminations and ours, we can never be certain that the learner has "the same" concept that we do. This is of course just a specific example of the fallacy of induction (Driver, 1983).

Conceptual Development

If *cognitive* development is primarily a matter of the unfolding of biological potential triggered by interactions with the environment, then *conceptual* development is basically due to learning which is contingent upon particular experiences. Conceptual learning in science is considered a largely iterative process: where available mental structures are used to interpret experience, and are modified according to that experience. This reflects the comments about Dewey's ideas above, and indeed common thinking about learning in science education tends to be considered "constructivist" in the sense that Dewey, Piaget, Kelly and Vygotsky (among others) are widely considered to be constructivist (Taber, 2009, pp. 22–33). That is, they see the development of personal knowledge as basically a building process: using existing knowledge as tools for forming new knowledge. This links too to the ideas of Gagné (1970), but with the important difference that where Gagné encouraged teachers to consider how the formal public knowledge structures of science are built up into coherent networks of ideas, constructivists in science education have been concerned with how learners tend to build up their own, often alternative, knowledge structures. Such research is considered to *complement* conceptual analysis of scientific knowledge in informing pedagogy.

Drawing upon Cognitive Science

Whilst science education researchers are in a strong position to explore and characterise student thinking, many of the constructs used in the field are ambiguous. Terms such as "alternative conception" are sometimes used to refer to a hypothetical mental structure, and are sometimes used to label the models researchers form to summarise findings from different informants (Taber, 2009, 188). Where conceptions (or intuitive theories or alternative frameworks or mini-theories, etc.) are posited as being located in learners' minds, it is often unclear what form they are understood to take. Indeed it might be suggested that just as students often operate with alternative technically dubious versions of science concepts, science education researchers have been exploring students' ideas using conceptual tools that are in their own way just as vague and imprecise as those of the students they are exploring.

Folk Psychology and Educational Research

In other words, educational research has often been based on a good understanding of the science concepts students are asked to learn, and a strong familiarity with the classroom context in which school and college learning takes place—but an *impoverished conceptual framework for interpreting cognition*. It may be ironic that science educators have worked hard to shift teachers away from operating with a "folk psychology" model of teaching (as the transfer of knowledge from teacher to student), whilst carrying out their own research from a similar folk psychology base (Taber, 2009, pp. 126–128).

For example such constructs as "ideas", "beliefs", "learning", "understanding", "thinking" and "memory" have often been taken for granted in studies, rather than seen as problematic to define and so recognise. This is not true of all studies, and it is clearly recognised that in any research certain starting points have to be taken as accepted givens. However, such implicit "taken-for-grantedness" may commonly lead to confusing what a researcher interpreted as the meaning of a students' speech utterance with what the student thought, and indeed then what they remembered and so what they may be considered to know. That is not to suggest that such distinctions are ever likely to be unproblematic in practice (Taber, 2009, 146), but lack of clarity in researchers' accounts only increases the potential for confusion.

Such confusions have characterised the debate about the nature of students' scientific thinking when different research evidence is drawn upon to argue that learners' ideas are coherent or piecemeal; or are stable or labile, etc. Whilst it would be naive to assume that this area of research can be significantly advanced by a simple clarification of terminology and tightening of language, the cognitive sciences, the "new science of mind", is now sufficiently developed to offer a good deal of valuable guidance (Gardner, 1977). The rest of this chapter will explain this position with some examples.

Thinking, Knowing and Ideas

One central feature of any model of student cognition drawing upon the cognitive sciences is the distinction between what a learner thinks (at any one time) and what they can be considered to "know". Thinking is a process, and the ideas that learners have (and may then express) are products of that process. Thoughts are transient, and draw upon both memory and immediately available perceptual information.

So, to take an extreme example, if a student locked in an isolated sensory derivation chamber thinks that uranium is the heaviest naturally occurring element, then we might feel that justifies assuming the student "knows" that information. (This ignores the issue of *how we know* what the student thinks: not a trivial consideration, especially in this set of circumstances!) However, we might have less confidence in thinking another student "knows" this same fact when they tell us this whilst reading a chemistry book. Indeed, if the student is Chinese and is just learning to read English, but has minimal English language comprehension, we might infer that any "thinking" is at the level of converting text to verbal output, and does not justify us assuming the student even "held the idea" during processing. My computer can convert text into "speech" in a similar way, but I do not consider it to think.

Often, as educators, we are less concerned with what ideas might be expressed in a specific unique context (such as when reading a pertinent text), but what ideas are likely to be reproduced reliably in a variety of contexts with limited environmental support. By the latter, I mean that educators traditionally judge student knowledge in formal education by what they express under test conditions where they have no access to reference materials and are not allowed to confer with others. We want to know what they remember: what they have "held in memory". Whilst such test conditions are seldom authentic reflections of how knowledge is applied in real life contexts, there seems to be widespread tacit acknowledgement that what is produced working alone in a test can be considered to offer a pragmatic assessment of what someone can remember with limited support—and so reflects what is "known".

Memory

However, memory is an area where folk-psychology notions may seem seductive (Claxton, 2005). Memory, on such an account, is a kind of storage space where we place things we may want to take out again later. When we remember, we take those same things back out of memory, and metaphorically blow off the dust as we re-examine them.

Here cognitive science has much to offer. For one thing, studies of memory have sharpened the distinction between working memory (where currently considered material is processed) and long-term memory. The rather severe limits of working memory have been used to explain some student learning difficulties in terms of tasks being beyond the capacity of working memory, although it has also been argued that this severe limitation is an adaptation to prevent our thinking becoming too labile for our own good (Sweller, 2007).

However, more significantly, cognitive science shows that long-term memory is based upon making structural changes in a substrate that can later channel thinking. The important point here is that the memory traces are different in nature to the ideas. This should perhaps be obvious to all, but the influence of the metaphors of everyday life should not be underestimated (Lakoff & Johnson, 1980). We do not put ideas into storage, *we code them in a very different format*.

Remembering is a reconstructive process whereby we use the memory traces to help build new thoughts that (we trust) are close to those we had that triggered the original trace. The process does not give perfect fidelity, so remembering is creative: it involves making sense of the available trace as best as possible. This explains, of course, why the same student seems to know something one day, but to have forgotten it the next: the same memory trace will be sufficient to generate thinking similar enough to the original thoughts under some conditions, but not others. It also explains how students can remember a teaching episode, but manage to recall it as supporting their own alternative conceptions, even when the teaching was specifically designed to challenge those very conceptions. Recalling (correctly) that the teacher showed us electrical circuits and measured the current flow at different points can be the basis of a (reconstructed) narrative where the real details are interpreted in terms of the students' understanding: so the student remembers (incorrectly) how the teacher showed that current decreases around the circuit (Gauld, 1989)—and has no awareness that only parts of the memory are based on the original events.

The important point here is that any simplistic notion of whether someone "knows" something or not will not do justice to human cognition. People will give reports of thinking that seem to indicate certain knowledge under some conditions when perceptual cues, and preceding thoughts, allow memory traces to generate ideas that will not be "recalled" under other conditions. This explains some of the variation sometimes found in research into students' scientific thinking.

Situated Knowledge and Distributed Cognition

There has been a good deal of work exploring "situated" knowledge, where a person can apparently demonstrate knowledge only in particular situations, such that the knowledge cannot be considered to reside in the individual as such, as in other contexts it is apparently not demonstrated (Hennessy, 1993). This again relates to what we mean by "having" or "holding" knowledge. Here we need to consider how a person's cognitive apparatus accesses both memory traces and perceptual cues in the environment when processing (thinking).

If familiar environments cue activation of particular memories, leading to behaviour (e.g. talking or writing) that we interpret as demonstrating knowledge and understanding, then we will find that the context dependence of performance varies between individuals—that is some will demonstrate knowledge at most times and places; others only when conditions closely match those of the learning episodes. This raises issues for assessing student learning.

Indeed the distinction between only being able to offer accounts we judge as demonstrating knowledge in certain contexts, and the ability of an individual to produce similar reports through reading information directly from a reference source may need to be seen as separate points on a continuum. When teachers adopt "scaffolding" approaches to support student learning in their "zones of next development" (Scott, 1998) they are in effect facilitating intermediate states between these points.

A related issue concerns the social aspects of learning. One major area of contention in research into learners' ideas in science has been the acceptability of studies that treat learners as if effectively isolated thinkers who develop knowledge individually without regard to the social context (Taber, 2009, pp. 191–193). There are indeed two issues here. One concerns the admissibility of treating the social context of learning as a complication that needs to be initially ignored to develop first-order models of student learning. This is something of argument about degree: both sides acknowledge the importance of the social dimension—but disagree about whether it should be a core focus of research, or a complexity best addressed later in the research programme.

However, there is also a school of thought, the construct*ionist* view, that questions whether it is ever sensible to consider that the individual is the locus of knowledge: believing that knowledge is always distributed across a social network. To those working in the personal constructivist tradition—exploring what *individuals* think, know and understand—such a position seems quite bizarre. Indeed it suggests that the objects of their research are a kind of epiphenomena, and are not sensible foci for study. That both sides tend to talk across each other in such debates may again be related to the common practice of researchers operating with common-sense folk psychology definitions of knowledge, knowing, understanding, etc.

Perception and Conception

Another useful area of cognitive science that can inform our understanding of student thinking and understanding is work on perception. An important feature of studies in this area is to erode another simplistic distinction—that between "pure" perception and thought. A simple model considers that perception is a process by which information from the environment is captured and presented to mind, where it can become the subject of thought. Work in cognitive science has demonstrated that perception involves multi-stage processing, so that the conscious mind seldom experiences anything close to "raw perceptual" data. As Gregory (1998, 9) reports in the case of sight: "the indirectness of vision and its complexity are evident in its physiology". As the Gestalt psychologists first suggested, what is presented to consciousness as the object of perception is usually a pattern that has *already been interpreted* (Koffka, 1967): we see a bird or a snake or a tiger: not just patches of moving colour and shadow.

A cognitive science perspective suggests that in modelling thinking, remembering is much like perceiving—in both cases the available "data" (electrical signals from sensory organs; electrical patterns modulated through memory "circuits") undergoes various processing ("interpretation") before being presented to consciousness. The evolutionary advantage of this is clear: quick responses—we can run or duck or attack before it is "too late". The cost is that we have to accept a fairly high rate of false positives—leading to people commonly seeing images of figures in toast or rock formations, or sending in photographs of their "rude" vegetables to television shows. This also leads to people seeing potential attackers in the dark and children seeing evil characters in wallpaper patterns at night. This is relevant to science learning, as it start to explain some of the common ways that people interpret phenomena that are at odds with scientific understanding.

Research is starting to explore where these effects are operating in the cognitive system. Some aspects of pattern recognition may actually be genetically determined. For example, humans appear to have evolved to be "hard-wired" to readily detect face-like patterns—and sure enough we see faces readily: not only the "man in the Moon", but even on a crater on Mars. We are able to effectively communicate the face with a simple emoticon, i.e. :-)

Other pattern recognition systems may develop in response to environmental stimuli. For example, Andrea diSessa (1993) has undertaken work to explore how what he terms *phenomenological primitives* channel student understanding and explanations according to common patterns that are abstracted, and has used this approach to offer explanations of many conceptions elicited from college students. This work has mainly been carried out in physics, but certainly has potential to inform learning in other sciences (García Franco & Taber, 2009) and probably beyond. It suggests that research that is able to identify the types of patterns that are readily abstracted from the perceptual field could help teachers design teaching to use, rather than be thwarted by, such mechanisms (Taber, 2008).

Constructing Knowledge

When thinking about the learning of complex conceptual material, work such as that of diSessa offers very useful insights, suggesting that processing elements in the pre-conscious part of the cognitive system may be highly significant for how learners come to understand science concepts (or those of other subject areas). In particular, it implies that we need to recognise that our brains hold some "knowledge" at intuitive levels: that is, that we make systematic discriminations based on processing elements that are well "below" conscious awareness. DiSessa believes that conceptual knowledge may be built upon networks of such intuitive knowledge elements.

A model developed by Annette Karmiloff-Smith (1996) posits at least four discrete levels of the cognitive system: one purely implicit level to which we have no access through introspection, and three more explicit levels. The highest of these levels allows us to access knowledge in verbal propositional forms: an elephant is a mammal; transitions metals can demonstrate a range of oxidation states in their compounds, and so forth. The intermediate levels do not reflect knowledge elements that are themselves "in" verbal, propositional form. This again links to science education research: for example about the role of visualisation in learning science (Gilbert, 2005).

Karmiloff-Smith's model (which informs Fig. 8.1) assumes that knowledge held in each level of the system can be (but is not necessarily) re-represented at the next level. Conceptual development involves this type of re-representation making knowledge more explicit over time. The student who replies to a question about the seasons by suggesting the Earth is nearer the Sun in summer could on diSessa's model be activating (at an intuitive level) a primitive knowledge element that (we can verbalise as) "effects are greater closer to the source", and applying this intuition to the specific question. However, it is also possible that such an intuition has over time been re-represented such that the learner actually has developed an explicit

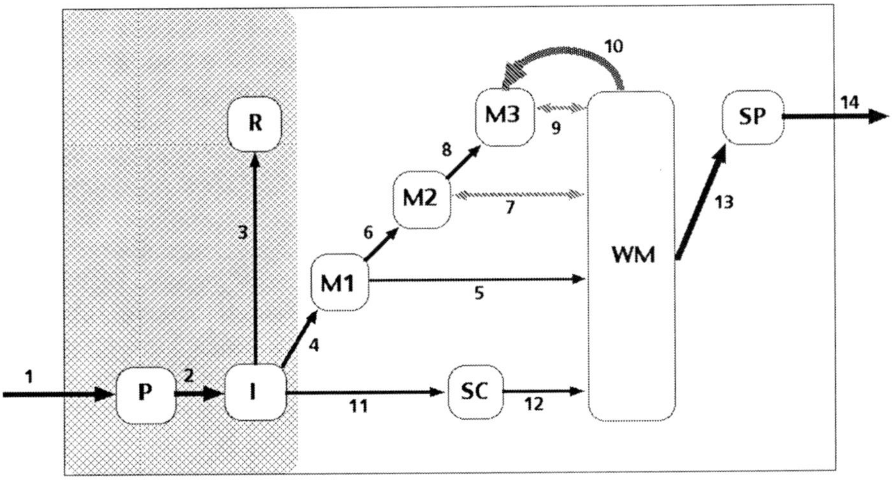

A highly simplified model of the cognitive system illustrating how ideas from cognitive science can inform thinking about student learning and thinking (drawing particularly on the ideas of Annette Karmiloff-Smith). 1. Sensory input is processed in hardwired perceptual elements (P) before ... 2. being interpreted by implicit pattern-recognition elements (I) that are not open to conscious awareness, but are able to... 3. signal other implicit units (R), e.g. to initiate the blink reflex. 4. Implicit 'knowledge' may be re-represented at an explicit level (M1) that is not open to conscious interrogation, but that can... 5. inform conscious thought (WM) without conscious awareness of the source. This leads to 'intuitive' knowledge. Implicit knowledge in this form can also be... 6, 8. re-represented at more explicit levels (M2, M3). Knowledge represented at level M2, is... 7. open to conscious introspection, but is not presented to consciousness in verbal form - e.g. running a mental simulation through imagery - and has to be verbalised before being reported. Knowledge represented at level M3 can be... 9. directly accessed in propositional form and is presented to consciousness verbally, i.e. as conceptions. 10. The outcome of thinking can be deliberately integrated in this representational form, allowing the development of extended conceptual frameworks of propositional knowledge. Patterns of sensory input recognised as carrying linguistic information can be... 11. processed in the brain's speech comprehension areas (SC), and then... 12. directly presented as language. The outcomes of processing in working memory (WM) can be... 13. processed in the brain's speech production centres (SP), which... 14. produce utterances that are interpreted by researchers as demonstrating intuitive theories, conceptions, conceptual frameworks etc.

Fig. 8.1 A scheme to explain the origins of different types of learner knowledge conception that the Earth is nearer the Sun during summer, which is accessed as propositional knowledge. Such distinctions are not purely academic: in the latter case answers on this topic are likely to be consistent, whereas in the former case, modifying the question may sometimes lead to a different primitive intuition being activated and a different answer generated. This model offers some explanatory value in making sense of the disparate characteristics reported for students' ideas in science.

Karmiloff-Smith also offers another possibility: that under some circumstances it is possible to short cut the process by which we build implicit intuitions of the world which through successive re-representation can become converted to directly accessible representations of propositional knowledge. She suggested that we are able to sometimes directly acquire knowledge at this level by interactions with others. This is of course reassuring to those working in school systems where much of teaching concerns presenting the concepts to be learned by verbalising propositional knowledge. However, the mechanism is not limited to true information: a student could through this mechanism learn the Earth is nearer the Sun during the summer if this is suggested by a classmate.

Here Vygotsky's distinction between spontaneous and scientific/academic concepts becomes very relevant. Vygotsky recognised the limitations of spontaneous concepts that could not be directly verbalised and applied in principled ways; but also that academic concepts would be rote learnt and meaningless unless related to existing knowledge grounded in personal experience. For Vygotsky (1934/1994), conceptual development was a process of developing linkage between these two types of concepts so that spontaneous concepts become available to operate on in principled ways, and academic concepts are understood (not just regurgitated). Vygotsky put great stress on the way those with access to cultural tools such as language could support the learning of the young during this process.

Conceptual Change

This brings us back to a pre-occupation of science education—how to bring about conceptual change (Taber, 2009, pp. 280–298). The natural process of conceptual development may well involve the slow building of explicit knowledge structures by re-representing more intuitive cognitive elements: but what when this leads to conceptions at odds with what teachers are asked to teach? Some approaches to cognitive change are based on persuasion, but seem to suggest that the learner is able to undergo conceptual change as a deliberate rational choice. It seems likely that teaching that encourages metacognitive sophistication may indeed support such processes in some cases. However, for those student conceptions that have been found to be most tenacious, persuasion has limited effect.

Sometimes this can actually be explained on rational grounds—from the students' perspective their own understanding is more coherent and has greater explanatory power (Thagard, 1992). In other cases research suggests that fundamental ontological category errors have been made: so that the type of *process* the teacher means by "heat" or "light" is just totally incompatible with the type of *stuff* the student understands "heat" or "light" to be (Chi, 1992). Research suggests in these cases the teacher really needs to start again and help build an alternative understanding from scratch, rather than challenge the students' ideas: that is the teacher needs to help the student acquire a totally new concept.

The knowledge-in-pieces approach based on diSessa's work suggests that at least with some concept areas a better knowledge of students' repertoires of intuitive knowledge elements will allow teachers to deliberately channel learning by building—and sometimes re-building—conceptual knowledge upon the most helpful intuitions in terms of match to desired target knowledge (Hammer, 2000). So thinking about the seasons in terms of throwing balls at targets at different angles to the direction of throw might activate suitable intuitions, rather than thinking in terms of getting closer to a fire.

Towards a Model of Cognition that Supports Research into Student Learning

This chapter has done little more than offer an overview of an interesting research issue in education, and a glimpse of how cognitive science can support our research into classroom learning and teaching.

The issue—deriving from science education but likely equally relevant in other subject areas—was the nature of learners' ideas in science. In particular, how several decades of work exploring student thinking and understanding of science concepts has led to an eclectic range of findings. Research has characterised learners' ideas along a range of dimensions (Taber, 2009, pp. 226–256), so that they:

- may reflect or contradict target knowledge in the curriculum;
- may be recognised as fanciful or conjectural, or may be the basis of strong commitments;
- may be labile and readily "corrected" or tenacious and resistant to teaching;
- may be highly integrated into complex frameworks or may be isolated notions with limited ranges of convenience;
- may be inconsistent, or show high levels of coherence across broad domains;
- may be unitary or manifold.

For a time, this led to much debate about *which* characterisations were actually correct. However, as research in science education has increasingly drawn upon ideas from cognitive science, it has become much clearer why thinking elicited from science students has such variety. A cognitive system with different types of knowledge elements at different levels of explicit access; a limited working memory; a long-term memory system that necessarily has to represent ideas in a physical substrate; etc., starts to explain why students sometimes offer inconsistent and changeable answers, but other times reliably offer accounts of complex well-integrated frameworks of conceptions. This is illustrated in Fig. 8.1. A single chapter can only offer a brief taster of how ideas from the cognitive sciences are supporting research into science education (and many of the ideas mentioned in this chapter are explored in more depth in Taber, 2009). It is certainly not the case that science educators now have a clear understanding of cognition that explains all we wish to know about learning in science, and how to support that learning more effectively. However, the adoption of a range of notions from the learning sciences is certainly offering the means to start clarifying some of the vague taken-for-granted ideas that have been common in the field, and is offering useful models of cognition that are helping us make much better sense of the disparate findings of research in this field.

References

Biesta, G. J. J., & Burbules, N. C. (2003). *Pragmatism and educational research*. Lanham, MD: Rowman & Littlefield Publishers.

Bliss, J. (1995). Piaget and after: The case of learning science. *Studies in Science Education, 25*, 139–172.

Bruner, J. S. (1960). *The process of education*. New York: Vintage Books.

Chi, M. T. H. (1992). Conceptual change within and across ontological categories: Examples from learning and discovery in science. In R. N. Giere (Ed.), *Cognitive models in science* (Vol. XV, pp. 129–186). Minneapolis, MN: University of Minnesota Press.

Claxton, G. (2005). *The wayward mind: An intimate history of the unconscious*. London: Little Brown.

diSessa, A. A. (1993). Towards an epistemology of physics. *Cognition and Instruction, 10*(2&3), 105–225.

Driver, R. (1983). *The pupil as scientist?* Milton Keynes: Open University Press.

Driver, R., & Erickson, G. (1983). Theories-in-action: some theoretical and empirical issues in the study of students' conceptual frameworks in science. *Studies in Science Education, 10*, 37–60.

Duit, R. (2007). *Bibliography – Students' and Teachers' Conceptions and Science Education*. Retrieved from http://www.ipn.uni-kiel.de/aktuell/stcse/stcse.html

Fensham, P. J. (2004). *Defining an identity: The evolution of science education as a field of research*. Dordrecht: Kluwer Academic Publishers.

Gagné, R. M. (1970). *The conditions of learning* (2). New York: Holt, Rinehart & Winston.

García Franco, A., & Taber, K. S. (2009). Secondary students' thinking about familiar phenomena: Learners' explanations from a curriculum context where 'particles' is a key idea for organising teaching and learning. *International Journal of Science Education, 31*(14), 1917–1952.

Gardner, H. (1977). *The mind's new science: A history of the cognitive revolution* (2). New York: Basic Books.

Gauld, C. (1989). A study of pupils' responses to empirical evidence. In R. Millar (Ed.), *Doing Science: images of science in science education* (pp. 62–82). London: The Falmer Press.

Gilbert, J. K. (2005). Visualization: A metacognitive skill in science and science education. In J. K. Gilbert (Ed.), *Visualization in science education* (pp. 9–27). Dordrecht: Kluwer Academic Publishers.

Gilbert, J. K., & Watts, D. M. (1983). Concepts, misconceptions and alternative conceptions: changing perspectives in science education. *Studies in Science Education, 10*, 61–98.

Glasersfeld, Ev. (1988). The reluctance to change a way of thinking [Electronic Version]. *Irish Journal of Psychology, 9*, 83–90. Retrieved from http://www.univie.ac.at/constructivism/EvG/papers/110.pdf.

Goswami, U. (2006). Neuroscience and education: from research to practice? *Nature Reviews Neuroscience*, *7*, 406–413.
Goswami, U. (2008). *Cognitive development: The learning brain*. Hove, East Sussex: Psychology Press.
Gregory, R. L. (1998). *Eye and brain: The psychology of seeing* (5th ed.). Oxford: Oxford University Press.
Hammer, D. (2000). Student resources for learning introductory physics. *American Journal of Physics*, *68*(7-Physics Education Research Supplement), S52–S59.
Hennessy, S. (1993). Situated cognition and cognitive apprenticeship: implications for classroom learning. *Studies in Science Education*, *22*, 1–41.
Herron, J. D., Cantu, L., Ward, R., & Srinivasan, V. (1977). Problems associated with concept analysis. *Science Education*, *61*(2), 185–199.
Hsu, Y. -S., Wu, H. -K., & Hwang, F. -K. (2008). Fostering high school students' conceptual understandings about seasons: The design of a technology-enhanced learning environment. *Research in Science Education*, *38*, 127–147.
Johnstone, A. H. (1991). Why is science difficult to learn? Things are seldom what they seem. *Journal of Computer Assisted Learning*, *7*, 75–83.
Karmiloff-Smith, A. (1996). *Beyond modularity: A developmental perspective on cognitive science*. Cambridge, MA: MIT Press.
Kelly, G. (1963). *A theory of personality: The psychology of personal constructs*. New York: W W Norton & Company.
Koffka, K. (1967). Principles of gestalt psychology. In J. A. Dyal (Ed.), *Readings in psychology: Understanding human behavior* (2, pp. 9–13). New York: McGraw-Hill Book Company.
Lakoff, G., & Johnson, M. (1980). Conceptual metaphor in everyday language. *The Journal of Philosophy*, *77*(8), 453–486.
Osborne, R. J., & Wittrock, M. C. (1983). Learning science: A generative process. *Science Education*, *67*(4), 489–508.
Piaget, J. (1972). *The principles of genetic epistemology*. (W. Mays, Trans.). London: Routledge & Kegan Paul.
Piaget, J. (1979). *Behaviour and evolution* (D. Nicholson-Smith, Trans.). London: Routledge & Kegan Paul.
Pretz, J. E., & Sternberg, R. J. (2005). Unifying the field: Cognition and intelligence. In R. J. Sternberg & J. E. Pretz (Eds.), *Cognition and intelligence: Identifying the mechanisms of mind* (pp. 307–318). Cambridge: Cambridge University Press.
Schmidt, H. -J. (1991). A label as a hidden persuader: Chemists' neutralization concept. *International Journal of Science Education*, *13*(4), 459–471.
Scott, P. (1998). Teacher talk and meaning making in science classrooms: A review of studies from a Vygotskian perspective. *Studies in Science Education*, *32*, 45–80.
Shayer, M., & Adey, P. (1981). *Towards a science of science teaching: Cognitive development and curriculum demand*. Oxford: Heinemann Educational Books.
Sugarman, S. (1987). *Piaget's construction of the child's reality*. Cambridge: Cambridge University Press.
Sweller, J. (2007). Evolutionary biology and educational psychology. In J. S. Carlson & J. R. Levin (Eds.), *Educating the evolved mind: Conceptual foundations for an evolutionary educational psychology* (pp. 165–175). Charlotte, NC: Information Age Publishing.
Taber, K. S. (1998). An alternative conceptual framework from chemistry education. *International Journal of Science Education*, *20*(5), 597–608.
Taber, K. S. (2006). Beyond constructivism: The progressive research programme into learning science. *Studies in Science Education*, *42*, 125–184.
Taber, K. S. (2007). *Classroom-based research and evidence-based practice: A guide for teachers*. London: SAGE.
Taber, K. S. (2008). Conceptual resources for learning science: Issues of transience and grain-size in cognition and cognitive structure. *International Journal of Science Education*, *30*(8), 1027–1053.

Taber, K. S. (2009). *Progressing science education: Constructing the scientific research programme into the contingent nature of learning science*. Dordrecht: Springer.
Thagard, P. (1992). *Conceptual revolutions*. Oxford: Princeton University Press.
Vygotsky, L. S. (1934/1986). *Thought and language*. London: MIT Press.
Vygotsky, L. S. (1934/1994). The development of academic concepts in school aged children. In R. van der Veer & J. Valsiner (Eds.), *The Vygotsky reader* (pp. 355–370). Oxford: Blackwell.
White, R. T. (1985). Interview protocols and dimensions of cognitive structure. In L. H. T. West & A. L. Pines (Eds.), *Cognitive structure and conceptual change* (pp. 51–59). London: Academic Press.

Chapter 9
An Analysis of Design Strategies for Creating Educational Experiences in Virtual Environments

Theresa Horstman[1] and Stephen Kerr[2]

[1] University of Washington, Seattle, WA, USA, e-mail: thorst@u.washington.edu
[2] University of Washington, Seattle, WA, USA, e-mail: stkerr@u.washington.edu

Introduction

In this chapter we analyze and compare e-learning instructional design methodologies with those of video game design methodologies to better understand how differences in design strategies shape the ways in which users engage with video games and e-learning. Although focused on the similarities and differences in design methodologies, we limit our topics to concepts specific to learning and content management. The purpose, through comparative exploration, is to discover potential design strategies that may improve the quality and effectiveness of e-learning courses through increased engagement.

Though we focus on content design choices we do not evaluate the difference in designing for different organizations or target audiences. The fundamental differences of designing a course for children versus adults or academic versus workplace remains intact—it is the process by which one designs for the technology that is under evaluation.

An important component that influences e-learning design that will not be covered in detail is the method of project management. How an e-learning course development cycle is managed has a significant impact on the degree in which technology can be integrated into the design. In some e-learning development organizations the project management process that guides the development of instructor-led training or classroom-based materials is the same for e-learning development. In other organizations, a different project management process, similar to software development, is used and tends to be more accommodating for integrating technology into courses. Given the scope of our topic we assume the project management cycle would adjust accordingly.

Lastly, this chapter does not include an analysis of board games or other forms of game play. This is to limit the focus on how content is treated and organized in

T. Horstman (✉)
University of Washington, Seattle, WA, USA
e-mail: theresahorstman@gmail.com

M.S. Khine, I.M. Saleh (eds.), *New Science of Learning*,
DOI 10.1007/978-1-4419-5716-0_9,

relation to the available technology in game design and e-learning. Though board games and other forms of play have a significant contribution to understanding effective instructional design, the interests here are specific to the technology and the comparison between two similar media types: video games and e-learning.

We have included a few assumptions about both e-learning and video games. The first is that standard practices exist for e-learning design and development methodologies, and that these are based on the current training and learning industry standards. As a result, in the instances where exceptions to these rules apply, some generalized statements are contestable. Although descriptions of practices are based on accepted standards and industry recommendations, they are made with the understanding that e-learning design and development practices are founded on general best practices and not entirely on hard-fast rules.

The second assumption is about play and learning. Though it may not always be appropriate to integrate the two together, it is assumed that learning and play are not mutually exclusive and that making a game educational does not automatically strip it of its game-like quality. However, whether or not it is fun, is another matter. It is with this assumption that it may be possible for e-learning to utilize video game methodologies for designing educational content.

The play and fun associated with video games has a wide array of connotations a few of which includes immersiveness, challenge, and engagement. These associations lend themselves to learning and can be considered a focal point for striving to create better e-learning. However, the drawback for linking immersive to fun is the assumption that if the activity is fun then the content cannot be taken seriously. Though we do not make recommendations for designing to specific content it is assumed that some content may not be appropriate for e-learning, regardless of design strategy.

Lastly, we assume that people learn from playing video games. The content learned may be specific to the game environment and game play, but learning does takes place. This is based in the demonstration of player progression through game play and that game progression cannot be solely attributed to external knowledge—the player must acquire some new set of knowledge in order to progress in game play. With this assumption, the question still remains, whether the learning that occurs in video games can be successfully transferred and measured to external circumstances.

The categories of topics are based on groupings of shared concepts between game design and instructional design for e-learning and reflect the concepts which may lend itself to better understanding how players and students interact with the medium. The four categories of comparison are; user-centered design, integration of content, visual representation of content, and motivation.

User-Centered Design

User-centered design in video games focuses on creating a unique and engaging user experience through game play and user interactions. This includes consideration of how the user is interpreting, interacting, creating meaning, and engaging with the application as the focal point of design decisions. For a game designer to try to separate user experience from game design is to lose game play itself. At each stage, game designers ask themselves, how does this decision impact the user experience in positive or negative way?

While the purpose of e-learning courses differs from that of video games, there is an important correlation between the two. E-learning courses can be user-centered, which is focused on the desired outcome of instruction—a successful transference of knowledge—and providing instruction in a meaningful and memorable way. The question e-learning designers ask themselves is, how does this design decision impact the effectiveness of the learning experience in a positive or negative way?

User-centered design is an important consideration in any application design that includes human–machine interaction because it shapes the quality of the user experience. The quality of the user experience influences a variety of outcomes, such as the likelihood of using the application again and the amount of interference experienced that prevents the user from achieving his or her objectives. However, e-learning and video games share the characteristic of striving to create a unique and purposeful user experience (as opposed to, for example, a word processing application which does not necessarily have a linear progression of events) and both games and e-learning are designed to fulfill a purpose in which the user gets from point A to point Z. The emphasis on the journey, rather than the destination, may vary amongst different types of games and courseware; both e-learning and games are structured for fulfilling specific objectives.

In this way, user-centered design shares many similarities with learner-centered design, where the design process focuses on creating an experience based on the learners' abilities and needs. This correlation between user- and learner-centered exists on many levels. To further illustrate, player progression in games is dependent on the player's ability to demonstrate skills, and these skills, including strategy, are acquired during the course of game play. Game designers are aware of the player experience—and even assume the role of the player—when designing game play progression in order to anticipate information gaps and to evaluate the effectiveness of the design. Learner-centered design also adopts the perspective of the learner and determines how best to present content based on the attributes and skill set of the target audience. These two approaches include an awareness of how the student/player acquires information, an awareness of the objectives, the ability to build upon existing knowledge, the student/player's ability to strategize, and consideration of the components that motivate the student/player to participate.

To further illustrate evidence of learner-centered design in video games, a typical design strategy in Role Playing Games (RPGs) is to present a few character skills in the beginning and allow the player to become familiar with each skill's limitations and capabilities through experience in less complex situations. As the player successfully completes simple challenges, more complex circumstances are introduced in which the player must figure out how to apply the same skills but in a different manner because the situations are different. For example, World of Warcraft (WoW), low-level characters are given only three to four combat skills.

In early situations, the consequences of using these skills inappropriately are less severe than at higher levels. The design expectation is that the degree of complexity of a situation is in proportion to the amount of practice and exposure the player has had with those particular skills. The same skills are present at higher levels but the consequences of misuse can be more severe, in part because the player has failed to demonstrate an understanding of the correct use of the skills.

With its potential to improve learner engagement and knowledge retention, one of the most important concepts that e-learning design may borrow from game design is to shift focus on user experience, not just from a content perspective but from a human–machine interaction perspective. User-centered design in game design, specifically which components are adapted and adjusted throughout the design and development process to create a successful game, may be a process e-learning designers and developers can apply to improve e-learning design.

To narrow the focus and help build a correlation between the objectives of e-learning design and video game design, we will focus on a few aspects concerned with successful transfer of information and the treatment of content. This includes design considerations of how the user translates and understands interactions, ease-of-use with the application in relation to the content, demonstration of comprehension of content, and how the user experiences the game as a whole system. User-centered design ensures the content necessary for game continuation is embedded properly within game play. This content not only needs to be accessible but also challenging and interesting to the player in order for the game to be successful. User-centered design pays attention to how the player perceives, translates, and comprehends the game content through interactions to ensure the games' success; the stronger the user-focus in the design process, the better the game play and more accurately game content is portrayed to the player because it is designed and tested through the player experience.

There are pivotal moments in game play when the player transitions from translating the game as interacting with or manipulating a machine to interacting with and responding to virtual objects in the game. This is evident in the manner in which players describe their in-game actions: "fighting mobs" instead of "clicking mobs" or "running" instead of "holding down the arrow key." This transition from external awareness of action to virtual projection of action is due, in part, to how the player translates and understands his or her interactions in the game in relation to the cohesiveness of the game environment and the player's awareness of his or her virtual relationship with the objects in the virtual space. Through the course of game design, objects are assigned meaning and the meaning is sustained and further developed through the actions of game play. Collectively, the cohesiveness of the objects and their meaning also sustain player engagement.

Transitioning a player from manipulating a machine to interacting with virtual objects is shaped not only by how the player perceives the interaction but also by the application's ease of use in relation to the content. Games that are difficult to use or have a user interface (UI) that does not fully support necessary interactions prevent the player from becoming immersed in game play. To help us clarify categories of different types of user interaction, Galloway (2006) identifies a quadrant of gamic qualities: diegetic and nondiegetic machine and operator acts. A diegetic machine act is atmospheric or ambience, contributing to the overall experience of a game and is classified as a process. A diegetic operator act is the player's movements or expressive acts—the actions of the player—which is classified as play. A nondiegetic machine act is a "disabling or enabling act," such as goals, leveling, or "game over" and is classified as code. Lastly, a nondiegetic operator act is a "configuration" act, where the player manipulates the game (machine) such as "pushing pause" to suspend the game. This is classified as algorithm (Galloway, 2006). Galloway's identification of game qualities, or what he calls "tendencies," suggests that specific combinations are better at sustaining the immersiveness of game play and other combinations may detract. Depending on the game content, a higher ratio of nondiegetic operator acts may not create as an immersive environment as diegetic operator acts because the player is focused on the external qualities of the game, the machine, rather than expressive acts. User-centered design is sensitive to the players' focal points that involve active participation and problem solving or passive interpretation *in relation to the purpose* of the game. This is not to say one combination is better than another; arcade games may utilize nondiegetic machine acts more readily than other genres because the game play and user interactions can support that type of design. For example, a "game over" function works best in replayable games that do not contain content where the player invests a lot of time; because loss of the investment may not make the game worth replaying. Considering the user experience in terms of these quadrants reveals the types and combinations of interactions in relation to the content that successfully engage players in game play. It also reveals that an unbalanced ratio applied to the wrong content type results in a poor user experience.

Considering the structure of the user experience through these terms, designers can identify the ways in which the player is engaged with the content and how the player is interacting with the game. One key component that shapes how the player interacts with the game is the UI. A UI that is difficult to use or that inconsistently represents content can deter player engagement because it prevents him or her from being able to predictably access information or perform actions necessary to succeed. As the toolset that facilitates the player's interaction with the game, the UI is also a vehicle that allows the player to demonstrate comprehension of content through the execution of the objectives.

For example, in a puzzle game such as Bejeweled, a player demonstrates comprehension of content through game progression; align similar gems which will award points, continue game play, and increase difficulty. The player's comprehension is further demonstrated as the player's strategy adapts to the difficulty of the puzzle, without which the game would not continue. In more complex game designs, such as an RPG, players demonstrate comprehension of in-game content by correctly modifying and using character skills in different situations. As the player successfully masters a circumstance or completes a quest, the situations become increasingly difficult, requiring the player to adjust strategies based on ability to incorporate new knowledge with that which was created in previous experiences, thereby demonstrating their comprehension again. Progression in game play requires the player to demonstrate an understanding of the components that comprise in-game content. More than just passing a test and moving on to the next section, it is virtual action demonstrated in a situational circumstance that encompasses the unique objectives to specific content. In addition, it ties different components of the content into a continuous progression of complex actions. This demonstration cannot be accomplished unless the UI supports the designed interactions of game play.

User-centered design is also addresses how all of the elements of a game work together to create the player experience as a whole. This is one of the enabling characteristics in which game design is an effective tool for communicating complex content because the design approach is concerned with incorporating a wide range of content into a cohesive structure. Part of this involves creating a user experience in an environment which is consistent with itself. This is achieved by designing the use of different game components, such as audio, animation, game play, logic, and scoring not only by their function but considering how they impact other components. The approach that considers the overarching user experience shapes design decisions and allows for content to be introduced that may have otherwise been considered unnecessary as isolated functionalities. For example, consider the audio track in a game; music may create a mood, but it is also serves as an implicit indicator of meaning. For example, when there is trouble nearby or a new challenge has begun, or as the player approaches a friendly nonplayer character (NPC). If this audio indicator is removed, another indicator would need to take its place, not because the music is important as an isolated function, but the information the music conveys in relation to the other components is necessary for the player to understand the content and continue game play.

E-learning design strategies could improve by considering the aspects of user-centered design outlined by game design practices but it requires a shift in thinking about how content is represented in virtual form. These improvements could include increased engagement because the learner transitions to being focused on interacting with the content rather than interacting with the machine. Attention to how the user translates and understands the interactions, the application's ease of use in relation to the content, demonstration of comprehension of content, and how the user experiences the course as a whole system are not new concepts for e-learning design; rather the execution, particularly the representation and organization of content is not the same. This may be due to different interpretations of what these aspects mean to learners as opposed to gamers and how they should be carried out.

In e-learning courses, how the user translates and understands the course interactions typically means to ensure the learner understands navigation, course layout and progression, and UI functionality. How the learner translates objects within the course is limited because much of the content is presented not as interactionable objects, but as interactionable, discrete processes, such as multiple-choice questions or branching scenarios. In contrast, game content is represented through interactionable objects; the player interacts with these objects based on the context of the purpose of the game. The very manner in which content is presented in e-learning inhibits immersive connectedness with its meaning because the learner is focused on the process rather than the object. If we examine the structure of e-learning courses through the lens of Galloway's terms, diegetic and nondiegetic machine and operator acts, e-learning courseware is comprised largely of all nondiegetic acts. The learner manipulates the machine, classified as algorithm, and the machine imposes its structure on the user, classified as code. These are mechanical functions of an application and alone lack the depth of meaning which in combination with the diegetic acts, produce. Creating an application without the qualities of expressive and atmospheric action imposes a structure not capable of creating meaningful engagement because the human–machine interaction is reduced to scripted function and not on integrating the meaning of the content or requiring the user to reflect on the meaning of his or her interactions.

This shift is subtle but significant, creating experiences in which the user engages with the content with limited awareness or focus on the functionality of the machine. If e-learning shifted the approach of content development to incorporate this level of engagement how much more effective would it be as an experiential learning tool? The objectives of e-learning would change to create a virtual environment where the learner is engaged with the content as object through expressive acts and not as process and manipulating a machine.

How users demonstrate comprehension of content in e-learning and video games is closely related to the manner in which they interact with the application. Demonstration in e-learning is often modeled after standardized testing methods, separating the assessment from the content that is learned. Demonstrating comprehension in video games is embedded throughout game play in an environment where player progression restricted without the demonstration of comprehension. In e-learning, part of the conceptual separation between content and demonstration of knowledge is due to not considering the user experience of a course as an integrated system; instead, it is viewed as a sequence of distinct events. The shift toward user-centered game design involves designing an e-learning course that occupies a virtual environment rather than a sequence or series of pages. Designing environments of content creates the perception of learning through creating situational experiences rather than completing a sequence of segmented tasks. Reading text is no longer considered the experience, but using reading as a means for contributing to a virtual experience is. In addition, through this process the learner is not being told what they need to know, but learning through virtual experience and discovery through interactions with objects. This requires an instructional design approach for creating a virtual learning environment where the learner perceives and responds to objects as the content and demonstration of knowledge acquisition is through interactions with these objects.

Transitioning from the e-learning design perspective to game design interpretation of user-centered game design is greatly determined by how the content is represented and organized. The first aspect of this will involve examining and comparing the instructional and game design methods of segmenting and consolidating content.

Integrating Content

In order for an instructional design approach to allow for creating a virtual learning environment where the learner perceives and responds to content as objects rather than a presentation of content, the method in which content is represented needs to be reexamined. How content is represented in both games and e-learning is a significant factor because it determines the type of interaction that can be created for the user experience, however, where e-learning may benefit from game design is by examination of integrated content management approaches. For example, in designing levels of game play, the designer considers which tasks must be successfully completed, how those tasks are represented to the player, and the actions the player must make in order to complete the tasks. Though content is segmented into distinct aspects of game play, scoring, types of interactions, skills, etc. game play itself integrates discrete objects or segmented content to relate to each other and ultimately back to game objectives. These distinct segments are easily identifiable, but it is during the course of game play that they appear to be part of an integrated experience because each segment is designed in relation to each other. This means not only designing the content that must be contained in the experience to support the game objectives but also tying it all together to create a cohesive experience. Content as object in video games fulfills two purposes: contributing unique content to the game while reinforcing the user experience as a whole. Designing content as object is affected by how content is represented (images, graphics, audio, types of interaction, text, scoring, etc.), how these representations work together, and the distribution of the content. Serving as the means by which the player receives information and feedback to continue play, these elements, if designed well, inherently improves user experience, retention, and learning effectiveness of in-game content.

In order to convey information to the player, the game designer must determine the best modes of representation and how the player will be able to understand the meaning of each representation. In addition, the representations of content must be consistent with itself and with the game environment. For example, in the first edition of WoW, in-game objects that pertained to quest completions were unmarked, the only information displayed in rollover text was the name and/or description of the object. Assuming the player is completing a new quest and using only in-game resources to problem solve, he or she would have to understand the information in the quest log, locate the correct location on the map, then identify and try the task(s). Once found, the correct combination triggers a tracking mechanism in the quest log, which informs the player of his or her progress. Though the type and complexity of content, actions, and locations may differ between quests, the basic problem-solving process remains intact for new quest completion. In a later release, this process changed and the in-game objects relevant to quest completion are marked. Not only does the rollover text display the name and/or description of the object, it also displays the name of the quest it pertains to and the number of tasks remaining until quest completion. Changing the meaning of the objects to include this new detailed information altered the problem-solving process, thus changing game play and how the player interacts with these objects. The player is no longer required to read the content of the quest log in order to figure out his or her next actions; he or she can rollover objects to determine whether they are necessary for the next course of action. Although the reason for making these changes is unique to the game play experience of WoW, it is an example of the many decisions that are significant to learning; the degree of difficulty is impacted by how the content is represented and the manner in which the player engages with the content.

Content that is inconsistently represented prevents the player from learning appropriate use of the skill and from developing for more complex challenges. Similarly, content that is under-represented prevents player progression as well. For example, in an RPG, a character skill such as healing is represented in many different ways: an icon or button to trigger the action, text to describe or identify the action, other actions to which this one is compared and contrasted, and finally, circumstances in which the action is used. If the content pertaining to healing is inconsistently represented or not explained within the context of the game, then it becomes too difficult to determine how to use this skill, increasingly so as the game develops into more complex scenarios.

Creating consistency also includes the mode by which the content is represented. In the previous example, if the rollover text for some quest objects did not indicate their connection to a quest, the mode of providing information to the player is unreliable and would require the player to rely on the previous process of problem-solving. From the player's perspective, this inconsistency detracts from immersiveness of game play because the player is focused on reconciling a discrepancy between game function and content.

How the representations of in-game content work together produces the context for game play. During game play the player discovers the meaning of each object through its relationship with other objects—in context. Sustaining this context during game play explains the relevance of the objects as experience, not just as a sequence of information. And though the logical organization of content for the game designer may look a lot like e-learning it is the relationship between the content, the interconnectedness of meaning that contributes to the immersive results. In any moment of game play there is a balance of indicators to help the player understand the context; music, audio narration, on-screen text, animations, and graphics. For example, in an First Person Shooter (FPS) if a player approaches a dangerous challenge, the design decision involves selecting the best representations or combination of representations to strike a balance between providing too much information or not enough information. Decisions include whether to create indicators such as ominous music, NPCs shouting a warning, a warning light in the HUD (head-up display), or a pulsating red glow around the periphery of the player's vantage point. The method of determining how danger is communicated to the player depends on desired difficulty of game play and is significant because the result of the decision impacts not only this single experience, but is also representative of a recurring type of information as it exists in context.

Designing content in context allows game designers to balance implicit and explicit content distribution. In the previous example, the player learns through the course of game play what each of those indicators mean, which opens the opportunity to embed more content implicitly. If the design decision is made to use a warning light in the HUD as a visual and text indicator of danger, this could encode any number of circumstances, from all dangerous situations to only one specific type of danger—determined by the game objectives and type of game play. This is important because game play consists of players figuring out strategies based on the information provided. Too little information and the game is too difficult; too simply communicated, and then the game's degree of challenge is forfeited.

A key factor for how representations of content work together is how the content is distributed within the game. As a standard design practice, the design recommendation for building e-learning includes segmenting and organizing content into chunks of information. The same is true for game design as the principles of cognitive load are still the same; it is the distribution that is different. Game content must be accessible and manageable by the player but in order to do so, the content is segmented, organized, and *distributed* across internal mechanisms within the game. This allows greater and more complex amounts of information to be integrated into the game without making it too difficult for the player to synthesize into action. For example, if the player must retain a large amount of poorly distributed or excessively detailed information over too long of a period of time, the game becomes too difficult.

UI design is an example of embedding content that a player may need to access in specific circumstances. This serves two purposes, the first is that the player is aware and knows each element of content might be needed for any particular circumstance and is therefore, in each situation, evaluating which content or combinations of are required for success. The second is that this mechanism also serves as an extension of the player as a tool for organizing and keeping accessible content necessary for game play. The UI as tool for distributed cognitive processes of the player, enabling him or her to incorporate more information into action than he or she could perform without it. In 3D games, the environment itself can act in the same capacity, where locations within the space serve the same purposes—a virtual location to store and access in times of need. For a literal example, bank locations are a common feature in RPGs where the player acquires items for a range of applications, some of which are used for very specific situations. Players store materials here and access them when necessary, but it remains up to the player to figure out which circumstances are appropriate for each item's use. This conceptual design of organizing pieces of content expands and deepens the players' knowledge of game content because of the volume in which is distributed to the banks.

An aspect of distributing content is also captured by scaffolding of content. The increase of complexity and difficulty of game play is integrated into game play progression. For game design this means balancing game play as a linear progression of events with an iterative progression of events. There are many ways to scaffold content in a game to achieve a balance between pace and the complexity of the content but the iterative game play process allows the player to engage with some content repeatedly although in new and different ways. For example, in RPGs, a character's set of skills may remain the same, yet the situations in which the skills are used vary and become increasingly difficult as the player successfully progresses. This provides an opportunity for the player to demonstrate an entry-level understanding of the skills as well as to develop an expert-level understanding of how the skills work together in different situations.

First, a notable difference between e-learning and video games is the difference in type of content. Generally speaking, game content is self-referential and self-contained. Although there are examples of external modes of information that enhance or are essential to game play, a majority of game design assumes that content necessary for success is contained within the game. In addition to this, it is also assumed that in-game content is not a requirement for any other external (out-of-game) experience. Therefore, external transference of content is not an objective of game designers whereas in e-learning transference of content to external circumstances is expected and measured. Does this difference mean that game design methods for organizing content are not applicable to e-learning?

In e-learning, segmenting content to align with learning objectives achieves a clear connection between the learner's task and the successful acquisition of the learning objective. However, oversegmentation of content may result in two defects; the oversimplification of the meaning of the content by removal from contextual experience and the experience of nondiegetic acts which remove the learner from the environment. Both result in reduced immersive qualities of the learning experience. To increase learner engagement in e-learning, one strategy may be to adopt the methods of integrating content into a virtual experience. Reconsider how content in e-learning is represented (graphics, audio, types of interaction, text, scoring, etc.), how these representations work together, and the distribution of the content. Through the lens of game design, consider the learning objectives as the defining parameters of the virtual space; everything created is for learner's success in demonstrating completion of the learning objectives. Rather than focusing on a sequence of pages, the designer could incorporate experiences or interactions each of which represent a learning objective, until all learning objectives are represented in a cohesive environment. The designer adjusts the design of the experiences so they are all interrelated and designs levels of difficulty for each experience. This includes, at the end, combinations of experiences that incorporate aspects of all the learning objectives in one experience.

Consider the example of role-play scenarios; reading a role-play scenario for learning is not the same experience as acting out a role-play scenario and the methodologies for designing these two experiences are very different. The first is the *documentation* of a progression of events and creating available choices; the second is a *representation* of events and creating available choices. Looking more closely at this example consider how the content for each role is represented in the reading and acting out a role-play scenario in a simple two-dimensional (2D) environment.

In reading a role-play scenario the descriptions of all the roles are embedded in the text. The degree of detail on each role's specific characteristics and the description of the circumstance and situation are dependent up on the length and quality of the text. In a 2D environment this might include iconic or avatar representation of characters. These representations could contain a large amount of information about each character utilizing the methods of content distribution in games; for example, rollover text to indicate name, role, and status, a symbol above the head to indicate emotional reactions, or changes in appearance to indicate user progression. A role-playing scenario could integrate any number of visual representation combinations to create a complex story for each character.

Though the differences in design strategies can be compared without considering graphics, visual representation of content is a significant component of game design and the approach of representing information in visual content also demonstrates a unique design approach from which e-learning could benefit from.

Visual Representation of Content

The visual element of video games is a major feature for communicating content, creating a seamless game play experience where the player is challenged and progresses while "reading" the information being presented in graphics. Game designers balance the meaning of the graphics so that players are not required to pay attention to all of the information all of the time but must understand what the visual information means so the player is able to focus selectively. A well-designed game distributes and manages visual content to prevent overload while teaching the correct interpretations of visual information through game play. There are two aspects of designing visual content for game design that may be useful for e-learning. A well-designed game uses visual representation of content as objects to provide explicit and implicit information that help instruct players through game play. In addition, the visual content of a game consolidates large amounts of content into accessible pieces of information.

An analysis of how successful games have embedded complex content to be more easily accessible and made meaningful through graphical representations is evident in successful game play. A visual icon can represent simple or complex content but the player develops an understanding of the meaning of the icon through its relationship with other objects in its environment and through player interaction with the environment—game play. For example, in RPG games, character types can represent a wide range of detailed information; race, class, skill sets, attitudes, languages, etc. The level of detail and amount of information assigned to a character representation depends on the type of game play, for instance, an NPC that represents an ongoing quest line will have more detail than an NPC where only a single player interaction is required. The amount of information assigned is also tied to the objectives of the game. An avatar in a puzzle game may only act as a vehicle for communicating specific instruction to the player directly, like a coach. How much content is assigned to a visual object is determined by the purpose of the object and how it fits in game play.

Graphical representations can have a profound impact on how the user perceives, understands, and interacts with in-game content. For example, in Warhammer Online, the areas where the player is to complete quests are highlighted on the map in red so the player needs only to reference his or her map to determine next steps with little or no planning. In WoW, the in-game map does not have this feature and requires the player to read the quests and pay attention to story details contained within the quest log and strategize based on his understanding of the game as played thus far—a system that requires the player to be able to read between the lines or reference previous tasks completed (though there are also online materials that do this for players). Though different in design, it should be noted that the neither one nor the other is recommended as "better" but only different and the strategy of game play is affected, which emphasizes different game play and player experience.

Embedding content and information graphically also allows games to incorporate, literal representations of content as well as figurative representations of abstract concepts. This is an important feature of game design, harnessing the ability to communicate abstract concepts through visual medium. For example, in some RPGs, choosing to select or interact with a specific object/character may align the player with a faction who represents a specific ideology, impacting the remainder of the game. Objects within the context of the game environment can be assigned abstract meanings such as specific ideologies, but the definition of the object is only meaningful to the player if the context of the game and game play reinforces and supports it. This requires the player interactions to reflect the consequences and rewards of the objects' assigned meaning.

The visual representation of content also provides an opportunity to consolidate a large amount of information and make it easily accessible to the player. Objects do not have to be as complex as a character in an RPG; a lot of information can be embedded in an icon, but like the complex representations, the meaning of simple objects to the player is also defined in relation to the environment and other objects. Examination of any portion of game play reveals how much information is conveyed through visual objects and as a result how the design of visual information supports and reinforces the user experience through this content. For example, in some RPGs a single icon represents a single character action, such as casting a specific spell. A series of icons represent a collection of character actions, such as a different spell for each icon. In one situation, perhaps icon A and B should be used, in another situation icon A, C, and D should be used. Although the player knows what each icon stands for, it is only within the context of these situations and through the action of choice does the player develop a deeper understanding of what each icon means. If the player misunderstands or does not know the meaning of the icon, assuming that knowing what the icons mean is a key learning objective for game progression, then the player fails until they are able to demonstrate otherwise. This potential for failure ensures that the player has an accurate understanding of the purpose and meaning of the icons without having to provide an explicit explanation.

Player interaction reveals which objects within the environment are symbols and representations of content. These reusable objects become the sort of "language" players begin to understand and determine how they can interact with them. Looking at content as representational allows the designers to create interactions and relationship between the player and the game. By doing so, the conceptual relationships created by user interaction with objects within the game become the building blocks for creating meaningful game play. Graphics in video games are not only artistic interpretations and representations of the environment but also a method for communicating content to the player. Visual objects reinforce the narrative, represent an environment, represent actionable objects, and display cinematic sequences and animation. While there is a range of image fidelity to match the content of each game type the value of visual representation of content is in creating a consistent experience for the player.

To consider how game designers begin to think about the visual representation of information, we have to look more closely at the initial scoping and design phase. The initial game concept includes a description about how the game will play, what it will look like, and what the user experience will be. How these elements are supported technically is determined by what the available resources are. From the onset the type of graphical interface and types of interactions are integrated when considering the objectives or purpose of the game. This approach creates a virtual space that allows designers an ongoing opportunity to evaluate the best methods for representing and interacting with the game content. The process for deciding how and which information is represented is defined by the user experience.

Perhaps the biggest conceptual transition for e-learning designers is to envision the content and learning objectives through graphical imagery and user interactions rather than by explaining content through text. The practice of segmenting graphics, text, and media elements into individual contributing factors prevents the practice of designing a virtual space for user experience because to envision content in a virtual space is to define it as an object, set of objects, interactions, within an environment. For e-learning, visual objects are also knowledge objects, the learning objects of a course represented as an object, set of objects, or interactions within an environment. The purpose of the content and how it fits in with the rest of the course is defined by the learning objectives as well as how those learning objectives are demonstrated by the learner. The learner demonstration of content is game play; interactions with the content objects in specific situations within the context of an environment.

E-learning design can capture the meaning and intent of the learning objective within an abstract representation and strategically place meaning within the virtual environment. It requires designers to envision how the interaction with the object will create meaning for the player and how the designer can shape the desired outcome. Rather than telling the learner what they need to know, shaping instruction as a form of visual story telling with interactions allows the learner to engage and discover it.

Motivation

Player motivation in video games can be said to be successful because of a combination of qualities, not because of a single characteristic. A single game can provide different motivating qualities and still create a cohesive game experience, which engages a range of players who may be motivated by different qualities of play. User interactions, feedback mechanisms, and goals are three motivating elements that are found in games and e-learning but for which design practices differ. The method of how these three elements are designed in games may be transferable to e-learning and improve learner engagement.

How the player interacts with the game, game play, is a key component to creating and sustaining motivation. Games with clumsy or difficult UI inhibit continuous game play. Similarly, repetitive or insufficiently challenging tasks cause the player to lose interest just as rewards that are not meaningful or require too much work from the player may decrease player motivation. Designing interactions in game play encompasses how the player plays the game, the meaningfulness of the content, and how the player interacts with game content.

Mechanically, interactions are restricted by the parameters of the machine, console, handheld, or computer; for example, clicking buttons or moving a mouse. In a game, however, these mechanical actions mean something more, represented by the meaning and consequences of the players' choices. This player interaction consists of two things simultaneously: the mechanical, such as clicking the mouse button; the representational, the in-game result of selecting an object. The focus of the designer is how to make the later engaging, and to do so, requires making interactions meaningful.

Making meaningful interactions is the distinction between interacting with the machine and interacting with the virtual environment of the game, or diegetic and nondiegetic acts. To give interactions meaning, the objects, the context, and the consequences must tie back to the game objectives and present a challenge for the player in which his or her decision has an impact on the virtual environment. Increasing the number of these expressive player interactions increases the player's involvement in game play. For example, in the design of a real-time strategy (RTS) game, the factors that can be influenced by the player are determined by the objective of the game. In one RTS, food, natural resources, and military are three categories of content, each of which requires specific user interactions to manage the development. In another RTS, the food could be broken down to subcategories of different crops; natural resources could consist of subcategories of different types of resources, and the military could consist of subcategories of personnel. As a result specific player interactions are designed to manage the development of each subcategory within each category. The level of detail in content is transferred to the level of detail in player interaction and their consequences. Each interaction has a result, reward, or consequence relative to the meaning and context of the game. For example, if the purpose of the game was to build several societies, the single layer of categories is sufficient whereas too many subcategories would result in unmanageable and unnecessary level of detail. The result of player interaction is another motivating aspect of game play as it represents adaptive feedback. Interactions allow the player to be tested on his or her ability and understanding of not only game mechanics, but the overall game purpose, and specific game objects.

Feedback is the reinforcing component of player interactions and provides information to help the player make decisions and strategize game play. Successful feedback mechanisms convey information at the right degree of difficulty and within the context of game play. Inadequate or inappropriate feedback can be disruptive for game play and detract from the immersive qualities by making the game too difficult or cause confusion. Feedback takes many forms as a reward or deterrent, it can be in any mode or form of media, and it can occur in a quick moment or persist over time; and may have any form of technology assigned to it. An important characteristic of feedback, however, is that it is embedded in game play which does not interfere with game play but enhances and sustains it by creating informed choices for the player. Embedded feedback in game play can provide information unique to the choices and decisions the player has made, up to that point, or through a specific sequence, adapting to player interactions. Feedback can be embedded in the narrative and portrayed as communication between characters, it can appear in the form of an objective within a quest, or it can be the response of NPCs after interacting with the player. Guitar Hero and Rock Band are examples of one method of embedding feedback into game play. The player receives a continuous stream of graphical feedback based on her or his performance. When the performance is exceptionally good or bad, audio of the crowd cheering or jeering is added as additional indicators. This type of feedback also enables the experience that the player is interacting with the content and not just the machine, which contributes to creating an immersive and engaging environment.

How feedback is embedded into game play is one design method that demonstrates evidence of learning in video games. Feedback provides information to the player that prompts the player to make decisions and take action. What creates and sustains the immersive and engaging quality of player feedback in games is that it is embedded seamlessly into the content and game play for a fully integrated game experience. When designing feedback, the purpose is to provide information to the player that guides him or her to continued and sustainable game while allowing the opportunity to adjust strategy. In WoW, when players form groups to attack monsters, typically the group tries to keep the monster focused on the one player who can sustain the highest amount of damage (the tank). The monster stays focused on the tank through a few different tactics depending on group configuration, but sometimes during this interaction the monster loses focus on the tank and focuses the attack on another player; when this happens, the player who is now the focus of the monster's attack hears a specific sound that indicates the change. This sound was added to allow the player enough time to respond appropriately (perhaps to cease previous action to lose monster focus), because the visual cues did not provide enough information to the player in a timely manner. This type of feedback mechanism, without explicit explanation to the player of its function, clearly indicates a complex piece of content; indicating to the player there is a change in environment due to his or her actions and the player needs to figure out the appropriate response to avoid failure.

Another aspect of game play that contributes to increasing and sustaining player motivation are goals. Goals provide a sense of accomplishment, track progression, indicate increase in difficulty, and organize game content in the form of objectives. For the player, completing a goal creates a sense the player has made decisions and taken action which led to the successful completion; the goal must contain a challenge for the player to overcome. Goals are a means by which the player tracks progression and is able to see a history of accomplishments. This history of progression can be used for reflection as well as preparing and scaffolding content to more complex situations. Goals are also an organizational function which helps to group content according to the objectives of the game.

Goals are represented in many different forms and can be used simultaneously, such as scoring mechanism, gear, leveling, and actions, and can provide different types of motivation for different players. The flexibility of goals in games can change over time and through the course of game play providing an opportunity to motivate different players for different reasons in the same game. However, whatever the game design, goals, and subgoals contribute toward the end goal and the feedback provided enhances the player's experience to understand the context of the game.

One essential difference in motivation between e-learning and video games is required and voluntary participation. Mandatory e-learning courses are not uncommon and video games rarely, if ever, are considered a requirement. For required courseware, the consequence of forced rather than voluntary participation may have a significant drawback on the effectiveness of game design methods over traditional e-learning design. Learning that takes place in commercial video game play is voluntary and quickly abandoned without consequence by players if it proves not to be a good fit. E-learning, when considered from this perspective, may be at a disadvantage. However, given this difference in participation, there are conceptual shifts in perspective as it pertains to motivation from which e-learning design could benefit from. While designing user interactions within context, embedding feedback and goal-based instruction are not new concepts to e-learning, the approach in the design of these elements could improve learner engagement through increased motivation.

How the learner interacts with the content of an e-learning course has just as much impact on the learner as it does in games. The difference in approach is learner interactions often consist of clicking "next." Even interactions such as a drag-n-drop exercise are mechanical because the learner interaction is segmented from the rest of the content, not embedded in a continuous flow of interactions cohered by an overall objective. This produces a detrimental difference in the learner interpretation of the interactions; when not interacting with the content, the learner is interacting with the machine. In games, nondiegetic actions are balanced with diegetic acts depending on the type of content, this controls the degree to which the player is aware of his or her interaction with the machine as opposed to the content. Designing interactions that are motivating in games is more than just defining the mechanical requirements for completing a task; the design also defines what the task means in the context of the virtual environment and the impact of the task to the player.

Reorganizing the content configuration of e-learning and designing content for the purpose of learner interaction may produce the same results, moving the learner focus away from machine acts and toward the interaction and understanding of the content and objectives. In practice, e-learning design often limits the participant's choices, rather than maximizing them, as it is feared that more choices will detract from the learning objectives. However, by limiting user interactions with the content, the learning may also be less effective because the opportunity for the learner to understand the content through interacting with the content is reduced. By increasing learner interactions there is also an opportunity to improve engagement and motivation. However, just as with games, adding disjointed and nonmeaningful interactions for the sake of interacting does not support the overall objective of a game or a course and is not representative of good design sense. Like games, the learning objectives are self-referential and the interactions should relate to the meaning and purpose of the content. In following this approach of content development through interactions, game designers have successfully managed to create an environment where the learning objectives of the game, if designed well, are transferred to the player.

Without reexamining the manner in which learners interact with the content of the course, feedback will remain to be designed as a mechanical feature of e-learning. Feedback in e-learning is typically explicit and takes the form of an assessment, praise, or coaching and is another segment of the course separate from the content. Separating feedback from content as a means of *correcting* learners' choices does not help create an immersive and engaging environment. Integrating feedback as a means of *communicating consequences* enables the learner to determine the correctness of his or her choices—thereby learning which the right choice was without having to be told so explicitly. If the same type of feedback used in games, could be used in e-learning to communicate the consequences of choices, it would in turn allow the learner to achieve a sense of accomplishment by completing challenges based on his or her problem-solving ability.

Lastly, goals in e-learning are often a direct representation of learning objectives just as goals in games are directly related the purpose of the game. However in games, goals are presented as problems to be solved, and the necessary information required to solve each goal is integrated into game play rather than submitted to the player as facts to be learned. Goal-based instruction for e-learning should be very much the same, constructing circumstances in which the learner must demonstrate acquired necessary knowledge in order to successfully complete the goal. In this type of design, the learner discovers the information required to complete the goal through interaction with the content within the context of the virtual environment. This allows the learners to demonstrate their knowledge in context and focus on accomplishing specific tasks that can progress the learner through increasing levels of difficulty. The conceptual shift for designing goals in e-learning design is connected to the manner in which content is represented and interactions are designed.

Conclusion

We examined game design methodologies of treating content through the lens of e-learning in an effort to garner a design perspective that might improve the quality and effectiveness of e-learning courseware. Examining game design methods enables e-learning designers to make a conceptual shift from how content is segmented and organized based on classroom- or instructor-led design to designing integrated content in a virtual space. This includes reconsidering the emphasis on user-centered design practices, integrating content into learner experiences, the visual representation of content in e-learning, and the motivational aspects related to content.

The shift toward user-centered design extends beyond learning objectives. In a game design process, *how* the learner experiences the game is just as important as *what* the player needs to know. E-learning focused on instructor or teacher-centered design, where *what* the learner needs to know is designed as a presentation, not as an experience. Therefore, the typical focus is on reducing the options for *how* the learner experiences the content through the perspective of the instructor/teacher. De-emphasizing the learner experience further inhibits the learner from experiencing potential engaging or immersive qualities of the course.

Content organization is another shift that may improve learner engagement and e-learning effectiveness. The common practice of segmenting content into distinct chunks of information and removing it from context may be influenced, in part, by the infrastructures that support e-learning courses, such as Learning Content Management Systems (LCMS). Segmenting and separating content for an LCMS allows institutions to organize and track courseware but also to organize the content in the courses for repurposing and rapid production with minimal rework. This method undercuts creating course content in context and reduces the options for creating engaging environments because it limits the amount and type of learner's interactions with the content. The reduction of learner options for various modes of interacting within the course also eliminates different ways of receiving information, thereby reducing the challenge—in short, e-learning minimizes the manner in which learners interact and receive information from the course. In game design an immersive and engaging environment requires a process which integrates content to create context and continuity, recognizing that oversegmented content reduces expressive acts of the player and therefore inhibits engagement.

In order to attain an integrated contextual environment, much of the content is represented visually, as objects defined by their relationship with other objects. Visual representation of content allows the player to perceive interacting with the environment and not just the machine. Visual representation can also consolidate and communicate complex amounts of information succinctly and quickly. With the appropriate course content e-learning may be able to improve engagement and learning effectiveness by shifting content design approaches toward visual representations instead of text-based interactions.

Lastly, the motivational features related to content include the types and frequency of interactions, the type of feedback mechanisms, and designing goals.

While including these elements is not a new feature for e-learning, designing them using game design methods is another example of a conceptual shift for designing content. Increasing the number and type of interactions the learner has with the content and embedding feedback within the goals enhances problem solving and encourages the learner's ability to learn content.

The concepts presented here are intended to prompt consideration between the differences in design methodologies and outline methods that can improve the quality of e-learning. These methods for creating more engaging and immersive e-learning require a shift away from traditional e-learning design methodologies and adopting the method of experiential learning inherent in game design. This shift also includes designing a virtual environment rather than discrete pages and focusing on user experience by placing instructional value on the objects, the relationships of objects for creating context, and user interactions within the environment. By comparing the design choices between e-learning and games, designers and developers can discover which decisions increase the likelihood of building an effective and engaging e-learning course that utilizes the full capabilities of the medium.

References

Age of Empires. (1997). Ensemble Studios, Microsoft Game Studios.

Apperley, T. H. (2006). Genre and game studies: Toward a critical approach to video game genres. *Simulation & Gaming*, *37*(1), 6–23.

Bejeweled. (2001). PopCap Games.

Bogost, I. (2006). *Unit operations: An approach to videogame criticism*. Cambridge, MA: MIT Press.

Clark, R., & Mayer, R. E. (2007). *E-learning and the science of instruction: Proven guidelines for consumers and designers of multimedia learning*. San Francisco: Pfeiffer.

Crawford, C. (1982). *The art of computer game design*. Retrieved 2008, from http://www.vancouver.wsu.edu/fac/peabody/game-book/Coverpage.html.

Dewey, J. (1916). *Democracy and education*. New York: The Free Press.

Everquest II. (2004). Sony Online Entertainment.

Frasca, G. (2003). Simulation versus Narrative: Introduction to Ludology. In M. J. Wolf and B. Perron, (Eds.), *Video game theory reader* (pp. 221–235). New York: Routledge.

Gaber, J. (2007). Simulating planning: SimCity as a pedagogical tool. *Journal of Planning Education and Research*, *27*(2), 113–121.

Galloway, A. R. (2006). *Gaming: Essays on algorithmic culture*. Minneapolis, MN: University of Minnesota Press.

Gee, J. P. (2003). *What video games have to teach us about learning and literacy*. New York: Palgrave Macmillan.

Gee, J. P. (2005). Learning by design: Good video games as learning machines. *E-learning*, *2*(1), 5–16.

Guitar Hero. (2006). Activision.

Juul, J. (2005). *Half-real: Video games between real rules and fictional worlds*. Cambridge: The MIT Press.

Neverwinter Nights: Shadows of Undrentide. (2003). Infogrames/Atari, MacSoft.

Piskurich, G. M. (2000). *Rapid Instructional design: Learning ID fast and right*. San Francisco: Pfeiffer.

Prensky, M. (2001). Digital natives, digital immigrants. *From On the Horizon*, *9*, 5.

Prensky, M. (2003). Digital game-based learning. *ACM Computers in En-tertainment, 1*, 1–4.
Prensky, M. (2008, November–December). The role of technology. *Educational Technology*. Retrieved January 2009, from http://www.marcprensky.com/writing/Prensky-The_Role_of_Technology-ET-11-12-08.pdf
Rankin, Y., McNeal, M., Shute, M. W., & Gooch, B. (2008). *User centered game design: Evaluating massive multiplayer online role playing games for second language acquisition*. 2008 ACM SIGGRAPH symposium on Video games (pp. 43–49). Los Angeles, USA.
Rock Band. (2007). Electronic Arts Studios.
Rollings, A., & Adams, E. (2003). *Andrew rollings and Ernest Adams on game design*. Berkeley, CA: New Riders.
Rollings, A., & Morris, D. (2004). *Game architecture and design: A new edition*. Indianapolis, IN: New Riders.
Shaffer, D. W., Squire, K. R., Halverson, R., & Gee, J. P. (2004). *Video games and the future of learning*. Retrieved 2008, from Academic ADL Co-Lab: http://www.academiccolab.org/resources/gappspaper1.pdf.
The Elder Scrolls IV: Oblivion. (2006). Bethesda Game Studios, 2 K Games, Bethesda Softworks.
The Sims. (2000). Electronic Arts.
Trauma Center: Second Opinion. (2006). Atlus.
Turkle, S. (1994). Construction and reconstructions of self in virtual re-ality: Playing in the MUDs. *Mind, Culture, and Activity, 1*(3), 158–167.
Warhammer Online. (2008). Electronic Arts.
World of Warcraft. (2004). Blizzard Entertainment.

Part II
Computers and New Science of Learning

Chapter 10
Redesigning Testing: Operationalizing the New Science of Learning

Zachary Stein[1,2], Theo Dawson[1], and Kurt W. Fischer[2]

[1] Developmental Testing Service, LCC, Northampton, MA, USA; Harvard University Graduate School of Education, Cambridge, MA, USA, e-mail: zas456@mail.harvard.edu
[2] Harvard University Graduate School of Education, Cambridge, MA, USA

Introduction: Testing

Every year, across the globe, tens of millions of children, adolescents, and adults from all walks of life take tests. In the USA, students may take anywhere from six to twenty standardized tests on their way from kindergarten to college, not counting the numerous summative and formative assessments employed by teachers. Imagine a high school student in Massachusetts who sits down to take a standardized test that will ultimately determine both her chances of graduation and the standing of her school. She participates in a large, complex, and polycentric educational testing infrastructure that transcends local, state, national, and international borders. At all points there are overlapping networks of connections with industry, government, and research. This international testing infrastructure is an unprecedented state of affairs, representing both a vast and incomparable example of "applied psychology" and a crucial force shaping educational systems. The goal of this chapter is to begin to reflect on this state of affairs, bring key issues to light, and report on specific avenues of research and design for building a new type of educational testing infrastructure that will bring greater benefit to greater numbers by serving more diverse purposes and populations.

The current state of educational testing is the outcome of a complex history of educational research, practice, and policy. In the first section we draw out key themes from this history, framing the discussions to follow. Tests and assessments have always been a necessary aspect of most educational situations—being part of the conversation between teacher, student, and curriculum. As broad social and cultural trends toward mass schooling emerged, educational practice began to assimilate the outputs of a newly professionalized psychology, fostering the development

Z. Stein (✉)
Developmental Testing Service, LCC, Northampton, MA, USA; Harvard University Graduate School of Education, Cambridge, MA, USA
e-mail: zas456@mail.harvard.edu

M.S. Khine, I.M. Saleh (eds.), *New Science of Learning*,
DOI 10.1007/978-1-4419-5716-0_10, © Springer Science+Business Media, LLC 2010

of a specific type of testing infrastructure. This late-modern approach to testing is relatively isolated from research about learning, emphasizing the use of tests as sorting mechanisms, and neglecting the use of tests as educative aids. More recently, in the USA in particular, this approach to testing has been wedded to sweeping educational policies mandating specific high-stakes uses, which has put testing at the center of many debates about schooling. This heightened awareness leads us to suggest that *now is the time* to ask foundational questions about what today's tests measure and how they are used.

In the second section, we begin a response to these foundational questions, suggesting that a testing infrastructure based on research into the nature of learning will be better able to meet the challenges facing educational systems in the twenty-first century. Arguments from a variety sources propose that the new science of learning should be at the heart of efforts to redesign testing infrastructures. Moreover, given the rapidly changing conditions to which educational institutions must respond, the values that shape test reform efforts should transcend outdated dichotomies about the function of testing and the purposes of education—moving beyond unproductive either/or commitments: either tests as sorting mechanisms or tests as educative aids; either tests of competencies or tests of content; either tests to train the work force or tests to foster reflective citizens. Tests should be based on research about how students learn and guided by explicit commitments to reshaping schools in positive new directions.

In the third and fourth sections, we outline our approach to test development, wherein new computer-based tools are wedded to advances in psychometrics and cognitive developmental psychology, thus bringing the new science of learning to bear in the design of a broad and flexible testing infrastructure that is both standardized and formative. For decades research in cognitive development has focused on the diverse *learning sequences* that characterize the acquisition of knowledge, capabilities, or skills. Recently, in the wake of Fischer's *Dynamic Skill Theory*, a common or general scale has been built, which can be used to research and understand development and learning along an almost endless variety of different learning sequences. The *Lectical™ Assessment System* is a psychometrically refined measure of this general scale, allowing for reliable and valid assessments of student performance and the concomitant construction of empirically grounded learning sequences. The *DiscoTest™ Initiative* embodies our general approach to test design, which combines this approach to researching and measuring learning—wherein diverse learning sequences can be understood in terms of a common scale—with advances in computer-based tools. The result is a radically new approach to testing, an approach that could form the foundation for *a mass customized testing infrastructure* that provides all the benefits of embedded, formative tests, with the kind objectivity and validity that are desirable in standardized tests. Moreover, as discussed in the conclusion, this new approach to test design reframes what is considered possible and preferable for the future of the testing infrastructures that shape educational institutions.

Historical Preamble: The Broad Function of Testing and the Birth of a Specific Testing Industry

Education, broadly construed, serves a basic function in fostering crucial skills and dispositions in younger generations, thus enabling the continuity and reconstruction of social structures and cultural traditions (Dewey, 1916; Habermas, 1984). Comparative psychology suggests that sustained and explicit teaching and learning are unique to our species. While some other species pass on acquired techniques, some argue that no other species fundamentally depends on mechanisms of cultural transmission to foster the maturity of its members (Tomasello, 1999). In a definitive way, to be human is to be educated. Importantly, educational processes of almost any type depend upon assessments, or tests.[1]

Tests, broadly construed, serve a basic educational function. They are a necessary part of a dialogue between the student, the teacher, and what is being taught. For as long as *Homo sapiens sapiens* has existed there have always been students and teachers because there have always been things to be taught. Thus, there have always been tests. Even before the invention of schooling, informal and formal tests of all kinds were used for educational purposes, from the passing on of food-procuring practices and culture-specific skills to apprentice workshops and religious training (Cremin, 1970). In order for teachers to provide instruction or guidance they must understand what the student has understood so far. How else can the teacher know what the student needs to learn next? Testing is one primary way that the intergenerational interactions constituting cultural transmission become explicitly and reflectively educative. Thus the use of tests to "measure" student understanding has a long history. Yet, as discussed below, questions of what is worth measuring have not figured prominently in modern test design.

After the invention of schooling, formal testing itself became an explicit component of educational systems of various sizes and types. As testing became explicit its uses became more varied. Classically, public debates and oral exams came to supplement ongoing educative assessments, serving to determine if students had learned sufficiently to assume the roles in society they were being trained to fill (e.g., the priesthood). Proficiency in reading and writing became a focus of testing as some elite segments of the population came to value and require literacy. Thus, early on, beyond serving as an educative aid, formal testing infrastructures came to

---

[1] Throughout this chapter we use the terms *test* and *assessment* somewhat interchangeably, more commonly using the former. Both terms are rich with connotations and there are liabilities accompanying the use of either. We feel that *testing* better conveys a formalized educational process, whereas *assessment* is a more general and ambiguous term, which includes research instruments and various noneducative measurements of capability. We realize that our usage of these terms cuts against the grain of some aspects of common usage, but we desire to redeem *testing* from its status as a term of derision.

function as mechanisms serving social goals and perpetuating specific social structures. The use of tests as sorting mechanisms has a long history, and the privileging of this usage is a key theme in modern test design.

The birth of democracies fueled ambitions for large-scale public educational systems, and the emergence of these institutions coincided with the emergence of psychology as a discipline (Karier, 1986). This is a coincidence of no small import in the history of testing. Around the turn of the twentieth century, psychologically informed testing procedures proliferated, spawning the field of psychometrics and the preliminary use of intelligence testing to administer mass schooling in France (Lagemann, 2000). Knowledge of IQ testing broke into public awareness during World War I, as the US Armed Forces pioneered large-scale administrative applications of psychological testing—applications that were immediately adopted for educational use (Sokal, 1990). Despite the lamentable misuses of IQ testing due to its ties to eugenics (Gould, 1981), by the end of World War II the Educational Testing Service had been founded, and our contemporary standardized educational testing infrastructure was beginning to take shape (Lemann, 1999).

The contemporary educational scene in most industrialized countries is dominated by a specific type of standardized testing infrastructure (Hursh, 2008; National Research Council, 2001). This is an infrastructure that has been shaped by the demands of rapidly growing public education systems with unprecedented influxes of students being educated for unprecedented amounts of time. Today's tests were built during radical social transformations that brought to light dire inequalities of educational opportunity and accomplishment. And, for the most part, the recent architects of our testing infrastructure have been adamant proponents of the fair distribution of educational opportunities and well aware of the important social function to be performed by the tests they designed (Lemann, 1999; Sokal, 1990).

However, our current testing infrastructure has been shaped by specific psychometric techniques and psychological commitments, criticized by one authority as "the application of twentieth century statistics to nineteenth century psychology" (Mislevy, 1993, p. 19). Moreover, this approach to psychological testing has always neglected the educative function of tests and emphasized their use as sorting mechanisms for allotting future educational opportunities and conferring credentials (Chapman, 1988). The use of tests as sorting mechanisms allows the testing infrastructure to serve a broad public function in overseeing social role allocation. Thus, what now exists is an infrastructure built and run by private companies but serving a public function (Lemann, 1999). This has led to concerns about the existence of a standardized testing industrial complex and other sociopolitical criticism of the testing industry, from inflammatory exposés (Nairn, 1980) to more carefully reasoned calls for reform (Hursh, 2008).

In the USA this testing industry has been coupled to legislative injunctions resulting in the near universal use of high-stakes tests, which serve as both accountability measures for schools and graduation requirements for students (Hess & Petrilli, 2006; NRC, 1999). This nationally mandated use of a specific form of testing in K-12 education represents a radical departure from prior US educational policy, which had traditionally left control of test use and design up to state and local officials. These recent developments have increasingly brought testing into the center of national debates about education. In particular, the Obama administration has drawn attention to the liabilities of the contemporary testing infrastructure—in both its specific details and broad impacts (Obama, 2008; White House, 2009).

Teaching to the tests as they currently exits means preparing students for life as if it were a set of multiple-choice questions. It would seem that the time is ripe for seriously questioning the foundations of our testing infrastructure, asking a series of very basic questions: *What is being measured with today's tests? What should be measured? How are today's tests being used? How should they be used?*

Reflecting on Testing: The Need for a Theory of Learning and Clarity About Values

Although it may not be apparent at first, questions about what we are measuring with tests and how they should be used hinge upon the way we conceive the nature of *learning* (NRC, 2001). The criticism of contemporary tests as the application of advanced statistics in service of simplistic psychology is to the point. In order to use tests effectively and knowledgeably, we need to understand the meaning of the score a student receives. Does a score mean something about a capability or trait processed by the student, or does it simply let us know how the student performs on a specific set of questions in relation to group averages? The latter claim—given that it remains strictly descriptive, positing no explanation for the score (e.g., IQ) or prescription for changing it—does not entail beliefs about specific psychological constructs; the former does.

Claiming that a test score reflects an underlying capability or trait—be it an aptitude, skill, or disposition—entails certain views about these psychological phenomena. More specifically, using such a claim about the meaning of a test score to guide actions, such as doling out remediation or rewards, entails some theory of *learning*. Imagine again the high school student from Massachusetts taking a standardized test. The use to which her scores will be put—determining graduation eligibility and school standing or quality—imply that the capabilities being assessed are the result of her individual effort and the school environment. That is, they assume a theory—however implicit—about how the capability being measured changes over time as a result of certain factors. Roughly speaking, theories about how psychological phenomena undergo change are theories of learning or development (Reisberg, 2001). Different theories of learning will give the same test score different meanings, and different theories of learning result in different forms of test design (NRC, 2001; see Fig. 10.1). Moreover, a test built without an explicit theory of learning—as many tests are—can serve only very limited functions.

For example, most standardized tests, like the one taken by the Massachusetts student, can serve *only* as sorting mechanisms because they are built without reference to an explicit theory of learning. No doubt, they are reliably and objectively measuring *something*, but it is unclear how this "something" relates to the

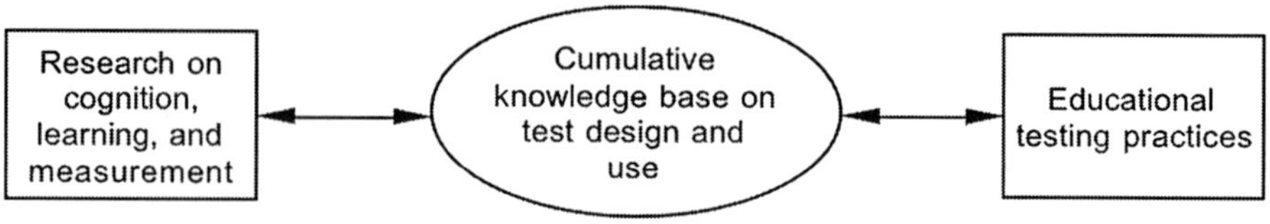

Fig. 10.1 Connections between research, test design, and practice. Adapted from National Research Council (2001, p. 295)

learning process. Thus, tests not carefully wedded to a theory of learning can be used to classify students and schools, to sort them, but such tests cannot be used as educative aids, because they provide no insight into the learning process per se. On the other hand, building tests around an explicit theory of learning increases the range of functions the test can serve, for example, allowing for insight into what a student has learned and could most benefit from learning next.

Contemporary theories of learning have become increasingly sophisticated due to advances in cognitive science and neuroscience. Likewise, advances in psychometrics have made it possible to reliably and validly measure a wider range of dynamic and meaningful constructs. As alluded to in the historical section above, the contemporary testing infrastructure, and the uses to which it is put, reflect these advances only in a very limited way, if at all. The rest of this chapter is devoted to outlining one approach that pulls together advances in the new science of learning and psychometrics to retool test design and educational practice.

Fischer's *Dynamic Skill Theory* (Fischer & Bidell, 2006) provides a comprehensive and empirically grounded approach to human development and learning. This approach has fostered methods for building empirically grounded learning sequences in a variety of domains, which can be aligned along a common underlying developmental dimension. This underlying dimension has been operationalized as a psychometrically refined metric, known as *The Lectical Assessment System* (the LAS: Dawson, 2008), which has been used to build unique and richly educative tests that are both standardized and customizable to different curricular frameworks (Dawson & Stein, 2008). The *Discotest Initiative* is the name given to our efforts in this direction. Below we discuss this approach to redesigning standardized testing infrastructures based on the new sciences of learning; we explain why it should be seen as a valuable alternative to the infrastructures currently in place.

However, the value of different testing infrastructures should not be determined solely on the basis of the manner in which they wed research about learning with test design and educational practices. Decisions must be made about the general shape of the educational system and the role that ought to be played by even the best-designed tests. These decisions are fundamentally evaluative. They touch on some of our broadest goals and commitments about how schooling fits into a shared vision of the good life and just society. Typically, a set of classic dichotomies have been used to frame this discussion: Should tests be used to sort individuals and make high-stakes decisions or should tests be embedded in the curricula as educative aids? Should tests assess broad competencies or specific knowledge? Should tests help us in training the workforce or in fostering critically minded citizens?

Below, we will show that these are false dichotomies. Advances in test design allow for a reevaluation of what is generally considered as possible and preferable for mass education and its testing infrastructure. After discussing the approach we have adopted for designing tests based on the new science of learning, we will return to some of the broad evaluative questions and discuss how we understand the implications of these innovations.

Advances in Developmental Science and the Birth of the DiscoTest Initiative

James Mark Baldwin (1906) was the first psychologist to offer a complex view of human development in which a variety of different *learning sequences* unfold across qualitatively distinct developmental levels. This set an important agenda for development science, wherein a *learning sequence* is defined as an empirically grounded reconstruction of the levels or phases undergone during the acquisition of a specific capability, concept, or understanding. Decades after Baldwin, Heinz, Werner (1957) and Jean Piaget (1932) would also offer theories of human development in which learning sequences figured prominently. Eventually, Kohlberg (1984) would build learning sequences in the moral domain, King and Kitchener (1994) in reflective judgment, Case (1992) in several knowledge areas, Watson and Fischer (1980) for social roles, and Siegler (1981) in mathematics, with many others following suit. For over a century researchers have been creating new methods and building empirically grounded models of specific learning sequences in a wide variety of domains. This general approach to researching development and learning continues to produce knowledge, with an increasing focus on individual differences and educational implications (Stein, 2009).

As a part of this tradition, Fischer's *Dynamic Skill Theory* (Fischer, 1980; Fischer & Bidell, 2006) has added a generative set of methods and concepts useful for researching and modeling learning sequences. First outlined in the 1980s, the General Skill Scale (Fig. 10.2) is the backbone of the general approach. The Skill Scale is a model of the basic structural transformations characteristic of skill development and has been empirically refined in light of decades of research. Importantly, in this context the term *skill* should be taken in a very general sense, as the basic or generic unit of psychological process. All skills are richly multidimensional, intrinsically involving emotion, cognition, context, and social support. Skills are built actively and dynamically by individuals in specific contexts and they are built hierarchically, with more complex ones transcending but including less complex ones. As individuals build unique skills in different domains, learning sequences unfold across the different tiers and levels: *actions* lay the groundwork for concrete *representations*, which serve eventually as the basis for the construction of *abstractions*. Within each tier, there is a series of levels, as the basic skill-type (action, representation, or abstraction) is coordinated into increasingly complex forms of organized behavior.

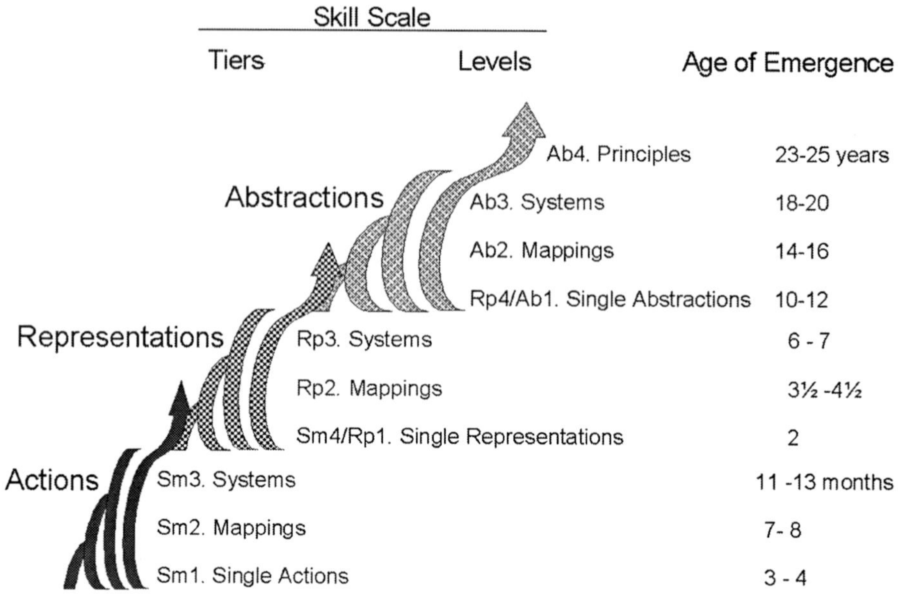

Fig. 10.2 Developmental scale for skill levels and tiers

Thus the Skill Scale is a model of the developmental dimension underlying the learning sequences that comprise development in almost all domains. This model has been used to guide researchers in their analysis of behaviors and performances, informing the dissection of the skill structure and thus locating performances along the developmental continuum specified by the general Skill Scale—a technique known as Skill Analysis. Analyzing the structure of diverse performances as they unfold over time in a given domain allows for the inductive reconstruction of learning sequences in that domain. This general technique has been used in a variety of domains, including mathematics (Fischer, Hand, & Russell, 1984), reflective judgment (Kitchener & Fischer, 1990), and self-in relationship (Fischer & Kennedy, 1997). Research informed by the Skill Scale has been paralleled by research involving comparable frameworks (Case, 1992; Commons, Trudeau, Stein, Richards, & Krause, 1998), which has reinforced the idea that the Skill Scale represents an important underlying developmental dimension.

Importantly, this research tradition has focused in large part on the diversity and dynamism of human development. Thus, the emerging consensus regarding a common scale should not be seen as a reworking of the simple ladder-like, growth-to-goodness models of development offered in the 1960s and 1970s. Instead, learning sequences are understood as sets of diverse pathways, which individuals traverse in unique ways—often toward common goals (Fischer & Bidell, 2006). Of course, some researchers have constructed learning sequences to serve as ideal types—simplifying the dynamics of development into set of static level descriptions. These idealizations can be useful only insofar as they frame an understanding of how individual learners work, *in medias res*, to construct unique paths through this empirically grounded but ideally represented space. Thus, focusing on individual differences does not entail neglecting invariance. The general Skill Scale represents an important confluence of research concerning certain invariant processes underlying the diversity and variability of real human learning in context.

In the wake of this confluence of research, Dawson (2008) confirmed the existence of a developmental dimension underlying a wide variety of learning sequences by applying a set of psychometric techniques. This resulted in a refinement of the basic principles of Skill Analysis—along with other comparable developmental assessment systems—and the construction of the most psychometrically validated and reliable developmental assessment system to date, the LAS. The LAS has been used to systemize the construction of learning sequences out of both longitudinal and cross-sectional data sets (Dawson-Tunik, 2004). This process for building learning sequences involves a three-step iterative method (described in detail elsewhere: Dawson-Tunik, 2004; Dawson & Stein, 2008).

Dynamic Skill Theory and the *Lectical Assessment System* represent fundamental advances both our understanding of learning and our methods for studying and measuring it. Importantly, the ability to build learning sequences about specific topics using a psychometrically sophisticated instrument allows for a radically new approach to test design. The DiscoTest Initiative seeks to build a new testing infrastructure around the basic advances provided by this broad approach to understanding and researching learning. Before getting into the details of how DiscoTests are built and used, we will briefly explain the guiding insights and goals.

As explained above, tests should be built around actual research into how students learn (NRC, 2001). The systematic construction of focused learning sequences provides valuable insight into student learning processes by allowing for a general characterization of the range of possible conceptions—the steps along the way from less sophisticated to more sophisticated understandings. This allows for tests that can place any given student performance in relation to the range of possible performances, and thus gives insight into what the student currently understands and what the student is likely to benefit from learning next. These tests can be integrated with curricula that are also informed by empirically grounded learning sequences, which also can provide the basis for richly educative feedback. Moreover, because the learning sequences are built around a psychometrically refined general metric, a test that is scored on that metric also serves as a standardized measure of student performance. Thus, the goal of the DiscoTest initiative is to build standardized tests that can be customized to different curricula and built around empirical research into how students learn, providing both educative feedback and psychometrically reliable scores.

DiscoTest: Building the Computer-Based Educational Testing Infrastructure of Tomorrow

The DiscoTest Initiative is a nonprofit, research-oriented effort to develop free, valid, reliable, standardized, and educative assessments of key skills and concepts.

These assessments can easily be embedded in curricula and can be employed without extensive training to track student development in classrooms, schools, districts, or nations. Each DiscoTest (also called a *teaser*—short for *brain teaser*) is developed by a team of researchers, content experts, and teachers who have come together as peers to study the development of a "big idea" or core skill (e.g., the physics of energy, conservation of matter, algebraic thinking, the scientific method, reflective judgment, leadership, or ethical reasoning) and then use the results to describe learning sequences for important concepts. These learning sequences are then used to inform curricula and construct low-inference scoring rubrics for one or more teasers.

The overarching objective of the DiscoTest Initiative is to contribute to the development of optimal learning environments by creating assessments that deliver the kind of educative feedback that learners need for optimal learning. Assessments of this kind determine where students are in their individual learning trajectories and provide feedback that points toward the next incremental step toward mastery. They function as standardized formative assessments.

Building tests with these qualities requires an entirely new approach—one that is discursive and iterative, bringing together educators, researchers, and domain experts as equal partners. The name "Disco" was chosen for this initiative because it is the Latin root of *discourse*. Coincidentally, it also evokes the image of joyful kinesthetic interactions with music, an image that sits well with the notion that learning is fun.

Naming the Disco initiative was the least of many challenges. Here are a few others: DiscoTests:

1. must be grounded in solid empirical evidence about the ways in which students learn specific concepts and skills. (To accomplish this goal, Dawson developed a new set of research and test development methods.)
2. must be composed of intriguing items that allow students to show how they think about what they have learned, rather than simply demonstrating that they can get a "right" answer.
3. must not waste students' time. In other words, every interaction with a DiscoTest must be a useful learning experience, and all DiscoTests must function as an integral part of the curriculum.
4. must provide students, teachers, and parents with a record of learning in which each milestone is meaningfully connected to specific knowledge and skills.
5. must have a long shelf-life, which implies that (1) they are of enduring importance and that (2) it should be very difficult to cheat on them, and (3) they should used in ways that make it seem pointless to cheat on them.
6. must provide data that researchers can use to continually refine our understanding of learning.

Although it is not possible to provide a detailed account of our approach to all of these challenges within the context of a brief chapter, in this section we show how several of them are addressed through the DiscoTest Initiative and the design of DiscoTests. First we describe the tests and how they are scored. Then we describe how we build them, and how they can be used.

Anatomy of a DiscoTest. Because teasers are designed to be tests in the sense described above, they must (1) provide students with an opportunity to engage in meaningful action on their knowledge and (2) offer useful feedback. These requirements forced us to rule out multiple choice items like the one shown in Fig. 10.3. This item asks the student to select one of five possible responses. There is one right answer. The other answers are intended to represent common misconceptions held by students. A number of assumptions accompany items of this kind. For example, it is assumed that students who get an item right either (1) know the answer or (2) have made a good guess. Also, it is generally assumed that students who get an item right without guessing know more than students who get an item wrong. If these assumptions held, items of this kind might provide information that could inform accurate feedback—but the assumptions do not hold.

Students who select the right answer (b) do so for several different reasons, many of which reflect partial knowledge or misunderstanding. Here are some of the explanations students have given for choosing the correct answer to the item in the example:

1. The right pan will not move because the amount of matter in a closed container remains the same no matter what chemical or physical changes take place (textbook response, could be memorized).
2. The right pan will not move because a gas was formed but nothing was destroyed (answer showing partial understanding).
3. The right pan will not move because not even bubbles can get out of a jar that is closed tight (answer showing that the student believed the jar was closed really tight).
4. The right pan will not move because the gas does not have any weight (answer showing partial understanding).
5. The right pan will not move because in a chemical reaction, atoms rearrange to make new substances, but none of them are destroyed (answer showing greatest level of understanding).

This phenomenon, which has been described by numerous researchers (Sadler, 2000), strongly suggests that multiple choice items are unlikely to provide the kind of information required to inform educative feedback. Sadler has shown how multiple-choice tests can be used more effectively, but multiple choice items, no matter how well they are constructed, still limit the learning functions of an assessment. Consequently, DiscoTests are composed of items that are open-ended and require short essay responses consisting of judgments and justifications that not only show (1) what students know, but also (2) how they understand what they know, and (3) how they can use their knowledge to deal with similar tasks and situations. The item in Fig. 10.3, stripped of its multiple-choice options, can function as a DiscoTest item, as shown in Fig. 10.4.

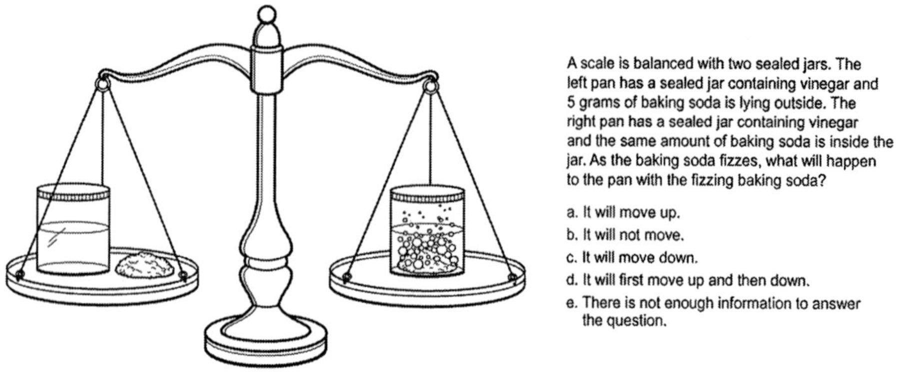

Fig. 10.3 Multiple choice vinegar and baking soda item

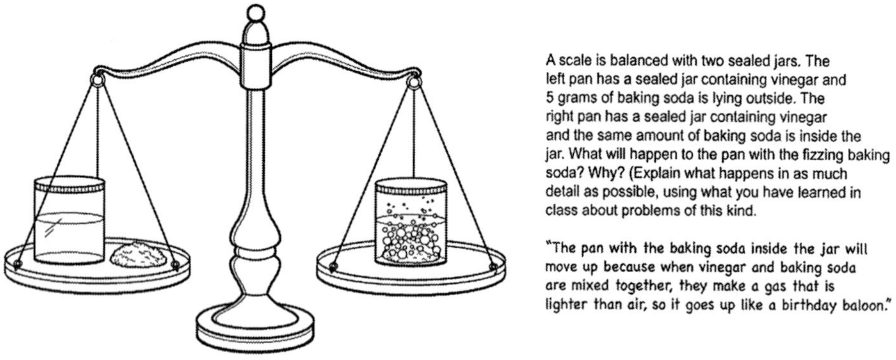

Fig. 10.4 Open-ended vinegar and baking soda item

Teasers are commonly composed of 5–7 items of this kind, which provide information that cannot be provided by multiple-choice items. For example, they can help teachers answer questions like the following:

1. What concepts is this student working with?
2. How does she understand these concepts?
3. What is her line of reasoning?
4. How well does she explain her thinking?

In addition to helping students consolidate new knowledge, items of this kind provide an opportunity to hone essential life skills like reasoning and writing.

Scoring and reports. After students submit their responses to a set of teaser items, they are directed to a coding page on which they are asked to match their own responses to options in a series of "pull-down" menus. These menus function as *low-inference* rubrics, and can be used effectively by students, teachers, and researchers.

For example, the following choices are offered in one of the coding menus for the item shown in Fig. 10.4:

- none of the codes are like statements made in this response
- the right pan will move because more (or less) stuff is in it
- the right pan will not move because nothing can get out
- the right pan will move because of something that happens when baking soda is mixed with vinegar
- the right pan will not move because nothing is created or destroyed
- the right pan will not move because new molecules have formed but the number of atoms is the same
- the right pan will not move because the mass of a closed system stays the same, no matter what kind of chemical reaction or state change takes place

Students simply choose the response that most closely matches their own. For students, coding is an important part of the learning process, because it allows them to reflect upon their own performances in light of a range of response options.

After their coding selections are submitted, students are redirected to a report that (1) portrays their score on Fischer's General Skill Scale (also known as the Lectical™ Scale), (2) describes what their performance suggests about their current level of understanding, and (3) provides suggestions for developmentally appropriate learning activities. (Examples can be viewed at DiscoTest.org.) In addition to viewing individual reports, students who have taken an assessment on multiple occasions can track their own developmental progress by viewing a figure that shows how their thinking has developed over time.

Of course, teachers can also code teasers, which provides students with an expert perspective on their performances and helps build teachers' knowledge about how students learn particular concepts and skills. Teachers can view individual student reports and classroom profiles that show the distribution of scores relative to the General Skill Scale.[2]

Uses of DiscoTests. In the classroom, DiscoTest teasers can be used in a number of ways. They can be used to assess students' preinstruction knowledge or stimulate student interest in a new subject area. They also can be used during or following instruction to (1) test how well students understand new ideas, (2) stimulate class discussion, and (3) help students integrate new concepts into their existing knowledge. They can be taken by single students, groups of students, or the entire class, and can be scored by individuals or groups.

DiscoTests are ideal for informing parents of their children's progress in school, because they provide specific information about how well their child understands class material and what he or she is most likely to benefit from learning next. In fact, the learning suggestions that are included in each report often consist of activities that parents and children can do together. For example, a student struggling to grasp

---

[2]Sample assessments and reports can be found at http://discotest.org.

the basic concepts might be asked to watch an online video where backing soda and vinegar are combined, or to try this at home. A more advanced student might be pointed to a university website where the principles of conservation of matter are applied to real life engineering problems.

Finally, because student performances remain in the system indefinitely, entire schools or districts can follow the development of individual students over time, providing a high-quality method for tracking student progress and evaluating curricula.[3] Moreover, cumulative evidence of growth over time and across several topics provides a basis for making judgments about student readiness to graduate or advance to a new level in their studies.

Building DiscoTests. Needless to say, constructing reliable and valid tests of the kind we have described requires methods that are not part of the toolkit of most test developers. The most fundamental hurdle has been working out a practical approach to describing learning sequences at a fine-enough grain to make them useful for diagnostic purposes. Our (still evolving) solution is a set of methods that make use of a developmental metric that can be used to measure progress along the General Skill Scale. This metric, the LAS, is a well-tested developmental scoring system that consistently produces scores that are reliable within about ¼ of a General Skill Level (known as a *phase*).[4] The LAS thus makes it possible to use a combination of longitudinal and cross-sectional data to construct accurate and detailed learning sequences.

Researchers and teachers use these methods to document the pathways through which students learn a specific skill or set of concepts, to build curricula, and to facilitate learning. The research process is iterative. We begin by designing a single interview instrument composed of a set of open-ended problems that can be used to study the thinking of children as young as 5. Then, making an effort to sample approximately 20 individuals performing in each phase represented in the age range from 5 to 20 or so (about 14 phases), we use the instrument to conduct probed, clinical interviews. These are independently (1) scored with the LAS to determine their developmental phase and (2) submitted to a comprehensive analysis of their content. When both analyses have been completed, analysts study the relation between the level of performance and their conceptual content, gradually constructing descriptions of understanding in each phase and connecting these to describe a detailed learning sequence. This process is described more thoroughly elsewhere (Dawson, 2002, 2003, 2004; Dawson & Gabrielian, 2003; Dawson, Xie, & Wilson, 2003; Dawson-Tunik, 2004).

The items from the interview instrument usually become items in the first version of a new DiscoTest. The newly described learning sequence and the interview data used to construct it provide the basis for initial versions of coding menus and student

---

[3] Although DiscoTest does not collect identifying information for students, the system is set up so that each student is associated with a unique identifier.

[4] In a given classroom for grades 7–12, the range of student performances is likely to be four to six phases (1.5 skill levels).

feedback. At this point, the new teaser can undergo a first round of testing. Two to three rounds of testing are required to refine coding menus, check the accuracy of the learning sequence, evaluate item functioning, and optimize reliability.

Unlike conventional tests, DiscoTests can be used indefinitely; students can take the same teaser several times without exhausting its potential to help them gain an increasingly sophisticated understanding of targeted concepts. This is because the items are deliberately constructed to be answerable at several different levels of sophistication. Moreover, because the primary role of DiscoTests is educative (and items do not have single correct answers) concerns about cheating are minimal. Furthermore, DiscoTests are both educative and standardized. All performances are placed on the same, domain independent, general scale. This makes it possible to compare learning across any range of subjects or contexts. Finally, DiscoTests double as data collection instruments. Eventually, they will yield large longitudinal databases that will allow researchers to construct increasingly refined accounts of the pathways through which students learn important skills and concepts.

New Tools Foster New Values: Revisioning Education and Testing

We have discussed the history of our contemporary testing infrastructure and explained the need for new approaches grounded in the science of learning. We have also provided an overview of one new approach that combines advances in basic research about learning with new techniques in psychometrics to build embedded formative assessments that are both standardized and richly educative. The DiscoTest initiative is engaged in building *a mass-customized testing infrastructure* wherein metrics that are informed by learning theory and research are used in the design of standardized tests that fit the needs of specific curricula and support learning. This way of designing tests has broad implications for what is considered possible and preferable for standardized testing infrastructures.

This approach to test design also allows us to transcend the dichotomies mentioned in the introduction and third section. First, by using a psychometrically refined developmental measure to research specific learning sequences and then using that same measure to assess student performance relative to the researched learning sequences, we transcend the dichotomy between educative and standardized assessment. Student performances are evaluated both in terms of where their performance is in relation to the Skill Scale and in relation to the learning sequence being assessed, a measurement that is simultaneously standardized and educationally relevant. Knowing where the student performs on the General Skill Scale provides all the benefits (and liabilities) of standardized testing (e.g., allowing for comparison between students, or between subject areas for the same student, or between groups of students). But knowing where a student performs relative to an empirically grounded learning sequence provides all the benefits of formative assessment; with rich information about what the student understands and could best benefit from learning next. With the right measures, research approach, and curricula, we no longer must choose between tests that are standardized and tests that are educative aids.

Secondly, the dichotomy between testing for general capabilities and testing for specific content is rendered moot. Research reveals that skills that are conventionally thought of as general skills, such as those for abstract reasoning, critical thinking, or academic writing, unfold along unique pathways *in specific content areas*. Thus, just as a score on a DiscoTest is both standardized and educative, it is also indicative of a range of general skills as they are exercised in specific content areas. These skills are demonstrated when students explain their thinking in written responses.[5]

Thirdly, DiscoTests overcome the dichotomy between testing to prepare the workforce and testing to foster critically minded citizens. This classic dichotomy is an artifact of an earlier era, before postindustrial conditions characterized large segments of the world and information technologies created a networked polyvocal global public sphere. Today, we face unique conditions that render traditional ideas about the nature of socialization and adult life obsolete. Patterns of parenting, friendship, work, marriage, and political involvement have shifted rapidly away from predictability toward diverse individualized pathways of socialization with multiple outcomes and divergent views of success (Arnett, 2004; Beck, 2001). This complexity and heterogeneity should be met by a flexible educational system capable of responding to the unique needs of an increasingly diverse population of students. Such a system, if it is to maintain rigor and efficacy, will need a testing infrastructure that is standardized and customizable, broad and flexible, one that integrates basic knowledge about learning into new contexts and applications—one that rewards good thinking rather than right answers. DiscoTests do not have right answers. They are designed to provide students with many opportunities to apply their knowledge to the kinds of problems they will face in the real world—messy, open-ended problems without simple answers.

We have thus touched on the philosophical issues at the heart of testing reform. The contemporary testing infrastructure set constraints on pedagogical options and structures the distribution of opportunities and resources. Moreover, as many have noted (e.g., Hursh, 2008; Dewey, 1916), the reward systems of schools act as proxies for the general values of society. Tests teach students—both indirectly and directly—what is deemed valuable in the sociocultural context they inhabit. Thus a new testing infrastructure will have wide ranging implications, from classroom practice to college admissions and beyond. Redesigning large-scale testing infrastructures means, in part, recasting how social values are operationalized. The possibilities for building fundamentally new types of tests, based on the new science of learning and human development, allows us to transcend narrow debates about the goals of schooling and to help people learn better.

---

[5] It is important to note that leaning disabled students or students whose native language is not the language of instruction and assessment will need appropriate accommodations, probably along the lines of the principles of *Universal Design For Learning* (see Rose & Meyer, 2002).

References

Arnett, J. (2004). *Emerging adulthood*. New York: Oxford University Press.

Baldwin, J. M. (1906). *Thought and things: A study in the development of meaning and thought or genetic logic* (Vols. 1–3). New York: Macmillan Co.

Beck, U. (2001). A life of one's own in a runaway world: Individualization, globalization and politics. In *Individualization* (pp. 22–30). London: SAGE Publications.

Case, R. (1992). *The minds staircase: Exploring the conceptual underpinnings of children's thought and knowledge*. Hillsdale, NJ: Lawrence Erlbaum.

Chapman, P. D. (1988). *Schools as sorters*. New York: New York University Press.

Commons, M. L., Trudeau, E. J., Stein, S. A., Richards, F. A., & Krause, S. R. (1998). Hierarchical complexity of tasks shows the existence of developmental stages. *Developmental Review, 18*, 237–278.

Cremin, L. (1970). *American education: The colonial experience*. New York: Haper & Row.

Dawson, T. L. (2002). A comparison of three developmental stage scoring systems. *Journal of Applied Measurement, 3*, 146–189.

Dawson, T. L. (2003). A stage is a stage is a stage: A direct comparison of two scoring systems. *Journal of Genetic Psychology, 164*, 335–364.

Dawson, T. L. (2004). Assessing intellectual development: Three approaches, one sequence. *Journal of Adult Development, 11*, 71–85.

Dawson, T. L. (2008, 11/1/04). The Lectical™ Assessment System. 1. Retrieved September, 2008, from http://www.lectica.info

Dawson, T. L., & Gabrielian, S. (2003). Developing conceptions of authority and contract across the life-span: Two perspectives. *Developmental Review, 23*, 162–218.

Dawson, T. L., & Stein, Z. (2008). Cycles of reseach and application in education: Learning pathways for energy concepts. *Mind, Brain, and Education, 2*, 89–102.

Dawson, T. L., Xie, Y., & Wilson, M. (2003). Domain-general and domain-specific developmental assessments: Do they measure the same thing? *Cognitive Development, 18*, 61–78.

Dawson-Tunik, T. L. (2004). "A good education is ..." The development of evaluative thought across the life-span. *Genetic, Social, and General Psychology Monographs, 130*(1), 4–112.

Dewey, J. (1916). *Democracy and education*. New York: The Free Press.

Fischer, K. (1980). A theory of cognitive development: The control and construction of hierarchies of skills. *Psychological Review, 87*(6), 477–531.

Fischer, K., & Bidell, T. (2006). Dynamic development of psychological structures in action and thought. In W. Damon & R. M. Lerner (Eds.), *Handbook of child psychology: Theoretical models of human development* (6th ed., Vol. 1, pp. 313–399). New York: John Wiley & Sons.

Fischer, K. W., Hand, H. H., & Russel, S. (1984). The development of abstractions in adolescence and adulthood. In M. L. Commons, F. A. Richards & C. Armon (Eds.), *Beyond formal operations: Late adolescent and adult cognitive development* (pp. 43–73). New York: Praeger.

Fischer, K. W., & Kennedy, B. (1997). Tools for analyzing the many shapes of development: The case of self-in-relationships in Korea. In K. A. Renninger & E. Amsel (Eds.), *Processes of development* (pp. 117–152). Erlbaum: Mahwah, NJ.

Gould, S. J. (1981). *The mismeasure of man*. New York: Norton.

Habermas, J. (1984). *The theory of communicative action: Reason and the rationalization of society* (T. McCarthy, Trans., Vol. 1). Boston: Beacon Press.

Hess, F., & Petrilli, M. (2006). *No child left behind*. New York: Peter Lang.

Hursh, D. (2008). *High-stakes testing and the decline of teaching and learning*. New York: Rowman & Littlefeild.

Karier, C. (1986). *The individual, society, and education: A history of American educational ideas* (2nd ed.). Chicago: University of Illinois Press.

King, P. M., & Kitchener, K. S. (1994). *Developing reflective judgment: Understanding and promoting intellectual growth and critical thinking in adolescents and adults*. San Francisco: Jossey Bass.

Kitchener, K. S., & Fischer, K. W. (1990). A skill approach to the development of reflective thinking. *Contributions to Human Development, 21*, 48–62.
Kohlberg, L. (1984). *The psychology of moral development: The nature and validity of moral stages* (Vol. 2). San Francisco: Jossey Bass.
Lagemann, E. (2000). *An elusive science: The troubling history of educational research*. Chicago: University of Chicago Press.
Lemann, N. (1999). *The big test: The secret history of the American meritocracy*. New York: Farrar, Straus and Grioux.
Mislevy, R. J. (1993). Foundations of a new test theory. In N. Frederiksen, R. J. Mislevy & I. I. Bejar (Eds.), *Test theory of a new generation of tests* (pp. 147–169). Hillsdale, NJ: Erlbaum.
Nairn, A. (1980). *The reign of ETS: The corporation that makes up minds*: The Ralph Nader Report on the Educational Testing Service.
National Research Council on the Foundations of Assessment . (1999). *High stakes: Testing for tracking, promotion, and graduation*. Washington, DC: National Academy Press.
National Research Council on the Foundations of Assessment . (2001). *Knowing what students know: The science and design of educational assessment*. Washington, DC: National Academy Press.
Obama, B. (2008) Speech to the 146th Annual Meeting and 87th Representative Assembly of the National Educational Association. Delivered July 5, 2008.
Piaget, J. (1932). *The moral judgment of the child*. London: Routledge and Kegan Paul.
Reisberg, D. (2001). Learning. In R. Wilson & F. C. Keil(Eds.), *The MIT encyclopedia of the cognitive sciences* (pp. 460–461). Cambridge, MA: MIT Press.
Rose, D., & Meyer, A. (2002). *Teaching every student in the digital age: Universal design for learning*. Washington, DC: ASCD Books.
Sadler, P. M. (2000). The relevance of multiple choice tests in assessing science understanding. In J. J. Mintzes, J. H. Wandersee, & J. D. Novak (Eds.), *Assessing science understanding: A human constructivist view* (pp. 249–278). San Diego, CA: Academic Press.
Siegler, R. S. (1981). Developmental sequences within and between concepts. *Monographs of the Society for Research in Child Development, 46*, 84.
Sokal, M. (Ed.). (1990). *Psychological testing in American society: 1890–1930*. New Brunswick, NJ: Rutgers University Press.
Stein, Z. (2009). Resetting the stage: Introduction to special sections on learning and development. *Mind, Brain, and Education, 3*, 2.
Tomasello, M. (1999). *The cultural origins of human cognition*. Cambridge, MA: Harvard University Press.
Watson, M. W., & Fischer, K. W. (1980). Development of social roles in elicited and spontaneous behavior during the preschool years. *Developmental Psychology, 16*, 484–494.
Werner, H. (1957). The concept of development from a comparative and organismic point of view. In D. B.Harris (Ed.), *The concept of development*. Minneapolis, MN: University of Minnesota Press.
White House office of the press secretary (2009) *Administration's statement on educational policy*. Retrieved, June, 2009, from http://www.whitehouse.gov/the_press_office/Fact-Sheet-Expanding-the-Promise-of-Education-in-America/ .

Chapter 11
Self-regulated Learning with MetaTutor: Advancing the Science of Learning with MetaCognitive Tools

Roger Azevedo, Amy Johnson, Amber Chauncey, and Candice Burkett

Cognition and Technology Research Lab, Department of Psychology, Institute for Intelligent Systems, University of Memphis, Memphis, TN, USA

Introduction

Learning about conceptually rich domains with advanced learning technologies requires students to regulate their learning (Jacobson, 2008). Current research from cognitive and learning sciences provides ample evidence that learners have difficulty learning about these domains (Chi, 2005). This research indicates that the complex nature of the learning content, internal and external conditions, and contextual environment requirements are particularly difficult because they require students to regulate their learning (Azevedo, 2008). Regulating one's learning involves analyzing the learning context, setting and managing meaningful learning goals, determining which learning strategies to use, assessing whether the strategies are effective in meeting the learning goals, evaluating emerging understanding of the topic, and determining whether there are aspects of the learning context which could be used to facilitate learning. During self-regulated learning (SRL), students need to deploy several metacognitive processes and make judgments necessary to determine whether they understand what they are learning, and perhaps modify their plans, goals, strategies, and effort in relation to dynamically changing contextual conditions. In addition, students must also monitor, modify, and adapt to fluctuations in their motivational and affective states, and determine how much social support (if any) may be needed to perform the task. Also, depending on the learning context, instructional goals, perceived task performance, and progress made toward achieving the learning goal(s), they may need to adaptively modify certain aspects of their cognition, metacognition, motivation, and affect (Azevedo & Witherspoon, 2009; Winne, 2005).

R. Azevedo (✉)
Cognition and Technology Research Lab, Department of Psychology, Institute for Intelligent Systems, University of Memphis, Memphis, TN, USA
e-mail: razevedo@memphis.edu

To appear in: In M. S. Khine & I.M. Saleh (Eds.), *New Science of Learning: Computers, Cognition, and Collaboration in Education*.

M.S. Khine, I.M. Saleh (eds.), *New Science of Learning*,
DOI 10.1007/978-1-4419-5716-0_11, © Springer Science+Business Media, LLC 2010

Despite the ubiquity of such environments for learning, the majority of the research has been criticized as atheoretical and lacking rigorous empirical evidence (see Azevedo, 2008; Azevedo & Jacobson, 2008; Jacobson, 2008). In order to advance the field and our understanding of the complex nature of learning with advanced learning technologies such as hypermedia-based environments, we need theoretically guided, empirical research regarding how students regulate their learning with these environments.

In this paper, we provide an overarching metaphor—"computers as MetaCognitive tools"—to highlight the complex nature of the use of computer-based learning environments (CBLEs) (Azevedo, 2005a). We also present an overview and basic assumptions of SRL models followed by a global description of SRL with hypermedia. This is followed by a synthesis of extensive product and process data from our lab regarding the role of key SRL processes and the role of adaptive scaffolding in designing an adaptive MetaTutor. We also provide an overview of MetaTutor, a hypermedia learning environment designed to train and foster high school and college students' learning about several biological systems. We present the results of an initial study aimed at examining the effectiveness of MetaTutor on the deployment of key SRL processes during learning. Lastly, we provide theoretically driven and empirically based guidelines for supporting learners' self-regulated learning with MetaTutor.

Metaphor: MetaCognitive Tools for Enhancing Learning

The history of CBLEs spans decades (see Koedinger & Corbett, 2006; Lajoie, 2000; Lajoie & Azevedo, 2006; Shute & Psotka, 1996; Shute & Zapata-Rivera, 2008; Woolf, 2009) and is replete with examples of multimedia, hypermedia, intelligent tutoring systems, and simulations used to enhance students' learning. However, their widespread use and rapid proliferation have surpassed our fundamental understanding of the scientific and educational potential of these tools to enhance learning. For example, researchers and designers are developing advanced learning technologies that integrate several technologies (e.g., adaptive hypermedia-based mixed-initiative tutoring systems with pedagogical agents) to train, model, and foster critical learning skills needed for students to remain competitive in the twenty-first century. This example illustrates the need for a framework that allows researchers, designers, and educators to understand the role of CBLEs and the multidimensional aspects associated with learning with CBLEs.

One approach to understanding the landscape and the various uses of CBLEs is to impose a metaphor—computers as MetaCognitive tools (Azevedo, 2005a, 2005b, 2008). The use of this term has at least two meanings. First, it is meant that current applications of CBLEs go beyond the development or training of cognitive skills (e.g., acquisition of declarative knowledge or the development of procedural knowledge), and that metalevel aspects of learning are critical for acquiring life-long skills.

The use of the term highlights the complex nature of the multitude of contextually bound learning processes. In addition, we also use "meta" to include metalevel (i.e., going beyond cognitive) aspects including metacognition as well as other internal (e.g., motivational and affective states) and external (e.g., assistance from external regulatory agents such as adaptive scaffolding) aspects of learning. Figure 11.1 provides a macroview of the critical aspects of the learning context, types of regulatory processes, task conditions, and features of the CBLE that comprise the foundation for the metaphor of computers as MetaCognitive tools.

We broadly define a computer environment as a MetaCognitive tool as one that is designed for instructional purposes and uses technology to support the learner in achieving the goals of instruction. This may include any type of technology-based tool, such as an intelligent tutoring system, an interactive learning environment, hypermedia, multimedia, a simulation, a microworld, or a collaborative learning environment. The characteristics explicitly stated by Lajoie (1993, p. 261) and several others (see Derry & Lajoie, 1993; Jonassen & Land, 2000; Jonassen & Reeves,

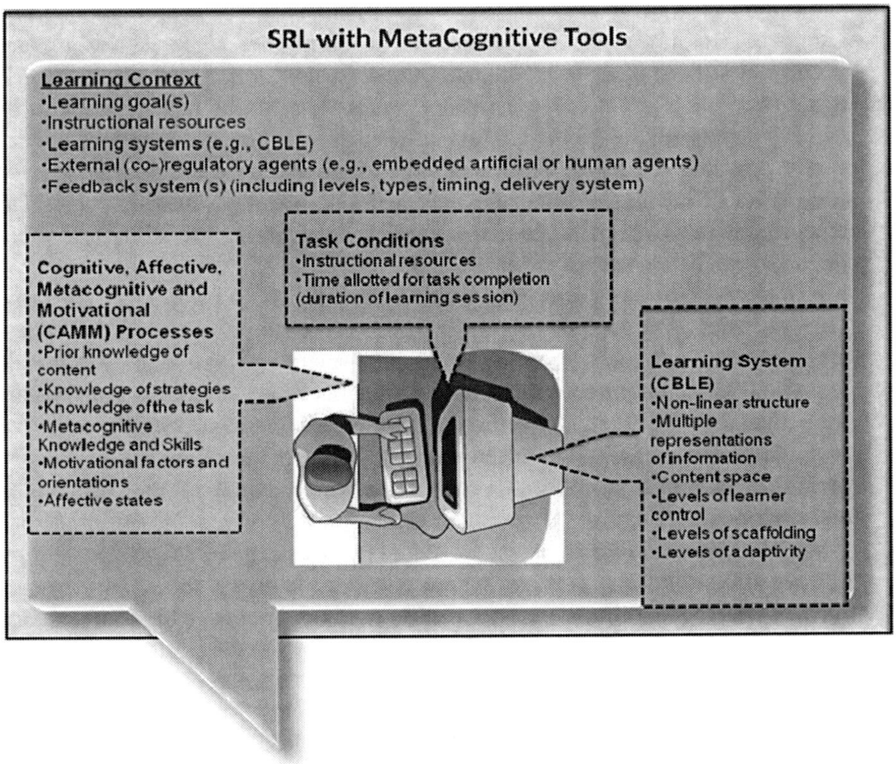

Fig. 11.1 A macroview of the variables associated with using computers as MetaCognitive tools for learning

1996; Lajoie, 1993, 2000; Lajoie & Azevedo, 2006; Pea, 1985; Perkins, 1985) serve as the foundational basis for the metaphor of computers as MetaCognitive tools. The definition subsumes the characteristics of a computer as a cognitive tool, in that the tool can (a) assist learners in accomplishing cognitive tasks by supporting cognitive processes, (b) share the cognitive load by supporting lower-level cognitive skills so that learners may focus on higher-level thinking skills, (c) allow learners to engage in cognitive activities that would be out of their reach otherwise because there may be no opportunities for participating in such tasks (e.g., electronic troubleshooting, medical diagnosis; see Lajoie & Azevedo, 2006), and (d) allow learners to generate and test hypotheses in the context of problem solving.

As such, a metacognitive tool is any computer environment, which in addition to adhering to Lajoie's (1993) definition of cognitive tool, also has the following additional characteristics:

(a) it *requires students to make instructional decisions regarding instructional goals* (e.g., setting learning goals, sequencing instruction, seeking, collecting, organizing, and coordinating instructional resources, deciding which embedded and contextual tools to use and when to use them in order to support their learning goals, deciding which representations of information to use, attend to, and perhaps modify in order to meet instructional goals);
(b) it is *embedded in a particular learning context* which may require students to make decisions regarding the context in ways that support and may lead to successful learning (e.g., how much support is needed from contextual resources, what types of contextual resources may facilitate learning, locating contextual resources, when to seek contextual resources, determining the utility and value of contextual resources);
(c) it *models, prompts, and supports learners' self-regulatory processes (to some degree)* which may include cognitive (e.g., activating prior knowledge, planning, creating subgoals, learning strategies), metacognitive (e.g., feeling of knowing[FOK], judgment of learning [JOL], evaluate emerging understanding), motivational (e.g., self-efficacy, task value, interest, effort), affective (e.g., frustration, confusion, boredoom), or behavior (e.g., engaging in help-seeking behavioral, modifying learning conditions, handling task difficulties and demands);
(d) it *models, prompts, and supports learners (to some degree) to engage or participate* (alone, with a peer, or within a group) in using task-, domain-, or activity-specific learning skills (e.g., skills necessary to engage in online inquiry and collaborative inquiry), which also are necessary for successful learning;
(e) it *resides in a specific learning context* where peers, tutors, humans, or artificial agents may play some role in supporting students' learning by serving as external regulating agents;
(f) it is *any environment where the learner deploys key metacognitive and self-regulatory processes prior to, during, and following learning*. As such, this involves capturing, modeling, and making inferences based on the temporal

deployment of a myriad of self-regulatory processes. The capturing, modeling, and inferences may occur at some level of granularity and be accomplished by the learner, environment, or some other external agent(s) (human, artificial). The capturing of these processes can occur at some level of specificity and be used for various instructional purposes (i.e., from understanding the development of these skills) to accurately model, track, and foster SRL, and perhaps also to make instructional decisions (at some level of specificity) on how best to support learning.

(g) It should also be noted that not all CBLEs include characteristics (a)–(f) and that the choice of which aspects to choose from is based on theoretical assumptions about the nature of learning, educational philosophy, the goal and purpose of the tool, and a fundamental conceptualization regarding the role of external agents (human or artificial).

Theoretical Framework: Self-regulated Learning

SRL has become an influential theoretical framework in psychological and educational research (Azevedo, 2007, 2008, 2009; Boekaerts, Pintrich, & Zeidner, 2000; Dunlosky & Metcalfe, 2009; Dunlosky & Bjork, 2008; Hacker, Dunlosky, & Graesser, 1998, 2009; Metcalfe, 2009; Paris & Paris, 2001; Schunk, 2008; Schunk & Zimmerman, 2008; Winne & Hadwin, 2008; Zimmerman, 2006, 2008; Zimmerman & Schunk, 2001, in press). *SRL is an active, constructive process whereby learners set learning goals and then attempt to monitor, regulate, and control their cognitive and metacognitive processes in the service of those goals.* We acknowledge that SRL also includes other key processes such as motivation and affect; however, we limit our research to the underlying cognitive and metacognitive processes during learning about complex science. The focus of SRL research over the last three decades has been on academic learning and achievement, with researchers exploring the means by which students regulate their cognition, metacognition, motivation, and task engagement (see Pintrich & Zusho, 2002; Schunk & Zimmerman, 2006; Wigfield, Eccles, Schiefele, Roeser, & Davis-Kean, 2006). With this context in mind, the current scientific and educational challenge is to investigate comprehensively the effectiveness of pedagogical agents (PAs) on SRL processes during learning with hypermedia-based, intelligent tutoring systems like MetaTutor.

Addressing our national science learning challenges requires a theoretically driven and empirically based approach (Pashler et al., 2007). Winne and Hadwin's (1998, 2008) model is currently the only contemporary model that provides phases, processes, and emphasis on metacognitive monitoring and control as the "hubs" of SRL. The model has been empirically tested in several complex educational situations (e.g., Azevedo et al., 2008) and makes assumptions regarding the (linear and iterative) nature and temporal deployment of SRL processes that fit perfectly with our current research (e.g., Azevedo, 2007, 2008; Witherspoon, Azevedo, & D'Mello, 2008). The model allows researchers to derive testable hypotheses regarding the complex nature of metacognitive monitoring and control, as well as the complex cycles that a learner and system undergo.

Winne and Hadwin (1998, 2008) posit that learning occurs in four basic phases: task definition, goal-setting and planning, studying tactics, and adaptations to metacognition. Winne and Hadwin's SRL model also differs from others in that it hypothesizes that an information-processing (IP)-influenced set of processes occurs within each phase. Using the acronym COPES, Winne and Hadwin describe each phase in terms of the interaction of a person's conditions, operations, products, evaluations, and standards. All of the terms except operations are kinds of information that a person uses or generates during learning. It is within this COPES architecture that the work of each phase is completed. Thus, the model complements other SRL models by introducing a more complex description of the processes underlying each phase.

Through monitoring, a person compares products with standards to determine if phase objectives have been met or if further work remains to be done. These comparisons are called cognitive evaluations; a poor fit between products and standards may lead a person to enact control over the learning operations to refine the product, revise the conditions and standards, or both. This is the object-level focus of monitoring. However, this monitoring also has a metalevel or metacognitive focus. A student may believe that a particular learning task is easy, and thus translate this belief into a standard in Phase 2. However, when iterating in Phase 3, the learning product might be consistently evaluated as unacceptable in terms of object-level standards. This would initiate metacognitive monitoring that determines that this metalevel information (in this case task difficulty) does not match the previously set standard that the task is easy. At this point, a metacognitive control strategy might be initiated where that particular standard is changed ("this task is hard"), which might in turn affect other standards created during the goal setting of Phase 2. These changes to goals from Phase 2 may include a review of past material or the learning of a new study strategy. Thus, the model is a "recursive, weakly sequenced system" (Winne & Hadwin, 1998, p. 281) where the monitoring of products and standards within one phase can lead to updates of products from previous phases. The inclusion of monitoring and control in the cognitive architecture allows these processes to influence each phase of self-regulated learning.

While there is no typical cycle, most learning involves re-cycling through the cognitive architecture until a clear definition of the task has been created. The next phase produces learning goals and the best plan to achieve them, which leads to the enacting of strategies to begin learning. The products of learning (e.g., understanding of the circulatory system) are compared against standards that include the overall accuracy of the product, the learner's beliefs about what needs to be learned, and other factors such as efficacy and time restraints. If the product does not fit the standard adequately, then further learning operations are initiated, perhaps with changes to conditions such as setting aside more time for studying. Finally, after the main learning process, students may make more long-term alterations to the strategies that make up SRL, such as the addition or deletion of conditions or operations, as well as changes to the ways conditions cue operations (Winne, 2001). The output (performance) is the result of recursive processes that cascade back and forth, altering conditions, standards, operations, and products as needed. In sum, this complex model leads to several assumptions that have guided the design and development of MetaTutor.

Theoretical Assumptions about SRL and MetaTutor

MetaTutor is based on several assumptions regarding the role of SRL during learning about complex and challenging science topics. First, learners need to regulate their SRL processes to effectively integrate multiple representations (i.e., text and diagram) while learning complex science topics in CBLEs (Azevedo, 2008, 2009; Jacobson, 2008; Mayer, 2005; Niederhauser, 2008). Second, students have the potential to regulate their learning but are not always successful for various reasons, such as extraneous cognitive load imposed by the instructional material (Sweller, 2006); lack of or inefficient use of cognitive strategies (Pressley & Hilden, 2006; Siegler, 2005); lack of metacognitive knowledge or inefficient regulatory control of metacognitive processes (Dunlosky & Bjork, 2008; Dunlosky & Metcalfe, 2009; Dunlosky, Rawson, & McDonald, 2002, 2005; Hacker et al., 2009; Schraw, 2006; Schraw & Moshman, 1995; Veenman, Van Hout-Wolters, & Afflerbach, 2006); lack of prior knowledge (Shapiro, 2008); or developmental differences or limited experience with instructional practices requiring the integration of multiple representations or nonlinear learning environments (Azevedo & Witherspoon, 2009; Pintrich & Zusho, 2002).

Third, the integration of multiple representations during complex learning with hypermedia environments involves the deployment of a multitude of self-regulatory processes. *Macrolevel processes* involve executive and metacognitive processes necessary to coordinate, allocate, and reallocate cognitive resources, and mediate perceptual and cognitive processes between the learner's cognitive system and external aspects of the task environment. *Mid-level processes* such as learning strategies are used to select, organize, and integrate multiple representations of the topic (Ainsworth, 1999, 2006; Mayer, 2001, 2005; Schnotz, 2005). These same mid-level control processes are also necessary to exert control over other contextual components that are critical during learning (Aleven, Stahl, Schworm, Fischer, & Wallace, 2003; Newman, 2002; Roll, Aleven, McLaren, & Koedinger, 2007). Researchers have identified several dozen additional learning strategies including coordinating informational sources, summarizing, note-taking, hypothesizing, drawing, etc. (Azevedo, 2008; Van Meter & Garner, 2005).

Fourth, little is understood regarding the nature of SRL processes involved in the integration of multiple external representations that are needed to build internal knowledge representations that support deep conceptual understanding, problem solving, and reasoning (Cox, 1999; Goldman, 2003; Kozma, 2003; Mayer, 2005; Schnotz & Bannert, 2003; Seufert et al., 2007; Witherspoon et al., 2008). Lastly, a critical issue centers on the development and effective use of cognitive and metacognitive processes in middle school and high school students (Baker & Cerero, 2000; Borkowski, Chan, & Muthukrishna, 2000; Lockl & Schneider, 2002; Pintrich, Wolters, & Baxter, 2000; Pressley, 2000; Schneider & Lockl, 2002, 2008; Veenman et al., 2006).

In sum, the last two sections have provided an overview of SRL, described the information processing of Winne and Hadwin, and followed up with a more detailed description of the SRL processes used when learning with a hypermedia learning environment. This leads to a synthesis of our extensive product and process data that was collected, classified, and analyzed, based on theoretical frameworks and models of SRL models.

Synthesis of SRL Data on Learning with Hypermedia

In this section, we present a synthesis of the research on SRL and hypermedia conducted by our team over the last 10 years, focusing explicitly on deployment of self-regulatory processes, and the effectiveness of different types of scaffolding in facilitating students' learning of complicated science topics. More specifically, we have focused on laboratory and classroom research to address the following questions: (1) Do different scaffolding conditions influence students' ability to shift to more sophisticated mental models of complex science topics? (2) Do different scaffolding conditions lead students to gain significantly more declarative knowledge of science topics? (3) How do different scaffolding conditions influence students' ability to regulate their learning of science topics with hypermedia? (4) What is the role of external regulating agents (i.e., human tutors, classroom teachers, and peers) in students' SRL of science topics with hypermedia? (5) Are there developmental differences in college and high school students' ability to self-regulate their learning of science with hypermedia?

In general, our empirical results show that learning challenging science topics with hypermedia can be facilitated if students are provided with adaptive human scaffolding that addresses both the content of the domain and the processes of SRL (see Azevedo, 2008 for effect sizes by type of scaffolding, developmental group, and learning outcome). This type of sophisticated scaffolding is effective in facilitating learning, as indicated by medium to large effect sizes (range of d = 0.5–1.1) on several measures of declarative, procedural, and inferential knowledge and mental models. In contrast, providing students with either no scaffolding or fixed scaffolds (i.e., a list of domain-specific subgoals) tends to lead to negligible shifts in their mental models and only small gains in declarative knowledge in older students.

Verbal protocols provide evidence that students in different scaffolding conditions deploy different key SRL processes, providing a clear association between these scaffolding conditions, mental model shifts, and declarative knowledge gains. To date, we have investigated 38 different regulatory processes related to *planning*, *monitoring*, *learning strategies*, methods of *handling task difficulties and demands*, and *interest* (see Azevedo et al., 2008 for a sample of the SRL processes and for details). These studies have shown some interesting developmental differences. Compared to college students, high school students tend to use fewer and less-sophisticated self-regulatory processes to regulate their learning with hypermedia. Specifically, they fail to create subgoals, monitor aspects of the learning environment (e.g., content evaluation, CE), or evaluate their own cognitive processes (e.g., feeling of knowing, FOK) or emerging understanding (e.g., JOL). Furthermore, they use less effective learning strategies such as copying information verbatim from the learning environment to their notes. The data also indicate that certain key self-regulatory processes related to planning, metacognitive monitoring, and learning strategies are not used during the integration process with multiple representations during hypermedia learning. This leads to declarative knowledge gains but failure to show qualitative mental model shifts related to understanding these complex topics.

Students in the fixed scaffolding conditions tend to regulate learning by monitoring activities that deal with the hypermedia learning environment (other than their own cognition), and use more ineffective learning strategies. By contrast, external regulation by a human tutor leads students to regulate their learning by activating prior knowledge and creating subgoals; monitoring their cognitive system by using FOK and JOL; using effective strategies such as summarizing, making inferences, drawing, and engaging in knowledge elaboration; and, not surprisingly, engaging in an inordinate amount of help-seeking from the human tutor (Azevedo et al., 2005a, 2006; Greene & Azevedo, 2009).

In a recent study, Azevedo and colleagues (2008) examined the effectiveness of SRL and externally regulated learning (ERL) on college students' learning about a science topic with hypermedia during a 40 min session. A total of 82 college students with little knowledge of the topic were randomly assigned either to the SRL or ERL condition. Students in the SRL condition regulated their own learning, while students in the ERL condition had access to a human tutor who facilitated their SRL. We converged product (pretest–posttest declarative knowledge and qualitative shifts in participants' mental models) with process (think-aloud) data to examine the effectiveness of SRL versus ERL. Analysis of the declarative knowledge measures showed that the ERL condition group mean was statistically significantly higher than the group mean for the SRL condition on the labeling and flow diagram tasks. There were no statistically significant differences between groups on the matching task, but both groups showed statistically significant increases in performance. Further analyses showed that the odds of being in a higher mental model posttest group were decreased by 65% for the SRL group as compared to the ERL group. In terms of SRL behavior, participants in the SRL condition engaged in more selecting of new information sources, rereading, summarizing, free searching, and enacting of control over the context of their learning. In comparison, the ERL participants engaged in more activation of prior knowledge, utilization of FOK and JOL, monitoring of their progress toward goals, drawing, hypothesizing, coordination of information sources, and expressing task difficulty.

In sum, our existing data stresses that learning about complex science topics involves deploying key self-regulatory processes during learning with hypermedia. These include several planning processes (creating subgoals, activating prior knowledge), metacognitive judgments (about emerging understanding, relating new content with existing knowledge), and learning strategies (coordinating informational sources, drawing, summarizing). In addition, the use of these processes can be facilitated by adaptive scaffolding by an external agent. In the next section, we describe the MetaTutor environment.

MetaTutor: A Hypermedia Learning Environment for Biology

MetaTutor is a hypermedia learning environment that is designed to detect, model, trace, and foster students' SRL about human body systems such as the circulatory, digestive, and nervous systems (Azevedo et al., 2008). Theoretically, it is based on cognitive models of SRL (Pintrich, 2000; Schunk, 2005; Winne & Hadwin, 2008; Zimmerman, 2008). The underlying assumption of MetaTutor is that students should regulate key cognitive and metacognitive processes in order to learn about complex and challenging science topics. The design of MetaTutor is based on extensive research by Azevedo and colleagues showing that providing adaptive human scaffolding that addresses both the content of the domain and the processes of SRL enhances students' learning about challenging science topics with hypermedia (e.g., see Azevedo, 2008; Azevedo & Witherspoon, 2009 for extensive reviews of the research). Overall, our research has identified key self-regulatory processes that are indicative of students' learning about these complex science topics. More specifically, they include several processes related to planning, metacognitive monitoring, learning strategies, and methods of handling task difficulties and demands.

Overall, there are several phases to using MetaTutor to train students on SRL processes and to learn about the various human body systems. Figure 11.2 has four screen shots that illustrate the various phases including (1) modeling of key SRL processes (see top-left corner), (2) a discrimination task where learners choose between good and poor use of these processes (see top-right corner), (3) a detection task where learners watch video clips of human agents engaging in similar learning tasks and are asked to stop the video whenever they see the use of an SRL process (and then indicate the process from a list) (see bottom-right corner), and (4) the actual learning environment used to learn about the biological system (see bottom-left corner).

The interface of the actual learning environment contains a learning goal set by either the experimenter or teacher (e.g., *Your task is to learn all you can about the circulatory system. Make sure you know about its components, how they work together, and how they support the healthy functioning of the human body*). The learning goal is associated with the subgoals box where the learner can generate several subgoals for the learning session. A list of topics and subtopics is presented on the left side of the interface, while the actual science content (including the text,

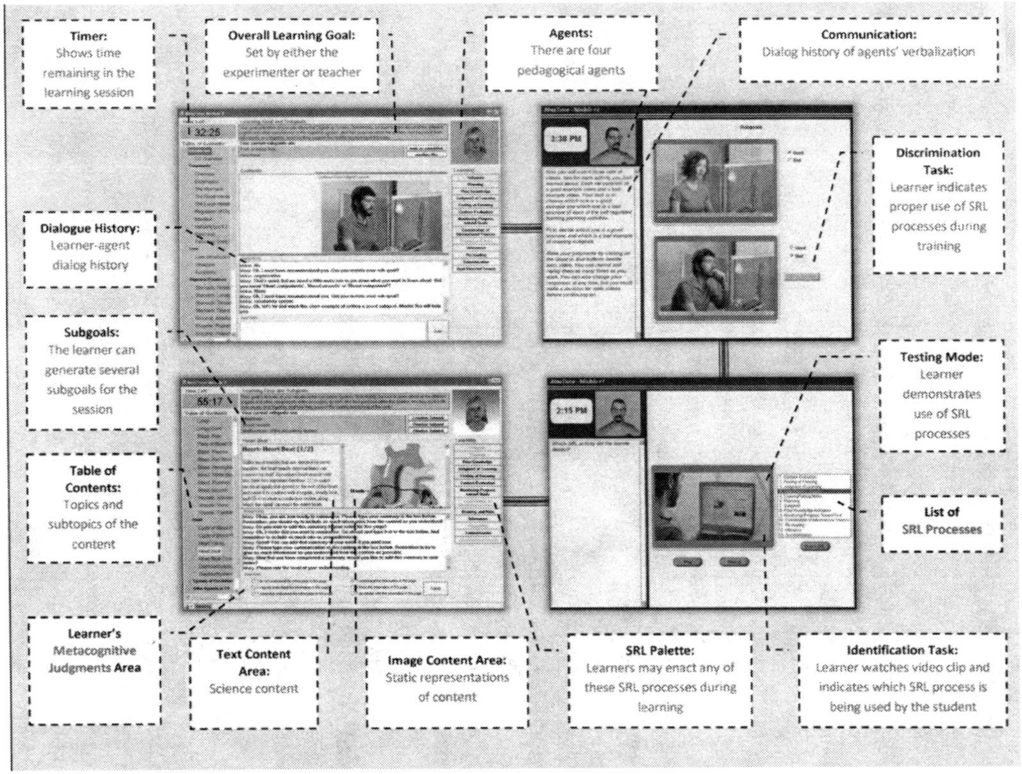

Fig. 11.2 Screenshots of MetaTutor

static, and dynamic representations of information) is presented in the center of the interface. The main communication dialogue box (between the learner and the environment) is found directly below the content box. The pedagogical agents are available and reside in the top right-hand corner of the interface. In this case, Mary the Monitor is available to assist learners through the process of evaluating their understanding of the content. Below the agent box is a list of SRL processes that learners can use throughout the learning session. Specifically, learners can select the SRL process they are about to use by highlighting it. The goal of having learners select the processes is to enhance metacognitive awareness of the processes used during learning and to facilitate the environment's ability to trace, model, and foster learning. In addition to learner-initiated SR, the agent can prompt learners to engage in planning, monitoring, or strategy use under appropriate conditions traced by MetaTutor.

The purpose of the MetaTutor project is to examine the effectiveness of animated pedagogical agents as external regulatory agents used to detect, trace, model, and foster students' self-regulatory processes during learning about complex science topics. MetaTutor is in its infancy, and thus the algorithms to guide feedback to the student have not yet been developed or tested. The challenge will be to provide feedback on both the accuracy of the content as well as the appropriateness of the strategies being used by the student. Current machine learning methods for detecting students' evolving mental models of the circulatory system are being tested and implemented (Rus, Lintean, & Azevedo, 2009), as well as specific macro- and microadaptive tutoring methods based on detailed system traces of learners' navigational paths through the MetaTutor system (Witherspoon et al., 2009). In the next section, we present data collected from an initial study using MetaTutor.

Preliminary Data on SRL with MetaTutor

During the past year we collected data using the current nonadaptive version with 66 college students and 18 high school students. The data show that the students have little declarative knowledge of key SRL processes. They also tend to learn relatively little about the circulatory system in 2 h sessions when they need to regulate their own learning (Azevedo et al., 2008, 2009). In particular, both college and high school students show small to medium effect sizes (d = 0.47–0.66) for pretest–posttest shifts across several researcher-developed measures tapping declarative, inferential, and mental models of the body systems.

Newly analyzed data from the *concurrent think-aloud protocols* with the non-adaptive version of MetaTutor show some very important results that will be used to design and develop the adaptive version. The coded concurrent think-aloud data from 44 (out of 60) participants are also extremely informative in terms of the frequency of use of each SRL class (e.g., monitoring) and the processes within each class (e.g., FOK and JOL are part of monitoring). Overall, the data indicate that learning strategies were deployed most often (77% of all SRL processes deployed during the learning task) followed by metacognitive judgments (nearly 16% of all

SRL processes). On average, during a 60 min learning session learners used approximately two learning strategies every minute and made a metacognitive judgment approximately once every 4 min while using the nonadaptive version of MetaTutor.

Figure 11.3 represents another approach to examining the fluctuation of SRL processes over time. This figure illustrates average frequencies of four classes of SRL over a 60 min learning session in our initial MetaTutor experiment. To examine trends and changes in SRL over time, the 60 min sessions were divided into six 10 min segments, as indicated by the *x*-axis. The *y*-axis indicates average frequency of the four classes of SRL: planning, monitoring, learning strategies, and handling task difficulty and demands. Learning strategies show the highest trend throughout the learning session, peaking in the first 20 min and gradually declining as the session progresses. Monitoring processes have the second highest frequency, although they appear to occur far less frequently than learning strategies (averaging fewer than five times for each time interval). Despite the low frequency of monitoring processes, it is still a step in the right direction to see learning strategies and monitoring occurring most frequently during the session, because these two classes are assumed to be the central hubs of SRL. Processes related to planning and handling task difficulty and demands occur least frequently, and do not occur at all in many time intervals.

A closer examination of the same data by SRL processes within each class is even more revealing. On average, these same learners are learning about the biology content by taking notes, previewing the captions, re-reading the content, and correctly summarizing what they have read more often than any other strategy. Unfortunately, they are not using other key learning strategies (e.g., coordinating informational sources, drawing, knowledge elaboration) that are associated with conceptual gains (see Azevedo, 2009; Greene & Azevedo, 2009). Another advantage of converging concurrent think-aloud data with time-stamped video data is that we can calculate the mean time spent on each learning strategy. For example, an instance of taking notes lasts an average of 20 s while drawing lasts an average of 30 s. Learners are

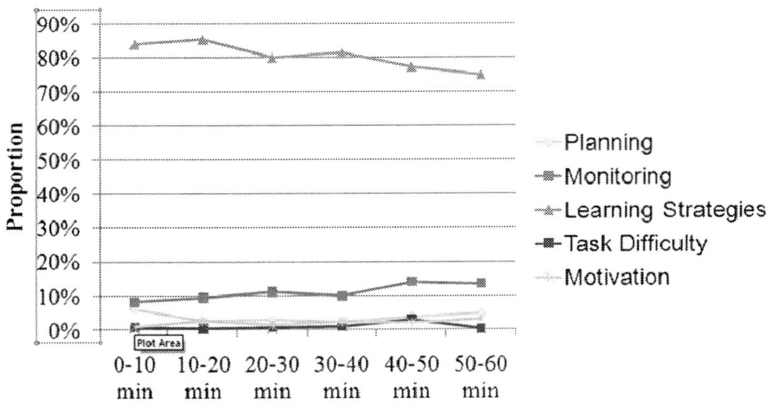

Fig. 11.3 Proportion of SRL processes (by class) during a 60 min learning task with MetaTutor

making FOK, JOL, and content evaluation more often than any other metacognitive judgment. These judgments tend to last an average of 3–9 s. Such data demonstrate the need for an adaptive MetaTutor, and will be useful in developing new modules.

The *log-file data* have also been mined to investigate the navigational paths and explore the behavioral signatures of cognitive and metacognitive processing while students use MetaTutor (Witherspoon, Azevedo, & Cai, 2009). It should be noted that MetaTutor traces learners' behavior within the environment and logs every learner interaction into a log file. These trace data are critical in identifying the role and deployment of SRL processes during learners' navigation through the science content. We conducted a cluster analysis using five navigational variables: (1) percentage of 'linear forward' transitions (e.g., p. 1 to p. 2); (2) percentage of 'linear backward' transitions (e.g., p. 2 to p. 1); (3) percentage of 'nonlinear' transitions (e.g., p. 3 to p. 7); (4) percentage of category shifts (from one subheading to another); and (5) percentage of image openings.

From this quantitative analysis, we found four major profiles of learners. One group tended to remain on a linear path within the learning environment, progressing from one page to the next throughout the session (average of 90% linear navigations). Another group demonstrated a large amount of nonlinear navigation (average of 36% of the time), while a third group opened the image a majority of the time (78% on average). The fourth group of learners was more balanced in their navigation, navigating nonlinearly on average 18% of the time, and opening the image accompanying the page of content 39% of the time. Further analysis revealed that learners in this fourth, "balanced" group scored significantly higher on composite learning outcome measures. An adaptive MetaTutor system should scaffold balanced navigational behavior.

A qualitative analysis of MetaTutor's traces of learners' navigational paths during each learning session was also performed (see Witherspoon et al., 2009 for a complete analysis). The work here is emphasizing the need to examine how various types of navigational paths are indicative (or not) of strategic behavior expected from self-regulating learners (Winne, 2005). Figures 11.4a and b illustrate the navigational paths of two learners from our dataset while they use MetaTutor to learn about the circulatory system. In Fig. 11.4a and b, the x-axis represents move x and the y-axis represents $x+1$. Figure 11.4a shows the path of a low performer (i.e., small pretest–posttest learning gains) while Fig. 11.4b illustrates the path of a high performer. These figures highlight the qualitative differences between a low and high performer in terms of the linear vs. complex navigational paths and reading times. For example, the low performer tended to progress linearly through the content until he got to a key page (e.g., p. 16 on blood vessels) and decided to return to a previous page. In contrast, the high performer's path is more complicated and is more consistent with a strategic, self-regulated learner by the complexity shown in Fig. 11.4b. This learner progresses linearly, at times makes strategic choices about returning to previously visited pages, and deploys twice as many SRL processes as the low-performing learner (i.e., 212 moves vs. 102 moves, respectively). This is symbolically illustrated in the figures by the difference between the "space" between the dots—i.e., more space between dots = longer reading times.

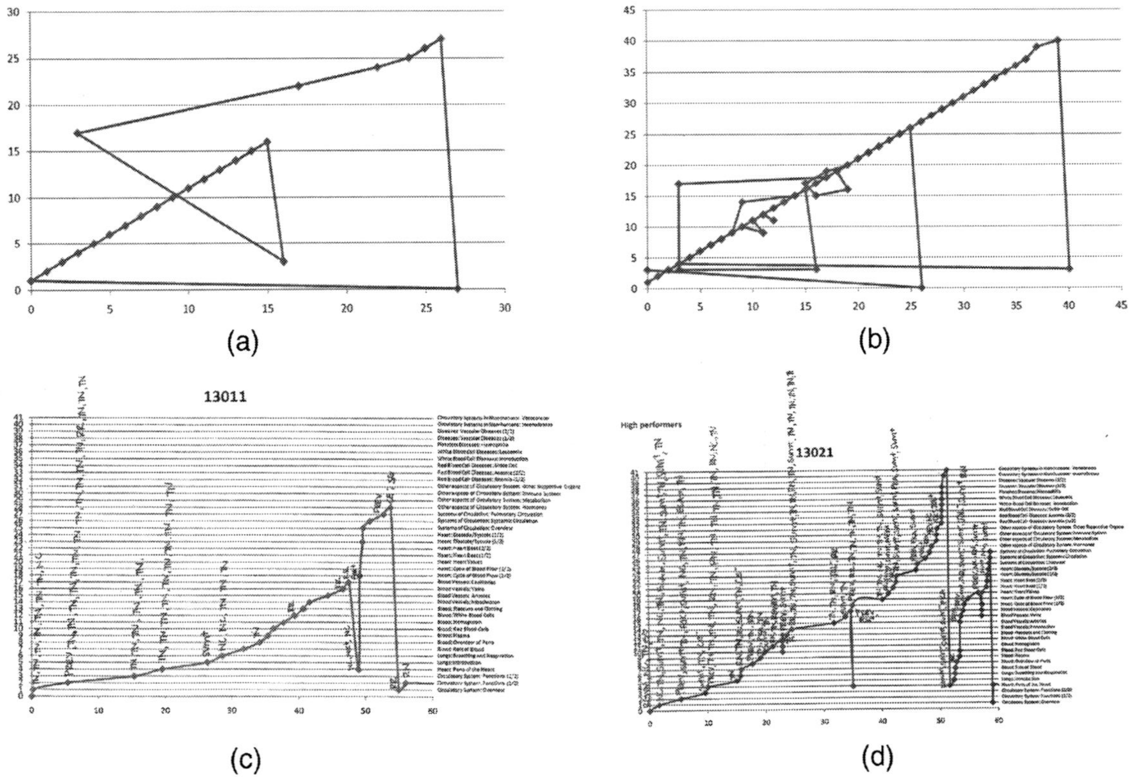

Fig. 11.4 Trace of a low–high mental model jumper during learning with hypermedia. (**a**) Navigational path of a low performer (#3011). (**b**) Navigational path of a high performer (#3021). (**c**) Navigational path of a low performer (#3011) with SRL processes annotated by hand. (**d**) Navigational path of a high performer (#3021) with SRL processes annotated by hand

The SRL processes deployed were handwritten on their navigational paths and presented in Fig. 11.4c and d. In Fig. 11.4c and d, the x-axis represents time (in minutes) within the learning session and the y-axis represents pages of content (and their corresponding titles). There are several key observations to highlight in terms of keeping with our goal of extracting information for the design of the adaptive MetaTutor. First, there is more complexity in the navigational paths and deployment of SRL processes as seen in the number of processes handwritten in the figures. Second, 70% of the low performer's SRL moves were coded as taking notes while the high performer only used 39% of his processes for taking notes. Third, one can infer (from the "space" between moves) that the low performer spent more time acquiring knowledge (reading the science content) from the environment while the high performer spent less time reading throughout the session. Fourth, the high performer used a wider variety of SRL processes compared to the low performer. A related issue is the nonstrategic move by the low performer to create a new subgoal near the end of the learning session. However, the high performer is more strategic in his self-regulatory behavior throughout the learning session. For example, he engages in what can best be characterized as "time-dependent SRL cycles." These cycles involve creating subgoals, previewing the content, acquiring knowledge from the multiple representations, taking notes, reading notes, evaluating content, activating prior knowledge, and periodically monitoring understanding of the topic.

Overall, these data show the complex nature of the SRL processes during learning with MetaTutor. We have used quantitative and qualitative methods to converge process and product data to understand the nature of learning outcomes and the deployment of SRL processes. The data will be used to design an adaptive version of MetaTutor that is capable of providing the adaptive scaffolding necessary to foster students' learning and use of key SRL processes. It is extremely challenging to think about how to build an adaptive MetaTutor system designed to detect, trace, model, and foster SRL about complex and challenging science topics. The next section will address these challenges in turn.

Implications for the Design of an Adaptive MetaTutor

In the next section, we highlight some general and specific design challenges that need to be addressed in order to build an adaptive MetaTutor system.

General challenges. Our results have implications for the design of the adaptive MetaTutor hypermedia environments intended to foster students' learning of complex and challenging science topics. Given the effectiveness of adaptive scaffolding conditions in fostering students' mental model shifts, it would make sense for a MetaCognitive tool such as MetaTutor to emulate the regulatory behaviors of the human tutors. In order to facilitate students' understanding of challenging science topics, the system would ideally need to dynamically modify its scaffolding methods to foster the students' self-regulatory behavior during learning. However, these design decisions should also be based on the successes of current adaptive computer-based learning environments for well-structured tasks (e.g., Koedinger & Corbett, 2006; Graesser, Jeon, & Dufty, 2008; VanLehn et al., 2007; Woolf, 2009), technological limitations in assessing learning of challenging and conceptually rich, ill-structured topics (e.g., Brusilovsky, 2001; Jacobson, 2008; Azevedo, 2008), and conceptual issues regarding what, when, and how to model certain key self-regulated learning processes in hypermedia environments (Azevedo, 2002). Current computational methods from AI and educational data mining (e.g., Leelawong & Biswas, 2008; Schwartz et al., 2009) need to be explored and tested to build a system designed to detect, trace, and model learners' deployment of self-regulated processes. Other challenges associated with having the system detect the qualitative shifts in students' mental models of the topic must be circumvented by using a combination of embedded testing, frequent quizzing about sections of the content, and probing for comprehension.

As for SRL processes, our data show that learners are using mainly ineffective strategies and they tend to use up to 45 min of the 60 min session using these processes. In contrast, the same data show learners use key metacognitive processes but they may last a short period of time (up to 9 seconds). The challenge for an adaptive MetaTutor is for it to be sensitive enough to detect the deployment of these processes and to accurately classify them. Aggregate data from state-transition matrices are also key in forming the subsequent instructional decision made by the system. All this information would then have to be fed to the system's students and instructional modules in order to make decisions regarding macro- and microlevel scaffolding and tailor feedback messages to the learner. Associated concerns include keeping a running model of the deployment of SRL processes (including the level of granularity, frequency, and valence; e.g., monitoring, JOL, and JOL–) and evolving understanding of the content and other learning measures. This history would be necessary to make inferences about the quality of students' evolving mental models and the quality of the SRL processes.

To be most effective in fostering SRL, adaptive hypermedia learning environments must have the capacity to both scaffold effective SRL and provide timely and appropriate feedback. In this section we focus on two specific and important modules for an adaptive MetaTutor that provide these critical components.

Scaffolding module. Scaffolding is an important step in facilitating students' conceptual understanding of a topic and the deployment of SRL processes (Azevedo & Hadwin, 2005; Pea, 2004; Puntabmbekar & Hubscher, 2005). Critical aspects include the agents' ability to provide different types of scaffolding depending on the students' current level of conceptual understanding in relation to the amount of time left in a learning session, and also their navigation paths and whether they have skipped relevant pages and diagrams related to either their current subgoal or the overall learning goal for the session. In addition, we need to figure in how much scaffolding students may have already received and whether it was effective in facilitating their mastery of the content. The proposed adaptive MetaTutor may start by providing generic scaffolding that binds specific content to specific SRL processes (e.g., intro to any section of content is prompted by scaffolding to preview, skimming the content, evaluating the content vis-à-vis the current subgoal, and then determining whether to pursue or abandon the content) versus a fine-grained scaffolding that is time-sensitive and fosters qualitative changes in conceptual understanding. This approach fits with extensive research on human and computerized tutoring (Azevedo et al., 2007, 2008; Chi et al., 2004; Graesser et al., 2008). One of the challenges for the adaptive MetaTutor will be to design graduated scaffolding methods that fluctuate from ERL (i.e., a student observes as the agent assumes instructional control and models a particular strategy or metacognitive process to demonstrate its effectiveness) to fading all support once the student has demonstrated mastery of the content. Our current data on SRL processes show that learners are making FOK, JOL, and content evaluation (CE) more often than any other metacognitive judgment. However, they are deploying these processes very infrequently. Thus, agents could be designed to prompt students to explicitly engage in these key metacognitive processes more frequently during learning. Another level of scaffolding would involve coupling particular metacognitive processes with optimal learning strategies. For example, if students articulate that they do not understand a certain paragraph (i.e., JOL–), then a prompt to re-read is ideal. In contrast, students who report that they understand a paragraph (i.e., JOL+) should be prompted to continue reading the subsequent paragraph or inspect the corresponding diagram.

Feedback module. Feedback is a critical component in learning (Koedinger & Corbett, 2006; VanLehn et al., 2007). The issues around feedback include the timing and type of feedback. Timing is important because feedback should be provided soon after one makes an incorrect inference or incorrectly summarizes text or a diagram. The type of feedback is related to whether the agents provide knowledge of results after a correct answer, inference, etc., or elaborative feedback, which is difficult to create because it requires knowing the student's learning history and therefore relies heavily on an accurate student model. For example, a key objective of this project is to determine which and how many learner variables must be traced for the system to accurately infer the students' needs for different types of feedback. We emphasize that feedback will also be provided for content understanding and use of SRL processes. The data may show that a student is using ineffective strategies, and therefore the agent may provide feedback by alerting the student to a better learning strategy (e.g., summarizing a complex biological pathway instead of copying it verbatim).

Summary

Learning with MetaCognitive tools involves the deployment of key SRL processes. We have articulated and explicitly described the metaphor of computers as MetaCognitive tools. We provided an overview of SRL and provided a description of the importance of using SRL as a framework to understand the complex nature of learning with MetaCognitive tools. We provided a synthesis of our previous work and how it was used to design the MetaTutor system. We then provided preliminary data on the MetaTutor and discussed how this data can be used to design an adaptive version of MetaTutor to detect, trace, model, and foster students' SRL about complex and challenging science topics.

Acknowledgments The research presented in this paper has been supported by funding from the National Science Foundation (Early Career Grant DRL 0133346, DRL 0633918, DRL 0731828, HCC 0841835) awarded to the first author. The authors thank M. Cox, A. Fike, and R. Anderson for collection of data, transcribing, and data scoring. The authors would also like to thank M. Lintean, Z. Cai, V. Rus, A. Graesser, and D. McNamara for design and development of MetaTutor.

References

Ainsworth, S. (1999). The functions of multiple representations. *Computers & Education, 33*, 131–152.

Ainsworth, S. (2006). DeFT: A conceptual framework for considering learning with multiple representations. *Learning and Instruction, 16*, 183–198.

Aleven, V., Stahl, E., Schworm, S., Fischer, F., & Wallace, R. M. (2003). Help seeking and help design in interactive learning environments. *Review of Educational Research, 73*(2), 277–320.

Azevedo, R. (2002). Beyond intelligent tutoring systems: Computers as MetaCognitive tools to enhance learning? *Instructional Science, 30*(1), 31–45.

Azevedo, R. (2005a). Computers as metacognitive tools for enhancing learning. *Educational Psychologist, 40*(4), 193–197.

Azevedo, R. (2005b). Using hypermedia as a metacognitive tool for enhancing student learning? The role of self-regulated learning. *Educational Psychologist. Special Issue: Computers as Metacognitive Tools for Enhancing Student Learning, 40*(4), 199–209.

Azevedo, R. (2007). Understanding the complex nature of self-regulatory processes in learning with computer-based learning environments: An introduction. *Metacognition and Learning*, 2(2/3), 57–66.

Azevedo, R. (2008). The role of self-regulation in learning about science with hypermedia. In D. Robinson & G. Schraw (Eds.), *Recent innovations in educational technology that facilitate student learning* (pp. 127–156). Charlotte, NC: Information Age Publishing.

Azevedo, R. (2009). Theoretical, methodological, and analytical challenges in the research on metacognition and self-regulation: A commentary. *Metacognition and Learning, 4*(1), 87–95.

Azevedo, R., & Hadwin, A. F. (2005). Scaffolding self-regulated learning and metacognition: Implications for the design of computer-based scaffolds. *Instructional Science, 33*, 367–379.

Azevedo, R., & Jacobson, M. (2008). Advances in scaffolding learning with hypertext and hypermedia: A summary and critical analysis. *Educational Technology Research & Development, 56* (1), 93–100.

Azevedo, R., & Witherspoon, A. M. (2009). Self-regulated use of hypermedia. In D. J. Hacker, J. Dunlosky, & A. C. Graesser (Eds.), *Handbook of metacognition in education* (pp. 319–339). New York, NY: Routledge.

Azevedo, R., Greene, J. A., & Moos, D. C. (2007). The effect of a human agent's external regulation upon college students' hypermedia learning. *Metacognition* and *Learning*, 2(2/3), 67–87.

Azevedo, R., Cromley, J. G., Winters, F. I., Moos, D. C., & Greene, J. A. (2006). Using computers as metacognitive tools to foster students' self-regulated learning. *Technology, Instruction, Cognition, and Learning Journal, 3*, 97–104.

Azevedo, R., Witherspoon, A., Chauncey, A., Burkett, C., & Fike, A. (2009). MetaTutor: A MetaCognitive tool for enhancing self-regulated learning. In R. Pirrone, R. Azevedo, & G. Biswas (Eds.), *Proceedings of the AAAI Fall Symposium on Cognitive and Metacognitive Educational Systems* (pp. 14–19). Menlo Park, CA: Association for the Advancement of Artificial Intelligence (AAAI) Press.

Azevedo, R., Witherspoon, A. M., Graesser, A., McNamara, D., Rus, V., Cai, Z., et al. (2008). *MetaTutor: An adaptive hypermedia system for training and fostering self-regulated learning about complex science topics*. Paper to be presented at a Symposium on ITSs with Agents at the Annual Meeting of the Society for Computers in Psychology, Chicago.

Baker, L., & Cerro, L. (2000). Assessing metacognition in children and adults. In G. Schraw & J. Impara (Eds.), *Issues in the measurement of metacognition* (pp. 99–145). Lincoln, NE: University of Nebraska-Lincoln.

Biswas, G., Leelawong, K., Schwartz, D., & the Teachable Agents Group at Vanderbilt. (2005). Learning by teaching: A new agent paradigm for educational software. *Applied Artificial Intelligence, 19*, 363–392.

Boekaerts, M., Pintrich, P., & Zeidner, M. (2000). *Handbook of self-regulation*. San Diego, CA: Academic Press.

Borkowski, J., Chan, L., & Muthukrishna, N. (2000). A process-oriented model of metacognition: Links between motivation and executive functioning. In G. Schraw & J. Impara (Eds.), *Issues in the measurement of metacognition* (pp. 1–42). Lincoln, NE: University of Nebraska-Lincoln.

Brusilovsky, P. (2001). Adaptive hypermedia. *User Modeling and User-Adapted Interaction, 11*, 87–110.

Chi, M. T. H. (2005). Commonsense conceptions of emergent processes: Why some misconceptions are robust. *Journal of the Learning Sciences, 14*(2), 161–199.

Chi, M. T. H., Siler, S., & Jeong, H. (2004). Can tutors monitor students' understanding accurately? *Cognition and Instruction*, *22*, 363–387.

Cox, R. (1999). Representation construction, externalized cognition and individual differences. *Learning and Instruction*, *9*, 343–363.

Derry, S. J., & Lajoie, S. P. (1993). *Computers as cognitive tools*. Hillsdale, NJ: Erlbaum.

Dunlosky, J., & Bjork, R. (Eds.) (2008). *Handbook of metamemory and memory*. New York: Taylor & Francis.

Dunlosky, J., & Metcalfe, J. (2009). *Metacognition*. Thousand Oaks, CA: Sage Publications, Inc.

Dunlosky, J., Hertzog, C., Kennedy, M., & Thiede, K. (2005). The self-monitoring approach for effective learning. *Cognitive Technology*, *9*, 4–11.

Dunlosky, J., Rawson, K. A., & McDonald, S. L. (2002). Influence of practice tests on the accuracy of predicting memory performance for paired associates, sentences, and text material. In T. J. Perfect & B. L. Schwartz (Eds.), *Applied metacognition* (pp. 68–92). Cambridge: Cambridge University Press.

Dunlosky, J., Rawson, K. A., & Middleton, E. L. (2005). What constrains the accuracy of metacomprehension judgments? Testing the transfer-appropriate-monitoring and accessibility hypotheses. *Journal of Memory and Language. Special Issue: Metamemory, 52*, 551–565.

Goldman, S. (2003). Learning in complex domains: When and why do multiple representations help? *Learning and Instruction, 13*, 239–244.

Graesser, A. C., Jeon, M., & Dufty, D. (2008). Agent technologies designed to facilitate interactive knowledge construction. *Discourse Processes*, *45*, 298–322.

Greene, J. A., & Azevedo, R. (2009). A macro-level analysis of SRL processes and their relations to the acquisition of a sophisticated mental model of a complex system. *Contemporary Educational Psychology*, *34*(1), 18–29.

Hacker, D. J., Dunlosky, J., & Graesser, A. C. (Eds.) (1998). *Metacognition in educational theory and practice*. Mahwah, NJ: Erlbaum.

Hacker, D., Dunlosky, J., & Graesser, A. (2009) (Eds.), *Handbook of Metacognition in Education*. New York, NY: Routledge.

Jacobson, M. (2008). A design framework for educational hypermedia systems: Theory, research, and learning emerging scientific conceptual perspectives. *Educational Technology Research & Development*, *56*, 5–28.

Jonassen, D. H., & Land, S. M. (2000). *Theoretical foundations of learning environments*. Mahwah, NJ: Erlbaum.

Jonassen, D., & Reeves, T. (1996). Learning with technology: Using computers as cognitive tools. In D. Jonassen (Ed.), *Handbook of research for educational communications and technology* (pp. 694–719). New York: Macmillan.
Koedinger, K., & Corbett, A. (2006). Cognitive tutors: Technology bringing learning sciences to the classroom. In R. K. Sawyer (Ed.), *The Cambridge handbook of the learning sciences* (pp. 61–77). New York: Cambridge University Press.
Kozma, R. (2003). The material features of multiple representations and their cognitive and social affordances for science understanding. *Learning and Instruction, 13*(2), 205–226.
Lajoie, S. P. (1993). Computer environments as cognitive tools for enhancing learning. In S. Derry & S. P. Lajoie (Eds.), *Computers as cognitive tools* (pp. 261–288). Hillside, NJ: Lawrence Erlbaum Associates, Inc.
Lajoie, S. P. (Ed.) (2000). *Computers as cognitive tools II: No more walls: Theory change, paradigm shifts and their influence on the use of computers for instructional purposes.* Mahwah, NJ: Erlbaum.
Lajoie, S. P., & Azevedo, R. (2006). Teaching and learning in technology-rich environments. In P. Alexander & P. Winne (Eds.), *Handbook of educational psychology* (2nd ed., pp. 803–821). Mahwah, NJ: Erlbaum.
Leelawong, K., & Biswas, G. (2008). Designing learning by teaching agents: The Betty's Brain system. *International Journal of Artificial Intelligence in Education, 18*(3), 181–208.
Lockl, K., & Schneider, W. (2002). Developmental trends in children's feeling-of-knowing judgments. *International Journal of Behavioral Development, 26*, 327–333.
Mayer, R. E. (2001). *Multimedia learning*. New York: Cambridge University Press.
Mayer, R. E. (2005). Cognitive theory of multimedia learning. In R. E. Mayer (Ed.), *The Cambridge handbook of multimedia learning* (pp. 31–48). New York: Cambridge University Press.
Metcalfe, J. (2009). Metacognitive judgments and control of study. *Current Directions in Psychological Science, 18*, 159–163.
Newman, R. S. (2002). What do I need to do to succeed ... When I don't understand what I'm doing!?: Developmental influences on students' adaptive help seeking. In A. Wigfield & J. Eccles (Eds.), *Development of achievement motivation* (pp. 285–306). San Diego, CA: Academic Press.
Niederhauser, D. (2008). Educational hypertext. In M. Spector, D. Merrill, J. van Merriënboer, & M. Driscoll (Eds.), *Handbook of research on educational communications and technology* (pp. 199–209). New York: Taylor & Francis.
Paris, S. G., & Paris, A. H. (2001). Classroom applications of research on self-regulated learning. *Educational Psychologist, 36*(2), 89–101.
Pashler, H., Bain, P., Bottge, B., Graesser, A., Koedinger, K., McDaniel, M., et al. (2007). *Organizing Instruction and Study to Improve Student Learning*. Washington, DC: National Center for Education Research, Institute of Education Sciences, U.S. Department of Education. NCER 2007-2004. Retrieved September 10, 2008, from http://ncer.ed.gov.
Pea, R. D. (1985). Beyond amplification: Using the computer to reorganize mental functioning. *Educational Psychologist, 20*, 167–182.
Pea, R. D. (2004). The social and technological dimensions of scaffolding and related theoretical concepts for learning, education, and human activity. *Journal of the Learning Sciences, 13*(3), 423–451.
Perkins, D. N. (1985). Postprimary education has little impact on informal reasoning. *Journal of Educational Psychology, 77*(5), 562–571.
Pintrich, P. R. (2000). The role of goal orientation in self-regulated learning. In M. Boekaerts, P. Pintrich, & M. Zeidner (Eds.), *Handbook of self-regulation* (pp. 451-502). San Diego, CA: Academic Press.
Pintrich, P., Wolters, C., & Baxter, G. (2000). Assessing metacognition and self-regulated learning. In G. Schraw & J. Impara (Eds.), *Issues in the measurement of metacognition* (pp. 43–97). Lincoln, NE: University of Nebraska-Lincoln.

Pintrich, P., & Zusho, A. (2002). The development of academic self-regulation: The role of cognitive and motivational factors. In A. Wigfield & J. S. Eccles (Eds.), *Development of achievement motivation* (pp. 249–284). San Diego, CA: Academic Press.

Pressley, M. (2000). Development of grounded theories of complex cognitive processing: Exhaustive within- and between study analyses of think-aloud data. In G. Schraw & J. Impara (Eds.), *Issues in the measurement of metacognition* (pp. 261–296). Lincoln, NE: University of Nebraska-Lincoln.

Pressley, M., & Hilden, K. (2006). Cognitive strategies. In D. Kuhn & R. S. Siegler (Eds.), *Handbook of child psychology: Volume 2: Cognition, perception, and language* (6th ed., pp. 511–556). Hoboken, NJ: Wiley.

Puntambekar, S., & Hübscher, R. (2005). Tools for scaffolding students in a complex learning environment: What have we gained and what have we missed? *Educational Psychologist, 40* (1), 1–12.

Roll, I., Aleven, V., McLaren, B., & Koedinger, K. (2007). Designing for metacognition—Applying cognitive tutor principles to metacognitive tutoring. *Metacognition and Learning, 2*(2–3), 125–140.

Rus, V., Lintean, M., & Azevedo, R. (2009). *Automatic detection of student models during prior knowledge activation with MetaTutor.* Paper submitted for presentation at the Biennial Meeting on Artificial Intelligence and Education, Brighton, UK.

Schneider, W., & Lockl, K. (2002). The development of metacognitive knowledge in children and adolescents. In T. J. Perfect & L. B. Schwartz (Eds.), *Applied metacognition* (pp. 224–257). Cambridge: Cambridge University Press.

Schneider, W., & Lockl, K. (2008). Procedural metacognition in children: Evidence for developmental trends. In J. Dunlosky & R. Bjork (Eds.), *Handbook of metamemory and memory* (pp. 391–409). New York: Taylor & Francis.

Schnotz, W. (2005). An integrated model of text and picture comprehension. In R. E. Mayer (Ed.), *The Cambridge handbook of multimedia learning* (pp. 49–69). New York: Cambridge University Press.

Schnotz, W., & Bannert, M. (2003). Construction and interference in learning from multiple representation. *Learning and Instruction, 13*, 141–156.

Schraw, G. (2006). Knowledge: Structures and processes. In P. Alexander & P. Winne (Eds.), *Handbook of educational psychology* (pp. 245–263). Mahwah, NJ: Erlbaum.

Schraw, G., & Moshman, D. (1995). Metacognitive theories. *Educational Psychology Review, 7*, 351–371.

Schunk, D. (2005). Self-regulated learning: The educational legacy of Paul R. Pintrich. *Educational Psychologist, 40*(2), 85–94.

Schunk, D. (2008). Attributions as motivators of self-regulated learning. In D. Schunk & B. Zimmerman (Eds.), *Motivation and self-regulated learning: Theory, research, and applications* (pp. 245–266). Mahwah, NJ: Erlbaum.

Schunk, D., & Zimmerman, B. (2006). Competence and control beliefs: Distinguishing the means and ends. In P. Alexander & P. Winne (Eds.), *Handbook of educational psychology* (2nd ed.). Mahwah, NJ: Erlbaum.

Schunk, D., & Zimmerman, B. (2008). *Motivation and self-regulated learning: Theory, research, and applications.* Mahwah, NJ: Erlbaum.

Schwartz, D. L., Chase, C., Wagster, J., Okita, S., Roscoe, R., Chin, D., & Biswas, G. (2009). Interactive metacognition: Monitoring and regulating a teachable agent. In D. J.Hacker, J.Dunlosky, and A. C. Graesser (Eds.), *Handbook of metacognition in education* (pp. 340–359). New York: Routledge.

Seufert, T., Janen, I., & Brünken, R. (2007). The impact of intrinsic cognitive load on the effectiveness of graphical help for coherence formation. *Computers in Human Behavior, 23*, 1055–1071.

Shapiro, A. (2008). Hypermedia design as learner scaffolding. *Educational Technology Research & Development, 56*(1), 29–44.

Shute, V., & Psotka, J. (1996). Intelligent tutoring systems: Past, present, and future. In D. Jonassen (Ed.), *Handbook of research for educational communications and technology* (pp. 570–600). New York: Macmillan.

Shute, V. J., & Zapata-Rivera, D. (2008). Adaptive technologies. In J. M. Spector, D. Merrill, J. van Merriënboer, & M. Driscoll (Eds.), *Handbook of research on educational communications and technology* (3rd ed., pp. 277–294). New York: Lawrence Erlbaum Associates, Taylor & Francis Group.

Siegler, R. S. (2005). Children's learning. *American Psychologist, 60*, 769–778.

Sweller, J. (2006). The worked example effect and human cognition. *Learning and Instruction, 16*(2), 165–169.

Van Meter, P., & Garner, J. (2005). The promise and practice of learner-generated drawing: Literature review and synthesis. *Educational Psychology Review, 17*(4), 285–325.

VanLehn, K., Graesser, A. C., Jackson, G. T., Jordan, P., Olney, A., & Rose, C. P. (2007). When are tutorial dialogues more effective than reading? *Cognitive Science, 31*(1), 3–62.

Veenman, M., Van Hout-Wolters, B., & Afflerbach, P. (2006). Metacognition and learning: Conceptual and methodological considerations. *Metacognition and Learning, 1*, 3–14.

Wigfield, A., Eccles, J., Schiefele, U., Roeser, R., & Davis-Kean, P. (2006). Development of achievement motivation. In W. Damon, R. Lerner, & N. Eisenberg (Eds.), *Handbook of child psychology* (vol. 3). New York: Wiley.

Winne, P. H. (2001). Self-regulated learning viewed from models of information processing. In B. Zimmerman & D. Schunk (Eds.), *Self-regulated learning and academic achievement: Theoretical perspectives* (pp. 153–189). Mahwah, NJ: Erlbaum.

Winne, P. (2005). Key issues on modeling and applying research on self-regulated learning. *Applied Psychology: An International Review, 54*(2), 232–238.

Winne, P. H., & Hadwin, A. F. (1998). Studying as self-regulated learning. In D. J. Hacker, J. Dunlosky, & A. Graesser (Eds.), *Metacognition in educational theory and practice* (pp. 277–304). Hillsdale, NJ: Erlbaum.

Winne, P., & Hadwin, A. (2008). The weave of motivation and self-regulated learning. In D. Schunk & B. Zimmerman (Eds.), *Motivation and self-regulated learning: Theory, research, and applications* (pp. 297–314). Mahwah, NJ: Erlbaum.

Winne, P. H., & Nesbit, J. C. (2009). Supporting self-regulated learning with cognitive tools. In D. J. Hacker, J. Dunlosky, & A. C. Graesser (Eds.), *Handbook of metacognition in education.* (pp. 259–277). New York, NY: Routledge.

Witherspoon, A., Azevedo, R., & D'Mello, S. (2008). The dynamics of self-regulatory processes within self- and externally-regulated learning episodes. In B. Woolf, E. Aimeur, R. Nkambou, & S. Lajoie (Eds.), *Proceedings of the International conference on intelligent tutoring systems: Lecture Notes in Computer Science* (LNCS 5091, pp. 260–269). Berlin: Springer.

Witherspoon, A., Azevedo, R., & Cai, Z. (2009). *Learners' exploratory behavior within MetaTutor.* Poster presented at the 14th international conference on Artificial Intelligence in Education, Brighton, UK.

Woolf, B. (2009). *Building intelligent interactive tutors: Student-centered strategies for revolutionizing e-learning*. Amsterdam: Elsevier.

Zimmerman, B. (2006). Development and adaptation of expertise: The role of self-regulatory processes and beliefs. In K. Ericsson, N. Charness, P. Feltovich, & R. Hoffman (Eds.), *The Cambridge handbook of expertise and expert performance* (pp. 705–722). New York: Cambridge University Press.

Zimmerman, B. (2008). Investigating self-regulation and motivation: Historical background, methodological developments, and future prospects. *American Educational Research Journal, 45*(1), 166–183.

Zimmerman, B., & Schunk, D. (2001). *Self-regulated learning and academic achievement* (2nd ed.). Mahwah, NJ: Erlbaum.

Zimmerman, B. & Schunk, D. (Eds.) (in press). *Handbook of self-regulation of learning and performance*. New York: Routledge.

Chapter 12
New Learning—Old Methods? How E-research Might Change Technology-Enhanced Learning Research

Peter Reimann and Lina Markauskaite

Faculty of Education and Social Work, The University of Sydney, Sydney, Australia,
e-mail: peter.reimann@sydney.edu.au; lina-markauskaite@sydney.edu.au

Introduction

We continue to be astonished how little has fundamentally changed in the technologies and practices of doing learning research around technology enhanced learning, compared to how dramatically the learning technologies themselves have changed. For instance, continuously produced learning traces closely mirroring the activity that learners enact are only occasionally considered for analysis (with exceptions such as in mobile learning and web-based learning). Further, most studies still are short term, including the time interval considered for observation and data recording, and analysis are performed by individual researchers, despite the fact that the single researcher, and even a small team of researchers, are often challenged by the amount and nature of data. This is not to say that researchers do not make use of modern research tools and technologies—generic software such as SPSS for quantitative analysis and NVivo for qualitative analysis are used in almost every social research study, and highly specialized applications are increasingly developed and trialed in various domains of social and behavioral research (described in journals such as *Social Science Computer Review* and *Behavior Research Methods*). Software tools indeed are often used. However, the inquiry approaches and the social organization of how research is being organized and conducted have changed only little, at least not as much as research practices in fields such as particle physics, medicine, astronomy, or molecular biology.

Moreover, the availability of an increasingly large number of technologies that are used at different stages of the inquiry cycle (from data capturing and analysis and writing up and publishing results) raises the question to which extent different tools yield comparable and compatible outcomes. This issue is gaining particular in importance as the software industry is moving from applications on individual computers to (web-based) services (Jacbos, 2005), allowing research practices to be more distributed and integrated than before.

P. Reimann (✉)
Faculty of Education and Social Work, The University of Sydney, Sydney, Australia
e-mail: peter.reimann@sydney.edu.au

M.S. Khine, I.M. Saleh (eds.), *New Science of Learning*,
DOI 10.1007/978-1-4419-5716-0_12,

There is, of course, no need to change practices for the sake of change. However, we argue that there are emerging needs that require revisiting some of our research approaches, routines, and technologies. Drivers for change are amongst others:

- "Mode II" knowledge production (Gibbons et al., 1994) in education—How to distribute research work across practitioners and researchers, with the Web 2.0 as a big enabler?
- "Rich and continuous data"—how to analyze process data streams and video as a data format, and publish how to publish on this?
- Accountability—how to establish trust in qualitative and quantitative research findings?

In this chapter we discuss the topic of technology-enhanced research at four levels. Section one introduces two complementary technological developments that are at the core of the present changes in research and scholarly practices: Grid technology/semantic networks that are primary enablers of "big science", and Web 2.0 and cloud computing that are primary enablers of new more democratic and social forms of scholarship. Section two discusses the need and possibilities for distributed and integrated learning research approaches and digital environments. We argue that such approaches and digital tools should link (real and online) classrooms and practice-based innovation into a larger system of educational knowledge, thus enabling new ways of building research upon earlier outcomes and of integrating research data and outputs for decision-making and policy. Section three discusses some of many other methodological developments and techniques—video analysis and process analysis—that we think have the biggest opportunities to enhance learning research. Finally, section four discusses a classic topic in epistemology—how to develop trust in research findings—from the perspective of provenance architectures. As research becomes more distributed, both socially (over people) as well as technically (over software services), the issue of trust in the data and the findings gains a new dimension, one that can be effectively addressed by computational approaches to provenance.

In short, this chapter discusses existing and emerging technological affordances and their possibilities to enhance learning research. Before starting this discussion we acknowledge that research technologies are evocative and open to many interpretations. How e-research will be taken up in education and what kinds of research practices it will support will depend on our interpretations and actions, aiming to shape and embrace it. Ours is only one out of many possible ways to address this potential.

Grids, Clouds, and Web 2.0 for Learning Research

In the last years we have seen two rather different, nevertheless complementary, technological developments, both yielding optimistic expectations to enhance and even dramatically change research practices. The first development is best known under the names Grid Computing, Semantic Grid, and Cyberinfrastructure, all pointing to big, systematically planned "top-down" e-research infrastructures. The second, even more recent development is best known under the umbrella terms Cloud Computing and Web 2.0, and is much more heterogenous in nature, but nevertheless aiming for integrated and interactive knowledge services that enable new forms of "social scholarship" (Cohen, 2007). We will turn to each if these in this section.

The availability of a wide range of specialized research tools in combination with the fact that the Internet is connecting all researchers to each other and a wealth of resources is the driving force behind the move toward e-research. While this is strongest in the natural sciences, the social sciences and the humanities are also seeing respective developments (Barjak et al., 2009). The Grid is a software infrastructure that enables "flexible, secure, coordinated resource sharing among dynamic collections of individuals, institutions and resources" (Foster, Kesselman, & Tuecke, 2001, p. 200). The core of the Grid architecture is a layered structure (see Fig. 12.1) formed of various interoperable protocols (Berman, Fox, & Hey, 2003; Foster et al., 2001 and Fig. 12.1).

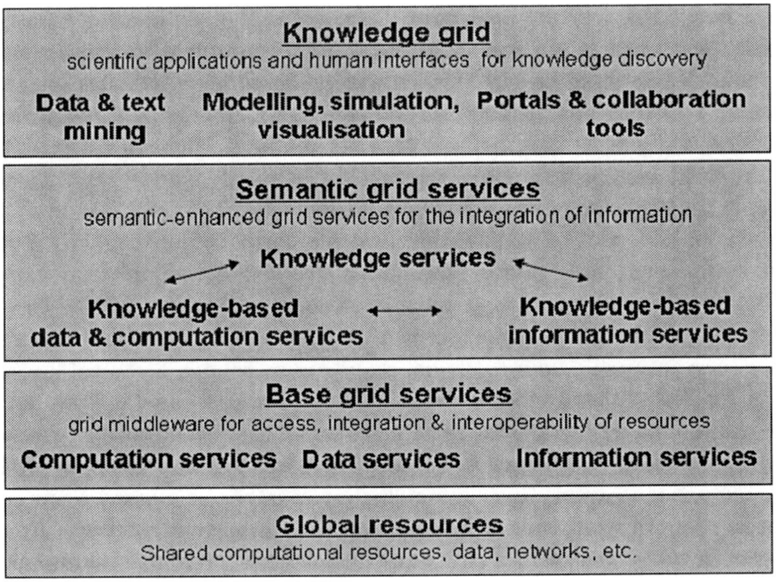

Fig. 12.1 Conceptual layers of the Grid (Markauskaite & Reimann, 2008)

The evolution of grids started in the early 1990s (De Roure, Baker, Jennings & Shadbolt, 2003). The first generation systems primarily focused on proprietary technological solutions for sharing high-performance computing resources at the bottom layer of the Grid model. The objective was to provide computational resources to a range of high-performance applications, primary for scientific discoveries in the life sciences. The second-generation systems focused on heterogeneity, scalability, and adaptability of computational resources and data. They introduced a layer of base Grid service software tools—called "middleware"—that provides users and applications with homogenous standardized interfaces. This Grid middleware layer has provided the means for interoperability and the integration of heterogeneous resources, and a significantly enhanced uptake of e-research in new research areas, including the humanities and the arts, which have started to compile large data archives.

The emerging third-generation systems have focused on the reuse of existing components and information resources, and the possibility of assembling these components in a flexible manner. At this stage, the Grid has started to evolve not only technologically, but has also been reconsidered organizationally. The emphasis has shifted from solely powerful and integrated technological tools, to an evolving infrastructure for transient multi-institutional "virtual organizations" (De Roure, Jennings, & Shadbolt, 2005). Dynamic and coordinated resource sharing and problem solving are the key features of the third-generation Grid. As De Roure et al. (2005) put it, this sharing "is not primarily file exchange, but rather direct access to computers, software, data, and other resources, as is required by a range of collaborative problem-solving and resource brokering strategies emerging in industry, science, and engineering" (p. 669). The key characteristics of the emerging Grid systems are service-oriented architecture and increasing attention to the "knowledge-based layer." This knowledge-based layer includes such aspects as resource description using metadata and ontologies, annotation using provenance information, and process descriptions, such as workflows. These developments have made the Grid increasingly more relevant for scholarly inquiry and knowledge creation in social sciences, arts, and humanities.

In the social sciences, including education, it is currently not so much the concept of Grid computing that is getting researchers involved, but rather the development of Web 2.0 and cloud computing (Greenhow, Robelia, & Hughes, 2009). This is certainly to a large extent due to the fact that the grid computing infrastructure has so far only been accessible with tools that require considerable technical knowledge, whereas the Web 2.0 and cloud computing tools, such as Google Docs, are readily accessible for everybody with basic understanding of web browser use and text processing. In addition, research in the social sciences and in humanities are highly contextualized and experiential, and a single researcher or a small team can still accomplish a lot of work without being involved in large collaborations. An exception is the development of infrastructures that address a research community as a whole, for instance, electronic repositories of cultural heritage, e-journal collections, and integrated distributed data repositories.

Increasing interest in social technologies and Web 2.0-enabled scholarship in education signal that Web 2.0 and cloud computing have the potential to be at least in the short run more transformative than the more radical large-scale visions behind grid computing (Greenhow et al., 2009). It is more likely that in the short term, the practice of individual and small team learning research will be more affected by del.icio.us and Facebook than by large institutional data repositories or scientific workflow applications, especially if these social technologies will be adapted to support researchers' knowledge practices and needs (Schleyer et al., 2008).

However, we would argue that grid computing and social technologies are not mutually exclusive. To the contrary, the concepts of grid computing, in particular of the semantic grid, are very relevant for moving from loose forms of cooperation to more integrated, large-scale research cooperation, incremental innovation, and dissemination. Grid computing is no longer (and never really has been) concerned solely with moving large amounts of scientific data around and crunching these data with numerical methods. Instead, the focus is on supporting research workflows, communication, and on semantic services for accessing and processing data. These technologies if integrated with more democratic Web 2.0 applications could be one of the (technical) enablers of new forms of the distributed research, which is the main focus of the next section.

Innovation and Inquiry Practices: Distributed Research[1]

Not only is it increasingly easier to connect a potentially large group of people with diverse professions and from different organizations for the purpose of conducting research, in education there is also a *need* to do so. It is increasingly acknowledged that traditional quantitative and qualitative educational research has failed to produce transferable and usable knowledge that, when it is acted upon, is likely to produce desirable outcomes in complex natural learning settings (Lagemann, 2002), and consequently failed to support sustainable innovation (Bereiter, 2002a). As Bereiter (2002a) reflecting on the retrospective of quantitative and qualitative educational research reasons,

> the direction of progress in both correlational and experimental research is toward increasingly fine separation of variables, moving farther and farther away from coherent design; most ethnographic researchers are naïve or uninterested in design improvement and most designers are untrained in ethnographic research, so that it is difficult to realise the potential of qualitative research for the advancement of educational innovation (p. 238).

The capacity and willingness of practitioners–innovators to engage in scholarly inquiry processes and conduct educational experiments are also limited (Bereiter, 2002a; Foray & Hargreaves, 2003). Schools, furthermore, are not a playground for testing pedagogical and technical innovation by trial and error and educational innovation must be grounded in research evidence. The basis for the production of innovation is to be found in teachers' design-based practices and teacher-led inquiry into their individual and organizational innovation practices. As Bereiter (2002a) argues, there is a need to create a "hybrid culture" that fuses educational "research culture" and "craft culture" of educational practice. In other words there

[1] This section is partly based on Markauskaite and Reimann (2008).

is a need to enable and support a hybrid model of practitioner and design-based research practice. One of the strengths of technological tools in learning technology research is that they could support not only isolated aspects of research but also integrate research with design and support smoothly all components of the inquiry cycle including problem formulation, design of digital learning artifacts, online data collection, analysis, and further improvement. In this section we discuss the nature of information and communication technology (ICT)-enhanced technological innovations and outline some possibilities of how technological affordances could enable and support such practices. Then, in order to illustrate how these conceptual changes could be linked to specific technologies, we sketch the elements of a high-level architecture for a teacher-oriented inquiry platform.

ICT for Educational Innovation

ICT in educational innovation plays a dual role: it is (a) a fundamental piece of equipment that has an important role in the concept and design of educational practices and (b) an enabler of new educational innovation and knowledge-building models and practices. While the roles of ICT *in* educational innovation are well realized and conceptualized, the potential of ICT *for* educational innovation is neither well understood nor utilized. One important function of ICT could be to overcome the fragmentation of knowledge caused by the multiple separated contexts in which educational knowledge is created.

Educational innovation is distributed in nature. Knowledge that contributes to innovations is generated by universities, schools, publishers, and others. The fundamental challenge is not only to empower all these potential sources of innovation to contribute, but also to integrate their distributed outputs, translate this knowledge into practice and feed it back into new innovation cycles. ICT, as a technological infrastructure, plays an important role for enabling effective organizational models for collaborative knowledge-building and sharing, such as “innovation networks” (Hargreaves, 2003). Web 2.0-based and other collaborative knowledge-sharing platforms can enhance collaboration and innovation uptake (Bentley & Gillinson, 2007). Additionally, new knowledge-creation platforms based on semantic grid technologies and e-research models, as developed in e-science (De Roure & Frey, 2007), can bring about a front-to-end digital chain of collaborative knowledge production—from research or innovation design to output. Further, these platforms can help with the integration and interaction of different kinds of evidence and knowledge produced in multiple case studies, research, and design projects. While it is not the case yet, numerous examples from other industry sectors show that integrated ICT-based platforms that support complex knowledge flows between research, practice, and decision-making could enhance teachers’ potential to engage in systematic inquiry as well as provide new types of evidence for educational decision-making, development, and further innovation (e.g., De Roure & Frey, 2007; Philip, Chorley, Farrington, & Edwards, 2007).

The central role in educational change and innovation is typically attributed to leading teachers who innovate in their everyday practices. Foray and Hargreaves (2003), however, identify two broad issues in the structure and dynamics of the professional knowledge base that impede the efficiency of innovations in classrooms. Firstly, linkages and feedback between formal research and practices are weak; and professional researchers rarely draw upon the practical knowledge of innovative practitioners. Practitioners' capacity and willingness to conduct educational experiments are also limited. Secondly, most of teacher practical knowledge remains tacit. Lack of knowledge codification impedes the accumulation of "know-how" and, as a result, information spillovers and dissemination are weak. Over the last decades, there has been an obvious growth in volume and interest in practitioner inquiry in education, e.g., action research (Cochran-Smith & Lytle, 1999; Dana & Silva, 2003). The outputs, however, vary greatly in quality and significance. Insufficient conceptual and methodological rigor, low generalizability of practice-oriented and heavily contextualized outputs, and lack of clear connection of practitioner research goals to larger social and political agendas are some typical areas of critique of teacher research (Cochran-Smith & Lytle, 1999).

Despite this, teachers' capacity to innovate is probably the most unexploited source for educational development. This capacity could be dramatically enhanced by improving links in the educators' professional knowledge base between scientific and practical knowledge and between tacit (implicit) practical knowledge and codified (explicit) abstract knowledge. This argument is in line with the ideas of other scholars who have advocated preparing teachers–researchers (Foray & Hargreaves, 2003) and creating the "hybrid culture" of research and practice (Bereiter, 2002b, p. 417).

There are a number of examples of less and more successful technology-enhanced research collaboration practices in education evidencing a range of different ways in which similar collaboration tools could support more distributed educational research (Borgman, 2006; Carmichael, 2007; Christie, et al., 2007; Laterza, Carmichael, & Procter, 2007; Procter, 2007; Strijbos & Fischer, 2007; Wilson, et al., 2007), but there are few examples and visions of how technologies could support the whole R&D chain.

From a technological point of view, research environments can provide important affordances and supports for creating, managing, and reusing information and knowledge. Special *innovation systems and e-inquiry platforms* can enhance in various ways individual, collaborative and systems' innovation capacities. Innovation and knowledge building in collaborative technology-supported environments have, however, a sociotechnical overhead, and it is challenging to achieve an alignment between technical and distributed human information systems (Ure, Procter, Lin, Hartswood, & Ho, 2007). For example, in order to make designs and data reusable, teachers need to describe their digital objects using metadata and shared domain ontologies and other annotations that could help others to understand, interpret, and repurpose their contributions in different contexts. Further, in our previous work we analyzed some social, cognitive, and technical aspects of teacher knowledge, collaborative work, and inquiry in digital environments and argued that research platforms should support teacher individual and social practices of knowledge construction (Markauskaite & Reimann, 2008). In other words, technical affordances should be aligned with and support cognitive and social knowledge creation practices.

Teachers as innovators and researchers need inquiry models that are better tuned to their everyday professional needs and allow creating trustworthy theory and research-inspired classroom innovations, thus combining the key strengths of practitioners' and researchers' inquiry approaches. The integration of the key epistemic strengths and steps of practitioner and design-based research could provide such models for teacher–researcher instructional innovations. We propose that such model could have a strong focus on a theory and research-based design, practitioners' reflection and sharing of outputs. In this way, design-based practitioner research model should have a strong focus on the following steps: (a) an initial definition of a learning problem; (b) identification and planning of theory and research-based solutions and actions; (c) design of the instructional interventions and other changes; (d) implementation and monitoring; (e) analysis and evaluation using scholarly qualitative and quantitative research techniques; (f) reflection and evidence-driven refinement of instructional strategies; and (e) communication and dissemination of innovations and research outputs.

A Teacher-Led Inquiry Platform

From sociotechnical perspective, the structure and the major elements of an e-inquiry environment for teacher innovation should not necessarily mirror, nevertheless support the above delineated model of knowledge construction. For example, Fig. 12.2 shows one of such possible designs of educational innovation and research platform. It includes three interconnected inquiry spaces: (a) *design, research, and reflection space* primarily designed for individual and small-team knowledge work; (b) *collaboration and knowledge sharing space* primarily designed for a broader community-based knowledge sharing and building; and (c) *knowledge dissemination and decision-making space* primarily designed for meta-level inquiries in shared innovation and research repositories.

The design, research, and reflection space includes a range of interconnected digital affordances that can help teachers to design, monitor, and evaluate ICT-enhanced innovations. Depending on the needs, this space could be used for individual or group innovations, but it primarily provides tools that are used for classroom innovation, research, and reflection and those inquiry tasks that are typically more individual or cooperative rather than collaborative, as it is common in classroom innovations, and do not require extensive synchronous interaction. For example, tools for instructional design allow to create new instructional resources repurposing available design patterns, learning objects and other resources. Tools for inquiry help to design and manage associated design-based practitioner inquiry studies. They can allow teachers to access and reuse standard design-based practitioner inquiry workflows, use various project management tools, integrate various documents, data, and other digital objects created at various stages of inquiry, and

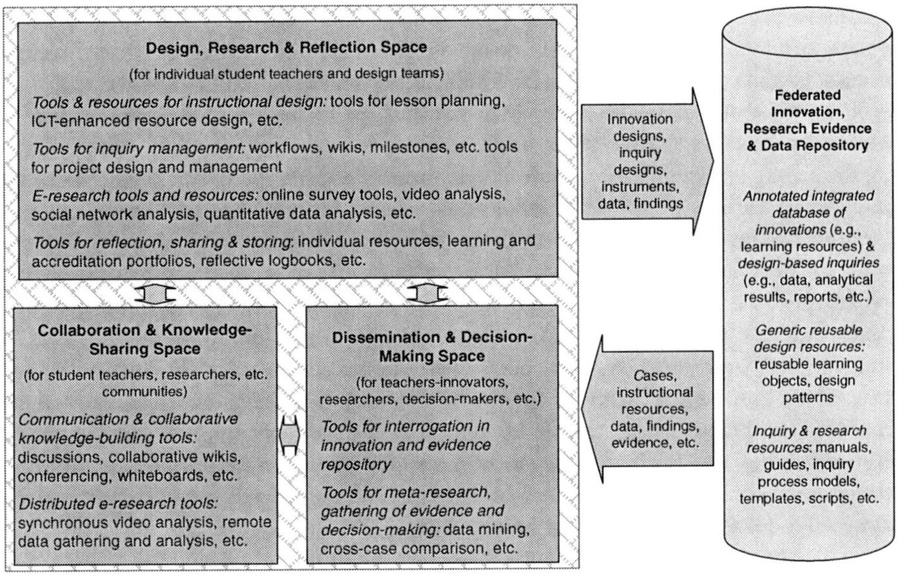

Fig. 12.2 A high-level architecture for an e-inquiry environment

generate reports for dissemination and sharing. Technological tools support various types of data analysis, including classroom video observations, automatic, and semiautomatic analysis of student online learning and interaction (e.g., CSCL [computer-supported collaborative learning], automatic essay analysis tools, and social network analysis). Such tools, based on the Grid technologies and semantic web architectures, can hide some complexity of educational data analysis, help to integrate various data sources (e.g., automatically captured data about student online learning and interactions with data collected in explicit ways, such as online surveys), and help teachers to use more robust and complex research techniques. Tools for reflection, sharing, and storing (e.g., e-portfolios or reflective logbooks) provide virtual spaces for storing created digital artifacts, help to document them and simplify knowledge sharing (e.g., add standard metadata to created instructional resources and collected evidence before teachers deposit them into public repositories).

The collaboration and knowledge-sharing space primarily provides support for collaborative research, knowledge-building, networking, and sharing. The tools in this space can serve different purposes. Collaboration tools provide affordances for intensive communication on designs and other questions within design-based inquiry teams and for involvement into knowledge-building process of other community members that are not core members of an inquiry team. They primarily include various synchronous and asynchronous communication means for discursive knowledge building, such as discussion boards, collaborative wikis, synchronous conferences, and shared whiteboards. Distributed e-research tools provide extensive possibilities for remote synchronous data analysis, such as distributed annotation and analysis of classroom video observations, remote synchronous access to data sets, and analysis. Tools allow teachers' collaboration with heterogeneous external professional communities, to include instructional designers, university researchers, and other professionals.

Knowledge dissemination and decision-making space provides possibilities for integrating various classroom innovations, related inquiry data and evidences into large shared innovation, and evidence repositories. This space provides a knowledge base for new innovations and decision-making. Firstly, shared repositories create opportunities for teachers interrogating such knowledge collections, finding inquiry cases that are relevant for their professional questions (including descriptions of innovations, their contexts, associated instructional resources, data, and evidences, i.e., what, how and why these innovations work). Teachers, building upon these resources and knowledge, can develop their new classroom innovations. Secondly, well-described small classroom innovations and inquiry data provide possibilities for conducting integrated analyses of raw data and meta-analyses of inquiry results at broader community or system levels.

ICT-enhanced educational innovations are modular in nature. Innovation systems and inquiry platforms can provide effective means for storing, sharing, and repurposing instructional resources (such as learning objects), design patterns, learning activity, and research workflows as well as other related digital artifacts and knowledge in *federated repositories*. Metadata with instructional contexts and provenance records, inquiry data, results, and evidence amended to the design-based innovations provide rich opportunities for integrating small-scale distributed classroom innovations and data into larger evidence repositories. This provides opportunities for reusing data in new meta-level studies using new data-driven methods (e.g., data mining). Such studies could generate new types of knowledge and generalized evidence that otherwise would be impossible to gain from individual inquiries.

Taken as a whole, such an e-inquiry infrastructure could support the entire digital life cycle of ICT-enhanced educational innovations and knowledge. Moreover, such platforms based on open service-oriented architectures allow flexible reconfiguration of spaces and tools to match specific needs of innovators, their knowledge structures, and knowing processes. And it provides a basis for distributing research on students' (and teachers') learning between the main actors, teachers, and full-time researchers. This will be essential, since it is unrealistic to assume that teachers will find the time to engage in extended research on top of all their other duties, even if they had the interest and the incentives.

Process Data Streams and Video Data

To illustrate specific applications (that could be seen as a part of the above discussed e-inquiry platform, but also independent areas of learning technology research), in this section we will focus on some specific methodological challenges in learning technology research and discuss emerging approaches and technologies helping to address these issues.

When Data is Flowing in Streams

With the ever-increasing use of mobile and web technologies for learning in- and outside of classrooms researchers gain potential access to quasi-continuous data "streams." This kind of data is invaluable given the current lack of process data that is available on a level close to students' learning activities. However, to capitalize on this potential a number of hurdles need to be overcome. Some of these are technical (how to represent, store, and access the data), some legal (data privacy, etc.), and some methodological: how to analyze process data, and along with that: how to theorize learning and development processes in pedagogical and psychological terms. We trust engineers to overcome the technical hurdles, and law and policy makers to deal with issues of privacy and governance. The methodological challenges we cannot delegate to others, however.

The methods potentially useful to analyze process data of individual and group learning as learners interact with technologies are too manifold to be surveyed here (see Langley, 1999; Olson, Herbsleb, & Rueter, 1994; Reimann, 2009 for a recent review specific to CSCL). Instead, we will focus on methods that are fully computational (or at least for which automatization is feasible) and are hence prime candidates for the (quasi-continuous) analysis of very large amounts of (quasi-continuous) data that are increasingly available in form of log files, for instance, from web-based learning environments and from "immersive" environments such as Second Life. For such amounts of data, stemming from learning situations that are rarely experimentally controlled, inductive data mining methods are helpful.

Data mining algorithms allow to analyze vast amounts of electronic traces, combined or not with complementary information (such as exam marks), and discover patterns that are not visible to the human eye (Ye, 2003). An important aspect of learner data is the *temporal aspect* of its events. A particular interesting question for understanding the quality of learning is whether there are some sequences of events that are more frequent within successful learners than within less successful ones (or vice versa). Sequential pattern mining (Srikant & Agrawal, 1996) is an example of algorithm that considers this temporal aspect and detects frequent sequences of items (here, events) appearing in a sequence data set a minimum number of times (called *support*). For example in the example given in Table 12.1, the sequence <a.d> has a support of 4 as it appears in all four sequences whereas <b,d> has a support of 2.

Applied to collaborative data, items such as a, b, c, and d become a representation of an atomic and multidimensional event (which typically would have the event's author, the time, the type of intervention, and possibly more information). Perera, Kay, Koprinska, Yacef, & Zaiane (2008), for instance, have built a variant of the

Table 12.1 Example of data used in sequential pattern mining

Sequence 1	<b,a,d,b>
Sequence 2	<a,b,b,d,c>
Sequence 3	<a,c,d>
Sequence 4	<a,c,c,d>

Generalized Sequential Pattern algorithm and applied it to collaborative learner data. The context was a senior software development project where students worked in teams of five to seven students and interacted over a collaboration tool comprising of a wiki, a task allocation system and a subversion repository. Perera and colleagues searched for sequential patterns within groups as well as within individuals and classified the results according to the "quality" of the group, based on marks, and on teachers' assessment of the group. Results pointed to the importance of leadership and group interaction, and they were able to identify patterns indicative of good and poor individual practice. An example of interesting patterns found was that well-performing groups used more heavily the task allocation system than the wiki, whereas weaker groups displayed the opposite characteristic.

Before forms of data mining such as just described can be conducted without human intervention, numerous decisions pertaining to issues such as data granularity (what should be considered to be a "event"?), model granularity (on which level to express learning and change: time series, event sequences, holistic structures such as textual summaries?), and regarding the tuning of the many parameters data mining methods come with need to be decided. Many of these decisions will depend on the *purpose* of the data analysis, of course constraint by the kind of data and the processing resources available. For instance, one might make different decisions when the purpose is monitoring of students' learning instead of finding a theoretically elegant description of regularities in the data.

Viewing individual or collaborative learning in terms of sequences of events makes few assumptions about the nature of the learning situation. For instance, we can look for sequences in classroom interactions as well as in informal learning situations. However, in situations where students' learning activities can be expected to follow at least partially a predefined structure, such as a group collaboration script (Kollar, Fischer, & Hesse, 2006), we can take into account this information by using process models representations of higher granularity, such as Finite State Machines or Petri Nets. Reimann, Frerejean, & Thompson (2009) for instance, made use of discreet event modeling techniques to represent group decision-making processes from chat log data in form of dependency graphs as illustrated in Fig. 12.3. The arcs on the right side of the boxes that point back at their own box indicate loops, meaning that statements of this type often occurred multiple times in a row. The numbers along the arcs show the temporal dependency of the relationship between two events, with the arrow pointing from a to be meaning that a is followed by b. The second number indicates the number of times this order of events occurred. The numbers in the boxes indicate the frequency of the respective event type.

Generalizing from this example, process mining approaches as developed so far mainly for enterprise computing could also play a role in educational e-research

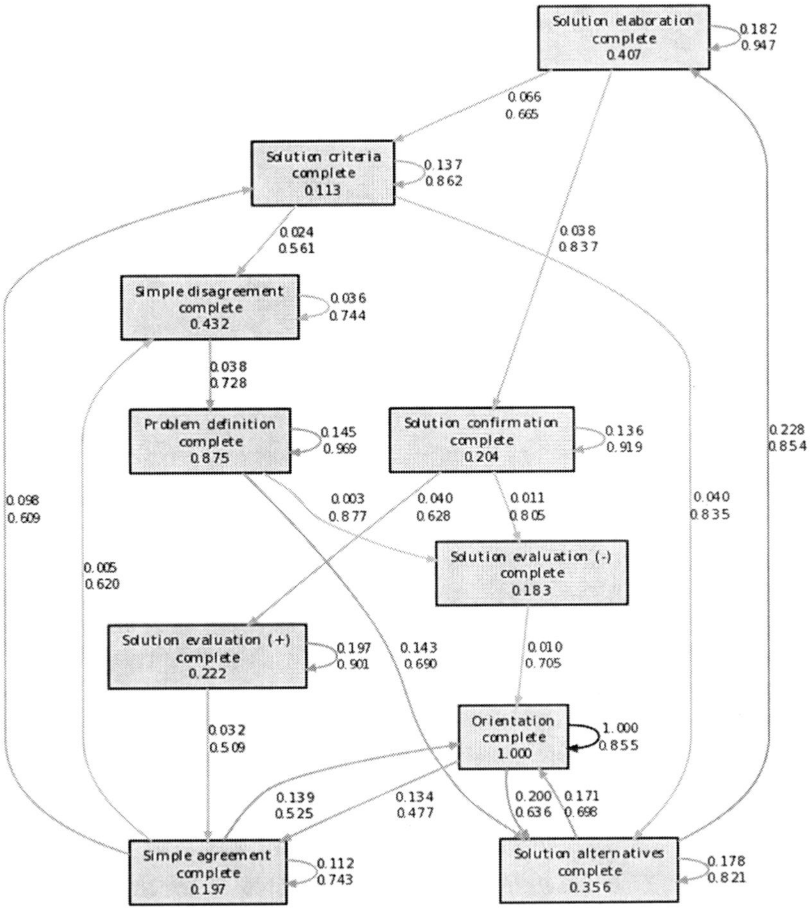

Fig. 12.3 Dependency graph as a visual representation of a group decision-making process

as illustrated in Fig. 12.4, process modeling can be used on data from event logs, which are typical for the kind of "continuous" data one gets from web servers and web applications. If the process mining algorithm is provided as service, then the even analysis can occur concurrently with changes in the event logs.

Process mining algorithms allow to analyze both structural aspects of a process—How are events/activities related to each? Who is interacts in realizing a process?—as well as performance aspects, for instance, related to the analysis of durations (see Van der Aalst & Weijters, 2005 for an overview). The output of a structural analysis can, for instance, be a dependency graph, depicting the structure of a (collaborative) process, such as shown in Fig. 12.3 for the case of decision-making processes as reflected in chat log files. Process mining can serve a number of purposes, among them:

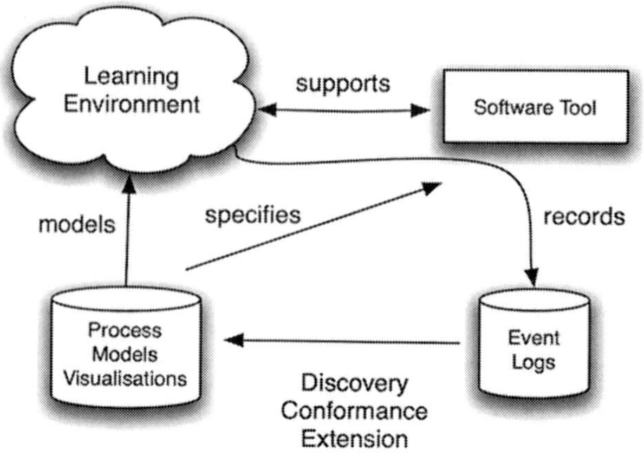

Fig. 12.4 Role of process modeling for analyzing event logs (modified after van der Aalst & Günther, 2007).

- Discovery—No a priori model exists. Based on a event log a model is constructed;
- Conformance—An a priori model exists. Event logs are used to determine the extent to which the enacted collaboration corresponds to the model.
- Extension—an a priori model exists. The goal is not to test but to extend the model, for instance, with performance data (e.g., durations of activities). Extended models can then be used for example to optimize the process (Van der Aalst & Günther, 2007).

To the extent that the algorithms can be sufficiently tuned to a specific area of individual or collaborative learning to deliver meaningful results, they could be run without human intervention and hence realize a (quasi-)continuous analysis of (quasi-)continuous data streams.

Collaborative Analysis of Video Recordings

Video as a data format to analyze and learn from is highly valued in education, both by practitioners as well as by researchers (Goldman, Pea, Barron, & Sharon, 2007). Like no other medium, video recordings (including audio) can store contextual information, which is particularly important for recording practices, such as classroom practices, which are not predominantly taking place in a textual medium. Since video recordings can store so much (but certainly not everything) of the context, they also allow the researcher to defer decisions as to which information to attend do in detail to later (thus contributing in no small measure the *data deluge* typical for qualitative research).

However, at this stage the analysis of video data is a very work-intensive practice. Depending on the questions asked and the analysis method employed, the relation between recorded time and analysis time can easily rich a proportion of 1 to several hundred units of time (Jordan & Henderson, 1995). In order to make video a data format that is a practical choice beyond a Ph.D. thesis, analyzing video invites collaboration, not only for practical reasons, but also because some methodologies require joint sense making of what is recorded. Roy Pea and colleagues have coined the term "video collaboratories" to highlight the special requirements for collaboration around video as data resources: "In research-oriented video collaboratories, scientists will work together to share video data sets, metadata schemes, analysis tools, coding systems, advice and other resources, and build video analyses together, in order to advance the collective understanding of the behaviors represented in digital video data" (Pea & Lindgren, 2008, p. 236).

The notion of collaboratively annotating video materials for the purposes of professional development and research-oriented analysis has become quite popular (for an overview, see e.g., Rich & Hannafin, 2009). For instance, Huppertz, Massler, and Plötzner (2005) have conducted a study whereby students and educators can provide online comments on short video clips delivered on the web. The short video clips can then be replayed with the comments and shared among the teachers and students. This digital learning environment has received positive feedbacks from students in the synthesis and analysis of video learning experience and related animation. The VideoPaper project at Tuft University (Beardsley, Cogan-Drew, & Olivero, 2007) has produced successful collaborations and interactions between learning sciences researchers, educators, and practitioners through digital video by encouraging reflection. The DIVER platform (Digital Interactive Video Exploration and Reflection, Pea, Mills, Rosen, Dauber, & Effelsberg, 2004), developed at the Stanford Centre for Innovation in Learning, allows researchers to easily edit and annotate collected video footage obtained from a panoramic camera, thus creating lightweight "dives" that illustrate some specific points or pieces of evidence. Dives can subsequently be exported to a Web site, so that other researchers have a chance to observe and comment on them. The web-based HyperVideo platform (Chambel, Zahn, & Finke, 2004) for collaborative learning, developed at the Computer Graphics Center/Darmstadt and the Knowledge Media Research Center/Tübingen, is based on the idea of selecting video segments from a source video and having spatio-temporal hyperlinks added by multiple users.

Another video annotation tool is EVA (web-based *E*ducation *V*ideo with collaborative *A*nnotation), developed at the University of Sydney (Wong & Reimann, 2009). It supports

- Real-time collaborative temporal video bookmarking and collaborative temporal HTML annotations associated with each video bookmark.
- Web-based video and annotation delivery with synchronization option for ease of presentation and viewing.
- Automatic indexation of the temporal video bookmarks and associated annotations for friendly navigation.
- Search facility of the time point of the video using matching information from the content of bookmarks and annotations.

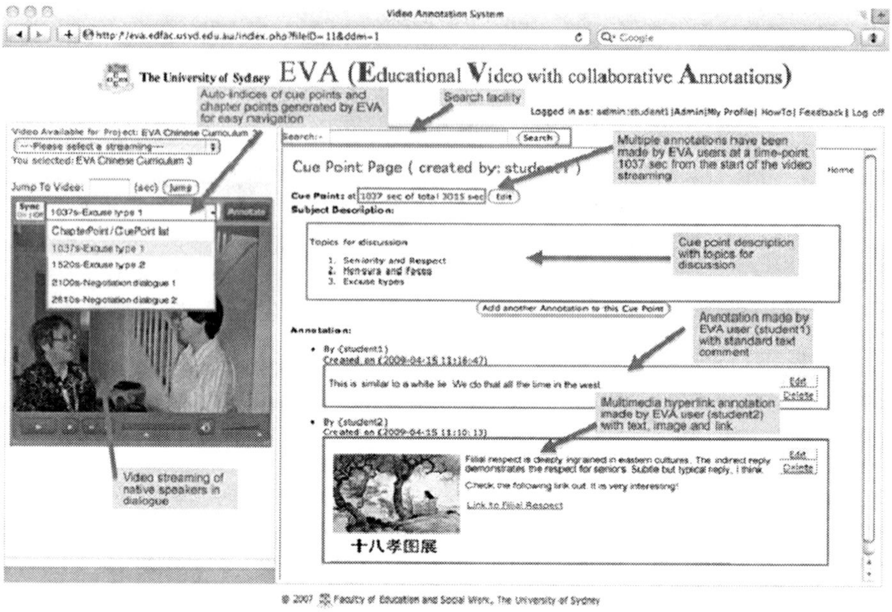

Fig. 12.5 Screenshot of the main interface of EVA

EVA contains two parts: a video streaming part and a part for displaying segments of video temporal bookmarks, called cue-segments, and their associated lists of users' annotations. Figure 12.5 illustrates the main user interface for EVA system showing both the video streaming on the left side and the list of annotations for a cue-point on the right side. At any time in a video, a user can create a comment that is pertinent to the context of the video at that particular time-point. EVA will generate a new cue-point and prompt for a cue-point description whenever a user tries to bookmark a new time-point. Otherwise, a user can append a new annotation to the list of annotations at a particular cue-point. The collection of cue-points forms a list of indices for user to navigate within the video content. Each annotation can be entered and modified by the owner of the annotation via a friendly WYSIWYG HTML editor and can contain images, diagrams, and other HTML hyperlinks. Each annotation can also be deleted and edited by the author. Because multiple users can annotate at each time-point of the video, each annotation is identified by the user, the time of creation, and the time of last modification.

Several pilot projects in teaching and learning using the EVA platform are currently being conducted at the University of Sydney in sport coaching, child development psychology, teacher professional learning, and social works. In sport coaching, each student coach videotaped both a live session of his/her coaching a team in an actual sport engagement and a live session of his/her private coaching of individual team member. Both videos were then uploaded onto the EVA platform for the teacher and peer student coaches for comments. The aim of the pilot is to promote microteaching, collaboration and reflective learning. In the teacher professional learning scenario, all keynote speakers from each professional learning seminar were videotaped and the videos were put onto the EVA repositories to be shared with and commented by other professional teachers. The objective is to cultivate professional communities of inquiry and practice based on the knowledge sharing and evolutionary growth paradigm (dePaula, Fischer, & Ostwald, 2001) where initial set of EVA videos can be viewed as initial knowledge seeds.

The responses from teachers and students toward the new form of video-based teaching and learning experience using EVA had been overwhelmingly positive. The users were excited about potential use of EVA teaching and learning experience. The users found the ability to interact with the video by constructing and sharing time-based commentaries very useful and refreshing for collaboration and reflection. Others perceived EVA activities as an effective process for collective knowledge construction and generation. All users liked the fact that they could annotate collaboratively, flexibly, and in real time.

While tools such as EVA are making it really easy to use video materials as resource for individual and collaborative reflection and knowledge creation in Higher Education settings, they also have the potential to lead to new forms of collaboration that build on new ways to distribute research work between various parties. This is addressed in Pea's notion of a "video collaboratory," but can go beyond the small team, involving mass collaboration around video sources, for instance by tagging. As is demonstrated by sites such as Del.icio.us and Flickr, mass tagging of artifacts—the emergence of *folksonomies*—can create valuable knowledge based on loose cooperation amongst the tag contributors, knowledge that can exploited for information management and research (e.g., Hotho, Jaeschke, Schmitt, & Stumme, 2006).

Mixed-Method Research: Establishing Trust in Findings

Many researchers in the field of technology-enhanced learning make use of mixed methods, combining qualitative and quantitative data. Qualitative methods play an important role because technology is a resource, not a causal factor in itself (Cohen, Raudenbush, & Loewenberg Ball, 2003): the effects of technology, like other resources, are dependent on its use by people, how they interpret a situation, and what technology could do for them. In the context of educational use of ICT, little can be learned about the effects of any technology on the school system without an analysis of teaching and learning processes. Furthermore, since technology is part of the larger context of a specific teaching/learning situation, it may in principle be impossible to separate the underlying (agentic or process) causality from the context (Maxwell, 2004).

There is a strong philosophical basis for agentic causation (for an overview, see Abell, 2004; Reimann, 2009) so that we do not have to be necessarily worried about the ontological underpinning of single-case causality. However, the epistemological question remains: How can we know that we have identified the correct causality in a single case or small N study? Or in other words (those of Kelly, 2004), how can we distinguish between the *contingent* and the *necessary*? Ideally, questions such as this could be answered at the level of the method, and would not have to be achieved on the level of a specific study, i.e., for each application of the method. What would need to be established for each application of the method is that it was realized with an acceptable quality standard. We can, hence, distinguish between the *argumentative grammar* (Kelly, 2004) of a method, the logic by which evidence is linked to claims (conclusions, interpretations, and recommendations), and the *provenance* of the data and claims (the manner they were brought about in a specific study). Together, these two aspects contribute to developing *trust* in the outcomes of a study: via the argumentative grammar, it is established that findings resulting from the application of the method are *in principle* warranted, and the provenance information can be used to establish that the method was applied correctly in a specific study. Since the argumentative grammar of the various methods used in learning research have been and continue to be extensively discussed (approaches and technological applications discussed in the section above have also focused on this level), we will focus here on the provenance aspect that underlies many methodologies and data, but has received little attention in learning research so far. It is also the aspect that could be addressed by information technology.

Provenance of Data and Findings

The term provenance is mostly used in Arts, where it is used to describe the history of ownership of a work of art. In computer science, Groth et al. (2006) define the provenance of a piece of data as "… the process that led to that piece of data"; as such, provenance is synonymous with data lineage, pedigree, or history and applies to quantitative as well as qualitative data. Reviews of related lines of research in computer and information science are provided by Bose and Frew (2005) and Simmhan, Plale, and Gannon (2005).

Provenance can relate to the use of data both within a study (e.g., How was the data created? How transformed? How did it enter into the conclusions?) as well as across studies (e.g., Which other studies refer to this data?). In this way, provenance can be used to assess data quality and reliability, to establish ownership of data, to establish an interpretation context, or to replicate a study (Chorley, Edwards, Preece, & Farrington, 2007).

The general architecture of a provenance system (Groth et al., 2006) relates provenance-processing services (such as for data audits) to the provenance records gained from an application environment (such as a number of qualitative and quantitative data transformation and analysis services) as shown in Fig. 12.6. In the general framework described by Groth et al., provenance information is represented as assertions (so-called p-assertions) made by an actor pertaining to a process. The

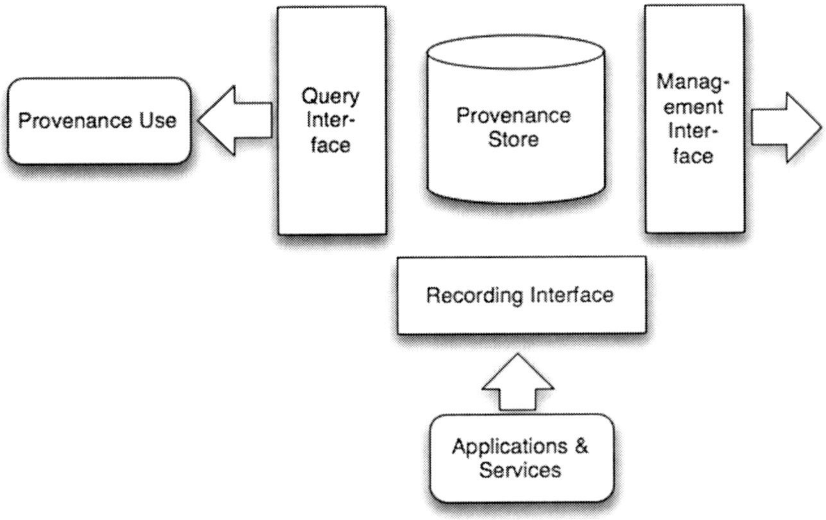

Fig. 12.6 Architecture of a general provenance system

central information stored in a provenance store is made up of process documentations, each consisting of a set of p-assertions made by the actors involved in the process.

Consider the hypothetical examples as shown in Fig. 12.7: a section in a video is coded by a rater using Transana for instance. The code is saved in the Transana database. At this stage, a provenance-enabled Transana would create a

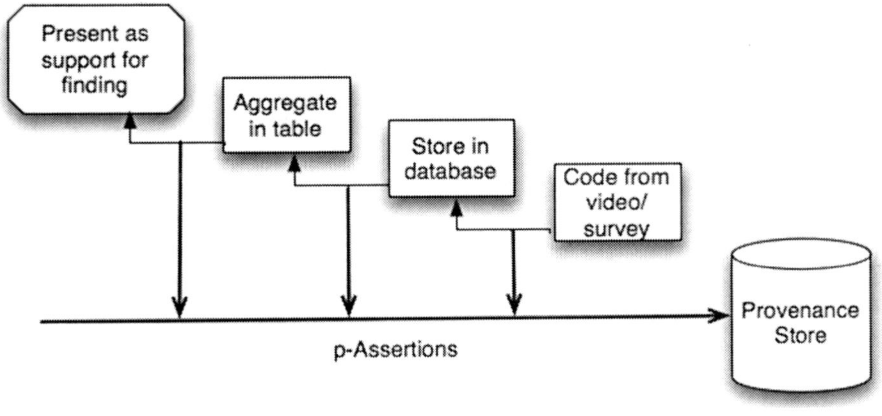

Fig. 12.7 Evidence chains examples

p-message and send it to a provenance system (outside of Transana), describing this coding event in some detail. Later, the same or a person different from the coder would retrieve a bunch of coded events from the Transana database and aggregate them into various counts, for instance using a spreadsheet program or a statistical package such as SPSS. The spreadsheet program, if provenance enabled, would create a p-assertion describing this operation. Finally, a word processor would be used to write a research report, using the frequency figures so support a specific claim about a finding. That part of the report would be linked back to the frequency table, and the word processor would issue a p-assertion to the provenance store describing this link. The graph shows a similar chain for the case of processing answers to a questionnaire or interview.

Having documented such chains of events in a provenance store, anybody interested in finding out how claims in the report are related to data could use the provenance system query interface to do so. To the extent that the outputs of the various steps are stored in some form digitally and are accessible through the Internet, the intermediate outputs can be displayed. To the extent that the applications are available as services, the process yielding the evidence chain can even be replayed.

A number of provenance systems have been developed in science e-research projects, for instance, *CombeChem* (Taylor et al., 2006) and *MyGrid* (Stevens, Robinson, & Goble, 2003). These tools track the experiment and analysis process and automatically create provenance record as well as allow researchers to annotate key research steps using controlled vocabulary or narrative descriptions. While in the social sciences the automatic tracking of data-producing processes is not as easy as in the scientist's laboratory, provenance approaches have been developed there as well, for instance, in the *PolicyGrid* project (Philip, Chorley, Farrington, & Edwards, 2007a).

In learning science research the provenance architectures must enable the capture of not only how data were created, but also the context in which data were originated. For design-based research, for instance, two key aspects of the provenance are important: (a) pedagogical or learning design provenance, related to the design of the pedagogical intervention; and (b) methodological or study design provenance, related to the accompanying study, data acquisition (observations, tests, etc.), and analysis. While structures and ontologies for representing science experiments can be adapted for methodology provenance (e.g., Taylor et al., 2006), new structures and ontologies need to be created to represent pedagogical designs.

Conclusions

In this chapter we introduced some existing and some emerging technologies and discussed the potential to enhance learning research. To repeat: technologies are evocative and open for many interpretations. How technology-enhanced research will be taken up, what kinds of research practices they will support, and for what kinds of tasks they will be utilized for is by large dependent on their use: Neither can technology determine our research practices nor can our research practices determine technologies; they are mutually coconstructed. This chapter presents just a few possible interpretations that have emerged from our own learning technology innovation and research practices as well as our engagement with research innovations in other disciplinary domains.

Research technologies and practices are created at and shaped by visions and actions at several levels. On the highest technological level a symbiosis of Grid and Web 2.0 computing could enable more integrated and collaborative research practices and new data-rich research methodologies. Growing attention of educational research community to social technologies might indicate that learning technology researchers will perhaps in the near future embrace these technologies in their research routines. While they offer great potential to democratize research and make it more transparent, other methodological advancements and innovations require more coordinated actions and more targeted solutions to technological challenges. For example, while our outlined e-inquiry platform could be seen as a bottom-up emerging social and technological space, its real potential rests on semantically well linked and integrated components. It would be hard to expect that such integration could be achieved without a priori coordination and agreement at least on some major technological specifications, such as for provenance and metadata.

There are many methodological issues in learning technology research that pertain to the limits of human abilities to process data without research instruments and currently provide a serious challenge for further research advancement. We are already recording much more data in learning research than are analyzed and reported; these data deluge offer great opportunity to investigate learning phenomenon on larger scales and greater levels of detail, but constitutes also a big methodological challenge (Borgman et al., 2008). We discussed just two methodological approaches—process analysis and multimedia data—where important advancements have been achieved over the last 10 years. This list by no means complete, with such approaches as educational data mining (Romero & Ventura, 2007), social network analysis (Wasserman & Faust, 1994), and virtual ethnographies (Beaulieu, 2004) being rapidly further developed and applied.

We discussed and emphasized some technological issues. In learning technology research, the phenomenon studied is by nature contextualized and often distributed. The ways in which the phenomena are studied are often based on interpretations that are deeply entrenched in our personal experiences. Under such circumstances, data about the inquiry contexts and how results were produced become an important part of research output and data. Questions of how to record and share contextual information are at the core for further advancement in learning technology research.

References

Aalst, W. M. Pv. d, & Günther, C. W. (2007). Finding structure in unstructured processes: The case of process mining. In T. Basten, G. Juhas & S. Shukla (Eds.), *Proceedings the 7th International Conference on Applications of Concurrency to System Design (ACSD 2007; Bratislava, Slovak Republic)* (pp. 3–12). Los Alamitos, CA: IEEE Computer Society Press.

Abell, P. (2004). Narrative explanations: An alternative to variable-centered explanation? *Annual Review of Sociology, 30*, 287–310.

Barjak, F., Lane, J., Kertcher, Z., Poschen, M., Procter, R., & Robinson, S. (2009). Case studies of e-infrastructure adoption. *Social Science Computer Review*, Online first, published on April 8, 2009.

Beardsley, L., Cogan-Drew, D., & Olivero, F. (2007). VideoPaper: Bridging research and practice for preservice and experienced teachers. In R. Goldman, R. Pea, B. Barron & S. Derry (Eds.), *Video research in the learning sciences* (pp. 479–493). Mahwah, NJ: Erlbaum.

Beaulieu, A. (2004). Mediating ethnography: reflections on ethnographic practices and the study of the internet. *Social Epistemology 18*(2-3), 139–163.

Bentley, T., & Gillinson, S. (2007). *A D&R system for education*. London: Innovation Unit.

Bereiter, C. (2002a). Design research for sustained innovation. *Cognitive Studies Bulletin of the Japanese Cognitive Science Society, 9*(3), 321–327.

Bereiter, C. (2002b). *Education and mind in the knowledge age*. Mahwah, NJ: Lawrence Erlbaum Associates.

Berman, F., Fox, G., & Hey, A. J. G. (2003). The grid: Past, present, future. In F. Berman, G. Fox & A. J. G. Hey (Eds.), *Grid computing: Making the global infrastructure a reality* (pp. 9–50). West Sussex: Wiley.

Borgman, C. (2006). What can studies of e-learning teach us about collaboration in e-research? Some findings from digital library studies. *Computer supported cooperative work, 15*(4), 359–383.

Borgman, C. L., Abelson, H., Dirks, L., Johnson, R., Koedinger, K. R., Linn, M. C., et al. (2008). Fostering learning in the networked world:The cyberlearning opportunity and challenge A 21st century agenda for the National Science Foundation. Report of the NSF Task Force on Cyberlearning. June 24, 2008.

Bose, R., & Frew, J. (2005). Lineage retrieval for scientific data processing: A survey. *ACM Computing Surveys, 37*(1), 1–28.

Carmichael, P. (2007). Introduction: Technological development, capacity building and knowledge construction in education research. *Technology, Pedagogy and Education, 16*(3), 235–247.

Chambel, T., Zahn, C., & Finke, M. (2004). *Hypervideo design and support for contextualized learning*. Proceedings of the IEEE international conference on advanced learning technologies (ICALT'04) (pp. 345–349).

Chorley, A., Edwards, P., Preece, A., & Farrington, J. (2007, October). *Tools for tracing evidence in social science*. Paper presented at the third international conference on e-social science, Ann Arbor, MI, USA.

Christie, D., Cassidy, C., Skinner, D., Coutts, N., Sinclair, C., Rimpilainen, S., et al. (2007). Building collaborative communities of enquiry in educational research. *Educational Research and Evaluation, 13*(3), 263–278.

Cochran-Smith, M., & Lytle, S. L. (1999). The teacher research movement: A decade later. *Educational Researcher, 28*(7), 15–25.

Cohen, L. (2007). *Social scholarship on the rise*. Retrieved August 11, 2009, from http://liblogs.albany.edu/library20/2007/04/social_scholarship_on_the_rise.html

Cohen, D. K., Raudenbush, S. W., & Loewenberg Ball, D. (2003). Resources, instruction, and research. *Educational Evaluation and Policy Analysis, 25*(2), 119–142.

Dana, N. F., & Silva, D. Y. (2003). *The reflective educator's guide to classroom research: Learning to teach and teaching to learn through practitioner inquiry*. Thousand Oaks, CA: Corwin Press.

De Roure, D., & Frey, J. (2007). *Three perspectives on collaborative knowledge acquisition in e-science*. Paper presented at the workshop on semantic web for collaborative knowledge acquisition (SWeCKa), Hyderabad, India.

De Roure, D., Jennings, N. R., & Shadbolt, N. R. (2005). The semantic grid: Past, present, and future. *Proceedings of the IEEE, 93*(3), 669–681.

De Roure, D., Baker, M. A., Jennings, N. R., & Shadbolt, N. R. (2003). The Evolution of the Grid. In F. Berman, G. Fox & A. J. G. Hey (Eds), *Grid Computing: Making the Global Infrastructure a Reality* (pp. 65–100). West Sussex: Wiley.

dePaula, R., Fischer, G., & Ostwald, J. (2001). *Courses as seeds: Expectations and realities*. Proceedings of the Second European Conference on Computer-Supported Collaborative Learning (Euro-CSCL 2001) (pp. 494–501). Maastricht, Netherlands.

Foray, D., & Hargreaves, D. (2003). The production of knowledge in different sectors: a model and some hypotheses. *London Review of Education, 1*(1), 7–19.

Foster, I., Kesselman, C., & Tuecke, S. (2001). The anatomy of the grid. Enabling scalable virtual organizations. *International Journal of Supercomputer Applications, 15*(3), 200–222.

Gibbons, M., Limoges, C., Nowotny, H., Schwartzman, S., Scott, P., & Trow, M. (1994). *The new production of knowledge: The dynamics of science and research in contemporary societies*. London: Sage.

Goldman, R., Pea, R., Barron, B., & Sharon, S. D. (2007). *Video research in the learning sciences*. Mahwah, NJ: Erlbaum.

Greenhow, C., Robelia, B., & Hughes, J. E. (2009). Web 2.0 and classroom research: What path should we take now? *Educational Researcher, 38*(4), 246–259.

Groth, P., Jiang, S., Miles, S., Munroe, S., Tan, V., Tsasakou, S., et al. (2006). *An architecture for provenance systems*. Retrieved from http://eprints.ecs.soton.ac.uk/12023/

Hargreaves, D. (2003). *Education epidemic: Transforming secondary schools through innovation networks*. London: Demos.

Hotho, A., Jaeschke, R., Schmitt, C., & Stumme, G. (2006). Information retrieval in folksonomies: Search and ranking. *The semantic web: Research and applications* (pp. 411–426). Berlin: Springer.

Huppertz, P., Massler, U., & Plötzner, R. (2005). v-share—Video-based analysis and reflection of teaching experiences in virtual groups. *Proceedings of the International Conference on Computer Support for Collaborative Learning*. Mahwah, NJ: Erlbaum.

Jacbos, D. (2005, July/August). Enterprise software as service. *Queue, 3*(6), 36–42.

Jordan, B., & Henderson, A. (1995). Interaction analysis: Foundations and practice. *The Journal of the Learning Sciences, 4*(1), 39–103.

Kelly, A. E. (2004). Design research in education: Yes, but is it methodological? *The Journal of the Learning Sciences, 13*(1), 115–128.

Kollar, I., Fischer, F., & Hesse, F. W. (2006). Collaboration scripts – a conceptual analysis. *Educational Psychological Review, 18*, 159–185.

Lagemann, E. C. (2002). *Usable knowledge in Education: a memorandum for the Spencer Foundation Board of Directors (Memorandum)*. Retrieved from http://www.spencer.org/publications/usable_knowledge_report_ecl_a.htm

Langley, A. (1999). Strategies for theorizing from process data. *Academy of Management Review, 24*(4), 691–710.

Laterza, V., Carmichael, P., & Procter, R. (2007). The doubtful guest? A virtual research environment for education. *Technology, Pedagogy and Education, 16*(3), 249–267.

Markauskaite, L., & Reimann, P. (2008). *Enabling teacher-led research and innovation: A conceptual design of an inquiry framework for ICT-enhanced teacher innovation*. Paper presented at the World Conference on Educational Multimedia, Hypermedia and Telecommunications 2008.

Maxwell, J. A. (2004). Causal explanation, qualitative research, and scientific inquiry in education. *Educational Researcher, 33*(2), 3–11.

Olson, G. M., Herbsleb, J. D., & Rueter, H. H. (1994). Characterizing the sequential structure of interactive behaviors through statistical and grammatical techniques. *Human-Computer Interaction, 9*(3/4), 427–472.

Pea, R., & Lindgren, R. (2008). Video collaboratories for research and education: An analysis of collaboration design patterns. *IEEE Transactions on Learning Technologies, 1*(4), 235–247.

Pea, R., Mills, M., Rosen, J., Dauber, K., & Effelsberg, W. (2004). The DIVER project: Interactive digital video repurposing. *IEEE Multimedia, 11*, 54–61.

Perera, D., Kay, J., Koprinska, I., Yacef, K., & Zaiane, O. (2008). Clustering and sequential pattern mining of online collaborative learning data. *IEEE Transactions on Knowledge and Data Engineering, 21*(6), 759–772.

Philip, L., Chorley, A., Farrington, J., & Edwards, P. (2007). *Data provenance, evidence-based policy assessment, and e-social science*. Paper presented at the Third international conference on e-social science, October 15, 2007, Ann Arbor, MI.
Procter, R. (2007). Collaboration, coherence and capacity-building: the role of DSpace in supporting and understanding the TLRP. *Technology, Pedagogy and Education, 16*(3), 269–288.
Reimann, P. (2009). Time is precious: Variable- and event-centred approaches to process analysis in CSCL research. *International Journal of Computer-Supported Collaborative Learning 4*, 239–257.
Reimann, P., Frerejean, J., & Thompson, K. (2009). Using process mining to identify models of group decision making processes in chat data. In C. O'Malley, D. Suthers, P. Reimann & A. Dimitracopoulou (Eds.), *Computer-supported collaborative learning practices: CSCL2009 conference proceedings* (pp. 98–107). Rhodes, Greece: International Society for the Learning Sciences.
Rich, P. J., & Hannafin, M. (2009). Video annotation tools. *Journal of Teacher Education, 60*(1), 52–67.
Romero, C., & Ventura, S. (2005). Educational data mining: A survey from 1995 to 2005. *Expert Systems with Applications, 33*(1), 135–146.
Schleyer, T., Spallek, H., Butler, B. S., Subramanian, S., Weiss, D., Poythress, L., et al. (2008). Facebook for scientists: Requirements and services for optimizing how scientific collaborations are established. *Journal of Medical Internet Research, 10*(3). Retrieved from http://www.pubmedcentral.nih.gov/articlerender.fcgi?artid=2553246 .
Simmhan, Y. L., Plale, B., & Gannon, D. (2005). A survey of data provenance in e-science. *SIGMOD Record, 34*(3), 31–36.
Srikant, R., & Agrawal, R. (1996). Mining sequential patterns: Generalizations and performance improvements. *Proceedings of Fifth International Conference on Extending Database Technology (EDBT),* Avignon, France.
Stevens, R., Robinson, A., & Goble, C. (2003). My-grid: Personalised bioinformatics on the information grid. *Bioinformatics, 19*(1), 302–304.
Strijbos, J.-W., & Fischer, F. (2007). Methodological challenges for collaborative learning research. *Learning and Instruction, 17*(4), 389–393.
Taylor, K., Essex, J. W., Frey, J. G., Mills, H. R., Hughes, G., & Zaluska, E. J. (2006). The semantic grid and chemistry: Experiences with CombeChem. *Journal of Web Semantics, 4*(2), 84–101.
Ure, J., Procter, R., Lin, Y. -W., Hartswood, M., & Ho, K. (2007). *Aligning technical and human infrastructures in the semantic web: A socio-technical perspective*. Paper presented at the third international conference on e-social science, October 7–9, 2007, Ann Arbor, MI, USA.
Van der Aalst, W. M. P., & Günther, C. W. (2007). Finding structure in unstructured processes: the case of process mining. In T. Basten, G. Juhas & S. Shukla (Eds.), *Proceedings the 7th International Conference on Applications of Concurrency to System Design (ACSD 2007; Bratislava, Slovak Republic)* (pp. 3–12). Los Alamitos, CA: IEEE Computer Society Press.
Van der Aalst, W. M. P., & Weijters, A. J. M. M. (2005). Process mining. In M. Dumas, W. M. P. van der Aalst & A. H. M. ter Hofstede (Eds.), *Process-aware information systems: Bridging people and software through process technology* (pp. 235–255). New York: Wiley.
Wasserman, S., & Faust, K. (1994). *Social Network Analysis: Methods and Applications*. Cambridge, UK: Cambridge University Press.
Wilson, A., Rimpiläinen, S., Skinner, D., Cassidy, C., Christie, D., Coutts, N., et al. (2007). Using a virtual research environment to support new models of collaborative and participative research in Scottish education. *Technology, Pedagogy and Education, 16*(3), 289–304.
Wong, W. Y., & Reimann, P. (2009). Web based educational video teaching and learning platform with collaborative annotation. In I. Aedo, N.-S. Chen, K. D. Sampson & L. Zaitseva (Eds.), *The Ninth IEEE International Conference on Advanced Learning Technologiies (ICALT 2009)* (pp. 696–700). Riga, Latvia: IEEE.
Ye, N. (Ed.). (2003). *The handbook of data mining*. Mahwah, NJ: Lawrence Erlbaum.

Chapter 13
Designing Higher Education Courses Using Open Educational Resources

Frank Rennie[1] **and Robin Mason**[2]

[1] Lews Castle College, University of the Highlands and Islands Millennium Institute, Stornoway, Isle of Lewis, Scotland, e-mail: frank.rennie@lews.uhi.ac.uk
[2] Open University, Milton Keynes, UK

Introduction

Over the last few years in particular, as a result of funding from the European Union Asia-Link Programme (Edushare, 2009) and the Edulink Programme (Sidecap, 2009) among others, we have been working with a number of universities in Asia, Africa, the Caribbean, and the South Pacific to assist the professional development of staff in the area of the design and support of distributed learning resources. It became obvious fairly quickly that all of these partners, to a greater or lesser extent, face severe technical and financial constraints in any attempt to introduce and/or expand educational technology within their institutions. In many cases it became apparent that even when pedagogic and technical skills were available, the costs of proprietary software, online journals and databases, and hardware/connection issues are sufficiently serious to prevent any significant progress. As we investigated potential solutions to improve the quality and flexibility of the curriculum with these partners, it led to a realisation that open access to, and the re-use of, educational resources to improve courses in higher education is a common problem shared by university staff in the "developed" and the "less-developed" countries, albeit that it is often viewed from different perspectives. This in turn led to a focus on skills training and "capacity building" of staff in the development and use of open educational resources (OER) in course design for distributed education. All of the institutions involved in these projects, including universities in the Maldives, Cambodia, Bhutan, Nepal, Turkey, Mauritius, the University of the West Indies, and the University of the South Pacific, have geographically distributed campuses. The three European partners in the project are all universities that are heavily involved

F. Rennie (✉)
Lews Castle College, University of the Highlands and Islands Millennium Institute, Stornoway, Isle of Lewis, Scotland
e-mail: frank.rennie@lews.uhi.ac.uk

Robin Mason tragically died before publication of this chapter

M.S. Khine, I.M. Saleh (eds.), *New Science of Learning*,
DOI 10.1007/978-1-4419-5716-0_13,

in distance teaching: the UK Open University, the University of the Highlands and Islands Millennium Institute (UHI), and Anadolu University in Turkey. There was therefore a need for course design solutions that could be networked between different campuses and which could be easily adapted to suit very different educational contexts of the various partner cultures.

Each of the partner universities practice different forms and levels of distance or distributed education and are at very different stages in the evolution of their design, delivery, and student support mechanisms. UHI is distributed in the sense that it is composed of 13 academic partners—colleges and research centres spread over a very wide geographical area of northern Scotland. Various combinations of technologies are used to deliver courses to students so that they do not need to physically re-locate in order to access higher education. Furthermore, staff can provide tuition to learners beyond the confines of the "home" campuses. The UK Open University can be called distributed in the sense that it too uses technology to deliver courses to students spread over the whole United Kingdom and beyond. Online and face-to-face tutorials are held to support students in their study of either print-based or web-based course materials. Anadolu is the largest distance teaching university in Turkey with over 1 million undergraduates and a strong distance learning programme.

Blended learning is another term which is often used to refer to practices similar to distributed education. Blended learning usually implies a combination of online and face-to-face teaching (Fig. 13.1). Distributed education usually implies a separation either in time or in space between the teacher and the taught and is normally regarded as utilising a range of different media resources for course delivery and communications between learners and tutorial staff. In any case, both concepts are addressing the need for greater flexibility and access to higher education than the traditional campus experience affords by providing resources and support for learners beyond the conventional fixed format of classroom attendance and face-to-face lectures.

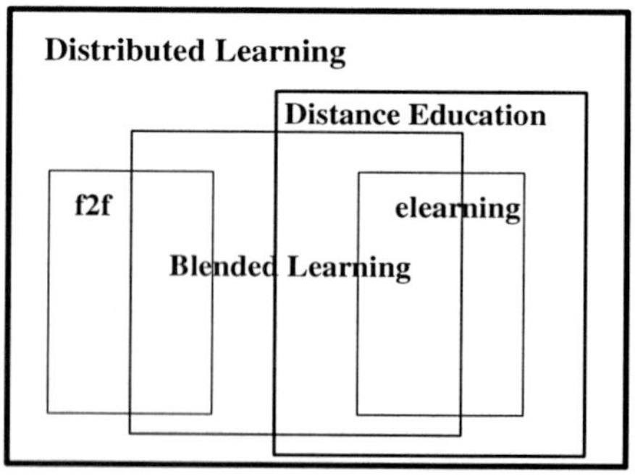

Fig. 13.1 The relationship of eLearning to distributed learning (Mason & Rennie 2006, p xvii)

After the initial orientation meetings to plan the structure, responsibilities, and timetable for the project partners, staff development workshops were held to assess the current (base level) status of the pedagogical systems of each of the partners and to agree to the extra "value-added" design skills to be acquired by each of the partner institutions. For all the partners, distributed education techniques (face-to-face, print, digital resources, and Internet technology) offer many benefits such as flexibility and new teaching resources; however, easy accessibility and equality of distribution continue to be problematic, and for this reason we explored digital offline resources as well as Internet-based solutions.

As examples of the contexts in which less developed countries are attempting to move from "conventional" face-to-face learning and memorisation towards the incorporation of educational technology to assist learning, the following might be considered. The Maldives are a collection of islands, or more correctly atolls, with small populations and little local access to higher education. Distance education is a priority for the Maldives College of Higher Education and their strategic plan involves the development of more flexible courses that can be offered at key centres throughout the islands. Both Bhutan and Nepal have a higher education system which could be called distributed, although they differ in the nature of the distributed components. In Bhutan there is a network of regional colleges throughout the country, each specialising in different subjects, but there is little experience of distance education or the use of new technology for supporting learners (Rennie & Mason, 2007). Nepal has a highly centralised higher education structure focussed on Tribhuvan University but has recently experimented with the introduction of some forms of technology-supported distance learning and is currently discussing the establishment of an Open University for Nepal. Internal travel is very difficult in both countries due to the mountainous terrain and the lack of infrastructure. Access to secondary education, much less higher education, is a major problem and only a small percentage of the total populations attend university. Separate campuses in different parts of the countries define their own structures and curricula. The same is true for the Cambodian partner, a private university called Build Bright University that has a very young staff and an energetic recent history of curriculum development, but with, at best, an intermittent quality of online access.

Online Versus Face-to-Face Teaching

Universities in countries with limited resources for e-learning face very difficult problems in trying to equip their students with the skills, experience, and online opportunities which the country needs to develop as a knowledge-based economy. In Asia the proportion of the total population participating in the Internet revolution is relatively small, but the rate of growth of mobile phone and Internet technology is rapid. In countries where the infrastructure is reasonably well developed, pressure is growing to use e-learning, partly because of the growing number of foreign universities offering online courses and partly as a perceived solution to offer access to mass education throughout the country. While in Europe online learning is growing in popularity and is increasingly accepted as a comparable alternative (or complement) to face-to-face education, in Asia ***all*** distance learning is still generally regarded with suspicion and is certainly not on a level of credibility with campus education. Blended learning, which combines on-campus and online education, is a far more acceptable alternative in Asia (Dean, Stahl, Sylwester, & Pear, 2001). In Europe, blended learning is becoming the new norm, just as it is in North America, and distributed educational resources, such as online texts or images, are commonly regarded as important components of most campus-based and distance-learning courses alike. A major challenge for the developing countries is how they can access and make use of such resources, and this thinking has converged with open courseware initiatives in some developed countries—such as the MIT OpenCourseware (2009) and the UK Open University OpenLearn initiative (2009).

The primary focus of our work stems from the need of the developing country partner institutions to improve the quality of their systems for teaching and academic administration and to do this in a more open and flexible format. In part, these problems arise from the lack of adequate finance for educational resources (e.g. up-to-date literature and new educational technologies) and in part due to the lack of maturity of the current educational systems. This work aimed to overcome these through specific training in the joint development of resources and the input of expertise in technology and educational systems. Particular emphasis was placed upon the use of (free or inexpensive) open source applications, open content materials, and other open-access freeware whose use can be maintained by the developing nations after the close of this particular project.

Open Educational Resources

The focus for the development of course content was the use of OER (See OER Handbook for Educators, 2009). These OER are digitised materials offered freely for educators and students to use and reuse for teaching and learning. There are over 3,000 open courseware course materials available currently, typically on the web as PDF files. The content is usually in text form, but may also involve images, sound, or video in digital format (CoL, 2009). We have taken a broad definition of OER to include learning objects, educational repositories, as well as articles in open access journals that can be embedded and/or linked then contextualised for use in various curricula. In most cases, a Creative Commons license applies to the use of the material; however, a recent OECD report on OER notes the following:

> There is a troublesome imbalance between the provision of OER and its utilisation. The vast majority of OER is in English and based on Western culture, and this limits their relevance and risks consigning less developed countries to playing the role of consumers (OECD, 2007, p. 14).

There may be minor difficulties in contextualising very specific resources, e.g. case studies, and also the search to locate, identify, and contextualise open-access, peer-reviewed, academic journal articles may initially be quite time consuming (Guttikonda & Gutam, 2009). Our projects aimed to address the issue of developing countries merely being passive users by embedding the practice of each partner adapting, reusing, and adding to the appropriate OER material. Furthermore, each partner was expected to do this in the context of their own culture and institutional context. In our experience, all of the partner universities taught in English, so the adaptation was not a translation, but a cultural refit, in order that the level and type of material is in keeping with the existing institutional curriculum. The OECD report also raises the issue of developing countries becoming dependent on externally generated content, rather than using OER content to produce locally relevant material (p. 105). The projects addressed this issue by focusing on three staff development processes in the use of OER: (1) adapting existing OER materials; (2) adapting existing material from the partner's own university; and (3) creating some new material to integrate them into a whole. In short, there was considerable practice in materials development that is both locally relevant and realistic in resource demands.

The authors have previous experience with the use of Open Access tools for community development (Mason & Rennie, 2007). This involved training in the community use of educational technology, the development of non-formal educational resources, and the detailed evaluation of the process to ensure transferability to other community education initiatives.

The Process

Using wikis and other social software, a number of activities were structured to support the partnership in contextualising existing content to fit their national curriculum. Wikis and a group-hub communications application were also utilised to disseminate and co-ordinate the detailed structure of the month-to-month project activities. Using the model of a "course module" around which all the other partner activities, resources, and skills are structured, we jointly developed higher education material on the general topic of "sustainable development and tourism" that could be re-purposed and subsequently delivered in some format in each of the partner institutions (not necessarily the same format for each academic partner). Each partner produced three types of content:

1. re-purposed existing open content resources
2. re-purposed existing institutional resources
3. new, short, wrap-around text to contextualise the materials to the locality.

We chose three ways of enabling student access to the learning resources:

(1) through a wiki publicly accessible to all learners.
(2) through OpenLearn—the Open University's application for distributed resource development and sharing.
(3) through a CD for distribution to students.

All academic partners received training in the use of a wide variety of media: video clips, photos, quizzes, and audio clips, in addition to text-based resources.

The primary intention was to facilitate the staff development of key personnel who were then charged with cascading the techniques and the pedagogy to colleagues at their own institution. There was therefore a double necessity, not simply to train the staff member in the relevant educational technology (and the pedagogical background to this) but to equip that person to be able to pass this training on to their peers when they returned to their normal duties. In addition, networked activities punctuated the project and were designed to explore the experience between and within partner institutions. A secondary aim was to develop a fuller understanding of the issues involved in adapting open content to local contexts, through practical tasks, evaluation exercises, and comparative analysis. A third aim was to develop flexible course materials that are to some extent customised and contextually relevant for these very different distributed university systems. An appreciation of the importance of contextualising and re-purposing of the resources is regarded as being of equal importance to the acquisition of the technical skills related to the educational technology applications. In order to be consistent with the "open access/open source" ethos, existing (free) training resources were used wherever possible (e.g. see Stannard, 2008).

The Conceptual Framework

The theoretical framework for the design of these courses using OER is to provide easy access to the course content (overview, teaching materials, digitised articles, relevant web sites, etc.) and to provide specific guidelines on the flexibility of delivery options for each course.

For instance (Fig. 13.2) the OER can be packaged together and contextualised by the tutor(s) to provide a common resource pool of learning materials. These would be freely available on the web and could either be embedded within the

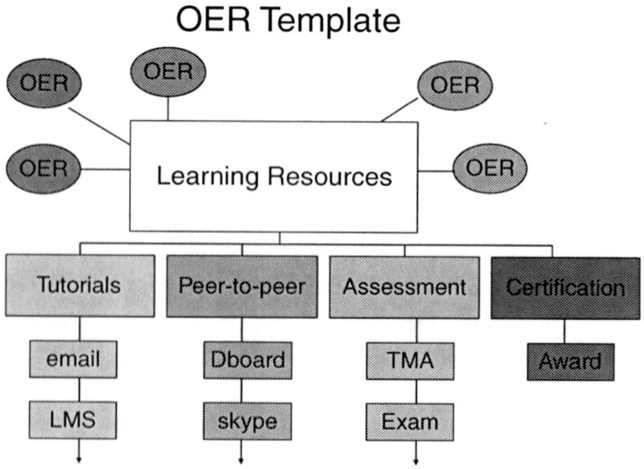

Fig. 13.2 The conceptual framework for networked OER use in course design

contextualised course or available as external links, depending upon copyright considerations. The course designers then specify the additional requirements for a learner to be able to utilise these learning materials in a structured manner that could lead to an academic award (but need not necessarily always do so). These additional requirements would include the following:

(1) a measure of peer-to-peer interaction;
(2) an amount of tutor support and supervision;
(3) an opportunity to be assessed on the course contents;
(4) an opportunity to obtain recognition (certification) for the assessed work.

A crucial factor is that in identifying these additional requirements (for each element of which the educational institutions may charge learners fees) the course designer does not need to proscribe a rigid form of learning delivery. (One of the consistent barriers to sharing and collaboration is that while institutions frequently exhort staff and students to use the virtual learning environment (VLE) or the e-portfolio, they really want them to use ***their*** version of the VLE or e-portfolio, which does not easily import/export with other such platforms). Instead, each educational institution could choose to use the common pool of learning materials, but to support their learners in ways that are consistent with their own existing educational procedures. An example from Fig. 13.2 would be that University X would utilise the common pool of learning materials but would use Moodle to provide email exchanges for the peer-to-peer interaction and computer conferencing for the class interaction with the tutor(s). The university would select a variety of online submissions as the assessment instrument of choice and would award a completion certificate that is consistent with their own quality assurance procedures. On the other hand, University Z might choose to utilise the same pool of common learning materials, but to teach the class only on a face-to-face basis, providing the web-based resources to assist supplementary learning, but with a final face-to-face formal exam. The common link is the shared pool of high-quality learning materials that have been structured for academic consistency and can be jointly updated and amended by the member academics participating in the different universities. Additions and improvements to the pool of teaching resources by one trusted expert would benefit all those using the open access resource pool—staff, students, and casual web-users.

Conclusions

Our initial interest in OER was sparked by some of the particular problems faced by universities in less-developed countries, mainly the lack of detailed benchmarked quality standards, the geographical and resource challenges in extending higher education to remote students, the need to provide educational opportunities for remote students, and the lack of know-how in effective course design for Internet-based teaching. In the course of investigation it became clear that most of these problems, for different reasons, are constraints in course design in many universities in the developed countries as well.

In testing the reality of this framework and the theory of course construction using OER, a number of early conclusions have been formed.

(1) Course design using OER is in a different sequence of activities from most "conventional" (i.e. "designed from scratch") courses. The key ***generic*** areas of importance for the OER course (or module) need to be identified first, with sufficient clarity to enable a coherent set of educational "lessons" (or key concepts) to be constructed, but not in such firm detail that the selection of the potential OER for re-use is unduly restricted.
(2) A thorough and comprehensive search of web-based resources and other open access resource repositories needs to be undertaken. A considerable number of such sources currently exist, but web browsers and tagging to search specifically for OER are in their infancy. The identification and contextualisation of open-access, peer-reviewed, academic journal articles may be particularly time consuming.
(3) Appropriate resources that can be used to assist the intended learning process are then grouped under the initial generic topic headings and in this manner a robust learning structure can be slowly developed through the re-use of existing learning resources.
(4) Naturally, not all of the resources that are appropriate for every course may be found in this manner, and at some stage it may be necessary to generate new learning resources, or to "wrap around" a (new) contextual explanation around the (pre-existing) learning resources in order to adapt the resources to the required context. It is expected that these new learning resources would then be added to the publicly accessible common pool of learning resources—perhaps by tagging them as "creative commons" resources (http://creativecommons.org/), etc.
(5) At this stage, having assembled the array of learning materials to be used on the course, decisions need to be taken on the presentational format of the course. We have so far used an interactive wiki, an open course repository in portable document format (pdf), and a simple MS Word document (all available open access via the web) and a hard copy version (CD) to enable learners in a variety of geographical locations to access the common pool of (open) learning resources.
(6) Consideration needs to be given to the issues of copyright (even with Creative Commons licenses) and what can be re-used, with or without modification. In this context there are pros and cons to providing external *links* to open access resources (avoids copying, acknowledges sources, consistent versioning, but requires constant checking for broken links) versus *embedding* the OER within the new document (more streamlined, self-contained, but may create multiple versions and may infringe copyright)
(7) Experiences with users has so far indicated three main types of users of open access courses: (i) independent learners and/or staff who use (download or read

online) the whole course/module unchanged from the initial course design (the majority); (ii) staff who adopt and contextualise open access courses, e.g. by adding a textbook or writing accompanying texts (apparently a small number); (iii) staff who download and contextualise the course/module by creating new OER and adding these to the global resource pool (currently a small minority of academics).

(8) Despite its early stage development, the use of OER in course design shows great promise for helping to provide wider access to more flexible higher education, through the design and sharing of the OER by trusted sources, and the methods for storing and locating OER in appropriate online repositories requires further development work (Fig. 13.3).

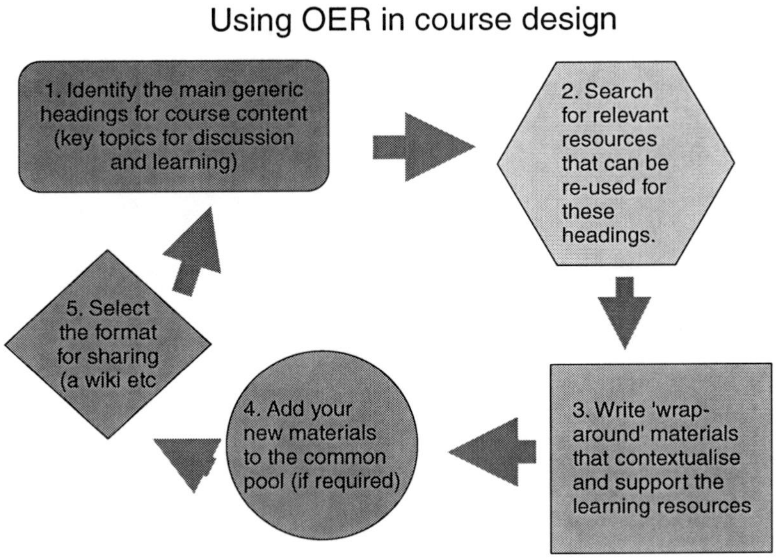

Fig. 13.3 Five steps in course construction using OER

References

CoL (Commonwealth of Learning). (2009). *Creating learning materials for open and distance learning: A handbook for authors and instructional designers. The Commonwealth of Learning*. Retrieved from, http://www.col.org/resources/publications/trainingresources/Pages/handbooks.aspx

Dean, P., Stahl, M., Sylwester, D., & Pear, J. (2001). Effectiveness of combined delivery modalities for distance learning and resident learning. *Quarterly Review of Distance Education*, *2*(3), 247–254.

Edushare. (2009). Project wiki. Retrieved from http://edushare.wetpaint.com

Guttikonda, A., & Gutam, S. (2009). Prospects of open access to Indian agricultural research: A case study of ICAR. *First Monday, 14*(7). Retrieved form, http://firstmonday.org/htbin/cgiwrap/bin/ojs/index.php/fm/article/view/2488/2238

Mason, R., & Rennie, F. (2006). *eLearning: The key concepts*. London: Routledge.

Mason, R., & Rennie, F. (2007). Using Web 2.0 for learning in the community. *The Internet and Higher Education, 10*(3), 196–203.

OECD. (2007). *Giving knowledge for free: The emergence of open educational resources*. Retrieved Centre for Educational Research and Innovation from, http://www.oecd.org/document/41/0,3343,en_2649_201185_38659497_1_1_1_1,00.html

OER Handbook for Educators. (2009). Retrieved from http://www.wikieducator.org/OER_Handbook/educator_version_one

OpenCourseware. (2009). *The landing page of the MIT Open Courseware initiative*. Retrieved from http://ocw.mit.edu/OcwWeb/web/home/home/index.htm

OpenLearn. (2009). *The Learning space of the UK Open University open courseware initiative*. Retrieved from http://openlearn.open.ac.uk

Rennie, F., & Mason, R. (2007). The development of distributed learning techniques in Bhutan and Nepal. *The International Review of Research in Open and Distance Learning, 8*(1). Retrieved form, http://www.irrodl.org/index.php/irrodl/article/view/339/765

SideCAP (2009) Project wiki. Retrieved from, http://sidecap.wetpaint.com

Stannard, R. (2008). *Teacher training videos*. Retrieved form, http://www.teachertrainingvideos.com

Chapter 14
The Evolution of an Automated Reading Strategy Tutor: From the Classroom to a Game-Enhanced Automated System

G. Tanner Jackson, Kyle B. Dempsey, and Danielle S. McNamara

University of Memphis, Memphis, TN, USA

Introduction

The implementation of effective pedagogical software is difficult to achieve. Indeed, a recent assessment of commercially available educational software illustrates this point (Dynarski et al., 2007). Unfortunately, many educational sites and programs focus on designing edutainment, by emphasizing the entertainment and engagement aspects of computer-based learning environments while expending significantly less effort to incorporate effective learning principles (Okan, 2003). Another problem plaguing educational software is that systems are often designed using a linear, sequential model (Pressman, 1997), in which case the software is programmed and implemented without being empirically tested in a real educational environment (Kennedy, 1998). Additionally, some educational software suffers due to inadequate implementations of established learning theories (Conole, Dyke, Oliver, & Seale, 2004), and even the lack of pedagogical principles entirely. These problems are typically more common to commercial software development, and various programming solutions have been discussed and implemented within the higher education research community (Anderson, Corbett, Koedinger, & Pelletier, 1995; Conole et al., 2004; Kennedy, 1998; Oliver, 2002). This chapter provides an example solution (similar to Anderson et al., 1995) and describes a successful implementation of effective pedagogical software, and details the development and evolution of the educational program.

One way to ensure that computer-based systems promote effective pedagogical principles is to model the system after an empirically proven training method and to then compare performance between the original and the adapted versions (Anderson et al., 1995; O'Reilly, Sinclair, & McNamara, 2004b). By beginning with an established training program, the effective pedagogical underpinnings remain essential to the computerized program, and the interface and engagement elements can be amended as needed (Anderson et al., 1995). This type of development

---

D.S. McNamara (✉)
University of Memphis, Memphis, TN, USA
e-mail: d.mcnamara@mail.psyc.memphis.edu

M.S. Khine, I.M. Saleh (eds.), *New Science of Learning*,
DOI 10.1007/978-1-4419-5716-0_14,

is often utilized in the field of intelligent tutoring systems (ITSs), and typically involves establishing training practices, developing automated instruction, and then amending motivational elements. While this development cycle can take years for completion because each step requires an iterative process of both execution and evaluation, it also has a greater chance of success. We illustrate such a cycle in this chapter in the evolution of an intelligent tutoring and gaming environment [i.e., interactive Strategy Trainer for Active Reading and Thinking-Motivationally Enhanced (iSTART-ME)] from an ITS (i.e., iSTART), which was originally conceived and tested as a human-delivered intervention (i.e., SERT).

The training programs discussed in this chapter (i.e., SERT, iSTART, and iSTART-ME) were designed with the common goal of improving students' ability to comprehend text. These interventions were inspired by previous research demonstrating that self-explanation improves comprehension and problem solving (Bielaczyc, Pirolli, & Brown, 1995; Chi, de Leeuw, Chiu, & Lavancher, 1994). Leveraging this research, a reading comprehension intervention, called Self-Explanation Reading Training (SERT), was developed to teach students self-explanation and reading strategies to improve their understanding of challenging texts. SERT was developed as a classroom based human-to-human training program, and evaluations have shown that it is effective at improving students reading comprehension (McNamara, 2004b; O'Reilly, Taylor, & McNamara 2006). SERT was found to produce significant improvement in comprehension and strategy use, however it lacked the potential to scale up to widespread use while maintaining effective instruction. Due to these limitations of the human-based SERT intervention, an ITS was developed. The iSTART is an ITS developed and adapted directly from the SERT pedagogical intervention. The transition from SERT to iSTART improved on both the pedagogy and social reach of the training. iSTART was also found to promote significant learning and improve students' ability to self-explain texts (O'Reilly et al., 2004a; O'Reilly, Sinclair, & McNamara, 2004b). The advancement of iSTART afforded students with individualized training on a widespread scale, however, after repeated exposure and sustained practice, students can become disengaged, they lack sufficient motivation to use the program effectively, and begin to display negative affect toward the learning task. Hence, iSTART-ME has been developed to remedy the motivational problems inherent to the long-term use of iSTART. This conversion preserves the iSTART pedagogy, but envelopes it within a gaming environment. The impetus behind each of these transitions has been to improve upon the efficacy of training by revising some aspects of the pedagogical implementation and rendering individualized training more accessible to students. The following chapter describes these programs, their success, and the changes from one to the next.

Self-Explanation Reading Training

SERT (McNamara, 2004b) is a human-to-human training program designed to teach students how to generate effective self-explanations by using effective reading strategies and, in turn, teach students reading strategies through the process of self-explanation. SERT was inspired by findings reported by Chi et al. (1994) indicating that self-explanation improves comprehension and problem solving, but that the benefits of self-explanation are reserved for those who do it well. At the same time, studies in the area of reading comprehension had pointed toward strategies that improve comprehension (e.g., Brown & Palincsar, 1982; Palincsar & Brown, 1984). SERT was designed to merge self-explanation and reading strategy training so that students could learn how to better self-explain texts and, at the same time, practice using reading comprehension strategies by self-explaining texts.

SERT was initially implemented within a one-on-one intervention program and eventually involved into a classroom-based intervention. The following sections describe these two programs and discuss studies investigating their effectiveness in improving students' comprehension of challenging text.

SERT: One-on-One

SERT (McNamara, 2004b) was first developed as a laboratory-based intervention, including two sessions and three testing sessions. The training was delivered to each student individually by an experimenter. Of course, one could imagine the same type of training being delivered by tutors to individual students.

SERT Introduction

The first phase of SERT is the introduction, which covers the use of self-explanation as a reading comprehension strategy and includes six reading strategies. For each strategy, the experimenter follows a script in which the strategy is defined and examples are provided of the strategies being used within self-explanations. The strategies include (1) *comprehension monitoring*; (2) *paraphrasing*, or restating information in their own words; (3) *prediction*, or predicting what information may be provided by the text next or what may happen next; (4) *bridging*, or making connections between the ideas in the text; (5) *elaboration* using their own domain knowledge; and (6) *logical inferences*, or using logic, general world knowledge, and common sense to make sense of the text. Within the introduction, students learn what the strategies are, why the strategies will help them with their reading comprehension, and examples of each of the strategies used in self-explanations.

SERT Practice and Demonstration

In the second phase of training, the students practice self-explaining four science texts. The student reads the text and self-explains aloud to the experimenter or tutor. The tutor scaffolds the student when additional self-explanation is necessary. After reading and self-explaining each text and answering questions about it, the student views a video of a peer-student self-explaining the same science text. The videos are stopped at various "stop points" and the student is asked to identify the strategy being used by the peer-student in the video. The student is also provided with a transcript of the video to refer back to when deciding which strategy or strategies were being used. The purpose of this phase is to provide the student with practice self-explaining and with a model of how the text might have been explained by another student. This provides the student with more examples of the strategies being used, and induces the student to reflect on what types of strategies can be used, and when.

Evaluation of One-on-One SERT

McNamara (2004b) examined the effects of SERT on comprehension and explanation quality in a study with 42 college students. Half of the participants received SERT and the remaining participants read aloud the four science texts (control condition). During the training phase, self-explanation, as compared to reading aloud, only improved comprehension for the most difficult of the four training texts. After training, all of the participants (SERT and control) were asked to self-explain a difficult text about cell mitosis. Those students who were prompted to self-explain (as in Chi et al., 1994) were compared to those who were provided with training to self-explain using the reading strategies (i.e., SERT). Those who received the additional training on reading strategies (i.e., SERT) showed significantly better comprehension than those who were merely prompted to self-explain.

Analyses of the self-explanations produced by the participants after training indicated that SERT's primary role was in helping the low-knowledge readers to use logic, common sense, or general knowledge to self-explain the text. Thus, the results showed that SERT helped the low-knowledge students to more effectively self-explain the text (using more effective strategies) and as a consequence they showed considerably better comprehension than the low-knowledge participants in the control condition who had not received training. Importantly, the low-knowledge participants who received SERT showed comprehension performance comparable to the high-knowledge participants.

Notably, these benefits only emerged on the text-based questions. The low-knowledge readers did not have sufficient domain knowledge to generate inferences to support a coherent situation model. Nonetheless, the use of paraphrasing along with the generation of inferences based on logic and general knowledge helped the readers to understand the basic ideas in the text and form a more coherent textbase level understanding. This is important educationally because a coherent textbase is a prerequisite to building knowledge.

McNamara (2000a) also reported on a study with middle school students (grades 6–8) who participated in a laboratory study with one-on-one SERT. These findings were never published in a refereed journal because the training did not yield a positive effect of SERT. There was no hint of a benefit of self-explanation and reading strategy training for these younger children. It seemed that they did not have sufficient basic skills in order to gain from the training. In particular, it seemed that they did not have sufficient paraphrasing skills and they did not have the ability to explain the text using knowledge. Rather than explaining the text and making connections between ideas in the text, their explanations tended to take them on tangents unrelated to the main points of the text. After this study, the youngest children for which SERT or iSTART has been used is grade 8 (e.g., McNamara, O'Reilly, Best, & Ozuru, 2006).

SERT: Group Training

SERT one-on-one provided encouraging results; yet it required extensive one-on-one tutoring with a human expert. This time and personnel intensive training had little hope of scaling up. Thus, the next iteration of SERT was revised such that it could be delivered in a classroom setting to groups of students. The group SERT training is similar to the one-on-one SERT tutoring, with the primary differences being the delivery/interaction method, pedagogical ordering of training components, and the use of collaborative learning sessions.

Group SERT Introduction

The group version of SERT incorporates the same lecture style introduction. However, the introduction section was adapted into a classroom-style lecture that could accommodate up to 20–30 students at a time. This introduction phase presents information and examples for the same set of six reading strategies and follows a similar script as was followed in SERT one-on-one. The examples are projected on a screen to the group, and each individual is provided with a handout containing the examples. This approach allows for discussion of the material as a group, though in fact, there are generally few questions and little discussion at this stage of training.

Group SERT Demonstration

The training components in group SERT were reconceptualized to more accurately implement modeling, scaffolding, fading and to implement an additional pedagogical principle of collaborative learning (McNamara, 2000b). In one-on-one SERT, students self-explain a text and then observe another student explain the same text. By contrast, in group SERT, the demonstration of the strategies in the video is presented before students attempt to apply the strategies to texts. As such, the demonstration section is used to scaffold the students as they advance their understanding from simple strategy descriptions to observing how they can apply these strategies in real contexts. During the demonstration phase of group training, students watch one of the videos used in one-on-one SERT. The video is paused at six specified points and the students are asked to write down the strategies being used by the student in the video (students are also provided with a transcript of the video). After the video is completed, all students engage in a group discussion of the strategies being used by the student in the video.

Group SERT Practice

After completing the video and discussion from the demonstration session, students are separated into pairs and are asked to practice using the strategies within their dyads. One student within each pair takes a turn self-explaining all of the sentences within a paragraph and the other student then gives a summary of the paragraph. Then, the students switch roles and swap who self-explains and who summarizes the paragraph. The summarization task is included to ensure that both students are attending to the text while also promoting further comprehension of the text. Although the student who is listening to the self-explanation is also asked to give feedback on the quality of the self-explanations, this rarely occurs.

Evaluation of Group SERT

There have been several evaluations of SERT delivered in classroom settings, both with college students and high school students. For example, Magliano et al. (2005) conducted a pretest-posttest study with 29 college students. They found that the students improved in their ability to answer true/false questions about science texts, and this gain was most apparent on the more difficult questions that required inferences to correctly answer the question. McNamara (2009, *Self-explanation and reading strategy training (SERT) improves low-knowledge students' science course performance*. Unpublished manuscript) compared the effects of SERT to a control condition on course exams with 265 college students enrolled in Introductory Biology (see also McNamara, 2004a; McNamara & Shapiro, 2005). The results showed that SERT had the largest benefit for the low-knowledge students. Moreover, the low-knowledge students who received SERT performed as well on the exams as did high-knowledge students who did not receive training.

SERT is also effective for high school students. O'Reilly et al. (2006) reported a study conducted with 465 students in grades 9–12 in rural, inner-city (urban), and suburban schools. They found that students who were provided with SERT in the classroom in comparison to a control condition improved in their ability to comprehend science text; however, the effects of training were significant only for students in the rural school. Students in the suburban school may have already been sufficiently familiar with the strategies before training, and the students in the urban school may not have possessed sufficient basic reading skills to gain from the training. The environmental conditions and prior skills of the students in the rural school, by contrast, were just right to gain from SERT.

O'Reilly, Best, and McNamara (2004) compared the effectiveness of SERT to a control condition and another commonly used training technique called *previewing* (or K-W-L). Previewing teaches students to preview specific parts of a chapter and then write what they know, want to know, and what they learned. The participants were 136 9th and 10th grade students in biology courses in an inner-city school. The students' ability to understand a science text was examined one week after training was administered. The results showed that low-knowledge students gained from SERT training in comparison to both the previewing and the control conditions, whereas the high-knowledge students did not. Previewing training had no effects on comprehension.

Discussion

Evaluations of both one-on-one SERT and group SERT found learning benefits for students who received some form of self-explanation training. Unfortunately, both of these SERT programs are limited to situations where an expert human teacher can provide the training. Also, the trainers must be trained. The requirement of having a trained human expert present to conduct the intervention means that SERT could be expensive to implement and might also have a limited impact (as the largest training group is 20–30 students at a time). It seemed unlikely at the time that this intervention could be successfully carried out as a teacher-training program.

Additional problems emerge from the collaborative aspects of the group SERT program. While the collaborative learning component to group SERT is an engaging method of training, it can also lead to problems of poor feedback quality, no feedback, and ineffective peer dyads. The group discussions heavily depend on the dynamics of the group. This can be challenging for the best of high school teachers. Moreover, creating an effective small group can be particularly difficult due to a number of factors. Specifically, maturity, romantic interests, friendships, rivalries, social survival, and many other social factors were observed to remove the focus away from the learning task. These anecdotal observations in high school classrooms suggested that a one-on-one training may be more conducive to learning within a high school environment, but this of course was entirely unrealistic if many students were to receive training. Ideally, a hybrid version of these two SERT programs would appear to be the most effective. That is, the ideal implementation of SERT would instruct students on an individual basis and also provide exposure to a larger number of students.

iSTART

This technology seemed to provide the best solution to the dilemma of how to provide SERT to a wide audience, and still provide tailored training. At the time that the initial one-on-one SERT evaluation projects were coming to a close, there was a growing recognition of algorithms such as Latent Semantic Analysis (LSA) to recognize the meaning of text (Hu, Graesser, & TRG, 1998; Landauer, Foltz, & Laham, 1998). Such algorithms were necessary in order to build a tutoring system that could interpret and respond to textual input such as self-explanations (Graesser, Wiemer-Hastings, Wiemer-Hastings, Harter, Person, & TRG, 2000; Wiemer-Hastings, Wiemer-Hastings, & Graesser, 1999).

Thus, iSTART was developed to instantiate SERT training within an ITS. iSTART is a web-based version of the SERT program that can potentially be deployed for use at any school, or for any individual with Internet access. This automated system was designed to address some of the limitations of the two SERT programs. Specifically, ITS technologies provided the means of providing individualized, adaptive, and engaging training to a wide-spread audience.

In order to transform a live intervention into an automated intervention, several choices needed to be made (McNamara, Levinstein, & Boonthum, 2004). The most important was how to deliver the material. One method would have been to film a live person and use real voice. Another would have been to use an animated agent, but use real voice. Neither of these options seemed viable because it was anticipated that the system would need numerous and frequent changes across time (and it did). And thus, a human voice could not be used because each small change could potentially necessitate re-recording the entire script. In terms of automated voices, one of our primary concerns was that schools be able to use the program, so this restricted selection to voices that were cost-free (and thus not high in quality). These restraints led us to using Microsoft Agent voices and characters.

The use of animated agents in iSTART allowed us to capitalize on several pedagogical techniques. SERT was transformed into three distinct iSTART modules: the introduction module, the demonstration module, and the practice module. These modules implemented the pedagogical principle of modeling, scaffolding, and fading, respectively. In addition, the implementation of the practice module afforded individualized practice with feedback. The following sections describe those modules as well as how the agents were used and the particular restraints of each module.

iSTART Modules

Introduction Module

The content of the iSTART introduction module is presented in SERT as a lecture on self-explanation and specific reading strategies. Having an animated agent deliver the same lecture content as a monologue risked being relatively boring and thereby losing students' attention. One question was how to deliver the initial lecture material without using a monologue. This was accomplished by taking advantage of what is referred to as vicarious learning (Cox, McKendree, Tobin, Lee, & Mayes, 1999). Vicarious learning is the notion that observing a learning process can be as effective as engaging in the learning process directly (Craig, Driscoll, & Gholson, 2004). This is frequently achieved by incorporating animated pedagogical agents that engage in interactive dialogues (e.g., Bransford, Brown, & Cocking, 2000; Graesser, Hu, & Person, 2001; Graesser, Hu, & McNamara, 2005; Louwerse, Graesser, & Olney, 2002). Hence, the iSTART introductory material is presented in the form of a trialogue comprising questions and answers between three animated agents, including two student agents (Mike and Sheila) and a teacher agent (Dr. Julie; see Fig. 14.1).

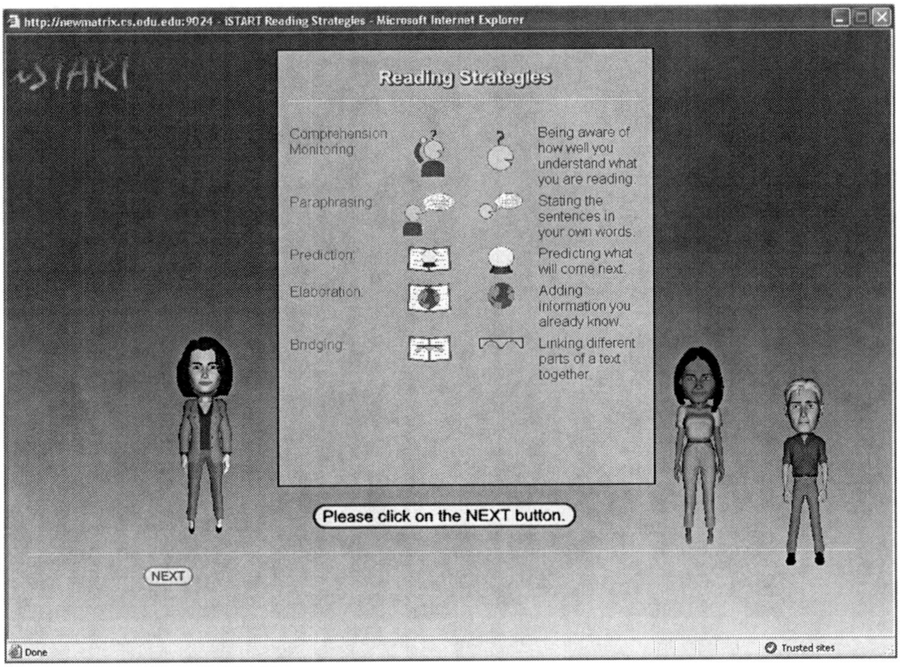

Fig. 14.1 Example screenshot of the iSTART Introduction Module. The teacher agent, Julie, is providing an overview of the strategies to be learned to the student agents, Sheila and Mike

Using dialogue allowed us to break up the material into bite-sized units and at the same time simulate the learning process via the two student agents.

The introduction module uses a classroom-like discussion that incorporates examples of both good and poor performances to model each of the target strategies. The interaction between the agents is modeled after the "lecture" portion from SERT, and thus it still exemplifies the active processing that a student should use when they provide their own self-explanations. During the interaction, the teacher agent describes a strategy and the student agents ask questions and provide various examples of that strategy (some good and some bad examples). The strategies included in this introduction module are the same as those within SERT, with one exception. In iSTART, the *logical inferences* strategy was combined within the *elaboration* strategy as part of using world knowledge and common sense. This change was implemented because the distinction between elaboration using common knowledge (i.e., logic) and domain knowledge (i.e., elaboration) was confusing to students. Thus, the strategies used within iSTART are as follows: *comprehension monitoring*, *paraphrasing*, *prediction*, *bridging*, and *elaboration*.

Formative quizzes were also incorporated after each of the strategies. After introducing a strategy, another agent (Merlin) asks a short series of questions that assess how well the student understood the strategy that had just been covered. The quizzes

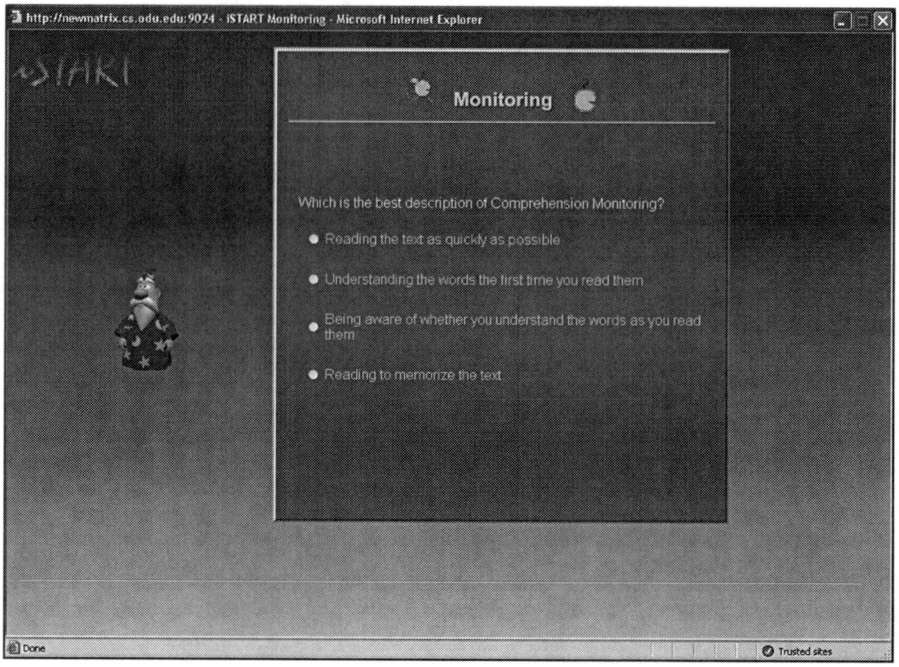

Fig. 14.2 Merlin poses formative comprehension assessment questions during the iSTART Introduction

are formative in the sense that the students are provided with hints and prompts when they incorrectly answer the questions. Because these quizzes do not require dialogue or vicarious learning, they were delivered by one agent (see Fig. 14.2).

Demonstration Module

The demonstration module is adapted from the demonstration video that students watched during the SERT training. This module is designed to scaffold the learner as they transition from acquiring strategy knowledge to applying those strategies with real texts. Instead of seeing a video with peers, the iSTART demonstration module uses two animated agents: a teacher/coach agent, Merlin, and a student agent, Genie. These agents interact with and guide the students as they analyze example explanations provided by the animated student agent (see Fig. 14.3). Genie acts as a student by reading a sentence aloud and providing an example self-explanation. Merlin provides feedback on Genie's explanation and then asks the learner to identify a strategy (or strategies) used within the explanation. Merlin may also ask the student to click on a part of the explanation to identify where a specific strategy was used. This interaction between Merlin and Genie is similar to the interaction

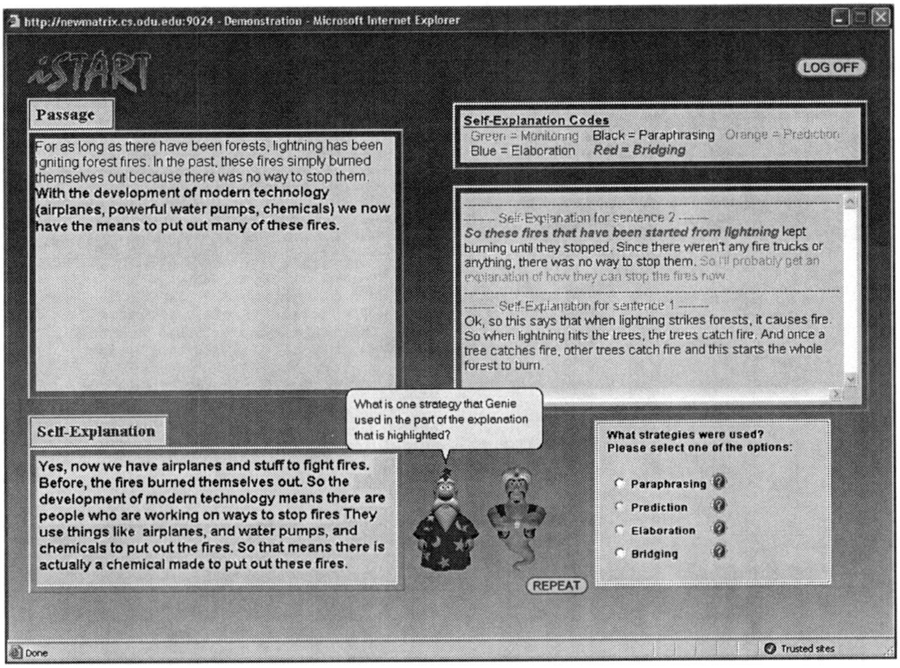

Fig. 14.3 Example screenshot of the iSTART Demonstration Module. Merlin provides feedback to the student agent, Genie, who is self-explaining a text about forest fires

that students will have with Merlin during the practice module. This module provides the same demonstration and content from the original SERT training, but now allows for students to progress through this automated training at their own pace.

Practice Modules

Lastly, the practice module required the most extensive adaptations in order to transform SERT from a live to an automated intervention. The practice module needed to be completely automated and provide timely, appropriate, and useful feedback to the students as they typed in their self-explanations (McNamara, Boonthum, Levinstein, & Millis, 2007; Muñoz, Magliano, Sheridan, & McNamara, 2006).

iSTART features two types of practice modules: regular and extended practice modules. The regular practice module is situated within the initial 2-h training session. That is, students typically go through the introduction, demonstration, and regular practice modules within 2 h. The regular practice module fades out direct instruction and provides the learner an opportunity to apply their newly acquired knowledge to two science texts. The extended practice module provides students the chance to read and self-explain a large number of new texts (either using texts

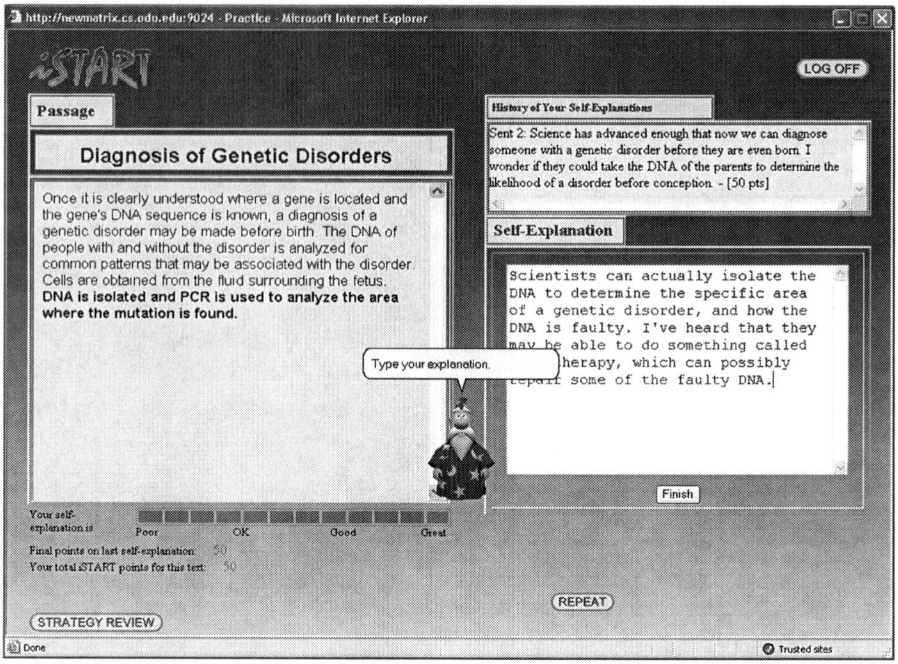

Fig. 14.4 Example screenshot of the iSTART Practice Module. Merlin provides feedback to the student, who is self-explaining a text about thunderstorms

already in the system or ones added by their teacher). Throughout both of these practice modules, an animated agent, Merlin, serves as a self-explanation coach and guides the learner as they generate their own self-explanations (see Fig. 14.4).

The regular practice module is the students' first chance to start generating their own self-explanations. This module utilizes two selected texts that allow iSTART to provide highly accurate assessments and targeted feedback (McNamara et al., 2007). Students are asked to read a sentence from the text and provide their own self-explanation. Each explanation is analyzed (using a combination of LSA and word-based approaches), and Merlin provides feedback to the learner. The feedback includes both qualitative assessments and offers suggestions on how to improve future explanations. For example, Merlin may say something like, "Okay, that's good. Next time try to connect information from different parts of the text." Merlin may also take the practice a step further by having students identify which specific strategies they used and where they were used. Throughout this practice module, Merlin adapts his responses to the quality of each individual explanation. In general, he provides a range of enthusiastic expressions for longer and more relevant explanations, but provides more scaffolding and support when explanations are short or irrelevant.

After completing the regular practice module, the students are automatically transitioned into the extended practice module where they can interact with varied ancillary texts (Levinstein, Boonthum, Pillarisetti, Bell, & McNamara, 2007). The extended practice module looks and functions exactly the same way as the regular practice module. This module is where students spend the majority of their time and are afforded the opportunity to apply the newly acquired strategy knowledge to new and varied science texts. These texts could be ones already present within the system or they could be newly added and assigned texts from their teacher. This extended practice module allows for a long-term interaction with iSTART and provides self-paced instruction at the individual level.

Providing Feedback in iSTART

Feedback on the content and quality of the self-explanation is a critical component of practice. This feedback needs to be delivered rapidly to the participant. During the practice phase, the agents' interactions with the trainee are moderated by the quality of the explanation. For example, more positive feedback is given for longer, more relevant explanations, whereas increased interactions and support are provided for shorter, less-relevant explanations. The computational challenge is for the system to provide the student appropriate feedback on the quality of the self-explanations within seconds. This evaluation comprises four steps: First, the response is screened for metacognitive expressions (such as "I don't understand what they are saying here"). Second, the remainder of the explanation is analyzed using both *word-based* and *LSA-based* methods (see McNamara et al., 2007). Third, the results from both methods' analyses are integrated with the metacognitive screening to produce feedback in one of the following six categories: (1) response to the metacognitive content; (2) feedback that the explanation appears irrelevant to the text; (3) feedback that the explanation is too short compared to the content of the sentence; (4) feedback that the explanation is too similar to the original sentence; (5) feedback that makes a suggestion for the following sentence; or (6) feedback that gives an appropriate level of praise.

Part of iSTART's evaluation procedure is based on LSA. The LSA method contrasts with the word-based evaluation, which calculates literal matching among words at a surface level. LSA is a computational method used to represent word meanings from a large corpus of text (Landauer & Dumais, 1997; Landauer, McNamara, Dennis, & Kintsch, 2007). The corpus of text is used to create a word by document co-occurrence matrix, which is then put through singular value decomposition to generate a high dimensional vector space. Within LSA, the conceptual similarity between any two language units (e.g., words, paragraphs) is determined by measuring the similarity of their representations within the multi-dimensional vector space (called a cosine). Empirical evaluations of LSA have shown comparable performance to human judgments of similarity of documents (Landauer & Dumais, 1997; Landauer et al., 1998), text coherence (Foltz, Kintsch, & Landauer, 1998; Shapiro & McNamara, 2000), grades assigned to essays (Landauer et al., 1998), and the quality of student dialogue contributions between human learners and computer tutors (Graesser et al., 2000; McNamara et al., 2007). LSA is used within iSTART to calculate the similarity between the student's explanation and a collection of words representing three different parts of the passage being explained: the target sentence, the title, and the prior content.

Evaluations were conducted to gauge the success of the assessment algorithms by computing linear equations based on a discriminate analysis of one data set and assessing its ability to predict ratings for a variety of data sets (McNamara et al., 2004, 2007; Millis et al., 2004). The *d*-primes in these studies have ranged from 1.0 to 3.0. Thus, across a number of evaluations, the iSTART algorithms have corresponded well to human ratings.

Evaluations of iSTART

Empirical studies on the effectiveness of iSTART have been positive. Studies at both the college (McNamara, 2004a; O'Reilly et al., 2004b) and the high school levels (O'Reilly et al., 2004; 2004a; O'Reilly et al., 2006; Taylor, O'Reilly, Sinclair, & McNamara, 2006) indicate that iSTART improves text comprehension and strategy use over control groups. Several studies have further confirmed that iSTART produces learning gains equivalent to those from the human-based SERT program (Magliano, Todaro, Millis, Wiemer-Hastings, Kim, &McNamara, 2005; O'Reilly et al., 2004b; 2004). It was also found that students who completed training with iSTART are significantly more effective at using self-explanation strategies (McNamara et al., 2006).

The effects of iSTART also depend on individual differences. One study investigated the effect of iSTART on adolescent students' comprehension and strategy use (McNamara et al., 2006; O'Reilly et al., 2004a). This study also examined whether the students' prior knowledge of reading strategies interacted with the benefits of strategy training (McNamara et al., 2006). Half of the students were provided with iSTART while the students in the control condition were given a brief demonstration on how to self-explain text. All of the students then self-explained a text about heart disease and answered text-based and bridging-inference questions. Results indicated that both iSTART training and prior knowledge of reading strategies significantly improved the quality of self-explanations. In turn, the quality of students' explanations of particular sentences was directly related to improved comprehension scores on questions tapping those sentences. In addition, it was found that benefits of reading strategy instruction depended on prior reading strategy knowledge. For low-strategy knowledge participants, the effects of iSTART were more pronounced at the more literal text-based level. Conversely, for high-strategy knowledge students, the effects of iSTART were evident on more difficult and integrative bridging inference questions.

Magliano et al. (2005; Experiment 2) found a similar pattern of results when they investigated whether and how the benefits of iSTART depended on the students' prior reading skill. In their study, college students read and self-explained two science texts before and after iSTART training. After reading the two texts, the students answered eight short-answer comprehension questions that corresponded to each text. Their reading skill was measured with the Nelson Denny Comprehension Test. Skilled readers answered more bridging questions correctly after training, whereas less-skilled readers improved on the text-based questions. Thus, more-skilled readers learned strategies that allowed them to make more connections within the text, and this ability was most apparent on the bridging inference questions. In contrast, the less-skilled readers learned the more basic level strategies (such as paraphrasing) that allowed them to make sense of the individual sentences.

Thus, it appears that many students benefit from iSTART, but in different ways, and according to their zone of proximal development (e.g., Vygotsky, 1978). Those students who possess more prior knowledge of reading strategies are able to engage in the more sophisticated processes (i.e., bridging inferences and elaborations), and therefore perform well on the subsequent bridging inference questions. In contrast, those students who have less knowledge of reading strategies struggle to develop a coherent understanding of the basic information and need to learn how to piece together the concepts from each sentence to form a coherent mental representation. Thus, students tend to make progress in their area of proximal development, and it appears that iSTART addresses at least two stages within reading comprehension development. First, readers must learn how to assemble a sufficient mental representation of the text-based information (i.e., how to fit together the information from each individual sentence). Once readers can create a conceptual representation, they move toward understanding the text at a deeper level. This deeper understanding comes from processing the relations between ideas and establishing links between the text and the student's world knowledge.

iSTART Discussion

iSTART was designed to address some of the constraints associated with SERT training. The human-based aspect of SERT-limited training to a single classroom at a time (and sometimes down to a single individual at a time). This design imposed physical constraints on the size of training groups and also made it more difficult to establish comparable groups for accurate evaluations. Through the invention of iSTART, it became possible to have an almost infinite number of students trained simultaneously, and each with training adapted to their individual pace and ability level.

Though iSTART is effective at producing learning gains and improving student's self-explanations, it comes with its own limitations. iSTART is effective at delivering the necessary self-explanation content to students. The animated agents are sufficiently engaging during the introduction, demonstration, and regular practice modules. However, during the long-term extended practice module students have been found to lose focus, disengage from the learning environment, and simply go through the motions to fulfill requirements. This is unfortunate because the extended practice module houses some of the largest practical benefits as it provides students an opportunity to apply knowledge by practicing the strategies, and a chance to actively transfer these skills to new texts.

iSTART-ME

iSTART-Motivationally Enhanced (Jackson, Boonthum, & McNamara, 2009) is an extension of the original iSTART program and is designed as a replacement for the extended practice module. The iSTART tutoring system was designed to tutor individual students over a long-term interaction, spanning across a full academic semester. This kind of repetitive exposure should greatly increase the learning and retention benefits of iSTART, however it seems to have the opposite effect on motivation and engagement. After interacting with the system for several weeks, the novelty of the animated agents wears off and the system becomes a toil. The iSTART-ME extension envelopes the extended practice module within a fully game-based environment to establish a better balance between education and engagement (Boyer, Phillips, Wallis, Vouk, & Lester, 2008; Jackson & Graesser, 2007). This new environment is specifically designed to address motivation, and should help to maintain students' interest and engagement over the long-term interaction.

iSTART-ME is designed as a hybrid environment that incorporates best practices from both ITSs and Game System Design. The synthesis of these two areas is expected to support effective learning, increase motivation, and sustain engagement during the long-term extended practice (Graesser, Chipman, Leeming, & Biedenbach, 2009; McNamara, Jackson, & Graesser, in press; Moreno & Mayer, 2005). In support of this expectation, research has shown that games have been linked with an increase in various motivational constructs, which may include self-efficacy, interest, engagement, and self-regulation (Gredler, 2004; Thomas, Cahill, & Santilli, 1997; Witmer & Singer, 1994). Additional research has shown that these motivational constructs are positively related to learning (Alexander, Murphy, Woods, Duhon, & Parker, 1997; Bandura, 2000; Csikszentmihaly, 1990; Greene & Azevedo, 2007). The hope is that the additional features in iSTART-ME will be sufficiently engaging and rewarding to enhance these various aspects of motivation, and will consequently have an indirect effect on overall learning (as in Ricci, Salas, & Cannon-Bowers, 1996).

iSTART-ME Modules

As previously mentioned, iSTART-ME is an extension of the original iSTART. Therefore the core components of iSTART remain the same (introduction, demonstration, and practice modules are left mostly unchanged), and it is only the extended practice module that has been modified extensively.

Extended Practice

The extended practice module has been updated to address some of the motivational concerns from the original iSTART. The basic functioning of extended practice remains very similar to its original iSTART implementation. That is, students have the opportunity to apply the self-explanation reading strategies and are asked to use these skills with a variety of texts. iSTART-ME extended practice uses the same assessment algorithms as the original iSTART, so students still receive feedback on each of their self-explanation attempts. However, in iSTART-ME extended practice, students also receive points based on the quality of their self-explanation. Students are rewarded with more points when they engage in consistently good practice performance and receive fewer points if they fluctuate between good and poor performance. Students accumulate points both within and across their interactions with texts. In between texts, students have the opportunity to use these points in various ways (see Fig. 14.5 for screenshot).

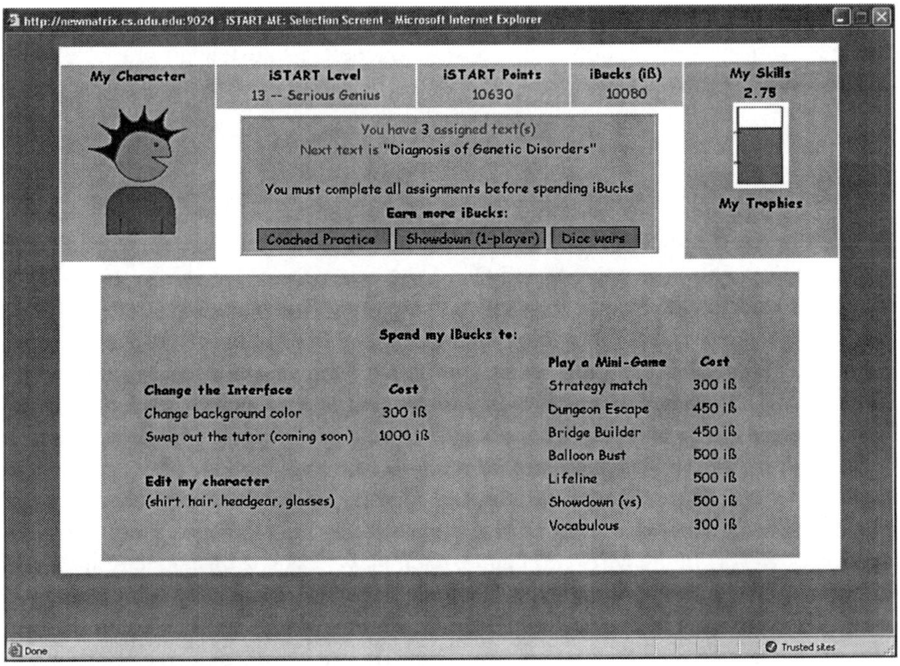

Fig. 14.5 Example screenshots of the iSTART-ME selection menu. The student is provided information on points earned while self-explaining texts during training and choices for how to spend points

The points in extended practice are the main component of a metagame and help to drive several of the other game elements in iSTART-ME. The iSTART-ME metagame primarily consists of earning points, advancing through levels, and purchasing rewards. As students accumulate more total points, they automatically advance through a series of labeled levels (e.g., "Serious Bookworm," "Expert Strategizer," "Ultimate Genius,"). Within the overarching metagame, students can redeem points for various in-system rewards: creating a personalized avatar, changing environment attributes, or playing an educational mini-game. Every student has a personal avatar to represent them within iSTART-ME, and students can spend points to customize their avatar with different hair, glasses, shirts, etc. Students may also choose to change the color scheme of iSTART-ME or to swap out the animated tutor for an alternative version. Lastly, students can redeem points to play an educational mini-game. A suite of short educational games (5–15 min play time) were designed for specific use within iSTART-ME. All of the mini-games incorporate similar features from existing games; however, the gameplay incorporates the strategies from iSTART and requires students to identify strategy use or generate self-explanations. Within these mini-games, students can earn points, advance through levels, and engage in active gameplay (e.g., popping balloons, building bridges, escaping a dungeon). Even though the points and levels within the mini-games do not transfer over into the iSTART-ME system, the students can still set high scores and compare performance among peers. All of these features work in combination to serve as the game-based extended practice within iSTART-ME.

MiBoard Game

In addition to the iSTART-ME adaptation of extended practice, there is also an online Multiplayer interactive Board Game (MiBoard Game; Dempsey et al., 2009) that gives students the chance to practice using the self-explanation strategies while competing against and collaborating with each other in a constructivist gaming environment. MiBoard is designed as an alternative form of extended practice within iSTART-ME. So rather than self-explaining a text to earn points, students can log into MiBoard Game and play a collaborative/competitive game with their peers.

MiBoard Game is designed so that three to four students can play and practice together by creating self-explanations and identifying the strategies used by other players. This is somewhat similar to the one-on-one peer practice from the group version of SERT. In the MiBoard Game, each player takes a turn generating a self-explanation for a provided sentence. Then all players try to identify what strategy or strategies were used in that self-explanation. Players obtain points when a majority of them agree on a specific strategy being used. If any players disagree on the strategies used in the self-explanation, then a discussion chatroom is activated. During the discussion, all players have the chance to provide a rationale for their original choice and can accrue points by convincing other players to change their strategy selection. After the discussion, all players get another opportunity to identify the strategies they think were used within the self-explanation. After all voting is complete, the players are brought back to the main board game screen. At this time the player who originally generated the explanation gets to roll the virtual die, and his/her token is automatically moved along the board. Then the next player will take a turn reading a sentence and generating a self-explanation, and so on. The game ends when one of the player tokens lands on the last board space, and a series of mini-awards are displayed for various in-game performance characteristics.

iSTART-ME Discussion

Situating iSTART within a game-based environment helps to address two limitations from the original design. This new game environment for extended practice should increase interest and engagement to help sustain the long-term interactions, and it hopefully provides a measuring stick by which students can gauge their own progress toward goals and even compare performance among peers. The addition of MiBoard, as an alternative to extended practice, offers the option of peer-to-peer collaborative learning with a game-based twist. The combination of iSTART-ME extended practice and MiBoard Game simultaneously capitalizes on the benefits found from previous training interventions, and attempts to address the aforementioned shortcomings of each.

The collection of game-based features in iSTART-ME was selected for implementation because they are positively associated with various aspects of motivation (McNamara, Jackson, & Graesser, 2009), they are easily implemented within the current iSTART system architecture (Jackson et al., 2009), and they allow for nearly infinite gameplay (unlike narrative or immersive environments where a plot dictates length of play).

General Discussion

Throughout this chapter we have focused on the evolution of a training program designed to teach students effective self-explanation strategies. This training program began as an individual human-to-human intervention (SERT one-on-one), incorporated that same training within a classroom-based collaborative learning environment (SERT group), transitioned into a highly distributable effective self-paced tutoring system (iSTART), and is currently being adapted into a game-based learning environment with collaborative peer-to-peer gameplay (iSTART-ME, with MiBoard). Each transition was designed to address potential limitations from a previous version and to improve upon the overall training effectiveness.

Each version of the training manipulated similar pedagogical principles. The goal of training has always been to teach students specific self-explanation strategies, and this skill acquisition has predominantly been achieved through the use of modeling, scaffolding, and fading. All training versions incorporate an introduction to the specific self-explanation strategies (modeling), a demonstration of someone else exhibiting both good and poor performance (scaffolding), and a practice session where each student applies the strategies to a text (fading). Despite the different implementations, all versions of the self-explanation training proved to be successful at promoting learning gains (i.e., improving reading comprehension).

Table 14.1 Comparisons of training components across self-explanation training techniques

	Introduction	Demonstration	Practice
SERT:one-on-one	Live direct lecture	Continuous video and worksheet	Short-term one-on-one with expert human tutor
SERT: Group	Live direct lecture	Partitioned video and group discussion	Short-term peer-to-peer practice with summarization
iSTART	Animated vicarious lecture	Animated vicarious discussion with interactive identification	Long-term one-on-one with animated coach
iSTART-ME	Animated vicarious lecture	Animated vicarious discussion with interactive identification	Long-term one-on-one with animated coach and game, and peer-to-peer game

Table 14.1 shows a summary of the different pedagogical implementations between versions.

Of course, there are other variations between the versions which are not listed in Table 14.1 (e.g., see Levinstein, Boonthum, et al., 2007), but the primary pedagogical changes involved computerization and availability of collaboration. For example, both the SERT transition from one-on-one to group and the iSTART transition from original to iSTART-ME consisted of a change from completely individualized training into a more hybrid environment that included some one-on-one interactions as well as collaborative learning. The other major transition, from SERT group to original iSTART, required automating each of the components. The original SERT materials had to be converted into electronic materials, most of which had to be re-conceptualized to fit within an animated script while maintaining the effectiveness of instruction.

This chapter has focused on the evolutionary changes of a training program as it has transitioned from human-based to computer-based and from individualized to collaborative. Each of these transitions helped to improve upon previous versions by addressing specific training limitations found during testing and evaluations. This is likely to be one of the many development trends in the future as our community continues to evolve into an era of electronic education.

Acknowledgments This research was supported in part by the Institute for Educational Sciences (IES R305G020018-02; R305G040046; R305A080589) and National Science Foundation (NSF REC0241144; IIS-0735682). Any opinions, findings, and conclusions or recommendations expressed in this material are those of the authors and do not necessarily reflect the views of the IES or NSF.

References

Alexander, P. A., Murphy, P. K., Woods, B. S., Duhon, K. E., & Parker, D. (1997). College instruction and concomitant changes in students' knowledge, interest, and strategy use: A study of domain learning. *Contemporary Educational Psychology*, *22*, 125–146.

Anderson, J. R., Corbett, A. T., Koedinger, K., & Pelletier, R. (1995). Cognitive tutors: Lessons learned. *The Journal of Learning Sciences*, *4*, 167–207.

Bandura, A. (2000). Self-efficacy: The foundation of agency. In W. Perig & A. Grob (Eds.), *Control of human behavior, mental processes, and consciousness: Essays in honor of the 60th birthday of August Flammer* (pp. 17–33). Mahwah, NJ: Erlbaum.

Bielaczyc, K., Pirolli, P. L., & Brown, A. L. (1995). Training in self-explanation and self-regulation strategies: Investigating the effects of knowledge acquisition activities on problem solving. *Cognition and Instruction*, *13*, 221–252.

Boyer, K. E., Phillips, R., Wallis, M., Vouk, M., & Lester, J. (2008). Balancing cognitive and motivational scaffolding in tutorial dialogue. *Proceedings of the Ninth International Conference on Intelligent Tutoring Systems* (pp. 239–249). Canada: Montreal.

Bransford, J., Brown, A., & Cocking, R., (Eds.) (2000). *How people learn: Brain, mind, experience, and school*. Washington, DC: National Academy Press. Retrieved form http://www.nap.edu/html/howpeople1/.

Brown, A. L., & Palincsar, A. S. (1982). Inducing strategic learning from texts by means of informed, self-control training. *Topics in Learning and Learning Disabilities*, *2*, 1–17.

Chi, M. T. H., de Leeuw, N., Chiu, M. H., & Lavancher, C. (1994). Eliciting self-explanations improves understanding. *Cognitive Science*, *18*, 439–477.

Conole, G., Dyke, M., Oliver, M., & Seale, J. (2004). Mapping pedagogy and tools for effective learning design. *Computers & Education*, *43*, 17–33.

Cox, R., McKendree, J., Tobin, R., Lee, J., & Mayes, T. (1999). Vicarious learning from dialogue and discourse. *Instructional Science*, *27*, 431–458.

Craig, S. D., Driscoll, D. M., & Gholson, B. (2004). Constructing knowledge from dialog in an intelligent tutoring system: Interactive learning, vicarious learning and pedagogical agents. *Journal of Educational Multimedia and Hypermedia*, *13*, 163–183.

Csikszentmihaly, M. (1990). *Flow, the psychology of optimal experience*. New York: Harper Collins.

Dempsey, K. B., Brunelle, J. F., Jackson, G. T., Boonthum, C., Levinstein, I. B., & McNamara, D. S. (2009). MiBoard: Multiplayer interactive board game. In H.C. Lane, A. Ogan, & V. Shute (Eds.), *Proceedings of the Workshop on Intelligent Educational Games at the 14th Annual Conference on Artificial Intelligence in Education* (pp. 113–116). Brighton, UK: AIED.

Dynarski, M., Agodini, R., Heaviside, S., Novak, T., Carey, N., Campuzano, L., et al. (2007). *Effectiveness of reading and mathematics software products: Findings from the first student cohort*. Washington, DC: U.S. Department of Education, Institute of Education Sciences.

Foltz, P. W., Kintsch, W., & Landauer, T. K. (1998). The measurement of textual coherence with Latent Semantic Analysis. *Discourse Processes*, *25*, 285–307.

Graesser, A. C., Chipman, P., Leeming, F., & Biedenbach, S. (2009). Deep learning and emotion in serious games. In U. Ritterfield, M. Cody, & P. Vorderer (Eds.), *Serious games: Mechanisms and effects* (pp. 81–100). Mahwah, NJ: Routledge, Taylor and Francis.

Graesser, A. C., Hu, X., & McNamara, D. S. (2005). Computerized learning environments that incorporate research in discourse psychology, cognitive science, and computational linguistics. In A. F. Healy (Ed.), *Experimental cognitive psychology and its applications: Festschrift in honor of Lyle Bourne, Walter Kintsch, and Thomas Landauer* (pp. 183–194). Washington, DC: American Psychological Association.

Graesser, A. C., Hu, X., & Person, N. (2001). Teaching with the help of talking heads. In T. Okamoto, R. Hartley, D. G. S. Kinshuk , & J. P. Klus (Eds.), *Proceedings IEEE international conference on advanced learning technology: Issues, achievements and challenges* (pp. 460–461). Los Alamitos, CA: IEEE Computer Society.

Graesser, A. C., Wiemer-Hastings, P., Wiemer-Hastings, K., Harter, D., Person, N., & the TRG (2000). Using latent semantic analysis to evaluate the contributions of students in AutoTutor. *Interactive Learning Environments*, *8*, 129–148.

Gredler, M. E. (2004). Games and simulations and their relationships to learning. In D. H. Jonassen (Ed.), *Handbook of research on educational communications and technology* (pp. 571–582). Mahwah, NJ: Lawrence Erlbaum Associates.

Greene, J. A., & Azevedo, R. (2007). Adolescents' use of self-regulatory processes and their relation to qualitative mental model shifts while using hypermedia. *Journal of Educational Computing Research, 36*, 125–148.

Hu, X., Graesser, A. C., & the Tutoring Research Group (1998). Using WordNet and latent semantic analysis to evaluate the conversational contributions of learners in tutorial dialog. *Proceedings of the international conference on computers in education, Vol. 2* (pp. 337–341). Beijing: Springer.

Jackson, G. T., Boonthum, C., & McNamara, D. M. (2009). *iSTART-ME: Situating extended learning within a game-based environment.* Proceedings of the 14th international conference on artificial intelligence in education.

Jackson, G. T., & Graesser, A. C. (2007). Content matters: An investigation of feedback categories within an ITS. In R. Luckin, K. R. Koedinger, & J. Greer (Eds.), *Proceedings of AIED 2007 Conference* (pp. 127–134). Amsterdam: IOS Press.

Kennedy, D. (1998). Software development teams in higher education: An educator's view. In R. M. Corderoy (Ed.), *ASCILITE '98. flexibility: The next wave?* Proceedings (pp. 373–385). Wollongong: ASCILITE.

Landauer, T., & Dumais, S. T. (1997). A solution to Plato's Problem: The latent semantic analysis theory of acquisition, induction, and representation of knowledge. *Psychological Review, 104*, 211–240.

Landauer, T., Foltz, P. W., & Laham, D. (1998). An introduction to latent semantic analysis. *Discourse Processes, 25*, 259–284.

Landauer, T., McNamara, D. S., Dennis, S., & Kintsch, W. (Eds.). (2007). *Handbook of latent semantic analysis*. Mahwah, NJ: Erlbaum.

Levinstein, I. B., Boonthum, C., Pillarisetti, S. P., Bell, C., & McNamara, D. S. (2007). iSTART 2: Improvements for efficiency and effectiveness. *Behavior Research Methods, 39*, 224–232.

Louwerse, M. M., Graesser, A. C., Olney, A., & the TRG (2002). Good computational manners: Mixed-initiative dialog in conversational agents. In C. Miller (Ed.), *Etiquette for human-computer work* (pp. 71–76). Falmouth, MA: Sea Crest Conference Center.

Magliano, J. P., Todaro, S., Millis, K., Wiemer-Hastings, K., Kim, H. J., & McNamara, D. S. (2005). Changes in reading strategies as a function of reading training: A comparison of live and computerized training. *Journal of Educational Computing Research, 32*, 185–208.

McNamara, D. S. (2000a). *Background knowledge assessment as a key to improving learning from text* (Project JSMF 95-56). Final report submitted to James S. McDonnell Foundation Program in Cognitive Studies for Educational Practice.

McNamara, D. S. (2000b). *Promoting active reading strategies to improve undergraduate students' understanding of science*. Final report submitted to the ODU College of Sciences and ODU Office of Academic Affairs.

McNamara, D. S. (2004a). Aprender del texto: efectos de la estructura textual y las estrategias del lector. *Revista Signos, 37*, 19–30.

McNamara, D. S. (2004b). SERT: Self-explanation reading training. *Discourse Processes, 38*, 1–30.

McNamara, D. S., Boonthum, C., Levinstein, I. B., & Millis, K. (2007). Evaluating self-explanations in iSTART: Comparing word-based and LSA algorithms. In T. Landauer, D. S. McNamara, S. Dennis, & W. Kintsch (Eds.), *Handbook of latent semantic analysis* (pp. 227–241). Mahwah, NJ: Erlbaum.

McNamara, D. S., Jackson, G. T., & Graesser, A. C. (2009). *Intelligent tutoring and games*. Proceedings of the 14th International conference on artificial intelligence in education.

McNamara, D. S., Jackson, G. T., & Graesser, A. C. (in press). Intelligent tutoring and games (ITaG). In Y. Baek (Ed.), *Gaming for classroom-based learning: Digital role playing as a motivator of study*. Plainsboro, NJ: IGE Global Press.

McNamara, D. S., Levinstein, I. B., & Boonthum, C. (2004). iSTART: Interactive strategy trainer for active reading and thinking. *Behavioral Research Methods, Instruments, & Computers, 36*, 222–233.

McNamara, D. S., O'Reilly, T., Best, R., & Ozuru, Y. (2006). Improving adolescent students' reading comprehension with iSTART. *Journal of Educational Computing Research, 34*, 147–171.

McNamara, D. S., & Scott, J. L. (1999). Training reading strategies. In M. Hahn & S. C. Stoness (Eds.), *Proceedings of the twenty first annual conference of the cognitive science society* (pp. 387–392). Hillsdale, NJ: Erlbaum.

McNamara, D. S., & Shapiro, A. M. (2005). Multimedia and hypermedia solutions for promoting metacognitive engagement, coherence, and learning. *Journal of Educational Computing Research, 33*, 1–29.

Millis, K., Kim, H. J., Todaro, S., Magliano, J. P., Wiemer-Hastings, K., & McNamara, D. S. (2004). Identifying reading strategies using latent semantic analysis: Comparing semantic benchmarks. *Behavior Research Methods, Instruments, & Computers, 36*, 213–221.

Moreno, R., & Mayer, R. E. (2005). Role of guidance, reflection, and interactivity in an agent-based multimedia game. *Journal of Educational Psychology, 97*, 117–128.

Muñoz, B., Magliano, J. P., Sheridan, R., & McNamara, D. S. (2006). Typing versus thinking aloud when reading: Implications for computer-based assessment and training tools. *Behavior Research Methods, Instruments, & Computers, 38*, 211–217.

Okan, Z. (2003). Edutainment: is learning at risk? *British Journal of Educational Technology, 34*, 255–264.

Oliver, R. (2002). Winning the toss and electing to bat: Maximizing the opportunities of online learning. In C. Rust (Ed.), *Proceedings of the 9th improving student learning conference* (pp. 35–44). Oxford: OCSLD.

O'Reilly, T., Best, R., & McNamara, D. S. (2004). Self-Explanation reading training: Effects for low-knowledge readers. In K. Forbus, D. Gentner, T. Regier (Eds.), *Proceedings of the twenty-sixth annual meeting of the cognitive science society* (pp. 1053–1058). Mahwah, NJ: Erlbaum.

O'Reilly, T., Sinclair, G. P., & McNamara, D. S. (2004a). iSTART: A web-based reading strategy intervention that improves students' science comprehension. In Kinshuk, D. G. S. & P. Isaías (Eds.), *Proceedings of the IADIS international conference cognition and exploratory learning in digital age: CELDA 2004* (pp. 173–180). Lisbon, Portugal: IADIS Press.

O'Reilly, T., Sinclair, G. P., & McNamara, D. S. (2004b). Reading strategy training: Automated verses live. In K. Forbus, D. Gentner, T. Regier (Eds.), *Proceedings of the twenty-sixth annual meeting of the cognitive science society* (pp. 1059–1064). Mahwah, NJ: Erlbaum.

O'Reilly, T., Taylor, R. S., & McNamara, D. S. (2006). Classroom based reading strategy training: Self-explanation vs. reading control. In R. Sun & N. Miyake (Eds.), *Proceedings of the 28th annual conference of the cognitive science society* (pp. 1887). Mahwah, NJ: Erlbaum.

Palincsar, A. S., & Brown, A. L. (1984). Reciprocal teaching of comprehension-fostering and comprehension-monitoring activities. *Cognition and Instruction, 1*, 117–175.

Pashler, H., Bain, P., Bottage, B., Graesser, A., Koedinger, K., McDaniel, M., et al. (2007). *Organizing instruction and study to improve student learning* (NCER 2007–2004). Washington, DC: National Center for Educational Research, Institute of Education Sciences, U.S. Department of Education.

Pressman, R. S. (1997). *Software engineering: A practitioner's approach* (4th ed.). New York: McGraw-Hill Companies Inc.

Ricci, K., Salas, E., & Cannon-Bowers, J. A. (1996). Do computer-based games facilitate knowledge acquisition and retention? *Military Psychology, 8*(4), 295–307.

Roy, M., & Chi, M. T. H. (2005). The self-explanation principle in multimedia learning. In R. E. Mayer (Ed.), *The Cambridge handbook of multimedia learning* (pp. 271–286). New York: Cambridge University Press.

Shapiro, A. M., & McNamara, D. S. (2000). The use of latent semantic analysis as a tool for the quantitative assessment of understanding and knowledge. *Journal of Educational Computing Research*, *22*, 1–36.

Taylor, R., O'Reilly, T., Sinclair, G., & McNamara, D. S. (2006). *Enhancing learning of expository science texts in a remedial reading classroom via iSTART*. Proceedings of the 7th international conference of learning sciences (pp. 765–770). Bloomington, IN.

Thomas, R., Cahill, J., & Santilli, L. (1997). Using an interactive computer game to increase skill and self-efficacy regarding safer sex negotiation: Field test results. *Health Education & Behavior*, *24*, 71–86.

Vygotsky, L. S. (1978). *Mind in society*. Cambridge, MA: Harvard University Press.

Wiemer-Hastings, P., Wiemer-Hastings, K., & Graesser, A. (1999). Improving an intelligent tutor's comprehension of students with Latent Semantic Analysis. In S. P. Lajoie & M. Vivet (Eds.), *Artificial intelligence in education* (pp. 535–542). Amsterdam: IOS Press.

Witmer, B. G., & Singer, M. J. (1994). *Measuring immersion in virtual environments* (Technical Rep. 1014). Alexandria, VA: U.S. Army Research Institute for the Behavioral and Social Sciences.

Chapter 15
Experiences in the Field: The Evolution of a Technology-Oriented Teacher Professional Development Model

M. Brooke Robertshaw, Andrew Walker, Mimi Recker, Heather Leary, and Linda Sellers

Department of Instructional Technology and Learning Sciences, Utah State University, Logan, UT 84322-2830, USA

Introduction

In the USA, as in many places in the world, there has been an increasing focus on integrating online/Internet communication technology into primary and secondary education. These rapid technological innovations offer a wealth of potential for transforming education. In science education, for example, students can now access real-time images from space exploration, or download data and partner with other students and scientists to analyze simulations of complex weather events. They can remotely participate in scientific explorations and events, including research trips to Antarctica or solar eclipses (Computing Research Association, 2005; Pea et al., 2008). In mathematics, students can interact with virtual tools and manipulatives that help make abstract concepts more concrete (Dorward & Heal, 1999).

In recognition of this potential, several large-scale initiatives being taken are developing repositories (or, *digital libraries*) containing catalogued *online learning resources*. Key objectives are to provide teacher and learner access to high-quality learning objects in order to help improve both the effectiveness and the efficiency of education (McArthur & Zia, 2008). In the USA, the National Science Digital Library (NSDL.org) offers a comprehensive collection of educational content and contains services to learners, educators, and academic policy makers. The NSDL contains over 2.5 million high-quality, catalogued science, technology, engineering, and mathematics educational online resources (NSDL.org, 2009).

However, these tremendous opportunities also come with a significant number of challenges. Chief among them is that most mid- and late-career teachers are not digital natives. While experienced teachers may possess a vast and effective repertoire

M.B. Robertshaw (✉)
Department of Instructional Technology and Learning Sciences, Utah State University, Logan, UT 84322-2830, USA
e-mail: brooke.robertshaw@gmail.com

M.S. Khine, I.M. Saleh (eds.), *New Science of Learning*,
DOI 10.1007/978-1-4419-5716-0_15, © Springer Science+Business Media, LLC 2010

of teaching strategies and lesson plans, these were typically designed around the notion of temporally and physically constrained resources (e.g., textbooks) within the confines of a single classroom. The distributed and limitless access provided by the Internet turns these assumptions on their head (Greenhow, Robelia & Hughes, 2009; Pea et al., 2008). In addition, while the resources may be available, accessible, and meet quality standards—particularly with respect to content they are not always ready for classroom use. In a very real sense, there is a gap between online learning resources produced by researchers and content experts, and the practitioners, with pedagogical expertise trying to adapt them for their own classrooms.

In the context of an 8-year research project, we have been focusing on two related strands of research to help address these challenges. First, we have developed a simple, Web-based software tool that provides an important connection between teachers, their teaching practices, and online learning resources. Begun in 2001, the *Instructional Architect* (IA.usu.edu) helps teachers quickly and easily find and assemble online learning resources to design learning activities for their students. Second, to support teacher usage of the IA while also supporting a broader goal of conducting research about the impact of using online resources in the classroom, we have been iteratively developing and refining a technology-focused teacher professional development (PD) model to support teachers in integrating twenty-first century teaching and learning skills in their classrooms.

The following chapter describes the IA and several iterations of our PD model, as informed by evaluation results and best practices in the literature. As we will describe, while our different PD models have been based on different instructional models, the one common feature has been the use of authentic design problems. The chapter concludes with a discussion of the impact of our work on teacher design activities, and their classroom practices.

Technology Context: The Instructional Architect

Ultimately, teachers use the IA to create activities for their students that incorporate online learning resources built by others—including content experts and researchers. We begin the description of the IA with two examples created by teachers using our tool (see Figs. 15.1 and 15.2). The foreground of each figure shows one of the teacher's selected online resources. The background shows the IA project itself, created by the teacher.

As is apparent from the figures, teacher-created IA projects are fairly simple. Typical teachers are not professional Web designers, nor should we expect them to be. Instead, they are teaching professionals attempting to efficiently and effectively address classroom and learning issues.

System description. From the home page of the IA, users can (1) *browse* IA projects, (2) *register* as a new user, or (3) *login* as a registered user or as guests with reduced functionality.

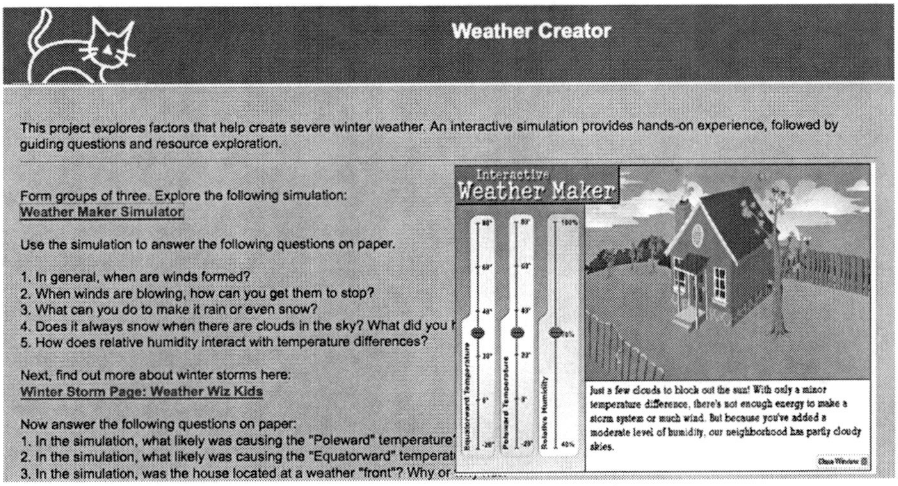

Fig. 15.1 An example of an Instructional Architect project about Weather for grade 3 with an overlay of the online resource linked to from the project

1. *Browse.* Currently, the IA has over 3,824 IA projects made publicly available by teacher users. Users can access IA projects by performing keyword searches or by browsing these IA projects by subject area, grade level, author's last name, or title.
2. *Register.* Users can create a free account, which provides them secure access to their saved resources and IA projects.
3. *Login.* After the end user logs in, the IA offers three major usage modes. First, with the "*My Resources*" tool, users can search for and select online resources available in the NSDL or anywhere on the Web.

Second, with the "*My Projects*" tool, they can create Web pages in which they sequence and annotate their selected resources in order to create learning activities (called "IA projects").

Finally, users can share their IA projects by *Publishing* them and setting permissions on them, such as (a) *user-only* view, (b) users and their students (*student* view), or (c) *public* view (anyone browsing the IA site). Users can also add basic metadata about their IA projects, including subject area, grade level, and core curriculum standard. These are then used to support browse and search of existing IA projects, as described above.

The design, development, and evaluation of the IA has been ongoing since 2002. From 2002 to June 2009, over 4,000 users have registered, 8,500 projects have been created, and 37,000 external online resources have been added to the database. Since mid-2006, IA projects have been viewed over 565,000 times.

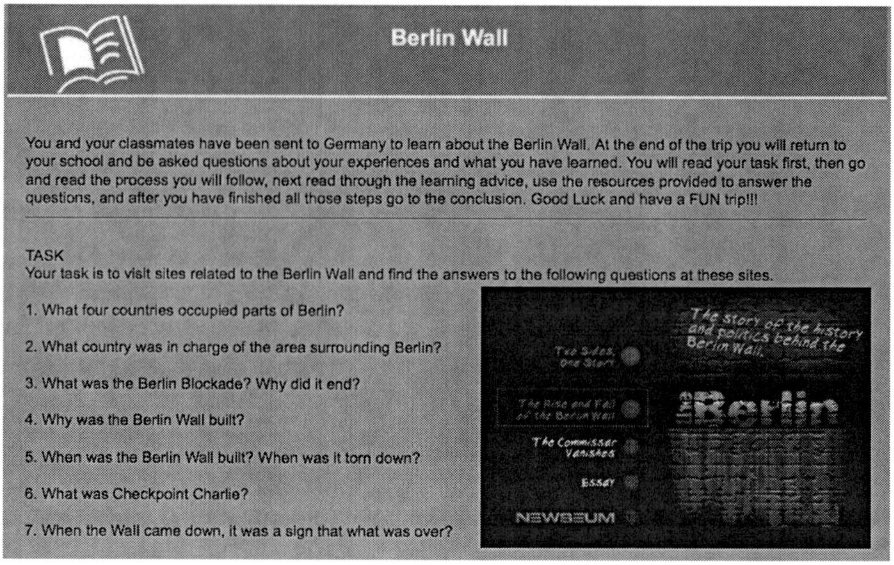

Fig. 15.2 An example of an Instructional Architect project about the Berlin Wall for grade 10 with an overlay of the online resource linked to from the project

Pedagogical Context: Problem-Based Learning

Problem-based learning (PBL) is a well-established inquiry-oriented instructional method, originally developed in medical education, and now used in K-12 and university settings (Savery, 2006). In PBL, learners acquire knowledge through engaging with authentic and challenging problems (Barrows, 1986, 1996; Savery, 2006). Typically, learners operate in small groups to solve these authentic problems using resources (including online resources) made available to them. The instructor acts as a facilitator and provides scaffolds and coaching. Each problem cycle concludes with a reflection phase, in which learners discuss the efficacy of the information obtained and their solution strategies.

Overall, research shows that PBL is successful in promoting student learning. Past meta-analyses show PBL students performing about as well on knowledge tests as their lecture-based counterparts (Gijbels et al., 2005). When asked to perform at a deeper level, for example, understanding the relationships and dependencies between concepts or applying knowledge, PBL students perform better (Walker & Leary, 2009). There is also uniform agreement across several meta-analyses that PBL students retain much more of what they learn (Barneveld & Strobel, 2009).

PBL findings specific to teachers are even more dramatic. For example, our own analysis of past work in teacher education that utilizes PBL (Derry et al., 2006; Gulseçen & Kubat, 2006; Shoffner & Dalton, 1998) shows a weighted effect size that is extremely high ($d = 1.14$).

Evolution of the Professional Development Models

The next section describes different iterations of the PD models used throughout the course of the research project (see Table 15.1). The hallmark of all iterations is the use of authentic design problems. Early in the workshop, PD participants are asked to select an authentic instructional problem or need in their classroom (e.g., a new curricular unit, a lesson students struggle with), and to design a solution using online learning resources and the IA. Participants were then asked to implement their design in their classrooms.

Table 15.1 Overview of models and implementation studies

Model	Model characteristics	Date	*N*	Delivery
1	Authentic problem, design-centered approach	Spring 2004	14	F2F workshop
		Spring 2007	20	F2F workshop
		Fall 2008	19	F2F workshop
2	Problem-based learning: simple-to-complex approach	Fall 2006	49	Online module
		Fall 2008	29	Online module
3	Problem-based learning: design approach	Fall 2008	24	F2F workshop
		Spring 2009	20	F2F workshop

Each iteration of the model was also evaluated. Evaluation studies focused on gauging the impact of the workshops on participants' technology knowledge and attitudes, and (short- and long-term) behaviors with regard to their use of and design with the IA. Finally, each evaluation measured participant satisfaction with the PD program.

Evaluation strategies and measures generally remained consistent across all PD workshops, although specific prompts and items evolved. At the start and end of the PD, participants completed online surveys, consisting of both open-ended and likert scale items. They also completed short reflection papers, describing their classroom implementation experiences. In addition, as the IA is a Web-based environment, Web-usage data were automatically collected during participants' online activities (called *webmetrics* (Khoo et al., 2008). Selected participants were also invited to participate in focus group interviews to provide more in-depth reports about their experiences.

Model 1: Authentic Problem and Design Centered

The first model that was developed was structured as face-to-face (f2f) workshops delivered as two 4-h workshops, separated by classroom implementation activities. This model consisted of the following six core activities:

1. A motivating example. An interesting learning resource from the NSDL (e.g., an interactive simulation of a frog dissection) is demonstrated to the participants.

The example also shows the use of a learning resource in an instructional setting. The specific example is modified to fit the target audience.
2. Instruction on how to find learning resources in the NSDL, including keyword and boolean searching, advanced searching, and browsing by collections. Depending on the technical expertise of audience, the amount of modeling is increased or reduced.
3. Participants identify an authentic instructional problem, need, or situation. They then practice search techniques to locate resources related to their selected objectives.
4. Participants design IA projects that address the identified problem. Examples include laboratories, assignments, interactive group work, research, resource lists, and homework.
5. Participants then implement their project in their classroom. Examples of implementation activities include working as a whole class group, having the project be one learning center of many, and having the students go through the project independently.
6. Participants reconvene in a second workshop to reflect on their experiences designing activities using online learning resources and discuss various methods and strategies for integrating online resources into their classrooms.

In addition, several aspects of the curriculum (e.g., the link to educational standards) were tailored to fit audience and institutional contexts. Finally, the amount of modeling was increased or decreased depending on the technical skill level of the audience.

Evaluation Findings

Evaluation findings for the model are presented from three f2f workshop implementations: teachers in a rural school district in the western USA in Spring 2004 ($N = 14$), teachers from a charter school in the state of Utah, USA in the spring of 2007 ($N = 20$), and finally science and math teachers in northern New York State, USA in the fall of 2008 ($N = 19$).

Spring 2004

This early evaluation of the workshop model focused on (1) knowledge of online resources for education and the NSDL, (2) attitudes about IA and technology use in the classroom, and (3) intended future use of IA in the classroom. Based on these three categories, over 90% of participants knew what online resources for education were prior to taking the workshops, while less than 20% were familiar with the NSDL. After the workshops 100% of the participants increased their knowledge of what the online resources for education were and what the NSDL was.

Attitudes about technology in the classroom and reported intentions to use the IA in the future were divided between teachers who reported (1) different levels of personal experience using online resources, (2) different levels of technology infrastructure in the school where they taught, and (3) either having or not having Internet access at home.

Spring 2007

Table 15.2 below shows participant responses on experience using online resources, experience creating online lessons, advantages of using technology in the classroom. Comparisons between the pre- and post-survey scores are made with Cohen's *d*, using the pooled estimate of the population standard deviation as the denominator. Cohen was understandable reluctant to come up with thresholds for something as complex as social science research but did say that effect sizes of 0.2 are relatively small, 0.5 are moderate, and 0.8 are large (Cohen, 1988).

Table 15.2 Likert scale survey item results, means, standard deviations, and effect sizes (scale from 0 = low to 4 = high), Spring 2007

	Pre-survey		Post-survey		
Likert scale survey item	Mean	SD	Mean	SD	Effect size (*d*)
I have experience using online resources in the classroom	3.20	0.72	3.50	0.67	0.44
I have experience creating online lessons	1.30	1.40	2.30	1.50	0.63

As seen in Table 15.2, all responses show increases from pre- to post-survey, with moderate to strong effect sizes. These results suggest a positive impact of the workshop experience. When asked about the future use of the IA on the post-survey, participants reported that they would use the IA in their classroom ($M = 3.80$, SD = 0.58) and would tell other teachers about the IA ($M = 3.80$, SD = 0.51).

Finally, site-usage statistics show that 35% of participants used the IA during the 2008–2009 school year.

Fall 2008

The evaluation of this workshop focused on (a) changes in the amount of experience using online resources, (b) difficulty in using online resources, and (c) self-report on the ability to use technology in the classroom.

Table 15.3 shows participants' response (mean, standard deviation, and effect sizes) on pre- and post-survey items. Results showed that by the end of the workshop experience participants reported a strong positive effect size in their experience creating online lessons, knowing how to effectively use technology in the classroom, knowing how to effectively teach with technology inthe classroom, and a moderate positive effect size in experience using online resources. Further, there was no change in attitudes toward difficulty of integrating online resources into the classroom.

Table 15.3 Likert scale survey item results, means, standard deviations, and effect sizes items (0 = very low; 4 = very high), Fall 2008

	Pre-survey		Post-survey		
Likert scale survey	Mean	SD	Mean	SD	Effect size (*d*)
I have experience creating online lessons	1.14	1.23	3.00	0.78	1.51
I have experience using online resources in the classroom	1.30	1.4	1.93	1.48	0.57
It is difficult to integrate online resources into my regular lesson plans	1.43	1.16	1.43	0.94	0
I know how to effectively use technology in a classroom setting	2.50	0.76	3.29	0.61	1.03
I know how to effectively teach with technology in the classroom	2.43	0.76	3.43	0.51	1.31

Finally, site-usage statistics show that 16% of the participants used the IA in the Spring semester of 2009, the most recent semester usage statistics are available at this writing.

Model 2: Problem-Based Learning: Simple to Complex Problems

The second model that was developed was created for a self-paced online delivery mode. It is based on a combination of PBL and van Marrienboer's Four Components/Instructional Design (4C/ID) model (van Marrienboer, Clark, & deCroock, 2002). van Marrienboer's 4C/ID model is similar to PBL, but rather than one large problem for learners to solve, learners solve more, and more complex problems related to the cognitive skills being learned (van Marrienboer, Clark, & deCroock, 2002). This model consisted of the following six core activities:

1. Use of authentic instructional problems, needs, or situations brought to the exercises by the students. They practice search techniques to locate resources and design IA projects related to their instructional objectives.
2. Instruction on how to use the IA including browsing and searching IA projects, searching for and storing links to resources within the IA, and designing and modification of IA projects.

3. Searching the NSDL and other sites for pertinent online learning resources. The instruction includes directions on using keyword and boolean searching, advanced searching, and browsing by collections.
4. Two different design exercises, the first being a simple design problem and the second being more complex. The first exercise simply asks students to design an IA project using three different online learning resources. The second exercise asks students to use three different resources from at least two different sources (e.g., the NSDL and National Geographic) and then to reflect on the differences and similarities between designing instructional materials using the IA and without using the IA.
5. The use of cognitive scaffolding (e.g., checklist, just-in-time help) to support the participants' learning. As the problems became more complex, as participants presumably gained more skill, the scaffolding decrease.
6. Use of a reflective phase (e.g., revising previous IA projects based on feedback from group members) asked them to summarize what was been learned and to integrate it with their prior knowledge.

Evaluation Findings

This model was implemented as an online module and evaluated with two groups of teachers in Fall 2006 ($N = 49$) and Fall 2008 ($N = 29$). Participants in both workshops came from a variety of professions, including K-12 teaching and library media, and were working on a graduate level degree. The Fall 2006 implementation was a part of a dissertation study which featured a treatment/control group methodology (Mao, 2007).

Fall 2006

The evaluation study used a two-group treatment/control group study. Treatment group participants were grade school, secondary school, post-secondary, and religious teachers. Each participant worked individually online in a self-paced manner on the workshop curriculum, while also being provided opportunities to share and discuss with his/her group members.

The evaluation focused on treatment group participants' knowledge and use with regard to the integration of online resources as a result of participating in a PBL-based workshop. Their data were compared to control group participants, who did not participate in the online workshop and simply completed the pre/post-survey.

Table 15.4 shows gains for the treatment group on all survey items. Results show that the treatment group felt that they had significantly more experience creating online lesson plans by participating in the online workshop, had presented more online resources to their students, and had students using online resources more than their counterparts in the control group. Table 15.5 shows significantly higher gains for the treatment group than the control group on a test of knowledge given to all participants.

Table 15.4 Likert scale survey item (0 = very low; 4 = very high) results related to use (mean, standard deviation, effect sizes; Fall 2006)

Likert scale question	Group	Pre-survey		Post-survey		
		M	SD	*M*	SD	Effect size (*d*)
Experience using online resources	Treatment	2.86	0.77	2.86	0.71	0
	Control	2.31	0.85	2.31	0.75	0
Experience creating online lesson plans	Treatment	1.27	1.20	2.14	0.83	1.04
	Control	1.69	1.31	1.23	1.16	–0.39
Presented online resources to students	Treatment	1.23	0.97	1.27	0.83	0.05
	Control	1.08	0.76	1.00	0.71	–0.11
Students used online resources	Treatment	0.68	0.65	0.91	0.92	0.25
	Control	1.00	0.71	0.92	0.64	–0.12

Table 15.5 Results of a test of knowledge given to participants

	Pre-test (*SD*)		Post-test (*SD*)		
	M	SD	*M*	SD	Effect size (*d*)
Treatment	3.32	1.04	5.14	1.46	1.24
Control	2.46	1.05	3	0.91	0.59

Finally, site-usage statistics show that 10% of participants used the IA during the 2008–2009 school year.

Fall 2008

In the Fall of 2008, participants moved through the material over a period of 2 weeks, as decided by the instructor of the class that they were taking. Again, participants came from a variety of professions and were seeking a graduate level degree.

As shown in Table 15.6, survey results showed a moderate to significant gain in the four areas reported. By the end of the workshop cycle, participants showed strong effect sizes in experience creating online lessons ($d = 0.71$) and using online resources in the classroom ($d = 0.55$). There was a strong effect size in participants' self-reports about being able to use technology in a classroom setting ($d = 0.87$) and a moderate effect size in their abilities to teach effectively with technology in the classroom ($d = 0.51$).

Finally, site-usage statistics show that 21%, of participants used the IA in the Spring semester of 2009, the most recent semester usage statistics are available at this writing.

Table 15.6 Mean, standard deviation, and effect size from selected survey questions (0 = very low; 4 = very high), Fall 2008

	Pre-test		Post-test		
Lickert scale item	*M*	SD	*M*	SD	Effect size (*d*)
I have experience creating online lessons.	2.32	1.38	3.10	1.10	0.71
In your last 2 weeks of teaching, how many times did you have students use online resources to aid them with an assignment or other learning activity?	1.89	1.59	4.00	3.86	0.55
I know how to effectively use technology in a classroom setting	2.89	1.15	3.42	0.61	0.87
I know how to effectively teach with technology in the classroom	2.89	1.05	3.26	0.73	0.51

Model 3: Problem-Based Learning: Authentic Design

The first model described above was centered around the use of an authentic problem, while the second model used a modified PBL approach. In 2008 the model was modified to be more aligned with the theory of PBL, as well as design centered. An additional instructional goal for the model was teaching participants to use PBL with their students in their classroom. It is delivered face to face in 2–3 sessions, each lasting 2.5–3 h in each session to elementary and secondary teachers. This model consisted of the following five core activities:

1. Use of an authentic instructional design activity to guide workshop participants through the basic steps to creating an IA project. Participants are taught to do a basic search of the NSDL, add resources from sources besides the NSDL, search and browse other IA projects, add found resources to the IA, and design, create, and modify a simple IA project.
2. Introduction to inquiry learning through participation in an inquiry-based learning activity using online learning resources with participants acting as students and then introduction to PBL as a form of inquiry learning.
3. Discussion of advantages and disadvantages of using a PBL in the classroom with the IA and online learning resources.
4. Design and implementation of one non-PBL-based IA project and one PBL-based IA project in the classroom between workshops.
5. Structured reflection individually, in small groups and with the large group, about the implementation of the different IA projects in their classrooms.

Model 3: Evaluation Findings

Evaluation findings for the model are presented from two f2f workshop implementations in the Fall of 2008 ($N = 24$) and Spring 2009 ($N = 20$). All participants in this workshop consisted of teachers and school library media specialists from a county school district in Northern Utah, USA. The county has a mix of rural and urban settings and technology access varies among the different schools in the district.

Fall 2008

Table 15.7 shows participant responses on pre- and post-surveys likert scale items, with all responses showing increases from pre- to post-survey, with moderate to strong effect sizes. Effect size computations show that participants had a strong positive effect size on experience creating online lessons, knowing how effectively use technology in a classroom setting, and knowing how to effectively teach with technology in the classroom. Results showed a small positive effect size on experience using online resources in the classroom.

Table 15.7 Likert scale survey items, means, standard deviations, and effect sizes (0 = very low; 4 = very high), Fall 2008

	Pre-survey		Post-survey		
Likert scale survey items	Mean	SD	Mean	SD	Effect size (*d*)
I have experience creating online lessons	1.64	1.4	2.89	0.94	0.89
I have experience using online resources in the classroom	2.92	1.15	3.11	0.94	0.17
I know how to effectively use technology in a classroom setting	1.88	1.05	2.84	0.96	0.91
I know how to effectively teach with technology in the classroom	1.92	1.08	2.95	0.78	0.95

Finally site-usage statistics show that 33% of participants used the IA during the Spring 2009 school semester (the most recent usage statistics available at this writing).

Focus group findings

A focus group was held at the end of the second workshop to solicit feedback directly from ten participants, about how the workshop model could be improved. The participants were divided into two groups and asked to examine the handouts and to provide feedback about what went well, what did not go well, and how the workshop could be improved. The two groups were brought back together to merge the feedback from the two groups.

Two main findings came from the participants:

- The workshop should be held over three meetings rather than two. One of the meeting times should be solely devoted to PBL.
- Teaching of the IA should be done through a direct instruction, step-by-step, approach.

Further, participants asked that they be allowed to form their groups, be shown more examples of IA projects, be given more time to reflect and share IA projects created by workshop participants, and be given more time to create their own IA projects. This feedback was taken into consideration and changes were made to the Spring 2009 workshop based on these findings, described next.

Spring 2009

Table 15.8 shows participant responses on pre- and post-survey likert scale items, with all responses showing increases from pre- to post-survey, with moderate to strong effect sizes. Effect size computations show that participants had a strong positive effect size on experience creating using online resources in the classroom and knowing how to effective teaching with technology in the classroom. Participants had moderate effect sizes on the experience creating online lessons, knowing how to effectively use technology in a classroom setting.

Table 15.8 Likert scale survey items results, means, standard deviations, and effect sizes (scale from 0=low to 4=high), Spring 2009

	Pre-survey		Post-survey		
Likert scale survey item	Mean	SD	Mean	SD	Effect size (*d*)
I have experience creating online lessons	2.81	1.22	3.25	0.93	0.47
I have experience using online resources in the classroom	1.44	1.46	2.75	0.93	1.4
I know how to effectively use technology in a classroom setting	1.75	1.13	2.63	1.31	0.67
I know how to effectively teach with technology in the classroom	1.75	1.13	2.75	0.93	1.08
I frequently use problem-based learning in the classroom	1.31	1.01	1.88	1.09	0.52
I will continue using problem-based learning in my classroom	–	–	2.63	1.31	–

Specific questions addressing the use of PBL showed a moderate gain in using PBL in the classroom. When asked on the post-survey if participants would continue using PBL in their classrooms, responses were mixed. This result perhaps shows the challenges of having large, sustained impact on teacher practice with PD workshop interventions.

Long-Term Impact

Many reviews of teacher PD have bemoaned the lack of long-term impact studies (Lawless & Pellegrino, 2007; Schlager et al., 2009; Wayne et al., 2008), be they months or even years later. These are expensive to conduct and, as such, data are scarce.

However, as the IA is a Web-based environment, Web-usage data can be automatically collected during participants' online activities [called *webmetrics* (Khoo et al., 2008)]. Table 15.9 shows a summary of usage activities to date and provides a hint of the impact of workshop activities on participants' long-term behavior. The results suggest that all participants used the IA and created several projects with many online resources. The high number of visits suggests that students accessed these projects, some many times. Note, also, the high standard deviations. These suggest that usage varied widely among participants.

Finally the last column shows the percent of participants still using the IA during the most recent school year, ranging from 10 to 35%. Again, since PD studies seldom report long-term impact data (Wayne et al., 2008), it is hard to know how these compare.

Conclusion

The impetus for this ongoing 8-year-long research project was to enable grade school and secondary education school teachers to have better access to the vast array of free online educational resources available to them. As technology has evolved, so has the focus of our work. At the beginning of the project our main concern was getting teachers to use online resources and we were not as concerned with the method by which they taught with them, nor were we as concerned with the long-term impacts of our workshop model.

The long-term nature of this project has showed us the difficulty of the task we have sought to undertake. Coupling basic technology skills training with design and pedagogical skills building increases the difficulty of the task but the integration of the three skill areas helps teachers to see the whole picture and thus are more likely to effectively integrate online resources into their classrooms.

The long-term nature of the project has also showed us that while we have tried to focus in on specific target audiences community (for example, teachers teaching grades 3–9 with a focus on math and science), as we have believed that this would

Table 15.9 Webmetrics data for workshops.

Model	Date	Number of logins per participant		Number of IA projects per participant		Number of online resources used per participant		Number of visits to project per participant		Percentage of users in 2008–2009 school year(%)
		M	*SD*	*M*	*SD*	*M*	*SD*	*M*	*SD*	
1	Spring 2004	Not available								
	Spring 2007	25.9	23	4.4	3.4	12	10.6	45	84.4	35
	Fall 2008	13	19.2	3.2	2.4	7.8	10	24.2	41	16
2	Fall 2006	19.3	28.5	3.8	4.1	21.2	34.7	103	186.4	10
	Fall 2008	13.8	11.3	3.9	2.3	17	12.4	35.6	100.5	21
3	Fall 2008	21.4	21.7	6.4	5.9	26.8	23.4	28.2	69	33
	Spring 2009	23.2	17.5	6.3	5.7	27	42.2	25.9	59.8	Not available

lead to the greatest long-term usage of the IA and skills we teach, our webmetrics analyses have shown us that our predictions are often wrong. We will continue to focus on specific target audiences with the understanding that the person who ends up utilizing the skills long term may not be the person we would have predicted.

Our plans for future research include exploring if there are substantive changes in the ways teachers engage in teaching and learning as a result of the workshop, and if changes do exist, what happens to student learning as a result of these changing teaching practices. Included in that is understanding how persistent the changes in teaching practices are.

We will also continue to learn more about our user base through the use of webmetrics and will be exploring why some users continue to come back and use the IA and why other users do not. We have IA users who have not had exposure to our workshop continue their use. We will persist, through the use of webmetrics and other methods, to learn about these users and then apply what we learn to our f2f workshops.

Lastly, one area of our research not mentioned within this chapter has been in understanding the types of knowledge that teachers use when developing lessons using online resources. We will continue this exploration and hope to create a measurement of this knowledge.

Suggestions for other future research include continued exploration of the use of PBL as a method for delivery of teacher technology PD workshops; further development of different models of how to incorporate both technological skills and different pedagogical skills, like PBL, into a PD workshop for long-term impact, and replication of our workshop model with the IA with different audiences around the world.

Acknowledgments This material is based on work supported by the National Science Foundation under Grants No. 0333818, 554440, & 0434892, and Utah State University. Any opinions, findings, and conclusions or recommendations expressed in this material are those of the author(s) and do not necessarily reflect the views of the National Science Foundation. We thank the teachers and student teachers who participated in our studies.

References

Barneveld, A. V., & Strobel, J. (2009). Is PBL effective? A meta-synthesis of meta-analyses comparing problem-based learning to conventional classroom learning. *Interdisciplinary Journal of Problem Based Learning*, *3*(1), 44–58.

Barrows, H. S. (1986). A taxonomy of problem-based learning methods. *Medical Education*, *20*(6), 481–486.

Barrows, H. S. (1996). Problem-based learning in medicine and beyond: A brief overview. *New Directions for Teaching and Learning*, *68*, 3–12.

Cohen, J. (1988). *Statistical power analysis for the behavioral sciences* (2nd ed). Hillsdale, NJ: Lawrence Earlbaum Associates.

Computing Research Association (2005). *Cyberinfrastructure for education and learning for the future: A vision and research agenda*. Washington, DC: Computing Research Association.

Derry, S. J., Hmelo-Silver, C. E., Nagarajan, A., Chernobilsky, E., & Beitzel, B. D. (2006). Cognitive Transfer Revisited: Can we Exploit new Media to Solve Old Problems on a Large Scale? *Journal of Educational Computing Research*, *35*(2), 145–162.

Dorward, J., & Heal, R. (1999). National library of virtual manipulatives for elementary and middle level mathematics. *Proceedings of Webnet, 99*, 1510–1512.

Gijbels, D., Dochy, F., Van den Bossche, P., & Segers, M. (2005). Effects of problem-based learning: A meta-analysis from the angle of assessment. *Review of Educational Research, 75*(1), 27.

Greenhow, C., Robelia, B., & Hughes, J. (2009). Web 2.0 and classroom research: What path should we take now?. *Educational Researcher, 38*(4), 246–259.

Gülseçen, S., & Kubat, A. (2006). Teaching ICT to teacher candidates using PBL: A qualitative and quantitative evaluation. *Evaluation, 9*(2), 96–106.

Khoo, M., Pagano, J., Washington, A. L., Recker, M., Palmer, B., & Donahue, R. A. (2008). *Using web metrics to analyze digital libraries*, 375–384.

Lawless, K. A., & Pellegrino, J. W. (2007). Professional development in integrating technology into teaching and learning: Knowns, unknowns, and ways to pursue better questions and answers. *Review of Educational Research, 77*(4), 575.

Mao, X. (2007). *The effects of professional development on teacher integration of educational digital libraries*. Unpublished dissertation, Utah State University.

McArthur, D. J., & Zia, L. L. (2008). *From nsdl 1.0 to nsdl 2.0: towards a comprehensive cyberinfrastructure for teaching and learning*. Paper presented at the Proceedings of the 8th ACM/IEEE-CS joint conference on Digital libraries.

NSDL.org (2009). Retrieved June 6, 2009, from http://www.nsdl.org .

Pea, R., Borgman, C. L., Ableson, H., Dirks, L., Johnson, R., Koedinger, K., et al. (2008). Fostering learning in the networked world: The cyberlearning opportunity and challenge, a 21st century agenda for the National Science Foundation. *NSF Report, June*.

Savery, J. R. (2006). Overview of problem-based learning: Definitions and distinctions. *The Interdisciplinary Journal of Problem-based Learning, 1*(1), 9–20.

Schlager, M. S., Farooq, U., Fusco, J., Schank, P., & Dwyer, N. (2009). Analyzing Online Teacher Networks: Cyber Networks Require Cyber Research Tools. *Journal of Teacher Education, 60*(1), 86.

Shoffner, M. B., & Dalton, D. W. (1998). Effects of Problem-Based, Networked Hypermedia, and Cooperative Strategies on Visual Literacy Instruction. *Proceedings of Selected Research and Development Presentations at the National Convention of the Association for Educational Communications and Technology*, St. Louis, MO, February 18–22, pp. 371–390.

Strobel, J., & van Barneveld, A. (2009). When is PBL More Effective? A Meta-synthesis of Meta-analyses Comparing PBL to Conventional Classrooms. *Interdisciplinary Journal of Problem-based Learning, 3*(1), 4.

Van Merriënboer, J. J. G., Clark, R. E., & De Croock, M. B. M. (2002). Blueprints for complex learning: The 4C/ID-model. *Educational Technology Research and Development, 50*(2), 39–61.

Walker, A., & Leary, H. (2009). A problem based learning meta analysis: Differences across problem types, implementation types, disciplines, and assessment levels. *Interdisciplinary Journal of Problem-based Learning, 3*(1), 12–43.

Wayne, A. J., Yoon, K. S., Zhu, P., Cronen, S., & Garet, M. S. (2008). Experimenting with teacher professional development: Motives and methods. *Educational Researcher, 37*(8), 469.

Chapter 16
A Dialogic Approach to Technology-Enhanced Education for the Global Knowledge Society

Rupert Wegerif and Nasser Mansour

Graduate School of Education, The University of Exeter, Exeter, UK

The Idea of the Knowledge Society

The claim that education needs to respond to the challenge of the emerging global knowledge society is now the common sense position in almost every government educational policy review (Jacoby, 2007). While we may not be surprised that relatively economically advanced countries like the UK, Germany, and the EU shape education policies to respond to the knowledge society e.g (European Council, 2000), Jacoby finds the same references to the need to compete in the knowledge society-shaping education policy in less-developed countries such as Bangladesh and Namibia. The interesting implication Jacoby draws from this is that the idea of the knowledge society now serves as a vision of a global future that is leading to a convergence of education policies. Whether grounded on an empirical analysis of changes in the economy or motivated by a shared vision of a global networked future, the idea that we are moving into a knowledge society now raises challenges for educational theories and educational practice and shapes educational policy across the world.

The basic idea behind the knowledge society is that we are in the midst of a new economic revolution in which the nature of work is shifting from the industrial stage dominated by the manufacture and exchange of physical goods towards the post-industrial "knowledge age" dominated by the manufacture and exchange of knowledge and ideas in a global context (Drucker, 1969; Bell, 1999; UNESCO, 2005). Manuel Castells, one of the most quoted commentators on the impact of new technology on society, extends Daniel Bell's earlier analysis of this shift in the economy and in society by bringing out the extent to which it is dependent on new information and communications technology. In his trilogy *The Information Age: Economy, Society and Culture* he analyses data on current trends to argue that there is a convergence towards a new form of social organization which he calls "the Network Society" defining this as "a society where the key social structures

R. Wegerif (✉)
Graduate School of Education, The University of Exeter, Exeter, UK
e-mail: r.b.wegerif@exeter.ac.uk

M.S. Khine, I.M. Saleh (eds.), *New Science of Learning*,
DOI 10.1007/978-1-4419-5716-0_16,

and activities are organized around electronically processed information networks" (Castells, 2001).

Thinking Skills for the Knowledge Age

Many have argued that education needs to respond to the accelerating rate of technological and social change associated with the knowledge age and globalisation. In particular a need is seen for more adaptability or "learning to learn" throughout the lifespan (e.g., Levin & Rumberger, 1995; Quisumbing, 2005). Castells supports this trend in arguing that this shift in the social economy "calls into question the entire education system developed during the industrial era" and demands that we develop a new pedagogy (Castells, 2001, p. 278). In the UK the influential Leitch report (2006) extrapolated the same trends to argue that to compete successfully in the global economy of the knowledge age we need to teach more Higher Order generic skills. The Leitch report defines these as "Level 4" skills but says little about their specific nature beyond the fact that they are associated with degree level qualifications. Bernie Trilling, head of Oracle Education, goes further and defines the skills we need for the knowledge age as the Seven Cs (see Table 16.1).

Table 16.1 Skills for the knowledge age as the Seven Cs

Seven Cs	Component skills
Critical thinking and doing	Problem solving, research, analysis, project management, etc
Creativity	New knowledge creation, "Best Fit" design solutions, artful storytelling, etc
Collaboration	Cooperation, compromise, consensus, community-building etc
Cross-cultural understanding	Across diverse ethnic, knowledge and organisational cultures
Communication	Crafting messages and using media effectively
Computing	Effective use of electronic information and knowledge tools
Career and learning self-reliance	Managing change, lifelong learning and career redefinition

(From Trilling & Hood, 2001)

While this is just one list it is reasonably representative of the range of lists articulating the skills needed to survive and thrive in the knowledge age (e.g., Bruns, 2007). With their focus on creative and critical thinking as well as on learning to learn, these lists are clearly a development in the same tradition as the teaching thinking skills movement, offering a new version of the sort of thinking that we should value and ought to teach more of because there is not enough of it about. However they do not entirely fit the cognitive assumptions that lie behind many more traditional approaches to teaching thinking. It is the argument of this chapter that the idea of the knowledge age and the kinds of skills, habits, and dispositions associated with it requires that we need to re-conceptualise what we mean by education and particularly education for higher order thinking skills.

A Dialogic Reconceptualisation of "Higher Order Thinking Skills"

Bakhtin, the main source of contemporary dialogic theory, is sometimes referred to in support of the claim that cognition is socially situated because for Bakhtin cognition occurs within dialogues in which all utterances are spoken by someone and have a specific addressee. However, it is interesting that for Bakhtin dialogic was also about escaping from what he referred to dismissively "the narrow space of small time" (Bakhtin, 1986, p. 167). He writes that:

> In order to understand it is immensely important for the person who understands to be located outside the object of his or her creative understanding – in time, in space, in culture (Bakhtin, 1986, p. 7)

Utterances in a dialogue, he pointed out, are never only directed at a specific addressee but also at a superaddressee, the ideal of a third party to the dialogue who has a capacity to understand what is really meant by the utterance even when the specific addressee cannot understand it due perhaps to his or her limitations (Bakhtin, 1986, p. 126). The superaddressee evokes for some the idea of God as a person who understands everything, but it is also similar to the ideal of an unsituated universal perspective aspired to by science and often referred to as a "God's eye point of view". This ideal of an unsituated perspective is understood by Bakhtin not as a real unsituated perspective but as a projection out of situated dialogues. The superaddressee mechanism in dialogues whereby every dialogue generates a "third" or "witness" position can help us to understand how dialogues teach thinking through an expansion of awareness. It is only by externalizing my thoughts to you on paper now, for instance, that I am able myself to see them clearly, question them, and move beyond them.

The phrase "Higher Order Thinking" originated in a distinction made between lower order skills such as remembering and higher order skills such as evaluating (Bloom, 1956). The sort of distinction being made by Bloom is suspect, but the phrase "Higher Order" is still useful to distinguish distinctively human creative thinking from the kind of "cognition" which has been ascribed to animals and to machines. The essential dialogicality of normal human thinking is increasingly pointed to by developmental psychology as a contrast to the more algorithmic cognition found in psychopathologies such as autism and in non-human contexts (e.g., Hobson, 2002; Tomasello et al., 2005).

The potential relevance of engagement in dialogue as shared enquiry to the tradition of teaching higher order thinking is evident if we adopt Resnick's definition of higher order thinking. Resnick chaired a US government commission into the teaching of thinking skills which took evidence from many practitioners and other experts. Her main conclusion was that:

> Thinking skills resist the precise forms of definition we have come to associate with the setting of specified objectives for schooling. Nevertheless, it is relatively easy to list some key features of higher order thinking. When we do this, we become aware that, although we cannot define it exactly, we can recognize higher order thinking when it occurs

The features that she then goes on to list are all characteristic of the kind of thinking found in complex real dialogues, for example:

- Higher order thinking is non-algorithmic. That is, the path of action is not fully specified in advance. Higher order thinking tends to be complex. The total path is not "visible" (mentally speaking) from any single vantage point.
- Higher order thinking often yields multiple solutions, each with costs and benefits, rather than unique solutions.
- Higher order thinking involves nuanced judgment and interpretation.
- Higher order thinking involves the application of multiple criteria, which sometimes conflict with one another.
- Higher order thinking often involves uncertainty. Not everything that bears on the task at hand is known (Resnick, 1987).

Although Resnick was conceptualising these as individual skills they are all evidently the kind of skills found in a complex open-ended dialogue (where a dialogue is defined with Bakhtin as a "shared inquiry" 1986, p. 168). Research findings on the effectiveness of teaching general thinking skills programmes suggest that the depth of dialogic engagement is relevant to evidence of learning that supports problem-solving and general thinking and learning skills and dispositions generally beyond the context in which they are learnt (e.g., Mercer et al., 2004; Wegerif et al., 1999; Trickey & Topping, 2004).

Whereas in the neo-Vygotskian socio-cultural tradition technology is often conceptualised as a mediating means for cognition, from this more dialogic perspective technology is seen as a facilitator opening and shaping dialogic spaces that would not otherwise be there. A dialogic perspective on cognition does not render the networked perspective on learning obsolete because dialogues always occur within networks. The dialogic perspective reveals, however, that the question "how can networks be made more intelligent?" is misleading and should be replaced with the very different question "how can networks open up, expand, deepen and generally resource creative dialogic spaces of reflection?"

Bahktin's dialogic principle of holding two or more voices together in tension without combining them into one thing characterises a type of creative non-identity. Bakhtin, some of whose own creative ideas sparked from dialogue with the ancient Greeks, sought to understand how voices from every age and culture could so fruitfully engage in dialogue with each other. He called the universal context of dialogue "great time". Teaching thinking on the dialogic model stimulated by Bakhtin is about drawing students from narrow concerns to the more universal thinking of "great time" which is the extraordinary space where all possible voices can talk together. This space cannot be characterised in positive terms; it does not have a fixed content such as a set of universal rational laws and it is the negative space of "difference" or the "gap" between identities and voices in a dialogue. The non-identity of dialogue is without a voice of its own yet it is pregnant with every possible voice. To learn to think is to move on a dimension from identification with limited images and limited objectives towards the impossible goal of identification with the non-identity of the space of dialogue. Another way of putting this is that the direction of growth implied is towards becoming more open to learning from others and from otherness in general.

We argue that movement in the direction of dialogue *as an end in itself* lies behind the teaching and learning of that Higher Order Thinking described by Resnick (1987) as an important goal for education. However, this dialogic understanding of "thinking" is no longer the individual cognition of traditional cognitive psychology. Thinking now is seen as embodied and situated in real dialogues. To learn thinking is to be drawn out into the space of dialogue which is a space of creative tension between different perspectives. Teaching for Higher Order Thinking, that kind of thinking which we value and want to see more of, can thus be translated into opening, expanding, and deepening dialogic spaces.

A Dialogic Foundation for the Design of Educational Technology

On a dialogic account of thinking the main aim is not to replace false representations with true ones so much as to augment understanding with new perspectives. In the rationalist tradition, represented by the thinking as computation metaphor that still dominates much cognitive psychology, there is a strong understanding of the vertical development of thinking from context-bound thinking towards universality through abstraction but little acknowledgment of the horizontal dimension of how different kinds of thinking are embedded in different ways of being. In the socio-cultural tradition, thinking is seen as the use of cultural tools in a social context so there is a strong understanding of the horizontal dimension in awareness of the variety of different kinds of thinking but no effective way to account for verticality. A model of learning to think as appropriating cultural tools and participating in cultural practices offers no way to say which tools or which practices are better in general, only in relation to a particular task already shaped by a community. This issue of verticality is important for education, which is inevitably about values and directions as well as processes. The metaphor of teaching and learning thinking as drawing students into spaces of dialogue across difference offers a vertical direction for the development of thinking without losing a sense of the horizontal. The direction of travel from narrow and local identifications that block dialogue towards increasing openness and engagement in universal dialogue is different from rationalism as it does not presuppose any overarching universal logical structures. The only universal presupposed "dialogic space", refers to the context of thinking rather than any specific content of thinking. It is also different from rationalism because the teaching of thinking, on this metaphor, does not just mean changing minds but also changing the world. If one side of dialogic space is transcendent and infinite, then the other side is embedded in the world. The task of teaching thinking by opening, deepening, and widening spaces of dialogue involves changing cultural practices and social structures.

Towards a Framework for the Design of Educational Technology that can Teach Thinking as Dialogue Across Difference

Converting the theoretical foundation for design argued for above into educational activities requires an intermediate framework for design consisting of flexible design principles, exemplars, and key questions to ask. Below we put forward a provisional framework for design based on (1) conceptual analysis of the components of an account of teaching and learning thinking understood as movement into dialogue across difference and (2) an assessment of what has worked in already tried and tested educational designs to promote creative dialogic thinking. Conceptually this model of teaching thinking assumes that thinking is limited by closed identities and monologic or systemic practices so the first aim must be to open dialogic spaces understood as spaces of internal freedom within the external constraints of a situation and the next aim is to improve the educational quality of these spaces drawing participants more completely into dialogue through deepening and widening these spaces.

Opening Dialogic Spaces

There are ways of using ICT in education which close down dialogic space and ways which open this up. Tutorial software used individually closes down dialogue when the same sort of questions and tasks given to a group will open up dialogic spaces within the curriculum. Simulations that encourage fast and furious engagement will close down dialogue when the same interfaces with a prompt for talking that interrupts the action will open up dialogic spaces (Wegerif et al., 2003). A singular affordance of new media technologies is the possibility of supporting new dialogic spaces anywhere and everywhere, from interactive blogs under exhibits in museums to texted exchanges between pupils in different classrooms. But the technological support alone does not make a dialogic space. One of the key findings from Wegerif's research with Neil Mercer, Lyn Dawes, Karen Littleton, and others on collaborative learning around computers in classrooms is that, for effective shared thinking, it is not enough just to place people in groups but they need to be prepared for working together in groups beforehand (Wegerif & Dawes, 2004). Applying discourse ground rules such as asking open questions and listening with respect to others opens up a creative dialogic space.

As well as the Thinking Together approach described by Wegerif and Dawes, Philosophy for Children also seems effective as a method of teaching for engagement in dialogic thinking. In one EC-funded study, "Philosophy Hotel", similar

Philosophy for Children pedagogy in different classrooms in several European countries was extended successfully to Internet-mediated philosophy discussions (a study by Steve Williams and Richard Athlone described in Wegerif, 2007, p. 267). The same principle that effective shared thinking needs to be positively taught emerges from reviews of collaborative learning in online environments (De Laat, 2006, p. 163).

Widening Dialogic Spaces

Baker, Quignard, Lund, and Séjourné (2003) distinguish between deepening and broadening a space of debate: Students broaden their understanding of a space of debate when they are better acquainted with societal and epistemological points of view, their associated arguments and value systems; they deepen it when they are able to go deeper into argument chains, to elaborate upon the meaning of arguments, and to better understand the notions involved. While the idea of dialogic space is broader than that of a space of debate, since it is not concerned only with explicit argumentation, the distinction between broadening and deepening remains useful. Broadening or expanding means roughly increasing the degree of difference between perspectives in a dialogue while maintaining the dialogic relationship. Broadening can be done through the use of the Internet to engage in real dialogues about global issues. An illustration of this is Oxfam's http://tv.oneworld.net/ site, where video stories from across the world are exchanged and discussed. Another example of pedagogical use of the potential of the Internet to support dialogue across difference can be seen in the development education site: http://www.throughothereyes.org.uk/

In practice this kind of resource may not support real dialogue unless used with a dialogic pedagogical approach, described above, that equips young people for questioning, listening to, and reflecting on the views of others. Broadening in the classroom can be done through structured web-quest-type activities where an issue is posed and learners are sent to different web-sites to explore it and to question the people behind different viewpoints.

Deepen Dialogic Space

Deepening refers to increasing the degree of reflection on assumptions and grounds. With the right pedagogy the broadening potential of Internet dialogues also becomes a deepening as students are led to reflect on the assumptions that they carry with them into dialogues. Talk in face-to-face dialogues exists only momentarily and only for those immediately present. Technologies that support drawing and writing can thus be thought of as a way of deepening dialogues, by turning transitory talk and thoughts into external objects that are available to learners for discussion and shared reflection (Goody, 1977). Computer documents can offer a kind of half-way stage between the evanescence of talk and the permanence of written texts. Harry McMahon and Bill O'Neill, the originators of Bubble Dialogue software, use the term "slow-throwness" to refer to the way that their tool can externalise the thoughts and feelings of the participants and also support reflection and the possibility of returning and retrospectively changing dialogues (McMahon & O'Neill, 1993; BubbleDialogueII, developed by Wegerif and Barrett, is available free from http://www.dialogbox.org.uk/intro.htm). Often deepening follows from widening where exposure to other ways of seeing things can lead one to question one's own framing assumptions. In this sense deepening is a form of "deconstruction" insofar as this means consciously exploring the key distinctions that frame constructions of meaning in order to become aware of how things might be otherwise. A specific form of deepening is to reflect on the process of dialogue and shared enquiry in order to become more aware of it and to refine it. Awareness tools to support collaborative learning online showing who is talking to whom and how much and what sort of things they are saying could serve this function. The most powerful example I have seen is the filming of groups of children talking together and then showing this back to them to support a discussion on what sort of behaviours are helpful and which are not.

Teach Content Through Induction into Fields of Dialogue

Interactivity makes it easy for software to simulate multiple points of view in a dialogue thus allowing learners to be inducted into a field of dialogue rather than into fixed "truths". Any content can be taught through engagement in dialogue between alternative points of view. In this way the student learns not only the current consensus view on a topic but also how to justify it and how to question it and so is inducted into knowledge as shared enquiry rather than as authoritative and final. The forum design whereby multiple voices speak on a topic and then a group of learners discuss what they think is easy to implement. What students learn from this is how to negotiate for themselves a position in a field of dialogue. The term "field of dialogue" here mediates between the completely open concept of dialogic space and the more circumscribed curriculum areas. A good example of a field of dialogue might be the range of views on global warming or on capital punishment.

From a dialogic perspective the Internet is not so much a "tool of tools" but a cacophony of voices offering countless opportunities for dialogic engagement with multiple perspectives on every topic. While these perspectives are mediated by technology, signs for the voices of the other, faces, voices, avatars, videos, and so on, are not best understood on the model of tools but as stand-ins for the face of the other or "epiphantic" signs that lead one to the voice of another person (Leimann, 2002). The issue for design is how to use these different ways of mediating the presence of the other to support dialogue across difference that issues in reflection and learning. Web quests offer one way of scaffolding dialogic encounters between voices. E-mail links between geographically distant groups are another. Dialogues via avatars in 3D virtual worlds are a further way (see Ligorio & Pugliese, 2004).

An Example of Broadening Dialogic Space

Computer-mediated dialogues generally expand the "space" of dialogue by spatialising time so that many can "talk" in parallel and their different voices can be represented by spatial differences in an interface. In web forums or e-mail in-boxes this different way of doing dialogue is represented in a kind of play-script with one utterance after another listed in a temporal sequence prefaced by the name of the participant. This linear list is a metaphor for the progression of moments in time, the line below being the utterance after the line above. Even this arrangement makes it easy to lose the context of the argument. The "dialogue maps" of more map-like graphical dialogue environments like Digalo are made up of boxes of different shapes and colours representing different types of contribution and links between them which can also be given a meaning. Digalo has mainly been used synchronously with boxes appearing and disappearing and being moved around and linked in real-time but the end result is not a temporal arrangement but a spatial arrangement (see Fig. 16.1).

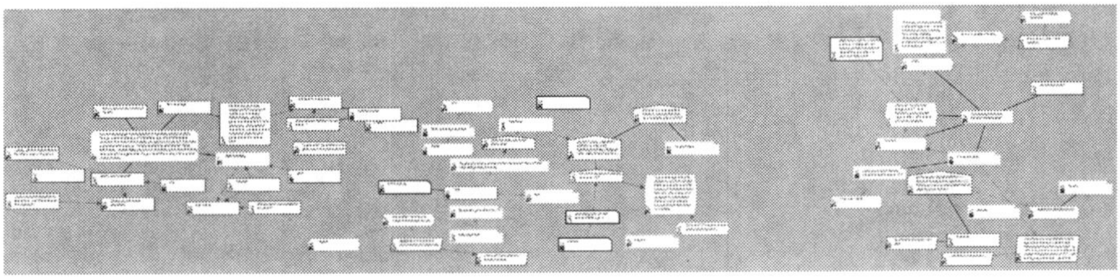

Fig. 16.1 Illustration of a Digalo map using 6 Hats technique

Figure 16.1 illustrates the potential for spatial arrangements of ideas looking at the patterning of messages rather than the content of messages. This is a map created by a group of university students using Edward de Bono's Six Hats technique to encourage them to look at an issue in a range of different ways. The dialogic process of exploring an issue through various perspectives, all of which are valid and none of which are ever simply "overcome" in a "synthesis," is well supported by the spatial representation of Digalo and its flexibility. Moving shapes around on the map supports reflection on the relationships between different perspectives. The development of dialogic reasoning is often signaled through the expression of openness of other points of view, through changes of mind and through inclusion of multiple voices in one "utterance" (see Fig. 16.2).

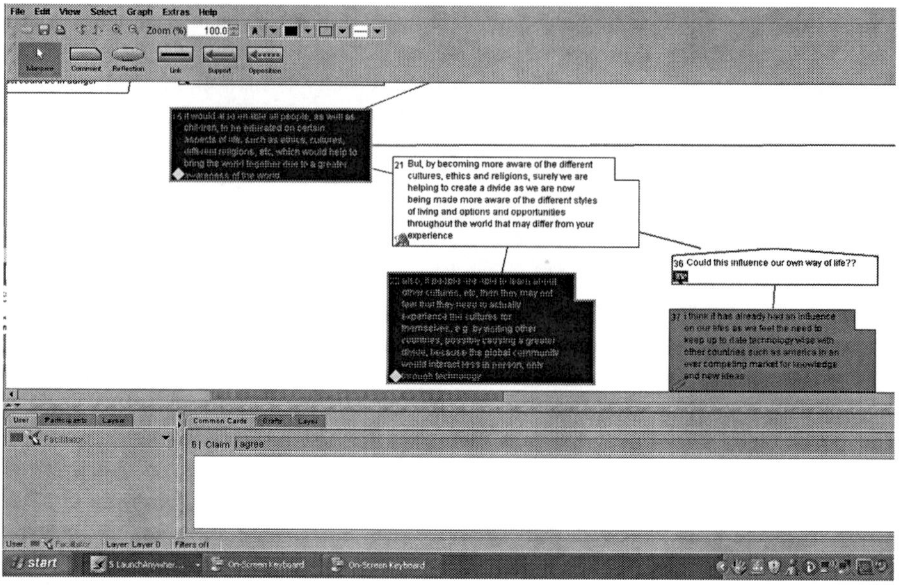

Fig. 16.2 A cluster of shapes around the emergence of a new perspective

Through combining a content analysis of the "maps" for the emergence of new perspectives with critical event recall we have explored the extent to which this tool affords creative reflection on multiple perspectives and so could be seen as a tool that supports that widening of dialogues (Wegerif et al., 2009).

ICT and Dialogue Between Media

Meaning can be explored using a variety of media. According to the dialogic across difference perspective I have outlined above, dialogues are not simply an exchange of words. They consist of a relationship between voices or perspectives motivating a flow of meaning. This flow of meaning is focused and articulated by signs and communications technologies but is not reducible to those signs or technologies. Exploring the dialogue between meanings in different modes has the potential to broaden dialogues, by giving access to new kinds of perspectives and to deepen dialogues, by encouraging one mode to reflect on another. For example asking students to reflect on musical representations of different arguments can give access to the emotions that are often implicit behind neutral seeming words in texts and so both broaden and deepen the dialogic space. This can be illustrated through a recent project in a school in the UK where the use of ICT was central. This was a creative workshop combining together music composition, dance movement and art-work using light to produce a response to an initial poem entitled "Light Shifts". The multi-modal result, presented in a powerpoint, is a powerful expression of

Fig. 16.3 Edited still from "Light Shifts" a multimodal powerpoint presentation (Cunliffe, 2008)

multi-media dialogue effectively evoking that "dialogic space" between and around different media that enables meaning to transgress and to transfer. Figure 16.3 gives an edited version still combining light and text but to this you have to add in imagination, movement, music, and voice.

Blogging as an Example of Induction into and Creation of Dialogic Space

The problem with neo-Vygotskian accounts of how we learn to think is that they focus on the tools within the dialogue rather than the space of dialogue itself. Some have argued in this neo-Vygotskian way, that writing provides a kind of cognitive technology for mediated thinking, especially through tools like tables and lists that make abstract formal thinking possible (e.g Goody, 1977). Walter Ong makes a different point when he describes how the initial custom of reading texts aloud in groups was gradually replaced by silent individual reading. This habit, combined with the sense of closure in printed texts as if thought could become a thing supported the development of a sense of a fixed inner self separate from the interplay of communal life. This was conceptualized as a new "inner space" from which individuals had the freedom to reflect critically on the culture around them (Ong, 1982). This kind of sense of an inner space of freedom that one carries around with one is the very model of the "autonomous self" that education systems still aim to produce (Biesta, 2006). Ong's careful and persuasive case offers a model for relating technologies to the development of embodied higher order thinking. On the whole, in the contexts of its use, electronic text is more immediately dialogic and communal than print technology. Yet, as writing, it continues, unlike oral dialogue, to endure over time and so it has the potential to support the disembedding of ideas from their contingent contexts that Ong attributes to writing. If electronic writing does support the kind of "inner space" of reflection away from the contingencies of time and physical context that Ong refers to, then this inner space is no longer the inert individualized space generated by earlier writing and reading practices but a collective and dialogic "inner space".

Ong's account of the way in which communicative practices associated with literacy led to the creation and deepening of individual inner space is applicable to analyzing the impact of new communicative technologies, not as tools that are internalized, but as new dialogic spaces that become part of the lifeworld of participants. In a recent talk the educational ethnographer, David Barton, described how he had put photos of the hills near his home in the North of England on Flickr and received comments from other amateur photographers in Japan and Germany. After that he described how he saw the same hills differently, as if through the eyes of the Japanese and the German photographers he was in dialogue with. This story illustrates how internet mediated dialogue can expand a space of reflection that is both individual and collective, both situated and transcendent. In a similar way the practice of blogging, for instance, can be a participation in a process of collective reflection. Events seem different when they are seen not only through one's own eyes but also through the eyes of the potential audience for one's blog. One course in Exeter University is assessed entirely through mutually visible multimedia blogs in a facebook-like web 2.0 environment and this has proved effective in creating a motivating shared reflective space. The majority of students report that seeing the views of others helps them to think and reflect and create new ideas.

Discussion and Conclusion

Both as a real shift in the foundations of economic and social life and as a vision of the future, the idea of the emerging global knowledge age challenges traditional approaches to education. New individual and collective skills and dispositions are required for thriving in the knowledge age. These have been described in terms of skills of communication, collaboration and creativity. Neither cognitive psychology, based on the computer metaphor of mind, nor socio-cultural approaches based on the metaphor of thinking as the use of cultural tools, can adequately account for how to teach effectively for these knowledge age skills. Dialogic theory can offer education a different vision which is a both trajectory of identity (like some socio-cultural theory such as that of Lave and Wenger (1991)) and also, like more rationalist and cognitivist accounts of education, a vertical development of thinking, since the trajectory is movement into the space of dialogue itself. This trajectory of learning is characterized by leaving behind narrow attachments and identities and becoming more open to otherness, both the otherness of different voices and the otherness of new ideas. This dialogic verticality is different from the verticality of the rationalists because it is a movement from identity into difference. At the end of the journey there are no universal structures of reason, only uncertainty, multiplicity and possibility. What could be more important in the emerging global network society than learning how to live constructively and creatively in a situation where there are always multiple voices with no possibility of an overview or a final true answer to any problem? In this Chapter we unpacked this dialogic theoretical perspective to turn it into a foundation for the design of education with technology and we tentatively put forward a framework for educational design based on the conceptual implications of the theory and on examples of activities that seemed to have worked in promoting movement into dialogic space. The concepts of opening, deepening, widening and resourcing dialogic space were used to analyze different educational designs. Some guiding principles were provided, such as the value of teaching content through drawing students into fields of dialogue and the importance of combining the use of technology with face-to-face pedagogies that actively teach the skills and social ground rules required for engagement in dialogue across difference. Although it remains weak on the details this framework offers a new way of understanding the role of the internet in teaching thinking. As well as the external relationships of voices situated in dispersed places and times, dialogue, it is claimed, offers the potential for internal relationships between voices. In mediating multiple voices in dialogue with each other the internet should be understood on the model of this internal dialogic space more than on the model of an external structure. The signs of the internet are perhaps best understood as stand ins or proxies for the "face of the other" described by Levinas as a kind of sign that signifies not content but a context for meaning (Levinas, 1978, p. 158, 1989, p. 90). This context for meaning is dialogue with others and with otherness in general. Whilst the internet is not itself dialogic space it appears to make possible the partial external realization of what has always been the internal intuition of dialogue: the ideal of all voices from all cultures and all times in dialogue together. As well as being an effective response to the need for workers who can thrive in a global knowledge economy, teaching thinking with the internet, understood as opening, widening and deepening dialogic space, is a practical proposal for how education could participate in the creation of a more peaceful future.

References

Baker, M. J., Quignard, M., Lund, K., & Séjourné, A. (2003). Computer-supported collaborative learning in the space of debate. In B. Wasson, S. Ludvigsen & U. Hoppe (Eds.), *Designing for change in networked learning environments: Proceedings of the International Conference on Computer Support for Collaborative Learning 2003* pp. 11–20. Dordrecht: Kluwer Academic Publishers.

Bakhtin, M. (1986). *Speech genres and other late essays*. Austin: University of Texas.

Bell, D. (1999). *The coming of post-industrial society*. New York: Basic Books.

Biesta, G. (2006). *Beyond learning: Democratic education for a human future*. Boulder CO: Paradigm Press.

Bloom, B. S. (Ed.) (1956). *Taxonomy of educational objectives: The classification of educational goals: Handbook I, cognitive domain*. New York, Toronto: Longmans, Green.
Bruns, A. (2007). *Beyond difference: Reconfiguring education for the User-Led Age*. Paper presented at the ICE 3 (Ideas, Cyberspace, Education) conference at Ross Priory, Loch Lomond, Scotland, 21–23 March 2007. Accessed on 10th August 2009 from http://snurb.info/publications.
Castells, M. (2001). *The internet galaxy: Reflections on the internet, business, and society*. Oxford: Oxford University Press.
Cunliffe, L. (2008). A case study: How interdisciplinary teaching using information and communication technology and supported by a creative partner impacted on creativity in an extra-curricular school activity. *International Journal of Education through Art, 4*, 1.
De laat, M. (2006). Networked learning. Apeldoorn: Politie Academy.
Drucker, P. F. (1969, April 24). The knowledge society. *New Society, 13*(343), 629–631.
European Council (2000). *Presidency conclusions of the council of the European Union*. http://www.europarl.europa.eu/summits/lis1_en.htm.
Goody, J. (1977). The domestication of the savage mind. Cambridge, England: Cambridge University Press.
Hobson, P. (2002). *The cradle of thought: Exploring the origins of thinking*. London: Macmillan.
Jacoby, A. (2007). The knowledge Society and global dynamics in education politics. *European Educational Research Journal, 6*(1), 39–45.
Lave, J., & Wenger, E. (1991). *Situated learning: Legitimate periperal participation*. Cambridge, UK: Cambridge University Press.
Leimann, M. (2002). Toward semiotic dialogism: The role of sign mediation in the dialogical self. *Theory and Psychology, 12*(2), 221–235.
Leitch, S. (2006). *Prosperity for all in the global economy world class skills*. Final report of the Leitch Review of Skills. London: HMSO/HM Treasury.
Levin, H., & Rumberger, R. (1995). Education, work and employment in developed countries: Situation and future challenges. In J. Hallak, & F. Caillods (Eds.), *Educational planning: The international dimension* pp. 69–88. UNESCO Bureau of Education, International Institute for Educational Planning. London: Garland.
Lévinas, E. (1978). *Autrement qu'être ou au-dela de l'essence*. Paris: Livre de poche.
Lévinas, E. (1989). Substitution. Translated by A. Lingis. In S. Hand (Ed.), *The levinas reader* pp 88–127. Oxford: Blackwell.
Ligorio, M. B., & Pugliese, A. C. (2004). Self-positioning in a text-based environment. *Identity: An International Journal of Theory and Research, 4*(4), 337–353.
McMahon, H., & O'Neill., W. (1993). Computer-mediated zones of engagement in learning. In T. Duffy, J. Lowyk & D. Jonassen (Eds.), *Designing environments for constructive learning* pp.37–57. Berlin: Springer-Verlag.
Mercer, N., Dawes, R., Wegerif, R., & Sams, C. (2004). Reasoning as a scientist: Ways of helping children to use language to learn science. *British Educational Research Journal, 30*(3), 367–385.
Ong, W. J. (1982). *Orality and literacy: The technologizing of the word*. London: Methuen.
Quisumbing, L. R. (2005). Education for the world of work and citizenship: Towards sustainable future societies. *Prospects: Quarterly Review of Comparative Education, 35*(3), 289–301.
Resnick, L. (1987). *Education and learning to think*. Washington, DC: National Academy Press.
Tomasello, M., Carpenter, M., Call, J., Behne, T., & Moll, H. (2005). Understanding and sharing intentions: The origins of cultural cognition. *Behavioral and Brain Sciences, 28*(5), 691–735.
Trickey, S., & Topping, K. J. (2004). Philosophy for children: A systematic review. *Research Papers in Education, 19*(3), 365–380.
Trilling, B., & Hood, P. (2001). Learning, technology and education reform in the knowledge age, or 'We're Wired, Webbed and Windowed, Now What?'. In C. Paechter, R. Edwards, R. Harrison, & P. Twining, (Eds.), *Learning, space and identity*. London, UK: Paul Chapman Publishing & The Open University, Also at: http://www.wested.org/cs/we/view/rs/654.

UNESCO (2005). *Towards Knowledge Societies: Unesco World Report.* [http://www.unesco.org/en/worldreport]

Wegerif, R. (2007). *Dialogic, education and technology: Expanding the space of learning*. New York, Berlin: Springer.

Wegerif, R., & Dawes, L. (2004). *Thinking and learning with ICT: Raising achievement in primary classrooms,*. London: Routledge.

Wegerif, R., Littleton, K., & Jones, A. (2003). Stand alone computers supporting learning dialogues in primary classrooms. *International Journal of Educational Research, 39*(8), 851–860.

Wegerif, R., McLaren, B. M., Chamrada, M., Scheuer, O., Mansour, N., & Mikšátko, J. (2009). *Recognizing Creative Thinking in Graphical e-Discussions using Artificial Intelligence Graph-Matching Techniques*. a paper presented at the 8th International Conference on Computer Supported Collaborative Learning (CSCL-09), June 8–13, 2009, University of the Aegean, Rhodes, Greece.

Wegerif, R., Mercer, N., & Dawes, L. (1999). From social interaction to individual reasoning: An empirical investigation of a possible socio-cultural model of cognitive development. *Learning and Instruction, 9*(5), 493–516.

Chapter 17
Conceptual Representation Embodied in Hypermedia: An Approach to Promoting Knowledge Co-Construction

Lei Liu[1] and Cindy E. Hmelo-Silver[2]

[1] University of Pennsylvania, Philadelphia, PA, USA , e-mail: Liulei_yzt@hotmail.com
[2] Rutgers, the State University of New Jersey, New Brunswick, NJ, USA

Conceptual Representations Embodied in Hypermedia: Promoting Co-Regulated Learning

Conceptual representations are often implicit in learning resources such as hypermedia. These representations serve as organizing frameworks that learners use to coordinate their knowledge. In particular, conceptual representations can be important for helping learners understand complex phenomena. Hypermedia can be a vehicle for conveying conceptual representations and can be useful for supporting individual understanding and metacognitive thinking (Jacobson & Archididou, 2000). However, little research has investigated how conceptual representations embodied in hypermedia may influence collaborative learning or how it affects the use of co-regulatory strategies. Using different external representations can guide and constrain collaborative learning discourse (Suthers & Hundhausen, 2003), and we would expect similar effects for conceptual representations.

Major challenges for learning about complex phenomena are student's cognitive, metacognitive, and self-regulatory processing (Hmelo-Silver & Azevedo, 2006). In this chapter, we will address how we have used conceptual representations to deal with the cognitive challenges. Manipulating the hypermedia structure may also affect self and co-regulation strategies. Our goal in this chapter is to examine the relationship between the conceptual representation used to structure hypermedia and the student's regulation of learning processes.

Hypermedia as a Representational Tool

Hypermedia can support learning about the facts, concepts, and principles of a domain (McManus & Segner, 1991). However, understanding also requires the integration of knowledge into framework consisting of relations among concepts

L. Liu (✉)
University of Pennsylvania, Philadelphia, PA, USA
e-mail: liulei_yzt@hotmail.com

M.S. Khine, I.M. Saleh (eds.), *New Science of Learning*,
DOI 10.1007/978-1-4419-5716-0_17,

and principles (Newton & Newton, 2000; Ruiz-Primo & Shavelson, 1996). The organization of hypermedia system can help learners develop such a framework. Hypermedia features such as links and cross-references can promote navigation patterns which model expert forms of knowledge organization (Jonassen, 1986; Nunes & Fowell, 1996; Park, 1991). Links enable semantically and logically related information to be tied together in conceptual webs and help learners to understand how ideas are interrelated. In other words, the nodes and links can be used to provide explicit conceptual representations to learners. It is the structure embedded in hypermedia, rather than the media and modalities in which they are presented, that are important for comprehension of complex systems (Hegarty, Narayanan & Freitas, 2002).

Conceptual representations refer to frameworks or models that people can use to organize their knowledge (Davis, Shrobe, & Szolovits, 1993). Such representations can highlight commonalities across different domains or systems (Novick & Hmelo, 1994) and may be used to guide students to see the common framework across different domains. In complex system learning, conceptual representations can promote developing a deep understanding by highlighting the key aspects of a complex system, such as the relationship among structural, functional, and behavioral levels of a system. One possible approach to helping students learn about complex systems is to provide instruction that focuses on the functional aspects of the system. We tested this idea with hypermedia as we investigated effects of two alternative conceptual representations on student understanding.

Structure–Behavior–Function as a Conceptual Representation

Conceptual representations provide organizing frameworks across domains. Collins and Ferguson (1993) refer to these as epistemic forms—target structures that are important in constructing knowledge and engaging in inquiry. These representations are useful in making sense of the world. Form and function analysis is a classic form of analysis in many fields of inquiry and is a canonical form of explanation in the life sciences (Bechtel & Abrahamson, 2005). Such an analysis produces an explanation of causal mechanisms as it stresses that understanding a form precedes and invites explaining mechanisms that account for that form's function.

Extending form and function analysis, Goel et al. (1996) designed the Structure–Behavior–Function (SBF) representation to allow computers to effectively reason about designed devices. The SBF theory provides a conceptual representation and sheds light on causal understanding of systems because of its focus on the dynamic nature and multilevel organization of the system, and the relationships between structures, functions, and behaviors (Goel et al., 1996). Structures refer to the elements of a system. Behaviors refer to the mechanisms within a system. Finally functions refer to outcomes or roles in a system. For example, the diaphragm would be one of the structures of the human respiratory system. The contracting and relaxing mechanism is an example of the behavior of the diaphragm. The function of the diaphragm is to create an air pressure differential inside the thoracic cavity so that the air can move in and out.

Structures are necessarily involved in the execution of behaviors that leads to particular functions. In complex systems, several structures might be involved in the same function. For example, the diaphragm, intercostal muscles, and ribs are all coordinated in the function of moving air into and out of the body. Similarly, the behavior of one particular structure often affects the behavior of other structures. For example, the blood vessels transport oxygen and nutrients throughout the body. However for this behavior to occur, the heart must pump the blood through the vessels.

The SBF representation also accounts for the expert–novice differences in complex systems domains (Hmelo-Silver & Pfeffer, 2004; Hmelo-Silver, Marathe, & Liu, 2007). Using clinical interviews, Hmelo-Silver and colleagues (2007) studied expertise in two complex systems domains: the human respiratory system and the aquarium systems. They found that novices tended to think about isolated structures whereas experts integrated behavioral and functional perspectives when asked to describe their understanding about these systems. For example, novices only talked about the surface components of the respiratory system, such as lungs, airway, ribs, and seldom mentioned the deep underlying mechanisms, such as how oxygen gets into the body or how diffusion occurs in the lungs. In comparison, experts explained about the underlying mechanisms, such as how the cellular respiration and the diffusion happen, which actually connected most of the components within the system. Furthermore, novices rarely mentioned those nonsalient elements that are either invisible or involved in complex causal mechanisms, such as the cellular respiration. In other research, Egan and Schwartz (1979) found that the functional aspect of conceptual representation might contribute to the distinctions between expert and novice understanding. They asked expert and novice electronic technicians to reconstruct symbolic drawings of circuit diagrams. They found that skilled technicians replicated the drawings based on the functional nature of the elements in the circuit (e.g., amplifiers, rectifiers, and filters). In contrast, novice technicians replicated drawing based more on the spatial proximity of the presented elements. Both studies suggest that a functional understanding is a characteristic of experts, consistent with Hmelo-Silver et al. (2007).

If functional understanding is characteristic of experts and a key form of domain reasoning in life sciences, then it also suggests that an emphasis on function and helping learners make connections across different SBF levels might be used to create instruction that will lead to a deep understanding. Liu, Hmelo-Silver, and Marathe (2005a) compared the effects of two alternative versions of hypermedia on the development of conceptual understanding of the human respiratory system. The function-oriented version emphasizes the "how" and "why" of the system and is consistent with both expert understanding and canonical biological explanations. The structure-oriented hypermedia emphasizes the "what" of the system, similar to most textbooks. The findings showed that the function-centered hypermedia helped students gain a deeper understanding of the system than the structure-oriented version. Moreover, the function-oriented version helped students learn about the normally nonsalient phenomena, such as alveoli, blood, capillaries, cellular respiration, red blood cells, and vascular system, that are important for the ultimate function of the system to support cellular respiration. This research demonstrated the positive effects of a conceptual representation for individuals but did not explore any potential benefits of using hypermedia in a collaborative learning context. As Azevedo and colleagues have repeatedly demonstrated, hypermedia poses challenges for students' self- and co-regulated learning (Azevedo, Cromley, & Seibert, 2004a; Azevedo, Moos, Greene, Winters, & Cromley, 2008; Azevedo, Winters, & Moos, 2004b).

Self-regulated and Co-regulated Learning

In hypermedia, students are given access to a range of nonlinear information. Such nonlinear organization provides not only new possibilities for teaching about the structure of domain knowledge but also challenges for self-regulated learning (SRL). SRL involves deploying and adapting cognitive tactics as well as making decisions about how to use metacognitive and motivational strategies (Weinstein & Mayer, 1986; Winne, 2001). Students need to set meaningful learning goals and engage in planning, monitoring, and evaluating their understanding and effort in relation to the task context (Winne, 2001; Azevedo et al., 2004a). Unfortunately students have difficulty in regulating their learning process (Azevedo et al., 2004a; Jacobson & Archidodou, 2000; Shapiro & Niederhauser, 2004). Research has shown that a significant difference between proficient learners and low-achieving learners as well as between experts and novices is their use of self-regulation strategies (Glaser, 1976; Schmitt & Newby, 1986). Often, learners do not know whether they are on the right track, what strategies to use, and when and how to use the strategies (Perkins, 1993). They may make poor decisions about what to study and in what order (i.e., selecting links) because they do not have sufficient prior knowledge or appropriate metacognitive ability (Cho, 1995). Recent research has suggested that learners have difficulty with self-regulation in hypermedia environments, but little research has explored the relation between hypermedia structure and self or co-regulated learning.

Collaborative learning environments can provide opportunities to deal with some of the SRL challenges by allowing regulatory activities to be distributed across participants. Like SRL, co-regulation concerns students' co-engagement in planning, monitoring, and evaluating strategies (the three major phases of self-regulation). Co-regulated learning emerges in the process of knowledge co-construction (Hickey & McCaslin, 2001). In the planning process, students set goals for their learning activity and keep attention focused on specific learning tasks. This process may affect the effectiveness of selected strategies to monitor learning progress toward the planned goals and evaluating their progress of learning (Pintrich & Zusho, 2002). In a classroom study of collaborative learning using hypermedia, Azevedo et al. (2004b) demonstrated that collaborative outcomes were related to the use of regulatory behaviors.

Although collaborative learning should promote positive outcomes, these do not always occur (Dillenbourg, 1999; O'Donnell & O'Kelly, 1994). Using hypermedia for collaborative learning can support knowledge co-construction. However, the structure of the hypermedia should affect how the students engage in collaborative knowledge construction (e.g., Suthers & Hundhausen, 2003). As noted earlier, the use of conceptual representations in hypermedia affects what students learn individually (Hmelo-Silver, 2004; Liu et al., 2005a). In this study, we try to understand the locus of this effect. One possibility is that organizing hypermedia around function helps problematize the ideas presented and requires learners to process the material more actively (Reiser, 2004). In addition, the function orientation may induce students to set goals that are more consistent with a deep approach to learning. In our study, we examine this in the context of dyads learning about the respiratory system using either a function-oriented or a structure-oriented hypermedia.

Method

Participants

Twenty participants from the educational psychology subject pool at a large public university participated. Participants received course credit for participating in the study. In each session, participants were grouped into dyads and randomly assigned to condition.

Materials

In this study we used two different versions of hypermedia (Liu, Hmelo-Silver, Marathe, 2005b) to teach about the human respiratory system: the function-oriented version (F-hypermedia) and the structure-oriented version (S-hypermedia) of hypermedia about the human respiratory system. Both versions present similar content; the major difference is in the underlying conceptual representations. In the function-centered hypermedia (F-hypermedia), our goal was to make the functional and behavioral aspects of the human respiratory system salient. The F-hypermedia guides student learning through an organizational structure that models how experts think about this biological domain (Collins, Brown, & Newman, 1989; Hmelo-Silver, 2006). Specifically, the F-hypermedia starts with two big functional–behavioral questions: "Why do we need oxygen?" and "How does oxygen get into the body?" (see Fig. 17.1). The answers to these questions require a holistic understanding of the human respiratory system and set the stage for future learning. The F-hypermedia is designed to help guide students in answering these two questions. For example, to guide answering the first question, we provided

Fig. 17.1 Opening screen of the function-oriented hypermedia

model explanations such as "cells need oxygen to burn food to produce energy," "blood carries oxygen and food to the cell," and "Breathing air from outside provides cells with oxygen". Thus, by clicking the first question, the students will be led to additional questions and information that help them make connections between external respiration (moving air into and out of the lungs) and internal respiration (occurring at the cellular level).

In contrast, the S-hypermedia presents information in much the same way as a traditional textbook. In S-hypermedia, students move from isolated elements of the system to their respective behaviors and functions. Learners start with a diagram of the human respiratory system with links to each component in the system (see Fig. 17.2) and then from the structure to the respective behaviors and functions. As in the F-hypermedia, the S-hypermedia provides links to other relevant information on each page.

Procedure

The first author ran all the sessions with each dyad in a laboratory setting. Each session lasted around 2 h. There was one Macintosh computer set up in the laboratory. Initially, each participant was asked to take a pretest on their conceptual understanding of the human respiratory system. Then the experimenter explained the purpose and procedures to the participants. The dyad was asked to explore the hypermedia collaboratively starting from the main page. Participants were told that collaboration meant that the participants needed to explain to their partner what the content meant to them and how it related to what already they knew about the human respiratory system. The dyads were also informed that their exploration needed to last

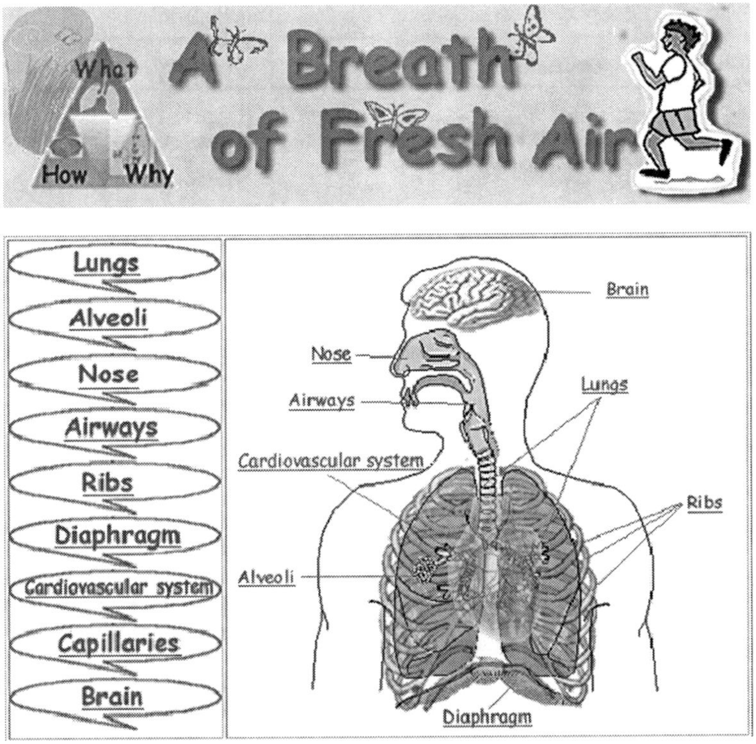

Fig. 17.2 Opening screen of the structure-oriented hypermedia

at least 40 min. After exploring the hypermedia, participants completed an individual posttest and a questionnaire on their attitude toward using the software and the collaborative learning activities. The dyads were both video- and audio-taped. The experimenter observed all sessions but would remind participants of the minimum 40-min limit if they worked too quickly.

Coding and Analysis

The tapes were transcribed verbatim, blind to condition. All transcriptions were marked with conversational turns. The coding categories used in this study were driven partly by Azevedo et al. (2004a) inclusions of SRL variables derived from students' self-regulatory exploration, and partly by a process of inductive analyses of our data. Table 17.1 illustrates all the coding categories (including respective definitions and examples) involved in this step of analysis, which may be grouped into four major categories: planning, monitoring, evaluation, and unrelated topics. The first three sets of categories refer to the major mechanisms involved in SRL (Karoly,

Table 17.1 Description of co-regulated coding scheme

Co-regulation	Definition	Example
Planning		
Expressing lack of knowledge	Feel the inadequacy of prior knowledge	"I didn't know..."
Explore Strategy		
–Free exploration	Select a link to read without explanation/justification	"Let's click this"
–Completion-driven	The selection of link is decided by identifying content that is new to them	"We did this before, let's do that"
–Specific question-driven	The selection of a link is to get info to understand a specific question/phenomena	"I want to know where cellular respiration process is. Let's go there"
Monitoring		
Check understanding		
–Reading	Verbatim reading of the hypermedia context	"There two main branches and they go smaller..."
–Elaboration	Extend meaning of the text and diagram by giving details or examples	"So the brain detects chemicals that the body needs, more or less, and then it controls the rate of breathing, by releasing other chemicals"
–Explanation	Clarify a cause-effect relation	"There is a little valve that when you eat it closes up. That's why you shouldn't talk when you eat because it opens"
–Raise question	Indicate uncertainty	"What are those brown things?"
–Simple answer	Give simple answers such as yes or no without elaboration or explanation	"Yes, it is heart"
–Agree	State agreement to an utterance	"I think that too"
–Disagree	State a different opinion	"But I think this was not like this"
–Feeling of knowing	State a sense of understanding	"I think I got it"
Check learning progress	Check whether they are making progress toward the goal	"I don't think this answered our question"
Evaluation/Reflection		
Content evaluation	Make comments on the content of the hypermedia	"I think here they should provide more info"
Strategy evaluation	Make comments on the strategy they used	"I think re-read this can help us find the answer"
Learning process	Recall and comment on how they learned	"We did see this and re-read it. Now I think I know what blood cells do in the system"
Learning product	Summarize what they learned	"Now both of us know how the system works"
Topic-unrelated Talk	Talk about things unrelated to the learning, such as social talk	"What's your major?"

1993). Planning includes expressing lack of knowledge and setting goals for exploring the hypermedia. Monitoring includes control of various strategies to reach goals such as students checking their understanding and learning process. To check their understanding, learners may apply strategies such as reading, elaborating, explaining, raising and answering questions, agreeing and disagreeing, expressing feeling of knowing. Evaluation involves making assessments of learning content, strategies, learning processes, and learning products. This mechanism is essential for students to select effective strategies and reflect on the relations between the strategies and the learning outcomes (Schoenfeld, 1987). The percentage of each co-regulated learning indicants were calculated and compared across conditions. A second coder was trained in the coding system and coded 20% of all data independently of the primary coder. The interrater agreement was above 90%. All the coding was completed blind to conditions. ANOVAs were used to compare the mean percentage of each indicator of co-regulated learning.

The student answers to pre- and posttest questions were analyzed using an SBF-based coding scheme (Hmelo, Holton, & Kolodner, 2000). For example, the mention of the lungs was coded as a structure, the mechanism of gas exchange as a behavior, and the need to provide oxygen as a function. A 2 × 2 mixed ANOVA with hypermedia condition as a between subjects factor and time as a within subjects factor was used to test the effect of hypermedia in terms of SBF.

Results

Quantitative Results

Co-regulated learning. The descriptive statistics for indicators of co-regulated learning are shown in Table 17.2 as mean percentages. Learners in the S-hypermedia condition were more likely than the F-hypermedia to express lack of knowledge ($F\,(1.18) = 12.09, p = 0.006$) engage in reading ($F\,(1.18) = 5.44, p = 0.04$), provide simple answers ($F\,(1.18) = 21.42, p = 0.001$) and raise question ($F\,(1.18) = 24.42, p = 0.001$). Learners in the F-hypermedia condition were more likely to engage in checking learning progress ($F\,(1.18) = 13.68, p = 0.004$), checking understanding ($F\,(1.18) = 5.38, p = 0.043$), and specific-question driven exploration ($F\,(1.18) = 6.36, p = 0.03$)

Learning outcomes. The results of pre- and posttests are shown in Table 17.3. The results indicate that both versions of hypermedia helped students learn about the human respiratory system. All students showed reliable gains in learning over time. Students using the S-hypermedia showed gains in understanding structures ($F\,(1.18) = 34.56, p < 0.001$), behaviors ($F\,(1.18) = 6.61, p = 0.03$), and functions ($F\,(1.18) = 16.67, p = 0.003$). Students using the F-hypermedia showed gains in understanding structures ($F\,(1.18) = 6.975, p = 0.027$) and behaviors ($F\,(1.18) = 16.16, p = 0.003$) in the posttest than in the pretest. Students who

Table 17.2 Mean percentage and standard deviations of co-regulated learning indicators

Co-regulation		F-condition	S-condition
Planning	Expressing lack of knowledge	2.02* (1.02)	4.21* (1.16)
	Explore strategy		
	–Free exploration	5.13 (6.91)	5.72 (4.29)
	–Completion-driven	4.11 (3.59)	5.78 (3.07)
	–Specific-question-driven	8.17* (5.20)	2.32* (2.27)
Monitoring	Checking understanding		
	–Reading	7.44* (2.72)	12.76* (4.88)
	–Elaboration	18.98 (3.63)	16.85 (4.48)
	–Explanation	4.72 (3.80)	1.85 (1.14)
	–Raise question	8.03 (3.03)	15.47* (2.09)
	–Simple answer	1.95 (1.34)	6.67 (2.10)
	–Agree	5.76 (2.27)	6.90 (2.54)
	–Disagree	0.62 (0.85)	0.75 (0.39)
	–Feeling of knowing	2.90 (3.76)	3.10 (1.98)
	Check learning progress	7.84* (2.87)	2.64* (2.17)
Evaluating	Content evaluation	2.57 (2.05)	2.55 (2.17)
	Strategy evaluation	1.80 (1.12)	0.67 (0.81)
	Learning process evaluation	3.71 (1.47)	2.35 (2.73)
	Learning product evaluation	2.98 (1.61)	1.75 (1.54)
Topic unrelated talk		11.26 (8.73)	7.64 (6.26)

The asterisk symbols show the items that have significant differences in the comparison statistics

used the F-hypermedia had significant gains in their understanding of nonsalient behaviors (F (1.18) = 10.76, $p = 0.01$), whereas students using the S-hypermedia did not. No other main effects or interactions were significant. However due to the small sample, it was hard to tell the differential impact of the underlying conceptual representations in the quantitative results.

Table 17.3 Means and standard deviations of pre- and post-tests across conditions reported by structures, behaviors, and functions

		Total			Nonsalient		
		S	B	F	S	B	F
F-hypermedia	Pre	8.70 (2.67)	1.50 (1.27)	4.30 (2.58)	2.80 (2.04)	0.30 (0.48)	1.40 (1.78)
	Post	10.80* (1.23)	3.20 (1.13)	5.90* (2.13)	4.40 (0.84)	1.00* (0.82)	2.60 (1.65)
S-hypermedia	Pre	7.90 (2.42)	1.90 (0.99)	3.70 (2.06)	2.10 (2.02)	0.10 (0.32)	1.30 (1.42)
	Post	11.70* (0.95)	3.10* (1.10)	7.10* (2.28)	4.90 (0.57)	0.50 (0.71)	2.80 (1.81)

Qualitative Results

The quantitative results represent one view of co-regulated learning, but we used the qualitative data to further enrich our understanding of how the different hypermedia structures affected students' co-regulated learning. To compare the discourse of dyads across the two conditions, we selected two successful dyads from each condition. The selection was based on the quantity and quality of the indicators of cognitive processing, such as elaboration and metacognition, that were observed in the collaborative discourse.

The focus of this analysis is on the three critical processes in co-regulated learning: planning, monitoring, and evaluation. There were qualitative differences in how dyads planned their exploration across conditions. Dyads who used the F-hypermedia planned their exploration based on specific questions. In other words, they selected links purposefully with goals of understanding particular phenomena. In contrast, dyads using the S-hypermedia mostly planned their exploration either to complete all the content in the hypermedia or without any clear goal. They first identified whether the content was explored before they made a decision on which link to click. In addition to the differences in planning strategies in co-regulated learning, dyads across conditions applied different strategies in the monitoring and evaluating processes. The following excerpts illustrated an example of how an F-hypermedia dyad (R and G) decided where they would go next in the hypermedia:

G: Why do we need oxygen?
R: Let's go there and find out.
G: But how does it do this?
G: Ok (reading hypermedia)
R: That is the only ATP cycle, rather complicated.
G: Which is basically what I said. I just...
G: Yeah, and you just store it to like where we need it
R: Yeah, well, other related needs... need for sugar, need for transporting oxygen and sugar

G: I guess click this thing over there... ok, we will go here and then go to other related needs.
R: Ok

This excerpt shows that R and G were planning their exploration based on the question: "Why do we need oxygen and how does the process go?" They selected the link to the ATP cycle and other related needs involved in this process. They used various strategies of connecting to their prior knowledge, for example, when G mentioned, "which is basically what I said" and paraphrasing the meaning of the content (e.g., G paraphrased that "...you just store it to like where we need it"). This excerpt also illustrated that this F-hypermedia dyad kept their attention focused on the questions they generated and judged whether the content was related to their questions. In this way, they had opportunities to explore the interrelationships among the functions and behaviors of various structures, which together comprise an aggregate system function.

For comparison, we present an example from an S-dyad, S and J, that demonstrates how they selected links during their exploration.

S: So this is like the nose itself, like basically...
J: Yeah... ahh trachea, that is how you spell it... there is also nose hairs that filter out
S: Did I do this? Right?
J: Yeah we did that one.
S: So let's go home...
S: Ok, so they are all go to the spine and it protects the lungs and the heart
S: Did we do?... Yeah, we did.
J: What else? We did ribs, the cardiovascular system, we did not do that one. Yeah, we did that one.
S: Ok, we did not do this one, yeah we did
J: Yeah, we did all this... I think we did everything.

This excerpt looks quite different from the one from the F-dyad, R and G. This dyads set their goal to finish exploring every page in the hypermedia. Such exploration may lead to intensive reading without deep reflection on the content. In contrast, R and G set their goal of exploration as to answer some specific questions, which may lead to deep reflection on the content to see whether the content answered their questions and whether it made sense. This S-dyad's focus was on task completion rather than on monitoring and evaluating their learning progress.

Other dyads in both conditions showed similar differences. The following excerpt displayed how another successful dyad from the F-hypermedia condition (N and V) planned their exploration strategy:

V: Yeah, the whole oxygen, carbon dioxide thing I am really not too sure about, I kind of thought we expelled carbon dioxide.
N: That's what I thought.
V: But I don't know if we push a button will it give us the answer?
N: Maybe... oh.

V: Oh it does, ok (Reading)
V: I don't think that answered the question.
N: Right, that didn't at all.
V: It just told us that we need cells to produce, cells use, that is it. It doesn't tell us anything about it.
V: Should we go back?
N: Can you click on the diaphragm?
N: Maybe if we go to "need for pump and vessels"

This example shows that both N and V were co-regulating to make decision on which link to click to understand how oxygen and carbon dioxide get in and out of the body. As the best F-dyad, they tended to connect their prior knowledge with the content they read (e.g., V mentioned "I thought we just expelled carbon dioxide"). It is notable that both N and V were questioning themselves as to whether the content answered their questions. Such reflection may help them to make sense of the content they read and monitor their progress toward learning goals. In contrast, the following excerpt showed that another dyad in the S-hypermedia condition (M and S) used a different strategy to plan their exploration:

S: So what exactly are we doing?
M: I don't know, I guess we just go back. I guess we just looked at each one of the things.
S: Oh, ok...
S: What about the oxygen with the... (reading). We missed all of that.
M: Oh yeah.

The above example showed that M and S did not come up with their own question to guide their exploration. Like the other dyad in the S-condition, M and S selected links by judging what they might have missed. Their exploration goal was to complete exploring the hypermedia instead of making meaning of it. There was little evidence of how they monitored and evaluated their learning progress and strategy use from this excerpt.

To summarize, dyads across conditions used different strategies in their co-regulated learning. Specifically, dyads in the F-condition used specific-question driven strategy to set up a goal for their exploration whereas dyads in the S-condition tend to set their major goal as to complete exploring the hypermedia. Such differences in goals lead to consequential differences in the monitoring and evaluation processes in co-regulated learning.

Discussion

Because of the small sample size, we must consider this to be an exploratory study. Nonetheless, the results of this study suggest that the underlying conceptual representation affects students' collaborative learning and the F-hypermedia promoted the use of more effective co-regulation strategies than the S-hypermedia did. They suggest that dyads using the F-hypermedia focused on understanding whereas dyads using the S-hypermedia were focused on completing the task. The dyads in the F-hypermedia condition used specific question-driven strategies when planning their exploration whereas the dyads in the S-condition applied task completion-driven strategies. Consequently, the dyads in the F-hypermedia condition checked their learning progress more often than the dyads in the S-hypermedia condition. The S-hypermedia dyads did more verbatim reading and, consequently, engaged in less constructive processing than the F-hypermedia dyads. Students in the F-hypermedia condition made greater improvement in understanding nonsalient phenomena than those in the S-hypermedia condition. This is particularly important because these nonsalient micro-level phenomena are key to understanding respiration at the cellular level. In prior research, novices never mentioned these aspects of the system (Hmelo-Silver et al., 2007).

Because the content was controlled across both versions of hypermedia, we argue that it was the alternative conceptual representations underlying the hypermedia that made such differences. It is important for students to be aware of their own thinking and to use such metacognitive knowledge to guide their learning plans and selection of learning strategies. Our findings suggest exploratory study indicate that the function-oriented conceptual representation helped problematize the content, encouraging students to set and monitor their learning goals as they explored the hypermedia. In addition, the functional emphasis can rock the cognitive boat (to paraphrase Reiser, 2004) and encourage students to engage in setting more specific learning goals that can be evaluated and to engage in greater constructive processing, which is important for learning (Chi, Siler, Jeong, Yamaguchi, & Hausman, 2001). More research is needed to better understand how different hypermedia organization affects how students regulate their learning.

Acknowledgments This research was funded by an NSF CAREER grant # 0133533 to the second author. Conclusions or recommendations expressed in this chapter are those of the authors and do not necessarily reflect the views of the National Science Foundation.

References

Azevedo, R., Cromley, J. G., & Seibert, D. (2004a). Does adaptive scaffolding facilitate students' ability to regulate their learning with hypermedia? *Contemporary Educational Psychology, 29*, 344–370.

Azevedo, R., Moos, D. C., Greene, J. A., Winters, F. I., & Cromley, J. C. (2008). Why is externally-regulated learning more effective than self-regulated learning with hypermedia? *Educational Technology Research and Development, 56*, 45–72.

Azevedo, R., Winters, F. I., & Moos, D. C. (2004b). Can students collaboratively use hypermedia to learn about science? The dynamics of self- and other-regulatory processes in an ecology classroom. *Journal of Educational Computing Research, 31*(3), 215–245.

Bechtel, W., & Abrahamson, A. (2005). Explanation: A mechanist alternative. *Studies in the History and Philosophy of Biological and Biomedical Sciences, 36*, 421–441.

Chi, M. T. H., Siler, S. A., Jeong, H., Yamaguchi, T., & Hausman, R. G. (2001). Learning from human tutoring. *Cognitive Science, 25*, 471–533.

Cho, Y. (1995). The nature of learner's cognitive processes in learner- and program-controlled hypertext learning environments. *UMI, DAI-A, 56/06*, 2207. Publication Number, AAT 9534749.

Collins, A., Brown, J. S., & Newman, S. E. (1989). Cognitive apprenticeship: Teaching the crafts of reading, writing, and mathematics. In L. B. Resnick (Ed.), *Knowing, learning, and instruction: Essays in honor of Robert Glaser* pp. 453–494. Hillsdale, NJ: Lawrence Erlbaum Associates.

Collins, A., & Ferguson, W. (1993). Epistemic forms and epistemic games: Structures and strategies to guide inquiry. *Educational Psychologist, 28*, 25–42.

Davis, R., Shrobe, H., & Szolovits, P. (1993). What is a knowledge representation? *AI Magazine, 14*, 17–33.

Dillenbourg, P. (1999). What do you mean by collaborative learning? In P. Dillenbourg (Ed). *Collaborative-learning: Cognitive and Computational Approaches* pp. 1–19. Oxford: Elsevier.

Egan, D., & Schwartz, B. (1979). Chunking in recall of symbolic drawings. *Memory and Cognition, 7*, 149–158.

Glaser, R. (1976). Components of a psychology of instruction: Towards a science of design. *Review of Educational Research, 46*, 1–24.

Goel, A., Gomez de Silva Garza, A., Grue, N., Murdock, J., Recker, M., & Govinderaj, T. (1996). Towards designing learning environments-I: Exploring how devices work. In C. Fraisson, G. Gauthier, & A. Lesgold (Eds.), *Intelligent Tutoring Systems: Lecture notes in computer science*. New York: Springer.

Hegarty, M., Narayanan, N. H., & Freitas, P. (2002). Understanding machines from multimedia and hypermedia presentations. In J. Otero, J. A. Leon, & A. C. Graesser (Eds.), *The psychology of science text comprehension*. NJ, Mahwah: Lawrence Erlbaum associates.

Hickey, D. T., & McCaslin, M. (2001). A comparative sociocultural analysis of context and motivation. In E. Volet (Ed.), *Motivation in learning contexts: Theoretical advances and methodological implications* pp. 33–55. Amsterdam: Elsevier Science Ltd.

Hmelo, C. E., Holton, D., & Kolodner, J. L. (2000). Designing to learn about complex systems. *Journal of the Learning Sciences, 9*, 247–298.

Hmelo-Silver, C. E. (2004). Problem-based learning: What and how do students learn? *Educational Psychology Review, 16*, 235–266.

Hmelo-Silver, C. E. (2006). Design principles for scaffolding technology-based inquiry. In A. M. O'Donnell, C. E. Hmelo-Silver, & G. Erkens(Eds.), Collaborative reasoning, learning and technology pp. 147–170. Mahwah, NJ: Erlbaum.

Hmelo-Silver, C. E., & Azevedo, R. (2006). Understanding complex systems: Some core challenges. *Journal of the Learning Sciences, 15*, 53–61.

Hmelo-Silver, C. E., Marathe, S., & Liu, L. (2007). Fish swim, rocks sit, and lungs breathe: Expert-novice understanding of complex systems. *Journal of the Learning Sciences, 16*, 307–331.

Hmelo-Silver, C. E., & Pfeffer, M. G. (2004). Comparing expert and novice understanding of a complex system from the perspective of structures, behaviors, and functions. *Cognitive Science, 28*, 127–138.

Jacobson, M. J., & Archodidou, A. (2000). The design of hypermedia tools for learning: Fostering conceptual change and transfer of complex scientific knowledge. *Journal of the Learning Science, 9*, 145–199.

Jonassen, D. H. (1986). Hypertext principles for text and courseware design. *Educational Psychologist, 21*, 269–292.

Karoly, P. (1993). Mechanisms of self-regulation: A system review. *Annual Review of Psychology, 44*, 23–52.

Liu, L., Hmelo-Silver, C. E., & Marathe, S. (2005a, April). *Function before form: An alternative approach to learning about complex systems*. Paper presented at annual meeting of the American Educational Research Association. Montreal CA.

Liu, L., Hmelo-Silver, C. E., & Marathe, S. (2005b). How representation matters: Comparing collaborative learning with alternative versions of hypermedia. In T. Koschmann, D. D. Suthers, & T. -W. Chan (Eds.), *Proceedings of CSCL 2005*, pp. 398–402. Mahwah NJ: Erlbaum.

McManus, W., & Segner, R. (1991). *Hypermedia in Construction Education*. Paper presented at the Associated Schools of Construction conference. Retrieved Aug 1, 2003,from http://asceditor.unl.edu/archives/1991/McManus91.htm

Newton, D. P., & Newton, L. D. (2000). Do teachers support causal understanding through their discourse when teaching primary science*? British Educational Research Journal*, *26*, 599–613.

Novick, L. R., & Hmelo, C. E. (1994). Transferring symbolic representations across nonisomorphic problems. *Journal of Experimental Psychology: Learning, Memory, and Cognition*, *20*, 1296–1321.

Nunes, J., & Fowell, S. P. (1996). Hypermedia as an experimental learning tool: A theoretical model. *Information Research New*, *6*, 15–27.

O'Donnell, A. M., & O'Kelly, J. O. (1994). Learning from peers: Beyond the rhetoric of positive results. *Educational Psychology Review*, *6*, 321–349.

Park, O. (1991). Hypermedia: Functional features and research issues. *Educational Technology*, *31*, 24–31.

Perkins, D. N. (1993). An *apple for education: Teaching and learning for understanding. Glassboro, NJ: The Educational Press Association of America.*

Pintrich, P. R., & Zusho, A. (2002). The development of academic self-regulation The role of cognitive and motivational factors. In A. Wigfield & J. Eccles (Eds.), *The development of achievement motivation* pp. 250–279. San Diego, CA: Academic Press.

Reiser, B. J. (2004). Scaffolding complex learning: The mechanisms of structuring and problematizing student work. *Journal of the Learning Sciences*, *13*, 273–304.

Ruiz-Primo, M. A., & Shavelson, R. J. (1996). Problems and issues in the sue of concept maps in science assessment. *Journal of Research in Science Teaching*, *33*, 569–600.

Schmitt, M. C., & Newby, T. J. (1986). Metacognition: Relevance to instructional design. *Journal of Instructional Development*, *9*, 29–33.

Schoenfeld, A. H. (1987). What's all the fuss about metacognition? In A. H. Schoenfeld (Ed.), *Cognitive science and mathematics education* (pp. 189–215). Hillsdale, NJ: Lawrence Erlbaum Associates.

Shapiro, A., & Niederhauser, D. (2004). Learning from hypertext: Research issues and findings. In D. H. Jonassen (Ed.), *Handbook of Research for Education Communications and Technology* (2nd ed). Mahwah, NJ: Lawrence Erlbaum Associates.

Suthers, D. D., & Hundhausen, C. D. (2003). An experimental study of the effects of representational guidance on collaborative learning processes. *Journal of the Learning Sciences*, *12*, 183–218.

Weinstein, C. E., & Mayer, R. E. (1986). The teaching of learning strategies. In M. C. Wittrock (Ed.), *Handbook of research on teaching* pp. 315–327. New York: Macmillan.

Winne, P. H. (2001). Self-regulated learning viewed from models of information processing. In B. J. Zimmerman & D. H. Schunk (Eds.), *Self-regulated learning and academic achievement: Theoretical perspectives* 2nd ed, pp. 153–189. Hillsdale, NJ: Erlbaum.

Chapter 18
Virtual Worlds for Young People in a Program Context: Lessons from Four Case Studies

Marina Umaschi Bers, Laura Beals, Clement Chau, Keiko Satoh, and Nauman Khan

Developmental Technologies Research Group, Eliot Pearson Department of Child Development, Tufts University, Medford, MA, USA

Introduction

In 2007 a report by the Pew Internet and American Life Project (Lenhart, Madden, Macgill, & Smith, 2007) revealed that 93% of Americans between the ages of 12 and 17 years are Internet users "and more of them than ever are treating is as a venue for social interaction—a place where they can share creations, tell stories, and interact with others" (p. i). In addition, the report found that 55% of online teens (ages 12–17 years) have a profile on a social networking site (e.g., Facebook or MySpace).

Prescott (2007) reported that of the five most frequented virtual worlds sites, four of them were youth focused[1] and furthermore, were ranked higher than adult-oriented equivalents such as *Second Life* and *World of Warcraft*. The Association of Virtual Worlds published a report entitled "The Blue Book: A Consumer Guide to Virtual Worlds" (Association of Virtual Worlds, 2008, August) in which descriptions, links, and categories for hundreds of virtual worlds are provided. A count of these worlds reveals that approximately 110 are categorized as for kids, 115 for tweens, and 140 for teens (some worlds, however, are designed for multiple age groups).

As examples of the increasing popularity of virtual worlds for children, the site Webkinz increased its visits by 1141% in a year (Prescott, 2007), and Club Penguin doubled in size, from 1.9 million to 4.7 million visitors (Shore, 2008). This popularity, however, for many of the sites is tied with commercial endeavors—for example, Club Penguin was acquired by Disney for $350 million (Barnes, 2007) and US retail sales of the Webkinz dolls in 2006 earned $45 million (Tiwari, 2007). As another

M.U. Bers (✉)
Developmental Technologies Research Group, Eliot Pearson Department of Child Development, Tufts University, Medford, MA, USA
e-mail: marina.bers@tufts.edu

[1] According to the report, the top five sites are Runescape, Webkinz, Neopets, Gaiaonline.com, and Club Penguin.

M.S. Khine, I.M. Saleh (eds.), *New Science of Learning*,
DOI 10.1007/978-1-4419-5716-0_18,

example, BarbieGirls.com, by Mattel, registered 4 million users in the first 3 months after its launch, with an average of 45,000 new girls a day.

From another perspective, KZERO Research, a UK-based company aiming to understand "the marketing dynamics relating to virtual worlds," examined the current state of virtual worlds by looking at the total registered accounts as of quarter two of 2008 and found how prevalent virtual worlds for youth are—the largest virtual world for adults (over age 20), has 13 million registered users, while the largest for children or youth has 90 million users (and there are six additional worlds with between 17 and 45 million users for people under 20 years). For a figure showing the year/month of the launch of the virtual world, its current size, and worlds that are currently in development, visit: http://www.kzero.co.uk/blog/wp-content/uploads/2008/05/virtual-world-numbers-q2-2008.jpg. As a final indication of the prevalence of virtual worlds for youth, eMarketer reports that 24% of the 34.3 million US child and teen Internet users will visit virtual worlds once a month in 2007, up to 34% in 2008 and by 2011, 53% (Williamson, 2008).

However, there are also popular virtual worlds with a less commercially focused approach. For example, ZulaWorld.com (though still based on the children's TV show Zula Patrol) focuses around math, science, and technology, and the Panwapa virtual world, immerses children "in a unique and novel exploration of self, community and cultures from around the world" in order to "empower a new generation of children, ages four to seven, to be responsible global citizens" (from the website). Other virtual worlds such as Quest Atlantis (Barab, Thomas, Dodge, Carteaux, & Tuzun, 2005), River City (Dede, Ketelhut, Clarke, Nelson, & Bowman, 2005; Dede, Nelson, Ketelhut, Clarke, & Bowman, 2004), Second Life in Education (http://sleducation.wikispaces.com/), MOOSE Crossing (Bruckman, 1996), Whyville (http://www.whyville.net/smmk/nice), 3DLearn (http://www.3dlearn.com/), Jumpstart (http://www.jumpstart.com/), and Zora (Bers, Chau, Satoh, & Beals, 2007; Bers, Gonzalez-Heydrich, Raches, & DeMaso, 2001a), to name just a few, are designed by researchers with the hope of engaging young people in learning and personal and social developments.

This chapter draws from experience in designing and evaluating the Zora virtual world for youth (Bers, 2001). Zora has been used since 1999 with several very different populations of young people, including those with end-stage renal disease undergoing dialysis treatment (Bers, Gonzalez-Heydrich, & DeMaso, 2003; Bers, Gonzalez-Heydrich, & DeMaso, 2001b), multicultural groups (Bers, 2008a; Bers & Chau, 2006), freshman in college (Bers, 2008a), posttransplant pediatric patients (Bers et al., 2007; Satoh, Beals, Chau, & Bers, 2007; Satoh, Blume, DeMaso, Gonzalez-Heydrich, & Bers, 2008), and participants in national and international after-school computer-based learning centers (Beals & Bers, under review).

Based on the differences of the sites and experiences, the chapter provides guidelines for understanding how to design and evaluate intervention programs that use virtual worlds for children by taking into consideration eight different dimensions: (1) curriculum, (2) mentoring model, (3) diversity, (4) project scale, (5) contact with participants, (6) type of assessment, (7) access environment, and (8) institutional context of usage.

First, we will describe the Zora virtual world and its design based on the Positive Technological Development framework (Bers, 2006, 2007). Then we will present four different case studies in which Zora was used which highlight different approaches to the eight dimensions presented earlier.

Zora: A Constructionist Multiuser Virtual Environment

Zora is a multiuser virtual environment that was first developed as part of Bers' doctoral work at the MIT Media Lab. The overarching goal of Zora is to provide a safe space for youth to explore issues of identity (Bers, 2001). The name Zora was inspired by one of the imaginary cities described by Italo Calvino: "This city is like a honeycomb in whose cells each of us can place the things we want to remember...So the world's most wise people are those who know Zora" (Calvino, 1972). The hope is that by engaging with Zora, children will also become wiser by knowing who they are.

Zora is designed upon constructionist learning principles that promote children's creation of their own personally meaningful objects and sharing them in a community (Papert, 1980). Constructionism, as both a theory of learning and a strategy for education, offers the framework for developing a technology-rich design-based learning environment in which children learn by making, creating, programming, and communicating (Resnick, Bruckman, & Martin, 1996). Constructionism is rooted in Piaget's constructivism, in which learning is best characterized as an individual cognitive process given a social and cultural context. However, while Piaget's theory was developed to explain how knowledge is constructed in our heads. Constructionism, developed by Papert, pays particular attention to the role of constructions in the world as a support for those in the head. Zora provides easy-to-use tools for children to design and inhabit a virtual city (see Fig. 18.1).

Users can populate the virtual city by making their own virtual places and interactive creations, including 3D objects, characters, message boards, and signs, as well as movies and sounds. Although Zora provides tools for creating objects, the focus is not on the aesthetics of the 3D objects, but on the meanings assigned to them. Thus, Zora encourages users to create stories and values for every object they make in the world. Upon logging into Zora, users encounter an initial blank 3D world. Their task is to create the virtual world's public and private spaces and populate it with interactive objects. While using building tools in Zora, users learn basic computer programming principles as well as gain technological fluency (Barron, 2004).

One of the design goals of Zora is to support children in their thinking about who they are, who they want to become and what kind of community they want to be part of. For this purpose, Zora provides opportunities for users to create models of identification and counteridentification (called heroes and villains in the virtual world), as well as personal and moral values linked to objects and a collaborative values dictionary. Furthermore, the community values dictionary prompts users to share

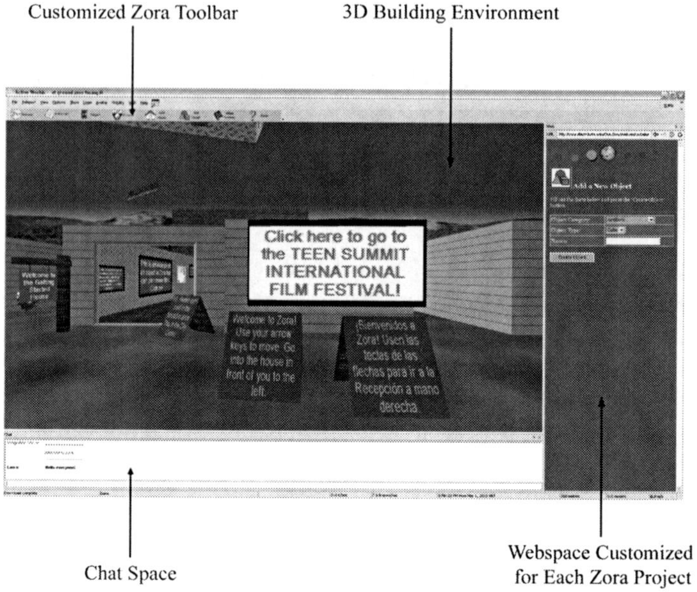

Fig. 18.1 The Zora virtual world

values and their multiple definitions, which are seen as personally meaningful as well as important to the community. The dictionary also reinforces discussions among community members about contrasting points of view for similar value entries or definitions (Bers & Chau, 2006).

In addition to making virtual objects and narratives, Zora provides a real-time chat system for participants to communicate with each other while navigating throughout the virtual world. The environment is purposefully designed to provide both synchronous and asynchronous modes of communication in order to accommodate different personalities and time zones, as well as to afford participants a chance to self-reflect on their narratives, values, and stories.

While the constructionist philosophy of learning informed the design of Zora as an environment for children to create their own virtual city, a most recently developed educational paradigm, computer-supported collaborative learning (CSCL), inspired the need to incorporate in Zora tools for community building and community scaffolding of learning (Koschmann & Kolodner, 1997; Preece, 2001). For example, the creation of theme houses and public spaces give grounds to develop social connections with others who share similar interests.

CSCL shifts the process of cognition as residing within the head of one individual, which was rooted in Piaget's theories, to the view of learning as a social process, which is rooted on Vygostskian's theory, and of cognition as situated within a particular community of learning or practice (Lave & Wenger, 1991). Thus the focus is on creating social environments in which constructionist types of learning activities using technologies can happen.

From a pedagogical perspective, Zora affords opportunities for developing educational interventions in which the curriculum can be emergent or explicit based on the needs and experiences of the population using Zora. For example, in terms of explicit curriculum, we have developed a system that provides online modules with activities aimed at exploring particular powerful ideas. The curricular modules and activities are designed by the researchers or practitioners running the project and can be setup on the basis of the population needs as well as the project goals. For example, each activity can be specified to be for individual or groups, for synchronous or asynchronous participation, for learning new content or engaging in social interactions. As users start to engage with the activities, the system automatically checks for status, updates the completed activities, and displays new ones based on what has been done previously. A rewards mechanism is also established to motivate youth to complete the activities. Each activity is associated with Zora-based online questionnaires to assess participant's learning as well as the activity itself.

From a technical perspective, the first version of Zora was developed in 1999 using the Microsoft Virtual Worlds development platform (Bers, 2001). The current version of Zora used in the *Active Citizenship through Technologies* (ACT) program has been revised and developed using the ActiveWorlds platform (Satoh, Mc Vey, Grogan, & Bers, 2006). This platform for developing educational multiuser environments is used by educational research projects such as Quest Atlantis (Barab et al., 2005) and River City (Nelson, Ketelhut, Clarke, Bowman, & Dede, 2005). Zora has similarities with the growingly popular Second Life® virtual world (Ondrejka, 2004) in presenting a 3D environment for users to develop a virtual community. However, unlike Second Life©, Zora is a secured and password-protected world in which only youth engaged with a particular research program can view the world and contribute to it. This provides a secure environment for children who are sharing emotionally charged personal situations (such as having a transplant or expressing personal opinions about political life) and for researchers who can have full access to the data.

Each action performed by the participants in Zora is logged into a database and analyzed with a customized log parser. The log parser is divided into four subcomponents: population demographics, search data, reports, and graphs. A search component provides access to various types of information about users, such as conversations, objects, number of times they logged into Zora, and the time spent on Zora, while also being able to filter for date ranges. Figure 18.2 displays a snapshot of the search page as well as a sample result page for objects created by a user. This information is not only displayed as a web page but it is also available in the form of an Excel worksheet. This facilitates researchers to perform further analysis on this data. The graphs component extends the results to a graphical format. Figure 18.3 shows the snapshot for the graph page and the data displayed in a graph. The reports component generates the reports for objects and conversations over time in the form of pdf documents.

From a theoretical perspective, Zora is designed upon Bers' Positive Technological Development (PTD) framework that addresses the question "how can we

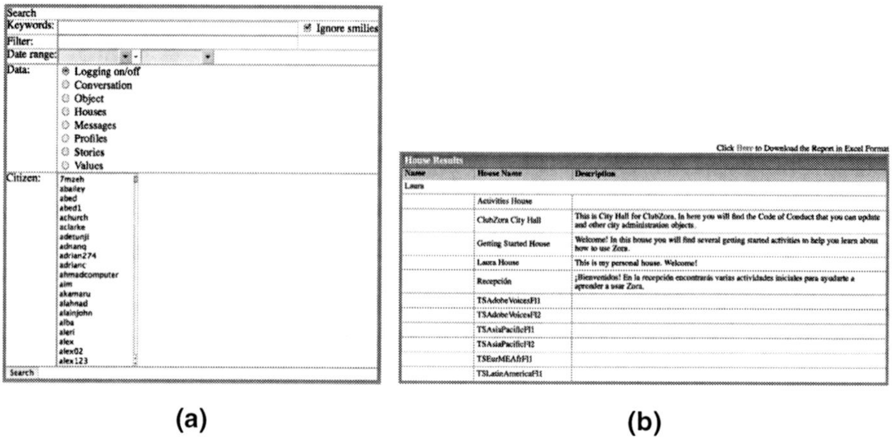

Fig. 18.2 (**a**) Log parser search page. (**b**) Results for query

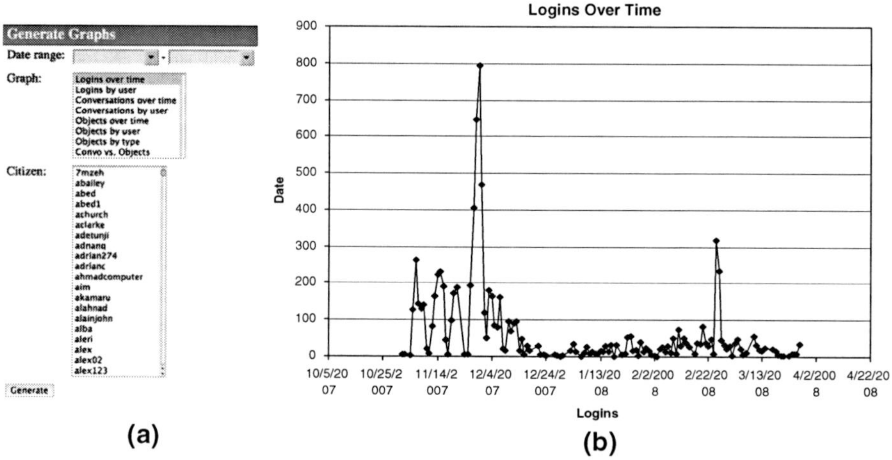

Fig. 18.3 (**a**) Log parser graphs page. (**b**) A sample graph of login time of all users over a time period

develop interventions to help children use technology in effective ways to learn new things, to express themselves in creative ways, to better communicate, to take care of themselves and each other, and to contribute in positive ways to self and society?" (Bers, 2006; 2008c). Informed by the strengths and assets of young people and by what goes right in children's use of technology, PTD focuses on supporting them in developing positive attitudes, predispositions, and skills for using technology with the goal of becoming contributors to their own personal growth and to society (Bers, 2008a, b).

In the following sections, we present four different case studies in which Zora was used since 1999: with a diverse group of children in a multicultural summer camp, with incoming freshman at a northeastern university, with transplant patients at Children's Hospital Boston, and with children in after school programs all over the world. By presenting each of the case studies, we focus on eight different dimensions of intervention programs that use virtual worlds specifically aimed for children's development and education: (1) curriculum, (2) mentoring model, (3) diversity, (4) project scale, (5) type of contact with participants, (6) type of assessment and evaluation, (7) access environment, and (8) institutional context of usage.

Case Study 1: Multicultural Summer Camp

This summer camp was held in a university lab during 3 weeks in 1999. Participants in the Zora summer camp were recruited through postings in different e-mailing lists. Interested candidates had to complete an application. The goal was to obtain a self-selected highly motivated group. It was made explicit to them that the goals of the workshop were "learning about computers as well as exploring issues about youth identity."

The selection process favored diverse cultural and religious backgrounds, gender balance, as well as the quality of the submitted biographies. Previous computer experience was not a factor for selection, but participants were required to have access to e-mail. There was a diverse group of 11 kids between ages of 11- and 15-years-old to participate in the summer camp, which was offered for free. Selecting a diverse population served two purposes. First, the educational goal of conveying to participants that to explore issues of identity and values, different voices need to be represented. Second, to observe if diversity would generate interesting discussions when conflict would surface, and how motivated participants would navigate those conflicts.

Eight of the participants came to the university lab and three of them worked remotely from their homes and met face-to-face only on the first and last days of the summer camp. An older child, Elisa, served as a mentor and helped to informally coordinate the activities. Elisa was only 1 year older than the oldest of the participants, but she had good social and technical skills and had had previous experience with Zora. Her role in the workshop was to mediate between the kids and the researcher and act as a peer mentor.

The workshop followed a flexible syllabus that helped Elisa guide the online activities. Kids worked on their virtual city at their own pace regardless of the activities planned in the syllabus. As the workshop evolved, kids proposed new activities. For example, they discussed and voted on rules to organize community life. Kids working remotely were able to connect during any other day and time, as well as during the workshop hours.

Overall, kids created a total of 33 virtual places divided into 12 personal homes and 19 public temples, such as the Jewish temple, the Sports arena, the Video game room, and the Dinosaur hall, and two community centers, the City hall and the Junk shop. Participants created an average of two temples and one personal home per person, with the exception of one of the kids working at home who created 10 virtual places but did not finish any of them. The Zora virtual homes evolved and dynamically changed as participant's developed different ways of understanding their identity through interactions with others community members. For example, the objects created by users became "tangible" representations of the multiple aspects of their identities. The use of storytelling helped kids to think about the personal and moral values associated with the self. (Bers, 2001).

During the last day of the workshop, every participant left a legacy with advice for future Zora users in the entrance to the city. Legacies were grouped into three categories. Those giving advice about technical issues, about how to design expressive artifacts and places, and about how to handle social issues in the community. For example, participants shared their differing points of view about death penalty, and then debated about the punishment they would implement in their virtual city.

Although Zora's design based on PTD enabled the participants to explore issues of self, Zora's design was not enough to make a successful learning experience. Other factors also had a positive influence and shaped the way the experience was conducted and the evaluation was made possible. These factors are organized in terms of the eight dimensions mentioned earlier.

(1) *Curriculum.* The curriculum used in the workshop focused exclusively on a child-centered approach to learning. This worked well because the participants were a highly motivated and self-selected group already thinking about issues of identity. The presence of a flexible, emergent curriculum provided Elisa, the mentor, with guidelines for possible activities based on children's interests. This curriculum was solely based on the possibilities for making objects and narratives afforded by Zora. For example, children could create personal and public spaces with objects and stories, values and definitions, models of identification ad counter identification. They could also engage in discussions about the social organization of their virtual city and the needed public spaces.

(2) *Mentoring model.* One of the goals of this work was to observe to what extent a virtual world with design features informed by theories of identity formation and moral development, such as Zora, would engage kids in exploration of identity and personal and moral values. Because the presence of an adult with background knowledge about this area and who would behave as coach or guide would bias the results, it was consciously avoided (Bers, 2001). Thus, the role of Elisa, the mentor, was conceptualized as someone of similar age who would work as a peer and who would also explore issues of identity and values while participating in the workshop. This model worked well in this experience in part because of the personality of Elisa, and in part because of the commitment of the participants. However, if the focus of the experience were to switch from a child-centered model of learning, such as the one taken in this case study,

to one where an adult has a more predominant role, new questions need to be answered. Should the adult indoctrinate learners about personal and moral values as the bag of virtues approach proposes (Chazan, 1985) Or should he or she be a neutral facilitator who does not interfere or reference personal or external values, but helps young people clarify their own values and engage in the valuation process such as "Values Clarification" argues for (Raths, Harmin, & Simon, 1978) For example, should the facilitator seed the Zora virtual city with particularly controversial cases to foster debate and be an advocate of moral content and a model of moral behavior or only a process facilitator? When and how a facilitator should intervene if participants decide to take an intolerant stance about a particular social, religious or racial group?

(3) *Diversity*. Since the goals for this study were to expose children to an environment in which conflict would emerge and interesting discussions about identity would happen, even more important than the curriculum was having a self-selected, highly motivated, and diverse group to work with, as was the case of the summer participants, who were screened during the application process. Although it was a diverse group in terms of ethnic, racial, religious, and socioeconomic composition, all participants spoke English and were first- or second-generation American. Thus, there all shared core characteristics and values, expectations, and demands, which made the work possible, even with such a diverse group.

(4) *Project scale*. The experience presented here is a small-scale intervention with only 11 participants and a mentor. Thus, there were no technological problems resulting from scalability, neither major issues in terms of self-organization and management of the experience. The small scale of the study allowed participants to be in control of most of the decisions regarding the virtual community without the need of institutionalization of policies. Since the virtual community was small, it was relatively easy for participants to reach consensus. What will happen when scaling up? What mechanisms need to be put in place?

(5) *Type of contact with participants*. Participants in the summer camp were self-selected, highly motivated, and went through an application process, namely, they all wanted to be there. Researchers had direct access to them and their families and were able to work with most of them face-to-face as well as online. This type of contact facilitated data collection via videotaped interviews and assured a 100% return rate in all questionnaires. Participants felt lucky to have been chosen to participate in Zora and were happy to attend the summer camp and to contribute to the research at the time this study was done in 1999, virtual worlds were not as popular as today.

(6) *Assessment*. In terms of evaluating the experience, the ethnographic approach with a natural observation method, analysis of system logs, pre- and postquestionnaires and a final extended personal interview was used. In order to avoid what Papert calls "technocentric questions," the evaluation was centered on what young people did with Zora and not what Zora did to them (Papert, 1987).

The topic of identity and values in education is controversial for a number of reasons. One has been that it is not easy to define what needs to be learned and how to evaluate the learning experience. A narrow definition of research questions and methods is hard to achieve, not to mention clear measures of success and failure. Thus the goal of this study was to show a range of fruitful possibilities with virtual environments such as Zora. However, this work only provided a window into children's thinking about identity and values and many questions are still unanswered: will the young people that participated in this experience carry their explorations of identity and values into the rest of their lives? Will the learning transfer to other contexts? How does the online experience compare with face-to-face only workshops? These questions are hard to answer and will require a different methodological approach.

(7) *Access environment*. The decision to use Zora in the context of an immersive summer workshop held at a university lab, instead of in a classroom or with all of the participants logging in from home was based on a reality. Zora makes special demands on time and technological infrastructure that were not always available in schools and homes in a reliable way back in 1999, when the workshop was held. As computers become cheaper and bandwidth for network became bigger, this problem was solved and other case studies reported in this chapter took on some of these new challenges. In the experience described in this case study, all the participants met face-to-face at least twice, and most of them were physically copresent when logged in. When difficult issues of socio-dynamics arose online, it was common for kids to go off-line to resolve them. What is the right balance between online and off-line activities? What kinds of issues require face-to-face interaction? Did the learners continue the kinds of conversations about controversial issues that they initiated online once they were face-to-face?

(8) *Institutional context of usage*. During the experience reported in this case study, the institutional context was given by the university lab that housed the Zora summer camp. Thus, the rules and policies were set up by researches to easily accommodate the research agenda and the needs of the project. For example, on an occasion the children chose to create a stripping bar. This originated as a result of one of the kids finding an online cartoon character that when clicked on would strip. Although there were no body parts exposed, the gesture of the character was clear at conveying the idea of stripping. The stripping issue kept being discussed all along the Zora summer camp, maybe due to the fact that kids were in the teens, an age in which talking about sex is particularly appealing. However, the stripping bar was never created and stripping was outlawed by decision of the Zora community members. The process of discussing this issue had a clear educational value, but the outcome might have turned out different. Since the institutional context was the university lab, researchers had the freedom to let this issue evolve so it could be solved by the children themselves, as opposed by an outside power structure or policy. This might not be the case in different institutional contexts.

Case Study 2: ACT

The *ACT* program was a 3-day orientation program for new first year students at our university. The program was first held in 2006 and then again in 2007 (Bers, 2008a, b; Chau & Bers, 2007). A flyer was included in the new student orientation packet during the summer prior to their arrival and all incoming students were eligible to participate in the ACT program. The flyer included information about program activities and the goal of the program to use a virtual environment to *design a campus of the future*. Interested students completed an online application form that collected demographic information including gender, age, hometown, and previous experience with various computer software programs. These questions were intended to help screen and select a student group to represent a variety of technological backgrounds. Because of the nature of university orientation programs, participants were a self-selected group of students who were interested in what the program offered.

Each year, 18 participants attended the ACT program. Participants ranged in age from 17 to 19 (mean = 18), and included three female students during the first year and four female students during the second year. All participants were fluent in English. Based on the background questionnaire, participants of both years represented technical competences ranging from basic word processing tasks and e-mail communication to web programming and graphic design. During postinterview, we also learned that while none of the first year students were familiar with the Active Worlds platform, two students from the second year program had had experience with Active Worlds environments as a user prior to the program.

During the ACT program, participants were divided into two groups who logged onto the ACT Zora world from separate computer labs on campus. Two peer leaders who were upperclassmen at the university guided each participant group through the ACT curriculum to build a *campus of the future* in the Zora world. Over the 3 days, participants logged onto Zora for ACT activities for approximately 26.5 h, and spent approximately 27 h in noncomputer orientation activities such campus tour, orientation lectures, dining out, and social activities. All Zora activities were recorded automatically using the Zora log system, and peer leaders documented out-of-computer activities with photographs and field notes. A researcher who did not take part of the Zora curriculum was also present during computer and noncomputer activities to observe and take field notes.

Throughout the ACT program, students use the Zora virtual environment to create a virtual campus of the future in which they graphically display information gathered from their visits around campus and the surrounding neighborhoods in the form of 3D virtual exhibits. They create virtual public and private spaces populated by objects, stories, and discussion cases, and engage in both synchronous and asynchronous discussions about a variety of civic and campus topics. In reflection of discussion cases, the activities on Zora encourage students to choose and work on the issues that are most personally meaningful to them and then share their ideas and data with others. This is a central tenet to the constructionist approach to learning (Papert, 1980) that has been carried to virtual communities designed with the constructionist framework (Elliott & Bruckman, 2002). At the end of the intensive program, students make a short digital video or infomercial about their virtual campus to share with their peers, faculty, and administrators. Each year participants host an open house in the semester following the preorientation program where they show their infomercials to the campus community and invite campus faculty, staff, and students to visit the *campus of the future* that they created during ACT.

Participants introduce the audience to their virtual creation and to learn about their ideas for building a stronger community within the campus as well as strengthening the relationships between campus and surrounding neighborhoods. This open house demonstrates students' work in Zora and invites participation and discussions in the virtual environment from guests from the wider academic community. As such, the ACT project provided students with an experience during the program to grapple with issues dealing with their civic life as they think through the design of the *campus of the future*, and it also served as an object to think with and talk about during the open house discussion. Much like the previous case study, Zora afforded an opportunity for these students to reflect and introspect through design and community building; in addition, the ACT program empowered participants by providing them an innovative tool to share their ideas with other members and faculties of the university.

From the participants' point of view, the ACT program might have seemed focused solely on their technology-based activities, in their research, and their design. However, participants' experience in the program was influenced by the many other activities included in the overall intervention, some that took part in outside of the computer labs, student's interaction with each other online and off-line, and the design of the overall 3-day program.

(1) *Curriculum.* The ACT curriculum was focused on the specific theme of designing the *campus of the future*, and peer leaders created a list of activities for students to explore and to guide their building of the *campus*. However, these activities were designed to be broad so that participant engagement remained flexible and open-ended. For example, in one activity participants were asked to consider the role of the university and its students in the lives of youth in the community surrounding the university. Some participants took the task to learn about the various early childhood education programs in the community and research about the different roles that university students could take to help educate young children; other students created objects and collected news articles to reflect on how campus and community police to work together to prevent rowdy college students to disturb community neighbors. While the curriculum had in its design specific topics that we wanted students to explore through the medium of discussion cases (e.g., youth programs, safety, equity, and private–public funds), participants were able to create the *campus* to reflect particular issues that they were most interested and felt most connected.

(2) *Mentoring model.* Because the ACT program was designed as an orientation program and its goal to guide participants to think about their role in the campus community, mentoring was a crucial element. Besides providing technical support and guiding participants through the activities, peer leaders took part in designing the curriculum and activities outside of the computer labs. For the ACT program, including peer leaders in the design process was critical in fostering the mentoring relationship between the peer leaders and participants. Peer leaders had the opportunity to share their experience of being upperclassmen with participants through the activities and experience they designed. This included simple topics such as which ice-cream store to visit after a group dinner, to which administrative office to contact to most efficiently learn about what campus dining did with leftover food. The intention throughout was to provide a genuine experience for both the peer leaders and the participants through which to build a mentoring relationship that could last beyond the 3-day program. The success of the ACT mentoring model was evident in that over half of the first year participants volunteered, without prompt, to return as peer leaders for the second year.

(3) *Diversity.* One of the first tasks of the program was to decide on selecting a group of 18 participants. The issue of diversity for this program rested in technical competency, previous experience with civic or community related activities, and exposure to the community neighboring the university. Unlike the first case study where racial and ethnic diversity purposefully played a major role in the participant selection process, this study aimed to select students from a range of technological experience, and from different types of communities. We also intended to include in the sample two to three international students each year to align with the student population at the university. Initially, we hoped to recruit an approximately equal sample of male students and female students; however, the lack of female applicants caused us to remove gender as a recruitment criterion. Through our analysis of the Zora log and field notes, we found patterns of Zora interactions that could be attributed to the diversity of participants' background. For example, participants who reported to be less social media savvy, including one participant who had a difficult time keeping up with typing in the chat, tended to create and build more objects. Log data showed that they were more likely to take directions and take others' discussion and turn them into objects and 3D exhibits.

(4) *Project scale.* Because of the context of ACT as an orientation program, we were not able to test the technical issues related to scalability. This issue was addressed in a different case study. Instead, the ACT program was piloted to test whether the university could uptake this and could offer portions of the program for all students on campus for extended projects or as part of the typical student life experience offered. Only 18 participants attended each year of the program and thus we focused the scalability issue on whether students could find an interest in using the Zora interface as a tool to communicate and form a network, and at the same time use it as a space for sharing ideas about their campus life with administrators. The mentoring model was one of the outcome questions

remained to be addressed. While at the program participants had direct and face-to-face interaction with peer leaders. One key concern would be to translate the face-to-face experience into the virtual space.

(5) *Type of contact with participants.* Unlike the other case studies described in this chapter and similar studies conducted by other researchers using virtual environments (Barab et al., 2005; Dede et al., 2005), the ACT program included approximately equal time for online and for face-to-face interaction. This was purposeful in design to reflect the overall goal of the program and the curriculum. We felt that in order for a small group to form a peer network that could successfully work together collaborative in very brief amount of time and with hope that these relationships could extend beyond the program, face-to-face time was deemed equally as important. Face-to-face time allowed more channels through which participants could easily form relationships quickly. And thus, we designed the program to maximize the relationship building aspects of the program (e.g., social activities, learning about the community, and the campus environment) to face-to-face, out-of-lab activities while focusing participants on the building and the *campus of the future* aspects of the curriculum.

(6) *Assessment.* Assessing participants' experience included multiple modes of data collection. Participants' activities on Zora were recorded automatically through the Zora log system, and raw data were analyzed by using the Zora Log Parser. Participants also completed the *Positive Technological Development Questionnaire* (Bers, 2006) before, after, and during a 3-month follow-up to the program to assess changes in their attitudes toward technologies and their competencies and experience as a result of the program. Results relating to these data are reported in Chau and Bers (2007). In addition, participants were interviewed after the program and during the follow-up to reflect on their experience, including technical, curricular, and program aspects. One of the most pertinent level of assessment, although less systematic, was their presentation of the *campus of the future* to administrators and other faculties during the open house events. Their enthusiasm was evident that they felt empowered by the process. However, methodological questions remain as to how to assess their enthusiasm systematically, and how to evaluate the level to which their interests and engagement with the ACT program and the Zora interface influenced their civic life on campus.

(7) *Access environment.* The advantage of the ACT program being held at monitored and supported computer labs on campus added to the smooth operation of the various activities. While Zora could be installed on most student computers, the decision to hold the program at the labs was to ensure reliability and consistency and to secure support from the university IT staff. The environment posed a different sort of collaborative space than other case studies presented in this chapter. It was evident from the field notes that although most curricular activities were conducted in the Zora virtual environment, there were certain interactions that participants found to be more efficient, or more possible, via face-to-face discussion. Because participants only had a brief amount of time allowed, they were rushed to gain fluency over the Zora interface and

to design a virtual exhibit. Certain elements about the *campus* that participants felt were less pertinent, such as placement of specific virtual houses or signs, they decided to work out through face-to-face interactions. Although at the time participants and peer leaders felt that these were less pertinent as data, participants' experience would undoubtedly be different they were not afforded the same opportunity. It could be that they were not able to organize a well-planned virtual map and thus houses could not be easily accessed or objects may not be placed appropriately as exhibits. These were in reality issues for other case studies presented in this chapter but the ACT program enjoyed certain privileges due to the access model inherent in the program.

(8) *Institutional context of usage.* The ACT program presents a unique case for discussing the institutional context of usage. As a program offered for university students, the ACT program did not face the same level of challenge as other case studies in terms of language, consent, and content appropriateness. Participants were expected to have at least a minimal level of technical competence that was sufficient for operating the Zora interface. And because it was held at a monitored space, we received adequate IT support throughout the program. However, due to the nature of an orientation program and the open-ended curriculum, participants were free to interact with each other and with the virtual space as they would like in Zora. This posed a problem for several participants who got distracted away from the curriculum. One participant, in particular, took pride in leaving behind 3D objects in places where other participants were creating their exhibits. Because the peer leaders were his peers and they did not feel comfortable "disciplining" this participant, the lead researcher had to step in and talk with the participant. Even so, he did not feel obligated to collaborate with other students because his felt that his ideas were not appreciated. The researcher ended up giving him very specific tasks to work on that could contribute to the overall design of the *campus* yet unobtrusive to other participants' parts of the virtual world. This and other similar events might not have been as delicate of an issue if this was part of a graded course or part of a program where inappropriate participants could be disciplined.

Case Study 3: Transplant Program

Virtual communities have the potential to support the personal and social development of youth with lifelong medical risk or chronic illness who due to their condition, may not be able to attend school regularly and thus have difficulty forming peer relationships (Bers et al., 2003). This case study examines how we can leverage youths' interests in online technologies to create a psychoeducational intervention to promote the overall well-being and health of pediatric posttransplant youth. The goals of the pilot study were to:

1. Facilitate peer networking building amongst same age pediatric posttransplant patients.

2. Encourage medical adherence through activities and environment that foster discussion, sharing of experience, and informal content delivery.
3. Support posttransplant patient's psychosocial adjustment to lifestyle changes by creating a community.

This research project started in late August of 2006 and ran through the summer of 2007 in collaboration with pediatric psychiatrists and medical staff in the pediatric transplant program at Boston Children's Hospital. Posttransplant patients were first referred to us by doctors based on their age (11–15) and health status. Those eligible patients and their families were then contacted and invited to participate in the project. Most participants used Zora from their homes (all over New England, and some other further states) and at times, during hospitalizations (Bers et al., 2007; Satoh et al., 2007; 2008).

Fifty-four patients were originally contacted through phone calls and mailings; 31 verbally agreed to participate and 25 returned the necessary consent and assent forms. Of these 25, we could not provide Internet to 3 due to their remote locations. Thus we worked with a total group of 22. Of the 22 patients, three never logged in into Zora, so our user group was composed of 19 children; however, 22 returned questionnaires. Forty-five percent of the participants were females and the average age at the start of the program was 13.7 years. Participants engaged in weekly online activities for the duration of the study. While they were free to log on at any time, the group activities followed a semistructured curriculum aimed at sparking conversations about transplant experiences by encouraging them to create virtual spaces such as a Health Museum and a Pharmacy.

During the project, each user logged into Zora an average of 60 times and spent an average of 39 h logged into the program. This represents almost 7 h more online than we had anticipated, as we had planned weekly online activities for 32 h. Users created a total of 4,027 objects and made 75 virtual houses. For example, they created a Legislature House where they put recommendations for hospitals to ease the stay of the patients, such as "soft pillows," "beds with comfortable mattress pads on them. . .especially in the cardiac cathlab, where you have to lay flat for 6 h," and suggestions for schools to ease transitions after prolonged hospitalizations, "so kids don't have to tell stories so many times" (Bers et al., 2007).

During the course of the study, three individuals underwent cardiac retransplantation. Their participation from the hospital both before and after the transplant added an extra dimension to group discussions. It also provided an opportunity for some of the participants to meet for the first time face-to-face.

During interviews, users reported positively about their experience with the project, especially about being able to meet other children who had received a transplant as made evident by a feedback from a participant:

> I believe that taking part in Zora did give me inspiration. I only had a liver transplant, and I cannot have tunnel vision that there's only me, but there are a multitude of other kids that have gone through similar experiences as myself. They inspired me to help educate others about organ donation, because there are kids like us whose lives have been saved through the gift of organ donation

Preliminary analysis of the data collected from the questionnaires reveal little change in the participants' medical adherence over the course of the Zora intervention primarily due to the fact that the participants were already exhibiting satisfactory level of adherence prior to participation in the project. However, it became clear that patients with high severity in their illness were the ones who used Zora the most and that participating in Zora helped in ameliorating children's fear of follow-up clinic visits. Based on log analysis and quantitative responses to questionnaires, we have also observed positive impact in terms of peer networking. For example, a social worker described Zora as providing ("something that none of [the patient's] Doctors or medical professionals could—a connection to other kids who knew exactly how he was feeling and experience the unpleasant things that go along with transplant each and every day").

In terms of the eight dimensions presented earlier, they played out in the following way in this study.

(1) *Curriculum.* As in the case of the multicultural summer camp, the curriculum for the study with the posttransplant patients was designed to be one of emergent nature. It provided guidelines for the mentors to facilitate activities throughout the 32-week intervention period on Zora. Besides activities meant to foster peer networking, other activities centered on the issue of medical adherence as well as getting the participants to become more comfortable discussing their transplant experience. For instance, when the moderator, a doctoral student in child development, noticed that the participants were starting to share experiences about their transplant history, she would encourage them to document these in a "Transplant House." When they would start sharing information about medication, she would encourage them to build a "Pharmacy" so they might post and share responses to questions such as "how do you remember to take your medication?"

While both the Transplant House and Pharmacy were included in the original curriculum, the moderator waited until she could see the online conversation naturally directed itself to one of these topics at which point she knew that participants were ready to talk about sensitive issues pertaining to their health. The components of the curriculum were conceived as general guidelines, and new ideas for projects coming directly from the patients were encouraged and welcomed. For example, during Halloween, participants chose to collaboratively build a Halloween virtual house with objects representing their own fears.

(2) *Mentoring model.* The facilitator was a child development doctoral student with experience in child health and a clear agenda in terms of the research and learning goals of the project. The facilitator coordinated weekly Zora online activities but spent most of her time, helping participants with the technical aspect of the program, from installing it to supporting creative uses. Although the goal was for the facilitator to progressively move toward getting the participants to help each other, this happened very slowly as children were on different schedules. Our mentoring model was composed of a facilitator and

several mentors, older teenagers who had had a transplant were identified as potential mentors for the Zora community and were invited to join. For example, when participants discussed online their worries about going to college and not having their mothers around to help them to remember to take their medications, we asked one of the mentors, a college student with a transplant, to come online to talk about his own experience. The long-terms plan is to have the participants, as they become older, to assume the role of mentors.

(3) *Diversity*. The diversity among this project's participants is found in terms of the type of organ they received, the types of medical situations that lead them to require an organ transplant, the time since transplant, and the severity of their condition. There were 13 participants from the heart transplant program, 3 from liver, and 6 from renal. Diversity is also present based on their location: 12 participants were from Massachusetts, 1 from Florida, 1 from Maine, 3 from New Hampshire, 2 from New York, and 3 from Rhode Island. They all had in common that they underwent the transplant procedure and received posttransplant follow-up treatment at Children's Hospital Boston. Regardless of their original ailment or organ received, they all share the experience of going through organ transplantation and thus were all committed to a life-long regimen of medications and follow-up invasive interventions.

(4) *Project scale*. Although 22 posttransplant patients signed consent forms, only19 used Zora and half of them participated on a regular basis. Although at the beginning of the project, scale was not an issue and children were happy to meet for the first time other posttransplant children, as the project evolved, children wanted to have more participants, as it was difficult to have synchronous activities and conversations. Throughout the study, we had to hold our weekly online meetings at two different times to accommodate different participants' schedules. In addition, the voluntary nature of the project meant that we could not enforce regular attendance. Thus there might be as few as one or two participants attending planned activities. However, participants would be online at other times to work on individual projects. Due to the "constant on" nature of this project, participants were welcomed to sign on at any time; however, our data showed that in many cases, a participant who logs on and finds that only one or two other members are on would sign off. This may be due to the lack of a minimum critical mass to sustain participants' engagement. Other researchers (e.g., Preece, 2000) have shared similar experiences for the need to have a minimum critical mass when building a social network or a virtual community. To increase the probability of having a minimum critical mass to sustain a discourse, we are increasing the overall user or participant pool by bringing on board a new site, Tufts Floating Hospital for Children.

(5) *Types of contacts with participants*. Besides regular online contact with the regular participants, we have made home visits to a few local participants' homes to gain an understanding of the environment and context in which Zora was being used. We also arranged to meet some patients at the time of their regular

hospital's clinical visits or while they were hospitalized for treatment. However, depending on the time since transplant, the frequency of the participants' routine visits to the hospital varied; therefore we could not arrange to meet every participant and their family. For those participants whom we could not visit either at home or at the hospital, interviews were conducted over the phone. In addition, users created a monthly newsletter, *Transplant Times*, that reported on some of the key activities that took place on Zora. The newsletter was printed and mailed to all participants, their families and hospital staff. At the end of the year, we organized a Zora group who would represent the virtual community of transplant patients at the hospital's annual fund raising walk. Five of the participants and their families joined for the walk which gave us, and them, the chance to meet other face-to-face.

(6) *Assessment.* Data collection included automatically generated logs that provided qualitative and quantitative data of user's online activities, self-report instruments, and semistructured interviews, as well as spontaneous feedback. We collected three sets of data: (1) data pertaining to Zora use and participant feedback through semistructured face-to-face or telephone interviews, as well as Zora logs, and home visits to check for fidelity in the way the system was used by the patients and the ways it was intended to be used; (2) data pertaining to the positive development of youth through the use of technology collected through questionnaires; and (3) data about patient's medical adherence and medical history provided by parents, medical staff, and children's themselves.

(7) *Access environment.* The participants were expected to log online from their computers in their homes. Since not every family had access to a computer suitable for using Zora, we provided computers to three families and also Internet service to one family. During hospitalizations, patients were able to participate from the hospital.

(8) *Institutional context of usage.* Participants were requested to sign a Code of Conduct which outlines some basic rules of Internet behavior (such as not disclosing personal information online) prior to logging into Zora for the first time. This was requested by the hospital IRB to ensure the safety of the participants. The initial items on the Code of Conduct signed by the participants are created by the researchers but once on Zora, we encouraged discussions about appropriate and inappropriate behavior on Zora (such as resolving issues of participants building on top of, or within someone else's "property" without notification). Once consensus was reached as a community, new items were added to the Code in the Zora world. The institutional complexity of hospitals and the interdisciplinarity of this work makes it difficult to be in full control of crafting an innovative educational intervention that, although might not meet the scientific review criteria of the medical field in terms of statistical significance of results, shows clear qualitative signs of having a positive impact. For example, based on feedback from participating children, parents, and medical staff, the CICU Cardiac Clinical Research and Education Fund at Children's Hospital Boston decided to continue funding the program as a free pilot clinical service, after the NSF funding finished, while we secured new funding.

Case Study 4: ClubZora: An International Network

The ClubZora project began in November of 2007 in collaboration with The Intel Computer Clubhouse Network (http://www.computerclubhouse.org/), whose mission is "to provide a creative and safe after-school learning environment where young people from underserved communities work with adult mentors to explore their own ideas, develop skills, and build confidence in themselves through the use of technology" (http://www.computerclubhouse.org/about1.htm).

Began in 1993, as a collaboration between the Computer Museum (now the Boston Museum of Science) and the MIT Media Lab, the Clubhouses serve youth between the ages of 10 and 18. Each Clubhouse has a paid coordinator and volunteer adult mentors who share their experiences and serve as role models. There are currently over 100 Clubhouses around the world, serving over 20,000 youth. Some Clubhouse locations are stand-alone buildings while others are located within community-based organizations, such as YMCAs or Boys and Girls Clubs; some are urban, and some are rural. Thus, they attract a wide variety of youth from many different backgrounds and experiences. Though the members are all part of this organization, there is little opportunity for them to interact with members from other cities or countries or to build community.

The two main goals of ClubZora were (1) to provide a virtual space for Computer Clubhouse members around the world to build a strong community and (2) to help youth from different cultures learn about each other. During the project, participants created almost 52,000 objects, recorded over 35,000 lines of chat, and logged in over 9,800 times. For example, a two-story fully decorated personal house by an 18-year-old citizen from Guadalajara, Mexico; a multistory replica of her Clubhouse by a 17-year-old participant from Colombia; "Area 34," a multihouse compound for the "Commander" created by several members of a Clubhouse in California; a complex maze system by a Clubhouse Coordinator in Columbia; and a pyramid with an internal meeting room, made by a Clubhouse Mentor from Costa Rica. In addition, a special "Teen Summit" space was created to celebrate the organization's bi-yearly gathering of youth and Coordinators in Boston, MA. For this space, the metaphor was an "International Film Festival" where each region served by the Clubhouses had their own house in which to display videos created by the Clubhouse members for the Teen Summit.

(1) *Curriculum*. The curriculum designed for the project was based on the goals of the project—to encourage a community of users and to explore issues of diversity. Using existing classroom social studies curriculums and based on our work in other settings, we designed a set of activities for ClubZora around the theme of culture. In addition, these activities were designed to facilitate interaction amongst ClubZora citizens as members of the Clubhouse Network. Example topics at the beginning of the project included Music, Country, Zora Entertainment Center, Faith/Beliefs, Holiday Celebrations, Values Dictionary, "Heroes & Villains," "Myself & Technology," Art Museum, School/Academics, Sports, "Language & Communication," Vacation, and

Community Service. However, these planned activities were just ideas—as with the other projects, the activities were designed to be emergent (i.e., based on the interests of the citizens).

In addition, each activity was designed with three parts—the first part related to the individual youth, the second part to the Clubhouse, and the third part to the whole Zora virtual city. For example, if the activity was about music, for the first part, the citizen might create a playlist of his/her favorite songs and post on a message board in his/her house. For the second part, the members of the Clubhouse would work together to create a display of their favorite artists and albums. In the final part, participants would visit the Zora city center and create a display of the favorite artists from around the world, including links to radio stations that Clubhouses might have. As another example, if the topic was about food, in the first part, the participant might post his/her favorite dish and recipe on a bulletin board in his/her virtual personal house. In the second part, the members of the Clubhouse would work together in the virtual Clubhouse to make a display of food that represents their region of their country. In the final part, participants would visit the other virtual Clubhouses and vote for their favorite dishes in the global "Zora Kitchen."

Finally, we wanted to encourage collaboration in Zora, not competition, so we designed a recognition system to motivate members to work and learn with each other. Each part of the activity, as described above, was linked to a level of recognition for that citizen. If the individual activity (Part 1) was completed, he/she was recognized with a planet in their account. If the Clubhouse activity is completed (Part 2), he/she will be recognized with a sun. If the global activity is completed (Part 3), he/she will be recognized with a galaxy. Users cannot see each other's amount of recognition, though Tufts administrators can. This recognition system was intended to be used to celebrate the accomplishments of the group—for example, a Clubhouse who has strong completion of Part 2 will be able to request a new 3D model to be added into the object library.

Although our planned activities are important, we encouraged each member and each Clubhouse to create and post their own activities to have fun together and learn about each other's culture. In addition, we provided an online form through which members could suggest activities. The members' whose suggestions were implemented were recognized within the body of the activity for their contribution.

From a technical perspective, as originally designed, each week a new activity was released online within Zora, to be accessed from the "Activities" page in Zora, with the user alerted about the new activity on the Zora "Home" page (i.e., so that it would be seen upon log on). Because the activities were released in this way, it did not matter when a member started with Zora—they could catch up with the activities through his/her personalized account. However, participants were able to use Zora whenever they wanted and they did not have to just complete the activities—the Zora world was always open for exploring and building.

(2) *Mentoring model*. There were two types of mentors for this project (called "Zora Ambassadors"): Ambassadors who went to the local Clubhouses and met the youth face-to-face and online Ambassadors who worked with the Clubhouse members virtually through Zora only. Ambassadors to the local Clubhouses were undergraduate and graduate students who visited once a week to help install Zora, teach members how to use the software, and encourage them to use Zora. At the end of each session, they submitted field notes, based on a template, to the project coordinator.

The online ambassadors for this project were bilingual (Spanish and English) and were assigned one afternoon each to be online for approximately 3 h at a time. They were comprised of undergraduate students, an alumna of the Devtech research group, and a high school student doing community service credit in Miami. For the online ambassadors, their primary task was to interact and get to know the youth. They were to facilitate communication amongst the youth about topics that we as a research team have deemed important—for this particular project, these topics include culture (getting to know about each other), values, and identity. They were also to encourage the youth to complete the activities and feedback surveys.

In addition, online ambassadors were encouraged to work with "their" group of youth (i.e., those who were on Zora their scheduled day) to plan projects within Zora or to come up with new ideas harnessing the youth's interests (e.g., making a movie of Zora, building a new community structure, coming up with a survey for everyone to take, or writing a newspaper). While the above tasks were the focus of their work, part of being an online mentor was monitoring for the safety of members. This included monitoring for inappropriate language, bullying, aggressiveness, and violations of the Zora Code of Conduct, which all members had to agree to before enrolling in the project. At the conclusion of each session, mentors were required to submit a set of field notes, also based on a template, to the project coordinator.

(3) *Diversity*. The nature of the organization in which we were working—the Intel Computer Clubhouse Network, which has over 100 Clubhouses located around the world—meant that the ClubZora citizens would be diverse. We enrolled over 570 citizens, including over 430 youth and 130 Clubhouse Coordinators. The enrolled citizens represented 84 Clubhouses, 19 countries, and all 8 regions of the world that the Clubhouse Network serves, including the USA, Asia Pacific, Europe, the Middle East-Africa, and Latin America. Of the youth, 37% were female and 63% male; 77% selected English as their primary language and 23% Spanish; and the average age was 14 years (range: 8–19 years). In addition, it is part of the mission of the Clubhouse to work with youth in underserved communities, meaning that there was also a range of socioeconomic backgrounds.

(4) *Project scale*. The ClubZora project was a large-scale intervention that was run completely virtually. We were not able, per IRB requirements, to link the "real life" Clubhouse member to their virtual persona. Thus, all contact with the citizens was done over email or within Zora itself. In addition, there

were citizens from a diverse range of time zones—since the project headquarters were in Boston, MA (EST), this meant that it was difficult to be online at the same time as many of the participants. In addition, the Zora-specific content, such as the activities, were supported in two languages—Spanish and English.

(5) *Type of contact with participants.* As mentioned in previous sections, contact with the citizens was done completely virtually, either through e-mail, from the organization's intranet, called *The Village* (which in many cases was not checked regularly by participants) or through Zora itself. Clubhouse members who had an account in The Village could request a ClubZora username and password via an online form in the Village. The project coordinator received these requests and examined them to make sure that they were only from Clubhouse members, in order to ensure the safety of the youth online. Participation in the project was completely voluntary and at the discretion of the youth to join.

(6) *Assessment.* Each part of an activity, as described in the curriculum section, was followed by a few questions that we invited participants to answer online. These questions related to the activity ("Did you like it?"), to the idea of positive development ("I believe that by using computer technologies people can find new ways to give back to their communities."), and to culture ("I like to learn about food from different cultures."). Participants were also encouraged to send feedback at any point during the project to the project coordinator. Finally, an online survey outside of Zora (in order to also reach those Clubhouse members who did not participate in Zora), in English and Spanish, was administered at the conclusion of the project to elicit feedback about the project as a whole. In addition, as described in the mentorship section, both local and online mentors were required to complete field notes at the conclusion of each of their sessions. Also, most activities within the software were logged and available for analysis using the Zora Log Parser.

(7) *Access environment.* While individual youth could request a Zora username and password, a Clubhouse Coordinator needed to install the software at the Clubhouse. All Clubhouses were invited to participate in the Zora project; however, there were two requirements: (1) The only supported languages were English and Spanish. Those speaking other languages were still able to participate, but support was only provided in those two languages. This included support documents, communication, and the Zora software itself (i.e., participants in those Clubhouses in which non-Latin characters were used had to switch to a Latin character set to be able to chat and modify text in Zora). (2) A high-speed consistent network connection was required. The software was only available as an online download and because of the heavy graphics load, a low-speed connection would have made it impossibly slow to use Zora.

(8) *Institutional context of usage.* Because this project was done within the larger context of an international organization, we had to be respectful and accommodating to their organizational rules and ideals. For example, in the online Zora Ambassador guide, we wrote:

> The culture of the Clubhouse is one in which "school-like" language or concepts as well as competition is not advised—for example, instead of the word "curriculum," the word "activities" is used. Instead of a "rewards" system we have a recognition system. Instead of "questionnaires" we ask for feedback. And, the word "research" is not used with the youth either. Remember, you are working with kids who are in a place that is not school (and specifically designed to be a non-school-like atmosphere)—we want Zora to be a fun and interesting place to be!

In addition, the Clubhouse Network provides access to a lot of extremely advanced and cutting-edge technology and is a testbed for many research projects that are competing to catch youth's attention and engage then in a sustained way.

Conclusion

This chapter shows the prevalence of virtual worlds in the lives of young people and presents four case studies of a diversity of programs that used a particular virtual world, Zora. Zora was designed and implemented to be used by researchers and practitioners developing psychoeducational interventions. However, in order to have successful learning experiences, the virtual world by itself is not enough While all programs presented in the case studies utilized the same virtual world, as shown in each of the above sections, they all took their own approaches to the eight dimensions that should be taken into consideration when designing and implementing programs that use virtual worlds: (1) curriculum, (2) mentoring model, (3) diversity, (4) project scale, (5) type of contact with participants, (6) type of assessment and evaluation, (7) access environment, and (8) institutional context of usage.

For example, in some projects such as the multicultural summer camp and the ACT program, the virtual world was used by participants who had face-to-face contact. The role of the technology was to provide another way for youth to engage in conversations about their learning. Because participants and program staff were in the same room, technological support was easily provided on-site. The face-to-face contract with participants also allowed for easier data collection, as pre- and postquestionnaires were distributed out by hand and included as part of the intervention and the participants were accessible for in-depth interviews.

In other projects, such as the work with posttransplant patients and the ClubZora project around the world, participants were only able to meet each other and work together through the virtual world. Technological support was done online. This posed challenges for both projects. For ClubZora, we had to conform to each Clubhouses' technological limitations and restrictions, often which included local firewalls (to protect Clubhouse members from certain types of Internet content) that often unintentionally blocked the Zora software. In addition, when Clubhouse Coordinators or members asked for technological help, they themselves did not have the authority to make changes to the Clubhouse technology (i.e., a technical consultant may be used), nor did they know the vocabulary with which to explain the problem, thus making remote troubleshooting difficult. In the case of the posttransplant patients, they were using Zora from their homes. The availability and technical knowledge of the parents varied and there was need for one-on-one face-to-face support as some of the children where young and did not know how to install software, troubleshoot, etc. In terms of data collection, both of these projects presented challenges in terms of missing data and lack of access to the participants for pre- and postsurveys. The ClubZora project presented a different challenge, but also yielded a lot of learning, as it was the first of the studies to be conducted on a very much larger scale than the other three.

As another example, in terms of institutional context of usage, while the summer camp and the ACT program where run at the researcher's universities, the other two studies involved a strong collaborative component with the home institutions, such as Children's Hospital Boston and The Intel Computer Clubhouse Network. This posed new challenges as both interdisciplinary perspectives and cultural organizational expectations and mandates needed to be negotiated on a frequent basis. In some cases, negotiations slowed down the program and hinder children's sustained engagement.

It is our hope that this chapter will provide insights from our experience that will help designers, implementers, and evaluators of programs that use virtual worlds specifically aimed for young people, to take into consideration that thinking needs to be done, not only about the design and implementation of the virtual world, but also in terms of how the curriculum and the mentoring model will play out, what the scale of the project and the diversity of the population will be, how the project evaluation will be conducted and how this will influenced by the type of contact with participants, and finally, how the participant's access environment and the institutional context of usage will have a profound impact in the type of intervention program that can be designed, implemented, and evaluated.

Acknowledgments We thank our collaborators at Children Hospital Boston and The Intel Computer Clubhouse Network, as well as at Academic Technologies, Tufts University. Finally, we thank the National Science Foundation for support of this research through an NSF Career grant #IIS-0447166 and the Tisch College of Public Service and Citizenship for a Faculty Fellowship. Any opinions, findings, and conclusions or recommendations expressed in this article are those of the authors and do not necessarily reflect the views of the National Science Foundation.

References

Association of Virtual Worlds (2008, August). *The blue book: A consumer guide to virtual worlds.*

Barab, S. A., Thomas, M., Dodge, T., Carteaux, R., & Tuzun, H. (2005). Making learning fun: Quest Atlantis, a game without guns. *ETR&D*, *53*(1), 86–107.

Barnes, B. (2007). Disney acquires web site for children [Electronic Version]. *The New York Times*. Retrieved August 2, 2007 from http://www.nytimes.com/2007/08/02/business/02disney.html?_r=1&oref=slogin.

Barron, B. (2004). Learning ecologies for technological fluency: Gender and experience differences. *Journal of Educational Computing Research*, *31*(1), 1–36.

Beals, L., & Bers, M.U. (2009). A developmental lens for designing virtual worlds for children and youth. *The International Journal of Learning and Media*, *1*(1), 51–65. </Devtech/publications/Beals–Developmental_Lens_for_Virtual_Communities.pdf>

Bers, M. U. (2001). Identity construction environments: Developing personal and moral values through the design of a virtual city. *The Journal of the Learning Sciences*, *10*(4), 365–415.
Bers, M. U. (2006). The role of new technologies to foster positive youth development. *Applied Developmental Science*, *10*(4), 200–219.
Bers, M. U. (2007). Positive technological development: Working with computers, children, and the internet. *MassPsych*, *51*(1), 5–7.
Bers, M. U. (2008a). Civic identities, online technologies: From designing civic curriculum to supporting civic experiences. Civic life online: Learning how digital media can engage youth. In W. L. Bennett (Ed.), The john d. And catherine t. Macarthur foundations series on digital media and learning (pp. 139–160). Cambridge, MA: The MIT Press.
Bers, M. U. (2008b). Virtual worlds as digital playgrounds. *EDUCAUSE Review*, *43*(5), 80–81.
Bers, M. U. (2008c). Blocks to robots: Learning with technology in the early childhood classroom. New York: Teachers College Press.
Bers, M. U., & Chau, C. (2006). Fostering civic engagement by building a virtual city. *Journal of Computer-Mediated Communication*, *11*, 3.
Bers, M. U., Chau, C., Satoh, K., & Beals, L. (2007). Virtual communities of care: Online peer networks with post-organ transplant youth. *Proceedings of the 2007 Computer Supported Collaborative Learning Conference*, New Brunswick, NJ.
Bers, M. U., Gonzalez-Heydrich, J., & DeMaso, D. (2001b). Identity construction environments: Supporting a virtual therapeutic community of pediatric patients undergoing dialysis. *Proceedings of the SIGCHI Conference on Human factors in Computing Systems*, Seattle, Washington.
Bers, M. U., Gonzalez-Heydrich, G., & DeMaso, D. (2003). Use of a computer-based application in a pediatric hemodialysis unit: A pilot study. *Journal of the American Academy of Child and Adolescent Psychiatry*, *42*(4), 493–496.
Bers, M. U., Gonzalez-Heydrich, G., Raches, D., & DeMaso, D. (2001a). Zora: A pilot virtual community in the pediatric dialysis unit. In V. L. Patel, R. Rogers & R. Haux (Eds.), *Studies in health technology and informatics* (Vol. 84, pp. 800–804). Amsterdam: IOS Press.
Bruckman, A. (1996). *Moose crossing: Creating a learning culture*. Paper presented at the Proceedings of the 1996 international conference on Learning sciences.
Calvino, I. (1972). Invisible cities. New York: Harcourt Brace.
Chau, C., & Bers, M. U. (2007). *Using a 3d virtual environment to foster college-community connections, 2007* American Educational Researcher Association Annual Conference. Chicago, IL.
Chazan, B. (1985). Models of moral education: Analyzing alternative theories. New York: Teachers College Press, Columbia University.
Dede, C., Ketelhut, D. J., Clarke, J., Nelson, B., & Bowman, C. (2005). *Students' motivation and learning of science in a multi-user virtual environment*. Paper presented at the American Educational Research Association Conference.
Dede, C., Nelson, B., Ketelhut, D. J., Clarke, J., & Bowman, C. (2004). Design-based research strategies for studying situated learning in a multi-user virtual environment. *Proceedings of the 6th International Conference on Learning sciences*, Santa Monica, California
Elliott, J., & Bruckman, A. (2002). No magic bullet: 3d video games in education. *Proceedings of the 2002 International Conference of the Learning Sciences*. Seattle, Washington.
Koschmann, T., & Kolodner, J. L. (1997). Technology and educational reform. *The Journal of the Learning Sciences*, *6*(4), 397–400. http://www.jstor.org/stable/1466778 .
Lave, J., & Wenger., E. (1991). *Situated learning: Legitimate peripheral participation*. Cambridge: Cambridge University Press.
Lenhart, A., Madden, M., Macgill, A. R., & Smith, A. (2007). *Teens and social media*. Pew Internet & American Life Project.
Nelson, B., Ketelhut, D. J., Clarke, J., Bowman, C., & Dede, C. (2005). Design-based research strategies for developing a scientific inquiry curriculum in a multi-user virtual environment. *Educational Technology*, *45*(1), 21–27.

Ondrejka, C. R. (2004). Escaping the gilded cage: User created content and building the metaverse. *Proceedings of the State of Play*, Los Angeles, CA.
Papert, S. (1980). *Mindstorms: Children, computers, and powerful ideas*. New York: Basic Books.
Papert, S. (1987). *Microworlds: Transforming education*. Norwood, NJ, USA: Ablex Publishing Corp.
Preece, J. (2000) *Online Communities: Designing Usability, Supporting Sociability*. Chichester, UK: John Wiley & Sons.
Preece, J. (2001). Online communities: Usability, sociability, theory and methods. In R. Earnshaw, R. Guedj, A. van Dam, & T. Vince (Eds.), *Frontiers of human-centred computing, online communities and virtual environments* (pp. 263–277). Springer Verlag: Amsterdam.
Prescott, L. (2007). Virtual worlds ranking—Runescape #1: Hitscape.
Raths, L. E., Harmin, M., & Simon, S. B. (1978). Values and teaching: *Working with values in the classroom*. Columbus, OH: Charles E. Merrill Publishing Co.
Resnick, M., Bruckman, A., & Martin, F. (1996, September/October). Pianos not stereos: Creating computational construction kits. *Interactions*, *3*(5), 40–50.
Satoh, K., Beals, L., Chau, C., & Bers, M. (2007). *Virtual community of learning and care at Children's Hospital, Boston*. In the symposium developmental technologies: Positive uses of technology for youth learning and development, Society of Research in Child Development Conference. Boston, MA.
Satoh, K., Blume, E. D., DeMaso, D. R., Gonzalez-Heydrich, J. M., & Bers, M. (2008). *A virtual community for post-transplant pediatric patients*, 28th Annual Meeting and Scientific Sessions of the International Society for Heart and Lung Transplantation. Boston, Massachusetts.
Satoh, K., Mc Vey, M., Grogan, D., & Bers, M. (2006). *Zora: Implementing virtual communities of learning and care*. Paper presented at the New Media Consortium (NMC)'s Regional Conference.
Shore, R. (2008). *The power of pow! Wham! Children, digital media, and our nation's future: Three challenges for the coming decade*. New York: The Joan Ganz Cooney Center at Sesame Workshop.
Tiwari, N. (2007). Webkinz: I fell in love with a cyber alley cat. CNET News.com.
Williamson, D. A. (2008). *Kids and teens: Virtual worlds open new universe*. Retrieved August 29, 2008, from http://www.emarketer.com/Report.aspx?code=emarketer_2000437&src=report_summary_reportsell

Chapter 19
New Technologies, Learning Systems, and Communication: Reducing Complexity in the Educational System

Helle Mathiasen[1] and Lynne Schrum[2]

[1]Department of Information and Media Studies, Aarhus University, Aarhus, Denmark, e-mail: hema@imv.au.dk
[2] College of Education and Human Development, George Mason University, Fairfax, VA, USA, e-mail: ischrum@gmu.edu

Introduction

Today education and enhanced information and communication technology (ICT) offer new possibilities for communication collaboration, interaction, and student-centered learning. Examining the potential impact of the new educational environment has become an important aspect of educational researchers' efforts. Much of this research and literature about ICT and learning has been conducted through the lens of sociocultural theories (e.g., Lave & Wenger, 1991), and theories about dialogism (e.g., Bakhtin, 1986). In this chapter we introduce a systems theoretical approach especially inspired by the German sociologist N. Luhmann, and examine the empirical and theoretical research on ICT through this lens.

Based on Luhmann's concepts of learning and teaching, which considers systems, communication, and learning, the chapter explores the ways in which new technologies have expanded classroom communication but also changed the nature of what learners and teachers may experience. Luhmann introduces the idea of complexity and contingency, and states, "Complexity means being forced to select; being forced to select means contingency; and contingency means risk" (Luhmann, 1995, p. 25). The interaction requires new ways of communicating and also challenges students' abilities to deal with their own ways of knowing. The concept of teaching is defined as a specific form of communication which intends to give students the opportunity to learn and construct knowledge; however, this presents new challenges for both learners and teachers. It represents inherent complexity, partly in the system and partly in the environment of the system. Thus, educators must learn to handle complexity as well as contingency.

H. Mathiasen (✉)
Department of Information and Media Studies, Aarhus University, Aarhus, Denmark
e-mail: hema@imv.au.dk

M.S. Khine, I.M. Saleh (eds.), *New Science of Learning*,
DOI 10.1007/978-1-4419-5716-0_19, © Springer Science+Business Media, LLC 2010

The chapter, through recent literature, offers analysis and implications of the ways complexity and contingency may impact teaching and learning. In particular, we call for ongoing research in communication and the conditions for learning in concrete educational settings, including development of learning resources and research projects focusing on new knowledge media and their learning potential. It is also essential, as the call for the use of ICT increases that the educational community begins to understand the requirements placed on the educator and the learners, as well as the interactions in which they participate. In particular, we must consider teachers, their ICT skills, and didactical/pedagogical skills they bring to their positions; educators must consider challenges in communication, design of educational environments, and the interplay that the ICT imposes on these requirements. The chapter concludes with the proposal of a research agenda to identify and begin to gain a conceptual understanding of learning and knowledge in this new environment.

Theoretical Framework

Introduction to Complexity in Education

In this section we present the key concepts which provide the framework of systems and environments, complexity, and learning and teaching. The definition of the concepts is inspired by systems theory and the concept of systems as operationally closed, self-referential, and autonomous (Luhmann, 1995). These system characteristics have consequences for the way we define learning and teaching. As a consequence of the above-mentioned systems' characteristics, we can infer that systems are observed to be nontrivial systems (Foerster & Pörksen, 2006; Luhmann, 2002).

We can describe these nontrivial systems as operationally closed, self-referential, autonomous, analytically indeterminable, unpredictable, and dependent on the previous operations and the concrete context. In principle, we can reject the idea of causality. In other words we cannot predict the outcome of a defined input. We do not know what happens in the system that is how the specific system operates in its self-referential mode. For example, when a student has listened to a lecture you cannot tell what the outcome is. While teachers' intentions about students' knowledge construction is one thing, the students' own construction of knowledge is another.

This approach to systems has consequences for the way we consider the possibility of the fulfillment of the required purposes of the educational system. Foerster concretizes this idea in by saying that nobody has the possibility to know what the students know, and because the student is regarded as a nontrivial system, the student is analytically inaccessible (Foerster & Pörksen, 2006, p. 67). Foerster proclaims in a polemic way that, for example, a test in schools does not really test the students' knowledge but actually tests the test. He offers the following theorem: "test test test" (Foerster & Pörksen, 2006, p. 67).

Thus we have to deal with complexity when systems, students, teachers, classes, universities, and the educational system as such are regarded as unpredictable, non-trivial systems dependent on the concrete context. That is the premise when we are talking about designing a teaching environment for the students, so the teachers must have the best (intended) possibilities to learn what is required in any specific context.

Systems and Environments

System is characterized by being operationally closed, but not closed in the sense that they function as autarchic systems. They are observing systems and get nourishment from their environment. A system and its environment are, in that sense, mutually dependent.

Hence the environment of a system is observed as potential nourishment for the system, and the environment is system specific in the sense that each system creates its own environment. A system observes its environment through the lens of the system that is actualized in the concrete context.

The starting point for the framework is therefore a basic systems theory model consisting of a system and its environment. Each system has a related environment that is specific to the system. Furthermore, a systems environment is always more complex than the system itself, so each system constructs, as it were, its environment due to the system's observing ability.

Complexity and Contingency

According to the nontrivial systems approach, we are dealing with complexity and not a cause–effect relationship. Luhmann writes, "Complexity means being forced to select; being forced to select means contingency; and contingency means risk" (Luhmann, 1995, p. 25). Complexity is therefore considered a surplus of possible options:

> We will call an interconnected collection of elements 'complex' when, because of immanent constraints in the elements' connective capacity, it is no longer possible at any moment to connect every element with every other element (Luhmann, 1995, p. 24)

Furthermore, systems observe their environment as more complex than itself, and that has consequences for the way we will observe and consider the nexus between learning and teaching.

> ... for each system the environment is more complex than the system itself. Systems lack the 'requisite variety' (Ashby's term) that would enable them to react to every state of the environment, that is to say, to establish an environment exactly suited to the system. There is, in other words, no point-for-point correspondence between system and environment [...] (Luhmann, 1995, p. 25)

The concept of complexity is inherent both in psychic systems and social systems, which are the two types of systems we are concerned about in this chapter. Social systems and psychic systems are observing systems based on meaning, implying that they choose to actualize something and leave other things alone. According to the system characteristics mentioned, the result is that in principle, the individual system's unique selection decides what the system chooses to actualize and therefore is contingent upon a premise for social systems' activities (based on communication) and psychic systems' activities (based on conscious activities, i.e., knowledge construction). The specific characteristics concerning psychic systems and social systems are unfolded below. A point at this moment is that the concepts and theoretical framework presented so far have consequences for the way the concepts of learning and teaching are defined, and that has further implications when we are talking about teachers as designers of environments for teaching and learning.

Psychic Systems and Social Systems

Psychic systems operate in and maintain themselves via conscious activities (e.g., thoughts, emotions, and intuitions). The concept of the human being is highly complicated (Luhmann, 1995, p. 40)

> A human being may appear to himself or to an observer as a unity, but he is not a system. And it is less possible to form a system of out of a collection of human beings. Such assumptions overlook the fact that the human being cannot observe what occurs within him as a physical, chemical, and living process. The living system is inaccessible to the psychic system; is must itch, hurt, or in some other way attract attention in order to stir another level of system formation – the consciousness of the psychic system – into operation (Luhmann, 1995, p. 40)

A psychic system designates a specific system of a "human being's" many systems, such as the neurological system and the digestive system. A psychic system is related to consciousness and consciousness makes use of thinking in a broad sense (Luhmann, 1988). In this theoretical framework, the learner (students as well as teachers) is observed as a psychic system, and this system operates in and maintains itself by means of conscious activities.

Communication

Social systems operate in and maintain themselves through communication. And the concept of communication is defined as the synthesis of three selections: (1) the selection of information, (2) the selection of utterance (selected by the utterer, e.g., the teacher), and (3) the selection of understanding (selected by the addressee, e.g., the student).

> If one conceptualizes communication as the synthesis of three selections, as the unity of information, utterance, and understanding, then communication is realized if and to the extent that understanding comes about. Every thing else happens "outside" the unity of an elemental communication and presupposes it. This is especially true for a fourth type of selection: for the acceptance or the rejection of the specific meaning that was communicated. One must distinguish the addressee's understanding of the selection of meaning that has taken place from acceptance or rejection as a premise of the addressee's own behaviour. This distinction is of considerable theoretical importance (Luhmann, 1995, p. 147)

Thus you need a minimum of two persons (psychic systems) to make a communication unit, hence a social system. We can observe the utterance but not the third selection. The selection of understanding is so to speak invisible; that is, it is operations internal to the specific psychic system. That has of course implications for the specific environment, designed for learning.

A main point is that communication can be successful if a *horizon of expectations* is established, and that can happen over time. These expectations might concern teacher and student roles and functions and how to behave in class and participate in a weblog or different discussion forums. It deals with routines, rules, and culture in its broadest sense. In the beginning, systems observe each other as black boxes, but over time systems build up expectations. This nevertheless does not mean that systems become transparent to each other over time (Luhmann, 2002).

Some teaching environments have more advantages than disadvantages depending on the concrete context (including intentions concerning, among other things, the aims and goals related to the concrete syllabus and curriculum as well as students' abilities). Furthermore, different communication forums can be suitable for different types of knowledge constructions. The challenge is to empower teachers to rethink their ways of organizing teaching in the light of the premise for communication, hence inherent complexity and contingency.

Learning and Teaching

We define learning as individual mental constructions and teaching as intended communication. The intention is to change the participants' mental structures. The teaching environment is seen as an environment where communication is intended to bring about students' attention, so the students have the opportunity to learn what is intended.

According to the theoretical frame, teaching and learning are two different modes attributed to different kinds of systems. A related point is that understanding requires someone with whom to communicate when it is a matter of testing one's own understandings.

Knowledge is seen as a result of learning processes in which communication is in focus. The theoretical framework therefore contains an important point, that exactly the specific communication/communication forum plays an important role when it comes to constructing different categories of knowledge. In this context, learning involves the individual mental constructions. A psychic system has to continue the communication process in order to realize the potential of grasping the other psychic system's selection of understanding; this iterative process deals with students' as well as teachers' selection of understanding. With that in mind we will focus on design of teaching environments.

Thoughts never leave psychic systems as thoughts, but are linguistic reconstructions. And the "risk," as mentioned, is that these linguistic reconstructions of thoughts may not be understood as intended. For example, the teacher just has to go on trying to grasp the students' way of understanding her utterance. The requirement on the part of the teacher is a pivotal point when designing teaching environments because learning cannot be organized or controlled by the act of teaching or by the teacher herself (cf. the systems theoretical basis) (Mathiasen, 2009). Learning develops from the selections made by the psychic system. The question is how to develop an environment, or communication forum, which supports and facilitates students' learning processes and knowledge constructions. In addition to the inherent complexity, we have to be aware of the systems theory approach, which means that each student has preferences about learning media, teaching contexts, and types of collaboration (Mathiasen, 2009).

The concept of teaching environment is a more precise indication than the concept of learning environment because communication is regarded as the "disturbing activity," as communication. Teaching environments are seen as communication forums, as social systems. We can only observe the first two selections in a communication unit, and not the third selection, which is a conscious activity. This is an important point to bear in mind when designing the actual teaching environment; that is, the specific communication forum plays an important role in communication. If the communication is productive, ongoing, and is focused on the theme in the concrete context, it can be seen as a possible way of facilitating learning and thereby knowledge construction. This applies in the face-to-face (f2f) context as well as in the many net-mediated communication forums (Mathiasen, 2007, 2008, 2009).

The determination of precisely which teaching environment (communication forum) best fulfills the concrete aims, goals, and requirements of the specific curriculum and syllabus is a job for the teacher, who is seen as the specialist. That does not mean that the students themselves cannot design and use communication forums instead of or concurrently to the institution determined conference system or learning management system, for example. This in fact is what the literature tells us. Moreover, the teacher has to reflect on the variety of learning media and their potential for facilitating learning, and then select learning media and test possibilities, here in the sense of testing understanding, which facilitates the intentions. The traditional lecture given by a teacher to a class does not necessarily contribute to an ideal teaching environment according to this theory of communication and learning, since the point of departure is that every psychic system is unique, which leads to highly complex environments when it comes to organizing the teaching environment.

Background

We will in the following section frame the field of research by introducing pedagogical and didactical parameters and some of their possible relations. The field in general is illustrated below from different perspectives and we start with Fig. 19.1, which is the simplest way of considering this complex area. As a domain, the figure can be seen, in all its simplicity, as being conditioned by a teacher role and related functions, a student role and related functions, and an issue (the theme). The relations between the acute angles are student to teacher, teacher to issue, and student to issue, respectively.

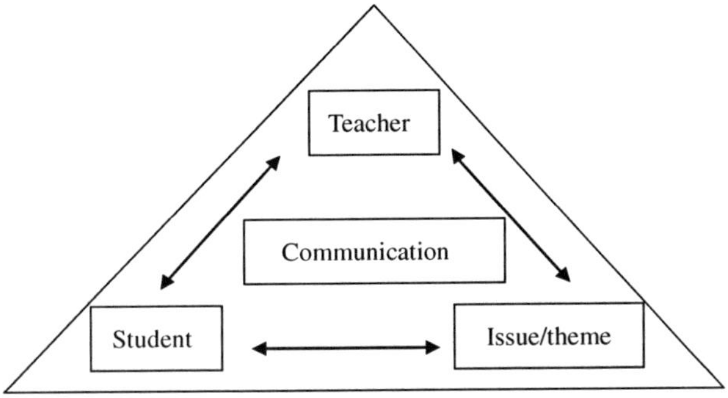

Fig. 19.1 The didactic triangle

This didactic triangle is not new. The very form of the figure is used in literature on educational theory in various theoretical frameworks, in which the concept of teaching or the concept of learning is used as the "foundation" rather than, as in the above figure, the concept of communication (Hopmann, 1997; Mathiasen, 2002). We focus on communication because this is a concept that in the presented theoretical framework is the brick and the fundamental element in the field of research.

The figure gives an idea of the domain, or the social system under which the different roles and functions play out. The figure illustrates teaching as communication about something—the issue/theme—and teaching in its self is observed as an operationally closed system in which the participants have specific roles and are assigned special attributions. The condition of communication is established as a consequence of the specific function of this system. It is thus the specialized form of communication which intends to change mental structures that constitutes this type of social system. In the present context, these types are characterized by interaction, as interactive f2f communication and net-mediated communication, as well as various combinations of these communications systems. Figure 19.1 may at first appear as a simple general model for the key parameters and their relations in a teaching setting. In this sense, the figure should either be developed by indicating the concrete context of use, where, for instance, the communication forum selected is made explicit, or by indicating that there are several teacher and student roles and teacher and student functions, and that these are, so to speak, mutually dependent, thereby indicating a built-in complexity in the system. We will unfold the figure by elaborating on the presented basis, including students, teachers, and issues.

The purpose is to illustrate the complexity which rules when it is about the educational system. The following figure (Fig. 19.2) is meant to be a point of departure, when we begin to consider the possibility of reducing complexity in the educational system. The figure illustrates some of the parameters in play and which every teacher must make decisions about, as she must decide what to select and what to deselect in the concrete context. And clearly, determining the concrete context must be the fundamental decision when preparing, planning, and organizing teaching.

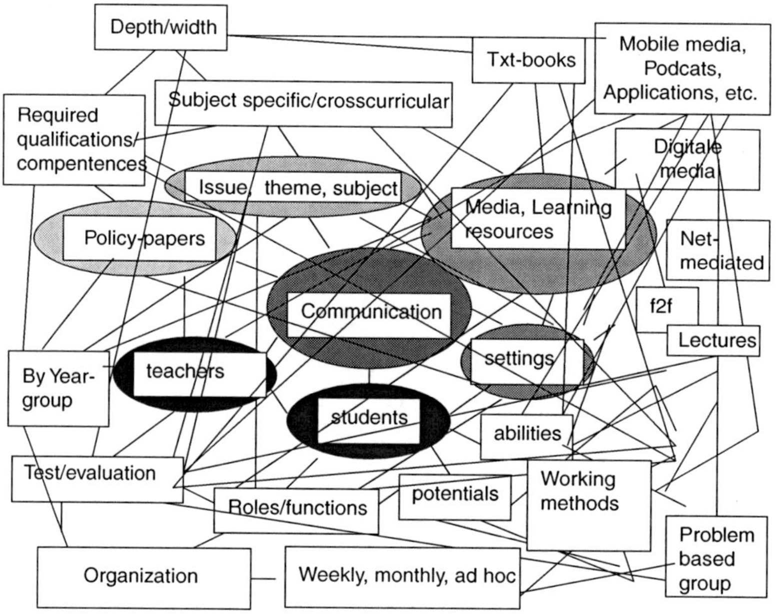

Fig. 19.2 The complexity of mutually depended didactic parameters

Thus, in Fig. 19.2 we present a complicated graphic of the many issues a current teacher must consider. The figure does not show all possible connections or interactions between and among the elements; rather, it shows a picture of the complexity the teacher has to deal with when making every decision concerning the parameters in play when organizing her teaching.

The next figure tries to look at the same domain but with a complexity reduced perspective using a lens focusing on a mix of relations. Thus, Fig. 19.3 offers a picture of relationships where temporality plays a role. Some of the arrows in the figure tell about present relation and mutual influences; other arrows demonstrate expected mutual influences.

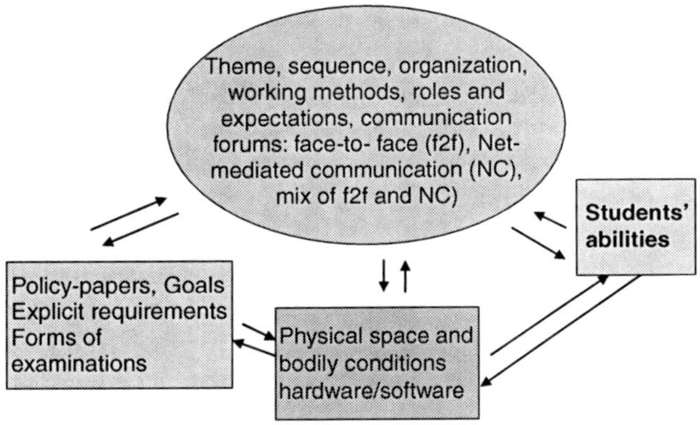

Fig. 19.3 Conditions for teaching planning

Figure 19.3 focuses on visualizing the different categories of selections in play and thus the teachers have to consider when planning their teaching. Some of the elements are basic in the sense that the teacher has no choices, found in the rectangle. The ellipse includes the elements which the teacher can consider, weigh, and has the liberty to choose. The square presents elements that either have a physical space and bodily frame, or condition that is more diffuse, like the students' present abilities.

The point is that the presented figures (Figs. 19.1, 19.2 and 19.3) are offered as reflection tools, each one with its specific advantages as a pedagogical reflection tool, from the simple model (Fig. 19.1) to the very complex model (Fig. 19.2) and from the complex model (Fig. 19.2) to a model focusing on both requirements, space, material, available hardware and software, and context (Fig. 19.3). Overall, all the figures have as a point of departure that the concrete context is in focus. The figures may tell a story of generalization but in fact the figures are meant to be very concrete reflection tools in the concrete planning. In other words, the concrete context must be in focus.

Challenges for the Educational System

In the following section we consider three foci regarding the research on (1) teachers, their ICT skills and their didactical and pedagogical skills in relation to use different types of learning resources, (2) different types of contexts including reflection on students' learning with media and technology, and (3) parameters concerning management, culture, and use of technology.

Focus 1: Teachers, Their ICT Skills, and Didactical/Pedagogical Skills

In general, one of our propositions is that teachers without strong and confident ICT skills will not be able to reduce complexity, the complexity which serves as the environment for the students. So instead of reducing the complexity of the teaching environment the teachers increase the complexity. Not that we advocate of reducing complexity as a purpose in itself; hence, students have to learn to cope with complexity and develop the ability to handle complexity. Rather, we suggest that teachers are of necessity expected to create opportunities to explore, develop, and interact with their peers and the content to begin to understand the affordances and challenges of their world.

We suggest that the role of a teacher is always as a designer of the teaching environment, which often (but not always) requires expanding on what is found in a textbook, and to substitute more authentic activities. This includes the wise use of the variety of "knowledge media" (digital media/textbooks, etc), working methods (traditional lectures, group work, net-based, mix of different methods, and organization of courses), and development of learning materials, assignments, and activities to promote anchored and structured experiences. These may be in whole group classes, self-organized group work, pair work, individualized one-to-one teaching; we assume most teachers will thoughtfully use all possible choices to promote appropriate student learning outcomes.

School and learning are different today in many respects. At one time memorization and recitation were the expectation and the efforts that earned rewards. These days, however, the world of learning is extremely different. Educators today are encouraged and even expected to use ICT to provide opportunities for their students to learn and think in new ways (Belland, Glazewski, & Richardson, 2008). These include an emphasis on solving ill-structured problems, employing problem- and cased-based learning, creating arguments that support students' knowledge and conclusions, demonstrating writing and development skills, collaborating with colleagues, and employing new methods of engaging with emerging technologies in educational environments (Cho & Jonassen 2002; Keys & Bryan 2001; Kyza & Edelson, 2005). Although access to these technologies has increased, Barron (2004) reminded us that access to technology does not necessarily equate to fluency. More importantly, Fragkouli and Hammond (2007) found that projects designed to develop and promote educators' use of ICT may have an impact on developing teachers' information technology skills and knowledge of information and communications technologies as a curricular tool, but the program had very limited impact on classroom practice. Putnam and Borko (2000) say that teacher learning is conceived as a social construction of knowledge, and that this must be the model that we consider in rethinking what it takes to be a teacher today.

The challenge for teachers then is to identify ways in which they can design instruction, employing current pedagogy and technology. However, the history of educational technology has suggested that teachers will abandon media that do not fit the social organization of schooling (Cuban, 2005). This may require more of an "interventionist" role and a "greater emphasis on an experimental culture of learning, rather than a culture in which curriculum and pedagogy is fully 'locked in' in advance of engagement" (McWilliam, 2008, p. 263). It is further essential that they understand what is required to authentically create the educational environment so that it recognizes the postmillennial world in which all learners now exist. Fischer

(2001) suggested that a new mindset is necessary where teachers see their role to make sure that they present knowledge as a goal for students to seek and to do so within personally relevant problems.

Zull (2002) describes the need for hands on, minds on experimentation and considers four stages in the cycle of learning. He describes that all learning requires a concrete experience, after which we develop reflective observation and connections, which in turn lead to the generation of abstract hypotheses, and finally, individuals will perform some type of active testing of those hypotheses. Any teacher who designs educational activities and a learning environment must be able to include these steps in those experiences. Lim (2008) suggests that "It is only when students are empowered to take charge of their own learning by co-designing their learning experiences with teachers and other students that they are more likely to engage in their learning process" (pp. 1002–1003).

Gerber and Scott (2007) examined the design of a learning curriculum and found that shifting focus to the specific rather than general principles of design was the key to being able to rethink and reassess the process. Their conclusion was that the diversity in many learner groups requires enhanced diligence and that "the relationship between teaching and learning is indirect. . ." (p. 475). And those differences are becoming more pronounced throughout the world. Rogers, Graham, and Mayes (2007), in an analysis of instructional design and cultural competence, suggest that "those assigned to accomplish this task are left with the great challenge of meeting the needs of learners who come from cultures that are foreign to themselves, and who often have very different abilities and experiences than originally assumed" (p. 197). Further, Sims and Jones (2003) emphasized that the roles of designer, teacher, and learner must strive to be interchangeable to take advantage of the information now widely available and the need to modify instruction rapidly.

In fact, Sims (2008) suggested that new models of teaching and the strategies required challenge the entire educational design team, including the teacher, the learner, and the materials. Some suggest (Oblinger, 2004; Sims, 2006; Siemens, 2007) that the new emerging technologies require educators to question the very essence of teaching and learning. Sims (2008) suggested that "while the technology has evidenced many new generations, our field continues to question and validate the dynamic between technology, teaching, and learning" (p. 155). Sims also suggests that a new model, Sims c3-learning—collaborative, contextual, and connected, could be the framework from which educators might design their instruction. He described them,

> Collaborative in that learners and teachers can engage in meaningful interactions that are dynamic and emergent. Contextual in that individual learners can focus on their own needs in their own situation as well as taking responsibility for contributing content relevant to those needs. Connected in that learners and teachers need not be constrained to the one classroom—there are many learning spaces and many willing to participate in those spaces (p. 162)

Oblinger and Hawkins (2006) reframed the debate by noting that "learning occurs as a result of motivation, opportunities, an active process, interaction with others, and the ability to transfer learning to a real-world situation" (p. 14). It is also worth noting the contributions of Siemens (2004) who postulated a learning theory for the digital age—connectivism. "Learning has changed over the last several decades. The theories of behaviourism, cognitivism, and constructivism provide an effect view of learning in many environments. They fall short, however, when learning moves into informal, networked, technology-enabled arena" (Siemens, 2007, p. 1).

A recent approach to educational development is that of *universal design*; as suggested by Rose and Meyer (2002), in that "barriers to learning are not, in fact, inherent in the capacities of learners, but instead arise in learners' interactions with inflexible educational materials and methods" (p. iv). Thus, it is important that when educators are designing their instructional activities, they include a combination of bottom-up (learner-prompted) and top-down (teacher-prompted) strategies. The hope then is that the adoption of universal design may lead to lead to designs that incorporate greater flexibility, multiple modalities, and an understanding of how different learners access learning. And Hedberg's (2006) comments, intended to consider online learning but appropriate in this context, argued for *disruptive pedagogies* which "involve the use of teaching strategies that exploit the currently underused capacities of technology options in such a way as to enable student engagement, motivation and higher order thinking skills" (p. 171).

Design of Environments for Teaching

Before design takes place, it is essential that teachers engage in reflection. Research into teacher development conceives teacher knowledge as highly contextualized and interpretive (Freeman & Johnson, 1998), drawing on the social contexts within which teaching takes place. This perspective draws on understandings of situated cognition in which the social context within which learning takes place is an integral part of the interpretation and application of that learning. Teacher learning involves engagement with questions about practice, about learners, and about their beliefs as teachers. Reflection is "a recognition, examination and rumination over the implications of one's beliefs, experiences, attitudes, knowledge, and values as well as the opportunities and constraints provided by the social conditions in which a teacher works" (Zeichner & Liston, 1996, p. 20).

And yet, what we are asking educators to do may not be intuitive or easy. In most situations (Wang, Nieveen, & Akker, 2007) educators are left on their own to determine the best ways to integrate technology into their curriculum. McWilliam (2008) goes on to describe her own four stages for teachers to unlearn the most typical instructional design strategies, and instead move to becoming not a sage on the stage or a guide on the side, but rather a "meddler in the middle" (p. 265). She intones teachers to spend less time giving instructions and more time being in the thick of the action, less time minimizing risks and more time being an experimenter and risk-taker, less time being a classroom auditor and more time being a designer, editor, and assembler; and finally, less time spent being a counselor and more time being a collaborative critic and authentic evaluator. As Sims (2006) "Rather the teacher, like the learner, needs to develop a skill set and ethos that allows him/her to become a participant in the one connected environment, where his/her experience and knowledge are a critical part of the learning environment, but not necessarily its foundation" (p. 262).

Another aspect of the design challenge is the need to scaffold and coach students (Sherin, Reiser, & Edelson, 2004). This includes the supports that may be in the form of reminders and help that the learner requires to carry out the task and gain the necessary skills. Stone (1998) suggested that the support provided is assumed to be temporary and withdrawn gradually, to transfer the responsibility in an appropriate manner, and Guzdial (1994) considered this withdraw to be akin to fading. The challenge of course is not to provide too many supports, but to also build on the "wisdom of the crowd" (Surowiecki, 2004), whose research suggested that when enough amateurs pool their knowledge they may come up with better answers than individuals.

Focus 2: Students' Learning with Media and Technology

We are well aware that each tool is not the same; it has certain affordances and constraints, plus, the ways in which it is used impact its value and helpfulness. The Each tool also has the possibility to change the interaction and as a result also "infects" conditions for learning and learning processes.

We know from Pink (2005) that one challenge is not just the ability to work in high-technology environments, but to utilize "high concept/high touch" abilities to make and remake our personal and professional environments in ways that serve both functional and aesthetic needs simultaneously. Kennewell and Beauchamp (2007) created a taxonomy of features that are inherent in digital media by describing two distinct types. They ascribed some things as intrinsic to the digital media itself, and those that are constructed by the hardware and software developers, and also those created by the teachers who are preparing resources for learning.

> These pedagogical features include the teacher (if present), other students, tools and resources, subject culture and classroom ethos. The features of the setting provide affordances which students may perceive as potential for action. At the same time, the features provide constraints which may structure the students' actions. The situation is not static, however, and the teacher's role is to orchestrate the features of the setting, using their knowledge of students' characteristics, in order that the goal may be achieved with some cognitive effort but without excessive frustration. Students, too, will orchestrate the features of the setting to support their pursuit of the goal (Kennewell & Beauchamp, 2007, p. 228)

Additionally, Kennewell and Beauchamp (2007) found that teachers did recognize the importance of their providing a variety of representations, particularly for complex ideas, and for offering a number of activities in which the same skills and concepts were involved. In other words, it is not enough to present complex ideas, or new ways of thinking in one or two opportunities or ways, but rather they concluded, "ICT activities were felt to add to the teacher's repertoire, even if they were not the most important ones. The degree of engagement and participation was felt to be increased; this was considered particularly important for the less able students" (p. 230).

A fundamental question in thinking about teaching and learning in the twenty-first century revolves around the notion of learners as different today, from those in previous generations, due in part to our media-centric world. Studies (Lenhart, Madden, Macgill, & Smith, 2007) have shown that students are capable, conscientious, concerned, and optimistic, and as a generation, determined to succeed. Over 90% of the students reported they value school plan to continue their education after secondary school, use computers and the Internet for school work and research, and spend more time using the Internet than watching television, and most create content on the Internet. In Lessig's (2001) terms, the user becomes the producer. Prensky (2001) stated that today's students do not just use, but rather assume and expect technology, are always "on," are skilled multitaskers, and significantly, embrace communities, collaboration, and social networking. Educators are told that it is their responsibility to inspire and engage students construct, perform, and become lifelong learners.

Authors such as Restak (2003) have done extensive investigation regarding how technology and biology are converging to influence the evolution of the human brain. He describes how we are now able to study the brain in real time, and even looks at how learning a new skill changes one's brain. From this comes the notion of cognition—the psychological result of perception and learning and reasoning (Merriam Webster, n. p.). He also discusses the ways in which the brain does have plasticity, but that it is also influenced by all sorts of technology around us; further he reflects upon the way humans face constant challenges to the ability to focus attention and how we have become more frenetic, distracted, fragmented, and even hyperactive. This reality has implications for the young learner who is perhaps less able to focus and discriminate between what is important and what is extraneous.

It is worth asking, however, if our students are really different in the ways they learn, remember, and solve problems. We can look to Cognitive Load Theory (Sweller, 1988) to think about what is required of a learner during knowledge acquisition process. Intrinsic load relates to the inherent difficulty of a task or idea, which extrinsic load relates to the impact of outside influences, including those imposed by the learning environment (e.g., interruptions, loud music, or poorly designed instruction). Kenny (2009) has investigated the notion that learners today are fundamentally different from those in the past, based on an abundance of popular treatises (Prensky, 2001) and anecdotal reports. He suggested that "At the forefront is the issue of which learner characteristics have changed, if any, and, accordingly, which evaluation tools are best suited to evaluate them" (p. 45). His strategy has been to go back to a well validated matching Familiar Figures Test (MFFT). Although it was developed over 30 years ago, its goal was to measure cognitive tempo on an impulsive–reflective axis. It may be considered a subgroup of cognitive style that works to identify differences in individual responses in the face of uncertainty in which subjects may opt to sacrifice speed for accuracy or vice versa. Two groups of K-12 students from different eras were investigated to determine if comparing cognitive tempos between subjects who took the original MFFT-20 to those who live in the current media-centric society provides any insights as to possible differences in the visual cognitive processing skills and preferences. Given that little has been done in the intervening years, Kenny concluded that results were tenuous at best, however, he did say:

> No one can deny that television viewing and computer usage have increased significantly over the past fifty years. But correlation is not causation. Further, no claims can be made that the cognitive processing characteristics being displayed by today's students are universal, or are caused solely by increases in viewing and usage habits. It is hard to dispute, however, that a cultural change is taking place in terms of a transition in which moving images are playing an ever-increasing role, and a correspondingly lessening role of text in the communicative and learning preferences and abilities of today's students (p. 56)

Kenny did report that "something interesting may be happening with regards to a propensity for and ability to accurately grasp and identify fast-paced, multiprocessed visual information on the part of today's youth" (p. 56). He further related these results to similar observations made in others' studies that evaluated processing speeds for various types of information presented in video format (Kenny, 2002; Papper, Holmes, & Popovich, 2004; Zillman & Brosius, 2000). In general, we do not yet know precisely what happens to learning and the nature of interactions in these new environments.

Focus 3: Management and Technology Issues

While the issues in this topic are not part of the design issues, it is important to consider them when discussing the complexity added to an educational environment with ICT. In investigations regarding reasons teachers do not use ICT for teaching, many barriers, both intrinsic and extrinsic (Zhao & Frank, 2003) have been identified. These include lack of time for professional development (McKenney, 2005), lack of teacher training in preservice education programs, general resistance by teachers to utilize technology (Collier, Weinburgh, & Rivera, 2004; Staples, Pugach, & Himes, 2005), and lack of technical support (Butler & Sellbom, 2002).

Schrum and Levin (2009) discuss the ways in which the larger culture and process of an institution impact the use of ICT, and they suggest that the role of the leader can either support or inhibit teachers' willingness to engage in this effort. We know from systems theory that the communication is directly affected and changed when ICT is introduced, but we cannot forget the other challenges that most teachers identify as reasons for not employing ICT. These include time, access, skills/knowledge, and support. If we consider the amount of effort and energy creating appropriate educational environments requires, then layer on the potential for ineffective or unsuccessful implementation, it is little wonder that individuals are reluctant.

We suggest that the context of the school in its entirety must work together for any real ICT implementation to take hold. If either the school leader or the teacher works in isolation, it is not likely to be meaningful over time. Both must be working synergistically; teacher-created teaching environments and leader-created or supported environments for teachers' creativity concerning rethinking and use of ICT are essential components. We propose that this is similar to Pandora's Box, or a Calder mobile, in which every level is related and mutually dependent with the other levels. Thus, the complexity of implementation may be reduced with common goals and share vision between the levels of decision making, resource allocation, and expected outcomes. Unfortunately, this is not always known or explicated.

Further Research—an Invitation

We have to deal with the fact that communication plays a key role in the construction of knowledge, and that it will be productive to reflect on and rethink teaching environments in the light of the presented theoretical framework. This includes rethinking and explicating teacher and student roles, in that each specific teaching environment has some, often implicit, expectations regarding teacher and student roles and related functions (Mathiasen, 2007).

If the presupposition is that different communication forums including digital and nondigital learning resources can be fruitful for knowledge constructions, the challenge is then to empower teachers to rethink their ways of organizing teaching including the use of ICT in the light of the premise of communication, complexity, contingency, and the risk involved. As a consequence of the presented theoretical frame and the research findings we suggest the following research questions as a part of the research agenda:

- Which communication forums facilitate which kind of knowledge construction and development of special and social competences, and what could be the repertoire of teacher and student roles?
- How can the use of different types of teaching environments, commonly seen as communication forums, facilitate each other?
- How can different learning resources, digital as well as nondigital, facilitate each students' learning and knowledge construction?

We invite the conversation around these topics and encourage research to explore the issues raised in this chapter. The voices that must be considered include those of the teachers, the learners, and the school leaders who help implement ICT in an effort to promote the goals of all educational systems. The educational community, and in particular the current and future learners, will all benefit from this collaborative conversation.

References

Barron., B. (2004). Learning ecologies for technological fluency: Gender and experience differences. *Journal of Educational Computing Research*, *31*(4), 1–36.

Bakhtin, M. (1986). The problem of speech genres (V. McGee, Trans.). In C. Emerson & M. Holquist (Eds.), *Speech genres and other late essays* (pp. 60–102). Austin: University of Texas Press.

Belland, B. R., Glazewski, K. D., & Richardson, J. C. (2008). A scaffolding framework to support construction of evidence-based arguments among middle school students. *Education Technology Research and Development (ETRD)*, *56*, 401–422.

Butler, D. L., & Sellbom, M. (2002). Barriers to adopting technology for teaching and learning. *Educause Quarterly*, *25*(2), 22–28.

Cho, K., & Jonassen, D. H. (2002). The effects of argumentation scaffolds on argumentation and problem solving. *Educational Technology Research and Development*, *50*(3), 5–22.

Collier, S., Weinburgh, M. H., & Rivera, M. (2004). Infusing technology skills into a teacher education program: Change in students' knowledge about and use of technology. *Journal of Technology and Teacher Education*, *12*(3), 447–468.

Cuban, L. (2005). *The blackboard and the bottom line: Why schools can't be businesses*. Cambridge, MA: Harvard University Press.

Fischer, G. (2001). Lifelong learning and its support with new media. In N. J. Smelser & P. B. Baltes (Eds.), *International encyclopedia of social and behavioral sciences* (Vol. 13, pp. 8836–8840). London, UK: Elsevier.

Foerster, Hv., & Pörksen, B. (2006). *Wahrheit ist die Erfindung eines Lügners. Gespräche für Skeptiker*. Heidelberg: Carl-Auer Verlag.

Fragkouli, E., & Hammond, M. (2007). Issues in developing programmes to support teachers of philology in using information and communications technologies in Greek schools: A case study. *Journal of In-service Education*, *33*(4), 463–477.

Freeman, D., & Johnson, K. E. (1998). Reconceptualizing the knowledge base of language teacher education. *TESOL Quarterly*, *32*(3), 397–417.

Gerber, S., & Scott, L. (2007). Designing a learning curriculum and technology's role in it. *Educational Technology, Research and Development*, *55*(5), 461–478.

Guzdial, M. (1994). Software-realized scaffolding to facilitate programming for science learning. *Interactive Learning Environments*, *4*, 1–44.

Hedberg, J. G. (2006). E-learning futures? Speculations for a time yet to come. *Studies in Continuing Education*, *28*(2), 171–183.

Hopmann, S. (1997). Wolfgang Klafki och den tyska didaktiken i Uljens, M (red). Didaktik. Lund: Studenterlitteratur.

Kennewell, S., & Beauchamp, G. (2007). The features of interactive whiteboards and their influence on learning. *Learning, Media and Technology*, *32*(3), 227–241.

Kenny, J. (2002). Managing innovation in educational institutions. *Australian Journal of Educational Technology*, *18*(3), 359–376.

Kenny, R. (2009). Evaluating cognitive tempo in the digital age. *Educational Technology Research and Development*, *57*, 45–60.

Keys, C. W., & Bryan, L. A. (2001). Co-constructing inquiry-based science with teachers: Essential research for lasting reform. *Journal of Research in Science Teaching*, *38*, 631–645.

Kyza, E., & Edelson, D. C. (2005). Scaffolding middle school students' coordination of theory and practice. *Educational Research and Evaluation*, *11*(6), 545–560.

Lave, J., & Wenger, E. (1991) *Situated Learning. Legitimate peripheral participation*. Cambridge: University of Cambridge Press.

Lessig, L. (2001). *The future of ideas: The fate of the commons in a connected world*. London: Random House.

Lenhart, A., Madden, M., Macgill, A. R., & Smith, A. (2007, December). Teens and social media. *PEW Internet & American Life Project*. Washington, DC: Pew Charitable Trusts. Retrieved January 3, 2008, from www.pewinternet.org/PPF/r/230/report_display.asp

Lim, C. P. (2008). Spirit of the game: Empowering students as designers in schools? *British Journal of Educational Technology*, *39*(6), 996–1003.

Luhmann, N. (1988). *Erkenntnis als konstruktion*. Berlin: Benteli Verlag.

Luhmann, N. (1995). *Social Systems* (Trans. J. Bednartz Jr. & D. Baecker). Stanford: Stanford University Press.

Luhmann, N. (2002). *Das Erziehungssystem der Gesellschaft*. Frankfurt: Suhrkamp.

Mathiasen, H. (2002). Personlige bærbare computere i undervisningen. Ph.d.-afhandling. Kbh: DPU's forlag.
Mathiasen, H. (2007). *Teaching and learning in a variety of communication forums*. In *iPED Conference 2007*, Coventry University Technocenter, UK, Coventry University Technocenter, UK.
Mathiasen, H. (2008). Is there a nexus between learning and teaching? In C. Holtham, & C. Nygaard (Eds.), *Understanding learning-centred higher education*. Denmark: Copenhagen Business School Press.
Mathiasen, H. (2009). *Can learning be organized?* ICELW, Conference, paper, New York, USA.
McKenney, S. (2005). Technology for curriculum and teacher development: Software to help educators learn while designing teacher guides. *Journal of Research on Technology in Education, 38*(2), 167–190.
McWilliam, E. (2008). *Unlearning how to teach. Innovations in Education and Teaching International, 45*(3), 263–269.
Oblinger, D. (2004). The next generation of educational engagement. *Journal of Interactive Media in Education, 8*(May), Retrieved June 12, 2009 from www-jime.open.ac.uk/2004/8
Oblinger, D. G., & Hawkins, B. L. (2006). The myth about No Significant Difference. *Educause Review, 41*(6), 14–15.
Papper, R., Holmes, M., & Popovich, M. (2004). Middletown media studies. *International Digital Media & Digital Arts Association, Association Journal, 1*(1)1–56. http://www.bsu.edu/icommunication/news/iDMAaJournal.pdf
Pink, D. H. (2005). *A whole new mind*. New York: Penguin.
Prensky, M. (2001). *Digital games-based learning*. New York: McGraw-Hill.
Putnam, R., & Borko, H. (2000). What do new views of knowledge and thinking have to say about research on teacher learning? *Educational Researcher, 29*(1), 4–15.
Restak, R. M. (2003). *The new brain: How the modern age is rewiring your mind*. New York: Rodale St. Martins Press.
Rogers, P. C., Graham, C. R., & Mayes, C. T. (2007). Cultural competence and instructional design: Exploration research into the delivery of online instruction cross-culturally. *Educational Technology, Research and Development, 55*(2), 197–217.
Rose, D. H., & Meyer, A. (2002). *Teaching every student in the digital age: Universal design for learning*. Alexandria, VA: Association for Supervision and Curriculum Development.
Schrum, L., & Levin, B. (2009). *Leading a 21st century school: Harnessing technology for engagement and achievement.* Thousand Oaks, CA: Corwin Press.
Sherin, B., Reiser, B. J., & Edelson, D. (2004). Scaffolding analysis: Extending the scaffolding metaphor to learning artifacts. *The Journal of the Learning Sciences, 13*(3), 387–421.
Siemens, G. (2004). *Connectivism: A learning theory for the digital age*. Retrieved April 1, 2009, from http://www.elearnspace.org/Articles/connectivism.htm
Siemens, G. (2007). *Description of connectivism*. Retrieved November 1, 2007, from http://connectivism.ca/about.html
Sims, R. (2006). Beyond instructional design: Making learning design a reality. *Journal of Learning Design, 1*(2), 1–9. Retrieved April 5, 2009, from http://www.jld.qut.edu.au/publications/vol1no2/documents/beyond%20instructional%20design.pdf.
Sims, R. (2008). Rethinking (e)learning: A manifesto for connected generations. *Distance Education, 29*(2), 153–164.
Sims, R., & Jones, D. (2003). Where practice informs theory: Reshaping instructional design for academic communities of practice in online teaching and learning. *Information Technology, Education and Society, 4*(1), 3–20.
Staples, A., Pugach, M. C., & Himes, D. J. (2005). Rethinking the technology integration challenge: Cases from three urban elementary schools [Electronic version]. *Journal of Research on Technology in Education, 37*(3), 285–311.
Stone, C. A. (1998). The metaphor of scaffolding: Its utility for the field of learning disabilities. *Journal of Learning Disabilities, 31*, 344–364.

Surowiecki, J. (2004). *The wisdom of crowds*. New York: Doubleday.
Sweller, J. (1988). Cognitive load during problem solving: Effects on learning. *Cognitive Science*, *12*, 257–285.
Wang, Q., Nieveen, N., & Akker, Jv. d (2007). Designing a computer support system for multimedia curriculum development in Shanghai. *Educational Technology Research and Development*, *55*, 275–295.
Zeichner, K. M., & Liston, D. (1996). *Reflective teaching*. Marwah, NJ: Lawrence Erlbaum Associates.
Zhao, Y., & Frank, K. A. (2003). Factors affecting technology users in schools: An ecological perspective. *American Educational Research Journal, 40*, 807–840.
Zillmann, D., & Brosius, H. -B. (2000). *Exemplification in communication: The influence of case reports on the perception of issues*. Malwah, NJ: LEA
Zull, J. E. (2002). *The art of changing the brain: Enriching the practice of teaching by exploring the biology of learning*. New York: Basic Books.

Part III
Collaboration and New Science of Learning

Chapter 20
Fostering Higher Levels of Learning Using Diverse Instructional Strategies with Internet Communication Tools

Heather Kanuka

University of Alberta, Edmonton, Alberta, Canada , e-mail: heather.kanuka@ualberta.ca

Introduction

For more than three decades now, the research on learning effectiveness and the use of Internet communication tools has been prolific, with persistence in passion and enthusiasm by many education researchers. Even though this research is extensive and rigorous, it has yet to reveal a consistent and reliable body of knowledge indicating that more effective learning is an outcome of the use of Internet communication technologies (e.g., Bernard et al., 2004). Moreover, it is difficult to ignore the studies that have revealed higher levels of thinking and meaningful learning are not being achieved through the use of text-based Internet communication tools (e.g., Gunawardena, Carabajal, & Lowe, 2001; Kanuka, 2005; Kanuka & Anderson, 1998; Nussbaum, Hartley, Sinatra, Reynolds, & Bendixen, 2002; Garrison, Anderson, & Archer, 2001 ; Rourke, 2005; Thomas, 2002). Hamilton and Feenberg (2005) observed that the generally disappointing research results coupled with the exaggerated and/or unsupported claims made about the use of text-based Internet group communication tools within the learning process presents a pressing need for exploring alternative pedagogical interventions.

Reasons offered in the literature that have disappointing findings have tended to revolve around the following explanations: (a) new educational frameworks are required for Internet communication technology (e.g., de Castell, Bryson, & Jenson, 2002; Garrison, Anderson, & Archer, 2000), (b) poor discussion moderation (e.g., Xin & Feenberg, 2005; Salmon, 2000;), or (c) a need for a progressive pedagogy in this highly mediated mode of learning (e.g., Bernard, de Rubalcava, & St-Pierre, 2000; Kirkwood & Price, 2005; Marra, Moore, & Klimczak, 2004). Building on the results of a prior study (Kanuka, Rourke, & Laflamme, 2007), this chapter explores the latter issue, focusing on the use of diverse instructional methods with text-based Internet group communication tools.

H. Kanuka (✉)
University of Alberta, Edmonton, Alberta, Canada
e-mail: heather.kanuka@ualberta.ca

M.S. Khine, I.M. Saleh (eds.), *New Science of Learning*,
DOI 10.1007/978-1-4419-5716-0_20, © Springer Science+Business Media, LLC 2010

Progressive Pedagogies

Progressive pedagogies are instructional methods which are deliberate and planned goal-oriented activities where the learning outcomes, the teacher's and the students' roles and activities are clearly defined, and described. Research on diverse uses of instructional methods in face-to-face settings have revealed that, under some conditions, it is possible to move learners from low levels of learning (e.g., rote learning/memorization of data and facts) to higher levels of learning (e.g., understanding of complex and abstracted phenomenon through critical, creative, and complex thinking skills). It has also been suggested that students who use active and diverse learning strategies are more likely to acquire sophisticated levels of understanding than students who do not use active and diverse learning strategies (Williams, 2002).

The progressive pedagogies explored in this chapter were diverse and intentionally selected instructional methods with the aim of providing students with some dilemma or perplexity as a result of an authentic problem (based on an actual event or events) and included the following components identified by Tenenbaum, Naidu, Jegede, and Austin (2001) as necessary to achieve higher thinking patterns: (1) arguments, discussions, debates, (2) conceptual conflicts and dilemmas, (3) sharing ideas with others, (4) materials and measures targeted toward solutions, (5) reflections and concept investigation, (6) meeting student needs, and (7) making meaning, real-life examples.

Following is a brief overview of each pedagogical intervention that was investigated for its effects on facilitating higher levels of learning. The Internet communication tool used to facilitate these pedagogical interventions was asynchronous, text-based group fora (WebCT group discussion).

The Nominal Group Technique. The nominal group technique is a democratic decision-building process designed to improve problem solving skills in a large group setting (Seaman & Fellenz, 1989). This pedagogical intervention typically begins with a presentation of a well-formed problem posed to students who are then asked to generate and prioritize their ideas about a solution. Students list ideas until their suggestions have been exhausted. The instructor then asks those students with extreme views to reconsider their ideas. Underpinning this instructional method is the assumption that a question and response technique, will prompt students to reflect on issues they might have disregarded as insignificant.

Debate. Debates are structured discussions in which reasons involving two or more opposing sides of an issue, proposition and/or proposal are presented. This is then followed by consideration of the implications of the issues presented, and sometimes a vote process ensues (Renner, 1999). The formal debate has an agreed upon set of rules and traditional procedures beginning with a presentation by two groups with opposing positions, followed by rebuttals from each group that both defend their own position and attack the position of the opposing team. This instructional method is designed to enhance students' confidence and ability to express viewpoints, as well as help develop coherent organization and precise expression of ideas (Kanuka & Kreber, 1999).

Invited Expert. Inviting an expert can be effective at helping students make authentic connections with the course content (Renner, 1999). An appealing aspect of an invited expert using communication technologies is the ability of Internet conferencing tools to gain access to experts who might be inaccessible through other forms of communication.

WebQuest. WebQuests are web-based inquiry activities in which information that the students use comes from resources on the Internet (Dodge, 1995). WebQuests have six critical attributes that include an introduction to a complex problem (or *case study*), engaging tasks (doable and interesting), a description of the process, multiple online sources and perspectives, followed by evaluation, and conclusions. WebQuests often also incorporate *role play* and *case studies* (described below) as an aspect of the tasks required of the students.

Case studies (required to introduce a complex problem within a WebQuest) supports a learning environment that seeks to present the complex reality of any issue with its concomitant ambiguity and multidimensionality thus providing a strong image of the multifaceted and complex nature of most subject areas (Lacey & Merseth, 1993). It has also been argued that the Web's hypertext linking ability (which is the defining attribute of a WebQuest) provides opportunities for students to gain access to complex concepts from multiple perspectives, for various purposes, and via different learning strategies (Lanza, 1991).

Role play (often used in webquests) is an effective way to help students become empathetic of others' worldviews (Renner, 1999). According to Hiltz and Turoff (1978), role playing is one of the most promising instructional methods for text-based computer-mediated conferencing due primarily to the anonymity inherent within the medium (see also Bonk & Reynolds, 1997; Collett, Kanuka, Blanchette, & Goodale, 1999; Paulsen, 1995). This anonymity (gained from the use of aliases) not only helps students to play their roles more convincingly, but also helps them to acquire an understanding of other worldviews.

Reflective Deliberation. Reflective deliberation is typically described as thoughtful mediation or contemplation, conceiving ideas and/or draw inferences expressed through critical dialogue (Kanuka et al., 2007). Reflective deliberation provides the opportunity for students to reflect on the abstracted material presented in academic settings and make it relevant to their own worlds (Laurillard, 2002).

Table 20.1 is an overview of each of the instructional methods used in this study with respect to structure, role of student, role of teacher, benefits, and limitations.

Guiding Theoretical Framework: The Practical Inquiry Model

Garrison et al. (2001) theoretical model of practical inquiry was used as a framework to guide the study that this chapter builds on, and assess patterns of cognitive presence. As Table 20.2 shows, the practical inquiry model asserts that there are five phases of critical thinking and cognitive presence.

Table 20.1 Overview of instructional methods

					WebQuest	
	Debate	Invited expert	Nominal group technique	Reflective deliberation	Role play	Case study
Structure	Highly structured	Minimally structured	Highly structured	Minimally structured	Highly structured	Moderately structured
Role of student	Students have a dominant role, which is demanding and aggressively challenges theirs, and others, understandings Students are required to search new information from not only their own perspective but also conflicting perspectives	Students are required to actively participate with the invited expert, but have minimal responsibility for the quality of their participation Students have minimal responsibility to explore diverse perspectives or actively explore new information	Students have a moderate amount of responsibility in that they are expected to make contributions (e.g., recommendation) Students have a moderate responsibility to explore diverse perspectives but not to actively explore new information	Students have a dominant role in that they must be able to generalize the course content, act on it, and then reflect on their actions Students are expected to explore new information but are not expected to actively explore other perspectives	Students have a dominant role and are responsible for providing well informed and well researched perspectives based on their assigned role Students are expected to explore new information and actively explore diverse perspectives	Students have a dominant role and are required to search for new information to justify plausible solutions to the case presented Students are expected to explore diverse solutions to the problem presented

Table 20.1 (continued)

	Debate	Invited expert	Nominal group technique	Reflective deliberation	WebQuest: Role play	WebQuest: Case study
Structure	Highly structured	Minimally structured	Highly structured	Minimally structured	Highly structured	Moderately structured
Role of teacher	The teacher has a dominant role in the careful planning and advanced preparation, including group formations—but is minimally involved in the activity	Minimal planning by the teacher is required in terms of disseminating background information about the invited expert; however, the teacher has a dominant role in moderating the discussion	The teacher has a dominant role in the planning and preparation; she also has a dominant role in moving the activities through a series of steps	The teacher has a minimal role in planning and preparation; however, she has a dominant role in the discussion	The teacher has a dominant role in planning and preparation—but is minimally involved in the activity.	The teacher has a dominant role in the careful advanced preparation of writing the case study and guiding questions—but is minimally involved in the activity
Benefits	Provides students with the opportunity to improve analytical communication skills through the need to formulate arguments, defend positions and critique counter arguments	The ability to pose probing questions, confront opinions, and evaluate responses that contribute the learners' own perspectives Minimal time required in terms of preparation	Prevents domination by a single perspective Forces passive group members to participate Results in a set of ranked solutions to a well-formed problem	Provides opportunities for students to clearly articulate their position, arguments, and interpretation on abstracted and complex phenomena Minimal time required in terms of preparation	Provides an opportunity to expose students to a variety of perspectives by asking them to assume the role of others with diverse view points	Facilitates the acquisition of analytical skills and the ability to think clearly in ambiguous situations

Table 20.1 (continued)

	Debate	Invited expert	Nominal group technique	Reflective deliberation	WebQuest Role play	WebQuest Case study
Structure	Highly structured	Minimally structured	Highly structured	Minimally structured	Highly structured	Moderately structured
Limitations	Time consuming to facilitate online Student resistance due to time-consuming group coordination and the need to research the topic (some team members may not assume their required responsibility)	The invited expert may not have moderating and/or teaching skills and/or be comfortable in an online discussion forum, which may leave learners to gain little benefit from the expert's experience(s)	Beginning with a well-formed problem eliminates the need for the students to discover for themselves the issues involved and, hence, removing the need to search for deeper understandings	Because roles and activities are not clearly specified, some students can dominate the discussion while others may choose not to participate Time consuming to moderate (without an active moderator discussions often get off topic)	Clear and articulate instructions are required for students to understand the purpose of role playing; without an understanding of the purpose students will not actively participate due to self-conciseness	Time consuming and difficult to write authentic case studies; if the students do not view the case as authentic and relevant it will not support lively discussions or generate plausible solutions

Table 20.2 Adapted from the practical inquiry model (Garrison et al., 2000)

Phases of cognitive presence	Description and evidence of process
Phase I&II: Triggering event and problem definition	Student activities begin with a triggering event (phase I) followed by problem definition (phase II) There is evidence of directed and purposeful thinking, with a focus on the problem that is introduced as the triggering event There is evidence of learners defining and redefining the problem presented A critical spirit and intellectual autonomy is present, whereby learners critically assess the issues explored and are open to alternative explanations
Phase III: Exploration	There is evidence that learners are searching for explanations of the problem presented and exploration of relevant ideas In addition to a critical attitude and expansive thinking, learners are divergently seeking for solutions; this is important in the development of critical thinking and problem solving, as ideas organize and make sense of contingent facts
Phase IV: Integration	There is evidence of a conceptualization of the problem presented Thinking is reflective and private, although reflection is socially shared with evidence of the individual tentatively making sense of the information that emerged during the exploratory phase There is evidence of judgments and decisions being made and focused on an idea or emerging hypothesis
Phase V: Resolution	The idea or hypothesis is tested. The testing begins with an initial process of sharing the idea or hypothesis with peers who, in turn, provide insights Learners become ready to act upon their understanding; if there is confirmation of the problem solution for resolution, understanding will result An unsatisfactory resolution will trigger a renewed search and the process will begin anew

The practical inquiry model was selected because of its ability to guide assessment for higher levels of learning, referred to as cognitive presence. Cognitive presence is understood by Garrison et al. (2001) as occurring within a critical community of inquiry in which participants "(re)construct experience and knowledge through the critical analysis of subject matter, questioning and challenging assumptions" (p. 7).

Integrating Progressive Pedagogies into the Learning Experience

High levels of learning and thinking are generally accepted as being the ideals and central aim of a university education. Accordingly, evidence of higher levels of learning and thinking should manifest within the senior undergraduate year. Premised on these assumptions, a fourth year university course was selected for this study; it was an optional bachelor of education course within an outreach program, cohort-based, and distance delivered using WebCT with an instructor who was experienced in both distance delivery and the use of asynchronous text-based Internet conferencing software.

Using the practical inquiry model to guide the course design, the first phase of the practical inquiry model (the triggering event) was introduced by the course instructor through the selected pedagogical interventions. The instructional methods explored varied in degree with respect to structure; though, they were all designed with explicitly stated learning outcomes, start dates, participation time lines, activity termination dates, contribution expectations, and group formation. Evaluation criteria for participation in the learning activities were provided in advance in the form of a grading rubric. The rubric was designed using the SOLO taxonomy (an orderly way of describing a hierarchy of complexity by which learners show mastery of academic work) (Biggs, 1999); the rubric was given to the students at the onset of the course (see Kanuka, 2005 for a full description of the SOLO taxonomy for this study). All assignments were set to invite higher levels of cognitive presence (e.g., extended abstract responses based on the highest level in the SOLO taxonomy); students were made aware at the beginning of the course that higher levels of thinking and learning were expected and grades were based on these criteria.

Quantitative Content Analysis (QCA)

Garrison et al. (2000) suggest a complimentary research technique—*quantitative content analysis* (QCA), along with their rubric (Table 20.3) for assessing the processes and outcomes of online discussion. The technique was originally defined by Berelson (1954) as the systematic, objective, and quantitative description of the manifest content of communication. Abstracting the salient steps, Garrison et al. (2001) describe it as a procedure that involves (1) segmenting conference transcripts into meaningful units, (2) classifying the units into one of the five phases of practical inquiry, and (3) summing the frequency of units in each phase.

The message was selected as the unit of analysis (though the matter of unitizing is unsettled in the distance and higher education literature, see Rourke, Anderson, Garrison, & Archer 2001, 2000; Fahy et al., 2000). Two graduate students were hired to segment and classify the content of the conference transcripts. The use of multiple coders permitted the determination of inter-rater reliability, which reflects the assumptions of QCA that communication content is manifest (not projective) and that the data analysis procedure is objective (not interpretive).

A coding scheme with categories based on the practical inquiry model was established prior to the data analysis. Representative samples were then gathered from the WebCT fora; this created a protocol for identifying and categorizing the phases

Table 20.3 Coding Scheme

Phases of cognitive presence	Indicators	Examples (drawn from the Debate forum)
Phase I: Triggering event Phase II: Problem definition	Evocative A. Problem recognition (information that culminates a question) B. Problem identification C. Puzzlement (questions that take discussions in new directions) D. Definition of problem E. Dissonance expressed F. Redefinition of problem G. Uncertainty exhibited H. Intellectual autonomy I. Appraisal	*[Name]—you used these statements as support of instructivist perspective—all we were doing was pointing out that the mission statement didn't necessarily tie into instructivist—so we weren't sure why you were bringing it into your position ...*
Phase III: Exploration	Inquisitive A. Divergence (unsubstantiated contradictions of previous ideas) B. Divergence (many different ideas/themes presented in one message) C. Information exchange (personal narratives/descriptions) D. Suggestions for consideration (explicit exploration) E. Brainstorming (adds to points but does not systematically defend) F. Leaps to conclusions (offers unsupported opinions) G. Explanation H. Identification of ideas I. Induction J. Deliberation	*You're right [name]. I think our group, with all the quotes, arguments and intellectual lingo, has forgotten the question.* *You have some really good points. And it's true, I agree with you, if the design isn't there and it doesn't catch the students attention, the learners won't keep coming back, or probably won't even sign up for the course. I've taken some distance courses, which because I needed the credits continued and finished them, but they were ugly in the design.* *I think our group was just trying to say, that instructivism is the process and the constructivism is the method that one might take. If you don't have the instructivist design of a course, then there is no structure, no way of measuring the learning, and basically a big "jelly fish" of a course ...* *... they may not agree with me, but that's how I've been interpreting this concept.*

Table 20.3 (continued)

Phases of cognitive presence	Indicators	Examples (drawn from the Debate forum)
Phase IV: Integration	Tentative A. Convergence (reference to message followed by substantiated) B. Convergence (justified, defensible, yet tentative hypotheses) C. Connecting ideas (integrating information from various sources) D. Creating solutions (explicit solution by participant) E. Reason analysis F. Make sense G. Reflection H. Commitment I. Implications considered J. Problem conception K. Problem resolution	*I too have been a big business corporate trainer for an international accounting firm and from that perspective my experience was that employees who could, or at least demonstrated that they could, think outside the box were the minority. Whether that is the fault of our education system or just the nature of people in general, I'm not sure. Whether profit goes up and expenses go down when we think outside the box is debatable. I think it depends on how that thinking is valued. It has been my experience that not all managers want employees who challenge the status quo because the managers themselves don't think outside the box.*

Table 20.3 (continued)

Phases of cognitive presence	Indicators	Examples (drawn from the Debate forum)
Phase V: Resolution	Committed A. Vicarious application to real world B. Testing solutions C. Defending solutions D. Ideas tested and confirmed E. New search F. Collaborative G. Uncertainty H. Problem perception I. Problem integration	"*. . . while the Mission Statement of [name of institution] is laudable, we are unsure how the opposing side has demonstrated that this Mission Statement is indicative of instructivism.*" *Rebuttal: It was never our intent to demonstrate that [name of institution] mission statement is indicative of instructivism.* *It is critical that a course design model be congruent with an institute's mission and vision statements, for without that key component, failure is sure to follow. However, that does not suggest that an institute's mission statement must be indicative of a particular educational design model. The Instructivist framework was adopted by [name of institution] NOT because it is "indicative" of their mission but because it is the one that supports their mission.*

for each instructional method and orientated the coders to use this protocol. See Table 20.3 for coding protocol.

Through the 13-week course and the five instructional methods, both coders segmented and classified all 1,014 of the students' messages. The number of messages posted by the students was highest during the WebQuest and lowest during the Reflective Deliberation (see Table 20.4).

Of the total 1,014 messages posted by the students, the coders determined that 572 (56.41%) contained signs of the processes associated with at least one of the five phases of cognitive presence. Aggregating the messages that were posted during all five instructional methods, we classified the highest frequency in the third phase of cognitive presence. As Table 20.5 shows, relatively few messages reached phase five (9.5% by coder 1 and 5.6% by coder 2), with the majority of messages falling in phase three (52% by both coders), the exploration phase, which is characterized by exchanging information.

Table 20.6 shows the minimum and maximum phases assigned for each instructional method. Table 20.6 also reveals the debate and WebQuest were the only two methods to reach phase 6.

Aggregating the classifications within instructional methods, it was found that the mode for the five phases of the practical inquiry model was highest during the WebQuest and lowest during the reflective deliberation (see Table 20.7).

Phase 3 is the highest mode (the one with the largest frequencies) across the coders and instructional methods.

Cohen's Kappa was used to determine reliability (Table 20.8). It has been suggested that a Kappa of higher than 0.61 represents reasonably good overall agreement (Kvalseth, 1989; Landis & Koch, 1977). As Table 20.8 reveals, the Kappas are

Table 20.4 Number of messages posted during each instructional method

Instructional method	Number of messages
WebQuest	444
Debate	348
Invited Expert	113
Nominal Group Technique	64
Reflective Deliberation	45
Total	1,014

Table 20.5 Frequency of postings in each phase of the practical inquiry model by raters (all instructional methods combined)

Practical inquiry model phase	Rater 1	Rater 2
1	1	2
2	61	90
3	305	308
4	149	144
5	56	33

Table 20.6 Minimum and maximum phases assigned for each instructional method

Instructional method	Minimum	Maximum
Nominal group technique	2	4
Debate	1	5
Reflective deliberation	2	4
Invited expert	2	4
WebQuest	2	5

Table 20.7 Frequency of postings in each phase of the practical inquiry model for Coders 1 and 2 broken down by instructional methods

	Debate		Invited expert		Nominal group technique		Reflective deliberation		WebQuest	
Phase	Coder 1	Coder 2	Coder 1	Coder 2	Coder 1	Coder 2	Coder 1	Coder 2	Coder 1	Coder 2
1	2	1	0	0	0	0	0	0	0	0
2	13	7	12	12	3	3	2	1	60	38
3	79	66	45	44	25	27	17	18	142	150
4	42	46	5	7	10	9	7	6	80	81
5	19	28	0	0	0	0	1	0	13	28
Totals	155	148	62	63	38	39	27	25	295	297

Table 20.8 Coder agreement of cognitive presence by instructional method (Cohen's Kappa and testing of independence between coders)

All groups	Debate	Invited	NGT	Reflective	Webquest
0.570 (9) = 626.64[a], $P < 0.001$*	0.557 $P^b < 0.001$*	0.638 $P^b < 0.001$*	0.230 $P^b = 0.214$	0.366 $P^b = 0.087$	0.590 (9) = 362.93[a], $P < 0.001$*

*Significant at 0.05 level.
[a]Fisher Exact's Test could not be computed due to insufficient memory.
[b]P-values were computed by Fisher's Exact Tests due to small expected cell sizes.

quite small for the nominal group technique and reflective deliberation methods (chance-corrected agreement is 23.0 and 36.6% respectively). For testing of independence between the coders for the nominal group technique and the reflective deliberation methods, Fisher's Exact Test P-values show they are not significant (Table 20.8). Although it has been argued that statistically unacceptable agreement between raters does not mean that the coding decisions are so inconsistent as to be worthless (Crocker & Algina, 1986), the data on nominal group technique in particular needs to be interpreted with caution as the coders strength of agreement is, at best, fair. An explanation for this result could be that because the nominal group technique was the first instructional method the coders analyzed they did not, yet, completely understand where the conceptual boundaries were for each of phase of the practical inquiry model. As the coders gained experience, the conceptual boundaries of the practical inquiry model became better understood by the coders. Well documented in the literature on content analysis is the need to train coders for this reason.

However, it is also important to acknowledge that an alternative explanation is also possible. Krippendorf (2004) (see also Rourke & Anderson, 2004) observed that when coders participate in the conceptual development of the boundaries for categories, it becomes difficult to determine whether they have gained greater proficiency at coding or, instead, have developed a new, group-specific unwritten consensus concerning what is expected of them. Hence, it is important to acknowledge that during the content analysis process boundaries may have been shifted by the coders until their meanings could accommodate what they were able to code with reliability and ease. Cognizant of this potential problem, an attempt to reduce the effects of boundary shifting between coders was achieved by having the coders code independently of each other. However, the coders did come together and debrief with the researcher once a week to discuss issues and problems during the analysis process and, as such, the alternative explanation for the satisfactory inter-rater reliability with the ensuing instructional methods could have been the result of conceptual boundary shifting, rather than greater coding proficiency by the coders.

Ecological Validity of the Coder's

Potter and Levine-Donnerstein (1999) maintain that when conducting a content analysis it is important to also demonstrate ecological validity. To achieve ecological validity, coders should come from the same social community as the eventual consumers of the findings. Acquiring ecological validity is important because the value of a study that uses content analysis (or any study for that matter) lies in how well the results resonate with the research consumers' experiences. In particular, even though the inter-rater reliability can provide credibility to content analyses, it does not tell the readers whether the patterns and observations found by the coders are likely to be the same ones that the readers would find. As such the coders for this study were selected because of their ecological validity: they were mature students in higher education and educational technology disciplines and had participated in online courses using text-based Internet communication tools. These characteristics are also characteristics of the consumers of this research and, hence, one can be reasonably certain that the coders' had ecological validity.

Discussion

This chapter explored the relationship between instructional methods and patterns of cognitive presence. The data revealed that students engaged in a WebQuest produced more messages that reflected the highest levels of cognitive presence than students engaged in (in order of effectiveness) debate, deliberative inquiry, nominal group technique, and invited expert. Table 20.1 in combination with the deindividuation theory and the Foucauldian metaphor of the panopticon may help to provide explanations for these results.

The theory of deindividuation asserts that being in a group provides a degree of anonymity that, depending on the size, allows one to avoid responsibility for actions (Zimbardo, 1969). The Foucauldian metaphor of the panopticon asserts that the mere knowledge of surveillance is enough to induce conformity without imposing force or physical confrontation (Foucault, 1977). Building on these theories, a similar line of argument has been put forward to analyze the effects of deindividualization and panopticon with online group communication. It can, and has, been argued that the absence of social and paralinguistic cues through the use of Internet communication tools, coupled with isolation at one's computer terminal and the ability of learning management systems to track student participation, results in a greater degree of deindividuation and panopticon (Spears & Lea, 1994). Hence, it is possible that anonymity and group conformity are actually being reinforced within online fora; this, in turn, could be a reason for why it is difficult for students to achieve high levels of learning using Internet-based communication tools. Specifically, the effects of anonymity and group conformity pressures may be inhibiting critical aspects to achieving higher levels of learning such as challenging, arguing, debating, and discussing of conceptual conflicts. It may be that certain pedagogical interventions, such as the WebQuest and debate, not only permit—indeed, require—students to actively challenge, argue, debate, and discuss the conceptual conflicts presented. As Table 20.1 illustrates—as well as the research this study builds on (Kanuka et al., 2007; Kanuka, 2005)—both the WebQuest and debate require students to confront conceptual conflicts and dilemmas, defend positions, make judgments, and question or rethink current assumptions of their own as well as their peers. In contrast, the invited expert, deliberative inquiry, and the nominal group technique are pedagogical interventions that are less confrontational in terms of argument formation and argument advancement, as compared to the debate and the WebQuest. The invited expert, deliberative inquiry, and the nominal group technique also do not require students to aggressively defend, challenge, rethink, or question positions.

These results are both insightful and useful in terms of contributions to identifying what activities are effective at facilitating online learning when the aim is to achieve high levels of cognitive presence. In particular, these results reveal that highly structured, planned, confrontational, and demanding activities that include directed roles and responsibilities for the students' contributions in the online classroom is a key element to moving students to higher levels of learning and meaningful thinking. Prior research has also found similar findings. Pawan, Paulus, Yalcin, and Chang (2003; see also Aviv, Erlich, Ravid, & Aviv, 2003), for example, found that "without instructors' explicit guidance and "teaching presence," [sic] students were found to engage primarily in "serial monologues" [sic]" (Abstract, ¶ 1). Further research investigating structure, student and teacher roles, and the use of argument from conflicting perspectives are promising directions for future research.

Conclusions

While the results of this study are encouraging in terms of gaining insights into effective use of text-based Internet communication tools, it is important to acknowledge that, overall, the levels of cognitive presence in this study remained mediocre with postings that tended to aggregate in Phase 3 (exploration of issues). The debriefing sessions with the coders may help to explain these findings. In particular, during the weekly debriefings the coders often brought up issues that revolved around a lack of trust formation and the absence of addressing conceptual conflicts (see Kanuka et al., 2007, for a full description of the coders reflective journals). It has been argued that these elements are necessary conditions for high levels of learning and achievement (e.g., Johnson & Johnson, 1999; Tenenbaum et al., 2001), which could be an explanation for why the postings tended to aggregate in Phase 3, rather than Phases 4 and 5.

The coders' observations are also comparable with similar research investigations. For example, their observations were analogous to Thomas' (2002) observation that "... the online discussion forum does not promote the interactive dialogue of conversation, but rather leads students towards interrelated monologues... Students interact not with another student, but with another student's writing" (p. 362). Particularly noteworthy is the observation by Thomas that "F2F *[sic]* discourse is fundamentally interactional in nature, while written discourse is generally transactional in nature" (p. 363), an observation very similar to one of the coder's observation of the online communication being "a desiccated document delivery system," rather than an interactive discussion—and similar to an observation made by Postman (1992). Postman maintained that oral communication focuses on group learning, cooperation, and a sense of social responsibility, while print communication focuses on individualized learning, competition, and personal autonomy. He further proposed that over four centuries education has achieved a pedagogical peace between these two forms of learning. Now comes text-based computer-mediated communication and Postman asks us "Will the widespread use of computers in the classroom defeat once and for all the claims of communal speech?" (p. 17). Some communication theorists (e.g., Baron, 2000) have argued that the written and spoken word is, indeed, merging in informal communication (e.g., blogs, twitter).

These observations and opinions should give us pause to ask: Is text-based communication a "discussion"? Or is text-based asynchronous communication, as both the coders and Thomas imply, "correspondence" between two or more persons? Is it dialogue? Or is it, in fact, as Pawan et al. (2003) and Thomas observe, a monologue? If we agree with communication theorists, that paralinguistic cuing is critical to the management and coordination of the conversational content (e.g., Clark & Brennan, 1991; Straus, 1997), then text-based asynchronous communication is *not* a discussion—which may be helpful in understanding why research on investigating higher levels of online learning that uses online "discussions" as the principal learning activity has, thus far, had some rather disappointing results.

Irrespective if one agrees or disagrees that text-based asynchronous communication is a discussion, the results of this study have shed light on certain pedagogical interventions that may contribute to higher levels of learning. Given the widespread use of text-based Internet communication tools within educational systems at all levels, research investigating pedagogical interventions requiring students to assertively confront conceptual conflicts and dilemmas, defend positions, make judgments, and question or rethink current assumptions of their own as well as their peers appears to be a promising route for further research.

References

Aviv, R., Erlich, Z., Ravid, G., & Aviv, G. (2003). Network analysis of knowledge construction in asynchronous learning networks. *Journal of Asynchronous Learning Networks, 7*(3), 1–13.

Baron, N. S. (2000). *Alphabet to email. How written English evolved and where it's heading*. New York: Routledge.

Berelson, B. (1954). Content analysis. In G. Lindzey (Ed.), *The handbook of social psychology: Theory and method* (Vol. 1, pp. 488–522). Cambridge, MA: Addison-Wesley.

Bernard, R. M., Abrami, P. C., Lou, Y., Borokhovski, E., Wade, A., Wozney, L., et al. (2004). How does distance education compare to classroom instruction? A meta-analysis of the empirical literature. *Review of Educational Research, 74*(3), 379–439.

Bernard, R. M., de Rubalcava, B. R., & St-Pierre, D. (2000). Collaborative online distance learning: Issues for future practice and research. *Distance Education, 21*(2), 260–277.

Biggs, J. B. (1999). *Teaching for quality learning at university*. Buckingham: SRHE and Open University Press.

Bonk, C. J., & Reynolds, T. H. (1997). Learner-centered Web instruction for higher-order thinking, teamwork, and apprenticeship. In B. Khan (Ed.), *Web-based Instruction* (pp. 167–178). Englewood Cliffs, NJ: Educational Technology Publications.

Clark, H. H., & Brennan, S. A. (1991). Grounding in communication. In L. B. Resnick, J. M. Levine, & S. D. Teasley (Eds.), *Perspectives on socially shared cognition*. Washington: APA Books.

Collett, D., Kanuka, H., Blanchette, J., & Goodale, C. (1999). *Learning technologies in distance education*. Edmonton, AB: University of Alberta.

Crocker, L., & Algina, J. (1986). *Introduction to classical and modern test theory*. Forth Worth, TX: Harcourt Brace Jovanovich College Publishers.

de Castell, S., Bryson, M., & Jenson, J. (2002). Object lessons: Towards an educational theory of technology. *First Monday, 7*(1). Retrieved August 5, 2005, from http://firstmonday.org/issues/issue7_1/castell/index.html

Dodge, B. (1995, 1997). *Some thoughts about Webquests*. Retrieved January 5, 2004, from http://edWeb.sdsu.edu/courses/edtec596/about_Webquests.html.

Fahy, P. J., Crawford, G., Ally, M., Cookson, P., Keller, V., & Prosser, F. (2000). The development and testing of a tool for analysis of computer mediated conferencing transcripts. *Alberta Journal of Educational Research, 46*(1), 85–88.

Foucault, M. (1977). *Discipline and punish*. Harmondsworth: Penguin.

Garrison, D. R., Anderson, T., & Archer, W. (2000). Critical inquiry in a text-based environment: Computer conferencing in higher education. *The Internet and Higher Education*, 2(2–3), 1–19.

Garrison, R., Anderson, T., & Archer, W. (2000). Critical inquiry in a text based environment: computer conferencing in higher education. *The Internet and Higher Education*, 2(2–3), 87–105.

Garrison, D. R., Anderson, T., & Archer, W. (2001). Critical thinking, cognitive presence, and computer conferencing in distance education. *The American Journal of Distance Education, 15*(1), 7–23.

Gunawardena, C., Carabajal, K., & Lowe, C. A. (2001). Critical analysis of models and methods used to evaluate online learning networks. (ERIC Document Reproduction Service No. ED456159).

Hamilton, E., & Feenberg, A. (2005). The technical codes of online education. *Techné, 9* (1), 97-123.

Hiltz, S. R., & Turoff, M. (1978). *The network nation: Human communication via computer.* London: Addison-Wesley Publishing Company.

Johnson, D. W., & Johnson, R. T. (1999). *Learning together and alone. Cooperative, competitive and individualistic learning.* Needham Heights, MA: Allyn and Bacon.

Kanuka, H. (2005). An exploration into facilitating higher levels of learning in a text-based Internet learning environment using diverse instructional strategies. *Journal of Computer Mediated Communication, 10*(3). Retrieved August 5, 2005, from http://jcmc.indiana.edu/vol10/issue3/kanuka.html.

Kanuka, H., & Anderson, T. (1998). On-line social interchange, discord, and knowledge construction. *Journal of Distance Education, 13*(1), 57–74.

Kanuka, H., & Kreber, C. (1999). Knowledge construction in the virtual classroom. *Proceedings of the Canadian Association for the Study of Adult Education,* June, 1999, Sherbrooke, Quebec.

Kanuka, H., Rourke, L., & Laflamme, E. (2007). The influence of instructional methods on the quality of online discussion. *British Journal of Educational Technology, 38*(2), 260–271.

Kirkwook, A., & Price, L. (2005). Learners and learning in the twenty-first century: What do we know about students' attitudes towards and experiences of information and communication technologies that will help us design courses? *Studies in Higher Education, 30*(3), 257–274.

Krippendorff, K. (2004). *Content analysis: An introduction to its methodology.* London: Sage.

Kvalseth, T. O. (1989). Note on Cohen's Kappa. *Psychological Reports, 65,* 223–226.

Lacey, C. A., & Merseth, K. K. (1993). Cases, hypermedia and computer networks: Three curricular innovations for teacher education. *Journal of Curriculum Studies, 25*(6), 543–551.

Landis, J. R., & Koch, G. G. (1977). The measurement of observer agreement for categorical data. *Biometrics, 33,* 159–174.

Lanza, A. (1991). Some guidelines for the design of effective hypercourses. *Educational Technology, 31*(10), 18–22.

Laurillard, D. (2002). *Rethinking university teaching.* London: Routledge Falmer.

Marra, R. M., Moore, J. L., & Klimczak, A. K. (2004). Content analysis of online discussion forums: A comparative analysis of protocols. *Educational Technology Research and Development, 52*(2), 23–40.

Neuendorf, K. A. (2002). *The content analysis guidebook.* London: Sage.

Nussbaum, M., Hartley, K., Sinatra, G. M., Reynolds, R. E., & Bendixen, L. D. (2002), *Enhancing the quality of on-line discussions.* New Orleans, LA: Paper presented at the annual meeting of the American Educational Research Association.

Paulsen, M. F. (1995). *Online report on pedagogical techniques for computer-mediated communication.* Retrieved August 5, 2005, from http://www.nettskolen.com/pub/artikkel.xsql?artid=123.

Pawan, F., Paulus, T. M., Yalcin, S., & Chang, C. -F. (2003). Online learning: Patterns of engagement and interaction among in-service teachers. *Language Learning & Technology, 7*(3), 119–140. [online]. Retrieved December 16, 2003, from http://llt.msu.edu/vol7num3/pawan/.

Postman, N. (1992). *Technopoly.* New York: Macmillan.

Potter, W. J., & Levine-Donnerstein, D. (1999). Rethinking validity and reliability in content analysis. *Journal of Applied Communication Research, 27,* 258–284.

Renner, P. (1999). *The art of teaching adults: How to become an exceptional instructor and facilitator*. Vancouver, BC: The Training Associates.
Rourke, L. (2005). *Learning Through Online Discussion*. Unpublished doctoral dissertation. University of Alberta, Edmonton Alberta.
Rourke, L., & Anderson, T. (2004). Validity in quantitative content analysis. *Educational Technology Research and Development*, *52*(1), 5–18.
Rourke, L., Anderson, T., Garrison, D.R. & Archer, W. (2001). Assessing social presence in asynchronous text-based computer conferencing. *Journal of Distance Education* *14*(21), 50–71.
Salmon, G. (2000). *E-moderating. The key to teaching and learning online*. London: Kogan Page.
Seaman, D. F., & Fellenz, R. A. (1989). *Effective strategies for teaching adults*. Columbus, OH: Merrill Publishing Company.
Spears, R., & Lea, M. (1994). Panacea or panopticon? The hidden power in computer-mediated communication. *Communication Research*, *21*, 427–459.
Straus, S. G. (1997). Technology, group process, and group outcomes: Testing the connections in computer-mediated and face-to-face groups. *Human-Computer Interaction*, *12*(3), 227–266.
Tenenbaum, G., Naidu, S., Jegede, O., & Austin, J. (2001). Constructivist pedagogy in conventional on-campus and distance learning practice: An exploratory investigation. *Learning and Instruction*, *11*, 87–111.
Thomas, M. J. W. (2002). Learning with incoherent structures: The space of online discussion forums. *Journal of Computer Assisted Learning*, *18*, 351–366.
Williams, C. (2002). Learning on-line: A review of recent literature in a rapidly expanding field. *Journal of Further and Higher Education*, *26*(3), 263–272.
Xin, C., & Feenberg, A. (2005). Pedagogy in cyberspace: The dynamics of online discussion. Special studies of the ACT Lab. Vancouver, BC: Simon Fraser University.
Zimbardo, P. G. (1969). The human choice: Individuation reason and order versus deindividuation impulse and chaos. In W. J. Arnold & D. Levine (Eds.), *Nebraska Symposium on Motivation* (Vol. 17, pp. 237–307). Lincoln, NE: University of Nebraska Press.

Chapter 21
Windows into Teaching and Learning Through Social Annotation Practices

Hope J. Hartman

School of Education, The City College of New York, New York, NY, USA; Educational Psychology Program, City University of New York Graduate Center, New York, NY, USA, e-mail: hhartman@ccny.cuny.edu

Web-based instruction is having a major impact on teaching and learning because of its pervasive access and ability to enhance meaningfulness by facilitating learner-centered approaches and social networking, the essence of Web 2.0 applications. WebQuests, Project-Based Learning, Wikis, and authentic multiuser virtual environments such as Active Worlds, River City, and Second Life allow learners to immerse themselves in intellectually stimulating, highly motivating social interactions as they learn from and with each other and experts.

HyLighter

Using innovative social annotation software, HyLighter, participants connect with each other, interacting as a virtual learning community. Multiple readers comment on selected areas or objects within a single document (or multiple documents), view each other's comments through a composite display, and comment on each other's comments thereby creating a collective annotation of the document (Lebow, Lick, & Hartman, 2008). This system enables teaching and learning to achieve greater breadth and depth as users collaboratively analyze information and share their thoughts and experiences. It operationalizes Brown and Duguid's (1995) conception of documents building and maintaining social groups as meaning is constructed and negotiated.

HyLighter, a hybrid social software and hypermedia annotation system, provides a unique learning environment. It is a *social networking software* which uses Internet applications to form online communities through computer-mediated communication. HyLighter's *hypermedia capabilities* enable users to add multiple linkages from comments tied to specific areas of a document or page to related segments of audio, video, graphic, or textual data. These affordances help HyLighter extend the capacity of the document as a medium for the social construction of meaning.

H.J. Hartman (✉)
School of Education, The City College of New York, New York, NY, USA; Educational Psychology Program, City University of New York Graduate Center, New York, NY, USA
e-mail: hhartman@ccny.cuny.edu

M.S. Khine, I.M. Saleh (eds.), *New Science of Learning*,
DOI 10.1007/978-1-4419-5716-0_21,

In the process, HyLighter can improve individual and group performance across domains, disciplines, and tasks. Through various practices, HyLighter can enhance the quality of instruction, and develop proficient, strategic, higher-level thinkers, and self-directed learners, who know when, why, where, and how to apply knowledge and learning strategies across tasks and content areas (Lebow et al., 2008; Hartman, 2001a).

For over 5 years I have used Hylighter as a form of distributed learning, primarily in teacher education courses: Psychology of Learning and Teaching, Child and Adolescent Development (graduate), and Adolescent Learning and Development (undergraduate and graduate). Dede (2002) defines "Distributed Learning" as educational experiences that combine face-to-face teaching with synchronous and asynchronous mediated interaction. Students, preservice and in-service teachers, used HyLighter for a variety of collaborative interactions including (1) analyzing and discussing assigned articles and case studies, (2) connecting assigned readings with course theories and concepts, (3) connecting course ideas and materials with students' prior knowledge, backgrounds, and experiences, (4) integrating Internet-based concept mapping with other hypermedia and multimedia environments, and (5) analyzing, developing, and refining lesson plans.

Permission was obtained from publishers to upload and annotate documents in HyLighter. Students were taught how to use this social annotation software in a college multimedia lab where I provided assistance and feedback. This involved making comments on ideas that were meaningful to them, they considered to be important, or that raised questions, and making connections from course content to their own prior knowledge, personal experience, beliefs, cultural background, and their professional experiences. In some courses, instead of administering a final exam, as a culminating experience and authentic assessment students presented their HyLighter projects to the class using a Smartboard.

Annotating documents online is comparable to paper and pencil annotations in which readers highlight text and make comments. Contributors use the cursor to block the text they want to comment on and a comment box opens for their input. HyLighter's editor allows contributors to include hyperlinks, color, insert pictures, and modify or delete their comments. Users can also record and play audio annotations. The Compare feature enables viewing others' comments with a unique color-coding system: yellow reflects a segment of text that the user commented on but no one else did ("mine"), blue reflects a segment commented on by one or more other people but not the person doing the comparison ("theirs"), and green reflects an overlap between self and others, meaning "we" marked up and commented on the same segment of text ("ours"). With blue and green, the more people who highlighted and commented on the same segment of text, the darker the color. This color coding creates a cumulative distribution of multiple readers' intellectual travels through a document. Readers can track their own journey through a document or compare theirs with the teacher's (the expert) and their peers. See Fig. 21.1 (Lebow et al., 2008). The table format, organized by text segments, is an alternative way to display highlighted text and comments, and is very useful for viewing the "big picture" of responses.

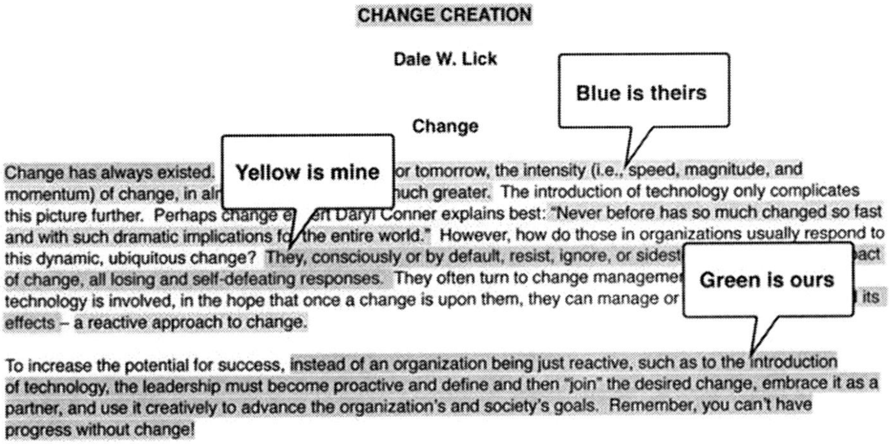

Fig. 21.1 Screen shot of color coding

In addition to commenting on text, users comment on each other's comments. This capability enables an asynchronous dialogue which reflects a key feature characterizing collaborative social annotations: feedback from peers and experts. This approach is an improvement over the more common threaded discussions which can easily lose focus on the text under discussion. Through social annotation, thinking becomes more transparent and users learn from and with each other. They become more aware of what they know and do not know, clarify comprehension, and evaluate and recognize their own strengths and weaknesses as teachers and as learners. These metacognitive processes enable users to apply this information reflectively for self-regulation, including self-diagnosis and self-correction. Consequently, learning and instruction are enhanced by acting on insights from collaboration-enhanced reflective analysis. Learning becomes more meaningful as prior knowledge and experience are activated and shared. Transfer is facilitated as learning is connected to past information, present understanding, and potential future applications. Social annotation also enables participants to develop broader and richer perspectives on content through sharing knowledge and strategies with others as members of a community of learners. Finally, both teachers and learners can become more motivated, have greater self-efficacy, and experience belongingness and collegiality as members of a reflective, interactive community focused on topics and activities of mutual interest.

Preliminary field tests of HyLighter at Tallahassee Community College and an online Masters Program at Florida State University identified the following benefits:

1. Increased participation, engagement, accountability, and completion rates in local and distance learning formats;
2. Development of active reading skills, enhanced learning from text, and improved writing skills;

3. Better quality of instruction;
4. Diagnosis of obstacles to learning;
5. Assessment of complex and higher-order cognitive skills;
6. Increased productivity of document-centered group work (Lebow, Lick, & Hartman, 2003–2004).

These findings indicate that HyLighter improved both teaching and learning. Applications of HyLighter discussed in this chapter validate and extend these findings.

Theoretical Underpinnings

A combination of complementary theoretical frameworks underlies this work. Dede's (2002) Distributed Learning emphasizes students' cognitive engagement with material in a broader social context than could occur in a classroom alone, because online learning facilitates interaction with students who do not participate in a face-to-face environment. Related work by Lefoe (1998) on design for web-based constructivist instruction is based on the rejection of teaching as knowledge transmission and acquisition in favor of an emphasis on learners' initiative and autonomy in constructing knowledge.

Vygotskyian Social Constructivism contributes to understanding the mechanisms and predicting benefits of the social annotation practices afforded by HyLighter. Feedback from peers and the professor scaffolds users within the Zone of Proximal Development from their actual to their potential levels of understanding and performance (Vygotsky, 1978). Using technology for scaffolding is a common theme in education today; animated pedagogical agents are another example.

At least three principles from Piagetian Cognitive Constructivism can explain the mechanisms and predict benefits of collaborative social annotation practices. First is active engagement in learning "...based upon personal need and interest" (Piaget, 1971 p. 152). Using individual experiences and values as a basis for selecting and commenting on text and reading others' comments encourages meaningful reflection on and reconceptualization of material rather than merely passively encoding it. Second is the role of social experience in intellectual development, which is among the mechanisms Piaget identified (1973). Social annotation exposes learners to multiple perspectives as they exchange ideas and collaborate on constructing thought, in this case about documents and videos, drawing on their diverse personal, cultural, and professional backgrounds. Third is equilibration, which emphasizes the role of conflict in promoting intellectual development. The varied perspectives encountered are sometimes discrepant or contradictory, engendering cognitive conflict. Meaning can be reconstructed, reconciling discrepancies, and resolving conflicts by thinking at new and higher levels.

The BACEIS model of improving thinking. (Hartman & Sternberg, 1993) is a comprehensive framework of factors internal and external to the student which affect

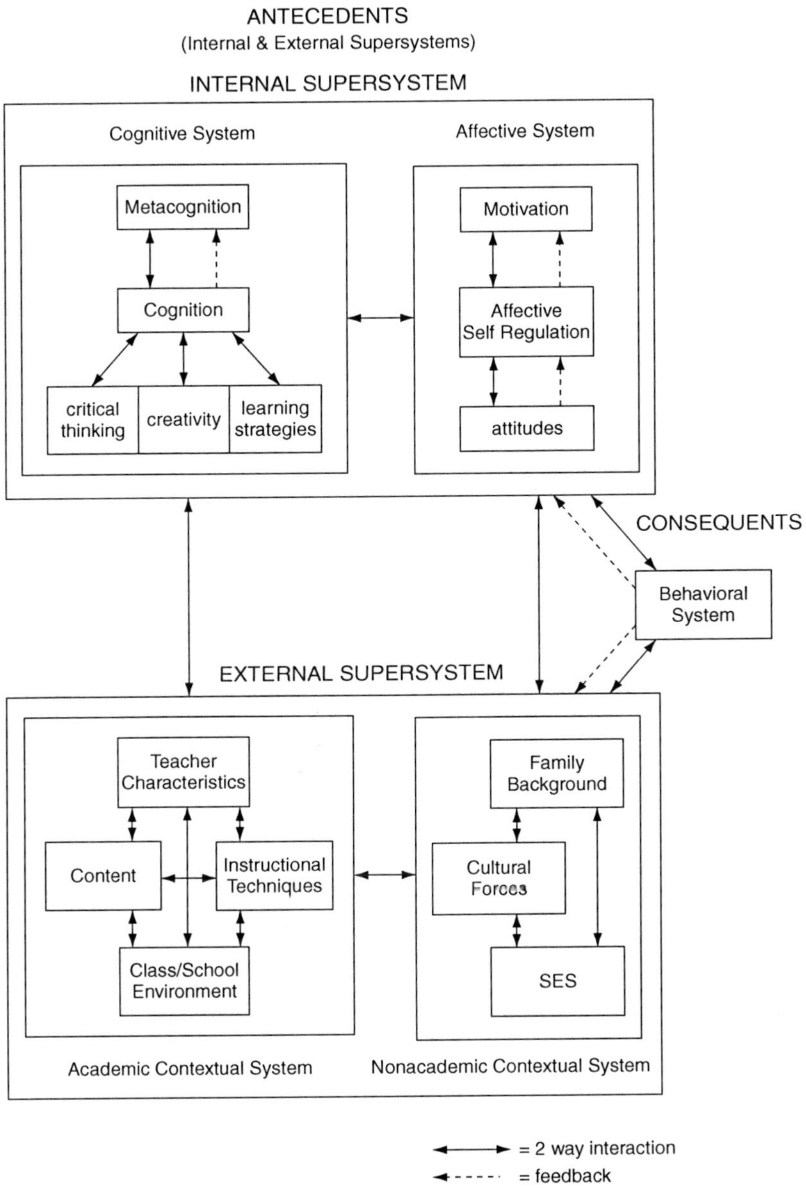

Fig. 21.2 BACEIS model components (Hartman & Sternberg, 1993)

a student's academic performance (Fig. 21.2). Factors internal to the student are cognition (thinking and learning) and affect (motivation and attitudes); factors external to the student are academic (e.g., school and classroom) and nonacademic (e.g., family, culture) environments. The BACEIS acronym represents: B = behavior,

A = affect, C = cognition, E = environment, I = interacting, S = systems. Internal and external components interact to impact intellectual and academic behavior.

In applying this theory to social annotation, the cognitive component is especially important. This includes metacognitive processes of reflecting on, activating, and applying prior knowledge and experience, and critical thinking about text. Considering the affective component, social annotation can be highly motivating as learners participate in an online community which can enhance attitudes such as self-efficacy, curiosity, and open-mindedness. Using this technology as an instructional strategy (academic environment) can encourage preservice and in-service teachers to incorporate cutting-edge technology into their own teaching. Finally, learners make connections between course documents and the nonacademic environment by relating coursework to their cultural, professional, personal, and family backgrounds. These connections often make coursework more interesting and meaningful, thus reflecting interactions between the academic and nonacademic environments and learners' cognition and affect.

Interactive Reading

HyLighter's Interactive Annotation enables students to learn from and with each other while engaged in course assignments including required reading of articles and case studies.

Articles

One article was "The Biology of Risk Taking" (Price, 2005). Tables 21.1 and 21.2 show segments of text spontaneously annotated by students. In Table 21.1 the annotated text is: "We now understand that adolescent turmoil, which we used to view as an expression of raging hormones, is actually the result of a complex interplay of body chemistry, brain development, and cognitive growth" (Buchanan, Eccles, & Becker 1992).

Table 21.1 Students' spontaneously annotated text on adolescent turmoil

Comments on this text	Interpretation of comments
"not hormones but still biological?"	Suggests need for clarification
"I am curious to understand more about adolescent development. it would provide insight to many difficult situations in the classroom"	Shows desire for more information and why it would be useful
"Now there's a better understanding of the complexities of factors affecting adolescent development"	Reflects understanding and appreciation of information in the text

Table 21.2 shows another example of comments and interpretations from spontaneously annotated text.

Annotated Text: "... the changes of puberty have long been understood to usher in adulthood; in many cultures, puberty and the capacity to conceive continue to mark entry into adulthood. In contrast, puberty in modern Western culture has become a multi-step entry process into a much longer period of adolescence" (King, 2002).

Table 21.2 Students' spontaneous comments on changes in puberty

Comments on this text	Interpretation of comments
"culture sees maturity as a time a lot like being younger. teenagers simply became more sexual. behavior not as disrespectful, or aggressive"	Shows preconceptions about puberty, oversimplification of text and writing flaws
"In many ways I am yet to consider myself an adult. I have only recently become self-sufficient, having lived by the benevolent generosity of my parents for many years	Reflects personal connection between text and own background, experience and perspective.
Puberty, and the changes it brings, have lost some importance in western culture. No longer does it signify the degree of adulthood that it once did. Children enter puberty in their early teens, but aren't really adults for many years after I think that as more and more people go to college and beyond, the age of adulthood increases. Self-sufficiency is a requirement of adulthood for my family. Puberty might signify the beginning of adolescence, but adolescence is a time period of varying lengths depending on an individuals maturity level and when they enter the working world"	Shows understanding of text and appreciation of the complexity of pubertal maturation
"The culture I came from defines adolescents as the middle point from acting as a child to acting as an adult. These adolescents who are going through puberty are going through changes physically, mentally and emotionally. They struggle to maintain their own identity while trying to fit in with their peers"	Shows connection to own culture. Reflects understanding the multidimensional components of puberty and recognizing an important problem that arises in the process.
"How do cultural influences extend or contract this adolescent period? Does the expectation of a crazy adolescence create one for Western teens?"	Reveals curiosity about the effects of culture on puberty and how expectations affect teenagers' performance

Examples in Tables 21.1 and 21.2 demonstrate students' comprehension, personal perspectives, curiosity, cultural differences, and variations in the scope and length of their spontaneous comments.

The author posed questions which students were instructed to highlight, answer and compare with their classmates' answers. One question was "Why do adolescents take risks?" Some students' answers were as follows:

- "I do not think that they are fundamentally different from young adults. However, I do believe that so many things are changing with their mental and physical development that they tend to experience more mood changes than adults. However, they are able to think and act very mature and stable as well."
- " they feel invincible."
- "Adolescents take risks sometimes as a way of testing the limits/boundaries of life. They need to learn some lessons of life the hard way. Sometimes it takes getting burned by fire to learn to respect its power. Part of the reason for the passion expressed by teens is the fact that they are experiencing so much for the first time. Everything is so exciting and new. They have not experienced the full set of consequences of living. The first time that you fall in love, you never imagine that it will eventually end. Experience and statistics will enlighten you at a later stage in your life. The same way that it takes time to learn how to cope with the effects of foreign substances in your body, it takes time to cope with changes in your internal body chemistry. In other words, getting used to determining how to cope with the effects of alcohol has some similarities with getting used to coping with changes in hormone levels. This is demonstrated throughout adulthood in terms of changes in the levels of hormones in males and females and the accompanying changes in behaviors, feelings and moods."

These examples show the striking variability in students' answers to the question posed by the author, and mirror the variability that typically occurred. By comparing their responses with their peers, students could self-evaluate the depth and complexity of their thinking and consider adolescent risk taking from the perspectives of everyone in the class, thereby enhancing thinking and meaningful learning. Class discussions rarely enable all students to answer the same question in detail, so this is a specific benefit of annotating text within the HyLighter environment.

HyLighter enables documents to be living, dynamic objects which teachers can tailor to the characteristics of particular courses and students. Although the author posed excellent questions in "The Biology of Risk Taking" to prompt more interactivity, reflection, and critical thinking, and require students to consider other issues, I embedded my own questions within the article. The questions were linked to specific sections of the article and included instructions for students to answer them and to read each other's answers.

One question that I embedded required students to reflect on and share views of adolescent maturity based on their cultural background. Activating and communicating this information was intended to prompt both meaningful learning and transfer. The question was "How does the culture that you came from view the maturity of adolescents?" Examples of students' answers are as follows:

- "The culture that I came from viewed adolescents as somewhat unable to function on their own, or dependent. Therefore their opinions were unimportant. "Seen, but not heard."
- "My cultural background is Austrian. My mother being a war bride after WWII came to this country with a very strict and authoritarian attitude as was in her

adolescent years from my grandparents. As an only child of working parents there was no room for silliness and foolishness in my family. I grew up independent and I rarely got into trouble, but I sure had lots of friends and lots of fun. Not quite what my parents was expecting to see on my report cards.

My adolescent years were a great time in my life. Being an only child, I had become very extraverted and outgoing. I grew up proud and I was always involved. I was very active into sports and socializing. I did grow up to fear my mother's wrath. She was not to be trifled with. I was always getting lectured from my mother up until I was age 50 when she past away.

My only times of trouble was getting arrested at age 14 with two of my best friends. We got caught shooting fireworks on July 3rd. July 4th the cops would have been too busy to bother with us. Your best friends are the ones sitting next to you in trouble and saying that sure was fun! The only other time I was in trouble was when I was 16 and my parents caught me sneaking off to the airport to take flying lessons. They found my log book and my mother was not too impressed.

My adolescent years were a more respectful time. Neighbors could be heard telling children, 'I'm gonna tell your mother.' There was much more respect in the school system from students and a fear of a teacher sending you to the principle. This is not so much the case today. The respect for elders is severely lacking."

- "As a third generation Lithuanian/Polish American with "old (European) school" parents, my puberty was only referred to nominally. I think my mother said "You're a woman now" when menses began. There certainly was no bat mitzvah or quince anos celebration. While my physical maturity was pretty much avoided as a topic of conversation, my intellectual maturity was engaged on a regular basis. The transition to adulthood was gradual as I was given increased social responsibility."

These comments show critical thinking and diverse perspectives about adolescent maturity, recognizing its complexity, and identifying strengths and weaknesses. Comments reflect students' transfer of course concepts regarding cognition and affect and influences from the nonacademic environment. Embedded questions prompt structured interaction and engagement with the material, bridging academic content, students' personal, cultural, and social lives, and their professional experiences. Responding to such questions makes learning more meaningful, helps learners connect new information with their prior knowledge, deepens thinking about the content and concepts, and shows nuances in their thinking. Questions open windows for students to look through and reflect on their own and each other's perspectives, experiences, and cultures. They reveal differences in the content and quality of students' thinking. Students who write short, simple responses might be surprised to see the depth and complexity of their peers' thinking, and vice versa. Also, questions invite critical thinking about students' cultural traditions and their own personal beliefs, values, and experiences.

From a professor's perspective, awareness of the variety of cultural backgrounds and similarities and differences in students' points of view and experiences provides a framework for better curriculum and instruction to respond to the unique characteristics of each class. Seeing the differences in their depth and complexity of thinking, and differential use of abstract generalizations and personal examples can facilitate teaching metacognitively by providing insights which guide planning, monitoring, and evaluating instruction for individual classes (Hartman, 2001b).

Students' responses externalize their thinking about course material so professors have the opportunity to learn what students have difficulty understanding, identify relevant prior knowledge that students can build on, identify and strategize to overcome misconceptions, see how students connect what they are reading to their own experiences, and assess their mastery of course material. Students are also able to help clarify each other's thinking by providing explanations and/or examples of confusing concepts. Meaning is thereby socially constructed through interactions of peers with each other and the professor.

In addition to questions, I embedded hyperlinks in the article so students could learn more about material by accessing Internet resources. One example was a link to details about "Tanner's 4 stages of pubertal maturation" which was mentioned as important, but not described.

Unpublished Document

In Fall 2008 I uploaded my Summary of Research on Parenting Styles so students could learn the content and practice using HyLighter for their major project of the semester, described later in this chapter. Fifty-one comments were made. Figure 21.3 is a screen shot from the beginning of the document showing some of the highlighting and comments.

Following are color-coded annotated excerpts from this screen shot with the corresponding comments. Contributors were identified online (see Fig. 21.3), but not here to preserve students' privacy.

Text: Diana Baumrind (1991) defined parenting style as the normal variations in parents' attempts to socialize and control their children. Baumrind studied 100 predominantly white, middle class preschool children (green, "ours") in California (1967, 1971).

Corresponding comments:

- "Baumind findings may not relate to all ethnic group."
- "While there may be interesting implications and findings from this study, the same study should be done in different settings using different populations (e.g., other ethnicities or socio-economic status (SES)). How interesting to then compare the results of the same study on different populations."
- (Me) "This makes the implications limited for our community because of our extensive ethnic and cultural diversity."

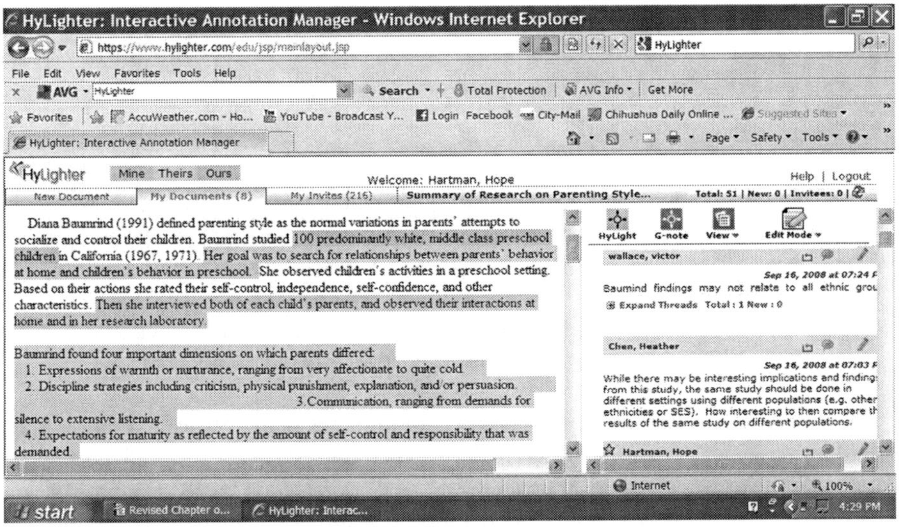

Fig. 21.3 Screen shot from annotated summary of research on parenting styles

- "I agree, the more cultural and ethnic diversity involved the more accurate the result of the research. People from different background tend to have different belief which shows up in the way they educate their children."
- "I agree with you too. I think that's why many students abilities are misinterpeted or there is misconceptions, because of the preconceptions that has been placed upon them."
- "I will have to agree, we live in a City that is very diverse, i feel that is the study would have been conducted with a more diverse group the results might have been a little diffrent since, diffrent cultures have diffrent morals & beliefs."
- "I would also have to agree. Hos would that work in NYC with all the diversity? I don't think it would."

These comments show students and me in a critical thinking dialogue about the research.

Text: Then she interviewed both of each child's parents, and observed their interactions at home and in her research laboratory. (yellow, "mine")

Corresponding Comment: Me: "Good methodology."

Although no students commented on this text segment, they could learn from the "expert" about the soundness of the research methodology.

Text: Baumrind found four important dimensions on which parents differed:

1. Expressions of warmth or nurturance, ranging from very affectionate to quite cold.
2. Discipline strategies including criticism, physical punishment, explanation, and/or persuasion.

3. Communication, ranging from demands for silence to extensive listening.
4. Expectations for maturity as reflected by the amount of self-control and responsibility that was demanded. (blue, "theirs")

Corresponding Comments:

- "In referencing the four (4) dimensions on which parents differed, it would be interesting to know what percentage of each parent/ mother and father, reflected what percentage of each category of the four dimensions, since both parents were interviewed, and what elements could have played a factor."
- "Baumrind's findings very useful. Refering to the statement that parenting styles vary with (SES), this is very true speaking from a personal point of view."

Students' comments, complete with spelling and grammar mistakes, show their thinking about the research. In addition to students reflecting on their own experience and learning about their classmates, making learning more meaningful, and eliciting critical thinking about the content, the comments elucidated my students' (1) backgrounds, (2) perspectives, (3) academic needs, for example, writing skills, and (4) interests, such as more detailed research results.

Case Studies

To prepare for annotating case studies in HyLighter, students were first required to annotate several case studies by hand in their case study text. Some made copies of cases rather than writing in the book. Others used Postits for comments instead of writing in the margins, a technique they learned in a literacy course. Then they annotated case studies in HyLighter.

Virtually all students successfully annotated assigned cases. Some students chose to read a case first and then went back and did the annotations. After using HyLighter for case study annotations, students met in small groups to discuss the case, how they decided what to highlight, and how their comments were influenced by their own backgrounds. Some chose not to read other peoples' comments until they were done with their own because they did not want to be influenced in their own annotations.

Annotations of the case study "A Teacher is Dedicated to Promoting Creativity in All Students" (Kowalski, Weaver, & Henson 1994) included the following text segment: "The continuing migration of other cultures to America is another factor that exacerbates the need for teachers to be committed to individualized learning." Following are corresponding comments:

- "one reason of teachers' individualized learning"
- "yes, in different ways and by using different approach to teach"
- "More heterogeneous groupings are formed as a result of the various cultural groups that generally make up classrooms today. This shows that teachers who

represent a more homogeneous group must be culturally sensitive to the needs of each student helping all students become successful."
- "Migration has lead to programs such as bilingual education and English as a Second Language (ESL)."
- (Me): "Increasing cultural diversity of classrooms creates additional challenges to teachers for understanding, accepting and assisting individual students. It also creates increasing opportunities for students from different backgrounds to learn from and about each other as individuals."

The first two comments suggest dialogue with the author and possibly each other. The third comment shows connections between the case study and concepts from our course, with a possible misconception of "homogeneous group." The fourth comment shows transfer from the case study to content learned in another course. My comment emphasizes a primary objective of what students are expected to learn in this course.

Outcomes

At the end of semester students evaluated their use of HyLighter for annotating articles and case studies. Results showed:

1. Many students reported that using HyLighter made them more active readers and that annotating and comparing annotations increased meaningfulness and memorability of what they read. A few students disliked highlighting but liked writing comments.
2. Some students thought about what they were highlighting for the first time.
3. Before this experience, some thought that all highlighting was of equal value and there were no better or worse ways to highlight; it was just a matter of personal style or preferences.
4. Two students did not highlight anything because they viewed everything as equally important. They failed to realize the importance of being selective.
5. Some students were relieved that they could highlight a section of text and did not have to comment in the dialogue box.
6. Most students liked comparing their highlights and comments with peers and the teacher to determine whether they missed anything important or focused on irrelevant details.
7. One student failed to use HyLighter when she heard there was a bug in the program because she thought that meant you would get a virus by using it!
8. Several students complained that the small size of the comment box made it hard to monitor their own writing.
9. Students generally persisted and enjoyed the HyLighter experience despite initial difficulties using it because of browser or other problems.
10. Virtually all students were fascinated by the differences between peers' highlights and comments.

11. Small group discussions about using HyLighter and students' background influences were extremely rich and enlightening, especially because about half of the class was born abroad.

Students' comments on articles and case studies, and their end of semester evaluations demonstrated collaborative, meaningful learning, thinking critically and metacognitively, and transferring from their own experience to what they learned in their coursework. Online dialogue about readings elicited participation of shy students who did not participate in class because they felt self-conscious and/or were insecure speaking in a nonnative language. Online they could take the time to look up spellings of words and did not have to worry about their pronunciation or speech speed, so they were more comfortable as contributing members of a community of learners.

HyLighter not only opened windows into students' perspectives and experiences, but also elucidated questions students had and topics they wanted to know more about, which was used to refine and extend instruction. I identified and corrected students' misconceptions through analyzing and responding to comments in the case studies. For example, one student thought that praise was an intrinsic motivator because it made the student feel good inside. Another student confused Kounin's classroom management principle "withitness" with his concept of "overlapping" and erroneously referred to "withitness" as "whiteness," perhaps because English was not her native language. By correcting these errors within the context of the case studies, learning occurred in a meaningful situation which facilitates comprehension, memory and transfer. The professor's and selected students' annotations were used as models to scaffold other students' development of effective highlighting and commenting skills.

Collaborative Concept Mapping

In Spring 2005, with cooperation from the Institute for Human and Machine Cognition, developers of CMAP, online concept mapping software, and David Lebow, developer of HyLighter, graduate, and undergraduate students in Adolescent Learning and Development collaboratively developed electronic concept maps using a combination of HyLighter and CMAP. A concept map is a knowledge representation with linking words specifying relationships between ideas and is designed to promote meaningful learning. "The meaning we acquire for a given concept is formed from the composite of propositions we know that contain that concept. The richness of meaning we have for a concept increases exponentially with the number of valid propositions we learn that relate that concept to other concepts." (Novak, 1998, p. 40). At the end of the semester, groups of students presented their collaboratively constructed concept maps to the rest of the class.

Combining HyLighter with Concept Mapping can have potential benefits including

1. facilitating and accelerating the development of structural knowledge
2. enabling coordinated group inquiry
3. supporting collaboration for reorganizing and synthesizing ideas from multiple sources
4. creating opportunities for new types of authentic learning and assessment activities
5. creating an alternative approach to concept mapping which ties nodes to annotations
6. expanding the concept of a knowledge model to include collective annotation. (Lebow & Lick, 2004).

Student-created concept maps integrating course readings with the theoretical framework underlying the course enabled students to construct their own big picture of course concepts and their interconnections. Students were able to link five course readings with their electronic concept maps: two chapters and three case studies. Case study topics included drug abuse, homework, teacher expectations, and assessment. Chapters were on metacognition in learning and in teaching. Additional course concepts, from How People Learn (2000), included expert versus novice teachers and scaffolding within the Zone of Proximal Development.

The BACEIS model, described earlier, is the theoretical framework underlying ideas in the courses, providing the "big picture" for students to connect what they learned though their readings and classwork (see Fig. 21.2). In addition to being trained in the use of HyLighter, as previously described, students were provided with detailed instructions on how to download and install CMAP and how to use it with HyLighter to create their own Concept Maps organized around the BACEIS model.

Before constructing CMAPS, students were required to generate propositions from course content that could be used to show connections between concepts, readings and the BACEIS model. Each student was required to individually create a set of propositions, which groups then synthesized for their project. The propositions appeared as a list in the CMAP work environment. Students used the concept maps to show their understanding of the concept label at each node and how the propositions were related to each other and the BACEIS model. Concept labels were linked to annotated course readings about the specific propositions. Propositions included:

1. cognition affects achievement
2. affect affects achievement
3. metacognition directs cognition
4. metacognition characterizes expert performance
5. inner speech guides thinking
6. domain-specific knowledge affects thinking
7. culture affects learning
8. feedback improves learning
9. scaffolding is based on the ZPD
10. teachers should model metacognition

Constructing CMAPS required students to discuss the readings and how key concepts from them connected to the propositions that they generated individually related to the BACEIS model. Reviewing the relationships between students' propositions and the readings helped them monitor their comprehension of the propositions as they fit them into their own conceptualization of the theoretical framework. Next, students negotiated which ideas and propositions to incorporate into the CMAP and how to structure it. Then they created hot links to corresponding ideas in the five readings annotated in HyLighter. When clicking on an icon located within a node (e.g., metacognition), a menu of all concepts linked to the selected node appeared. Clicking on a concept term opened a window with a list of all highlighted excerpts matching the selected proposition extracted from all five documents in the database. Consequently, students collaboratively synthesized course concepts and materials and coconstructed a three–dimensional (3D) knowledge structure. This process and product had the unique benefit of integrating and contextualizing important concepts.

Following (Figs. 21.4 and 21.5) are two examples of student-generated, collaboratively annotated CMAPS. These two were selected for inclusion here because of their size. Most of the CMAPS were too big and detailed for readability in a book. Conversely, online, you can easily change their size so they are readable, but with static print you cannot. Consequently, the richest, most thorough and detailed CMAPS could not be displayed in this chapter effectively!

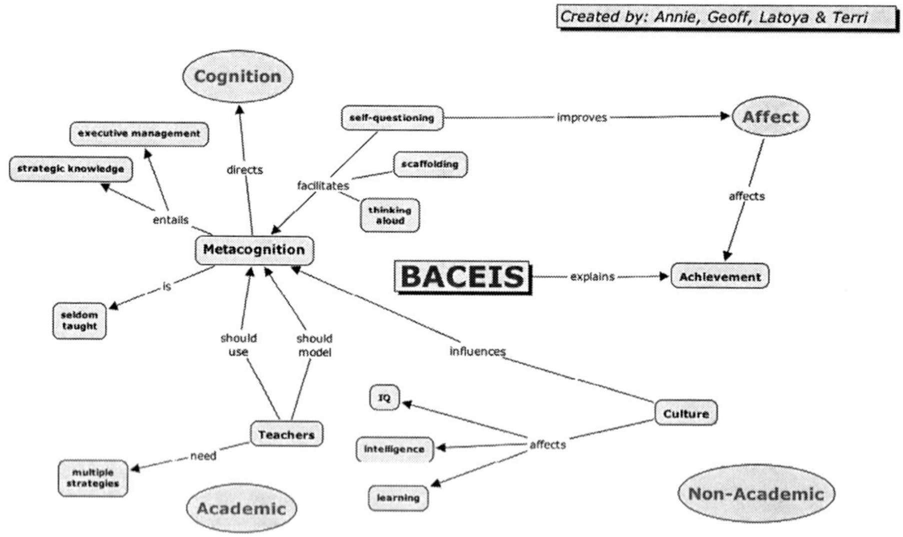

Fig. 21.4 Student-generated HyLighter enhanced 3D CMAP

From a teaching perspective, the individual propositions students created and the resulting group 3D CMAPS showed how many and which ideas students considered most important, how they understood the relationships between ideas and recognized connections between their readings and the BACEIS model. Some students'

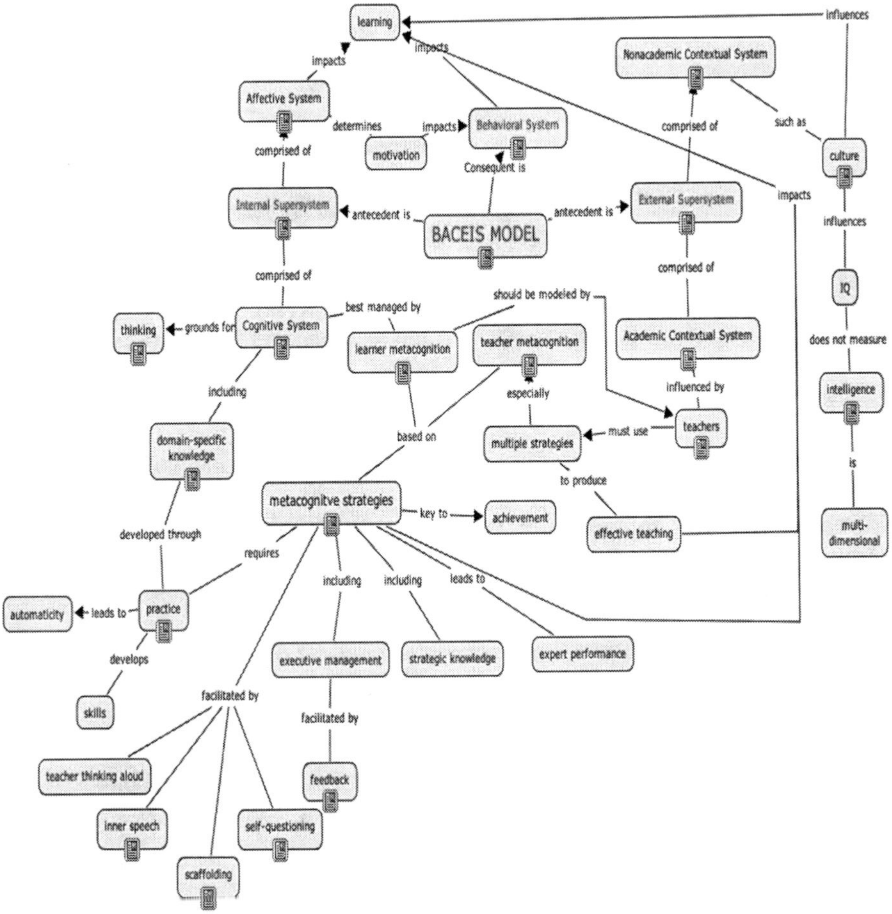

Fig. 21.5 Student-generated HyLighter-enhanced 3D CMAP

appreciation of the logic and complexity of interrelationships was impressive. Sometimes it was disappointing to see the oversimplification of information from readings and connections with the theoretical framework. However this feedback was important for planning my teaching for the next semester—more frequently and explicitly highlighting the complexities and interrelationships. Also, subsequently I stopped uploading long, technical chapters in HyLighter because students found their annotation tedious and too time consuming. Conversely, students enjoyed annotating the short case studies.

Another illuminating observation was that while most students mastered the requisite technologies for this project, some students were overwhelmed by them, in part because they had limited experience with computers and did not have them at home. These students were allowed to create a hand-drawn concept map and tell about connections between the readings and the BACEIS model. The Digital Divide persists, and affected the performance of some students on this project.

Hypermedia-Enhanced Lesson Plans

This project was intended to help preservice and in-service teachers use a combination of technologies in order to apply what they learned in their coursework to an actual lesson. InTime, http://www.intime.uni.edu, has a comprehensive database of pedagogically sound, technology-enhanced, multimedia lessons across the curriculum from prekindergarten through high school. A Hypermedia Lesson Plan has hot links embedded within it. The InTime lesson plans include links to national standards and to definitions of terms from their pedagogical model. "Hypermedia-Enhanced" means that the hypermedia lesson plans include elaborations, here by annotating connections to course concepts and theories, and identifying and linking relevant video clips illustrating the connections.

The following were project goals:

- Synthesize ideas from the course as they applied to a particular exemplary lesson from InTime.
- Enhance abilities to make connections between ideas from the course and resources available on the Internet.
- Demonstrate deep understanding of principles of effective learning, teaching, and development.
- Connect lesson plans and course material to required fieldwork experiences.
- Become part of a community of teachers and learners who learn from and with each other to improve their teaching and learning.

The project focused on five out of ten parts of InTime's "Technology as Facilitator of Quality Education Model": Learning, Information Processing, Democracy, Teacher Knowledge, and Teacher Behavior, each of which had corresponding probing questions and a video.

Students had three main tasks: First, to select a lesson plan to work on individually or in a group and answer the pre- and postvideo observation questions. The purpose of answering the questions was to increase meaningfulness and deepen their understanding of the lesson. The procedure followed for each of the five parts of the model was as follows:

1. Individually answer each prevideo viewing question.
2. Synthesize answers to prevideo viewing questions as a group.
3. View the video.
4. Individually answer each postvideo viewing question.
5. Synthesize answers to postvideo viewing questions as a group.

Second, students annotated connections between InTime lesson plans, videos, course material, and fieldwork experiences. After individually annotating the lesson plans with these connections, identifying and explaining them, and making links to corresponding video clips, groups discussed and synthesized their connections and selected video clips. Some of these connections and videos were presented at the end of semester. As the semester progressed, students had increasing opportunities to make connections from readings, coursework, and their fieldwork. To help students make relevant connections, they were provided with these examples: activating students' prior knowledge of a topic, teaching strategies (e.g., use of scaffolding, cooperative learning, and culturally responsive teaching); transfer to different subjects, transfer to everyday life, theories from our course, students' metacognitive knowledge, strategies, and skills; students' motivation and self-perceptions; teachers' attitudes; and influences of the nonacademic environment such as parents' attitudes, behavior, and school involvement.

Third, during our final class, groups selectively presented their annotated questions, lesson plans and video clips to the class from HyLighter using a Smartboard. Presentations required shifting back and forth between the HyLighter-based questions and lesson plans and the InTime videos though hyperlinks. Students were graded on their answers to the probing questions, the connections and videos identified, and their class presentation.

Students benefited from this project in numerous ways including (1) They learned from each other when discussing answers to the pre- and postvideo viewing questions in their groups; (2) Their ability to apply course concepts was enhanced by reading each other's lesson plan annotations, discussing the course connections based on their readings, coursework and fieldwork; and negotiating which were best illustrated in the lesson and most important to include in their final group products and presentations. For example, students analyzing the InTime lesson "Introduction to Black Studies" made connections to course concepts such as open-mindedness, and they critically analyzed the teacher's and students' performance, including racial stereotyping and problem solving. They connected the lesson to course theories, including practical intelligence (Sternberg, 1985) and interpersonal intelligence (Gardner, 1985); (3) Through this activity they obtained teaching experience as they presented their final group annotated questions, lesson plans, and corresponding videos to the class and learned from other groups who made presentations on different lesson plans. Finally, all students benefited from their experiences working with these cutting-edge technologies: the sophisticated InTime model and lesson plan database, HyLighter, and a Smartboard. These benefits provided students and me with windows into both learning and teaching. Students had deeper understanding of themselves and each other as learners, how to design effective lesson plans, and how to use technology to enhance instruction. I identified differential values and difficulties learning and applying various course concepts and theories and learned how to more effectively design technology-based group projects.

Collaboratively Developed Lesson Plans

Early in Fall 2008, students learned and practiced using HyLighter to prepare for their major project of the semester: collaborative development of lesson plans. Feedback from the Hypermedia-Enhanced Lesson Plan project the previous semester showed that although students greatly benefited from their collaborative lesson plan analysis, they would have rather collaboratively developed their own lesson plans.

Depending upon which course preservice and in-service teacher education students were taking, they learned about and applied either the Universal Design for Learning (UDL; Crawford, 2008) or Rich Instruction Model (RIM; Hartman & Sternberg, 1993) to the development of lesson plans. In the undergraduate Adolescent Learning and Development course, students applied the UDL to developing a single lesson plan; in the graduate version of that course students applied UDL to developing a 5-day unit. Graduate students in the Psychology of Learning and Teaching course applied the RIM to the development of a single lesson plan. In all courses each student was responsible for developing a lesson plan, but worked collaboratively in a group to help each other apply what they learned in our course to refine and improve their lesson plan designs.

Classes met in the Multimedia Lab for guidance as they uploaded the first drafts of their lesson plans in the end of October. Beginning then and continuing in November students were required to provide members of their subject content-based groups (e.g., science group) with feedback. Three reasons for the feedback component of the assignment, half the project grade, were to help their group members (peers) develop effective unit/lesson plans; to help students self-evaluate and improve their own unit/lesson plans; and to learn and practice applying research-based principles of effective feedback.

Students were given the following research-based feedback guidelines for making comments on each other's lesson plans (Bruner, 1966; Hartman, 2009):

- Teach learners to reflect on their performance and give themselves feedback. Ask about their perceptions of what and how well they are doing.
- Present feedback in a useful way for learners.
- Time feedback carefully for maximum impact, for example, when they can use it to correct their mistakes or otherwise improve their performance.
- Ensure learners are in an appropriate frame of mind for receiving feedback, for example, not when upset or anxious.
- Translate feedback into the learner's mode or way of thinking to maximize its potential use.
- Provide some encouraging feedback as well as criticism. If learners feel some areas of strength and degree of success, they are more likely to be motivated to improve their performance than if they feel that everything they do is wrong.
- Avoid overloading learners with criticism. We all have limited capacities for taking in information, especially criticism, so be selective and focus on the most important points rather than a comprehensive account of all flaws at once. Too much negative feedback can overwhelm learners and decrease their motivation to improve their performance.
- Structure feedback in a way that will encourage independent learning so that learners do not become dependent upon your feedback. For example, instead of telling the correct answer, pose a question which will lead learners to think in

the correct direction, and give guidance for self-correction so they can find the answer on their own.

I also provided each student with feedback so they could develop better lesson/unit plans.

The first week in December students uploaded their second drafts and again were required to provide each other with feedback. I also gave a second round of feedback to each student so they could make further improvements. Table 21.3 summarizes the feedback students gave each other.

Table 21.3 Analysis of students' feedback to each other

Category	Types of feedback
Questioning or explaining	• Why particular teaching methods and instructional materials were selected • Demographics of the target students in terms of grade/achievement level, and linguistic/cultural background • Purpose of the unit/lesson • Support students will need to complete assigned tasks • How effective the planned lesson would be in achieving the identified objectives • Amount and level of material to be covered • Prior knowledge/skill/experience needed for the unit/lesson • How students should approach a task • How to make the unit/lesson plan more consistent with the prescribed model • Connection to a theory studied in the course
Recommending	• Elaborations on the planned lesson • Alternative approaches to the lesson or alternative materials • How lesson content or skills could be transferred to everyday life experience • How to make the lesson more interesting or exciting • Ways to assess students' performance or judge their work
Other	• Praising good teaching methods and instructional materials • Correcting invalid information • Clarifying a concept, explanation or approach

Some students engaged in a dialogue about the lesson, responding to each other's and my comments and questions, and guiding each other to supplemental Internet or print resources. Additionally, some students used HyLighter metacognitively to make notes to themselves about changes to make in their plans. Most commonly the feedback I provided was to improve the alignment of the lesson design with the assigned model and to make more and more specific connections between their lessons and our coursework.

Following lesson presentations, a discussion of students' reactions to this assignment resulted in these conclusions: (1) working collaboratively on lesson plan design helped them better understand and apply the assigned model; (2) occasionally collaboration was unbalanced as some members of a group provided extensive and useful feedback to their peers while others provided minimal and/or superficial feedback; (3) the lesson design models were valued ways to conceptualize development of a lesson or unit; (4) collaborating on lesson/unit plan development was highly motivating and enhanced their feelings of self-efficacy; (5) using the HyLighter environment facilitated asynchronous collaboration; and (6) annotating lesson plans in HyLighter helped preservice and in-service teachers learn and learn to teach more metacognitively.

Limitations

The Digital Divide affected some of my students' abilities to engage in social annotation for various reasons: because they did not have computers at home, had no Internet access, had computers with dial-up connections, or had out-of-date browsers.

Other limitations were resistance to using any instructional technology, objection to being required to use a new technology or impatience with the learning process. A final disadvantage was working with this software during Beta testing, while there were still bugs in the system. A few students expressed resentment for being "guinea pigs" while the software was under development. However, in most cases these feelings were relatively minor compared to students' experience of the profound educational benefits of HyLighter's social annotation, both as learners and as teachers.

Conclusions

HyLighter used technology to create, support, and mediate relationships among learners and between the professor and the students while making learning deeper, broader and more meaningful. It enhanced complex cognition and metacognition, such as critical thinking, self-regulation, and self-directed learning, which contributed to learners transferring what they learned from one situation to another. Also it made learning more enjoyable, satisfying, and memorable, thereby enhancing motivation and feelings of self-efficacy. The social network feature has the potential to maintain relationships so students can continue to learn from and with each other in the future, as both students and as teachers.

In my classes, social annotation opened windows into learners' own and each other's thinking. It made learning meaningful while working both independently and in groups as they activated and applied prior knowledge from their own backgrounds and experiences and transferred what they learned from coursework. Students continuously compared and contrasted their knowledge, developing understanding, experience, and interpretations of what they read in the lesson plans, articles, and case studies and what they saw in the videos, with peers and the teacher. These activities facilitated self-reflection: helping students use various metacognitive reading strategies, including self-questioning, reviewing, monitoring their comprehension, clarifying confusing terms or concepts; thinking about content critically, and making connections to our coursework (Hartman, 2001a). Examining each other's comments and giving each other feedback helped students analyze course material, evaluate it in terms of its relevance to assigned tasks, and decide how to apply it. It enabled learners to monitor and evaluate their performance on academic tasks and assess their progress in connecting what they read with their prior knowledge, personal experiences, and professional situations. Preservice and in-service teachers also used what they learned from annotating readings, videos, and lesson plans to analyze real life classrooms—their own or in their fieldwork.

Learners' structured interaction with the material (cognitive activity) and each other (social activity), created engagement with the material (affective—motivational state). HyLighter-enabled practices deepened their understanding of texts and professional artifacts such as classroom videos, concept maps, and lesson plans. Communities of learners analyzed and synthesized information and connected it to personal, cultural, and professional background knowledge and experiences. Social annotation of the various information sources, and collaborative development of concept maps and lesson plans through social annotation, facilitated self-regulation of learning, and created a cohesive community of "teacher–learners" with peer networking about how to enhance their own, each other's, and their students' learning and development.

Observing students' comments on readings, videos, and lesson plans and their connections to course concepts facilitated teaching metacognitively because it provided me with valuable information. This feedback helped me to identify and overcome obstacles such as confusing concepts, misconceptions, and difficulties learning new instructional technologies. This feedback improved the quality of my instruction by enabling me to evaluate my own thinking as I monitored and assessed their learning, memory and transfer of course concepts and theories. Consequently, I was better able to plan how to meet the needs of current and future students. Also, social annotation products enabled more authentic assessment of learning than traditional final exams.

Future research should study how social annotation experiences increase preservice and in-service teachers' self-efficacy by giving them greater confidence in their ability to plan effective units/lessons, give effective feedback, and work collaboratively with diverse colleagues as members of a teaching community. Future research should also compare social annotation with other innovative Web 2.0 social networking practices to assess their relative impact on improving both learning and instruction.

References

Baumrind, D. (1967). Child care practices anteceding three patterns of preschool behavior. *Genetic Psychology Monographs, 75*, 43–88.

Baumrind, D. (1971). Principles of ethical conduct in the treatment of subjects: Reaction to the Draft Report of the Committee on Ethical Standards in Psychological Research. *American Psychologist, 26*, 887–896.

Baumrind, D. (1991). The influence of parenting style on adolescent competence and substance use. *Journal of Early Adolescence, 11*(1), 56–95.

Brown, J. S., & Duguid, P. (1995). *The Social Life of Documents.* Resource Document. http://www2.parc.com/ops/members/brown/papers/sociallife.html. Accessed June 11, 2009.

Bruner, J. (1966). *Toward a theory of instruction.* New York: W. W. Norton.

Buchanan, C. M., Eccles, J. S. & Becker, J. B. (1992). Are adolescents the victims of raging hormones? Evidence of activational effects of hormones on moods and behavior at adolescence. *Psychological Bulletin. 111*, 62–107.

Crawford, G. B. (2008). *Differentiation for the adolescent learner.* Corwin Press: Thousand Oaks, CA.

Dede, C. (2002). Designing and Studying Learning Experiences That Use Mulltiple Interactive Media to Bridge Distance and Time. Draft Chapter Prepared for: *Charalambos Vrasidas and Gene V Glass, (Eds.). Current Perspectives on Applied Information Technologies.* Vol. 1: Distance Education. Resource Document. http://www.lesley.edu/faculty/tbrownlb/T502/MultipleMedia.htm. Accessed July 30, 2009.

Gardner, H. (1985). *Frames of mind.* New York: Basic Books.

Hartman, H. J. (2001a). Developing students' metacognitive knowledge and skills. In H. J. Hartman (Ed.), M*etacognition in learning and instruction: Theory, research and practice* (pp. 33–68). The Netherlands: Kluwer.

Hartman, H. J. (2001b). Teaching metacognitively. In H. J. Hartman (Ed.), *Metacognition in learning and instruction: Theory, research and practice* (pp. 149–172). The Netherlands: Kluwer.

Hartman, H. J. (2009). *A guide to reflective practice for new and experienced teachers.* New York: McGraw-Hill.

Hartman, H. J., & Sternberg, R. J. (1993). A broad BACEIS for improving thinking. *Instructional Science: An International Journal of Learning and Cognition, 21*(5), 401–425.

King, R. A. (2002). Adolescence. In M. Lewis (Ed.) *Child and adolescent psychiatry.* (pp. 332–342). Philadelphia: Lippincott Williams & Wilkins.

Kowalski, T. J., Weaver, R. A., & Henson, K. T. (1994). *Case studies of beginning teachers.* White Plains, NY: Longman.

Lebow, D. G., & Lick, D. W. (2004). *Integration of HyLighter with Concept Mapping Software.* Unpublished Manuscript. Tallahassee, FL.

Lebow, D. G., Lick, D. W., & Hartman, H. J. (2003/2004). HyLighter and interactive annotation: New technology to develop higher-order thinking skills. *Inquiry: Critical Thinking Across the Curriculum, XXIII*(1 & 2), 69–79.

Lebow, D. G., Lick, D. W., & Hartman, H. J. (2008). New technology for empowering virtual communities. In M. Pagain (Ed.)., *Encyclopedia of multimedia technology and networking* (2nd ed., pp. 1066–1071). Information Science Reference. Hershey, PA: IGI Publications.

Lefoe, G. (1998). *Creating Constructivist Learning Environments on the Web: The Challenge in Higher Education.* Resource Document. ASCILITE http://www.ascilite.org.au/conferences/wollongong98/asc98-pdf/lefoe00162.pdf Accessed June 18, 2009.

National Research Council (2000). *How people learn: Brain, mind, experience and school.* Expanded Edition. Washington, DC: National Academy Press.

Novak, J. D. (1998). *Learning, creating and using knowledge.* Mahwah, NJ: Lawrence Erlbaum Associates.

Piaget, J. (1971). *Science of education and the psychology of the child.* New York: Viking Press.

Piaget, J. (1973). *To understand is to invent: The future of education.* New York: Penguin.

Price, L. (2005). The biology of risk taking. *Educational Leadership, 62*(7), 22–26.

Sternberg, R. J. (1985). *Beyond IQ: A triarchic theory of human intelligence.* New York: Cambridge University Press.

Vygotsky, L. (1978). *Mind in society: The development of higher psychological processes.* Cambridge: Harvard University Press.

Chapter 22
Orchestrating Learning in a One-to-One Technology Classroom

Jitti Niramitranon, Mike Sharples, and Chris Greenhalgh

Learning Sciences Research Institute, University of Nottingham, Nottingham, England,
e-mail: ttxjn3@nottingham.ac.uk

Introduction

Researchers in the field of technology enhanced learning have developed a number of approaches in using personal, portable, wirelessly-networked technologies to enhance teaching and learning both inside and outside the classroom (Sharples, 2000). The low cost and ease of integration into everyday classroom routines make mobile devices attractive for school learning (Chan et al., 2006). The educational potential of a one-to-one classroom where each child has access to a personal computer has prompted researchers to investigate effective strategies and scenarios for learning mediated by the technology. For example, classroom response systems such as EduClick, ClassTalk, and Clicker can aggregate anonymous responses from students (e.g., to choose a correct answer in a multiple choice question) and to display the results on a shared screen in front of the class (Liu, Liang, Wang, Chan, & Wei, 2003; Lowery, 2005). Subject-specific software applications running on handheld devices have been shown to be effective in supporting children to learn mathematics in classrooms (Roschelle, Rafanan, Estrella, Nussbaum, & Claro, 2009).

Computer-Supported Collaborative Learning (CSCL), built on a foundation of learners collectively forming a meaningful context to purposefully seek and construct knowledge (Koschmann, 1996), is another field of research that can be applied to a face-to-face classroom mediated by mobile technologies. Research in this area aims to design and develop software for mobile devices to support collaborative activities amongst students for individual, small group, and whole class learning (Roschelle & Pea, 2002; Zurita, Nussbaum, & Shaples, 2003; Pinkwart, Hoppe, Milrad, & Perez, 2003). CSCL scripts such as ArgueGraph, MURDER, and Social script can structure and orchestrate effective learning collaborations (Kobbe et al., 2007).

J. Niramitranon (✉)
Learning Sciences Research Institute, University of Nottingham, Nottingham, England
e-mail: ttxjn3@nottingham.ac.uk

M.S. Khine, I.M. Saleh (eds.), *New Science of Learning*,
DOI 10.1007/978-1-4419-5716-0_22, © Springer Science+Business Media, LLC 2010

Another area of current interest is in supporting teachers to prepare lessons for a technology-mediated classroom. Tools to specify lessons and design learning interactions include Educational Modelling language (EML) & IMS LD (Koper & Tattersall, 2005), LDL (Ferraris, Martel, & Vignollet, 2007) and LAMS (Dalziel, 2003).

Thus, one-to-one classroom technology is founded upon several research disciplines and one central aim is to integrate the methods and tools for personalised learning into a learning environment for the design and management of effective learning in a one-to-one classroom. This chapter presents a system, called SceDer, to design and orchestrate classroom learning. The design of the SceDer system has drawn upon a number of domains in order to provide: a pedagogical model for the design of lessons to support individual, group and whole class interactions; an intuitive authoring tool; an intermediate language and exchangeable learning object; a distributed learning environment to support a wide range of learning scenarios; progress, monitoring and control tools to harness learning in the one-to-one classroom.

CSCL Scripts in Face-to-Face Classroom Learning

Research on collaborative learning has shown that learners often do not collaborate well spontaneously because they tend not to participate equally, they often engage only in low-level argumentation, and they rarely combine their knowledge and converge on a shared answer (Kollar, Fischer, & Hesse, 2006). Based on such findings, CSCL scripts were developed with the aim of enabling a higher quality of both collaborative learning processes and individual learning outcomes in settings that include face-to-face, web-based as well as mobile contexts (Fischer, Kollar, Mandl, & Haake, 2007). Examples of collaboration scripts include the MURDER Script (Kobbe et al., 2007), Social Script (Weinberger, Ertl, Fischer, & Mandl, 2005), Collpad (Nussbaum et al., 2009), Universánt Script, and ArgueGraph Script (Jermann & Dillenbourg, 1999). The ArgueGraph Script (Dillenbourg & Crivelli, 2009) and the Collpad (Nussbaum et al., 2009) scenarios have a similar form of collaboration process which is separated into three phases: (1) learners form individual opinions or make individual responses; (2) learners form pairs or small groups with differing opinions and discuss their views; and (3) everyone in the group agrees to a joint answer which is presented to the teacher or to the whole class for further discussion.

In brief, collaboration scripts comprise a set of instructions that prescribe or guide how students should form groups, how they should interact and collaborate and how they should solve a problem (Dillenbourg, 2002). Scripts consist of two main parts: script components and script mechanisms. Script components contain at least five elements: (a) participants; (b) activities; (c) roles; (d) resources; and (e) groups (Kobbe et al., 2007). Script mechanisms are used for describing the distributed nature of scripts, that is, how activities, roles and resources are distributed across participants (task distribution), how participants are distributed across groups (group formation) and how tasks and groups are distributed over time (sequencing).

While CSCL scripts can provide a formalism for researching and designing successful learning, there is also a need to develop and implement tools that help to structure and manage learning within the classroom.

Learning Design and Delivery Tools for One-to-One Scenarios

The aims of learning design (LD) are to improve education by involving learners in structured learning activities. Such activities are sequenced carefully and deliberately in a learning work flow to promote effective learning. A successful LD can be shared, re-designed and re-used (Britain, 2004). IMS LD is a standard published by the IMS consortium based on the Educational Modelling language (EML) that is claimed to formally describe the design of teaching and learning for a wide range of pedagogical approaches (Koper & Tattersall, 2005). IMS LD provides benefits for e-learning stakeholders that include re-using learning units from one system to another, and supporting interoperability of courses to the market of e-learning more appealing (Koper & Tattersall, 2005).

However, IMS LD does not provide sufficient support to model group based, synchronous collaborative learning activities, artefacts, dynamic features, complicated control flow and varied forms of social interaction (Miao, Hoeksema, Hoppe, & Harrer, 2005; Niramitranon, Sharples, & Greenhalgh, 2009). It also has difficulties in expressing some aspects of a lesson plan, for instance: a scenario in which students pass a piece of work from one person to another within a group; how to provide a randomization mechanism; how to dynamically form groups when a lesson has already started (van Es & Koper, 2006). IMS LD also poses a difficult task for teachers in using complex technical specifications and modelling collaborative characteristics. To address these problems software tools such as Collage have been developed to help teachers in the process of creating collaborative learning scenarios by reusing and customizing patterns (Hernández-Leo et al., 2006).

LAMS (Learning Activity Management System) is an activity-based learning software which has embedded a design tool with its own delivery system. Teachers use an intuitive visual authoring environment to create learning activities in sequences by using tools provided in LAMS itself (e.g. vote, question and answer, forum). The output of the LD is executed and run under its own delivery system (Dalziel, 2003). Although LAMS does not implement IMS LD (Dalziel, 2006), it is widely used in education due to the ease of use in practice (Britain, 2004) and LAMS users have their own online community in an attempt to share design lessons and best practices (Laurillard, Oliver, Wasson, & Hoppe, 2009). However, LAMS has some issues, for example: the possible learning scenarios in LAMS are constrained by the available tools provided by LAMS itself; the mechanism of activity sequencing does not cover the fine detail of interaction and workflow, for example, Group 1 completes task A and passes to Group 2, then Group 2 completes the task and sends it back to the whole class.

To conclude the discussion of LD, IMS LD was originally designed to industrialise the creation of distance-learning activities, not for organising learning activities in the classroom (Ferraris et al., 2007), while LAMS has shown promise for classroom practice. However, LAMS has limitations on the tools it offers for creating learning activities and it does not have a mechanism to create the conditions in which effective individual, group and whole class interactions are expected to occur, to match those of CSCL Scripts.

What We Mean by One-to-One Classroom Orchestration and a Proposed Framework

To define the scope of classroom orchestration and to create a framework for design of new tools, we have studied both pedagogical and technological aspects to discover the needs of relevant stakeholders such as researchers, practitioners (teachers and students), educational technologists and software developers, as well as the affordances and constraints of the technology itself. The key findings for classroom orchestration can be described as follows:

- Practitioners: teachers and students without computer expertise should have a straightforward and simple system. The software tool should allow the teachers to design a wide range of effective learning scenarios (Anastopoulou et al., 2008).
- Researchers: a learning environment should be integrated with activities at various social levels (individual, group, class), to some extent across different contexts (museum, field trip, home, etc.), with multiple media (text, picture, drawing, video, etc.). The learning should not only focus only on individual learning activities but also on a level of productive interaction that can promote collaborative knowledge construction.
- Educational technologists and developers: the development of educational software should be based on a shared platform or standard, so that learning designs and lessons can be re-designable, interchangeable and may be executable in other delivery systems.
- Technologies: mobile computing devices (handheld computers, ultra mobile PCs, Tablet PCs, etc.) can offer valuable educational affordances such as portability, social interactivity, and context sensitivity (Naismith, Lonsdale, Vavoula, & Sharples, 2004). These should be exploited to facilitate learning in classroom practice.

From these requirements, the key elements of a one-to-one classroom orchestration model are effective learning scenarios; tools that are easy to use; rapid design; interactions for scaffolding personal, group or class collaboration across multiple learning activities; interoperability of mobile and wirelessly connected devices. We have further explored relevant learning design techniques, specifications and runtime environments, to investigate whether or not they are able to enact and efficiently support teaching and learning in a one-to-one context. The findings of the study have revealed that to be effective, a system needs to be supported by an educational modeling language (such as IMS LD) providing graphical authoring of learning design, for scenarios that are relevant to a one-to-one classroom, coupled with an appropriate execution environment that exploits networked collaborative learning. Orchestrating one-to-one classrooms not only relates to the aspect of learning design, but covers all aspects that could bring pedagogy and technology together.

We have proposed a system architecture as shown in Fig. 22.1. The system, called SceDer, consists of three main parts: a scenarios designer, named SceDer Authoring; an intermediate language, named Classroom Orchestration Modelling Language (COML), and a delivery, control, monitor and management system. Although we have addressed the concerns of educational technologists by embedding intuitive structures to support interoperability in our framework, we have not developed SceDer to comply with any existing learning standard. Since the learning design standards such as IMS LD and Virtual Learning Environments or players such as Moodle, Sakai or .LRN (dotlrn) are still missing important features for collaborative learning (Asensio-Pérez et al., 2008), we mainly focused on the *effectiveness*, *usefulness*, *expressiveness* of the system and its value for teaching and learning in a one-to-one classroom.

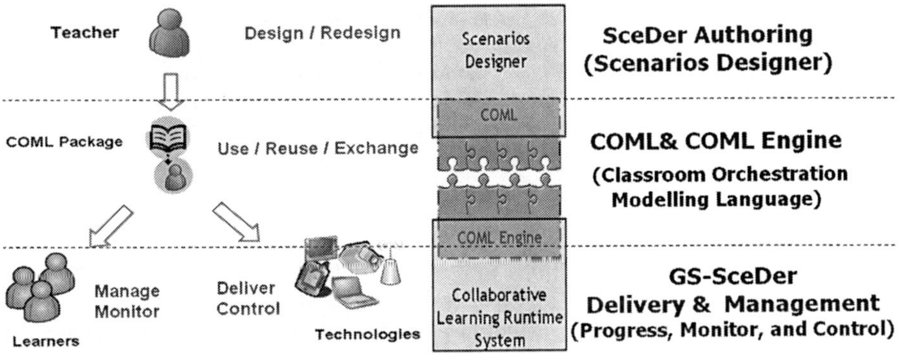

Fig. 22.1 SceDer system architecture for classroom orchestration

Example Scenarios for the One-to-One Classroom

We studied the effective one-to-one scenarios selected by Roschelle, Schank, Brecht, Tatar, and Chaudhury (2005). They identified 41 scenarios from the literature and selected a set of 13 as high priority because these scenarios: (a) were deemed most important for use especially in science classes; (b) had been tried in classrooms and worked well and (c) clearly leveraged technology i.e. can not be easily enacted with paper and pencil (Roschelle et al., 2005). Some example scenarios are as follows:

- Boomerang, students generate questions and a teacher collects and organises them for class discussion;
- ImageMap, a teacher sends as image out to the class, presents a question, and students respond by marking up the image;
- Question Answering, students in a small group all get one multiple choice question and each enters their individual answer. If everyone in the group agrees, they move on, otherwise they talk together to resolve differences.

Apart from the scenarios, we also studied the technique of Zurita and Nussbaum (2004) for how they exploited the use of PDAs to scaffold collaborative learning in classrooms. From these techniques and a set of the 13 scenarios, we formed many possible effective lessons for our further analysis stage, for example:

> In a chemical class, a teacher asks the whole class of students verbally "Please draw the molecular formula and electron dot of Nitrous oxide, Carbon dioxide, and Carbon monoxide". Each student answers the teacher by drawing a molecular form (N_2O, CO_2, CO) and electron dot (chemical representation form of electrons) on their personal computing devices and then submitting back to the teacher. The teacher groups answers both right and wrong, for each chemical substance. The teacher then divides students into three groups, passes each group the previous work (a group of right and wrong answers in the same formula), and asks them to choose or reproduce the correct chemical formula and electron dot of that substance. Group 1 works out Nitrous oxide. Group 2 works out Carbon dioxide and Group 3 works out Carbon monoxide. In each group, members discuss to choose or reproduce the joint answer and then send it back to the teacher. The teacher then reviews the work of each group and shows a prepared image of the correct molecular formula and electron dot to the whole class.

This lesson consists of a combination of "Boomerang", "Question Answering", and "Draw My Molecule" scenarios. It also represents one of the challenging one-to-one scenarios for both pedagogical and technological aspects because this scenario:

- requires various scaffolding phases to: create differences of ideas ("Boomerang" scenario), group the conflict opinions and assign them to work together for a joint answer ("Question Answering");
- requires technical workflows between activities, for example, the outputs of chemical formula generated by the whole class students has to be passed back to groups of students. Students may choose the correct one to send back again to the teacher;
- cannot be easily replaced by pen and pencil because it requires a rapid change of transition between each activity;
- requires more than a text or image display based delivery system. The learning environment has to provide drawing, annotating, grouping and graphical coordinating tools to the participants.

A Scenarios Designer for a One-to-One Technology Classroom

We studied a set of effective scenarios and how to manage collaboration in one-to-one classroom (see Section "Example Scenarios for the One-to-One Classroom") which is aimed at extracting and identifying commonalities of interaction patterns between human and technology. The processes of the analysis were carried out by breaking down the scenarios into *use case*, *activity* and *interaction* diagrams. As a result, we found common components such as *actors* (people), *learning activities*, *pre-prepared*, *in-class learning electronic artefacts*, *virtual working environment* which were then defined as elements of the formal notation.

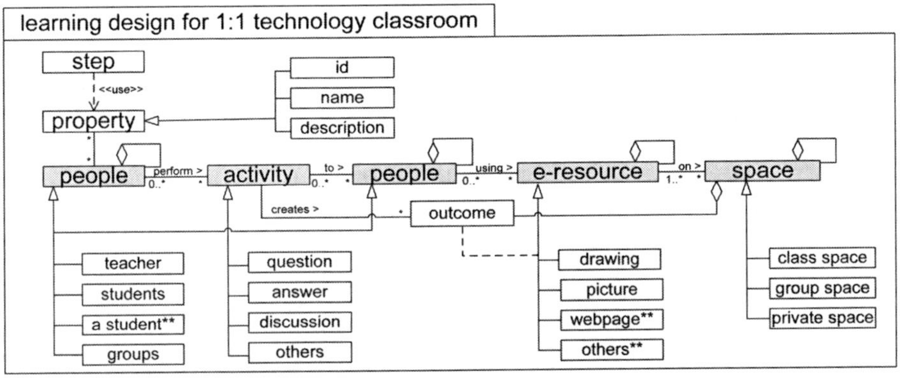

Fig. 22.2 Semantic model representing a learning design unit

The semantic model of learning design for one-to-one classroom shown in Fig. 22.2 can be summarised as follows: a lesson consists of a sequence of steps. In each step, people can be either a teacher, or a student (group or individual), to perform an activity. (Asterisks ** refer to an element that is ready in the design but has been disabled in SceDer Authoring, since the delivery system (GS-SceDer) has not yet implemented that feature). Frequently used activities such as questions, answers, discussions and other, user-defined, activities are provided. An electronic resource or an output of an activity performed by any person can be sent to other people in a specific working space such as personal space, a whole class space, or a group space. From the semantic model, learning design in our framework focuses at the level of the effective scenarios of use in the face-to-face classroom, not at a level of a complete course design or higher. In terms of supporting technological and pedagogical aspects, there are advantages of the proposed design technique of COML as follows:

- It allows design at a low granularity of interaction, that is: *one actor creates an activity for another actor with a tool or resource in an environment*. For example, a teacher sends a picture to a whole class. We regard one interaction like this as a "step". A series of "steps" is then sequenced as a scenario. A lesson may consist of one or more scenarios. These components (people, group, resources, activities, etc.) enable the construction of a rich collaboration.

- The system is able to support users at the right time with the right tool and an appropriate privilege (e.g. "read", "write" or "create"). For instance, one step in a complete lesson might be: Group 1 replies to a whole class by drawing on Public Space 1. For this step, the software shows an appropriate input type (drawing tool) to the members of Group 1 (as a *deliver*) and grants a privilege "write" to the space where the members of Group 1 jointly submit the created artefact. The artefact is then shown on the designated area, Public Space 1, where the privilege "read" (but not "write") is granted to the whole class. This technique has the implication of implementing a technical *role* and *privilege* for each user in each interaction, so that the technology can scaffold an environment to meet expected interactions for collaboration.
- At the level of interaction, teachers can flexibly handle the unplanned events in a real classroom setting, such as when members of a group are missing at a particular time, quitting engagement with an activity so that the a teacher can monitor a progress of the activity and go back to any previous step. The technology provides an appropriate environment to re-visit and repeat activities. A mechanism of monitoring can be applied to the level of interaction by checking whether or not the artefact created by a "deliver" has been submitted to a "space".

SceDer Authoring and COML

Based on our proposed model of one-to-one classroom interaction, a scenario authoring, named SceDer Authoring, was then developed with graphical user interface (Niramitranon, Sharples, & Greenhalgh, 2006; Niramitranon, Sharples, Greenhalgh, & Lin, 2007). It allows teachers to design learning scenarios for individual, group and whole class activities. The example scenario in Section "Example Scenarios for the One-to-One Classroom" can be designed by SceDer Authoring as shown in Fig. 22.3. The meaning of the scenario design shown in Fig. 22.3 from the first to the sixth row can be interpreted as the following:

- 1st row: a teacher asks students verbally "Please draw the molecular formula and electron dot of Nitrous oxide, Carbon dioxide, and Carbon monoxide";
- 2nd row: all students answer the teacher by drawing on their personal computing devices and all answers are then shown on the public presentation space "Public";
- 3rd row: the teacher splits the students into three groups and passes "Group 1" the "Output Step 2" to work out for the correct for the molecular formula and electron dot of Nitrous oxide, in the group working environment "Group 1" (an environment for the group to work collaboratively which could not be seen by other groups);
- 4th row: the teacher passes "Group 2" the "Output Step 2" to work out for the correct answer of Carbon dioxide in the group working environment named "Group 2".

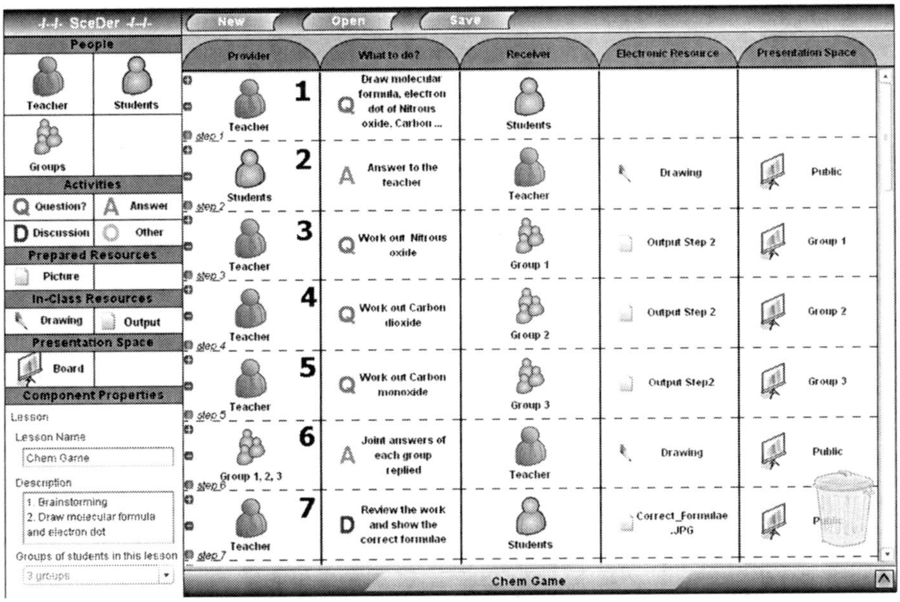

Fig. 22.3 SceDer authoring with the design of example scenario

- 5th row: the teacher passes "Group 3" the "Output Step 2" to work out for the correct answer of Carbon monoxide in the group working environment named "Group 3".
- 6th row: in each group, members discuss, choose or reproduce a new answer by using the drawing tool, then submit a joint answer to the public presentation space named "Public".
- 7th row: the teacher reviews each group's work, and also shows the picture of the correct answer "Correct-Formulae.JPG" on the public presentation space named "Public".

As shown in the design diagram, each step does not need to be associated with technology (e-resource, and presentation space). For example, in Step 1, the teacher verbally asks students to draw molecular formula of each chemical substance, in this case, the designed diagram has only three components for this step that are: a *teacher* icon is placed on the *deliver* column; a *question* icon is placed on *activity* and a students icon is placed on *receiver*. As a result, during the lesson when a teacher progresses to this step, the technology prevents the students from interacting with the system, so they can focus their attention on the teacher.

From Fig. 22.3, the designed diagram is then exported to COML, a lightweight language based on a generic XML description derived from our proposed semantic mode (see Fig. 22.2). COML is packed together with all the electronic resources needed for a lesson into a single ZIP file called a COML package. COML (Fig. 22.4) is currently intended to be a lightweight language to model classroom orchestration rather than a full learning design specification.

Fig. 22.4 A sample of the Classroom Orchestration Modelling Language (COML)

```
<step id="7">
  <name>Conclusion</name>
  <description>Last step of the lesson</description>
   <deliver type="teacher"></deliver>
   <activity type="discussion">
     <name>Review the work and show the correct formulae</name>
     <description>1.Review the work of all three groups.
                  2.Guide for the correct answers for a whole class.
     </description>
   </activity>
   <receiver type="student"></receiver>
   <resource type="preparedFile">
     <data isFile="true" resourceName="Correct_Formulae.JPG" />
   </resource>
   <space type="presenter">
     <name>Public</name>
     <target isPublic="true" />
</space>
</step>
```

Using SceDer to teach a lesson, a teacher begins by designing a lesson with SceDer Authoring (e.g. Fig. 22.3) and then exports the design to a COML Package. In the class, the teacher loads the COML Package into GS-SceDer which contains the COML interpreter engine. On the teacher's screen, there is a "Step Navigator Bar" and a "Monitoring Panel" where the teacher can begin a lesson, progress to next step, or navigate to all steps in a lesson. The teacher can also monitor the actions responded by each student at each step. At any step that requires group formation, the COML interpreter engine embedded in Group Scribbles randomly allocates students into groups and creates a working space (board) for each group.

GS-SceDer Learning Environment: A Learning Space for One-to-One Scenarios

In developing the specification for SceDer we studied the runtime environments of CopperCore, LRN and LAMS for their techniques to deliver a lesson, as well as general-purpose learning interface software such as Group Scribbles, regardless of whether they comply with any formal learning design specification. We found that Group Scribbles (Roschelle et al., 2007), a system developed by SRI International based on an ink improvisation concept, has shown potential as a delivery tool to support a wide range of learning scenarios. The concept of Group Scribbles was developed from the "Tuple Space" architecture designed to coordinate work across multiple computers in a classroom and there has been in interest for researchers in using "Tuple Space" to support flexible integration of existing algorithms with modern learning environments and interfaces (Giemza, Weinbrenner, Engler, & Hoppe, 2007). In terms of collaboration, a distributed learning environment considers students, rather than their computers, to be the distributed processor that can be utilised to engage and coordinate the learning activities (Roschelle et al., 2005).

Group Scribbles software is a general purpose graphical interface system where users manage their private spaces. With a pen tablet PC, users can draw, annotate and type on the provided sheets and labels in private spaces shown in Fig. 22.5. The users can drag any sheet or label from a private space and drop it onto a public space, or group space, where it can be seen, moved, or even taken back to a private space by other people. For example, to create a voting scenario in LAMS, students cast their votes in a web-style tool provided. In Group Scribbles, students just draw the vote of their choice on a sheet, and then drop them on a public space. The teacher and others in the class can then see these responses. This delivery mechanism, based on a Post-it^{TM} notes metaphor is very supportive of exploring new learning scenarios.

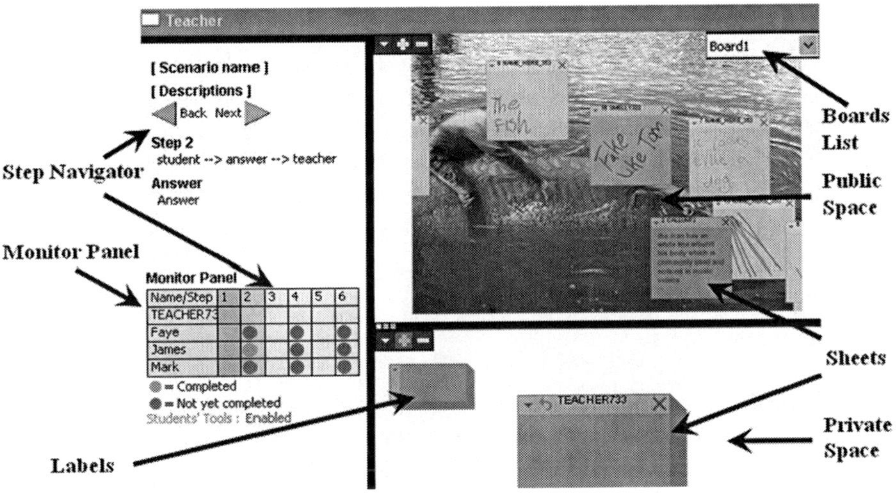

Fig. 22.5 GS-SceDer embedded in group scribbles while running a lesson

The GS-SceDer distributed learning environment is an extension of Group Scribbles which was embedded with a COML interpreter engine, graphical progress and monitoring bar. The system allows a teacher to step through a sequence of learning tasks that has been previously designed with the SceDer Authoring tool. Although only image files can be displayed and writeable sheets are the only objects that than can be passed along these spaces, the system architecture has been made ready for implementing other media, such as videos, audio and webpages. The distributed learning environment regards these resource files as objects which can be passed around spaces. To execute these files, they can be opened either by relevant software which is installed on that computer or by software which is integrated in a delivery system.

Therefore, we can describe how the SceDer design works with the delivery system (GS-SceDer) as shown in Fig. 22.6. On the *provider* column, the system enables an appropriate tool for people to create (for *in-class resources*) or to execute (for *prepared resources*) corresponding to the type of e-resources. The *activity* shows the description of the step which is typed in by the teachers when they create a lesson in order to remind them what to do at that step. On the *receiver* column, the system enables these people to be able to access to the *presentation space*. For

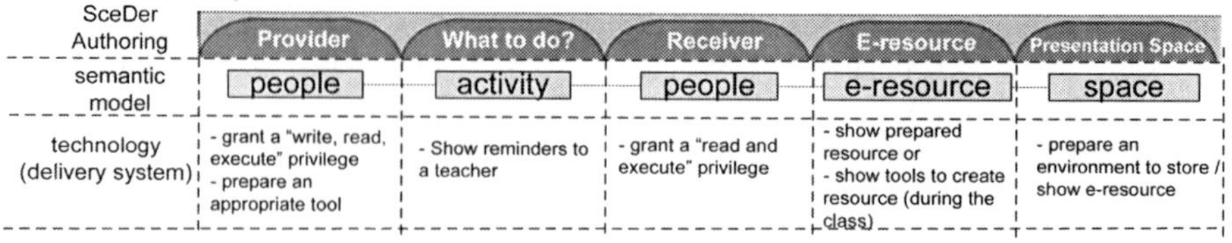

Fig. 22.6 A conceptual mapping between the semantic model and a distributed learning environment (Group Scribbles)

the last column, *presentation space*, the delivery system enables this environment to be accessible by the people who are appeared in both the *provider* and *receiver* columns. It can be also interpreted that, for a certain *presentation space*, the system grants a "write" privilege to the people in the *provider* column; provides an appropriate tool for them to create or show an e-resource, and grants a "read" privilege for the people in the *receiver* column.

Results

We have carried out a pilot study with 18 master students in three classes to establish proof of concept and to identify usability problems. After modifications to SceDer based on the problems found in the pilot study, we carried out the main evaluation with four classes of 20–30 students (aged 11–14) at a school where all students routinely used tablet PCs in the classrooms.

The results have been analysed for three main aspects: *usability*, *usefulness*, and *expressiveness*. The first session had the aim of evaluating teaching and learning with Group Scribbles alone by asking the two teachers to carry out lessons without using SceDer. The second session was to evaluate the combined GS-SceDer by asking the two teachers to design and conducts lessons and use GS-SceDer. Data collection included video observations of the learning activities in the classroom and interviews with teachers and students. The example scenarios designed by the two teachers are as follows:

Charles designed a lesson for Year 7 students which aimed to teach them powers of two (i.e. 2^2, 2^3, 2^4,...) based on a game play. The format of the game was that each group had to place answers in turn on chess board cells displayed as a background image. The answer in each cell had to be $2n + 1$, where n starts with 1, on the first cell. The teacher divided students into groups. The students who were sitting around the same table were in the same group.

Dan designed a lesson to teach Year 9 students, which aimed to ask students' opinions of a series of pictures. For example, Dan showed students a picture, a man riding a big fish (see Fig. 22.5), and asked whether or not this photograph was genuine and why. This lesson consisted of three pictures and the pictures were placed as a background image on each board. The purpose of the lesson was to explore differences through argument and to enable students to learn from the opinions of others.

The *usability* evaluation, shown in Table 22.1, revealed some minor issues of robustness, for instance a frozen screen on some occasions, and drawing pads that were too small. There were no reported problems regarding the tablet PCs or wireless network.

Table 22.1 Summaries of *usability*

	GS only		SceDer and GS-SceDer	
	Pros	Cons	Pros	Cons
The teachers	– Easy to use – Good to have a separate public and private area	– Crashes – Cannot estimate what is the size of images when they are placed on the board	– Learning to design within 15–20 min	– Drawing disabled message perhaps too small, (because students still keep trying to draw)
The students	– Can draw, see photos – Can see/learn other opinions – Can work with others – Enjoy the lesson – No training required, can learned in a short time	– Crashes – Other people move/delete my sheets – Size of sheets too small to draw – Zoom option not good enough	– Did not have to ask friends or teachers which board they are working on	– Stops students drawing (note: system has disabled them from drawing in order to prompt them to listen to the teachers

In terms of *usefulness*, shown in Table 22.2, students and teachers reported that they enjoyed the lessons, as they can see other people work and learn from their opinions, especially in the mathematics classes. With regard to pedagogical aspects, the teachers were able to use SceDer Authoring to design their scenarios without formal training. We provided them with only two example scenarios on a printed paper. In the aspect of continuity of scaffolding students to expected activities, the system can provide a fluid transition between individual, group, and whole class learning activities. For example, when the teachers proceeded to the next activity with a different working environment (board), the technology showed the corresponding board to the students. There were some occasions when the teachers needed to repeat steps in lessons and the technology enabled them to step back and repeat that activity. In contrast, when using Group Scribbles alone, if the teacher proceeded to the next activity, it took some minutes for all students to switch to the particular board and prepare for the next activity. Some students continued to play with the

Table 22.2 Summaries of *usefulness*

	GS only		SceDer and GS-SceDer	
	Pros	Cons	Pros	Cons
The teachers	– Good potential for collaborative learning – Support a wide range of scenarios	– If the software is installed inside a firewall, it could not be accessible from home	– SceDer has a graphical design, straight forward to create lesson – If students get lost or just entered, the teacher can click next or back to resume to the current screen – Can switch to any board and students are also sync'ed – Lessons are editable and reusable	– Have to walk to the laptop to use the control bar i.e. to click next, back or stop students using drawing tool
The students	– Able to learn from other people work		– Don't get lost when the teacher proceeds to any step	

previous activity on the tablet PCs and they needed to be verbally asked again by the teacher to switch to the correct board.

In terms of *expressiveness* of SceDer Authoring, apart from the actual scenarios enacted by teachers in the school, we have simulated a virtual class and found that SceDer Authoring is able to enact 9 out of the 13 scenarios selected from those by Roschelle and colleagues. The scenarios which are not currently supported involve a role play or a pair turn-taking activity.

Conclusion

From the results, although we found some technical problems, SceDer (SceDer Authoring, COML, and GS-SceDer based on Group Scribbles) has clear potential for orchestrating learning in one-to-one classrooms. The design technique of SceDer Authoring and COML seems to be efficient in modelling interactions to promote collaboration in one-to-one classroom. This is because COML is able to define the workflow, e-resource, a virtual distributed working environment and combines two sequences of activities of the design based on IMS LD into one process. As a result, SceDer Authoring also works more or less similarly to CSCL Script designer. For example, if Group 1 completes task A and passes that work to Group 2, these are two separate activities designed in IMS LD: (1) Group 1 completes task A; (2) Group 2 continues working on the task A. IMS LD or LDL does not explicitly define the workflow but makes use of an activity which has been completed at a different time (e.g. Group A finishes then Group B starts).

Group Scribbles, as a delivery system has shown great potential for supporting a wide range of effective scenarios, with ease of use. However, a well-structured lesson design may be required for a larger class (more than 20 students) due to the more complex information flow. For instance, in a brainstorming scenario, if the teacher asks 25 students for two answers each on one board, there will be 50 sheets on the screen which would be a time consuming process for the teacher to meaningfully arrange.

For future work, integrating SceDer Authoring and Group Scribbles together might augment the usefulness of a seamless application (Authoring and Player are integrated to advantages in LAMS). For even faster design, effective scenario-based templates (e.g. Brainstorming, ImageMap, etc) might be embedded, so that teachers can choose an appropriate scenario and use it instantly. At a lower lever of detail, the teachers could still customise the components (deliver, activity, receiver, e-resource, space) for each step of the interaction. SceDer has provided an initial demonstration of the value of teacher-designed orchestration of learning activities in a one-to-one classroom. Future work will show whether this can be extended to other learning scenarios and contexts.

References

Anastopoulou, S., Sharples, M., Wright, M., Martin, H., Ainsworth, S., Benford, S., et al. (2008). *Learning 21st century science in context with mobile technologies*. In B. C. Traxler John. Riordan (Ed.), Mlearn 2008 conference (pp. 12–19).

Asensio-Pérez, J., Bote-Lorenzo, M., Vega-Gorgojo, G., Dimitriadis, Y., Gómez-Sánchez, E., & Villasclaras-Fernández, E. (2008). *Adding mash-up based tailorability to VLEs for scripted collaborative learning*. In Proceedings of the first international workshop on mash-up personal learning environments(mupple08) (Vol. 388, pp. 14–17).

Britain, S. (2004). A review of learning design: Concept, specifications and tools. JISC report, 20.

Chan, T W , Roschelle, J., Hsi, S., Kinshuk, K., Sharples, M., Brown, T., et al. (2006). One-to-one technology-enhanced learning: An opportunity for global research collaboration. *Research and Practice in Technology Enhanced Learning, 1*, 3–29.

Dalziel, J. (2003). *Implementing learning design: The learning activity anagement system (LAMS)*. In Proceedings of the ascilite 2003 conference, Adelaide (p. 25).

Dalziel, J. R. (2006). *Lessons from LAMS for IMS learning design*. In Sixth international conference on advanced learning technologies (p. 1101–1102).

Dillenbourg, P. (2002). Over-scripting CSCL: The risks of blending collaborative learning with instructional design. In P. A. Kirschner (Ed.), Three worlds of CSCL. Can we support CSCL (pp. 61–91). Heerlen: Open Universiteit Nederland.

Dillenbourg, P., & Crivelli, Z. (2009). A model of collaborative learning scripts instantiated with mobile technologies. *International Journal of Mobile and Blended Learning, 1*(1), 36–48.

Ferraris, C., Martel, C., & Vignollet, L. (2007). LDL for collaborative activities. In L. Botturi & T. Stubbs (Eds.), Handbook of visual languages in instructional design: Theories and practices (pp. 226–253). Hershey, PA: Idea Group. Chapter XII.

Fischer, F., Kollar, I., Mandl, H., & Haake, J. M. (2007). Scripting computer-supported collaborative learning (Vol. 6). Boston, MA: Springer US.

Giemza, A., Weinbrenner, S., Engler, J., & Hoppe, H. U. (2007). *Tuple spaces as a flexible integration platform for distributed learning environments*. Supporting Learning Flow Through Integrative Tech-nologies, 313-320.

Hernández-Leo, D., Villasclaras-Fern_andez, E., Jarrín-Abellán, I., Asensio-Pérez, J., Dimitriadis, Y., Ruiz-Requies, I., et al. (2006). COLLAGE, a collaborative learning design editor based on patterns. *Educational Technology & Society*, *9*(1), 58–71.

Jermann, P., & Dillenbourg, P. (1999). *An analysis of learner arguments in a collective learning environment*. In Proceedings of the 1999 conference on computer support for collaborative learning.

Kobbe, L., Weinberger, A., Dillenbourg, P., Harrer, A., Hämäläinen, R., Häkkinen, P., et al. (2007). Specifying computer-supported collaboration scripts. *International Journal of Computer-Supported Collaborative Learning*, *2*(2), 211–224.

Kollar, I., Fischer, F., & Hesse, F. W. (2006). Collaboration scripts a conceptual analysis. *Educational Psychology Review*, *18*(2), 159–185.

Koper, R., & Tattersall, C. (2005). Learning design: A handbook on modelling and delivering networked education and training. Netherlands: Springer.

Koschmann, T. (1996). CSCL, theory and practice of an emerging paradigm: Theory and practice of an emerging paradigm. Mahwah, NJ: Lawrence Erlbaum.

Laurillard, D., Oliver, M., Wasson, B., & Hoppe, U. (2009). Implementing Technology-Enhanced learning. Technology-Enhanced Learning: Principles and Products, 289–306.

Liu, T. C., Liang, J. K., Wang, H. Y., Chan, T. W., & Wei, L. H. (2003). *Embedding educlick in classroom to enhance interaction*. In Proceedings of international conference on computers in education (ICCE) (p. 117–125).

Lowery, R. C. (2005). *Teaching and learning with interactive student response systems: A comparison of commercial products in the higher education market*. In Annual meeting of the southwestern social science association and its affiliates, march (p. 2326).

Miao, Y., Hoeksema, K., Hoppe, H. U., & Harrer, A. (2005). *CSCL scripts: Modelling features and potential use*. In Proceedings of the 2005 conference on computer support for collaborative learning: Learning 2005: The next 10 years! (pp. 423–432). International Society of the Learning Sciences.

Naismith, L., Lonsdale, P., Vavoula, G., & Sharples, M. (2004). Literature review in mobile technologies and learning. A Report for NESTA Futurelab. ISBN: 0–9548594.

Niramitranon, J., Sharples, M., & Greenhalgh, C. (2006). COML (Classroom orchestration modelling language) and scenarios designer: Toolsets to facilitate collaborative learning in a One-to-One technology classroom. Selected Papers from the Kaleidoscope Convergence Workshop: Amsterdam, The Netherlands.

Niramitranon, J., Sharples, M., & Greenhalgh, C. (2009) (Paper accepted). *Designing and orchestrating collaborative learning in a one-to- one classroom*. In The 17th international conference on computers in education, ICCE 2009, Hongkong.

Niramitranon, J., Sharples, M., Greenhalgh, C., & Lin, C. (2007). SceDer and COML: Toolsets for learning design and facilitation in one-to- one technology classroom. In U. S. Hirashima T.Hoppe (Eds.), ICCE′07 (pp. 385–391). Netherlands: IOS Press.

Nussbaum, M., Alvarez, C., McFarlane, A., Gomez, F., Claro, S., & Radovic, D. (2009). Technology as small group face-to-face collaborative scaffolding. *Computers & Education*, *52*(1), 147–153.

Pinkwart, N., Hoppe, H. U., Milrad, M., & Perez, J. (2003). Educational scenarios for cooperative use of personal digital assistants. *Journal of Computer Assisted Learning*, *19*, 383–391.

Roschelle, J., & Pea, R. (2002). *A walk on the WILD side: How wireless handhelds may change CSCL*. In Proceedings of CSCL (Vol. 2) Boulder, CO.

Roschelle, J., Rafanan, K., Estrella, G., Nussbaum, M., & Claro, S. (2009). *From handheld collaborative tool to effective classroom module: Embedding CSCL in a broader design framework*. In Proceedings of computer supported collaborative learning practices (pp. 395–403). Rhodes, Greece: ISLS.

Roschelle, J., Schank, P., Brecht, J., Tatar, D., & Chaudhury, S. R. (2005). *From response systems to distributed systems for enhanced collaborative learning*. In Proceeding of the 13th international conference on computers in education (ICCE 2005) (pp. 363–370).

Roschelle, J., Tatar, D., Chaudbury, S. R., Dimitriadis, Y., Patton, C., DiGiano, C., et al. (2007). Ink, improvisation, and interactive engagement: Learning with tablets. *Computer, 40*(9), 42–48.
Sharples, M. (2000, April). The design of personal mobile technologies for lifelong learning. *Computers & Education, 34*(3–4), 177–193.
van Es, R., & Koper, R. (2006). Testing the pedagogical expressiveness of IMS LD. *Journal of Educational Technology and Society, 9*(1), 229.
Weinberger, A., Ertl, B., Fischer, F., & Mandl, H. (2005). Epistemic and social scripts in computer supported collaborative learning. *Instructional Science, 33*(1), 130.
Zurita, G., & Nussbaum, M. (2004). Mcscl: Mobile computer supported collaborative learning. *Computers and Education, 42*(3), 289–314.
Zurita, G., Nussbaum, M., & Shaples, M. (2003). Encouraging face-to-face collaborative learning through the use of handheld computers in the classroom. Lecture Notes in Computer Science, 193–208.

Chapter 23
Designing Online Learning Environments for Professional Development

Kedmon Hungwe

Michigan Technological University, Houghton, MI, USA, e-mail: khungwe@mtu.edu

Introduction

Web-based Internet technologies afford expanded options for the design of online learning (Nipper, 1989; Breivik & Gee, 2006; Mitra & Hall, 2002; Fishman & Davis, 2006). The premise of this work is that the design of online professional development for teachers should encourage reflections about practice through participation in networks of peers. Bruner (1996) has argued that reforms in education must contend against deeply entrenched pre-understandings that may have to be replaced or modified. Teachers tend to innovate ad hocly, piecing together ideas and activities picked up from textbooks, colleagues, workshops, and conferences. This results in instructional practices that lack an adequate conceptual base and structure (Berns & Swanson, 2000). Bruner has therefore proposed that the starting point of reform should be to gain some insight into teachers' prior understandings. The use of online learning to support teacher learning and reflection may contribute to this.

In the USA, the primary impetus for professional development has been the No Child Left Behind (NCLB) Act of 2001, which is the cornerstone of federal K-12 education reform. The act requires that states ensure the availability of high-quality professional development for teachers and administrators. The law also establishes student-testing guidelines that are used for judging school effectiveness and specifies consequences for school failure.

The National Science Education Standards provide guidelines for curriculum reform in science (National Research Council, 1996). A key component of the reform agenda in science is universal scientific literacy, to be achieved by reforming practice so that it is meaning oriented. Education should foster creativity, inquisitiveness, and a deep understanding of concepts and their interconnectedness within and across the disciplines. The methodology proposed for achieving these goals is classroom inquiry. Classroom inquiry is both a way to teach science and a way

---

K. Hungwe (✉)
Michigan Technological University, Houghton, MI, USA
e-mail: khungwe@mtu.edu

M.S. Khine, I.M. Saleh (eds.), *New Science of Learning*,
DOI 10.1007/978-1-4419-5716-0_23, © Springer Science+Business Media, LLC 2010

of thinking about the nature of science (National Research Council, 2000). The National Research Council (2000, p. 25) describes the outcomes of inquiry in terms of five essential attributes:

1. Learners who are engaged by scientifically oriented questions.
2. Learners who give priority to evidence, which allows them to develop and evaluate explanations that address scientifically oriented questions.
3. Learners who are able to formulate explanations from evidence to address scientifically oriented questions.
4. Learners who are able to evaluate their explanations in light of alternative explanations, particularly those reflecting scientific understanding.
5. Learners who are able to communicate and justify their explanations.

The success of the reform agenda will depend on teachers who understand these goals and are able to transform them into classroom practice (Lederman, 1999; Johnson, 2006). Although teachers have been recognized as primary change agents, they generally lack clarity about the meaning of the reform concepts and how they can be translated into classroom practice within the complex culture of the school (Wee, Shepardson, Fast, & Harbor, 2007; Wallace & Kang, 2004). The success of these reforms will depend on teacher learning that is continuous and extends beyond initial teacher certification (Borko, 2004; Ball & Cohen, 1999; Villegas-Reimers, 2003; McGrath, 2008). Providing and sustaining professional development can be difficult. Teachers face barriers to access such as commitments to full-time jobs, family and community responsibilities, as well as distance from learning centers.

Conceptual Framework

As adult learners, teachers bring a considerable reservoir of prior knowledge when they enroll in professional development programs (Knowles 1978, 1980). Nevertheless, there is evidence that teachers generally find reforms difficult to implement even when they participate in professional development programs (Wee et al., 2007; Davis, 2003). We do not have an adequate understanding of how teachers conceptualize reform, how the conceptions are formed and sustained in specific contexts of practice (Windschitl, 2004). These limitations reflect inadequacies in how teacher knowledge is conceptualized. Teacher knowledge has tended to be understood from a cognitivist perspective (Kelly, 2006). Cognitivism discounts or marginalizes contexts and treats knowledge solely as a property of isolated individuals. Professional development will be more effective when it affords participants opportunities to critically reflect on knowledge in the context of their practices. One way of achieving this is to incorporate participatory and interactive design elements that privilege dialogue and meaning making. The emergent capabilities of web-based digital technologies afford design opportunities that are consistent with these principles (Mitra & Hall, 2002).

Exploring the Foundations of Design with Digital Media

Evolution of distance education: Digital technologies and the Internet represent, arguably, the most radical changes in communication media since Johannes Gutenberg's invented the printing press in the fifteenth century. They have emerged out the convergence text, video, sound, graphics, and images. These media have different historical trajectories (Fig. 23.1). Distance education operations have evolved through several generations tied to changes in technology. Taylor (2001) has proposed five generations of change, primarily distinguished by the levels of flexibility and interactivity they afford the user. Interactivity refers to the extent to which the media affords opportunities to respond to questions, contribute content, and network with others. Users may interact synchronously (in real time) as well as asynchronously. Audio conferencing and video conferencing are interactive, while print is not.

Flexibility is defined in terms of (1) place (i.e., the extent to which the medium permits the user to be flexible in their location–print is flexible, while video conferencing is not); (2) time (i.e., the extent to which the user can determine when to use the media—radio broadcasts are not flexible, while audio cassettes are flexible); (3) pace (i.e., the extent to which the user can control the pace of delivery—print is flexible, while satellite broadcasts are not).

Historically, a defining characteristic of distance education has been the separation in space and time of students from other students, and of students from instructors. Separation can compromise the quality of learning experiences (Prater & MacNeil, 2002). The capacity of the Internet technologies for networking is a significant development toward bridging separation in time among geographically dispersed persons.

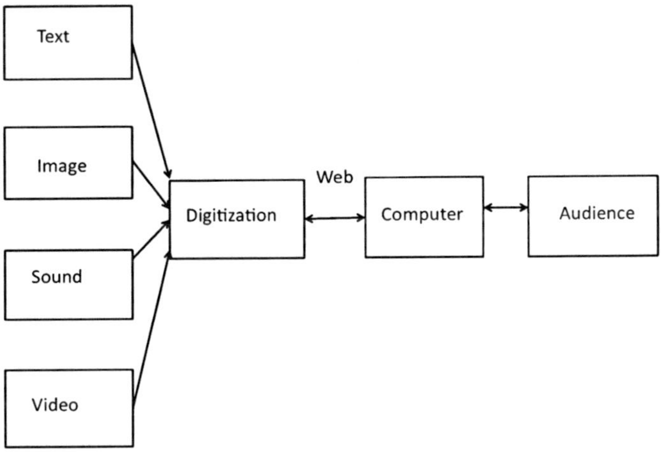

Fig. 23.1 Convergence of communication technologies with distinct histories through digitization of information

It has been argued that we are at the fringes of the next generation of distance education associated with the wide use of mobile-learning technologies. It will be characterized by greater flexibility and interactivity, with individuals able to learn from "anywhere." It will also be associated with greater capabilities for establishing virtual learning communities and social networks, and the uses of technologies such as electronic portfolios, logs, and wikis (Connolly & Stansfield, 2006; The New Media Consortium & EDUCAUSE Learning Initiative, 2009).

Perspectives on learning and development: Studies of teacher learning have been shifting from a focus on individual teacher understandings, toward research into the ways in which understandings are developed in social contexts (Peressini & Knuth,1999; Nichols & Tobin, 2000; Horn, 2005; Kelly, 2006). Sociocultural theory provides a conceptual foundation for this shift. Sociocultural approaches define mental actions in terms of the cultural, historical, and institutional settings in which they occur (Vygotsky, 1978; Wertsch, 1991). Mental action is therefore mediated by social contexts. One of the foundational constructs of sociocultural theory is the zone of proximal development (ZPD). It was introduced by Vygotsky as a basis for studying how individuals learn in social contexts. The ZPD is the gap between a learner's current level of development when not socially supported, and the learner's potential development when placed within a relationship with a more knowledgeable other. The concept of the ZPD is applicable to dyads (i.e., relations between two persons) and to learning communities. Learning communities are constituted by individuals with a mutual interest. They draw on each other's experiences and make collective use of cultural resources to scaffold learning (Moll & Whitmore, 1993). Learning is supported by simultaneously establishing and sustaining multiple zones of proximal development of the members (Daniels, 2001).

Bakhtin provides a complementary perspective to Vygotsky (Wertsch, 1991). A basic premise of Bakhtin's work is that no voice is isolated and each person is influenced by others in an inescapably intertwined way. He therefore believed that truth was dialogic in the sense that it was constructed out of the engagement of a multiplicity of voices, and through a commitment to the context of real-life events. The quest for understanding should be at the point of dialogic contact between people engaged in discourse (Honeycutt, 1994). Bakhtin drew distinctions between authoritative and dialogic discourses (Wertsch, 1991). Authoritative discourses are closed to interpretation and transmit fixed meanings (Scott, Mortimer & Aguiar, 2006). By dialogic, Bakhtin meant discourses where meanings are discursively negotiated and created. Dialogic discourses provide a firmer foundation for establishing truth claims than authoritative discourses. Daniels (2007) has suggested that dialogic discourses may be supported by promoting constructive discussion, questioning, criticism, and negotiation of meaning as an integral part of practice.

A more expansive view of learning: Learning entails more than changes in knowledge and skill. A more adequate view of learning should factor in the consideration that there are changes is self-understandings that are usually associated with changes in knowledge and skill. As an example, changes in role and function within organizations are emotionally charged with consequence and are anxiety-producing (van Maanen & Schein, 1979). Rather than seeking change, individuals tend to be motivated to reduce anxiety by avoiding situations that change the functional requirements of their roles (Dahl, 1984; Hungwe, in press). Understanding the connection between knowledge changes and learners' self-understandings is of critical importance when the goal of learning is to effect changes in professional practices. The prior experiences of adult learners may become a barrier to learning if they entail changes in the roles and functions. An adequate theoretical perspective on learning will seek to anticipate and account for such changes. Nevertheless, learning is often narrowly construed in terms of knowledge or mental change. However, changes in knowledge may generate changes in self-understanding and identity as an integral part of learning (Packer, 1993; Litowitz; 1993; Hungwe, in press). Litowitz expands on this, arguing that:

> Mastering activities and establishing a sense of oneself are not two distinct lines of development but are rather, intertwined in complex ways—that one can not study one without the other (p. 184).

Adult learners participating in professional development programs are, by virtue of their backgrounds, established in careers where their positions are defined in terms of specific competencies and roles. New learning experiences always have the potential to introduce some disequilibrium into those roles and competencies. The design of instructional programs for adult learners should therefore provide opportunities to reflect on personal concerns about change as an integral part of the teacher-learning process.

Overview of Course Design

The course on which this work is based was originally designed by faculty at Michigan Technological University in 2002. The course was motivated by a desire to provide professional development to certified science teachers in the state of Michigan. The objective was to engage teachers with the discourse on the theory and practice of classroom inquiry and to provide them an opportunity to reflect on the methodology in the context of their practices. The goals did not include implementation of classroom inquiry on the part of the teachers. That aspect would be addressed subsequently, through a different professional development experience. Although the course was originally designed for teachers in the state of Michigan, teachers from Hawaii, Florida, Massachusetts, and Canada have also taken the course.

The duration of the course was seven weeks. Web Courseware Tools (WebCT) was adopted as the platform. WebCT has been acquired by Blackboard and has been re-named Blackboard Learning System. It features, among other tools, (1) a centralized Web page where students can locate course-related resources such as a calendar and a syllabus; (2) a flexible gradebook that allows students to check their own grades; and (3) communication tools including discussion forums, chat rooms, and Internal private mail.

Design Elements

There were three primary considerations in designing the course. First, a flexible design was adopted. The teachers logged onto the course at their convenience, within a specified timeframe. Second, the participants were required to read and respond to literature that has defined the formal (official) discourse on classroom inquiry. To that end, the book, *Inquiry and the national science education standards* (NRC, 2000) was used as the main text for the course. The book introduces the reader to the theory and practice of classroom inquiry, connecting the goals of classroom inquiry to the national science education standards and the discourse on educational reform. It also provides vignettes that illustrate the applications of classroom inquiry, using age-appropriate examples. The text was supplemented by other readings. Third, a discussion forum was created as a way of establishing and sustaining a learning community of course participants. WebCT uses threaded discussions, which is a group of messages related to a single message. The forum provided the teachers with opportunities to converse among themselves, and to reflect on their learning, making sense of the course content in terms of their own professional backgrounds and goals. The asynchronous design afforded the participants time to read each other's responses, formulate their own ideas, and produce thoughtful responses.

To encourage accountability in discussions, the participants were required to complete the readings assigned each week, and take an online quiz, before contributing to the discussions. The readings provided a form of intellectual scaffolding, providing teachers with the background knowledge to discuss inquiry, as well as the linguistic tools to talk about reform. Accountability for discussions was also built into the course by assigning 30% of the course grade to discussions.

The weekly quiz: The quiz was made up of six multiple choice-type questions, and one essay-type question. The following are examples of essay type questions that were posed:

- The two scenarios provided in chapter 1 describe inquiry in science and inquiry in the classroom. What is one way that these two inquiries are similar? What is one way that they differ?
- Provide an example from your own teaching of the change elements (at least two) necessary to support inquiry-based teaching in your school.

Discussion topics: The goal of the weekly discussions was to encourage teachers to interpret the themes emerging from the course in terms of their own experiences, and to learn from each other. The instructor (who is also the author), participated in the discussions, commenting on the teachers' contributions. However, the primary interactions were between the teachers. The weekly topics and related discussion topics are listed in Table 23.1.

Final project: The teachers conducted a critical review of instructional materials that they were using or were contemplating using to explore ways in which they could be used as is, or adapted for classroom inquiry. This aspect of the course is

Table 23.1 Themes and discussions over the 7-week period of the course

Week	Theme	Discussion question
1	Introduction to classroom inquiry	Why would you not want to use inquiry?
2	Inquiry in the national science education standards	What is one myth about inquiry that you can especially relate to?
3	Images of inquiry in the K-12 classroom	How important is it for students to be able to think logically and critically about the world around them?
4	Preparing for inquiry-based teaching	When was your first introduction to inquiry?
5	Making the case for inquiry	What is the best way to use research when making decisions about the incorporation of inquiry into the curriculum?
6	Frequently asked questions about inquiry	Why is the debate about inquiry versus vocabulary important?
7	Supporting inquiry-based teaching and learning in the classroom and in the school	Where are you with respect to concerns about change?

not discussed in this chapter. The focus is on the discussions, which are used to provide insights into how teachers interpreted their experiences.

Participants

The data are derived from 19 teachers who participated in the course over the period 2004–2006. The teachers participated in three cohorts of five in 2004, five in 2005, and nine in 2006. The teaching experiences of the teachers ranged from 2 to 17 years, with an average of 6.9 years and median of 5 years (see Table 23.2). The teachers were drawn from rural, suburban, and urban public school districts and participated from their schools, with no face-to-face meetings.

Data Sources and Analysis

WebCT captures a record of all interactions and contributions by participants. The discussions have been analyzed using a phenomenological hermeneutical approach (Lindseth & Norberg, 2004). This entails applying an iterative process of reading, interpreting, and re-reading texts. Teachers' discussions were understood as constituting a text of shared speech. The full range of discussions were printed and read several times in order to grasp their meaning as a whole. Emerging understandings of the text were regarded as conjectures to be validated or re-interpreted through subsequent analysis. Following the initial readings, the text was summarized into condensed units that were abstracted to form themes, and sub-themes tied to the

Table 23.2 List of participants

Name	Year course taken	Teaching experience
Lindsay	2004	2
Mark	2004	11
Mariya	2004	10
Alex	2004	5
Judy	2004	17
Andrew	2005	3
Susan	2005	4
Cindy	2005	10
Bill	2005	2
Trisha	2005	3
Kim	2006	17
Emily	2006	5
Mike	2006	10
Beth	2006	3
Jill	2006	6
Laura	2006	2
Jack	2006	5
Jessica	2006	6
Erin	2006	12

focus questions. A theme, as defined by Lindseth & Norberg (2004), is "a thread of meaning that penetrates different parts of the text, either all or just a few" (p. 149). The whole text was re-read to validate, or re-interpret the summaries and themes. The interpretations were also read in conjunction with relevant literature on reform and classroom inquiry. The literature provided a theoretical foundation for revising, widening, and deepening understanding of the text.

Emerging Issues

Teachers' Conceptions of Classroom Inquiry

At the outset, the teachers expressed concerns about inquiry that stemmed from two inter-related misconceptions. First, the reform agenda was understood as advocating that *all* science subject content should be taught through inquiry; second, the teachers believed that inquiry was a *unitary method* of teaching that required that students should generate and pursue their own questions. Implementing inquiry would most likely result in a loss of control over instructional time, curriculum content, and students. "We all like things to be orderly and quiet," Jill (2006)[1] wrote. "Inquiry is neither. One never knows what baskets of problems will be encountered within the process." Laura (2006) wrote:

[1] Dates designate the year in which the contribution was made.

> I shudder to think about some of my students being put in charge of coming up with their own questions or investigations. I think inquiry would be a great method of learning for my higher ability students, but I do not think many of my lower ability students would really get it.

For Mike (2006), teaching through inquiry was uncomfortable because it meant following an "unknown" path.

> If I teach a traditional lesson I know, based on past experience, how long the lesson will take and what I need to teach the lesson. With an inquiry lesson it is much more difficult to know what time frame it will take to teach the lesson and exactly what I will need to support the students.

Classroom inquiry, as it has been discussed in the reform literature is neither a method, nor a set of methods. It can best be described as a *methodology*. The term methodology, as used here, refers to more than a set of methods; rather it refers to the rationale, assumptions, as well as methods that underlie a particular pedagogical approach (Webster's New Collegiate Dictionary, 1973). The course readings were the primary resource for addressing the teachers' misconceptions. Classroom inquiry was presented as a multifaceted approach with variations in the degree of teacher direction. Thus inquiry can be "guided" or "open" or "full" or "partial" depending on the extent to which the teacher structures learning experiences. While inquiry was a "central part of the teaching standards," it was not the only recommended approach. It was therefore a "myth" that the national standards advocate the use of inquiry for all subject matter (NRC 2000, p. 36). For some teachers, this provided some validation for their instructional goals and practices. Jill (2006), for example, wrote: "I'm always innovating something to try to engage more kids so they want to find the answers. I have found out that there was a name to what I was trying to do with the kids all these years!..inquiry." Alex (2004) had started out lukewarm about inquiry because he believed that "supporters of inquiry want inquiry-based learning to be exclusive in the classroom." He could not account for the source of his belief. "I'm not sure if I just listened to the wrong people when I first learned about inquiry, or if I simply didn't listen," he commented. Inquiry, as he had understood it, had "seemed like a huge time consumption, and a source of frustration for me in trying to cover content standards." He continued, "Honestly, this is a big part of why I was hesitant to embrace inquiry." As he reflected on the readings he had concluded that his own perspectives were consistent with inquiry.

> I knew that in my class I wanted to use 'open' inquiry some of the time, and to use what I now know is called 'guided inquiry' more often. Little did I realize that what I was seeking is just what the national standards call for, and that they have cool names for the varying levels of inquiry.

The course experience validated the teachers' perspectives, but only up to a point. Jack (2006) conceded that he felt "a little insecure about cutting the students loose." He continued, "My class and I swim on the shallow end of the pool, trying to muster the courage for an occasional foray into the deep end. It becomes a delicate balance between achieving my academic agenda and allowing the students a richer learning experience."

The teachers' conceptions of classroom inquiry had been acquired informally. Vygotsky (1987) made an analytical distinction between *everyday* and *scientific* (or spontaneous) concepts. Everyday concepts are acquired casually and spontaneously during social interaction, while scientific concepts are acquired through experience and reflection, and most typically through instruction. Scientific concepts are more abstract and more general than everyday concepts. They serve as tools for investigation and conceptual development. Everyday concepts, on the other hand, are connected to experience in a direct and relatively ad hoc manner. Dewey (1916) characterizes a scientific concept as a "system of attributes, held together on the basis of some ground, or determining, dominating principle" (p. 148). The teachers' pre-understandings can be characterized as informal, rather than scientific knowledge. This is consistent with Bruner (1996) and Windschitl (2004) views about how teachers acquire knowledge in practice. The professional development course was essential to clarify their thinking and begin to move them toward a systematic view of classroom inquiry. Mark's contribution captures the essence of the teachers' more comprehensive perspective that emerged from the course. He wrote:

> It is important that inquiry is not looked at in the small sense as an isolated activity and is viewed more in a curricular perspective as being integrative and comprehensively sustained by both traditional and inquiry-based teaching methods.

Teachers' Self-Understandings as Agents of Change

A commitment to inquiry entails embracing changes in roles and functions for both teachers and students. Success will depend on teachers who understand the meaning and rationale for inquiry and who are also willing to make commitments to the changes that it entails. Concerns about change may hinder reform, even when practitioners understand its meaning and rationale. The teachers concerns about inquiry were of two kinds. They did not believe that classroom inquiry was a priority in their districts. Laura, for instance, noted: "I still don't feel like there is a big push for teachers to use inquiry-based methods in my district. This is mostly due to our obsession with aligning curriculums across our district." They were under intense pressure from their school districts to raise and maintain high test scores. Trisha (2005) remarked: "I know you shouldn't teach to the test. However, our scores are consistently high and our district's philosophy is 'you don't screw with results." Erin (2006) believed that classroom inquiry would undermine her capacity to cover the curriculum. "If we don't cover everything in the curriculum the kids won't do well on the test," she wrote. Laura (2006) contributed to the same theme, writing, "Committing a large chunk of time to an inquiry based unit, where there may be many dead ends explored is no less than terrifying." Jack believed that classroom inquiry might "burn up precious time" (Jack, 2006).

The teachers were also anxious about their knowledge base for implementing classroom inquiry. Mariya (2004), for example, wrote: "There are some areas of science that I know little about and I find myself teaching in these areas sometimes.

So if we were doing an inquiry lesson, what happens to me if I can't answer questions or direct students to the right answer? It could be uncomfortable for me and potentially embarrassing."

The goals of classroom inquiry appeared to resonate with values that the teachers held about student learning. At the same time, the values were in tension with the teachers' understanding of what was required of them in their school districts. Table 23.3 summarizes the tensions between the traditional and the reform paradigms. The tensions generated a sense of anxiety among the teachers, as well as a lack of self-efficacy. As the course ended, Laura (2006) reflected on the matter as follows:

Table 23.3 Traditional and reform conceptions of practice

Traditional conceptions of practice	Reform conceptions of practice
Teaching primarily interpreted in terms of teacher adaptation to tradition	Teaching primarily understood in terms of teacher autonomy, creativity and commitment to reform
Premium on student performance	Premium on learning and conceptual development
Foregrounds role of teacher as subject expert and knowledge source	Foregrounds role of teacher as mentor and learner
Curriculum planning is content centered to which is brought to bear methods and problems	Curriculum planning is problem centered, to which is brought to bear content and methods
Classroom management principles privilege teacher direction and external regulation of students	Classroom management principles privilege learner self-direction and self-regulation of students

> Reading about all of these fancy inquiry projects depresses me. I go home with lessened self-esteem and confidence in my teaching ability. I honestly feel like I do not have the time, the support, or the resources. Not because I work for a horrible district but because all of the wonderful people I work with, and for, are just as busy as me and the last thing they have time to do is listen to my little idealistic plan to become the best darn science teacher in North America. I realize I am writing this at the risk of sounding like a complete basket case.

The argument for reform resonated with Laura's ideals about teaching. At the same time, the case for reform was not sufficiently compelling to cause her to want to change course.

Beth (2006) expressed an interest in aligning her teaching more with inquiry and "to stray from the 'recipe' labs that I am most familiar with." She toyed with the idea of changing her instructional approach. At the same time, she believed that her teaching approach was aligned with the expectations in her school district, and for that reason, she preferred to continue with the status quo. "I think that *if my school would agree to inquiry teaching,* then I would try to find a textbook that better fits into the inquiry process." (emphasis added).

The majority of the teachers were from districts that "tested well" on standardized tests. The tests provided validation for their work. Consequently, accountability based on standardized testing militated against reforms by encouraging conservative tendencies among teachers. The situation was more complex for urban teachers where student performance on standardized tests was below the national average. These teachers were more critical of the uses of tests for accountability. A case in point was Jill (2006), who wrote:

> People in suburban or rural districts seem to go upon this fallacy that teachers or adults who work in urban districts are awful at their jobs, therefore 'the district is bad,' because the kids test poorly. We who work in the city get tired of being blamed. We feel we are working twice as hard as those in rural and suburban districts. I've worked in all types of districts so I feel I can give a valid point of view. We feel looked down upon by the other districts as if we are not good enough for them. Yet we in the city are proud of stepping up to the plate and fighting for these kids that no one else outside of the city will fight for.

In summary, the course helped teachers to understand the meaning of classroom inquiry. Yet, as they came to appreciate its rationale and potential for improving the quality of learning, they also expressed some anxieties about the change.

The Problem of Validity

The course readings helped teachers to understand the meaning of inquiry. At the same time, they tended to be skeptical about the claims made in the official course readings. They characterized some of the vignettes and examples as impractical and not applicable to "normal" classrooms. They taught in diverse classrooms where some students had reading disabilities, others had cognitive impairments, and behavioral issues. They were often short of equipment. There were a range of factors that made them wary of the positive accounts that were presented in the readings. Laura's response to one vignette illustrates a case in point. She wrote:

> The classroom inquiry example in this week's reading was just delightful. How lovely to have students actually vocalize such an interesting question and then have the wherewithal to follow through and investigate it. Do things like this really happen in classrooms?! I'm being a little sarcastic, but I fear I may teach for thirty years and never have an experience like that in my own classroom.

The teachers were also concerned that students had been socialized to learn traditionally, and would be resistant to changes in instructional approach. "There are so many students that just want an answer handed to them–heaven forbid, they may actually need to think," Alex wrote. Lindsay concurred, observing that, "Students are more interested in the outcome more than in the process."

The participants were keen to hear what their peers thought. While they acknowledged the value of the readings, they were eager to have their peers validate their interpretations. One idea that resonated with them was that of constructing "replacement lessons," which means identifying lessons that are normally taught traditionally, and could be adapted to inquiry, one lesson at a time. By definition, the replacement lesson is small in scope. It allows the teacher to experiment cautiously.

Over time, larger units of the course can be adapted to inquiry. Kim shared that she had begun to design a replacement lesson. The readings and discussions had helped her "to understand better how more inquiry can be done in my classes." She was planning "to increase the amount of inquiry-based methods in the future." Cindy was more hesitant, describing the goals of classroom inquiry as "lofty" and "frustratingly difficult" to achieve. She was nevertheless encouraged to make a start."I truly believe that helping to develop these skills needs to be a educational goal for all of us," she concluded. For some teachers, the readings and discussions validated their intuitive notions about good teaching. Mark believed that the best way to learn inquiry would be "by experiencing it and by talking to other teachers who have adopted it into their classrooms." The course had advanced his "bolstered" confidence and "validated some of my teaching techniques that I just did because I thought it was the right thing to do."

In summary, the teachers' skepticism of official sources was a potential barrier to learning. The readings stimulated critical thinking, helping them to clarify and extend their thinking. The dialogue with peers helped to validate the teachers' understanding of inquiry.

Effectiveness of the Course Design

The course provided a forum for teachers to engage key reform ideas, and critically discuss them with peers. The participants displayed a high degree of engagement and candor. The level of contribution averaged 550 words per person, each week. In her concluding message, Judy (2004) wrote: "Thanks to all of you for sharing your ideas and experiences and contributing to our community of learners that has been as a source of inspiration for me!" One cohort was surveyed for comments on the course design. Among the comments were

- The readings were quite helpful. They helped me think about how I could improve my teaching.
- I *really* liked the flexibility of the course. The timeframe to read, discuss, and take quizzes was very doable in my extremely busy schedule. Online classes in general are difficult because we don't have a lot of interaction with our professors, but the course design worked very well for me. E-mail responses to my questions were prompt, the discussion board was very interactive. It is nice to have that kind of interaction.
- The discussions were nice to participate in because they allowed me to realize that there are many others out there that have the same concerns and issues as I do.
- I think I learned a better definition of what inquiry really is. I feel like I have been practicing inquiry, but not systematically. I think this course will really help to make my discovery lessons more student based so that I can really target *all* aspects of inquiry

These findings affirm the view that Internet-based technologies are an effective resource for meaningful discourse on educational reform among practitioners.

Conclusions

Practitioners construct everyday (informal) professional knowledge based on their work experiences. While adult learners bring a rich repertoire of knowledge to new learning, the knowledge should be problematized by examining its nature and assumptions, and the personal and contextual factors that account for it. Internet-based social networks provide an avenue for connecting geographically dispersed professionals. They have the potential to encourage critical reflection and reconstruction of informal knowledge on scientific foundations (Vygtsky, 1987).

Anxieties about change are a potential barrier, undermining practitioner's commitment to change, even when they understand the meaning and rationale for change. They arise because changes in knowledge and skill often entail changes in how individuals understand who they are, as well as their roles. One way to address this dimension of learning is through dialogue within a supportive community of peers. Internet-based technologies have the capabilities to support such learning communities.

References

Ball, D. L., & Cohen, D. K. (1999). Developing practice, developing practitioners: Toward a practice-based theory of professional education. In L. Darling-Hammond & G. Sykes (Eds.), *Teaching as the learning profession* (pp. 3–31). San Francisco, CA: Jossey-Bass.

Berns, B. B., & Swanson, J. (2000). *Middle school science: Working in a confused context*. Paper presented at the annual meeting of the American Educational Research Association, New Orleans, LA (Eric Document Reproduction Service No. ED444944).

Borko, H. (2004). Professional development and teacher learning: Mapping the terrain. *Educational Researcher*, *33*(8), 3–15.

Breivik, P. S., & Gee, E. G. (2006). *Higher education in the internet age: Libraries creating a strategic edge*. Westport, CT: Greenwood Publishing Group.

Bruner, J. (1996). *The culture of education*. Cambridge: Harvard University Press.

Connolly, T., & Stansfield, M. (2006). Using games-based elearning technologies in overcoming difficulties in teaching information systems. *Journal of Information Technology Education, 5*, 459–476

Dahl, J. (1984). Structured experience: A risk-free approach to reality-based learning. *Journal of Nursing Education*, *23*(9), 34–37.

Daniels, H. (2001). *Vygotsky and pedagogy*. New York: Routledge Falmer.

Daniels, H. (2007). Pedagogy. In H. Daniels, M. Cole, & J. Wertsch (eds.), *The Cambridge companion to Vygotsky* (pp. 307–331). New York: Cambridge University Press.

Davis, K. (2003). "Change is hard": What science teachers are telling us about reform and teacher learning of innovative practices. *Science Education*, *87*, 3–30.

Dewey, J. (1916). "Data and meanings". Chapter 4. In *Essays in experimental logic* (pp. 136–156), Chicago: University of Chicago.

Fishman, B. J., & Davis, E. A. (2006). Teacher learning research and the learning sciences. In R. K. Sawyer (Ed.), *The Cambridge handbook of the learning sciences* (pp. 535–550). New York: Cambridge University Press.

Honeycutt, L. (1994). *What hath Bakhtin wrought? Toward a unified theory of literature an composition.* Master of Arts thesis. University of North Carolina at Charlotte. Accessed at: http://www.public.iastate.edu/~honeyl/bakhtin/thesis.html

Horn, I. S. (2005). Learning on the job: A situated account of teacher learning in high school mathematics. *Cognition and Instruction, 23*, 207–236.

Hungwe, K. (in press). Identity, self-interpretation and workplace change: An investigation of the work activity of machining. *Journal of Adult Development.*

Johnson, C. C. (2006). Effective professional development and change in practice: Barriers science teachers encounter and implications for reform. *School Science and Mathematics, 106*, 150–161.

Kelly, P. (2006). What is teacher learning? A socio-cultural perspective. *Oxford Review of Education, 32*, 505–519.

Knowles, M. (1978). *The adult learner: A neglected species.* Houston: Gulf Publishing.

Knowles, M. S. (1980). *The modern practice of adult education.* Chicago: Association Press/Follett.

Lederman, N. (1999). Teachers' understanding of the nature of science and classroom practice: Factors that facilitate or impede the relationship. *Journal of Science Teacher Education, 36*, 916–929.

Lindseth, A., & Norberg, A. (2004). A phenomenological hermeneutical method for researching lived experience. *Scandinavian Journal of Caring Sciences, 18*, 145–153.

Litowitz, B. E. (1993). Deconstructing the zone of proximal development. In E. A. Forman, N. Minick, & C. A. Stone (Eds.), *Contexts for learning* (pp. 184–196). New York: Oxford University Press.

McGrath, S. (2008). Developing teachers and teaching. *International Journal of Educational Development, 28*, 1–3.

Mitra, A., & Hall, A. (2002). Distance education as a discursive practice: Voice, discourse and pedagogy. In G. Richards (Ed.), *Proceedings of World Conference on E-learning in Corporate, Government, Healthcare, and Higher Education 2002* (pp. 2683–2684). Chesapeake, VA: AACE.

Moll, L. C., & Whitmore, K. F. (1993). Vygotsky in classroom practice: Moving from individual transmission to social transaction. In E. Forman, N. Minick & C. Addison Stone (Eds.), *Contexts for learning* (pp. 19–42). New York: Oxford University Press.

National Research Council (1996). *National Science Education Standards.* Washington, DC: National Academy Press.

National Research Council. (2000). *Inquiry and the national science education standards.* Washington, DC: National Academy Press.

New Media Consortium & EDUCAUSE Learning Initiative (2009). The 2009 Horizon Report. New Media Consortium. http://wp.nmc.org/horizon2009/

Nichols, S. E., & Tobin, K. (2000). Discursive practice among teachers co-learning during field-based elementary science teacher preparation. *Action in Teacher Education, 22*, 45–54.

Nipper, S. (1989). Third generation distance learning and computer conferencing. In R. Mason & R. Kaye (Eds.), *Mindweave: Communication, computers and distance education* (pp. 53–73). Oxford: Pergamon.

Packer, M. J. (1993). Away from internalization. In E. A. Forman, N. Minick, & C. A. Stone (Eds.), *Contexts for learning* (pp. 254–265). New York: Oxford University Press.

Peressini, D. D., & Knuth, E. J. (1999). Why are you talking when you could be listening? The role of discourse and reflection in the professional development of a secondary mathematics teachers. *Teaching and teacher education, 14*, 107–125.

Prater, D. L., & MacNeil, A. J. (2002). The use of collaborative groups in traditional and online courses. In C. D. Maddux, J. Ewing-Taylor & D. LaMont Johnson (Eds.), *Distance education: Issues and concerns,* (pp. 67–76). Binghamton, New York: Howarth Press.

Scott, P., Mortimer, E. F., & Aguiar, O. G. (2006). The tension between authoritative and dialogic discourse: A fundamental characteristic of meaning making interactions in high school science lessons. *Science Education, 90*, 605–631.

Taylor, J. (2001). Fifth generation distance education. *e-Journal of Instructional Science and Technology* http://www.usq.edu.au/electpub/e-jist/docs/old/vol4no1/2001docs/taylor.html

Van Maanen, J., & Schein, E. H. (1979). Toward a theory of organizational socialization. In B. M. Staw (Ed.), *Research in organizational behavior* (pp. 209–264). Greenwich, CT: JAI.

Villegas-Reimers, E. (2003). *Teacher professional development: An international review of the literature*. Paris: UNESCO Institute for Educational Planning.

Vygotsky, L. S. (1978). *Mind and society: The development of higher psychological processes*. Cambridge, MA: Harvard University Press.

Vygotsky, L. S. (1987). Thinking and speech. In R. W. Rieber and A. S. Carton (Eds.), *The collected works of L.S. Vygotsky, Volume 1: Problems of general psychology* (Trans. N. Minick). New York: Plenum.

Wallace, C. S., & Kang, N. (2004). An investigation of experienced secondary teachers' beliefs about inquiry: An examination of competing belief sets. *Journal of Science Teacher Education, 41*, 936–960.

Webster's New Collegiate Dictionary (1973). Springfield, MA: G. & C. Merriam Company.

Wee, B., Shepardson, D., Fast, J., & Harbor, J. (2007). Teaching and learning about inquiry: Insights and challenges in professional development. *Journal of Science Teacher Education, 18*, 63–89.

Wertsch, J. (1991). *Voices of the mind*. Cambridge: Harvard University Press.

Windschitl, M. (2004). Folk theories of "inquiry." How pre-service teachers reproduce the discourse and practices of an atheoretical scientific method. *Journal of Research in Science Teaching, 41*, 481–512.

Chapter 24
Knowledge Building/Knowledge Forum®: The Transformation of Classroom Discourse

Thérèse Laferrière[1] and Mary Lamon[2]

[1] Laval University, Quebec, Canada, e-mail: tlaf@fse.ulaval.ca
[2] Lamon Consulting, Toronto, Canada, e-mail: mlamon@sympatico.ca

Background

Classroom Discourse

Several studies have indicated that meaningful discourse is the most relevant classroom variable for learning; but is not pervasive in North American schools (Applebee, 1996). Traditionally, and unlike conventional conversation or dialogue in research or professional communities, classroom discourse typically conforms to a participation structure controlled by the teacher. Teachers ask most questions, call on students to answer, and allocate turns (Greenleaf & Freedman, 1993). The discourse between teacher and students is then limited to a format with the purpose of transmitting information where the teacher already knows the answer. The typical classroom discourse structure has three turns (Sinclair et al., 1975; Mehan, 1979; Cazden, 1988) and is composed of the following moves: teacher initiation (e.g., ask a question) (I), student response (R), and teacher feedback/comment (F) or evaluation (E) of the student's response (IRF/IRE). According to Wells (1993), the IRF structure accounts for as much as 70% of all classroom talk, and is typical of classroom discourse (Lemke, 1990; Wells 1999). The use of Flanders' (1970) framework for studying classroom interaction has led to another observation: one that stresses that the teacher speaks for 60–80% of the time.

Ways of diversifying classroom discourse have been sought (Christie, 2002). For instance, Wells (1993, 1999) built on the "IRF" structure, one in which the teacher uses assisting questions, ones that encourage learners to think as well as participatory methods that actively engage students in their own learning either individually or in small groups. The community of learners model (Brown, 1994, 1997) and the knowledge-building community model (Scardamalia, Bereiter, & Lamon, 1994; Scardamalia & Bereiter, 2007) have arisen as powerful models for organizing the learning environment in ways that are especially respectful of research advances

T. Laferrière (✉)
Laval University, Quebec, Canada
e-mail: tlaf@fse.ulaval.ca

M.S. Khine, I.M. Saleh (eds.), *New Science of Learning*,
DOI 10.1007/978-1-4419-5716-0_24, © Springer Science+Business Media, LLC 2010

in the learning sciences (Bransford, Brown, & Cocking, 1999; Chan, & van Aalst, 2008; Sawyer, 2005; Zhang, Scardamalia, Reeve, & Messina, 2009). Unlike Brown and Campione's learning communities approach, knowledge-building communities make use of information and communication technology because it not only affords communication without restrictions of time and space, it also allows dialogue that can become more reflective, democratic, and collaborative.

Idea improvement is the central concept of Bereiter and Scardamalia's knowledge-building epistemology (Scardamalia et al., 1994). Other variants include the notions of dialogue (Wegerif, 2007), exploratory talk (Mercer, 2000), accountable talk (Michaels, O'Connor, Hall, & Resnick, 2002), and depth of understanding (Woodruff & Meyer, 1997). Knowledge building is a collaborative effort directed toward creating and improving theories, designs, and problem solving. Ideally, ideas get out into the whole community in a form that allows all to create new artifacts, to identify problems of understanding, to gather and critique information from authoritative sources, to design experiments and to create theories, explanations, historical accounts, problem formulations, or solutions. Familiar examples come from scientific research laboratories, expert jazz bands, and Olympic teams. These communities encourage individual and collective expertise, while continually advancing the frontiers of knowledge. Knowledge-building communities function then as second-order learning environments—cultures that support progressive problem solving (Bereiter & Scardamalia, 1993). Knowledge-building communities are guided by a system of twelve values or principles (Scardamalia, 2002) (Table 24.1). They are:

Table 24.1 Knowledge-building principles from Scardamalia (2002)

Knowledge-building principles	Definitions
Real ideas and authentic problems	Knowledge problems arise from efforts to understand the world. Ideas produced or appropriated are as real as things touched and felt. Problems are ones that learners really care about—usually very different from textbook problems and puzzles
Idea diversity	Idea diversity is essential to the development of knowledge advancement, just as biodiversity is essential to the success of an ecosystem. To understand an idea is to understand the ideas that surround it, including those that stand in contrast to it. Idea diversity creates a rich environment for ideas to evolve into new and more refined forms
Improvable ideas	All ideas are treated as improvable. Participants work continuously to improve the quality, coherence, and utility of ideas. For such work to prosper, the culture must be one of psychological safety, so that people feel safe in taking risks—revealing ignorance, voicing half-baked notions, giving and receiving criticism
Knowledge-building discourse	The discourse of knowledge-building communities results in more than the sharing of knowledge; the knowledge itself is refined and transformed through the discursive practices of the community—practices that have the advancement of knowledge as their explicit goal

Table 24.1 (continued)

Knowledge-building principles	Definitions
Epistemic agency	Participants set forth their ideas and negotiate a fit between personal ideas and ideas of others, using contrasts to spark and sustain knowledge advancement rather than depending on others to chart that course for them. They deal with problems of goals, motivation, evaluation, and long-range planning that are normally left to teachers or managers
Democratizing knowledge	All participants are legitimate contributors to the shared goals of the community; all take pride in knowledge advances achieved by the group. The diversity and divisional differences represented in any organization do not lead to separations along knowledge have/have-not or innovator/non-innovator lines. All are empowered to engage in knowledge innovation
Community knowledge/collective responsibility	Contributions to shared, top-level goals of the organization are prized and rewarded as much as individual achievements. Team members produce ideas of value to others and share responsibility for the overall advancement of knowledge in the community
Embedded transformative assessment	The community engages in its own internal assessment, which is both more fine-tuned and rigorous than external assessment, and serves to ensure that the community's work will exceed the expectations of external assessors
Constructive use of authoritative sources	To know a discipline is to be in touch with the present state and growing edge of knowledge in the field. This requires respect and understanding of authoritative sources, combined with a critical stance toward them .
Rise—above	Creative knowledge building entails working toward more inclusive principles and higher-level formulations of problems. It means learning to work with diversity, complexity and messiness, and out of that achieve new syntheses. By moving to higher planes of understanding knowledge builders transcend trivialities and oversimplifications and move beyond current best practices
Pervasive knowledge building	Knowledge building is not confined to particular occasions or subjects but pervades mental life—in and out of school
Symmetric knowledge advances	Expertise is distributed within and between communities. Symmetry in knowledge advancement results from knowledge exchange and from the fact that to give knowledge is to get knowledge

Online Discourse

Collaboration tools in this study were Knowledge Forum and a web-based videoconferencing system, thus combining asynchronous written online classroom discourse with synchronous oral discourse. Although we believe that hybrid learning environments are most effective (Laferriere, Lamon & Breuleux, in press), this paper deals with online discourse only. Lossman and So (2008) identified a "tendency to a higher diversity of verbal interactions online as compared to the more didactic teacher-centered discourse used in the classroom." (p. 1). Bordage (2007) found that written discourse was more conducive toward explanatory discourse than the verbal face-to-face context in which no collaborative technologies were used. Cazden (2001) alluded to computer-supported collaboration as leading to variations in the IRE/F (teacher initiation–student response–teacher evaluation/feedback) basic classroom discourse structure. Cazden recognizes (2001) that online discourse is more public, a characteristic often stressed by Bereiter and Scardamalia since 1994. Cazden (2001) and Scardamalia, Bereiter, Hewitt, and Webb (1996), stressed non-traditional discourse in which collaborative explanations are encouraged. The latter emphasizes the role of online collaborative spaces to this end.

Knowledge Forum is an asynchronous discourse medium that consists of contributions or notes embedded in views to a community knowledge base. A simple Knowledge Forum note, text, graphic, or other media consists of a single idea; however, the author of the note labels it with a problem and with "scaffolds." Both serve to give the note a place in more extended work with ideas such as theory refinement, evidence gathering, argumentation, or literary interpretation. Additionally, each note is embedded in one or more views. The views are graphical representations of higher-level conceptual structures constructed by participants to give greater meaning to the notes they contain (Scardamalia, 2002) (see Figs. 24.1 and 24.2).

This chapter presents teachers' boundary-spanning activity as they practiced a knowledge-building pedagogy and integrated the software into their teaching. Were they successful in transforming the IRF/E basic classroom discourse structure? To what extent? To document this working hypothesis, we first provide contextual and methodological background, especially in the presence of explanation as a key indicator of knowledge building. Second, the methodology for analyzing classrooms' online discourse is described. Third, the results of studies are presented. Fourth, the discussion highlights next research steps, and educational implications.

Methodology

When Mehan (1979) conducted his well-cited ethnographic study, he studied classroom interaction in one elementary classroom. Cazden's study was also an ethnographic one (1988, 2001). Currently, ethnography can be conducted online and more specifically through classroom discourse analysis. The unit of analysis was set in reference to the IRE/F sequence as we focused on sequences with at least a third turn/move or more.

From looking at the data and referring to previous analyses of Knowledge Forum databases, we thought that we had the possibility to document at length and in-depth the presence of a different kind of classroom discourse when students engage in knowledge building. Idea improvement, central to knowledge building, indicates that questions asked (I) in relation to problems of understanding and student responses (R) presenting explanations (Hakkarainen, 2003; Lipponen, Rahikainen, & Hakkarainen, 2002; Woodruff & Meyer, 1997; Zhang, Scardamalia, Lamon, Messina, & Reeve, 2007) are central. "Explanation-seeking why and how questions are especially valuable for progressive inquiry, whereas fact-seeking questions not embedded in genuine inquiry tend to produce fragmented pieces of knowledge" (Hakkarainen, 2003, p. 1073). Zhang et al. (2007) refined the explanation framework in ways that deepen the understanding of student responses (R). As for the "E" (teacher evaluation), one of the knowledge-building principles extends its meaning to (1) students providing responses to one another, ones found to be lengthy at times, and, in some cases, explanation-oriented ones (see Lee, Chan, & van Aalst, 2006).

For knowledge-building discourse to unfold an inquiry process must be triggered: Chan & van Aalst (2008) referred to collaborative inquiry, and Hakkarainen (2003) to "progressive inquiry"; Zhang et al. (2007) suggested the "inquiry thread" as a new unit of analysis when tracing ideas across views. The collaborative inquiry process is to be a lengthy one, centered on idea improvement and not task-centered and encompassing problems of understanding for knowledge building to occur (Scardamalia & Bereiter, 2006).

Our hypothesis was that we would find evidence of an inquiry-oriented basic pattern in Knowledge Forum databases. Contrary to synchronous classroom discourse where either one person speaks at a time (I, R, F/E) or all students are expected to provide the same answer (R), the asynchronous online discourse allows for multiple and diversified responses (Rs). The online classroom discourse sequence, tentatively conceptualized as IRFI, would then be the following one: an initiation question (I), one that would spark responses (Rs) leading, in a number of instances, to further inquiry (FI).

Participants

The presence of the IRFI pattern in the online discourse of classrooms using Knowledge Forum as their main collaborative technology was analyzed in the 2007–2008 online discourse of twelve classrooms from rural schools part of the Remote-Networked School initiative, sponsored by the Quebec Department of Education, Leasure and Sport (Canada). This enduring initiative (2002–2010) aims at enriching the learning environment of rural schools using advanced collaborative tools. Knowledge Forum is used for written discourse within and between schools and desktop videoconferencing for oral discourse. It is a multi-level innovation (classroom, school, school district, university-school partnership, ministry of education) in the context of a province-wide education reform informed by the new science of learning. Among other collaborative activities, teachers engaged students in online discourse on climate change mostly, but not exclusively, during science education classes. Some classrooms participated in the Knowledge Building International Project (KBIP), which also included classrooms from Barcelona, Hong Kong, Mexico, and Norway in 2007–2008. KBIP teachers were learning to inform their pedagogy using the knowledge-building principles when engaging students in written discourse on Knowledge Forum.

Here the discourse of the 8 teachers and 115 students from Quebec who had their classrooms collaborate using Knowledge Forum and desktop videoconferences during KBIP 2007–2008. Basic indicators that these classrooms engaged in discourse were the following ones: 19 views (see illustrations, Figs. 24.1 and 24.2) were developed by students and 1,547 notes were written in the 66 inquiry sequences analyzed. Between 65 and 73.5% of all sequences had three turns or more, and 28% of all sequences qualified as idea improvement sequences because they were found to contain notes that (1) improve the preceding note(s), (2) challenge the preceding note(s), and (3) move forward the questioning/explaining process (Hamel, 2007; Laferrière et al., 2008).

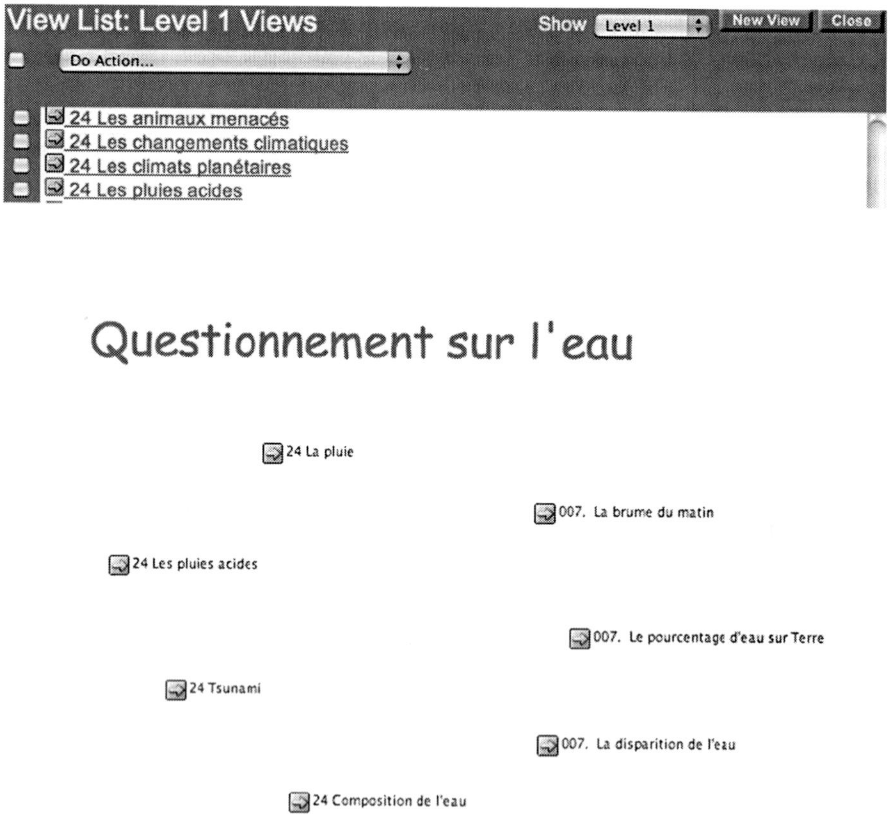

Fig. 24.1 Exemplars of some of the views developed by emerging knowledge-building communities

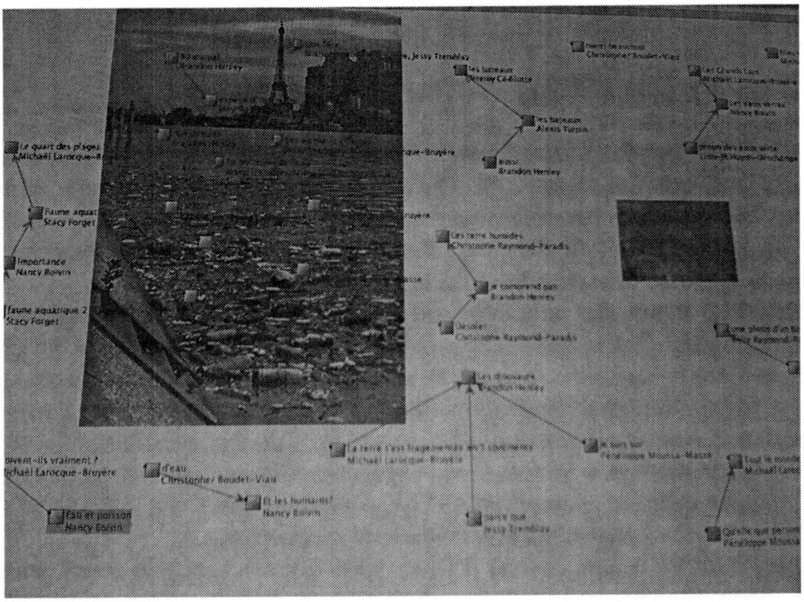

Fig. 24.2 Exemplar of a view developed by an emerging knowledge-building community

Data Analysis

To observe the presence of the IRFI pattern we focused on questions and explanations. For the analysis of questions asked, we used Hmelo-Silver and Barrows' (2008) grid, one developed for the study of groups engaged in collaborative problem-based learning[1]; Their grid distinguishes between questions that are task-oriented/meta level questions (group dynamics, monitoring, self-directed learning, need clarification, request/directive), short-answer questions (verification, disjunctive, concept completion, feature specification, and quantification), and long-answer questions (definition, example, comparison, interpretation, causal antecedent, causal consequence, enablement, expectation, and judgmental). Questions asked by teachers or students were distinguished.

[1] Scardamalia and Bereiter (2006) distinguish knowledge building from problem solving in that knowledge building focuses on complex generalizable problems and problem-based learning is context specific. However, Hmelo-Silver and Barrow's grid is applied to the resolution of complex problems, and was thought to be suitable for the task-at-hand.

Results

An Ongoing Questioning Process

A total of 209 questions were identified and classified (Table 24.2). Task-oriented or meta-level questions were 21%. Questions calling for short answers were 6%. Almost four questions out of five were ones likely to generate long answers (73%). Students asked 55% of all questions. This was a first indication that the classroom discourse might be departing from the basic IRF/E structure.

Table 24.3 shows that only one-third (29%, $n = 61$) of all 209 questions were asked during the first turn (I). These questions were asked four times out of five (79%, $n = 48$) by teachers. At times, these questions were the result of a classroom process of question identification, the teacher writing the question for a matter of convenience. Almost all questions (97%) were long-answer questions.

One-fourth (26%, $n = 54$) of second turn/moves (R) were questions (Table 24.4). Long-answer questions comprised 65%, and students asked the majority of these questions. Students also asked task-oriented/meta questions.

In the third move and beyond (FI), students and teachers also asked questions (Table 24.5). Students asked 68% ($n = 64$) of the questions, and one-fourth (24.5%) of their questions were task-oriented or meta-level ones. Most of their questions were long-answer questions (42.5%, $n = 40$), and almost none (1.1%) were short-answer questions.

Table 24.2 Types of teachers' and students' question moves

	Task-oriented/meta questions	Short-answer questions	Long-answer questions
Total 209 questions	(43) 21%	(13) 6%	(153) 73%
Teachers: 95	Teachers' questions: 9	Teachers' questions: 5	Teachers' questions: 81
Students: 114	Students' questions: 34	Students' questions: 8	Students' questions: 72
Students	e.g., Self-directed learning e.g., Need clarification	e.g., Verification e.g., Disjunctive	e.g., Example e.g., Interpretation e.g., Causal consequence
Teachers	e.g., Request/directive	e.g., Concept completion	e.g., Definition e.g., Comparison

Table 24.3 Teachers' and students' questions as initiation (I) moves

	Task-oriented/meta questions	Short-answer questions	Long-answer questions
First-turn questions (I) 61	1 (2%)	1 (2%)	59 (96%)
Teachers 48 (79%)	1 (2%)	0 (0%)	47 (76%)
Student(s) 13 (21%)	0 (0%)	1 (2%)	12 (20%)

Table 24.4 Teachers' and students' questions as response (R) moves

	Task-oriented/meta questions	Short-answer questions	Long-answer questions
Second-turn questions (R) 54	12 (22%)	7 (13%)	35 (65%)
Teachers 17 (32%)	1 (2%)	1 (2%)	15 (28%)
Student(s) 37 (68%)	11 (20%)	6 (11%)	20 (37%)

Table 24.5 Teachers' and students' questions as third move and beyond

	Task-oriented/meta questions	Short-answer questions	Long-answer questions
Third-move and beyond questions (FI) 94	30 (32%)	5 (5%)	59 (63%)
Teachers 30 (32%)	7 (8%)	4 (4%)	19 (20%)
Student(s) 64 (68%)	23 (25%)	1 (1%)	40 (42%)

Figure 24.3 represents the distribution of questions during the online classroom discourse. Teachers were active in the first move; but recall that in some cases teachers wrote a question following a discussion with their students regarding a question that might be of interest to inquire into. Moreover, we examined the moves (I, R, FI) variable 1 in relation to the types of questions, variable 2. Students' types of questions (task-oriented/meta, long-answer and short-answer questions) across moves revealed a significant difference ($\chi^2 = 14.102$, d.f. $= 4$, $p = 0.007$); the same regarding teachers' types of questions ($\chi^2 = 17.944$, d.f. $= 4$, $p = 0.001$). The space taken by students in the classroom discourse after the teachers' initial moves is substantial, and FI moves stand out.

Figure 24.4 shows where question-oriented action was concentrated: Almost no short-answer questions, and teachers did not direct the progressive inquiry as FI questions were dominated by the students. In addition, long-answer questions asked by teachers led to short-answer questions asked by students.

		Initiation (I)	Response (R)	Further Inquiry (FI)
Task-oriented/meta questions	Students	0	11	23
	Teachers	1	1	7
	Students	12	20	40
Long-answer questions	Teachers	47	15	19
	Students	1	6	1
Short-answer questions	Teachers	0	1	4

Fig. 24.3 Distribution of questions during online classroom discourse

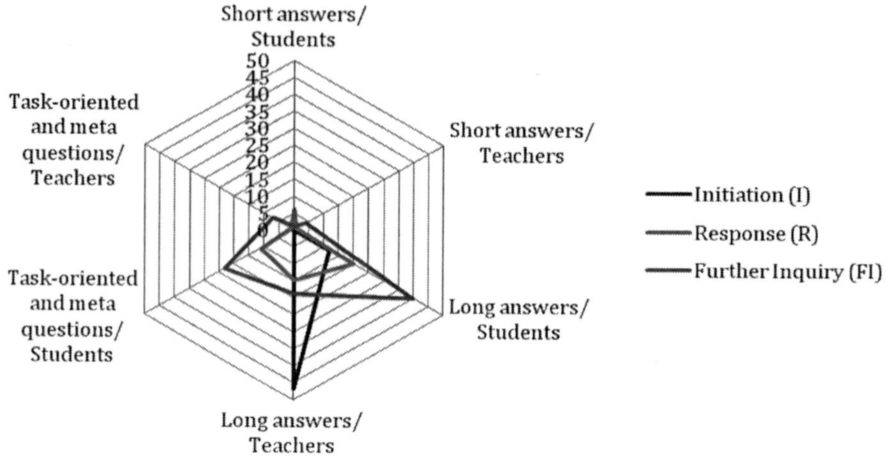

Fig. 24.4 A dynamic representation of teachers' and students' distribution of questions

Here is an illustration of one of these sequences that were analyzed: First, the teacher wrote the question and then students wrote notes. They were encouraged to use the scaffolds provided in Knowledge Forum.

1. Our Starting Question by Teacher using the scaffold *Let's put our knowledge together*

What causes climate changes?

1.2. Heat by A [2007, Oct 26]: Scaffold *My theory*

It is that it's caused by heat because it is warmer than usual.

1.2.1. Glaciers and Animals by B [2007, Oct 26]: My theory, I would say that it is true because in the North, the glaciers are melting and breaking and the animals are struggling to survive.

1.2.1.1. animals by C [2007, Oct 26]: Scaffold: *New information*

I completely agree with both of you that animals are struggling for their survival amid these climate changes. If their source(s) of food disappears, they could die; therefore, these animals are on the brink of extinction.

1.2.1.2. Why? by D [2007, Oct 26]: Scaffold: *I need to understand* why the animals are struggling to survive. Elaborate.

1.2.1.3. What? by E [2007, Oct 26]

I don't understand the link behind your theory; help me understand the link between your theory and Claudia's.

1.2.2. Heat by F [2007, Oct 26] Scaffold: *I need to understand*

Why is it warmer than usual?

1.2.2.1. Heat by G [2007, Oct 26]

My theory, because with pollution, the ozone layer gradually shrinks each year, so the sun takes less time to reach the earth, which in return causes the planet to heat up more rapidly.

1.2.2.1.1. the Ozone Layer is recovering by H [2007, Nov 13] Scaffold *Let's put our knowledge together.* You are right. I just want to add that the ozone layer is gradually recovering, thanks to our efforts. But, we shouldn't go back to our old habits.

1.3. Global Warming by G. [2007, Oct 26] Scaffold *My theory*

I think that global warming comes from carbon gas produced by car and truck motors which evaporates in the atmosphere and causes the planet to heat up.

1.3.1 The Ozone Layer by H. [2007, Oct 26] Scaffold *New information*

It's true. But, we shouldn't forget that if the planet is getting warmer, it's because the ozone layer is smaller and we have less protection against sunbeams.

1.3.1.1. Ozone Layer? by F [2007, Oct 26] Scaffold *Let's put our knowledge together.* So, if I understand completely, the sunbeams are able to reach the planet's surface much easier through the holes in the ozone layer. If the sunbeams come in, then they must surely go back out. What do you think?

1.3.1.2. You are Right! by B [2007, Nov 13] Scaffold *New information*

It's true, you are right. Because of all the pollution we are making, the ozone layer is now pierced and we are therefore less protected against sunbeams!

Overall, questioning was an ongoing distributed process rather than first-turn questions as in the IRF/E structure: Both teachers and students asked questions but questions differed in their potential to induce explanations. Explanation was distributed among students, and the above illustration is a clear example of that.

An Emerging Explanatory Process

Questions asked at one move or another led to a variety of ideas. Progressive discourse of an explanatory nature was likely to begin by a note presenting a student's initial understanding. In the illustrative sequence presented above, a student wrote on October 26th the following using the scaffold *My theory*: It is that its caused by heat because it is warmer than usual. Later in November, another student wrote, as a fifth move, the following note (Fig. 24.5):

Relevant explanations stressed specific problems and their causes. Figure 24.6 is an estimate of the level of explanation, using Hakkarainen's grid, observed in the sequences according to students' responses. Level 3 is clearly underdeveloped

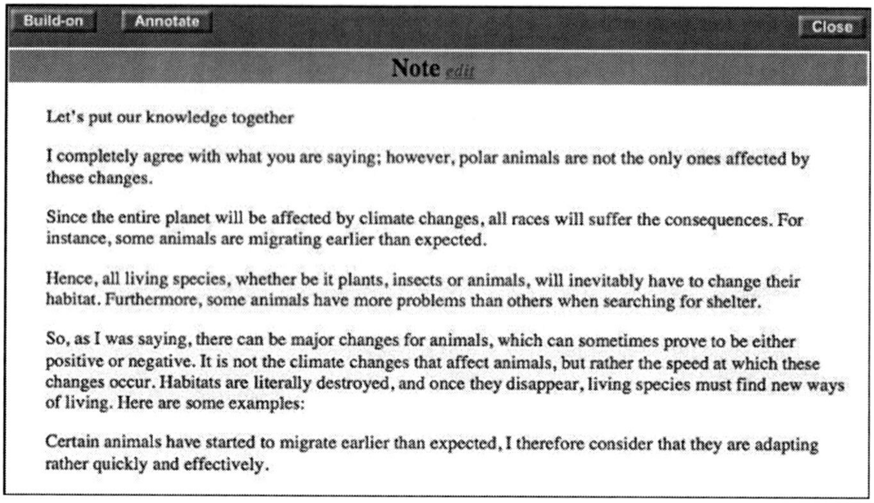

Fig. 24.5 Examples of explanations formulated by students involved in KBIP

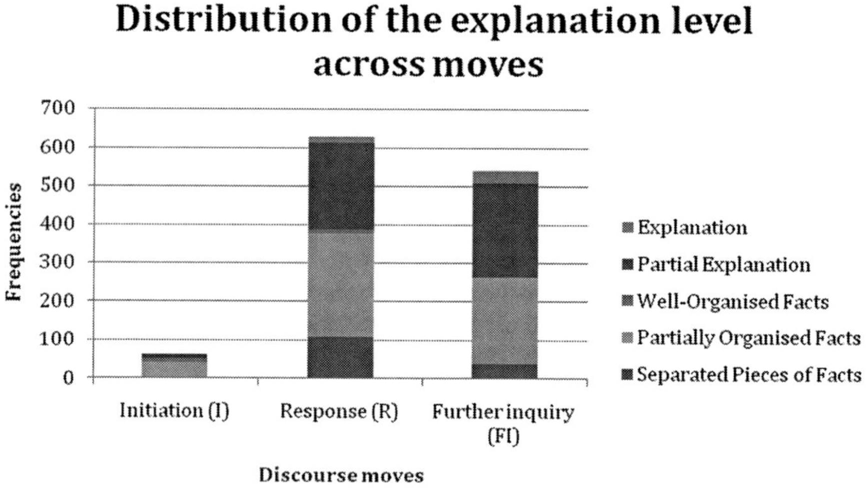

Fig. 24.6 Estimate of the level of explanation observed in the sequences

compared to Level 2. The Partial explanation category (Level 4) is high compared to Well-Organized Facts (Level 3).

These results seem to provide a clear indication that more complete explanations are to be sought (see, for instance, explanations in Fig. 24.6). To this end, and having in mind what could be instructive for teachers to know, we looked at the types of explanations in relation to the discourse moves. Figure 24.7 presents a distribution of the nature of the explanations across discourse moves.

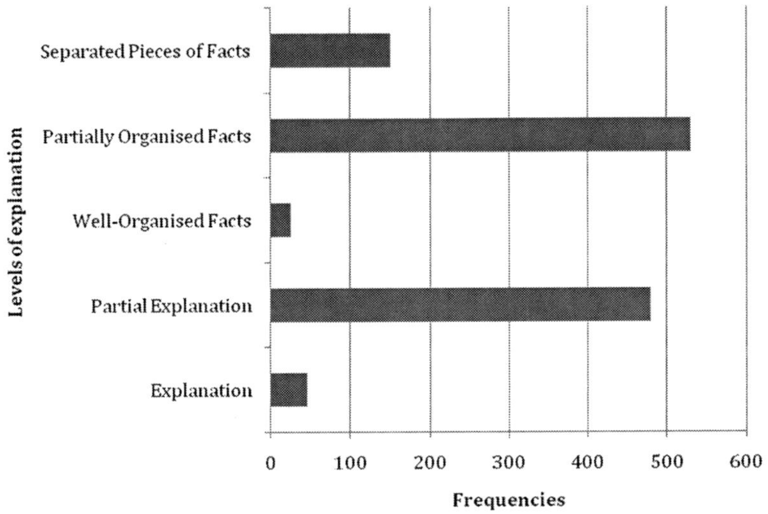

Fig. 24.7 Distribution of the explanation levels across discourse moves

The level of explanation varies significantly ($\chi^2 = 160.604$, d.f. $= 8$, $p = 0.000$) across discourse moves. Given this result and looking at Fig. 24.7, one may interpret that as discourse moves on, more partial and complete explanations are present and well-organized facts diminish.

Discussion, Pedagogical Implications, and Future Steps

Teachers were the ones who wrote up the first question regarding climate change, with or without preliminary discussion with students. Contrary to the basic IRE/F classroom discourse structure identified in the late seventies, questions kept being asked throughout discourse sequences, and it is clearly demonstrated that students asked FI questions in their third move and beyond. This is substantive evidence that what Cazden saw as the potential of technology being realized (2001): classroom online discourse using Knowledge Forum, inspired by a knowledge-building pedagogy, modifies the basic discourse structure of the classroom.

IRFI is therefore suggested as the structure of progressive online discourse provided it is guided by a pedagogy that emphasizes authentic questioning and values collaborative inquiry within and between classrooms with the support of a powerful electronic forum (e.g., Knowledge Forum).

Some of the students' short-answer questions followed teachers long-answer questions. It was as if teachers' questions prompted students to ask specific questions. We do not know yet how the combination of long-answer and short-answer questions can be articulated for progressive online discourse. More investigation is needed regarding questions most likely to engage students in an inquiry process. Our analysis benefited from the works of Hamel (2007), Hakkarainen (2003), Lee et al. (2006) and Zhang et al. (2007) but more needs to be known regarding the nature of online questions (e.g., levels of structuring and abstraction).

We argue that not all online collaborative spaces afford progressive discourse. For instance, Knowledge Forum has affordances to this end: it has built-in scaffolds, which can be modified by the teacher in the pursuit of specific goals regarding students' online work and chosen by students (metacognitive acts) as a way to identify the nature of their contribution. Another research step for better informing teachers would be to analyze the scaffolds used by students across discourse moves.

Online discourse in which FI is also what the new science of learning is recommending. For the past decade, the learning sciences have been presenting research results that are rich in new conceptual tools to the professional community of educators. These results go beyond what was learned reading Dewey, Piaget, and Vygotsky, although all three would be delighted with how we have built on their work.

One advance is a knowledge-building community. Students construct their knowledge when they are learning from books or through inquiry. Here, we want to point out some important differences between learning and knowledge building. Because education and society in general is struggling to cope with the demands of the new economy, there is some interest in restructuring school activities and classroom discourse so that they resemble the workings of high-performing research groups—where a team is investigating real questions and members are trying to contribute to progress on those questions. This is knowledge building. Learning occurs in all activities directed toward gaining personal knowledge; knowledge building is activity directed toward constructing new knowledge for a community through theory construction and revision. Explicitly formulating "my theory" makes possible comparisons to other theories, tried out on relevant problems, subjected to criticism and continuous idea improvement.

What is particularly distinctive about a knowledge-building community is the use of the twelve KB principles informing pedagogy, and using collaborative technologies. Online discourse in Knowledge Forum became integral in classrooms' progressive inquiry. Providing students with a cumulative database, as well as a means of recording information and ideas, is pivotal. It acts as a tool for making thinking explicit, encouraging creative thinking—the making of inspired hypotheses, the articulation of probing questions, the blending of others' findings with one's own, and the intensive attempt to solve authentic problems.

Project-based learning has been the way that teachers have integrated the computer and the Internet in their classrooms when applying a more active and collaboratively oriented pedagogy (see Kozma, 2003). It might be helpful to distinguish knowledge building from project learning; the essential difference is that students' work is not driven by the idea of creating a product. For instance, in Caswell & Lamon (1999) although students did create a video documentary, the idea of sharing what they knew with the rest of the school emerged from their work; it was not the starting point.

Moreover, knowledge building engages student in accountable talk (Michaels et al., 2002). Accountable talk encompasses three broad dimensions: one, accountability to the learning community, in which participants listen to and build their contributions in response to those of others; two, accountability to accepted standards of reasoning, talk that emphasizes logical connections and the drawing of reasonable conclusions; and, three, accountability to knowledge, talk that is based explicitly on facts, written texts, or other public information. These kinds of accountable talk share similarities with knowledge-building principles: the first, accountability to the community, is akin to collective cognitive responsibility: team members produce ideas of value to others and share responsibility for the overall advancement of knowledge in the community; the second kind of accountable talk is like knowledge-building discourse in that the knowledge itself is refined and transformed through the discursive practices of the community; and the third is akin to constructive use of authoritative sources: To know a discipline is to be in touch with the present state and growing edge of knowledge in the field. Taken together, research from the last 30 years (Cazden, 1988), to research on the effects of accountable talk (Wolf, Crosson, & Resnick, 2006) and knowledge building along with research from the learning sciences (Graesser, Gernsbacher, & Goldman, 2003), as well as the present results are persuasive in arguing for a more collaborative classroom discourse aimed at progressive inquiry.

References

Applebee, A. N. (1996). *Curriculum as conversation: Transforming traditions of teaching and learning*. Chicago: University of Chicago Press.

Bereiter, C., & Scardamalia, M. (1993). *Surpassing ourselves: An inquiry into the nature and implications of expertise*. Chicago and La Salle, IL: Open Court.

Bordage, J. (2007). Construction sociale de connaissances dans trois contextes scolaires distincts. Doctoral dissertation. Québec, Canada: Université Laval.

Bransford, J. D., Brown, A. L., & Cocking, R. R. (1999). *How people learn: Brain, mind, experience, and school*. Washington, DC: National Academy Press.

Brown, A. (1994). The advancement of learning. *Educational Researcher, 23*(8), 4–12.

Brown, A. L. (1997). Transforming schools into communities of thinking and learning about serious matters. *American Psychologist, 52*(4), 399–413.

Caswell, B., & Lamon, M. (1999). The development of scientific literacy: The evolution of ideas in a knowledge building classroom. In J. Leach & R. E. Moon (Eds.), *Learners & Pedagogy* (pp. 183–185). London: Paul Chapman.

Cazden, C. B. (2001, 1988). *Classroom discourse: The language of teaching and learning* (2nd ed) (pp. 140–157). Portsmouth, NH: Heinemann (Original work published 1988).

Chan, C. K. K., & van Aalst, J. (2008). Collaborative inquiry and knowledge building in networked multimedia environments. In J. Voogt, & G. Knezek (Eds.), *International handbook of information technology in primary and secondary education* (pp. 299–316). Dordrecht, the Netherlands: Springer.

Christie, F. (2002). *Classroom discourse analysis: A functional perspective*. London: Continuum.

Dillon, J. T. (1990). *The practice of questioning* (pp. 11–47). NY: Routledge, Chapman and Hall, Inc.

Flanders, N. A. (1970). *Analyzing teaching behavior*. Reading, MA: Addison-Wesley Publishing Company.

Graesser, A. C., Gernsbacher, M. A., & Goldman, S. (Eds) (2003). *Handbook of discourse processes*. Mahwah, NJ: Erlbaum.

Greenleaf, C., & Freedman, S. W. (1993). Linking classroom discourse and classroom content: Following the trail of intellectual work in a writing lesson. *Discourse Processes*, *16*(4), 465–505.

Hakkarainen, K. (2003). Progressive inquiry in a computer-supported biology class. *Journal of Research in Science Teaching*, *40*(10), 1072–1088.

Hamel, C. (2007). *The third contribution in a thread: Nature and patterns? The case of the Remote Networked Schools (RNS) Initiative*. Poster session presented at the Knowledge Building Summer Institute, OISE/UT, Toronto.

Hmelo-Silver, C. E., & Barrows, H. S. (2008). Facilitating collaborative knowledge building. *Cognition and Instruction*, *26*(1), 48–94.

Kozma, R. B. (Ed.), (2003). *Technology, innovation and educational change: a global perspective. A report of the IEA Second Information Technology in Education Study – Module 2*. Eugene, OR: International Society for Technology in Education (ISTE).

Laferrière, T., Allaire, S., Breuleux, A., Hamel, C., Turcotte, S., Gaudreault-Perron, J., et al. (2008). *L'école éloignée en réseau*. Research report, phase III, CEFRIO, Québec. Retrieved June 4, 2009, from http://www.cefrio.qc.ca/upload/L_Ecole_eloignee_en_reseau_Phase3_Final%20isbn.pdf

Laferrière, T., Lamon, M., & Breuleux, A. (in press). Blended learning environments. In P. Resta (Ed.), *Teacher development in an e-learning age: A policy and planning guide*. Paris, France: UNESCO.

Lee, E. Y. C., Chan, C. K. K., & van Aalst, J. (2006). Students assessing their own collaborative knowledge building. *International Journal for Computer-Supported Collaborative Learning*, *1*, 277–307.

Lemke, J. (1990). *Talking science: Language, learning, and values*. Norwood, NJ: Ablex.

Lipponen, L., Rahikainen, M., & Hakkarainen, K. (2002). Effective participation and discourse through a computer network: Investigating elementary students' computer supported interaction. *Journal of Educational Computing Research*, *27*(4), 355–384.

Lossman, H., & So, H. J. (2008, June). *A comparative discourse analysis of online and offline Knowledge Building activities*. Paper presented at The 8th International Conference on the Learning Sciences (ICLS), Utrecht, The Netherlands.

Mehan, H. (1979). *Learning lessons: Social organization in the classroom*. Cambridge, MA: Harvard University Press.

Mercer, N. (2000). *Words and minds: How we use language to think together*. London: Routledge.

Michaels, S., O'Connor, M. C., Hall, M. W., & Resnick, L. B. (2002). *Accountable talk: Classroom conversation that works* (3 CD-ROM set). Pittsburgh: University of Pittsburgh.

Sawyer, K. (Ed.) (2005). The *Cambridge handbook of learning sciences*. Cambridge University Press: New York, NJ.

Scardamalia, M. (2002). Collective cognitive responsibility for the advancement of knowledge. In B. Smith (Ed.), *Liberal education in a knowledge society* (pp. 67–98). Chicago: Open Court.

Scardamalia, M., & Bereiter, C. (1994). Computer support for knowledge-building communities. *The Journal of the Learning Sciences*, *3*(3), 265–283.

Scardamalia, M., & Bereiter, C. (2003). Knowledge building. In J. W. Guthrie (Ed.), *Encyclopedia of education* (pp. 1370–1373). New York: Macmillan Reference.

Scardamalia, M., & Bereiter, C. (2006). Knowledge building: Theory, pedagogy, and technology. In K. Sawyer (Ed.), *Cambridge handbook of the learning sciences* (pp. 97–118). New York: Cambridge University Press.

Scardamalia, M., & Bereiter, C. (2007). Fostering communities of learners and knowledge building: An interrupted dialogue. In J. Campione, K. Metz, & A. Sullivan Palincsar (Eds.), *Children's learning in laboratory and classroom contexts* (pp. 197–212). New York: Lawrence Erlbaum Associates.

Scardamalia, M., Bereiter, C., Hewitt, J., & Webb, J. (1996). Constructive learning from texts in biology. In K. Fischer & M. Kirby (Eds.), *Relations and biology learning: The acquisition and use of knowledge structures in biology* (pp. 44–64). Berlin: Springer-Verlag.

Scardamalia, M., Bereiter, C., & Lamon, M. (1994). The CSILE project: Trying to bring the classroom into World 3. In K. McGilley (Ed.), *Classroom lessons: Integrating cognitive theory and classroom practice* (pp. 201–228). Cambridge, MA: MIT Press.

Sinclair, J., Mc, H., & Coulthard, M. (1975). *Towards an analysis of discourse: The English used by teachers and pupils*. London: Oxford University Press.

Wegerif, R. (2007). *Dialogic, education and technology: Expanding the space of learning*. New York: Springer.

Wells, G. (1993). Reevaluating the IRF sequence: A proposal for the articulation of theories of activity and discourse for the analysis of teaching and learning in the classroom. *Linguistics in Education*, *5*(1), 1–37.

Wells, G. (1999). *Dialogic inquiry: Toward a sociocultural practice and theory of education*. Cambridge: Cambridge University Press.

Wolf, M. K., Crosson, A. C., & Resnick, L. B. (2006). *Accountable talk in reading comprehension instruction* (CSE Technical Report 670). Los Angeles: National Center for Research on Evaluation, Standards, and Student Testing (CRESST). Retrieved June 26, 2009, from http://www.eric.ed.gov:80/ERICDocs/data/ericdocs2sql/content_storage_01/0000019b/80/1b/e0/be.pdf

Woodruff, E., & Meyer, K. (1997). Explanations from intra and inter group discourse: Children building knowledge in the science classroom. *Research in Science Education*, *27*(1), 25–39.

Zhang, J., Scardamalia, M., Lamon, M., Messina, R., & Reeve, R. (2007). Socio-cognitive dynamics of knowledge building in the work of 9- and 10-year-olds. *Educational Technology Research and Development*, *55*(2), 1042–1629.

Zhang, J., Scardamalia, M., Reeve, R., & Messina, R. (2009). Designs for collective cognitive responsibility in knowledge building communities. *Journal of the Learning Sciences*, *18*(1), 7–44.

Chapter 25
Digital Video Tools in the Classroom: How to Support Meaningful Collaboration and Critical Advanced Thinking of Students?

Carmen Zahn[1], Karsten Krauskopf[1], Friedrich W. Hesse[1], and Roy Pea[2]

[1] Knowledge Media Research Center, Konrad-Adenauer-Strasse 40, D-72072, Tuebingen, Germany
[2] Stanford Center for Innovations in Learning, 450 Serra Mall, Wallenberg Hall, Stanford, CA 94305, USA

Introduction

Whether in the arts, at home, or in the workplace—digital video and web-based video systems have brought about a large variety of filmic expression in many areas. For example, in entertainment we use DVD movies that are partitioned into chapters or scenes (including additional scenes that were not shown in the original movie), which enable the viewer to systematically access specific contents of interest. In the workplaces, digital video technology is used for professional video analyses (e.g., in the area of professional sports Cassidy, Stanley, & Bartlett, 2006; Eckrich, Widule, Shrader, & Maver, 1994, or teacher education, e.g., Moreno & Ortegano-Layne, 2008; Petrosino & Koehler, 2007), as well as computer-supported collaborative work (e.g., in medicine, Sutter, 2002). Additionally, in the realm of Web 2.0 and the Semantic Web, users can actively participate by creating and broadcasting their own digital videos (Alby, 2007) and by designing complex information structures based on video. The annotation feature of YouTube constitutes a very recent example for this development. It enables users to add audiovisual or text-based commentaries, or to add hotspots to videos and then publish the results. In sum, in our everyday life we find many examples of video tools that include the selection of single scenes or objects from existing video information, and even the direct integration of video scenes with e-communication tools, so that the "constructive" use of video (in a constructionist sense, e.g., Papert, 1993) has become widely available.

As a result, the ways in which people "watch" video today are in the process of being reshaped (Cha, Kwak, Rodriguez, Ahn, & Moon, 2007). Concurrently new specific *skills* grow more important for people, so that they can use the new (audio)visual media to participate in societal communication processes, and

C. Zahn (✉)
Knowledge Media Research Center, Konrad-Adenauer-Strasse 40, D-72072, Tuebingen, Germany
e-mail: c.zahn@iwm-kmrc.de

M.S. Khine, I.M. Saleh (eds.), *New Science of Learning*,
DOI 10.1007/978-1-4419-5716-0_25,

to express themselves. Otherwise people will be limited in their opportunities to solve complex problems in the future. Current research in education has repeatedly emphasized that contemporary literacy concepts cannot be restricted to individual skills of reading and writing static texts, tables, graphs, but must now be extended toward complex visual media (e.g., Stahl, Zahn, Schwan, & Finke, 2006). These skills can be summarized as visual literacies (Messaris, 1994, 1998) for visual communication (Messaris, 1998), on the one hand, and new media literacies for participatory cultures and for community involvement (Jenkins, Clinton, Weigel, & Robison, 2006), on the other. The *visual literacies* model defined by Messaris (1994) refers to four skills levels, ranging from simple understanding of audio-visual content to sophisticated critical film analysis. Analysis is accomplished by using general film analysis methodology to de-compose and to evaluate the source, thereby developing a critical stance and aesthetic appreciation of visual communication. Visual literacies include productive communicative skills, too (Baacke, 1999a, 1999b). According to Jenkins et al.'s (2006) notions of *new media literacies*, emphasize active participation and include the abilities to interact meaningfully with media content and advanced cognitive tools ("appropriation" and "distributed cognition"), skills to interact and collaborate with others, and skills "to pool knowledge and compare notes with others toward a common goal" ("collective intelligence", p. 4) among other abilities.

However, such advanced skills of understanding and working creatively with (audiovisual) media need to be developed. They provide new challenges for school-based education, and for both students and teachers alike. Schools—especially in the sectors of history, politics, ethics, language, and media education—are challenged to provide opportunities for students to participate and to develop such visual and communication skills. This, in turn, requires radically changing the role of digital video and computers in classroom learning.

Digital Video in Education

Video has long been acknowledged in school-based education as a didactical means to pursue a variety of learning goals in many domains. However, empirical findings on its effectiveness for knowledge acquisition is somewhat inconsistent (e.g., Park & Hopkins, 1992; Salomon, 1983, 1984; Wetzel, Radtke, & Stern, 1994) with clear positive effects only for interactive video (McNeil & Nelson, 1991). Also, empirical findings on the use of video in the classroom show a limited variety and limited goal orientation among the teachers (Hobbs, 2006).

The pedagogy associated with educational media is in a way prefigured in the technical properties or the "affordances" (Norman, 1988) of the technologies in use. Audiovisual media, which are in the focus of this chapter, underwent drastic changes in their educational potential and in their technological "evolution": When films had to be mounted in projectors and played for a large public, education could not be achieved by having learners interrogate film-as-data, much less design, construct, or edit films. The educational value was limited to simply having students watch a film and derive information from what they saw. Alternative pedagogies for using audio-visual recordings emerged with interactive video technology (see Wetzel et al., 1994) or interactive DVDs—and more recently with constructive video technologies. These new developments add to the cognitive functions of film (Salomon, 1994) and enable new forms of active video-based learning. In interactive video, the learner is interacting with videos that others have captured, structured, and sequenced (e.g., as in an instructional video designed to learn challenging nautical knots: Schwan & Riempp, 2004). Interactive video activities are supported by various technologies, including digital video players (such as Adobe Flash Player, Apple Quicktime™, RealPlayer™, Windows MediaPlayer™), DVD-menus, embedded hotspots and dynamic hyperlinks). Research has shown that people learn from interactive videos when video-related actions (such as the use of video player functions or dynamic hyperlinks) accompany effective usage strategies. For example, in the Schwan and Riempp (2004) study, the participants learned to tie nautical knots from video clips by using the stop or slow motion functions to adapt the speed and flow of video information to their individual cognitive needs while they were working out the knot-tying procedure. Likewise, in a study of Zahn et al. (2004), participants interacted with dynamic hyperlinks plus stop, rewind, and fast forward functions in a hypervideo and used them strategically to structure and monitor their information input according to their cognitive capacities while processing the information on "lakes as ecological systems." In both studies, the learning outcome was shown to be closely related to individual usage patterns. As Schwan and Riempp summarize, the video-related usage strategies of learners can be thought of as "epistemic actions" in the sense that they support cognitive activities during the learning process and are of central importance for learning. Similar arguments are made by Spiro, Collins, and Ramchandran (2007) in their comprehensive reflections on video usage based on cognitive flexibility theory. The authors focus on the learning of complex problems in ill-structured domains and they sketch out how (nonlinear) digital video can be used to avoid oversimplifications and to support the understanding of complexity and multidimensionality, for example, in the domain of history. Taken together, these findings indicate that effective learning with digital videos actually may depend on new media skills (here: "the ability to interact meaningfully with tools that expand mental capacities," Jenkins et al., 2006, p. 4).

For constructive video, learners are not only interacting with video, they are creating "their own" video materials by either capturing video themselves and/or selecting from pre-captured video assets in order to edit and re-sequence them for purposes of critical reflection or communicating to an audience. By creating a video and sharing it with others, learners engage in the processes of collaborative problem-solving (de-composition, selection, evaluation of information in teams). The conjecture is that people can learn from constructive video because they "design" them with audience needs in mind thereby being supported by a given video tool. Examples include tools for de-composing and annotating video, (e.g., Smith & Reiser, 2005); creating video hyperlinks, (e.g., Zahn & Finke, 2003); or "diving" into video in order to create new points of view onto a source video and to share them within a knowledge community (Pea et al., 2004; Pea, Lindgren, & Rosen, 2006). Each of these tools provides specific affordances designed to support cognitive and socio-cognitive activities of people who use them to create new video content. Having students edit videos as an authentic "visual design problem" with the direct involvement of video tools puts students in the active role of designers *and* helps to foster the deep understanding of the topic. This active process also helps them to develop what Carver, Lehrer, Connel, and Erickson (1992) called organizational, representational, and presentational skills.

However, until today, creating scripts and storyboards, shooting and film-editing (not to mention video annotation or hypervideo construction) have not yet been considered key competencies in our educational systems, even though writing and editing texts are skills which are supposed to be promoted by instructional means. In short, with the exception of some basic experiences with home videos, YouTube, or similar platforms, skills for creating and designing video footage are lacking.

In the research to be reported here, the potential educational value of constructive video is investigated empirically by experimental studies in the laboratory and in the field. In particular, the cognitive and technical conditions necessary for effective video-supported collaboration and acquisition of (visual) literacy skills in student groups are studied. The overarching questions we are trying to answer are: How can digital video technologies be implemented in educational learning processes? How can they be implemented broadly and without an overall amount of effort that would render a widespread application very unlikely? This means, finally, that the curricular and classroom context must be taken into account when trying to practically pave the way for realizing this way of learning as a part of "normal" classroom activities.

In the remainder of this chapter, we present research that tackles these questions. First, we present two exemplary types of digital video tools with specific affordances that might be used to guide students in collaboration, design, and learning. Then, we will describe the concept of collaborative visual design as a theoretical framework that informed the development of a constructivist task for secondary school education. Finally, we will present our initial research on students' performance in a collaborative visual design task in a classroom setting and offer our conclusions from the results.

Tools and Tasks for Learning with Digital Video—an Integrated Approach

Video Tools to Guide Collaboration

Specific video tools were developed for educational purposes but have so far been minimally appropriated yet in K-12 education (Pea et al., 2006; Zahn et al., 2005). Two of these tools will be presented in the following two sections: The tools are designed to support group knowledge processes. They can enable collaborative analysis and collaborative design of visual communication, like editing, re-sequencing, and annotating video to create new multimedia products. What needs to be considered, however, is that each of these tools affords specific cognitive and socio-cognitive activities. Our understanding of such affordances is related to the concept of "representational guidance" in collaborative problem solving (Suthers, 1999, 2001). It describes the implicit impact on social interactions that tools for students' productions of representational artifacts may have. Suthers and Hundhausen (2003) found, for example, that the salience of information in external representations can have important effects on students' interactions during collaborative problem solving (representational bias). These effects are based on both experimental data and a classroom study. Thus, we need to take into account that the form of external representations and the corresponding tools used in collaborative design scenarios can shape the interactions between learners and should therefore be included in the related research.

Tools for Collaborative Observation and Analysis

The DIVER/WebDIVER™ system was developed by the Stanford Center for Innovations in Learning (SCIL) and is based on the notion of a user "diving" into videos. "Diving" refers to creating new points of view on a source video by using a virtual camera that can zoom and pan through space and time within an overview window of the source video. The virtual camera can take a snapshot of a still image clip, or dynamically record a video "path" through the video to create a dive™ (which we also call a WebDIVER™ worksheet, see Fig. 25.1 below). These can be

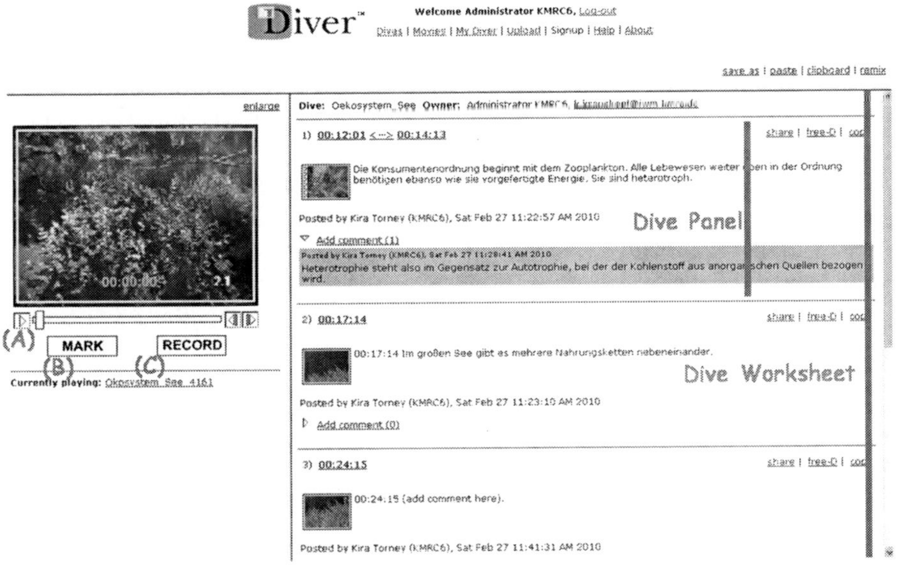

Fig. 25.1 WebDIVER™ worksheet. (**a**) Button for playing and pausing the source video, (**b**) mark-button for capturing still images, (**c**) record-/stop-button for capturing sequences

commented on by writing short text passages or codes (Pea et al., 2004). A dive is made up of a collection of re-orderable "panels," each of which contains a small key video frame that represents a clip, plus and a text field and room for comments to be added to this dive. Diving into video performs an important action for establishing common ground that is characterized as "guided noticing" (Pea et al., 2006). The use of the virtual camera for the framing of a focus within a complex and dynamic visual field directs the viewer's attention to notice with particular attention what is being framed. Thus the viewer is guided to that noticing act from a particular point of view. While one can guide another to notice a video referent with a certain interpretation by pointing and speaking about it, this is a *transient* act. As a new tool for supporting guided noticing interactions, DIVER™ makes pointing to video moments and making interpretive annotations a *persistent* act that is then replayable as an artifact Pea, Lindgren & Rosen (2006). In this way, DIVER™ can be used as a tool to promote the development of "professional vision" in learning within disciplinary domains (Goodwin, 1994).

Originally, DIVER's primary focus was on supporting research activities in the learning sciences (such as interaction analysis: Jordan & Henderson, 1995), and in teacher education, where video analyses play a major role for understanding one's own behavior and reflecting on it in relation to the behavior of others. There are two different ways users work with video using the DIVER™ approach. In the first, after creating a dive using the desktop DIVER™ application, the user can upload it onto WebDIVER™, a website for interactive browsing, searching, and displaying of video clips and collaborative commentary on dives. In an alternative version of the WebDIVER™ system, one can dive on streaming video files that are made accessible through a web server over the Internet. Using WebDIVER™ in either of these ways, a dive can be shared over the Internet. Thus it can become the focus of knowledge-building exchanges, which can be argumentative, tutorial, assessment, or general communicative exchanges. With DIVER/WebDIVER™ it becomes obvious that digital video technology may not only amplify existing kinds of activities and communication, but that it might augment our spectrum of activities and initiate entirely new forms of learning (Pea, 1985; Beichner, 1994). For related prior work see also Goldman-Segal (1998) and Stevens, Cherry, and Fournier (2002). In our research we aim to provide empirical data specific to these theoretically implemented affordances to advocate their use in education by empirical data.

Tools for Collaborative Hypervideo Structuring

Other tools for video-based collaboration are based on the idea of hypervideo, i.e., the selection of video segments from a source video and creation of spatio-temporal hyperlinks (see Fig. 25.2) to video by multiple users. For example, in the hypervideo system originally developed at the Computer Graphics Center (ZGDV) in Darmstadt, Germany, and presented by Zahn and Finke (2003), (1) information is mainly presented by video, (2) knowledge can be collaboratively expanded by means of both dynamic links and written e-communication, and (3) the construction process of joint knowledge representation is reflected in a resulting hypervideo.

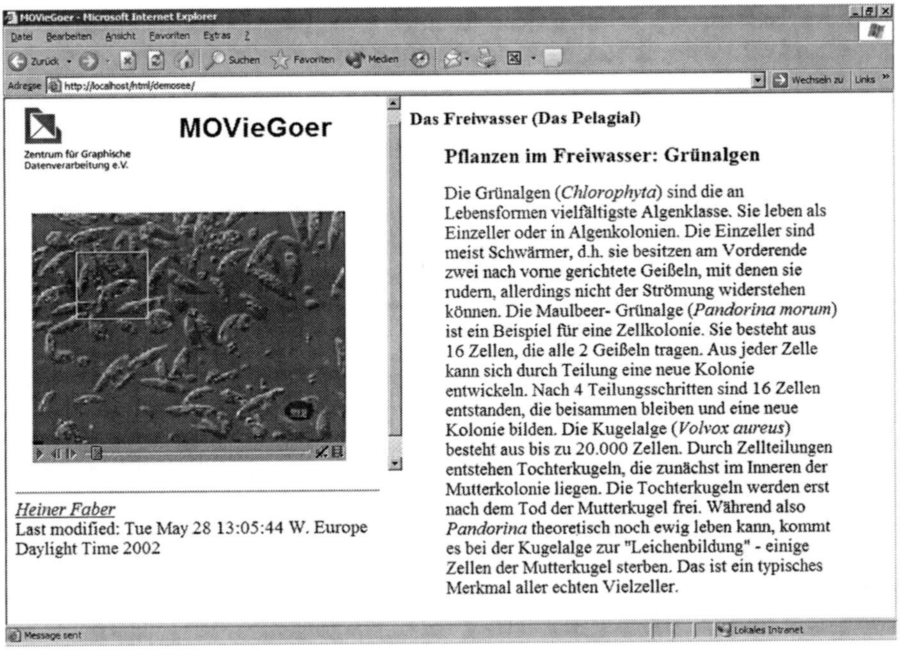

Fig. 25.2 Graphical user interface of a hypervideo system (see also Zahn & Finke, 2003). A dynamic sensitive region, "hotspot" within the video (white frame on the *left*) is connected via multiple links to other materials (e.g., a text document, on the *right*)

Hypervideo is thus denoted as a "dynamic information space" of a collaborating group (*DIS*, Zahn & Finke, 2003; Chambel, Zahn, & Finke, 2005).The system was first developed for unspecified learning or work situations. The basic idea was that structuring hypervideos by dynamic links can serve to promote both learning to integrate different information elements and developing nonlinear knowledge structures by collaboratively designing information and discussion links. Users of this hypervideo system can create their own dynamic sensitive regions ("hotspots") within video materials and add multiple links to these sensitive regions. Links can consist of data files uploaded from a local computer, as well as URLs. The links (or associated information elements, respectively) can then be discussed by means of an integrated e-communication tool. Thus, both randomly accessing videos and adding one's own new information and knowledge becomes possible. The web-based graphical user interface (see Fig. 25.2) allows the adaptation due to different GUI layouts and consists basically of a video player that visually displays the spatio-temporal hyperlinks within the video frame and offers functionalities in order to create new video annotations. Newly created video annotations are immediately transferred from the client to the server in order to be instantly shareable by the community. An example of a similar digital tool is the web-based application Asterpix (http://video.asterpix.com/). Users can, after creating a free account (a professional version is available for purchase that offers more features, like automatic object tracking for hotspots), select a video from the web either by search or by pasting the exact URL. After editing basic descriptive information of the video, it opens in the Asterpix hypervideo browser and hotspots can be added and edited. Hotspots can contain a text commentary, links to other web-videos or websites, and tags that help to identify an object referred to by the hotspot. This web application is of special interest, because, in contrast to YouTube, where only personally uploaded videos can be annotated, Asterpix enables viewers of digital videos on the Internet to share their thoughts and knowledge by re-"designing" the source video instead of being either limited to a written commentary or forced to upload a new video. As an example of a Web 2.0 application that represents the new paradigm of participation mentioned above.

On a generic level, the video systems described above can be seen as cognitive/collaborative tools that enable "pointing to video" (DIVER/Web DIVER^{TM}) and "linking video information" (hypervideo, Asterpix), to enhance the probability that in collaborative problem-solving processes, external representations help to focus joint attention and relate associated knowledge items so that negotiations of meaning between participants in a conversation will build upon a common ground. This form of communication with video is important for tapping powerful potentials (and some challenges) of video-enhanced learning in the classroom. The *potentials* can be seen in a more active and situated use of videos in many subject areas. Active and situative learning (Greeno, 2006), in turn, is the basis for sustainable knowledge and skills acquisition.

We take the approach of integrating these exemplary *tools* (and their affordances) as described above with a perspective of *design as problem solving* (e.g., Dillon, 2002). Therefore, a design problem involving constructive video was developed that allows for predictions of positive effects on learning outcomes (here: new media literacies and visual skills including an advanced understanding of video sources in the domain of history). As a heuristic for building the design task and for our research, we relied on the cognitive framework described in the next section.

Collaborative Visual Design—a Cognitive Framework

From a cognitive perspective, a design task is defined as a specific type of rhetorical problem (Stahl, Finke, & Zahn, 2006). *Visual* design consists of creating and structuring *visual* content for an anticipated audience according to the aesthetic standards of *visual* (or audiovisual) media. Our definition of visual design as problem solving is firmly based on three major lines of research from cognitive psychology: First, we note earlier findings by Goel & Pirolli, (1992), who demonstrated that design is a process of problem solving of an ill-defined and complex problem to be structured by the designer. Seitamaa-Hakkarainen (2000) provided further evidence for "dual space search" processes in such design. Second, we note influential cognitive approaches to text production (e.g., Flower & Hayes, 1980, 1986; Hayes, 1996), which explain writing for an audience as a complex problem-solving process, where intensive interactions between a content problem space and a rhetorical problem space lead to knowledge transformation (Bereiter & Scardamalia, 1987). Finally, we note the constructionist approach of *learning through design* (e.g., Kafai & Resnick, 1996), which has been applied in pedagogy and approved by many case studies ranging from K-12 education to university and adult education levels. Particularly, multimedia design problems using the services of emerging computer technologies for the support of active learning and media skills acquisition have become popular. Examples include contextualized multimedia design in elementary biology (e.g., Beichner, 1994), software design in mathematics (e.g., Harel, 1990; Kafai, 1996), hypermedia design in history and the humanities (e.g., Carver et al., 1992; Bereiter, 2002; Stahl & Bromme, 2004), and designing instruction in simulations in physics (Vreman-te Olde, 2006). These examples all involve generative activities of (a) integrating various media and (b) structuring information for others. In this context, Erickson, Lehrer, and colleagues (Erickson & Lehrer, 1998; Lehrer, Erickson, & Connel, 1994) emphasized the importance of sub-processes in design problem solving, such as planning, transformation, evaluation, and revision in hypertext design for history learning (see Fig. 25.3).

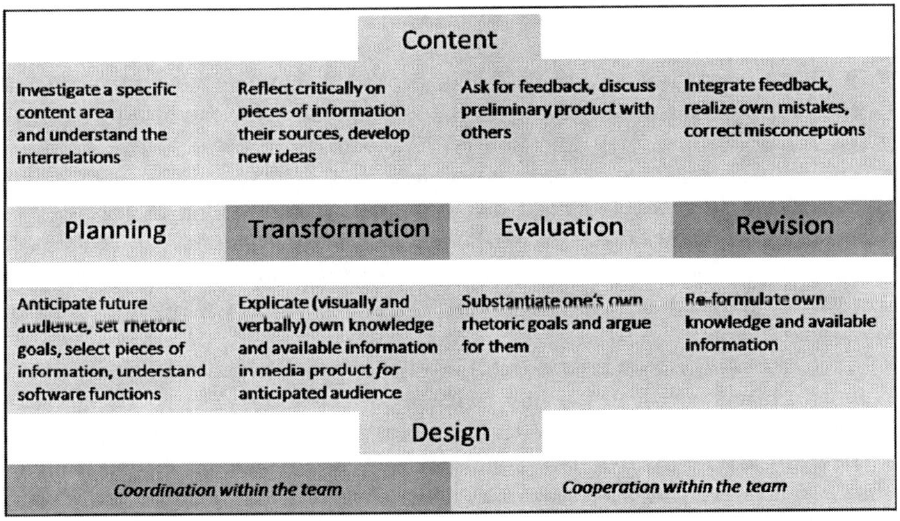

Fig. 25.3 Visual design as problem solving: cognitive and socio-cognitive processes during learning by designing, accentuating aspects of content, design, and teamwork (see also Zahn, 2009)

These cognitive perspectives are adopted in our works on learning by hypervideo authoring and creating digital video (Stahl et al., 2005; Zahn et al., 2005). We assume that students who design digital (hyper)videos, simultaneously have to take into account both visual content and style of their design product. Thereby they have to establish a joint dual problem space (for *joint problem spaces*, see Roschelle & Teasley, 1995) being distributed over the cognitive systems

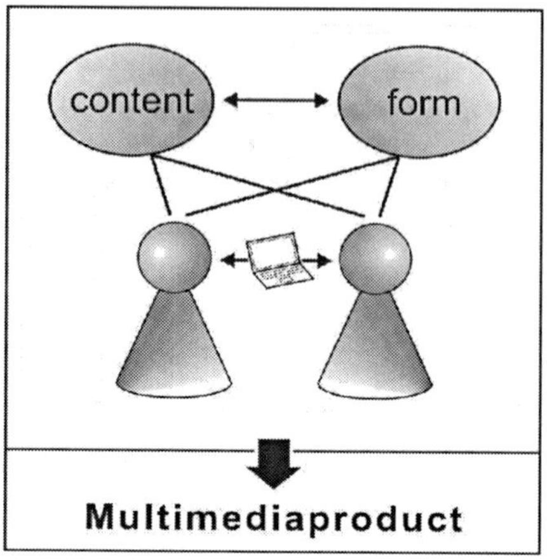

Fig. 25.4 Collaborative design activities as joint dual problem space involving content and form

of *at least two people* (see Fig. 25.4). The participants (students in our case) have to cooperate, when they decide *what* to say/show and *how* to say/show it, when they plan, transform, evaluate, and revise their video product. Thereby they have to negotiate shared design goals and their understanding of content (see Fig. 25.3). This adds not only to the educational value but also to the complexity of problem solving (see Barron, 2003; see also Lowry, Curtis, & Lowry (2004) who assume that in order to write a text in collaboration with others, students have to share and negotiate their content knowledge, as well as task schemas, genre knowledge, task goals, and task relevant strategies). In sum, we perceive collaborative visual design as complex problem solving that eventually can lead to deep understanding of content and new literacy skills acquisition in students.

This framework serves for conducting systematic research concerning the real (as opposed to the theoretical) learning potentials of collaborative visual design tasks. Scientific reports confirming the effectiveness of visual design that would go beyond the level of assumptions or case studies are very rare. However, this research has shown that in *realistic* scenarios (e.g., university seminars), student performance depends on situational factors including instructional support of the problem solving process (e.g., Stahl, Zahn, Schwan, & Finke, 2005). Hence, from a pedagogical perspective, the additional question arises *how* to instructionally support the complex process of collaborative visual design in class. Similar questions have inspired educational research approaches, such as for example, Kolodner's (e.g., 2003) influential works on Learning By Design^{TM} in science classes. The present endeavor reflects our scientific interest in providing new experimental work based on the theoretical considerations described above, to shed light on the application of visual design in an instructional framework.

Instructional Framing of Collaborative Visual Design: Approaches, Results, Problems

The cognitive models of writing and design on which we partly base our theoretical framework consider both individual and environmental factors as determinants for text production (e.g., Hayes, 1996). Individual factors incorporate motivational and affective states of the person who is writing, her or his working memory, long-term memory, and prior knowledge (e.g., task schemas, topic knowledge, genre knowledge, audience knowledge). Environmental factors incorporate the physical environment (e.g., the media or tools in use) and social factors (e.g., the collaborators in the writing process). Thus, visual design tasks, too, will be contingent upon interactions of cognitive and environmental factors present in a concrete classroom situation. *Cognitive factors* in our specific case include task schemas about video production, topic knowledge, and rhetorical concepts about digital video and filmic styles. *Environmental factors* in our case include peer–peer interactions and teacher–student interactions, as well as interactions with the digital video tools in use (affordances).

Empirical research concerning these possible influencing factors (to our knowledge) is virtually nonexistent. However, for our context, we can rely on a specific result reported by Stahl and Bromme (2004) who developed a set of instructional units for secondary students designing hypertexts and to help students in dealing one by one with the specific demands that the features of hypertext present for knowledge transformation. They argue that due to the novelty of the medium hypertext, student designers cannot be assumed to have firmly established media-related rhetorical concepts. Thus they developed a course program to tackle this specific problem by instructional means and compared two metaphors epitomizing rhetorical concepts about hypertext (space vs. book metaphor) in a case study. Results revealed a superiority of the space metaphor for learning by hypertext design.

For our purposes, we primarily look at media-related concepts in relation to "representational guidance" in collaborative problem solving (Suthers, 1999, 2001, see section about video tools). Our specific empirical investigations tap the following questions:

- How would students approach collaborative visual design tasks in a real, "noisy" classroom setting?
- How do students use the affordances of video tools for collaborative visual design?
- Where, precisely, do students need instructional support?

To find answers to these open questions, we developed a prototypical task for German secondary education (history and/or German language art lessons), i.e., designing a web page for a virtual history museum, and we conducted a field experiment.

Pursuing Instructional Goals and Developing a Student-Centered Learning Task

Relating to our framework described above, our task involves collaborative visual design based on a video resource showing a historical newsreel on the 1948 Berlin blockade (Fig. 25.5) andusing digital video tools (see tools section above). Students are asked to act as a team of online editors who design a web page for a popular German virtual history museum. The explicated overall design goal is to comment on the video showing the historical newsreel, for publication in the virtual history museum for future visitors. This product is based on the collaborative analysis of the source video by integrating additional information applying one of the digital video tools. Learners are explicitly made aware of the audience they are designing for (i.e., museum visitors) and the purpose the product should serve for this audience: Namely, the future visitors of the virtual museum should be able to develop a good understanding of both the content and the filmic codes/style of the historical newsreel.

Fig. 25.5 Landing of a Douglas C-54 of the US Air Force at the airport Berlin Tempelhof in July 1948. The supply of West Berlin with goods by the air forces of the Western Allies during the Berlin Blockade (June 1948—May 1949) by the Soviet Union represents one of the largest humanitarian operations in history. It is an important topic in Germany's postwar history as studied in secondary education. Henry Ries/DHM, © New York Times

Following our theoretical considerations the task includes an individual inquiry phase for planning, where learners first watch a digital video showing the historical Berlin-Blockade newsreel from 1948, then visit the virtual history museum LEMO, and finally familiarize themselves with the specific period of German history. Participants have to acquaint themselves with the contemporary use of newsreels as well as basic information on general filmic codes and style. Then, students explore the functions of the digital video tool fitting for the respective experimental condition with a thematically unrelated, instructional video clip. In the subsequent transformation phase students pair up together and collaboratively design elements for the web-museum using one computer. When working with the digital video tool, students are always free to evaluate and revise their evolving product.

Our major concern was a design task realizable within the constraints of an average lesson. One thing we did to accomplish this was to relate the content of the task to educational goals relevant to the teachers and students. We chose the described topic (historical content and visual/media competence) to satisfy curricular demands. Another equally important aspect was to adapt to the structural time prerequisites. Our prototypical research task was adapted to the standard German time-frame devoted to a subject in one day (two subsequent units of 45 min each). With regard to technical resources, we acted on the anticipation of how schools (at least in southwest the South-West of Germany) will be equipped in a few years from now, due to certain governmental programs. Thus, we are able to investigate several generic aspects of the learning processes that we assume to take place during learning with collaborative visual design tasks in the near future. Among these are the elaboration of content and visual information, the transfer of visual literacy skills to the analysis of other video sources, and the collaborative negotiation of meaning during the design activities.

The task was created to be applicable to German language arts and history learning. The former is the domain traditionally concerned with enhancing the levels of students' literacy and their skills for cooperative learning (e.g., Blell & Lüdtge, 2004).[1] The latter represents a domain where working with constructive video is considered highly preferable while also providing a challenge for students and teachers (Krammer, 2006; Smith & Blankinship, 2000). In addition to the new literacies described above, in history learning, factual knowledge is closely intertwined with specific thinking skills, like de-composing, evaluating, analyzing, and critically reflecting on historical sources—together with (re-)constructing knowledge. These are necessary skills for a full understanding of historical topics (e.g., Wineburg, 2001); however, they are difficult to teach in most traditional history lessons at schools. In line with these educational goals (which correspond to Jenkins et al.'s, 2006, notions of social and cultural skills for community involvement) our experimental collaborative task for history learning involves the following components: Critical analysis, judgment, collaborative problem solving, and appropriation. Precisely, the students could learn to use modern digital video tools for critical

[1] Reference models relating to the levels of proficiency in language learning and (media) literacy which are relevant for our work include the "Common European Framework of Reference for Languages" (Goethe-Institut/Inter Nationes, 2001), or the PISA concepts of "literacy" and "reading competence" (OECD, 2001, 2003). Further on, the general educational standards for the German Gymnasium include the ability to apply the basic terms of film analysis and to compare film composition with other formal strategies, for example, in literature (Core ideas for skills acquisition in German secondary education, *Gymnasium*, for grades 9 and 10, Ministry of Culture, Youth, and Sports of Baden-Württemberg, 2004).

analysis and discussion of archive video material, they could learn using general film analysis methodology to de-compose and to evaluate the video source, thereby developing a critical stance and understanding of the diversity of ideas during their collaboration. Furthermore, they could learn to design a web page, to present their own ideas on the Berlin-Blockade and work creatively with them.

Our task was first tested in a pilot laboratory experiment (Zahn, Pea, Hesse & Rosen, in press) with a sample of psychology students. We investigated both the general effectiveness of the task and the specific effects of how students use the digital video tool DIVER/WebDIVER™, in contrast to a control condition using "simpler" technology (video-player and text-editor). We examined the possible implicit impact of the different technologies on design products, dyads' conversations, and individual learning and skills acquisition. According to our underlying assumptions, the video tools were considered to be prototypical examples of either providing specific support in terms of technical affordances for the dyads' activities and socio-cognitive efforts (WebDIVER™) or not providing such support (video player and text editor). The results revealed generally high appraisal of the task and significant positive effects of the WebDIVER™M video tool concerning design, knowledge, and visual skills acquisition. The affordances of WebDIVER™ thus enhanced the quality of participants' design activities. Moreover, the influence of the video tools extended to the learners' socio-cognitive processes and focused their interactions on the task.

Integration into "Noisy" Classroom Settings—Initial Results from a Field Study

What follows are results from a field experiment (see Zahn, Krauskopf, Hesse & Pea, submitted) with 234 students in four German secondary schools. The same task was applied with 10th grade students (70% female, age $M = 15.9$ years, $SD = 0.8$). A 2×2 factorial experimental design was applied to test impacts of digital video technology, on the one hand, and shared media-related goals, on the other. More precisely, concerning the first factor, we again compared DIVER/WebDIVER™ with a Player & Text condition, as in our lab experiment. Concerning the second factor of the impact of shared media goals, we compared two different task goals provided with the instructions for "creating Dives" vs. "creating annotated movies". The media goals were based on the findings of Stahl (2005) that metaphors guide text-based construction of hyper-structures. As dependent variables we considered students' collaborative design activities, design products, dyads' conversations, motivation and knowledge and visual skills acquisition.

The procedure was divided into four steps (see Fig. 25.6), of which steps 2 and 3 should support collaborative problem solving: In step 1, students completed a questionnaire assessing 'participants topic- related prior knowledge, general interest in history, prior computer experiences, and knowledge about media production. In step 2, a phase of individual inquiry followed, where the students watched a

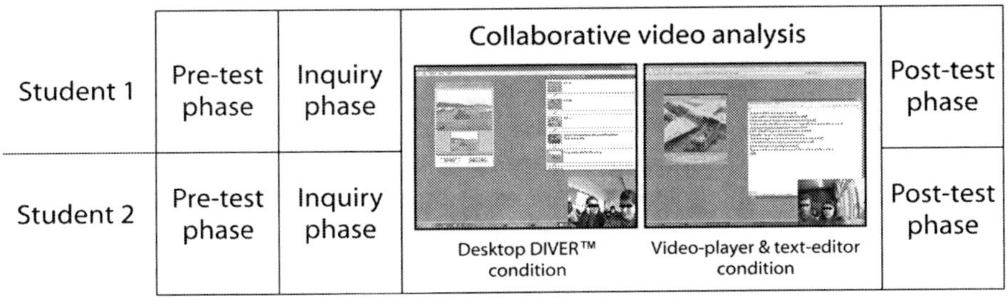

Fig. 25.6 General procedure of prototypical task and experimental design

digitized historical newsreel on the Berlin-Blockade from 1948 and consulted additional material on the respective historical context and filmic codes and style. In step 3, the design task was introduced and students were randomly joined in dyads to work with the computer in a face-to-face setting. After briefly practicing the respective digital processes, they were asked to analyze and comment on the historical newsreel, so that their product could be published in a virtual history museum. Working time for the video-based design task was restricted to half an hour. When students were finished, they proceeded to step 4, in which a post-experimental questionnaire tapped their appraisal of the design task and the group collaboration, and a multiple choice tested what knowledge about the topic had been acquired.

While the limited amount of time in the experiment needs to be discussed with regard to the space it leaves for processes of knowledge building to unfold, our field data (Zahn, Krauskopf, Pea & Hesse, submitted) show that participants' knowledge significantly increased during the design task ($F(1, 106) = 42.2$; $p < 0.01$, partial $\eta^2 = 0.29$). These cognitive outcomes were not differentially affected by the different conditions. In all conditions the design task proved to be interesting for the students and applicable in regular classroom situations. Replicating findings from the prior lab study, the affordances of DIVER significantly increased the quality of design products and influenced design processes positively by focusing the learners' interactions on task-relevant, conversations. Students working with DIVER considered design-related issues significantly more often than dyads working with the combination of Player & Text and displayed a tendency towards fewer help requests. Additionally, working with DIVER influenced the collaborative interactions within dyads indicating more autonomous design activities when working with DIVER. The digital tools did not further students' general problem solving behavior, which in all conditions was rather action-oriented and lacked thoughtful planning and evaluation (less than 3% of the time on the task was devoted to planning and less than 1% on evaluation).

In order to provide further qualitative evidence of process, we also conducted additional analyses focusing on how the dyads used and integrated technology affordances during their design-related interactions. The aim was to replicate corresponding findings from the pilot study that identified processes of "guided noticing" (Pea et al., 2006; Zahn, Pea, Hesse & Rosen, in press). There, interaction patterns were observable in dyads working with DIVER/WebDIVER^{TM} mirroring how dyads' elaborations on the source video are guided by the tool affordance when they create interpretive annotations. As expected, exemplary episodes for these patterns (*design cycles*, Zahn et al., in press) were also found in the field data. Overall, such exemplary episodes illustrate the kinds of processes possibly lying behind the quantitative indicators reported above and give an impression of how learners' socio-cognitive processes are impacted and complement quantitative findings.

Conclusions

At the beginning of the chapter, we were posing the following questions:
How can digital video technologies be implemented in educational learning processes to foster new media literacy skills? How can they be implemented broadly and without an overall amount of effort that renders a widespread application very unlikely?

We sought answers to these questions by introducing an integrated approach to computer-supported learning with constructing digital video in history and German language art lessons. We presented an a cognitive approach where digital video tools are used in the context of collaborative visual design tasks to foster advanced literacy skills and the construction of shared interpretations in students. We demonstrated in a field experiment that the approach can be successfully realized. Predictions of positive effects on learning with digital video in class derived from our cognitive framework (collaborative visual design) were empirically supported.

More precisely, in the empirical studies we asked: How would students approach collaborative visual design tasks in a real "noisy" classroom setting?

How do students use the affordances of video tools for collaborative visual design?

Where, precisely, do students need instructional support?

Concerning the first question, we find in the field study that substantial knowledge and (visual) literacy skills acquisition takes place during a collaborative visual design task, even when students spend only a short period of time with the video material. Students well understood and appreciated the task as being interesting. These results are a strong support for the interpretation that students approach visual design tasks in the style of our exemplar as a valuable and practicable way of learning.

Concerning the second question, our results indicate that digital video technologies can act as powerful cognitive tools supporting the learning processes during collaborative visual design tasks. We found effects of different tools that afford different learning activities, which also extend their impact to the socio-cognitive level. Furthermore, the findings suggest that when explicit instructional guidance is limited, technological affordances implicitly guide students' task-related and socio-cognitive actions. Our data also indicate that subtle attempts to support the design process by providing metaphors to help learners structure their design problem space are easily overshadowed by the strong effects of tool affordances.

Concerning the third question, we found that tools do not support the overall design process (e.g., the amount of time devoted to planning, acting, evaluating, and revising), thus leaving the need of and room for explicit instructional modulation by an educator—especially the support of planning, evaluation and revision of design products by students.

Concerning the practical implications of our findings, we infer that constructive video tools can be directly integrated into regular educational practice and respective curricula support learning processes and new media/visual skills acquisition. However, the effects of implicit guidance by technological affordances need to be considered as an important factor in computer-supported learning by teachers with regard to the educational goals and applied teaching strategies. Studying them also means providing information for effective integration in the classroom, namely, the instructional integration of such tasks by the teacher who can make use of a tool's affordances for the learning goals. According to Oser & Baeriswyl, 2001), an educator's profession is to orchestrate teaching and learning processes. In line with this, learning activities and socio-cognitive processes afforded by the educational technologies in use can be seen as supportive to both these instructional aspects. As a result, in future studies we will seek to investigate the when and how of explicit instructional support of teachers and thus address their role as facilitating catalyst for (a) optimizing learners' problem solving within the joint problem space of a complex visual design tasks, as well as for (b) successful integration of these tasks into classroom instruction.

Acknowledgments This work was partly supported by a grant from the National Science Foundation (NSF REC 0354453) and the Deutsche Forschungsgemeinschaft [German Research Foundation] (DFG ZA 524/1-1). Any opinions, findings, and conclusions expressed in the chapter are those of the author and do not necessarily reflect the views of the sponsoring agencies. Thanks to Benjamin Klages, Julia Vowinkel, and Alla Trofimovskaja for helping during the field experiment. Any correspondence concerning this chapter should be addressed to Dr. Carmen Zahn, Knowledge Media Research Center, Konrad-Adenauer-Strasse 40, D 72072 Tuebingen, Germany, phone: +49 (0)7071-979-225. Electronic mail may be sent to c.zahn@iwm-kmrc.de.

References

Alby, T. (2007). *Web 2.0: Konzepte, Anwendungen, Technologien*. Muenchen: Hanser Fachbuchverlag.

Baacke, D. (1999a). Medienkompetenz als zentrales Operationsfeld von Projekten. In D. Baacke, S. Kornblum, J. Lauffer, L. Mikos, & G. A. Thiele (Eds.), *Handbuch Medien: Medienkompetenz – Modelle und Projekte* (pp. 31–35). Bonn: Bundeszentrale für politische Bildung.

Baacke, D. (1999b). Projekte als Formen der Medienarbeit. In D. Baacke, S. Kornblum, J. Lauffer, L. Mikos, & G. A. Thiele (Eds.), *Handbuch Medien: Medienkompetenz – Modelle und Projekte* (pp. 86–93). Bonn: Bundeszentrale für politische Bildung.

Barron, B. (2003). When Smart Groups Fail. *Journal of the Learning Sciences*, *12*, 307–359.

Beichner, R. J. (1994). Multimedia editing to promote science learning. *Journal of Computers in Mathematics and Science Teaching*, *13*, 147–162.

Bereiter, C., & Scardamalia, M. (1987). *The Psychology of written composition*. Hillsdale, NJ: Lawrence Erlbaum Associates.

Bereiter, C. (2002). Emergent versus presentational hypertext. In R. Bromme & E. Stahl (Eds.), *Writing as design: Hypermedia and the shape of information space* (pp. 73–78). Amsterdam, Boston, London, New York, Oxford, Paris, San Diego, San Francisco, Singapore, Sydney, Tokyo: Pergamon/Elsevier Science.

Blell, G., & Lüdtke, C. (2004). Sehen, Hören, Verstehen und Handeln. Filme im Fremdsprachenunterricht [Seeing, hearing, understanding and acting – Films in foreign language education]. *Fsu*, *6*(402–405), 445.

Carver, S. M., Lehrer, R., Connell, T., & Erickson, J. (1992). Learning by hypermedia design: Issues of assessment and implementation. *Educational Psychologist*, *27*, 385–404.

Cassidy, T., Stanley, S., & Bartlett, R. (2006). Reflecting on Video Feedback as a Tool for Learning Skilled Movement. *International Journal of Sports Science & Coaching, The Sport Coach as Learner*, *1*, 279–288.

Cha, M., Kwak, H., Rodriguez, P., Ahn, Y., & Moon, S. (2007). I Tube, you tube, everybody tubes: Analyzing the world's largest user generated content video system (pp. 1–14). San Diego CA, US.

Chambel, T., Zahn, C., & Finke, M. (2005). Hypervideo and cognition: Designing video-based hypermedia for individual learning and collaborative knowledge building. In E. M. Alkhalifa (Ed.), *Cognitively informed systems: Utilizing practical approaches to enrich information presentation and transfer* (pp. 26–49). Hershey, PA: Idea Group.

Dillon, A. (2002). Writing as design: Hypermedia and the shape of information space. Conceptual and empirical approaches. Advances in learning and instruction series. In R. Bromme & E. Stahl (Eds.), *Writing hypertext and learning* (pp. 63–72). Amsterdam: Pergamon.

Eckrich, J., Widule, C. J., Shrader, R. A., & Maver, J. (1994). The effects of video observational training on video and live observational proficiency. *Journal of Teaching in Physical Education*, *13*, 216–227.

Erickson, J., & Lehrer, R. (1998). The Evolution of critical standards as students design hypermedia documents. *Journal of the Learning Sciences*, *7*, 351–386.

Flower, L., & Hayes, J. R. (1980). The cognition of discovery: Defining a rhetorical problem. *College Composition and Communication*, *31*, 21–32.

Goel, V., & Pirolli, P. (1992). The structure of design problem spaces. *Cognitive Science*, *16*, 395–429.

Goethe-Institut/Inter Nationes/Council of Europe (2001). *Gemeinsamer Europäischer Referenzrahmen für Sprachen: Lernen, Lehren, Beurteilen. [A Common European Framework of Reference for Languages]*. Retrieved June 12, 2009, from http://www.goethe.de/z/50/commeuro/deindex.htm

Goldman, R. (1998). *Points of viewing children's thinking: A digital ethnographer's journey*. Mahwah, NJ: LEA.

Goodwin, C. (1994). Professional vision. *American Anthropologist*, *96*, 606–633.

Greeno, J. G. (2006). Learning in activity. In R. K. Sawyer (Ed.), *The Cambridge handbook of the leanring sciences* (pp. 79–95). Cambridge: Cambridge University Press.

Hayes, J. R., & Flower, L. S. (1986). Writing research and the writer. *American Psychologist*, *41*, 1106–1113.

Hayes, J. R. (1996). A new framework for understanding cognition and affect in writing. In C. M. Levy & S. Ransdell (Eds.), The science of writing. *Theories, methods, individual differences, and applications* (pp. 1–27). Mahwah, NJ: Erlbaum.

Harel, I. (1990). Children as software designers: A constructionist approach for learning mathematics. *Journal of Mathematical Behavior*, *9*, 3–93.

Hobbs, R. (2006). Non-optimal uses of video in the classroom. *Learning, Media and Technology*, *31*(1), 35–55.

Jenkins, H., Clinton, K., Weigel, M., & Robison, A. J. (2006). *Confronting the Challenges of Participatory Culture: Media Education For the 21st Century*. Retrieved October 1, 2008 from http://www.newmedialiteracies.org/files/working/NMLWhitePaper.pdf.

Jordan, B., & Henderson, A. (1995). Interaction analysis: Foundations and practice. *Journal of the Learning Sciences, 4*, 39.
Kafai, Y. B. (1996). Learning design by making games. Children's development of design strategies inthe creation of a complex computational artifact. In Y. B. Kafai & M. Resnick (Eds.), *Constructionism in practice* (pp. 71–96). Mahwah, NJ: Lawrence Erlbaum Associates.
Kafai, Y. B., & Resnick, M. (Eds.) (1996). *Constructionism in practice: Designing, thinking, and learning in a digital world* (pp. XII, 339S). Mahwah, NJ: Lawrence Erlbaum Associates.
Kolodner, J. L., Camp, P. J., Crismond, D., Fasse, B., Gray, J., Holbrook, J., et al (2003). Problem-based learning meets case-based reasoning in the middle-school science classroom: Putting learning by design^{TM} into practice. *Journal of the Learning Sciences, 12*, 495–547.
Krammer, R. (2006). Filme im Geschichtsunterricht – Analysieren-Interpretieren-Dekonstruieren. *Historische Sozialkunde, 3*, 26–33.
Lehrer, R., Erickson, J., & Connell, T. (1994). Learning by designing hypermedia documents. *Computers in the Schools, 10*, 227–254.
Lowry, P. B., Curtis, A., & Lowry, M. R. (2004). Building a taxonomy and nomenclature of collaborative writing to improve interdisciplinary research and practice. *Journal of Business Communication, 41*, 66–99.
Mc Neil, B., & Nelson, K. (1991). Meta-analysis of interactive video instruction: A 10 year review of achievement effects. *Journal of Computer-Based Instruction, 18*(1), 1–6.
Messaris, P. (1998). Visual aspects of media literacy. *The Journal of Communication, 48*, 70–80.
Messaris, P. (1994). *Visual literacy – image, mind & reality*. Boulder, San Francisco, Oxford: Westview Press.
Ministerium für Kultur, Jugend und Sport Baden-Württemberg [Ministry of Culture, Youth, ans Sports of Baden-Württemberg] (2004). *Bildungsplan 2004. Allgemein bildendes Gymnasium [Education plan 2004. General university-track secondary Education]*. Stuttgart.
Moreno, R., & Ortegano-Layne, L. (2008). Do classroom exemplars promote the application of principles in teacher education? A comparison of videos, animations, and narratives. *Educational Technology Research and Development, 56*, 449–465.
Norman, D. A. (1988). *The psychology of everyday things*. New York. Basic Books.
OECD (2001). *Knowledge and Skills for Life: First Results from PISA 2000*. Retrieved June 12, 2009, from http://www.pisa.oecd.org/document/46/0,2340,en_32252351 _32236159_33688686_1_1_1_1,00.html
OECD (2003). *The PISA 2003 Assessment Framework: Mathematics, reading, science and problem solving knowledge and skills*. Retrieved June 12, 2009, from http://www.pisa.oecd.org/document/46/0,2340,en_32252351_32236159_33688686_1_1_1_1,00.html
Oser, F., & Baeriswyl, F. (2001). Choreographies of teaching: Bridging instruction to learning. In V. Richardson (ed.). *Handbook of research on teaching*. 4th edition, (pp. 1031–1065). Washington, D.C.: American Educational Research Association.
Papert, S. (1993). *The children's machine -rethinking school in the age of the computer*. New York: Basic Books.
Park, O., & Hopkins, R. (1992). Instructional conditions for using dynamic visual displays: A review. *Instructional Science, 21*, 427–449.
Pea, R. D., Lindgren, R. W., & Rosen, J. (2006). *Computer-Supported Collaborative Video Analysis*. Bloomington, US. Retrieved July 10, 2008, from http://hal.archives-ouvertes.fr/hal-00190631/fr/.
Pea, R. D., Mills, M. I., Rosen, J., Dauber, K., Effelsberg, W., & Hoffert, E. (2004). The DIVER^{TM} project: Interactive digital video repurposing. *IEEE Multimedia, 11*, 54–61.
Pea, R. D. (1985). Beyond amplification: Using the computer to reorganize mental functioning. *Educational Psychologist, 20*, 167.
Petrosino, A. J., & Koehler, M. J. (2007). Teachers as designers: Pre an in-service teachers' authoring of anchor video as a means to professional development. In R. Goldman, R. Pea, B. Barron, & S. Derry (Eds.), *Video research in the learning sciences* (pp. 411–423). Mahwah, NJ: Lawrence Erlbaum Associates.

Roschelle, J. M., & Teasley, S. D. (1995). The construction of shared knowledge in collaborative problem solving. In C. O'Malley (Ed.), *Computer supported collaborative learning* (pp. 69–97). Berlin: Springer.

Salomon, G. (1983). Television watching and mental effort: A social psychological view. In J. Bryant (Ed.), *Children's understanding of television: Research on attention and comprehension* (pp. 181–198). New York: Academic Press.

Salomon, G. (1984). Television is "easy" and print is "tough": The differential investment of mental effort in learning as a function of perceptions and attributions. *Journal of Educational Psychology, 76*, 647–658.

Salomon, G. (1994). *Interaction of media, cognition and learning: An exploration of how symbolic forms cultivate mental skills and affect*. Mahwah, N.J. Lawrence Erlbaum Ass. Inc.

Schwan, S., & Riempp, R. (2004). The cognitive benefits of interactive videos: Learning to tie nautical knots. *Learning & Instruction, 14*, 293–305.

Seitamaa-Hakkarainen, P. (2000). *The weaving-design process as a dual-space search* (Research Report 6). Helsinki: University of Helsinki, Department of Home Economics and Craft Science.

Smith, B. K., & Blankenship, E. (2000). Justifying imagery: Multimedia support for learning through explanation. *IBM Systems, 39*, 749–767.

Smith, B. K., & Reiser, B. J. (2005). Explaining behavior through observational investigation and theory articulation. *The Journal of the Learning Sciences, 14*(3), 315–360.

Spiro, R. J., Collins, B. P., & Ramchandran, A. (2007). Reflections on a Post-Gutenberg epistemology for video use in ill-structured domains: Fostering complex learning and cognitive flexibility. In R. Goldman, R. Pea, B. Barron, & S. Derry (Eds.), *Video research in the learning sciences* (pp. 93–100). Mahwah: Lawrence Erlbaum Associates.

Stahl, E., Zahn, C., & Finke, M. (2006). Knowledge acquisition by hypervideo design: An instructional program for university courses. *Journal of Educational Multimedia and Hypermedia, 15*(3), 285–302.

Stahl, E., Zahn, C., Schwan, S., & Finke, M. (2006). Knowledge acquisition by designing Hypervideos: Different roles of writing during courses of "new" media production. In L. Van Waes, M. Leijten, & C. Neuwirth (Eds.), *Writing and Digital Media*, Studies in Writing (pp. 77–88). Oxford: Elsevier.

Stahl, E. (2005). Is a hypertext a book or a space? The impact of different introductory metaphors on hypertext construction. *Computer Education, 44*, 115–133.

Stahl, E., & Bromme, R. (2004). Learning by Writing Hypertext: A Research Based Design of University Courses in Writing Hypertext. In *Effective Learning and Teaching of Writing* (pp. 547–559). Retrieved July 10, 2009, from http://dx.doi.org/10.1007/978-1-4020-2739-0_37.

Stevens, R., Cherry, G., & Fournier, J. (2002). *Video Traces: Rich Media Annotations for Teaching and Learning*. In Proceedings of the CSCL 2002 Conference on Computer Supported Collaborative Learning. Boulder, CO.

Suthers, D. D. (2001). Towards a systematic study of representational guidance for collaborative learning discourse. *Journal of Universal Computer Science, 7*, 254–277.

Suthers, D. D., & Hundhausen, C. D. (2003). An experimental study of the effects of representational guidance on collaborative learning processes. *Journal of the Learning Sciences, 12*(2), 183–218.

Suthers, D. D. (1999). *Effects of alternate representations of evidential relations on collaborative learning discourse*. In Proceedings of the 1999 conference on Computer support for collaborative learning (pp. 611–620). Palo Alto, California: International Society of the Learning Sciences. Retrieved July 10, 2009, from http://portal.acm.org/citation.cfm?id=1150240.1150314.

Sutter, B. (2002). Instructional Artefacts. In G. Stahl (Ed.), *Computer support for collaborative learning: Foundations for a CSCL community – Proceedings of CSCL 2002 Boulder, Colorado, USA, January 7-11 2002* (pp. 72–81). Hillsdale, N.J: Lawrence Erlbaum Associates, Inc.

Vreman-de Olde, C. (2006). *Look – experiment – design. Learning by designing instruction.* Enschede: Gildeprint Drukkerijen.

Wetzel, C. D., Radtke, P. H., & Stern, H. W. (1994). *Instructional effectiveness of video media*. Hillsdael, NJ: Lawrence Erlbaum Associates.

Wineburg, S. (2001). *Historical thinking and other unnatural acts: Charting the future of teaching the past*. Philadelphia: Temple University Press.

Zahn, C. (2009). Gestaltendes Lernen:"Learning by design" im Schulunterricht?. *LOG IN Informatische Bildung in der Schule, 156*, 27–35.

Zahn, C., & Finke, M. (2003). Collaborative knowledge building based on hyperlinked video. In R. B. B. Wasson (Ed.), *CSCL 2003 – commuity events. Communication and interaction* (pp. 173–175). Bergen, NO: Intermedia.

Zahn, C., Barquero, B., & Schwan, S. (2004). Learning with hyperlinked videos–design criteria and efficient strategies for using audiovisual hypermedia. *Learning and Instruction, 14*, 275–291.

Zahn, C., Krauskopf, K., Hesse, F. W., & Pea, R. D. (2009). *Constructive video in the classroom – A field experiment on the role of computer technology and metaphors in complex problem solving performed by school students*. Manuscript submitted for publication.

Zahn, C., Pea, R., Hesse, F. W., & Rosen, J. (2009). *Knowledge building through collaborative construction of digital video: A comparative experimental study on the role of thechnology in complex problem solving*. Manuscript submitted for publication.

Zahn, C., Pea, R., Hesse, F. W. & Rosen, J. (in press). Comparing simple and advanced video tools as supports for complex collaborative design processes. *The Journal of the Learning Sciences*.

Zahn, C., Pea, R., Hesse, F. W., Mills, M., Finke, M. & Rosen, J. (2005). Advanced digital video technologies to support collaborative learning in school-based education and beyond. In: T. Koschmann, D. Suthers & T. W. Chan (Eds.) *Computer Supported Collaborative Learning 2005: The next 10 years*, (pp. 737–742). Mahwah, N. J. Lawrence Erlbaum Ass. Inc.

Chapter 26
Technology for Classroom Orchestration

Pierre Dillenbourg and Patrick Jermann

Swiss Federal Institute of Technology Lausanne (EPFL), Lausanne, Switzerland

Introduction

On a regular basis, new metaphors emerge in the field of learning technologies. Are they "old wine in a new bottle" or do they convey a novel idea? Is "inquiry-based" learning more than "learning from simulations"? Is "educational data mining" different from "student modelling"? Is "orchestration" just a new buzzword? It probably is, but nonetheless this chapter argues that the idea of "orchestration" conveys a new approach to the relationship between classrooms and technologies. First, we explain why this relationship should be analyzed in terms of classroom life and not only in terms of learning outcomes. Then, we decompose this relationship by extracting 14 "design factors," first from the metaphor of "orchestration" (see "The 'Orchestration' model") and then from the idea of viewing a classroom as an "ecosystem" (see "The 'Ecosystem' model"). These factors relate pedagogical and technological design choices with classroom life. In the next three sections, we illustrate these factors with three learning environments we have developed and tested in real contexts. Our conclusions revisit orchestration as the management of constraints systems.

This analytical chapter is restricted to the domain of formal education in co-present settings. It does not deny the interest of research on informal learning as well as on distance education but stresses the social responsibility of our research community to contribute to schooling.

"It Works Well (In My Class)"

As most scholars in learning sciences, we are not only researchers but also teachers in our own university. Surprisingly, these two roles sometimes co-exist almost independently from each other.

P. Dillenbourg (✉)
Swiss Federal Institute of Technology Lausanne (EPFL), Lausanne, Switzerland
e-mail: pierre.dillenbourg@epfl.ch

M.S. Khine, I.M. Saleh (eds.), *New Science of Learning*,
DOI 10.1007/978-1-4419-5716-0_26, © Springer Science+Business Media, LLC 2010

As teachers, we sometimes have the nice feeling that the method we are using is "working well." What this often means is that students are engaged in the activities: they attend the course, they pay attention to our talk, they argue with each other, they ask questions, they make suggestions, etc. in short, they are "with us." "It works well" is just a personal feeling, a subjective opinion, not an objective measure. This opinion may rely on cognitive cues: the students' answers indicate that they understand, they come with original solutions or new ideas, they deliver satisfactory assignments, they do well at the exam, etc. Finally, "it works well" also means that the method is compliant with our constraints: the students' workload is reasonable, our teaching workload is acceptable, there is no main bug in the technology, the teaching material can be reused next year, the students are satisfied (as shown by the course evaluation), as well as the director and the students' parents. As teachers, we have to care about many of these constraints that we do not really conceptualize as researchers: homework, parents, discipline, room size, friendship, security, etc. In summary, there are many conditions for a method to "work well" and we, as teachers, are happy when it happens.

As researchers, we did not pay that much attention to things that "work well." A first obvious critique is that the teacher's opinion that it "works well" may be unfounded. It may be that students were actually bored while the teacher perceived them as engaged. It may be that students were highly engaged but did not learn much through the activity. For instance, the LOGO environment "worked well" for many years but did not reach its promises in terms of learning outcomes (Pea, 1983; Tetenbaum & Mulkeen, 1984). Similarly, many colleagues stick to lecturing because, from a classroom viewpoint, it "works well," that is, it satisfies many of the constraints we will analyze in this chapter. Educational research reached its maturity when it replaced stories about methods that supposedly "work well" by empirical evidence of learning gains (pre-post). The fact that teachers feel their method "works well" is probably a necessary condition for success, at least for sustainability of the method, but certainly not a sufficient condition. The second critique against this idea is that "it works well" refers to a broad beam of interweaved factors that can hardly be disentangled in a formal experiment. Rigorous experiments may not address more than a few independent variables while "it works well" refers to many parameters. While design-based research leads to pedagogical methods that "work well," they still face founded criticisms with regard to the generalizability of their findings.

Can we reconciliate the viewpoint of teachers who need methods that "work well" and the viewpoint of researchers for whom "it works well" can hardly be viewed as a scientific statement? Wouldn't we be extremely happy as researchers to know that the teachers involved in our empirical studies continue to use—on a voluntary basis—the methods we experimented in their class? Wouldn't we be upset as teachers to experiment for these methods that don't work very well? The gap between the teachers' and researchers' viewpoint is related to the difference of scale in their preoccupation. On the one hand, the researcher has to narrow down his focus to a specific activity or process (e.g. peer tutoring), hopefully isolated from any other source of influence which would be considered as a bias. It is interesting—yet dramatic—to note that the "teacher effect" is often viewed as an experimental bias. On the other hand, the teacher has to consider the broader scope of what's happening inside the class and to some extent also outside the class. So, there is a difference of scope in the concerns of each side. The new models we analyze in this chapter are compatible with these two levels since they articulate in a single picture individual cognitive processes, social interactions and the class life. We hence refer to them as "*integrative models*" versus other models that have a more local scope (e.g. the zone of proximal development, the repair theory, etc.),

Integrative models are not learning theories. They do not predict how learning may result from specific activities. Instead, their strength is to be rather "agnostic" with regard to learning theories. Theories provide us with a particular lens to grasp the complexity of learning in classrooms, but they are somehow exclusive. Isn't it legitimate to combine them, for instance to reason on the metacognitive skills that can be internalized through social interactions (Blaye, 1988)? Isn't it legitimate to design activities that combine self-explanation and socio-cognitive conflict? Teachers don't have to choose among Bloom, Vygostky and Piaget. Researchers don't have to choose either. Students have a single brain; they don't switch between brains when moving from individual to social activities. When two peers perform a classification task, individual induction and social argumentation are deeply intertwined. The interest of the models we discuss hereafter is to pay attention to the multiple levels that enter into play when explaining that a method "works well." It is also their weakness: by addressing many aspects, they remain quite abstract. We hence attempt to extract more specific factors but these models do not predict learning effects, they are ways to think about the reality for which we design learning environment. We analyze very broad models, orchestration and ecosystems, and then instantiate them with homemade specific models ["split where interactions should happen" (SWISH) and "Der Erfahrraum"]

The "Orchestration" Model

Many scholars have used "orchestration" to refer to the design and real-time management of multiple classroom activities, multiple learning processes and multiple teaching actions (Brophy & Good, 1986; Tomlinson, 1999; DiGiano & Patton, 2002; Fischer, Wecker, Schrader, Gerjets, & Hesse, 2005; Gravier, Fayolle, Noyel, Leleve, & Benmohamed, 2006; Dillenbourg & Fischer, 2007; von Inqvald, 2009). The metaphor is appealing. Both music writers and teachers have to harmonize multiple "voices." They need a fine-grained control of time. They translate a global message (emotions, knowledge) into a sequence of atomic actions (notes, interactions). Rothstein-Fisch and Trumbull (2008) explain that they use the word "orchestration" instead of "management" because it "denotes bringing about harmony" (p. 101). Moon (2001) justifies the use of the word "orchestration" to mean "the process of managing a whole learning group in such a way as to maintain progress towards the learning outcomes and improvement of practice for all" (p. 120)

Unfortunately, the classroom "orchestration" seems to have a different meaning than its musical counterpart. In music, orchestration refers to writing the score that an orchestra will play. It does not refer to the activity of the conductor when the orchestra is playing. The metaphor is applied in a more orthodox way to computer science where "service orchestration" (Peltz, 2003) refers to the definition of some workflow or architecture that will automatically connect different systems (namely web services). Applied to the educational context, the proper meaning of "orchestrating" would correspond to instructional design and not to the real time management of class activities.

Nevertheless, metaphors don't have to be perfect to be inspiring. The key difference between music orchestration and classroom orchestrations is that, when orchestrating a classroom, the score has often to be modified on the fly. Could we imagine that orchestra players read their score on a computer display (rather than on paper) and that this score changes dynamically, depending for instance on the audience's emotional state? Good teachers perform "reflection in action," i.e. they are able to change the score as they are playing it. A good learning environment should let good teachers modify the score as often as necessary. The words *dynamic orchestration* could convey the combination of design/planning and real-time adaptation. However, "dynamic" does not mean free improvization but a certain degree of freedom around the instructional plan.

Is that stretching the model of orchestration too far? Metaphors are not correct or incorrect; the question is whether they are useful or not. In HCI, designers have used metaphors such as the desktop, the cockpit, the window, etc.. Instructional designers also developed metaphors such as "frames" (Merrill, Li, & Jones, 1992) or, "anchored" instruction (Bransford, Sherwood, Hasselbring, Kinzer, & Williams, 1990). A metaphor is "useful" if it helps the designer/teacher to take decisions, namely because it provides a global structure to articulate multiple local decisions. A metaphor creates an *educational flavour* that local design principles do not convey. We analyse now why "orchestration" does convey flavours that a concept such as "classroom management" would not convey. We try to operationalize these flavours by extracting a certain number of design factors.

Teacher-Centrism

Orchestra players religiously follow the movements of the conductor. This quasi-mimesis is an exaggeration of the message it should convey but it stresses the importance of the teacher's role. In the last decades, many colleagues have redefined the role of teachers as facilitators (Carey, 1994) along the common place slogan "from a sage on the stage to a guide on the side." Orchestration has a different flavour: teachers are not on the side, they are the conductors, they are driving the whole activity. They are managing in real time the activities that occur at multiple planes. They share their passion for the content. Their body language conveys their interpretation (speed, intensity, etc.) to the musicians.

> Factor 1. *Leadership.* Teachers act as the drivers of the whole scenario and lead the collective (i.e. class-wide) activities.

Our community has somehow confused constructivism with "teacherless" (Dillenbourg, 2008). Let us state clearly that promoting the role of teachers as orchestrators does not imply that they have to lecture intensively or that they have to make a show. Orchestration would be compatible with "teacher-centric constructivism": it is the students who have to learn through their activity but teachers have the leadership of the whole scenario: lectures may be integrated into constructivist perspective for several purposes as in the 3 examples below.

- *Debriefing* lectures "work very well": these are not simple feedback sessions but lectures that address *new* course contents through the data produced by the students themselves (experiment results, projects, assignments,...). The drawback is that these lectures have to be prepared after receiving the students' contribution which require last minute preparation or even some improvization.
- There is a "time for telling" (Schwartz & Bransford, 1998): lectures "work well" in terms of learning when students have previously acquired some experience of what the lecturer is going to say; when they have the meanings but not the words.
- Lectures enable teachers to "qualify" the knowledge for instance to explain to students why an equation is beautiful, why a theory is somehow obsolete, why these results are surprising,... This "personal touch" or meta-knowledge can hardly be made explicit without over-simplification. It's the beauty of human presence to be able to convey these subtle cues.

Providing teachers with a strong leadership implies that they have the power to drive the system and not to be prisoners of an instructional plan. Acknowledging the role of teachers does not simply mean to let them tune some options or parameters but to empower them with respect to technology. This implies that teachers are allowed to bypass decisions taken by the system and to flexibly rearrange their own scenario. However, we will see that flexibility has some limits described in "Implications for learning technologies."

Factor 2. *Flexibility*. Teachers have the possibility to change the learning scenario on the fly, as far as it makes sense.

As leaders of a class, teachers have the responsibility of what students do in this class. They don't have the same degree of control that the orchestra conductors have over their musicians, but they still have to be "in control" of their class. A method "does not work" if students become distracted, if they talk to each other when the teacher speaks to them, if they read their email while they should interact with a simulation. Some methods may reduce the authority of teachers because some students start to do silly things while waiting for late groups, because teachers lose face when encountering technical bugs.

Factor 3. *Control*. Teachers maintain in the classroom the level of interest and concentration necessary for the on-going activities.

A method that "works well" facilitates teachers' task of maintaining interest and concentration among their audience. The class behaviour is not a main concern in learning sciences research but it is a major issue for teachers (especially new teachers), directors, parents and even students.

Cross-Plane Integration

In computer-supported collaborative learning (CSCL), the idea of "script" emerged as a method that shapes the way collaboration will occur within a team (Dillenbourg, 2002). More precisely, scripts aim at triggering specific types of interactions that are known to generate learning gains such as providing explanation, solving conflicts or mutually regulating each other. For instance, to increase conflicts within a team, some scripts, referred to as micro-scripts, will prompt peers to provide counter-evidence against the claims made by the other (Weinberger, Ertl, Fischer, & Mandl, 2005). Another approach is to detect people who have opposite opinions and ask them to perform a task together, or to give peers different documents to read so that they end up with different opinions (Jermann & Dillenbourg, 1999). These so-called macro-scripts (Dillenbourg & Hong, 2008) also include individual activities (read, summarize, write, etc.) and class-wide activities (introductory lectures, vote, debriefing, etc.) in addition to small group activities. We also refer to them as "integrative" scripts (Dillenbourg & Jermann, 2007) in the same way we talk here about "integrative" models.

Factor 4. *Integration* refers to the combination, within a consistent scenario, of individual, small group and class-wide activities, as well as activities beyond the class.

Anecdotically, we have used a notation (Fig. 26.1) that is very similar to music scores. Time is represented from left to right. Lines refer to what Vygostky designed as planes: the intra-psychological plane (level 1 in Fig. 26.1: individual cognition), the interpsychological plane (level 2: small group interactions) and the social plane (level 3: where culture is located). It is clear that the mental activities defined by Vygostky occur most of the time at the three levels in parallel. The "notes" placed on the score do not represent cognition but concrete activities.

These levels constitute an arbitrary segmentation of a social scale continuum. However, looking at practices, most classroom activities occur along these three levels: solo, class or in between. We added three levels that can be encountered: (level 4) activities with other classes in the school; (level 5) activities with local community (parents, correspondents, local fieldtrips, etc.) and (level 6) activities with the anonymous world via Internet (e.g. on-line newspapers, polls, etc.).

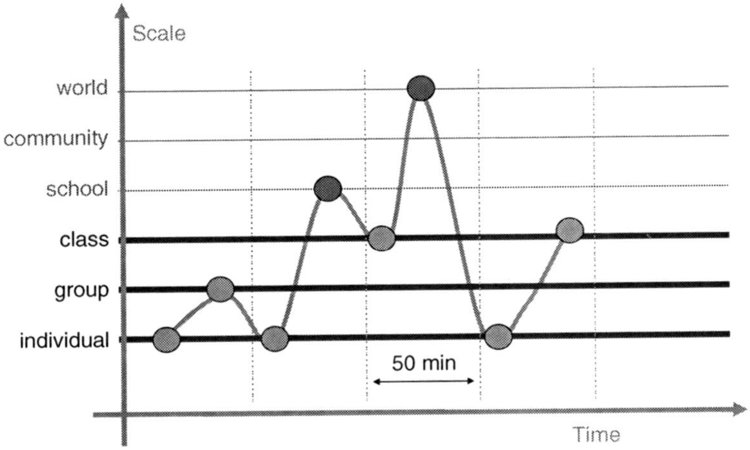

Fig. 26.1 A musical notation for integrated scripts

Again, this segmentation is very pragmatic: level 5 adds logistics and security concerns to perform out of school the activities that are performed in the school at level 4.

Sequentiality

A piece of music is more than a set of notes, the sequence makes it all. A method that "works well" is not just a random sequence of activities; there is something in the sequence that turns discrete activities into a consistent whole, there is a scenario.

Orchestration has a flavour of linearity. Some verses or refrain can be moved and repeated, but nonetheless, the idea of orchestration refers to some sequentiality. In terms of learning, the order of activities partly determines the cognitive process. Whether a concept definition is introduced before or after the examples will switch between an inductive and a deductive approach. Letting students evaluate their solution before or after providing a feedback changes it all. The order matters. For many years, non-linearity has been perceived as an educational plus, e.g. when moving from linear programmed instruction to branched programmed instruction or when moving from texts to hypertexts. It was a new feature offered by technologies that certainly facilitates adaptation to individual needs. But, despite being the enemy of individualization, linearity has pedagogical advantages. It may lighten teachers' cognitive load of orchestration by streamlining activities. It simplifies issues of data consistency at the technical level. It also creates a class atmosphere by knowing that all students experience the same thing more or less at the same time. Of course, there is design trade-off with factor 2, since flexibility should enable teachers to escape from linearity, but the favour of linearity is quite strong.

Factor 5. *Linearity*. Most scenarios are simple sequences of activities that almost all students will perform at almost the same period. It is easy to explain to the students.

The notion of scenario implies continuity across activities: the groups remain the same, the students keep their roles or rotate in a predictive way, the activities concern the same objects or issues (as in problem-based learning or project-based learning). Technically, this continuity may be implemented as a workflow: the output of an activity is used as input for subsequent activities.

Factor 6. *Continuity*. The successive learning activities are articulated around the same data structures (objects, groups, assignments, etc.) that circulate via a workflow.

A method that "works well" is not emotionally flat. It includes phases of tension, where energy is accumulated, and phases of relaxation, where accumulated energy is exploited. It is difficult to report this from a scientific stance, but the best methods are salty.

Factor 7. *Drama*. The emotional state of students varies across activities, with highest moments that trigger engagement for the rest of the scenario.

Time Management

One of the main constraints that teachers have to cope with is time. Not only is teaching time limited, but moreover it is segmented into time slices. The flexibility of this segmentation depends on the system; classes with a single teacher being of course more flexible. A method will only be described as "working well" if most of the following timing issues can be orchestrated.

A method that "works well" must be reasonable in terms of total time necessary. Time for learning has always been a critique against constructivist approaches and an easy argument in favour of lecturing since the rate of content per minute is very high. The time necessary must be proportional to the importance of the domain to be taught within the year curriculum. This importance is measured in terms of credits in higher education or class-contact hours in lower school levels. This means that the time available depends upon the curriculum relevance of the topic (see "Selection").

Factor 8. *Relevance*. The total time that a method requires to teach X should be proportional to the importance of X as specified in the curriculum

A method that "works well" must be flexible in terms of time segmentation. Should the next activity require a full period or can it be segmented into two periods? Should the teacher stop 15 min before the break because it is not worth starting a new activity for 15 min? Can students save and reuse intermediate work states?

Factor 2 (again). *Flexibility*. Teachers have the possibility to adapt the next pedagogical activity to fit the time slice available.

The dynamics of a method that "works well," the feeling of drama, require the right intervention at the right time. This is a trivial statement but isn't true that the best joke can be destroyed by a bad timing? This means that some activities must be set up when the students are hot, when the energy is present. This new instance of factor 7 will be illustrated in "The 'SWISH' model and the ManyScripts environment."

Physicality

Finally, conducting an orchestra is rather physical. It is not a virtual action in a virtual space. The conductor is physically engaged. The spatial layout of the room and the location of each musician are very important. The orchestration of classroom activities encompasses the spatial organization of tables, chairs and tools. This layout must facilitate the transition between the different forms of grouping in the scenario and depicted in Fig. 26.1. It must enable students to move when they have to move, for instance because they are switching roles within a group or switching between groups as in some Jigsaw scripts (Aronson, Blaney, Sikes, Stephan, & Snapp, 1978). The teacher must be able to pass between groups and be present across the space. The students' and teachers' location must enable them to see what they are supposed to see.

Factor 9. *Physicality*. Compared to previous models that stressed virtual learning spaces, orchestration refers to the concrete layout of the physical space in the classroom and to the physical movements of the different actors.

The "Ecosystem" Model

It is very tempting to describe as an ecosystem any dynamic system, i.e. any system with multiple circular causal components (Copeland, 1979, Stoll & Fink, 1996; Dillenbourg, 2008). This metaphor has been applied outside the field of environmental sciences for instance to describe a city or a society as an ecosystem. Some authors such as Resnick (2002) or Brown and Adler (2008) use the word ecosystem to refer to the global learning space outside the school, namely the digital sphere. As for "orchestration," these metaphors are used in a shallow way. Nonetheless, is it interesting to consider a classroom as an ecosystem when one designs learning technologies? Does it help to understand why some methods "work well"? Actually, the notion of ecosystem is quite different from the "orchestration" since an ecosystem does not include a central orchestrator (unless some divinity is considered as orchestrator). Nonetheless, some authors in natural sciences talk about "orchestrating an ecosystem" such as a Sequoia Forest (Brigg, 2001). The word "orchestration" is then used in a broad sense as a synonym of "management." The ecosystem model has also been applied to business cases. For instance, the study of various communities using the SAP environment is described as the orchestration of an ecosystem (Iansiti & Lakhani, 2009). We prefer to restrict "orchestration" to a specific type of management, as described by the factors identified so far.

Species

In an ecosystem, one cannot start feeding the rabbits without considering the impact on foxes. As any ecosystem, a classroom shelters the interactions between several animal species: students, teachers, teaching assistants (TAs), special support staff, directors, inspectors, parents, etc. This has trivial implications which are nonetheless worth mentioning.

Methods that "work well" don't only have to be designed for learners and, as mentioned in "Teacher-Centrism," for teachers, but also for parents, directors, etc. For instance, the learning technologies our community is developing rarely pay attention to the homework and, through it, to the role of parents. Technologies could improve the integration of homework in the flow of learning and enable parents to follow what their children have done. Isn't it strange that, while many scholars on learning technologies are parents, we behave as researchers as if we were not? Some ethical arguments may explain why researchers neglect these possibilities: homework increases the effects of social disparities (Ferguson, Ludwig, & Rich, 2001); not all parents have Internet access; parents might interfere too much with the teachers' job. However, the reality is that parents and homework are part of the ecosystem.

> Factor 4 (again). *Integration* of homework and parents' interaction in the educational workflow.

Each species includes a large variety of animals whose features (size, fitness, etc.) follow more or less a Gaussian distribution of animals. There can be a rabbit that is 1 m long but not many. A method that "works well" cannot be generalized if it is designed for exceptional teachers simply because the researcher was lucky to find one exceptional teacher, for instance teachers who cope easily with situations where there is some chaos in the classroom. The very fact that teachers accept to participate in our experiments is an unavoidable bias in the representativity of these volunteers. The trivial implication is that pedagogical methods must be adaptable to differences between teachers. Our point goes further: designing for the ecosystem means that most teachers should be able to apply our method, not only a few of them.

Factor 10. *Design for all.* The method can be conducted by most skilled teachers, not only by exceptional teachers

Selection

A method that "works well" in an education ecosystem has to pay respect to the rules that govern life and death within the ecosystem.

Teachers are not free to teach what they want; they have some degree of freedom in primary school, almost no freedom in secondary schools and a bit more at university level. Our community has been quite creative in designing activities that address skills that are not in the curriculum or only in the "meta"-section with transversal skills. An extra-curriculum investment from teachers and students is acceptable for a short duration (the time of an experiment), but such an environment will not be used over long term if it is justified by the importance of its learning objectives within the curriculum.

Factor 11. *Curriculum relevance.* How important are these learning objectives within the curriculum of these students?

Whether we like or not, the educational ecosystem is shaped by large-scale evaluations such as PISA or TIMSS. Our research community tends to neglect or even disregard these assessments. Instead, we should contribute to the improvement of the quality of these measures. Meanwhile, these large assessments and more generally all exams are part of the educational ecosystem. A method that "works well" is a method that does not put teachers, directors or ministers in an undefendable position when the results of evaluations are published. At the university level, we don't have large-scale assessments, but the same argument applies: a method will not "work well" if the students don't perceive this method as useful for passing the course exam.

Factor 12. *Assessment relevance.* Is the method compatible with the different assessments that students will have to pass?

In theory, curriculum relevance should guarantee the assessment relevance, but in practice there are gaps: the specific way of measuring skills and knowledge may differ from the way they are taught, the national or international assessments may differ from local curricula, etc.

Legacy

Given the complexity of causal relationship within an ecosystem, external interventions have to be minimalist. The same applies to the classroom ecosystem. The learning environments we design do not land in an empty world. Every class has its legacy of methods, tools and resources that have been used so far. A new method cannot wash out the past. For instance, a method that "works well" should be compatible with the main book used in the course; otherwise teachers would be in a very difficult position of explaining why they do not use the book that has been bought. Another example is that every student or teacher has a legacy of habits with respect to computational tools. If the learning environment proposes a specific email tool or a specific chat tool, it will suffer from a strong competition with the email and chats that students are using, i.e. the ones that already include all their contacts, their histories, their goodies, etc. The obvious implication is to design a minimalist intervention that respects this legacy, namely to design a learning environment that is limited to the functionalities strictly required by the pedagogical method. This means design should resist the temptation to provide a fully integrated learning environment (with yet another agenda, yet another forum, etc.).

Factor 13. *Minimalism.* The functionalities offered by the learning environment are only those specific to the learning scenario and those are not provided by the tools (books, software, etc.) already in use by the students

However, minimalism has drawbacks: an integrated environment enables interconnection between tools, for instance a link between chat utterances and graphical objects on the display (as in ConcertChat, Mühlpfordt & Wessner, 2005) or a link between a forum and a spreadsheet (as in http://www.sense.us). Despite emerging standards and multiple APIs, it remains a technical challenge to provide this kind of interactions between the environment we design and multiple existing tools (e.g. with the five most popular chat systems). In other words, there is a trade-off between minimalist intervention and integration, but the ecosystem model is rather on the first end.

Sustainability

The classroom has limited energy resources as any ecosystem. The energetic efficiency of a pedagogical method is a key factor to claim that it "works well." The energy that students will invest is of course limited; it is actually measured in terms of time (i.e. credits). For instance, it happens that a very exciting project concentrates all the students' energy on one specific course, leading them to fail other courses. But, most importantly, we refer here to the teachers' energy. A method based on teachers' heroic investment over a few months is not a method that will "work well" for several years. Teachers and their team will do it well the first year, even better the second year and then the investment will inevitably decrease over the following years.

> Factor 14. *Sustainability*. The energy required to run the method can be maintained over several years

We should not forget that teaching is a long-term repetitive activity: researchers do an experiment once in a classroom but teachers have to repeat it for many years. A method that "works well" has to have realistic energy expectations. It may for instance be that groups of two are better than groups of four for the targeted interaction but they require twice more energy for grading the assignments. Design is always a trade-off.

The "SWISH" Model and the ManyScripts Environment

This section and the two next ones illustrate how the factors mentioned actually shape the design of technologies used in the classroom. We report the local design models used for building these environments, their implementation and how they relate to the 14 factors.

The "SWISH" model

A macro-script is a pedagogical method that aims to trigger specific interactions during teamwork (Dillenbourg & Jermann, 2007). Here are two scripts we want to relate to our 14 factors. Their score-like representation is reported in Fig. 26.2.

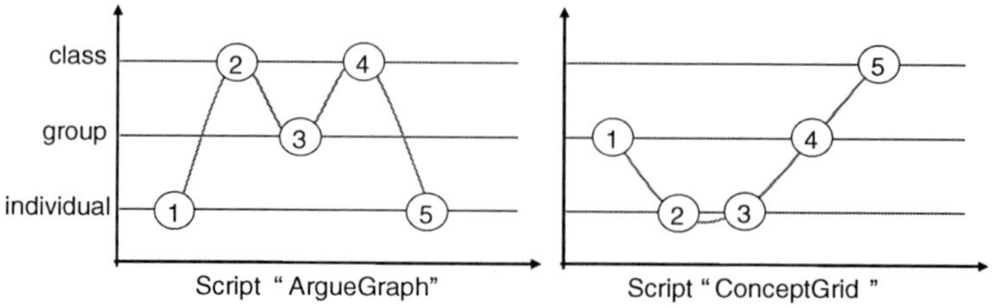

Fig. 26.2 Integration of activities in two macro-scripts

- ArgueGraph (Dillenbourg, 2002) aims to trigger argumentation by forming pairs of students with conflicting opinions. It is run in five stages: (1) individuals answer a questionnaire; (2) the system computes their opinion by compiling their answers and locates them on a map that is projected in the classroom and discussed collectively; (3) groups are formed with individuals to maximize their distance on the map; they have to answer the same questionnaire as in the first phase; (4) the teacher gives a debriefing lecture based on the answers provided by individuals and pairs; (5) students have to write a summary of the arguments. Typical ArgueGraph sessions last 3–4 h depending on the number of questions. Experiments showed that the ArgueGraph conflict mechanism leads students to express more elaborated arguments (Jermann & Dillenbourg, 1999)
- The ConceptGrid script (Dillenbourg & Jermann, 2007) aims to trigger explanations. (1) each team has a set of papers to read and a set of definitions to produce; students distribute their work within teams; (2) students individually read the papers they have been assigned to; (3) students individually enter the definition of the concepts that they have been assigned; (4) teams have to build a grid of concepts in such a way that they are able to explain the relationship between two neighbours on the grid (by entering a short text in the system); (5) the teacher gives a debriefing lecture based on the grids built by students. A typical ConceptGrid sessions lasts 2–3 weeks, including the time for their readings. Experiments showed that ConceptGrid forces students to elaborate upon each other's explanations (Dillenbourg & Hong, 2008).

These examples of macro-script rely on the same design principle that makes the team interactions more difficult than if the teacher let them freely collaborate. Collaborative learning is often described as the side effect of the effort engaged to build a shared understanding of the task at hand. This effort is represented as Δ on Fig. 26.3: there is a natural divergence in teams at the beginning ($\Delta 1$) and the script actually increases this divergence ($\Delta 2$) in order to increase the intensity of interactions required to finally minimize this divergence ($\Delta 3$). In ArgueGraph, the effort necessary to reach agreement is higher since we pair students who disagree. In ConceptGrid, the effort necessary to build a consistent grid is increased by the fact that no student has enough knowledge to do it; they have to explain it to each

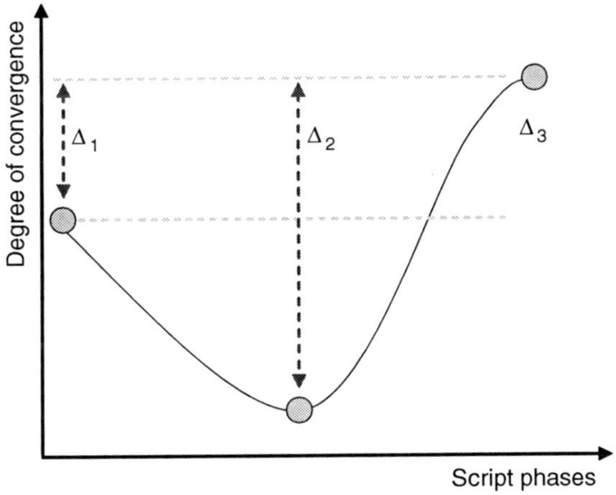

Fig. 26.3 Macro-scripts reduce team convergence to increase the effort to be engaged

other. Both scripts increase the collaborative effort by "splitting" the team in terms of opinions and knowledge, respectively. The nature of this split determines the type of interactions that student will need to engage in order to complete the task. Hence, the design principle was termed SWISH. Other examples are provided in Dillenbourg & Hong (2008).

The ManyScripts Environment

The two examples of scripts are available in a web-based platform. Teachers can select a script (ArgueGraph, ConceptGrid, etc.), edit the contents, set up the groups and tune some parameters. Figure 26.4 presents a snapshot from the ArgueGraph script in the ManyScripts platform: the system synthesizes all the justifications that individuals and pairs have associated to their answers. Teachers use this display during his debriefing lecture (Phase 4).

Design Factors

In both scripts, the teacher has a salient role (factor 1: Leadership) especially during the debriefing phase. These are not genuine lectures but "organic" lectures based on what students have produced. The drawback is that these lectures cannot be prepared in advance. We usually had one coffee break between the duo answers and the debriefing phase in ArgueGraph. This semi-improvization is against factor 10 (DesignforAll) since many teachers don't like to improvize, even if in this case the lecture is facilitated by the environment (Fig. 26.4). In ConceptGrid, we usually asked students to complete their grid 1 or 2 days before the debriefing lecture, which requires less improvization but nonetheless heavy work to analyse all grids the

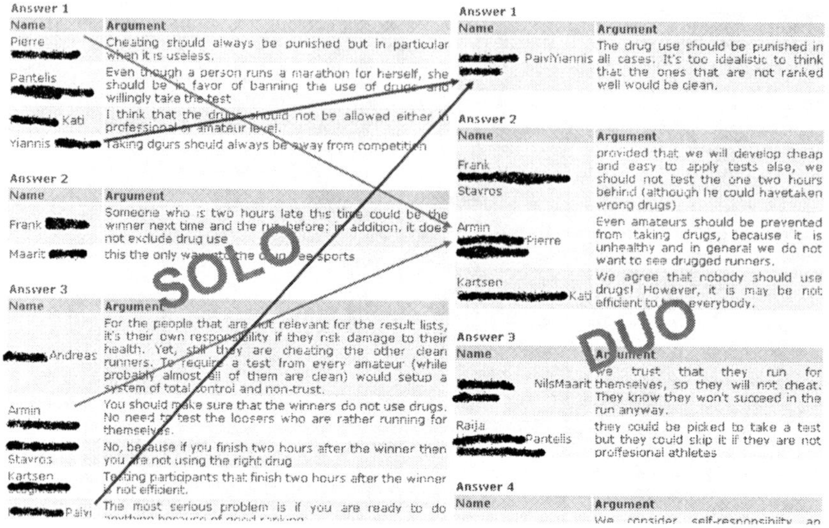

Fig. 26.4 Annotated snapshot of ManyScripts (names are deleted; arrows have been added to indicate how the teacher compares answers)

night before the course. This stressful preparation work reduces the sustainability (factor 14).

Both scripts illustrate factor 4 (integration) since they integrate individual, small group and class-wide activities in a meaningful way. They are linear (factor 3) and based on a workflow that provides continuity (factor 6): for instance, data from individual answers (ArgueGraph, phase 1) are automatically processed to form conflicting pairs (phase 2); individual and pair answers (phase 3) are collected for debriefing (Phase 4).

Drama (factor 7) is embedded in the SWISH model. However, smaller design elements make the drama higher in ArgueGraph than in ConceptGrid. The conflict phase triggers a degree of engagement that goes beyond the "didactic contract" (Brousseau, 1998): in many cases, we had to tell students "Stop arguing now with you friend even if you have not convinced him, this is just a didactic game." In the ArgueGraph script, we also noticed the following phenomenon. When being asked to choose between answers A and B, many students expressed their frustration not to be able to answer some mix of A and B. This frustration pushed them to stand up literally during the debriefing session (phase 4) to defend themselves. They seemed to feel a pressing need to explain that they answered B but actually wanted to answer something slightly different. Their frustration raised their level of participation. Once, we modified the interface of the environment and let the student express subtle choices (e.g. to answer "in some cases" instead of "yes" or "no"), and this completely destroyed the drama factor. Finally, we found that the energy generated by this design was very fragile. It depends upon the timing (factor 7) of the script. Once, we did the debriefing activity one week after the argumentation phase instead of right after, and all energy had disappeared from this debriefing session.

The time flexibility (factor 2) was crucial in ArgueGraph. We had bad experiences with an early version of the environment in which all students were expected to provide their individual answers before moving to the group formation. The whole class was stuck if one student left the room or lost the Internet connexion. Now, ManyScripts offers the possibility to move on to phase 2 even if all answers from phase 1 have not been provided. In terms of timing, teachers actually make sure that the delay between the first student who completes the questionnaire and the last one is not too high. If many students have to wait for other, it quickly generates all sorts of undesirable behaviour (factor 3: Control).

Since ConceptGrid has a duration of several weeks, we had to implement flexibility (factor 2) in terms of group formation. Once a group of students is formed, what happens if a student drops out the class? If the teacher decides to make groups of four, what happens if the number of students in the class is not a multiple of 4? ManyScripts implements two functionalities for coping with these accidents (Dillenbourg & Tchounikine, 2007). If a student is missing in a group, the teacher may turn on the "SPY" feature which enables the group in which role X is missing to borrow the definitions produced by the students who play role X in any other group of the class. This makes sure that all students have the same workload (factors 12 and 14). Conversely, if the group has for instance five students for four roles, the teacher may activate the "JOKER" function: a "joker" student may provide a definition that belongs to any other role. These functionalities are not perfect solutions but ways to carry on the script despite an imperfect situation. A method that "works well" should survive to these common accidents in everyday classroom life. Finally, ConceptGrid pays attention to factor 12 (assessment relevance) by connecting the script to the course exam: the environment includes a button to print all the work produced by a team so that they could use it during the exam.

The "Erfahrraum" Model and the TinkerLamp Environment

The "Erfahrraum" Model

The initial vocational education is structured as a dual system in Switzerland and other German-speaking countries: students spend about 4 days per week in a company and 1 day per week at school. These apprentices are between 16 and 20 years old and represent 69% of the teenagers in the educational system.[1] Vocational education constitutes a specific ecosystem, with its culture, its laws, its actors (e.g. the companies, the corporate associations), quite different from general education. Our main research hypothesis was that technologies may play a specific role in a dual system as a bridge between what apprentices do at their workplace and what they

[1] http://www.bfs.admin.ch/bfs/portal/fr/index/themen/15/04/00/blank/uebersicht.html

do at school. The model of "Erfahrraum" combines two ideas into a German name that reflects the socio-cultural context in which this model emerged. "Erfahrung" means "experience." Learning from experience is of course not a new idea: it is rooted in Dewey's work. Experiential learning is defined by Keeton and Tate (1978) as learning "in which the learner is directly in touch with the realities being studied" (p. 2). A dual training system combines this direct experience with some distanciation, more abstract activities in the classroom. Learning technologies are envisioned as ways to capture the apprentices' experience in order to exploit it during these more abstract activities in the classroom. "Raum" means room, as we insist on the physical orchestration of the room (factor 9).

The model has been implemented by different technologies in three different contexts. In the first context (Gavota, Schneider, Betrancourt, & Richle, 2008), we capture workplace experience of dental assistants by asking them to write down their experience in a wiki-like environment. The school activities, peer commenting and text revision exploit the diversity of experiences across a class of 20 apprentices: some work in small cabinets with a single dental surgeon, some in large cabinets with several surgeons, some with old-fashioned technologies, other with high-tech cabinets, etc. In the second project, J.-L Gurtner (University of Fribourg) captures workplace experience life in the context of car mechanics and pastry making. They call apprentices on their workplace on the phone and/or ask them to take pictures. Later on, this raw material feeds classroom activities. Finally, we instantiated the Erfahrraum approach in the context of logistics (Jermann, Zufferey, & Dillenbourg, 2008). Our observations of logistics apprentices in their warehouse revealed a gap between what apprentices are asked to do in their warehouse and what they are supposed to learn. While the official curriculum specifies that they should acquire logistics skills, the apprentices mainly follow their boss' instructions (e.g. "move this boy over there"). They are rarely involved in decision making such as flow optimization, warehouse layout or storage management. We refer to this as the "abstraction gap," i.e. the difference in the degree of abstraction between the tasks they experience and the tasks they should master. In school, the apprentices encounter more abstract logistics problems but the drawback is that they do not connect these tasks to their warehouse experience.

The TinkerLamp Environment

The TinkerLamp is an augmented reality system designed to run tabletop tangible simulations. The simulation which we developed in close collaboration with teachers from a professional school allows logistics apprentices to build a warehouse model by placing small-scale shelves on the table. Besides shelves, users can place tangibles which represent architectural constraints (e.g. pillars to sustain the roof of the warehouse, loading docks, offices and technical service rooms). The building elements for the model are scaled to allow the construction of a realistic warehouse (32 by 24 m in reality).

Fig. 26.5 TinkerLamp: a tabletop tangible simulation in the domain of logistics. *Left*: four TinkerLamps used concurrently in a classroom. *Right*: a closeup of a small-scale warehouse designed by apprentices. Information is projected on the floor and on *top* of the shelves

The physical small-scale model is augmented through a video projector placed above the table (Fig. 26.5). All objects (shelves, pillars, cardboard) are tagged with fiducial markers (similar to a 2 dimensional bar code) which enable a camera to track their position on the table (Fiala, 2005) and enable the system to project graphical representations (augmentations) on top and around the objects. The physical layout of the warehouse is used as input to configure a simulation. Projected forklifts represent the movement of goods in and out of the warehouse.

The simulation is controlled by a paper-based interface called TinkerSheets (Fig. 26.6). Small tokens can be placed on a paper form which is recognized by the system and allows users to set parameters like the type of warehouse management, the number and type of forklifts, or the type of augmentation which is displayed. Master sheets allow setting the main parameters relevant for a particular logistic

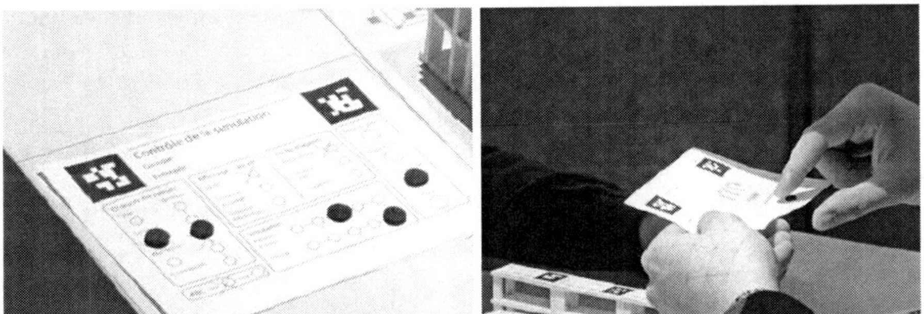

Fig. 26.6 TinkerSheets. *Left*: a master sheet from the official curriculum is used to parameterize the warehouse simulation. *Right*: a companion sheet is used by an apprentice to visualize different types of surfaces in the warehouse

concept and companion sheets either allow setting supplementary parameters or to visualize general simulation output (summarized numbers, graphs, etc).

The TinkerLamp is used on a regular basis in four different classes in two Swiss schools. Teachers are enthusiastic and describe it as an environment that "works well." More formal evaluation has shown the positive effects of the tangibles on learning (Schneider, Jermann, Zufferey, & Dillenbourg, submitted), but the usability of TinkerSheets has not been empirically proved.

Design Factors

The TinkerSheets offer interesting opportunities with respect to our 14 factors. First, they make curriculum relevance (factor 11) very tangible. The official curriculum—jointly designed by public authorities and the relevant corporate association—has the form of a large binder. Teachers may simply take one sheet from this binder and place it under the TinkerLamp in order to set up the activities described in the sheet. In addition, teachers may annotate these sheets with personal comments (e.g. which simulation parameters work better for this activity) that will be very useful for the next year reuse of this activity (factor 14: sustainability).

These sheets can also be used for designing homework (factor 4: Integration), for instance by printing a warehouse performance sheet at the end of a warehouse design activity. Teachers may then ask apprentices to perform some analysis at home and to come back for the next week with new simulation parameters. Their homework could typically be assessed by putting the homework sheet under the TinkerLamp and see how the warehouse performs.

What is interesting here is that continuity across activities (factor 5) becomes tangible: what connects successive activities is not an invisible workflow, but a concrete sheet of paper that is passed from hand to hand between the different phases of the activity. This "tangible workflow" has advantages: it is simple and concrete, publicly visible, documents can be annotated, shown to echo other, etc. Actually, the virtual workflow still exists since any sheet is associated to a fiducial marker that connects it to a data structure, but this invisible data set has a concrete clone in the physical world.

The physical orchestration (factor 9) of the activities was initially not trivial. Controlling the simulation required teachers to use finger-driven menus that were not easy to use. This difficulty did not empower teachers as drivers (factor 1). We replaced these menus by TinkerSheets that have a much better usability. Once they are laid out around the display area, they constitute some kind of cockpit in which it is relatively easy to see all available options. Initially, we used a very large version of the TinkerLamp (the TinkerTable, $1.5 \times 2\ m^2$), which occupied a large space for only five students. What would then happen with the students who are not working (factor 3: control)? Working with a subset of the class is acceptable for one experiment but not sustainable on the long term (factor 14). One teacher came with an innovative idea: while one team was working on the table, he projected their work on a screen placed elsewhere and on which he could discuss with the rest of the class what one group was saying. The new tool was then integrated in the "legacy" environment of a whiteboard and a beamer (factor 13). Later on, we produced a smaller simulation environment (40 × 50 cm) in such a way that four groups can work simultaneously in the same class under four different TinkerLamps.

The Shelve and Lantern Environments

The Recitation Section Model

Recitation sections are managed in our university in a way similar to many other places: the students receive a set of exercises to be carried out with the help of TAs, mostly PhD students. The sessions gather between 20 and 60 students in a room with two or three TAs. The students work in groups of two to four; some prefer to stay alone. They raise their hand to attract the TA's attention who joins the group and provides help for a few minutes. Occasionally, if several teams face the same difficulty, the TA gives a collective explanation on the blackboard.

The Lantern Environment

We observed several recitation sessions and noted several regulation problems: students spend a lot of time chasing the TA instead of working on their assignments; TAs do not necessarily come in a "fair" way (first asker is not first helped), some students ask help from the very beginning of the exercises without even trying seriously to solve it, most students do not complete all exercises while exam items have a level of difficulty similar to the last exercises of the session (factor 12), etc. (Alavi, Dillenbourg & Kaplan, 2009). To help the TA to orchestrate the session, we developed two awareness tools. The "Shelve" (Fig. 26.7) is a central display where teams indicate with a remote control device which exercise they do and when they need help. The "Lantern" (Fig. 26.8) is a small device that teams put on their table and which they use to provide the same information either by turning it (to indicate their move through the exercises) or by pushing on its top (to ask TA's help). Both the Lantern and the Shelve display the same information: which team is working

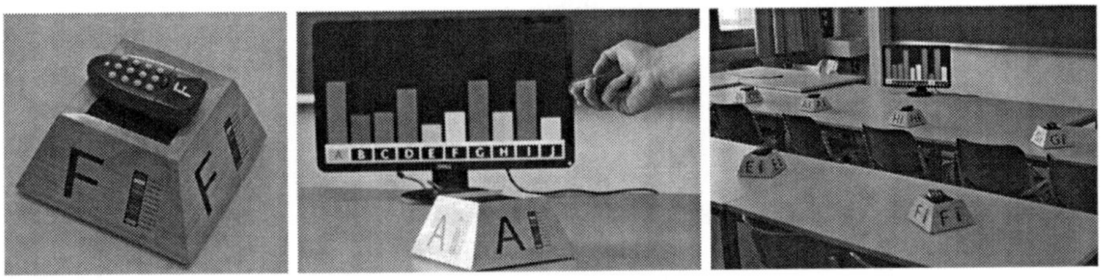

Fig. 26.7 The Shelve environment

Fig. 26.8 The Lantern (*left*) and its use during orchestration

on which exercise (each exercise has a different colour), how long they have been working on that exercise (the height of the colour bar), do they need help (it blinks) and for how long (it blinks faster).

Design Factors

The Lantern helps tackling the problems of time management (factor 7) and control (factor 2). The main difficulty for the orchestrator is to manage multiple teams of different sizes working at different speeds and requiring different types of help at different times. The experiments (Alavi et al., 2009) showed that students using the Lantern or the Shelve spend less time chasing the TA: once they push their device to ask for help, they can concentrate on their exercises. Control (factor 3) is improved because teams do not simply wait doing nothing.

Overall, this environment illustrates the physicality of orchestration (factor 9). The only difference between the Lantern and the Shelve is the spatial layout. Besides the fact that Shelve is centralized and Lantern is geographically distributed, both devices display the same information in the same way. The Lanterns connect spatially the information displayed (exercise being done, time in exercise, waiting time) with the team being concerned by this information. Yet, this single difference led to different interaction patterns in the class. The central display induced more comparison between groups, independent of their location, while the distributed version led to the emergence of clusters, i.e. sets of 2–3 small groups, located close to each other, and which interact with each other (e.g. a group A helps group B because A sees that B has been waiting for help at an exercise that A has completed, Alavi et al. (2009).

Conclusions

Implications for Learning Technologies

We presented three examples of technologies developed in our lab but many other colleagues have developed environments that are close to the orchestration model and inspired us, such as the NIMIS classroom (Hoppe et al., 2000), personal response systems, classroom scenarios based on handhelds (DiGiano & Patton, 2002; Zurita & Nussbaum, 2004) or even on multiple mice (Infante, Hidalgo, Nussbaum, Alarcon, & Gottlieb, 2009)

Our goal in presenting these examples was to show that the orchestration model, although being somewhat abstract and metaphorical, can be turned into concrete implementation choices. We hereafter list several technological choices that are more or less directly connected to the orchestration model.

1. Orchestration technologies are different from distance education since they are designed for classroom life. They may include on-line activities but the most salient part of the scenario occurs in face-to-face interactions.
2. A part of e-learning technologies are document-centric, whereas the orchestration technologies mostly support activities (e.g. the simulation for TinkerLamp) and overall diverse forms of interactions (as in ArgueGraph or Lantern).
3. Orchestration technologies should have a high usability for the teacher. Of course, the usability also concerns the students but the idea of orchestration is that teachers may easily interact with the technology despite being overloaded by other tasks such as managing groups, lecturing, etc.
4. These technologies make orchestration quite physical, i.e. they have to cope with the spatial organization of the classroom and other spaces as well as with the location and movements of students and teachers. The development of human-computer interaction (HCI) towards location-aware services is hence also pushing learning technologies towards orchestration.
5. These technologies make orchestration very concrete, i.e. something that can be manipulated by the actors (the tangible aspects) and also something that can be perceived by all actors (the ambient dimension). The development of HCI towards concrete elements (tangibles, roomware) is supporting the pedagogical evolution towards orchestration.
6. Since orchestration technologies have to integrate different activities into a scenario, they need to include some workflow functionality, i.e. the storage and reuse of data between activities. These activities can be performed with heterogeneous software which makes the workflow more complex to implement.
7. Combining the two previous points, when these digital data are represented as physical objects, the workflow management becomes a public task and hence becomes easier. This applies to the TinkerSheets but also to explain why walking to someone with a personal digital assistant (PDA) to share is richer than sending him the data by WiFi (Roschelle & Pea, 2002).
8. Implementing flexibility is a complex design issue. First, a learning environment that would be completely open, where teachers can change everything, would not convey anymore a pedagogical idea. For instance, in ArgueGraph, changing the group formation criteria from "pair students with opposite opinions" to "pair students with similar opinions" is technically easy but pedagogically meaningless. We refer to this as intrinsic constraints because they correspond to the core idea

of the script (Dillenbourg & Tchounikine, 2007). Flexibility can be increased by reducing extrinsic constraints which are implemented for technical reasons (e.g. data consistency problems if one student drops out) or sometimes simply because the designer did not consider leaving this choice open. Designing environments with a clear scenario but which still allow for flexibility remains a challenging trade-off for which new software architectures would be interesting.

9. The integration of a new learning technology in the classroom legacy (factor 13) is important. It takes ages to convince a student who is used to chat on-line with system X to move to system Y. There is a need to design our learning environments from the very beginning either as very open systems that can interact with any other web service or simply to consider our learning environment as web services. The advent of "cloud computing" may push learning technologies towards a better technical integration

Implications for Design-Based Research

Design-based research (DBR) (Collins, 1992; Sandoval & Bell, 2004) relies on prototyping-testing cycles with the participation of all classroom actors. If this participatory design is carefully conducted, it should produce methods that "work well." However, the generalizability of the method and hence of the associated learning effects is arguable. Despite our conviction that DBR is the best method for studying classroom orchestration, we must acknowledge that the generalization remains a problem. Conjecture maps help the interpretation of results and their potential generalization. Conjectures embed the relationship between interventions and expected learning outcomes or expected process changes and are not very different from experimental hypotheses. One solution we have chosen for the logistics project was to complement the DBR approach by a more formal experiment with a control group. When a method "works well," it means that it is compliant with the many constraints of the context where it has been tested. It's never "it works well universally" but "it worked well in my class this year." Understanding which constraints were satisfied and why the method satisfied them is the condition to generalize the DBR results. This generalizability is not only for the sake of science but also because it is our social duty to come up with methods that "work well" beyond a single context (even if no method will "work well" universally). We elaborate this in the next section.

Orchestration as Constraints Management

Teachers who have to orchestrate the classroom and its technologies actually face a multi-constraints management problem.

1. Curriculum constraints: how relevant is the topic with respect to the learning objectives listed in the curriculum, will these students be motivated by this topic?
2. Assessment constraints: are my learning activities compatible with summative evaluation exams, large-scale assessments studies, etc.?
3. Time constraints: how much time is necessary, how much time is available (see constraint 1) and how much flexibility do we have around these two factors?
4. Energy constraints: how much time and energy must teachers engage to prepare and run this method, how long can they sustain it, etc.?
5. Space constraints: do I have the space necessary in my classroom to set up these activities, is the classroom layout compatible with the interaction I expect to trigger, etc.?
6. Safety constraints: Can I keep control of my class? Can I be sued in court because some accident may occur during the field trip?

There are of course other constraints such as financial constraints (obviously), cultural constraints (the Tinker lamp simulation fits well the specific culture of warehouse workers), teachers' personality constraints (e.g. risk-aversive versus pioneers), motivational constraints (a method that "works well" should boost the teacher's self-esteem), etc. Overall, we could add the prerequisites constraints: no method "works well" if students don't have the prerequisites. We could build a long list of constraints; these factors have nicely been explored by Bielaczyc (2006). Our point here was to have a shorter list of constraints and to underline which ones are particularly relevant to the concept of orchestration.

Final Word

It is true that "it works well" is a subjective feeling and not a rigorous statement. However, it is a social reality. No successful empirical study will lead to any generalization if the teachers do not acquire the conviction that "it works well." It is hence a key item on the agenda of learning sciences to understand what teachers mean by "it works well." It is a key challenge to improve research methods so that they combine this concern with generalizability.

Acknowledgements The environments listed in this paper have been developed by Fabrice Hong, Guillaume Zufferey, Son Do-Lenh, Bertrand Schneider, Hamed Alavi, Frédéric Kaplan and Olivier Guédat. We thank the students and teachers who have been involved in the various experiments. The work on the TinkerLamp is supported by Dual-T, a leading house funded by the Swiss Federal Office for Professional Education and Technology. The work on the Lantern is supported by the Swiss National Science Foundation (Grant PDFM1-118708). The work on ManyScripts was supported by Swiss Center for Innovation in Learning (St Gallen) and a group of KALEIDOSCOPE, a former European Network of Excellence. The work on orchestration is the theme of a group within STELLAR, a new European Network of Excellence on learning technologies.

References

Alavi, H., Dillenbourg, P., & Kaplan, F. (2009) Distributed Awareness for Class Orchestration. *Proceedings of the Third European Conference on Technology-Enhanced Learning* (EC-TEL09). Nice France, Sept. 2009

Aronson, E., Blaney, N., Sikes, J., Stephan, G., & Snapp, M. (1978). *The jigsaw classroom*. Beverly Hills, CA: Sage Publication.

Bielaczyc, K. (2006). Designing social infrastructure: Critical issues in creating learning environments with technology. *Journal of the Learning Sciences*, *15*(3), 301–329.

Blaye, A. (1988) Confrontation socio-cognitive et résolution de problèmes. *Doctoral dissertation*, Centre de Recherche en Psychologie Cognitive, Université de Provence, France.

Bransford, J. D., Sherwood, R. D., Hasselbring, T. S., Kinzer, C. K., & Williams, S. M. (1990). Anchored instruction: Why we need it and how technology can help. In D. Nix & R. Spiro (Eds.), *Cognition, education and multimedia: Exploring ideas in high technology* (pp. 115–141). Hillsdale, NJ: Lawrence Erlbaum.

Brophy, J., & Good, T. (1986). Teacher behavior and student achievement. In M. C. Wittrock (Ed.), *Handbook of research on teaching* (3rd ed.). New York: McMillan.

Brousseau, G. (1998). *Théorie des situations didactiques*. Grenoble: La Pensée Sauvage.

Brown, J. S., & Adler, R. P. (2008). Minds on fore: Open education, the long tail and learning 2.0. *Educause Review*, *43*(1), 16–32.

Carey, D. M. (1994). Teacher roles and technology integration: Moving from teacher as director to teacher as facilitator. *Computers in the Schools*, *9*(2), 105–118.

Collins, A. (1992). Toward a design science of education. In E. Scanlon &T. O'Shea (Eds.), *New directions in educational technology* (pp. 15–22). New York: Springer-Verlag.

Copeland, W. D. (1979). Student teachers and cooperating teachers: An ecological relationship. *Theory into Practice*, *18*(3), The Complex Classroom: A Research Focus, 194–199.

DiGiano, C., & Patton, C. (2002). Orchestrating handhelds in the classroom with SRI's ClassSync™. In G. Stahl (Ed.), *Computer support for collaborative learning 2002* (pp. 706–707). Hillsdale, NJ: Lawrence Erlbaum Associates, Inc.

Dillenbourg, P. (2002). Over-scripting CSCL: The risks of blending collaborative learning with instructional design. In P. A. Kirschner (Ed.), *Three worlds of CSCL. Can we support CSCL?* (pp. 61–91). Heerlen: Open Universiteit Nederland.

Dillenbourg, P. (2008). Integrating technologies into educational ecosystems. *Distance Education*, *29*(2), 127–140.

Dillenbourg, P., & Fischer, F. (2007). Basics of computer-supported collaborative learning. *Zeitschrift für Berufs- und Wirtschaftspädagogik*, *21*, 111–130.

Dillenbourg, P., & Hong, F. (2008). The mechanics of CSCL macro scripts. *International Journal of Computer-Supported Collaborative Learning*, *3*(1), 5–23.

Dillenbourg, P., & Jermann, P. (2007). Designing integrative scripts. In F. Fischer, H. Mandl, J. Haake & I. Kollar (Eds.), *Scripting computer-supported collaborative learning – cognitive, computational, and educational perspectives* (pp. 275–301). Computer-Supported Collaborative Learning Series. New York: Springer.

Dillenbourg, P., & Tchounikine, P. (2007). Flexibility in macro CSCL scripts. *Journal of Computer Assisted Learning*, *23*(1), 1–13.

Ferguson, R. F., Ludwig, J., & Rich, W. (2001). A diagnostic analysis of black-white GPA disparities in shaker heights. *Ohio Brookings Papers on Education Policy*, *4*, 347–414.

Fiala, M. (2005). ARTag, A Fiducial Marker System using Digital Techniques. *IEEE Proc. CVPR*. San Diego, CA, June 2005.

Fischer, F., Wecker, C., Schrader, J., Gerjets, P. H., & Hesse, F. W. (2005, August). *Use-inspired basic research on the orchestration of cognition, instruction and technology in the classroom*. Paper presented at the SIG Invited Symposium "Instructional design and empirical research: Experiments and/or design experiments" at the 11th Conference of the European Association for Research on Learning and Instruction (EARLI), Nicosia, Cyprus.

Gavota, M., Schneider, D., Betrancourt, M., & Richle, U. (2008). A technology-enhanced learning environment to support learning by sharing professional experience in writing. In *Proceedings of World Conference on Educational Multimedia, Hypermedia and Telecommunications 2008* (pp. 2883–2892). Chesapeake, VA: AACE. Retrieved from http://www.editlib.org/p/28774

Gravier, C., Fayolle, J., Noyel, G., Leleve, A., & Benmohamed, H. (2006), Distance Learning: Closing the Gap between Remote Labs and Learning Management Systems, *Proceedings of IEEE First International Conference on E-Learning in Industrial Electronics*, Hammamet, Tunisie, December 18–20, pp. 130–134.

Hoppe, H. U., Lingnau, A., Machado, I., Paiva, A., Prada, R., & Tewissen, F. (2000). Supporting Collaborative Activities in Computer Integrated Classrooms - the NIMIS Approach *Proc. of 6th International Workshop on Groupware*, CRIWG 2000. IEEE CS Press, Madeira, Portugal.

Iansiti, M., & Lakhani, K. R. (2009) SAP AG: Orchestrating the Ecosystem. HBS Case No. 609-069; *Harvard Business School Technology & Operations Mgt. Unit.* Available at SSRN: http://ssrn.com/abstract=1408558

Infante, C., Hidalgo, P., Nussbaum, M., Alarcon, R., & Gottlieb, A. (2009). Multiple mice based collaborative one-to-one learning. *Computers & Education, 53*(2), 393–401.

Jermann, P., & Dillenbourg, P. (1999). An analysis of learner arguments in a collective learning environment. C. Hoadley et J. Roschelle (Eds.), *Proceedings of 3rd Computer-Supported Collaborative Learning Conference*, pp. 265–273, Stanford.

Jermann, P., Zufferey, G., & Dillenbourg, P. (2008) Tinkering or Sketching: Apprentices' Use of Tangibles and Drawings to Solve Design Problems. *Proceedings of the Third European Conference on Technology Enhanced Learning (EC-TEL 2008),* pp. 167–178, Maastricht (The Netherlands), September 16–19. Lecture Notes in Computer Science, Springer.

Keetoon, M. T., & Tate, P. J. (1978). The bloom in experiential learning. In M. T. Keeton and P. J. State (Eds), *Learning by experience – what, why, how* (pp. 1–8). San Francisco: Jossey Bass.

Merrill, M. D., Li, Z., & Jones, M. K. (1992). An introduction to instructional transaction theory. In S. A. Dijkstra, H. P. M. Krammer & J. J. G. van Merrienboer (Eds.), *Instructional models in computer-based learning environments.* NATO ASI Series F (Vol 104, pp. 15–41). New York: Springer-Verlag.

Moon, J. (2001). *How to improve the impact of short courses and workshops* (2001). Training & Professional Development. London: Kogan Page.

Mühlpfordt, M., & Wessner, M., (2005). Explicit Referencing in Chat Supports Collaborative Learning. In *CSCL'05, 6th International Conference on Computer-Supported Collaborative Learning,* Lawrence Erlbaum Associates, 662–671.

Pea, R. (1983). *Logo programming and problem solving* (Technical Report No.12). New York: Bank Street College of Education, Center for Children and Technology.

Peltz, C. (2003). Web Services Orchestration and Choreography. *Computer, 36*(10), 46–52.

Resnick, M. (2002). *Rethinking learning in the digital age.* In G. Kirkman (Ed.), The global information technology report: Readiness for the networked world (pp. 32–37). Oxford: Oxford University Press.

Rigg, C. M. (2001). Orchestrating ecosystem management: Challenges and lessons from sequoia national forest. *Conservation Biology, 15*(1), 78–90.

Roschelle, J., & Pea, R. (2002). A walk on the WILD side: How wireless handhelds may change computer-supported collaborative learning. *International Journal of Cognition and Technology, 1*(2), 145–168.

Rothstein-Fisch, C., & Trumbull, E. (2008) *Managing Diverse classrooms.* ASCD. http://www.ascd.org

Sandoval, W. A., & Bell, P. L. (2004). Design-based research methods for studying learning in context: Introduction. *Educational Psychologist, 39*(4), 199–201.

Schneider, B., Jermann, P., Zufferey, G., & Dillenbourg, P. (submitted). Benefits of a Tangible Interface for Collaborative Learning and Interaction. IEEE Transactions on Learning Technologies.

Schwartz, D. L., & Bransford, J. D. (1998). A time for telling. *Cognition and Instruction*, *16*(4), 475–522.

Stoll, L., & Fink, D. (1996). *Changing our schools*. Philadelphia: Open University Press.

Tetenbaum, T. J., & Mulkeen, T. A. (1984). Logo and the teaching of problem solving: A call for a moratorium. *Education Technology*, *24*(11), 16–19.

Tomlinson, C. A. (1999). The Differentiated Classroom: Responding to the Needs of All Learners, ASCD. http://www.ascd.org

von Inqvald, E. (2009). *Teachers' implementation and orchestration of Cabri: Initial use of a dynamic geometry software package in mathematics teaching*. Saarbrücken: VDM Verlag.

Weinberger, A., Ertl, B., Fischer, F., & Mandl, H. (2005). Epistemic and social scripts in computer-supported collaborative learning. *Instructional Science*, *33*, 1–30.

Zurita, G., & Nussbaum, M. (2004 A constructivist mobile learning environment supported by a wireless handheld network. *Journal of Computer Assisted Learning*, *20*, 235–243.

Chapter 27
Knowledge Building in Society 2.0: Challenges and Opportunities

Jingyan Lu, Ming Lai, and Nancy Law

Division of Information and Technology studies, Faculty of Education, The University of Hong Kong, Pokfulam Road, Pokfulam, Hong Kong

Introduction

Approaches to and understandings of learning have changed substantially in recent decades, particularly with the advent of information technology. Learning has changed from that of imparting knowledge from teachers to learners in traditional school systems to that of constructing knowledge collectively among learners, teachers, and others, across various contexts, like schools, families, community, and technology supported learning environments. Although, traditional notions of education are well suited to industrialized economies which require workers who have mastered specific bodies of knowledge and have acquired specific sets of skills, the emergence of knowledge-based economies are confronting educators with new challenges of how to prepare students for the knowledge age (Drucker, 1994). Knowledge-based economies shift the focus from the mastery of knowledge to the creation of knowledge. Everyone, not just the elites, is now required to engage in creating knowledge or in adding value to existing knowledge (Scardamalia & Beretier, 2003). Carl Bereiter and Marlene Scardamalia (2003) have proposed "knowledge building" as a theory for organizing school education to meet the challenges of the knowledge age.

Knowledge building is the process by which societies expand the frontiers of knowledge. It occurs in scientific communities and in companies where members focus on advancing community knowledge. Individuals learn by contributing to the knowledge of the communities they belong to. Recent reports on the implementation of knowledge building in schools suggest that even elementary students have the ability to engage in activities similar to those of knowledge workers. For instance they are able to advance knowledge by identifying inadequacies in current states of collective knowledge (see e.g., (Hakkarainen, 1998; Scardamalia, Bereiter, & Lamon, 1994; Zhang, Scardamalia, Lamon, Messina, & Reeve, 2007).

J. Lu (✉)
Division of Information and Technology studies, Faculty of Education, The University of Hong Kong, Pokfulam Road, Pokfulam, Hong Kong
e-mail: jingyan@hlucc.hku.hk

M.S. Khine, I.M. Saleh (eds.), *New Science of Learning*,
DOI 10.1007/978-1-4419-5716-0_27,

Various technology-based learning environments support collaborative knowledge building (Chan & van Aalst, 2006; Hoadley & Kilner, 2005; Lai & Law, 2006; Scardamalia & Bereiter, 1994). Recently, web 2.0 is being applied in education (Alexander, 2006; Bryan, 2006; Collis & Moonen, 2008), and several studies have discussed its contribution to knowledge building (Cress & Kimmerle, 2008; Mark & Lee, 2008). Thus, both web 2.0 and knowledge building view knowledge as artifacts that people can construct, change, and improve. Building knowledge at web 2.0 is what we call society 2.0.

While web 1.0 focused mainly on supporting reading, web 2.0 emphasizes collective intelligence by supporting participatory, collaborative, and dynamic online learning (O'Reilly, 2007). In this chapter, we explore how web 2.0, with its focus on collaboration, provides support for the cognitive, communicative, social, and emotional needs of knowledge builder. We argue that to use web 2.0 technologies in the design of learning environments that support knowledge building they must be rooted in appropriate theories of learning and pedagogical practices.

This chapter will first introduce how knowledge building has been used as a pedagogy to develop classroom communities; second, web 2.0 is introduced briefly with respect to how it transforms perceptions of knowledge as artifacts and how it is spawning modes of collaborative knowledge creation rooted in knowledge building; third, contemporary learning theories that support the understanding and application of web 2.0 are introduced; fourth, web 2.0 technologies, such as blogs, wikis, and social bookmarking, are discussed with respect to how their design can be informed and enhanced by knowledge building theories of learning; finally, the challenges and opportunities of web 2.0 for advancing our understanding of the new sciences of learning are discussed.

Knowledge Building

The theory of knowledge building is founded on Popper's (1972) differentiation of three worlds: the physical world (World 1), the mental world (World 2), and the world of human knowledge and ideas (World 3). Popper (1972) held that knowledge is not entirely dependent on individual knowers. Rather knowledge can be treated as an object for others. Learning can be differentiated from knowledge building. Thus, the former occurs in World 2 and focuses on the mental contents of individual knowers, while the latter occurs in World 3 and focuses on the advancement of knowledge (Bereiter, 2002). Traditional theories of learning focus mainly on improving the mental content of individual learners, while knowledge building focuses mainly on the advancement of knowledge within communities of knowledge builders. Thus in school settings, it is important for learners to work as members of communities, with the collective goal of advancing the frontier of community knowledge. It is important for learners to experience knowledge not as entirely located inside of their heads but as an artifact that everyone can work on, contribute to, improve and ultimately create.

In schools, it is important for students to work in communities and to work on advancing community knowledge. They need to experience knowledge building as a dynamically evolving, collectively shared adventure. Bereiter and Scardamalia (2003, 2006) identify two modes of working with knowledge: the belief mode and the design mode. The belief mode is concerned with making ideas true and the design mode is concerned with creating and improving ideas. Bereiter and Scardamalia (2003) argue that traditional pedagogies operate mainly in the belief mode. They focus on what learners believe or ought to believe. In contrast building knowledge depends on the design mode. The belief mode highlights three questions: (1) what are ideas good for? (2) what do ideas do or fail to do? and (3) how can ideas be improved? (Bereiter & Scardamalia, 2006) Thus in school settings, it is important for learners to generate their own research questions, articulate their own theories or ideas, and to continuously improve them (e.g., Hakkairenen, 2003; Zhang et al., 2007).

The principles of knowledge building have been realized in some well-designed platform, e.g., Knowledge Forum (Scardamalis, 2004). However, due to technical requirements, its use has been somewhat limited. More recently web 2.0 and its associated technologies have been responding to the pedagogical needs of knowledge building. Web 2.0 is providing the tools and support learners need to engage in such fundamental knowledge building processes as social interaction, dialogue, and sharing (Paavola, Lipponen, & Hakkarainen, 2004). Given that the goal learning in Society 2.0 is for learners and other knowledge workers to create and generate ideas, concepts, and knowledge (Rogers, Liddle, Chan, Doxey, & Isom, 2007), this chapter argues that web 2.0 is uniquely well appointed to support knowledge building in a much wider space, transcend the traditional limit of schools, communities, and traditional subject domains. However, the efforts to use web 2.0 to advance knowledge building needs to be integrated into and informed by relevant theories of learning

Web 2.0 and Knowledge Building

Web 2.0 consists of a collection of technologies or social tools. These social tools support not only social interactions but also have the "flexibility and modularity that enables collaborative remixability—a transformative process in which the information and media organized and shared by individuals can be recombined and built on to create new forms, concepts, ideals, mashups and services" (McLoughlin & Lee, 2007, p. 665). Web 2.0 tools are designed to bring minds, thoughts, feelings, and ideas together. In addition to sharing, communication, and information searching, and in line with the design mode requirements of knowledge building, web 2.0 technologies support users in co-creating and adding value to knowledge (McLoughlin & Lee, 2007). The openness and democracy of web 2.0 allows users to collaboratively mix, amend, recombine, revise, and comment on each other's ideas. Web 2.0 technologies thrive on the concept of collective intelligence

(Rogers et al., 2007), which acknowledges that communities that work cooperatively and share ideas are significantly more productive than individuals working alone.

Web 2.0 technologies emphasize connectivity, active participation, and collaboration in sharing and creating knowledge and ideas. Web 2.0 tools such as blogs, wikis, social networks, tagging systems, and content-sharing sites exemplify the new user-centric information infrastructure supporting these activities. Because web 2.0 technologies are designed to serve the social and networking needs of society 2.0, they differ from past technologies rooted in more traditional theories of learning. However, the philosophy behind the design of web 2.0 is well aligned with such contemporary theories of learning as communities of practice, social constructivism, situated learning, knowledge building, and collective intelligence. Research in the learning sciences has traditionally situated itself in particular theory-driven technology-based learning environments. How should learning science researchers use web 2.0 technologies, such as blogs, wikis, and social bookmarking, to meet educational and research purposes? How should web 2.0 technologies be used to facilitate knowledge building? How can such theories of learning, particularly social learning theories, support the learning in web 2.0? The following section discusses several social learning theories and its connection with web 2.0 application.

Social Learning Theories Supporting Web 2.0

In general, two groups of theories support web 2.0 learning. One group focuses on the cognitive or social-cognitive aspects of learning, such as thinking and reflection and includes such theories as social constructivism, situated cognition, shared cognition, and distributed cognition. The other group focuses on the socio-cultural aspects of learning, such as communication, participation, and interaction and includes communities of practice, and social cultural and cultural historical theory. Knowledge building has the advantage of combining and deepening the basic principles of both groups of theories. This section introduces the two groups of theories and discusses their connections with web 2.0.

Learning Through Thinking and Reflection

Social constructivism holds that forms of knowledge, such as language, values, rules, morality, and symbol systems, can only be acquired through interactions with others (Piaget, 1926). In his later work on structuralism, Piaget (1970) argued that humans are not born with essential structures of thought but rather construct them through a long process of psychological development which includes both maturation and interaction with the world. Inspired by Piaget's theory and findings, Dosie and Mugny (1984) undertook a systemic empirical investigation of how social interactions affect individual cognitive development. They found that individual development and social interaction are interdependent. Children construct knowledge through their interactions with others, especially through socio-cognitive conflicts (Dosie & Mugny, 1984). Today, conflict theory is used in the design of collaborative learning environments to stimulate interaction. Social constructivism has also been used to guide the design of various teaching and learning settings, especially for collaborative technology-supported learning environments where multiple forms of communication support interactions among learners and teachers. Web 2.0 supports constructive learning by providing opportunities for students to publish artifacts of their learning and to provide feedback and reflections on the artifacts of their peers.

Situated cognition argues that learning is a function of the activities, contexts, and cultures in which it occurs (Lave, 1991). Language learning, tool using, and *cultural adaptation* should be situated (Brown, Collins, & Duguid, 1989). From this perspective, cognitive tasks cannot be separated from social tasks. Environments are integral parts of cognitive activities and not merely sets of circumstances in which context-independent cognitive processes unfold. Situated cognition views learning in terms of the process of entering a communities of practice. These processes involve groups of learners working together to accomplish common goals. This usually involves collaboration between learner with different roles and experiences (Brown et al., 1989; Clancey, 1995). As newcomers move from the peripheries of communities to their centers, they become more actively engaged in community culture and increasingly assume the roles of experts (Lave & Wenger, 1991). Learning, both in and out of school, advances through collaborative social interaction and the social construction of knowledge. Web 2.0 can put the theory of situated cognition into practice by providing environments for pedagogical activities in which knowledge is dynamically and collaboratively constructed.

Shared cognition emphasizes the fact that socially shared meanings cannot be reduced to representations in the minds of solitary learners, but rather as arising through social interactions among groups of learners (Resnick, Levine, & Teasley, 1991). These interactions include both verbal and non-verbal communication and the resulting artifacts. Shared cognition specifies that knowledge and skills are acquired in the contexts in which they are exercised (Brown et al., 1989; Lave & Wenger, 1991). Thus, shared cognition and situated cognition are highly intertwined. Shared cognition views collaborative learning as the process of building and maintaining shared understandings in authentic learning environments (Roschelle & Teasley, 1995). The principles of shared cognition are often realized in collaborative learning. They guide the design of knowledge building on web 2.0. However, the needs of team members must be clearly defined. That is, the notion of "shared" in shared cognition needs to be operationalized. Advancements such as web 2.0 offer opportunities for investigating notions of "sharedness" beyond traditional face-to-face communication.

Distributed cognition argues that cognition in not only in the head but is also distributed among learners and tools (Hutchins, 1995). Distributed cognition is distributed because the knowledge and effort required to solve problems are distributed among learners and environments. There are several views of how cognition is distributed (Salomon, 1993b). For instance, Saloman (1993a) sees cognition as rooted in psychological, social, and cultural processes. Thus learning is distributed across learners, through artifacts and shared languages. Three themes have emerged in distributed cognition: (a) the increasingly important role that technology plays in handling intellectual tasks to ease individual cognitive load, (b) the emphasis of Vygotsky's socio-cultural theory which describes how social interactions and externally mediated actions make explicit processes that are then internalized, and (c) the dissatisfaction with the view of cognition as residing in the minds of individual learners. Pea (1993) argues that cognition is not a quality of solitary minds but rather the product of relationships among mental structures and culturally constructed intellectual tools. Distributed cognition is represented in tools, modes of presentations, and other artifacts that are created by offloading heavy cognitive demands. In Pea's view, external resources change the nature and function of systems from which activities arise. The principles of distributed cognition are often applied in the design of artificial intelligence or computer-based learning environments in order to reduce the cognitive load of learners. Web 2.0 social technologies embody and facilitate the distribution of cognition across environments, artifacts, and communities.

Learning Through Communication, Participation, and Interaction

Communities of practice are defined as "groups of people who share a concern, a set of problems, or a passion about a topic, and who deepen their knowledge and expertise in this area by interaction on an ongoing basis" (Wenger, McDermott, & Snyder, 2002, p. 4). Members of communities care about common domains and how they interact and collaborate (Laferrière et al., 2004). Therefore, membership in communities of practice is derived from mutual engagement (Wenger, 1999). Practice is what members of the community are developing to be effective in their domain. That is, "practice is a set of frameworks, ideas, tools, information, styles, language, stories and documents that community members share" (Wenger et al., 2002). Practices comprise shared repertoires, which are defined as "routines, words, tools, ways of doing things, stories, gestures, symbols, genres, actions, or concepts that the community has produced or adopted in the course of its existence, and which have become part of its practice" (Wenger, 1998, p. 83). Practices also include discourse practices which are shared among members in practice as well as the styles which express the forms of membership and member identities.

A *cultural-historical theory* of learning focuses on social interaction and its relation with the internalization of cognitive developments. Learning has a cultural-historical origin. It begins in social interaction and is then internalized. Vygotsky (1978) proposed that cognitive development should be explored as social, cultural, and historical processes. His concept of the zone of proximal development (ZPD) is particularly useful for understanding the mechanisms of social learning. According to Vygotsky, peer interaction, scaffolding, and modeling are important ways of facilitating individual cognitive development and knowledge construction. ZPD can involve both individuals at different levels of expertise such as students and teachers and artifacts such as books, computers, and scientific tools.

Like Vygostky's cultural-historical approach, *socio-cultural theories* propose that individuals' cognitive developments are embedded in the socio-cultural activities through which they engage in mutually constituting relationships (Rogoff, 1998, p. 686). Learning involves transformations through participation in socio-cultural activities which are taken as the units of analysis. *Appropriation*, which exemplifies Rogoff's socio-cultural theory, occurs when two or more people are jointly involved in solving a problem; their understanding of the problem may change as a result of each other's contributions (Rogoff, 1991).

Connecting Two Strands of Theories—Agency and Collective Cognitive Responsibility

Promoting agency in learning is an important theme in the learning sciences. The notion of agency emerged with constructivism but has varied levels of involvement according to different theories (Scardamalia & Bereiter, 1991). Piaget's notions of constructivism attributes agency entirely to children who were regarded as natural born scientists. Vygotosky's cultural historical theory and his notion of the ZPD treats student's active knowledge construction in terms of social interactions with more knowledgeable others. Students assume varying levels of agency in their learning, especially given the extent to which technology supports learning contexts and promotes collaborative interaction. Collective cognitive responsibility is an important aspect to understand the social and cognitive contributions in knowledge creation society. It includes reviewing and understanding the state of knowledge in the broader world, generating and receiving constructive criticism, sharing and synthesizing multiple perspectives, anticipating and identifying challenges and solving problems, and collectively defining knowledge and emergent goals.

Agency and collective cognitive responsibility are complementary elements of learning. A certain level of agency determines the level of collective cognitive responsibility which further promotes higher levels of agency. Web 2.0 users possess new degrees of agency in managing their engagement with resources and other users and it is easy to interact in and with social and technological networks. Because web 2.0 is inherently social, users are central to both the content and the form of all material and resources (Hardey, 2007). The next section will introduce three web 2.0 technologies: blogs, wikis, and social bookmarking.

Applications of Web 2.0 Technologies

Blogs

Blogs are "easy-to-use website[s] characterized by dated entries displayed in reverse chronological order" (Stefanac, 2006, p. 230). Bloggers post online diaries, photos, and opinions to which readers can respond by posting comments and feedback.

Blogs have the general web 2.0 advantages of encouraging individual ownership, responsibility and identity (Godwin-Jones, 2003). and ease of use (Downes, 2004). Blogs are also lightweight and cost-efficient (Fiedler & Cantoni, 2004), versatile and flexible (Nardi, Shiano, Gumbrecht, & Swartz, 2004), interactive (Williams & Jacobs, 2004), and RSS equipped (O'Reilly, 2007). Blogs combine self-expression with social interaction (Richardson, 2006) and support both individualistic and collaborative activities (Huffaker, 2005). Blogging motivates users by providing them with a forum in which to express oneself online by documenting one's life, articulating ideas and opinions, expressing feelings and emotions while forming and maintaining community bonds (Brooks, Nichols, & Priebe, 2003; Nardi et al., 2004).

Blogs were originally used to promote communication, information sharing, and entertainment. Recently, they have been extended to academic, educational, and research settings to promote the sharing of opinions, to facilitate teaching and learning, and to support collaborative learning. Blogging provides learners with opportunities to write for readers beyond their immediate classmates. The opportunity to participate in discussion forums and to self-publish one work fosters a sense of ownership and responsibility among learners, who may focus more attention on what they say and how they say it when "they know they are writing for a real audience. This same degree of personal responsibility is lacking in discussion forums." (Godwin-Jones, 2003, p. 13). Moreover, by allowing for the confrontation of thoughts and ideas contributed by collaborating learners, blogging fosters higher levels of feedback, comment, and reflection among participants (Huffaker, 2005; Richardson, 2006). Blogs have been found to be effective in getting teachers to reflect on their own practice (Ray & Coulter, 2008; Stiler & Philleo, 2003). Blogs have also been found to increase levels of meaningful intellectual exchange among MBA students (Williams & Jacobs, 2004) and to support learning communities though sharing resources and ideas, reflecting on personal experiences and networking with others (Loving, Schroeder, Kang, Shimek, & Herbert, 2007). In addition to cognitive applications, blogs also serve social and emotional purposes. Blogs are often forums in which users engage in emotional projection (Farmer, 2004; Nardi et al., 2004) or can serve as outlets for venting and releasing stress (Brescia & Miller, 2006).

Learning science theories connecting blogging with knowledge building include social constructivism and communities of practice. Social constructivism emphasizes the construction of knowledge through the interactions among knowledge workers, tools, and other artifacts. Social interactions and cognitive conflicts are essential components of cognitive development, and blogging expands the opportunities for strangers to interact in relevant ways. Blogging involves sharing information, providing comments, and suggesting resources. Blogs are far more accessible and easy to use than earlier bounded learning technologies which need specific access rights. Diverse ideas, critiques, and questions can lead to cognitive conflicts which inspire further exploration and inquiry.

Blogs and blogging promote the formation of communities of practice or blogging communities. Blogging is inherently interactive and blogging communities form spontaneously when bloggers share interests, domains knowledge, and forms of discourse. Shared interests and knowledge attracts people to blogging communities while blogs afford the development of distributed expertise by allowing bloggers to contribute new and potentially useful facts, judgments, and comments. Knowledge and practice are advanced during communities of practice.

Wikis

Wiki are systems (tools) that allow a number of users to construct corpuses of knowledge in a set of interlinked web pages, using a process of creating and editing pages (Franklin & Harmelen, 2007). Wikis have been used for both individual and collaborative purposes in education. They allow individual learners to write, edit, and revise their own thoughts and over time to monitor, alter, and reflect on them. Wikis also allow groups of learners to collaborate on writing, shaping, designing, and managing wikis on diverse topics.

Wikis can promote process-oriented as opposed to a product-oriented collaborative writing (Lamb, 2004) by lending to it a degree of seriousness and a sense of permanence (Godwin-Jones, 2003) and by allowing for open access with unrestricted collaboration in contributing and editing tests (Hsu, 2007). Wikis also allow for incremental knowledge creation and enhancement (Cole, 2009), do not impose pre-defined structures unlike blogs (Bryant, 2006), and are easy to use (Ebersbach, 2008). Wikis enable users to trace the history of their collaboration (Bower, Woo, Roberts, & Watters, 2006). Wikis allow for concrete tasks requiring the negotiation of meanings where the identity of the contributors is not essential to the task (Bower et al., 2006). Wiki users are motivated by perceived incongruities between their own knowledge and the amount of information available on the wiki.

Because wikis allow users to create and collaboratively revise texts, research on wikis has focused on writing skills and collaboration. Users can create content and then add, delete, or change any parts they want. Learners have reported that they were able to improve their writing and critical thinking skills by working on wikis (Wheeler, Yeomans, & Wheeler, 2008). The central group work spaces offered by wikis have been found to facilitate group collaboration and communication (Bower et al., 2006). Cognitive conflicts, assimilation, and accommodation have been used to account for knowledge building in wikis (Cress & Kimmerle, 2008). In addition to eliminating inconsistencies, appropriation also reflects mutual engagement in building knowledge. Users demonstrate higher levels of agency than bloggers since their contributions will be demonstrated by their writings. Higher levels of collective cognition may derive from the competitive as opposed to collaborative basis of wiki involvement. The sense of mutual engagement in wikis should be stronger among communities of practice because in so far they emphasize mutual engagement. Participants learn to expand knowledge and improve practice by interacting and sharing community goals.

Social Bookmarking/Tagging

Social bookmarking is a method for Internet users to define, store, organize, search, and manage bookmarks of web pages (Millen, Yang, Whittaker, & Feinberg, 2007). Unlike old ways of using folders to organize bookmarks, social bookmarking uses tags that collectively and/or collaboratively form folksonomies or *social tagging*, that the process by which many users add information in the form of keywords to share content (Yew, Gibson, & Teasley, 2006).

Three elements of social bookmarking, users, resources and tags, are organized into two dimensions: information management and social networking. Social bookmarking acts as an "outboard memory," for storing links that might be lost, scattered across different browser bookmark settings, or distributed among emails, printouts, and web links (Alexander, 2006). Rather than assigning bookmarks to one category, tagging enables users to assign bookmarks to a number of tags corresponding to different dimensions. Tags can refer not only to subject domains but also to levels of usefulness and interest and individual website can be assigned multiple tags. Web links can be hierarchically organized under multiple tags based on how many people have tagged them. Social tagging systems rely on shared and emergent social structures and behaviors, as well as the related conceptual and linguistic structures of user communities (Marlow, Naaman, Boyd, & Davis, 2006). Well-know examples are del.icio.us, citeulike, and digg.com. Social bookmarking also helps users to connect through the same bookmarking. Using tags can help users find not only interesting weblinks but others who share the same interest. While bookmark collections are personally created and maintained, they are typically visible to others. Users benefit by getting pointers to new information from others while getting a general sense of other people's interests (Millen et al., 2007).

Shared understanding is the basis of social bookmarking. Social bookmarking facilitates knowledge building and knowledge management. It provides representations of knowledge that is associated with old and new collaboratively negotiated knowledge. Social tagging has been found to enable *processes* of group knowledge formation and content labeling (Yew et al., 2006). It enables students not only to interact through shared vocabularies but also to develop common sets of norms and practices. Social bookmarking supports lightweight information sharing or knowledge management within organizations (Millen et al., 2007). Tagging has also been found to promote social connection in business organizations (Marlow et al., 2006) and to provide a common language for communication (Yew et al., 2006). The idea of a shared vocabulary is crucial to the formation of group knowledge as it can promote processes of establishing mutual beliefs and assumptions to support group communication which is essential for the formation of cohesion (Clark & Brennan, 1991).

Conclusion

Web 2.0 fosters learning in society 2.0 in which there are no clear boundaries between consuming and producing of knowledge and where learners participate in self-organizing communities by creating and sharing knowledge. Web 2.0 supports learning "based on the premise that our understanding of content is socially constructed through conversations about that content and through grounded interactions, especially with others, around problems or actions" (Brown & Adler, 2008, p. 18). Web 2.0 technologies reflect contribution-oriented activities and empower learners by enabling them to share in the creation of their own learning resources (Collis & Moonen, 2008). By providing opportunities for connecting the learning sciences with knowledge building web 2.0 significantly advances and extends learning activities from classroom into society 2.0 at large.

Web 2.0 technologies support not only cognitive processes but also socio-emotional processes by involving students in "getting to know each other, committing to social relationships, developing trust and belonging, and building a sense of on-line community" (Kreijns, Kirschner, & Jochems, 2003, p. 342). Web 2.0 technologies not only address the educational needs of learners, but their social and psychological needs as well because communities of practice are affectively, cognitively, and socially structured. Building affective structures entail processes of "affiliation, impression formation, and interpersonal attraction to induce and promote social relationships and group cohesion" (Kreijns et al., 2003, p. 342).

Web 2.0 technologies support learning environments that require new skills such as searching, sorting., and synthesizing wide varieties of information. "Working in virtual reality also requires a variety of new skills, as one... becomes an agent in its creation, or at least collaborating with others in shaping it" (Moore, 2007, p. 180). Unfortunately, web 2.0 does not come with a manual, telling learners how to use it to its fullest potential. Recent and ongoing research has succeeded in identifying a few guidelines for use and in identifying a number of unsuccessful applications. For instance, blog-enabled conversations are distributed and fragmented and there are no tools enabling learners to keep track of the flow of arguments (Efimova & de Moor, 2005). Interaction through hyperlinking and commenting on blogs are limited and asymmetrical (Hsu, 2007; Nardi et al., 2004). Lack of organization and structure in wikis can result in unmanageable outputs (Ebner, Kickmeier-Rust, & Holzinger, 2008; Hsu, 2007), and anonymous contributions can discourage feelings of authorship and pose problems for evaluating the quality of wiki content (Boulos, Maramba, & Wheeler, 2006). Social bookmarking and tagging are plagued by uncontrolled vocabularies which can cause ambiguity and chaos in the system. Users may use the same tag in different ways or different tags in the same way (Mathes, 2004; Yew et al., 2006).

How can researchers and educators work together to motivate and support students in building knowledge in society 2.0? While the design of learning technologies in the past was based on fixed models and theories, the design of web 2.0 technologies is based on openness and flexibility and can overcome the constraints of space and time, context, and hierarchy, thereby allowing learners to participate more actively in building knowledge together. However, greater freedoms and opportunities carry greater risks and greater responsibilities Research and evidence from the classroom reveal that lack of structure and guidance can cause these applications to fail (Cole, 2009; Ebner et al., 2008; Wheeler et al., 2008). How can we meet these challenges and take advantage of these opportunities? How can we strike a balance between that which is structured and that which is open?

We have witnessed great changes in educational technology. For instance, computer-assisted learning, intelligent tutoring system, computer-based learning environments, computer-supported collaborative learning, computer-supported knowledge building, and computers as cognitive tools all refer to underlying changes in educational philosophy. Because information technology typically evolve faster than pedagogy they cannot guarantee the success of learning applications and web 2.0 is no exception. We hypothesize that web 2.0 technologies have the potential to facilitate knowledge building, but these technologies need to be guided by theories of learning that are task and context relevant. We hope this chapter can serve as an enabling framework that educators, instructional designers, and researchers can use, adapt, and apply to their work to meet these challenges.

References

Alexander, B. (2006). Web 2.0: A new wave of innovation for teaching and learning? *EDUCAUSE Review*, *41*(2), 32–44.

Bereiter, C. (2002). *Education and mind in the knowledge age*. Mahwah, NJ: Lawrence Erlbaum Associates.

Bereiter, C., & Scardamalia, M. (2003). Learning to work creatively with knowledge. In E. De Corte, L. Verschaffel, N. Entwistle & Jv. Merriënboer (Eds.), *Powerful learning environments: Unravelling basic components and dimensions* (pp. 55–70). Amsterdam: Pergamon.

Bereiter, C., & Scardamalia, M. (2006). Education for the knowledge age: Design-centered models of teaching and instruction. In P. A. Alexander & P. H. Winne (Eds.), *Handbook of educational psychology* (2nd ed, pp. 695–713). Mahwah, NJ: Lawrence Erlbaum Associates.

Boulos, M. N. K., Maramba, I., & Wheeler, S. (2006). Wikis, blogs and podcasts: A new generation of web-based tools for virtual collaborative clinical practice and education. *BMC Medical Education*, *6*, 41.

Bower, M., Woo, K., Roberts, M., & Watters, P. (2006). *Wiki pedagogy – A tale of two wikis*. Chapter presented at the Conference on Information Technology Based Higher Education and Training.

Brescia, W. F., Jr., & Miller, M. T. (2006). What's it worth? The perceived benefits of instructional blogging. *Electronic Journal for the Integration of Technology in Education*, *5*, 44–52.

Brooks, K., Nichols, C., & Priebe, S. (2003). Remediation, genre, and motivation: Key concepts for teaching with weblogs. *Into the blogosphere: Rhetoric, community and culture of weblogs* Retrieved September 20, 2007, from http://blog.lib.umn.edu/blogosphere/remediation_genre_pf.html

Brown, J. S., & Adler, R. P. (2008). Minds on fire: Open education, the long tail, and learning 2.0. *EDUCAUSE Review*, *43*(1), 16–32. %U http://connect.educause.edu/Library/EDUCAUSE+Review/MindsonFireOpenEducationt/45823.

Brown, J. S., Collins, A., & Duguid, P. (1989). Situated cognition and the culture of learning. *Educational Researcher*, *18*(1), 32–42.

Bryan, A. (2006). Web 2.0: A new wave of innovation for teaching and learning? *EDUCAUSE Review*, *41*(2), 32.

Bryant, T. (2006). Social software in academia. *Educause Quarterly*, *29*(2), 61–64.

Chan, C. K. K., & van Aalst, J. (2006). Computer-supported knowledge building in teacher education: Experience from Hong Kong and Canadian teachers. *Teaching Education*, *17*, 75–90.

Clancey, W. J. (1995). A tutorial on situated learning. In J. Self (Ed.), *Proceedings of the International Conference on Computers and Education* (pp. 49–70). Charlottesville, VA: AACE.

Clark, H. H., & Brennan, S. E. (1991). Grounding in communication. In L. B. Resnick, J. M. Levine & S. D. Teasley (Eds.), *Perspectives on socially shared cognition* (pp. 127–149). Washington, DC: American Psychological Association.

Cole, M. (2009). Using wiki technology to support student engagement: Lessons from the trenches. *Computers & Education, 52*(1), 141–146.

Collis, B., & Moonen, J. (2008). *Web* 2.0 tools and processes in higher *Education*: Quality perspectives. *Educational Media International, 45*(2), 93–106.

Cress, U., & Kimmerle, J. (2008). A systemic and cognitive view on collaborative knowledge building with wikis. *International Journal of Computer-Supported Collaborative Learning, 3*(2), 105–122.

Dosie, W., & Mugny, W. (1984). *The Social development of the intellect*. Oxford: Pergamon Press.

Downes, S. (2004). Educational blogging. *EDUCAUSE Review, 39*(5), 14–26.

Drucker, P. F. (1994). The age of social transformation. *Atlantic Monthly, 274*(5), 53–80.

Ebersbach, A. (2008). *Wiki: Web collaboration* (2nd ed.). Berlin; New York: Springer.

Ebner, M., Kickmeier-Rust, M., & Holzinger, A. (2008). Utilizing wiki-systems in higher education classes: A chance for universal access? *Universal Access in the Information Society, 7*(4), 199–207.

Efimova, L., & de Moor, A. (2005). *Beyond personal webpublishing: An exploratory study of conversational blogging practices*. Chapter presented at the 38th Annual Hawaii International Conference on System Science (HICSS'05), Los Alamitos.

Farmer, J. (2004). *Communication dynamics: Discussion boards, weblogs and the development of communities of inquiry in online learning environments*. Chapter presented at the Beyond the comfort zone: Proceedings of the 21st ascilite conference, Perth.

Fiedler, S., & Cantoni, L. C. M. (2004). *Introducing disruptive technologies for learning: Personal webpublishing and weblogs*. Chapter presented at the Ed-Media 2004, Lugano, Switzerland.

Franklin, T., & Van Harmelen, M. (2007). *Web 2.0 for content for learning and teaching in higher education*. Retrieved from http://www.jisc.ac.uk/media/documents/programmes/digitalrepositories/web2-content-learning-and-teaching.pdf

Godwin-Jones, R. (2003). Emerging technologies. Blogs and wikis: Environments for on-line collaboration. *Language Learning & Technology, 7*(2), 12–16.

Hakkarainen, K. (1998). Epistemology of scientific inquiry and computer-supported collaborative learning. Unpublished doctoral dissertation, University of Toronto.

Hakkarainen, K. (2003). Emergence of progressive-inquiry culture in computer-supported collaborative learning. *Learning Environments Research, 6*(2), 199–220.

Hardey, M. (2007). The city in the age of web 2.0: A new synergistic relationship between place and people. *Information, Communication and Society, 10*(6), 867–884.

Hoadley, C. M., & Kilner, P. G. (2005). Using technology to transform communities of practice into knowledge-building communities. *SIGGROUP Bulletin, 25*(1), 31–40.

Hsu, J. (2007). Innovative technologies for education and learning: Education and knowledge-oriented applications of blogs, wikis, podcasts, and more. *International Journal of Information & Communication Technology Education, 3*(3), 70–89.

Huffaker, D. (2005). The educated blogger: Using weblogs to promote literacy in the classroom. *AACE Journal, 13*(2), 91–98.

Hutchins, E. (1995). *Cognition in the wild*. Cambridge, MA: MIT press.

Kreijns, K., Kirschner, P. A., & Jochems, W. (2003). Identifying the pitfalls for social interaction in computer-supported collaborative learning environments: A review of the research. *Computers in human behavior, 19*(3), 335–353.

Laferrière, T., Breuleux, A., & Erickson, G. (2004). Telecollaborative communities of practice in education within and beyond Canada. In A. Brown & N. Davis (Eds.), *World Yearbook of*

Education 2004: Digital technology, communities & education (pp. 264–276). New York, NY: RoutledgeFalmer.

Lai, M., & Law, N. (2006). Peer scaffolding of knowledge building through collaboration of groups with differential learning experiences. *Journal of Educational Computing Research, 35*(2), 121–142.

Lamb, B. (2004). Wide open spaces: Wikis, ready or not. *EDUCAUSE Review, 39*, 36–49.

Lave, J. (1991). Situated learning in communities of practice. In L. B. Resnick, J. M. Levine & S. D. Teasley (Eds.), *Perspectives on socially shared cognition* (pp. 63–82). Washington, DC: American Psychological Association.

Lave, J., & Wenger, E. (Eds.) (1991). *Situated learning: Legitimate peripheral participation*. Cambridge, England: Cambridge University Press.

Loving, C. C., Schroeder, C., Kang, R., Shimek, C., & Herbert, B. (2007). Blogs: Enhancing links in a professional learning community of science and mathematics teachers. *Contemporary Issues in Technology and Teacher Education, 7*(3), 178–198.

Mark, J. W., & Lee, C. M. A. C. (2008). Talk the talk: Learner-generated podcasts as catalysts for knowledge creation. *British Journal of Educational Technology, 39*(3), 501–521.

Marlow, C., Naaman, M., Boyd, D., & Davis, M. (2006). *HT06, tagging chapter, taxonomy, Flickr, academic article, to read*. Chapter presented at the Proceedings of the seventeenth conference on Hypertext and hypermedia.

Mathes, A. (2004). Folksonomies – Cooperative classification and communication through shared metadata *Adammathes.com* Retrieved July 18, 2009, 2009, from http://www.adammathes.com/academic/computer-mediated-communication/folksonomies.html

McLoughlin, C., & Lee, M. (2007). *Social software and participatory learning: Pedagogical choices with technology affordances in the Web 2.0 era*. Chapter presented at the ascilite, Singapore.

Millen, D. R., Yang, M., Whittaker, S., & Feinberg, J. (2007). Social bookmarking and exploratory search. In *ECSCW* (pp. 21–40). Ireland: Limerick.

Moore, M. G. (2007). Web 2.0: Does it really matter? *American Journal of Distance Education, 21*(4), 177–183.

Nardi, B. A., Shiano, D. J., Gumbrecht, M., & Swartz, L. (2004). Why we blog. *Communications of the ACM, 47*(12), 41–46.

O'Reilly, T. (2007). What is Web 2.0: Design patterns and business models for the next generation of software. *Communications & Strategies, 65*, (Jan), 17–37.

Paavola, S., Lipponen, L., & Hakkarainen, K. (2004). Models of innovative knowledge communities and three metaphors of learning. *Review of Educational Research, 74*(4), 557–576.

Pea, R. D. (1993). Practices of distributed intelligence and designs for education. In G. Salomon (Ed.), *Distributed cognitions: Psychological and educational considerations* (pp. 1–46). Cambridge, UK: Cambridge University Press.

Piaget, J. (1926). *The child's conception of the world*. Paris: Alcan.

Piaget, J. (1970). *Structuralism* (C. Maschler, Trans.). New York: Basic Books.

Popper, K. R. (1972). *Objective knowledge: An evolutionary approach*. Oxford, HK: Clarendon Press.

Ray, B. B., & Coulter, G. A. (2008). Reflective practices among language arts teachers: The use of weblogs. *Contemporary Issues in Technology and Teacher Education, 8*(1), 6–26.

Resnick, L., Levine, J., & Teasley, S. (Eds.) (1991). *Perspectives on socially shared cognition*. Washington DC: APA Press.

Richardson, W. (2006). *Blogs,wikis,podcasts and other powerful web tools for classrooms*. Thousand Oaks, CA: California Corwin Press.

Rogers, P. C., Liddle, S. W., Chan, P., Doxey, A., & Isom, B. (2007). Web 2.0 learning platform: Harnessing collective intelligence. *Turkish Online Journal of Distance Education, 8*, 3.

Rogoff, B. (1991). Social interaction as apprenticeship in thinking: Guided participation in spatial planning. In L. Resnick, J. Levine & S. Teasley (Eds.), *Perspectives on socially shared cognition*. Hyattsville, MD: American Psychological Association.

Rogoff, B. (1998). Cognition as collaborative process. In W. Damon, D. Kuhn & R. S. Siegler (Eds.), *Handbook of child psychology: Cognition, perception, and language* (pp. 679–744). Cambridge, UK: Cambridge University Press.

Roschelle, J., & Teasley, S. D. (1995). The construction of shared knowledge in collaborative problem solving. In C. E. O'Malley (Ed.), *Computer-supported collaborative learning* (pp. 69–97). New York: Springer-Verlag.

Salomon, G. (1993a). Editor's introduction. In G. Salomon (Ed.), *Distributed cognitions: Psychological and educational considerations* (pp. xi–xxi). New York, NY: Cambridge University Press.

Salomon, G. (Ed.) (1993b). *Distributed cognition: Psychological and educational considerations*. New York, NY: Cambridge University Press.

Scardamalia, M., & Bereiter, C. (1991). Higher levels of agency for children in knowledge building: A challenge for the design of new knowledge media. *Journal of the Learning Sciences, 1*(1), 37–68.

Scardamalia, M., & Bereiter, C. (1994). Computer support for knowledge-building communities. *Journal of the Learning Sciences, 3*(3), 265–283.

Scardamalia, M., & Beretier, C. (2003). Knowledge building. In J. W. Guthrie (Ed.), *Encyclopedia of education* (pp. 1370–1373). New York: Macmillan Reference.

Scardamalia, M., Bereiter, C., & Lamon, M. (1994). The CSILE project: Trying to bring the classroom into World 3. In M. Kate (Ed), *Classroom lessons: Integrating cognitive theory and classroom practice* (pp. 201–228). Cambridge, MA: MIT Press/Bradford Books. xvi, 317 pp.

Scardamalis, M. (2004). CSILE/Knowledge Forum. In A. Kovalchick & K. Dawson (Eds.), *Education and technology: An encyclopedia* (pp. 183–192). Santa Barbara, CA: ABX-CLIO Inc.

Stefanac, S. (2006). *Dispatches from Blogistan: A travel guide for the modern blogger*. Berkeley, CA: New Riders.

Stiler, G. M., & Philleo, T. (2003). Blogging and blogspots: An alternative format for encouraging reflective practice among preservice teachers. *Education, 123*(4), 789–798.

Vygotsky, L. S. (1978). *Mind in Society*. Cambridge, MA: Harvard University Press.

Wenger, E. (1999). *Communities of practice: Meaning, and identity*. Cambridge: Cambridge University Press.

Wenger, E., McDermott, R., & Snyder, W. M. (2002). *Cultivating communities of practice: A guide to managing knowledge*. Boston, MA: Harvard Business School Press.

Wheeler, S., Yeomans, P., & Wheeler, D. (2008). The good, the bad and the wiki: Evaluating student-generated content for collaborative learning. *British Journal of Educational Technology, 39*(6), 987–995.

Williams, J. B., & Jacobs, J. (2004). Exploring the use of blogs as learning spaces in the higher education sector. *Australasian Journal of Educational Technology, 20*(2), 232–247.

Yew, J., Gibson, F. P., & Teasley, S. D. (2006). Learning by tagging: The role of social tagging in group knowledge formation. *Journal of Online Learning and Teaching, 2*(4), 275–285.

Zhang, J., Scardamalia, M., Lamon, M., Messina, R., & Reeve, R. (2007). Socio-cognitive dynamics of knowledge building in the work of 9- and 10-year-olds. *Educational Technology Research and Development, 55*, 117–145.

Chapter 28
Innovations in Culturally Based Science Education Through Partnerships and Community

Megan Bang[1,2], Douglas Medin[3], Karen Washinawatok[4], and Shannon Chapman[5]

[1] TERC, Cambridge, MA, USA
[2] American Indian Center of Chicago, Chicago, IL, USA, e-mail: megan_bang@terc.edu
[3] Northwestern University, Evanston, IL, USA
[4] Menominee Language and Culture Commission, Keshena, WI, USA
[5] Menominee Tribal School, Neopit, WI, USA

Introduction

In what follows we describe a program of educational research aimed at improving science achievement among Native American children. This ongoing project builds on previous work but is distinctive in two ways. First, it involves a coalition of community members and teachers developing science curricula. Second, it represents the cooperative efforts of reservation-based tribal institutions, an urban tribal institution, and a major research university. On numerous grounds this is an unlikely combination, so the synergies growing out of this project will repay careful attention.

Background

Our long-term goal is to improve science learning and school achievement for Native American children. Student achievement in science education is a well-rehearsed problem, particularly for those groups of children who have historically been placed at risk. This problem is particularly acute with Indigenous populations. The high school graduation rate is at just 51.1% for Native youth (Orfield, Losen, Wald, & Swans, 2004). Only 6% of the population that does go on to college receives a bachelor's degree (NSF, 2007; Pavel, Curtin, & Whitener, 1998). Nowhere is the problem more apparent than in science learning. Over the past 10 years, Native people have represented an average 0.63% of the total number of bachelors degrees and

D. Medin (✉)
Northwestern University, Evanston, IL, USA
e-mail: medin@northwestern.edu

M.S. Khine, I.M. Saleh (eds.), *New Science of Learning*,
DOI 10.1007/978-1-4419-5716-0_28, © Springer Science+Business Media, LLC 2010

an average of 0.48% of the doctorates awarded in Science and Engineering (NSF, 2007), The 2,000 census found that about 1.5% of the US population identified themselves as American Indian or Alaskan Native. Thus, these figures indicate that Native people are about 60% under-represented at the college level and 67% under-represented at the doctoral level (even without taking into account the younger age distribution of Native Americans).

To make these numbers more concrete, over the past 10 years a total of only 14 doctorates have been awarded to Native scholars in Computer Science, 10 in Physics, 5 in Astronomy, 3 in Ocean Sciences, and 1 in Atmospheric Sciences (NSF, 2007); in the biological sciences, 108 doctorates have been awarded to Indian scholars. Yet these numbers only represent 0.3% of the total number of degrees awarded (NSF, 2007). These numbers represent an increase in representation from earlier decades, albeit a minimal one.

The issue of achievement in STEM (science, technology, engineering, math) fields is far more significant than just a matter of representation; it centrally involves power, particularly in light of real socioscientific problems facing the world—such as global warming and other environmental issues. The lack of degreed expertise within Indigenous communities contributes to, and perpetuates, struggles with sovereignty and survival, education and educational achievement, economic development, the enhancement of community health, community-based governance of resource management, and the cultural vitality of Native communities. In short, Native people both on and off reservations continue to struggle for cultural and sovereign survival. To improve the circumstances that affect Indigenous communities in ways that are likely to have a sustained impact requires that we improve the educational experience and attainment of Native people, especially within STEM education.

Understanding the widespread lack of achievement in STEM education and developing possible solutions poses critical challenges, in light of cognitive science research, and community-based research, which suggest that the problems with achievement are more complicated than simply knowing or not knowing "science content" (see Demmert & Towner, 2003, for a review). A growing body of educational research is demonstrating the need to understand the complexities that (culturally) diverse ways of knowing create for teaching and learning environments, particularly if we are to improve school achievement for those groups of students who have historically been placed at risk (i.e., Warren et al., 2001; Gutiérrez & Rogoff, 2003; Gutierrez, 2006).

Challenges to and the Need for Innovation

We are far from the first to point out the under representation of Native scholars in science and science education. But there are a number of significant barriers to progress in addressing these issues. First of all, we are not optimistic that large-scale studies of the correlates of achievement will provide constructive advice.

We see three problems with this approach: (1) It reifies the status quo because innovations will likely be buried in the noise after large-scale predictors are regressed out, (2) The large-scale factors are likely to be variables such as family income, parent formal education, and number of books in the home, variables that are difficult to turn into interventions, except for the implicit, pernicious suggestion that everyone should be white and middle class, and (3) The units of analysis (e.g. Native Americans) are often too broad to reveal the relevant dynamics (see Chandler & LaLonde, 1998 for a compelling example involving suicide rates among First Nations peoples of British Columbia).

A second barrier to constructive engagement of science education research with Native communities is the physical, social, historical, and power distance between major research universities and tribal institutions. Universities tend to be in urban areas and though more Native Americans live off reservations than on them, Indian children are usually scattered throughout urban schools and an Indian child is often the only Native American in the classroom. Although the more recent development of tribal colleges and universities is a positive development, the primary mission of these tribal institutions has been education, not (educational) research.

A third barrier (or perhaps an amplification of the second) is the status of both education and research in tribal communities. We will not rehearse the boarding school era and the enduring historical trauma associated with it and other assimilationist efforts that have been integral to schools and schooling. Perhaps it suffices to say that the history of formal education in American Indian communities documents the consistent attempts to undermine the sovereignty, as well as cultural and intellectual vitality of Indigenous peoples. Control over the education of Indigenous children and even the parenting of Indigenous children was systematically and intentionally manipulated as a way to "solve the Indian problem."

Although the most pernicious aspects of the boarding school era have been confronted and displaced, they have been replaced by more subtle, but ultimately equally damaging, power structures that organize learning in terms of the values and practices of the dominant culture. The everyday practices of teaching and learning have not been in the control of or in many cases even implemented by Indian people. For many community members, memories of school are very unpleasant. Although they wish for their own children to have better experiences, it is hard for them not to conceptualize schools as a "necessary evil," let alone as a positive resource for community values.

There is a corresponding history of exploitation in research conducted in Indian communities. The polite expression of this attitude is the belief that "we have been studied too much." More analytic responses point to the unequal benefits of research—the Indian informants get coffee and donuts and the graduate student researcher gets a Ph.D. or the Professor gets a book published. And with annoying frequency, the research report is disparaging of the community being studied. Who needs that?

In summary, there are very significant barriers to efforts to address underrepresentation in science and science education in Native American communities. Pretty clearly significant changes in orientations and innovations are needed to address them. On the other hand, we could be accused of failing to recognize the significance of the development of tribal colleges and universities and other efforts of tribal entities to assert sovereignty. As will be seen, however, we embrace both perspectives.

Innovation: Partnerships and Communities

Overview. Our project is a collaborative effort involving Northwestern University, TERC, the American Indian Center (AIC) of Chicago, and various institutions on the Menominee reservation in Wisconsin, including the Menominee tribal school and the Menominee Language and Culture Commission. We began by describing our current interdisciplinary research team and then give a brief history of our collaboration.

The majority of our research team consists of Native American educators who have close ties to the communities being studied. Bang, Director at the AIC of Chicago, has been a member of and working in the Chicago Indian community for more than 12 years, and has been working with the Menominee community for the past 7 years. Washinawatok has a lifetime of experience on the Menominee reservation, having served as Tribal Chair, as a member of the Tribal Legislature, as Dean of NAES College (Native American Educational Services), Menominee campus, and she has been a research partner for the past 5 years. She is currently Director of the Menominee Language and Culture Commission and a member of the Menominee Indian School District Board. Chapman is lifelong member of the Menominee community, has been a logging contractor, and is currently Assistant Principal at the Menominee tribal school. Chapman has recently replaced Carol Dodge, who took over the Menominee component of this project when Washinawatok was serving as Tribal Chair. Medin (Northwestern) has worked with the Menominee community for more than 12 years and with the Chicago Indian community for 7 years. He has taught courses at NAES, Chicago campus, NAES, Menominee campus, and the College of the Menominee Nation. More recently teachers and researchers associated with the project have been able to receive Northwestern graduate and undergraduate credit for courses offered by Medin at the AIC and on the Menominee reservation.

Our collaboration has been designed to be an equal partnership. Rather than having Northwestern University control all research funds or having Northwestern as the primary institution issuing subcontracts to tribal entities, whenever possible we have sought to submit grants with a single project description and three independent budgets, independently administered. Our goal is also to match the budgetary sharing with equal sharing in research design and evaluation, taking into account the different skills collaborators bring to the project. Shortly, we will provide a bit more by way of the history of our collaboration but first we briefly describe the community component of our project.

Our project has two other crucially important goals: (1) to strengthen the capacity of Native communities to improve student learning and achievement and

(2) to increase Native undergraduate and graduate student participation in research. In our previous work we have actualized these goals in two ways: through a general process of collaborative praxis that builds the research skills and administrative infrastructure within Indian communities and through a collaborative design process we have been developing and refining. We call this design process *community-based design* (CBD), the foundation of which rests on the comprehensive participation of community members, including teachers, elders, parents, community experts, researchers, and youth in all aspects of the research, including the conceptions of the problems, project design and implementation, and data collection and analysis.

The above description offers a snapshot of our research partnership and goals. The remainder of this chapter is organized as follows. We first describe the benefits of our partnership by outlining how it addresses the barriers outlined above. In doing so, we will need to provide more background information. Next, we provide some examples of our CBD in practice and its effects on the communities. Then, we briefly outline more of the history of our project, because it may be relevant to other efforts at forging research partnerships. Finally, we summarize with lessons we have learned from our partnership.

Research in Indigenous Communities: Background and Organization

Since the 1970s there has been a growing effort for Indigenous people to be running schools in Indian communities. Most of the progress made on this front, however, has been at the administrative level, not at the classroom level. The majority of Indian children both on and off reservations have non-Indian teachers. The design of this research project recognized this and intentionally proposed engaging teachers and community members in the design of a learning environment integrating levels of classroom, content, and pedagogy. The intent was to begin to create a space where community members engaged in reclaiming the classroom level of teaching and learning for Indigenous children (Smith, 1999).

The design of our methods has been based on an understanding of appropriate research methods for working with American Indian communities. There is a long history of research in American Indian communities that has often not been in their best interest, a legacy that has made many Native communities suspect of research. Over the years indigenous researchers themselves have worked to develop appropriate methods and criteria for conducting research (Hermes, 1999; Smith, 1999; Mihesuah, 1998; Guyette, 1983). There are some general lessons that have driven the approach to this work. First, all of literature generally agrees that the *participatory action research (PAR)* is the best framework of inquiry. PAR has generally been defined as an integrated approach that relies on the participation of community members to investigate the issues at hand while building local skills for the purpose of increasing autonomy through a process of praxis (Hermes, 1999). PAR includes the following criteria: elder input, use of traditional language, community participation in research agenda, staff selection, and budget, community payoff, respect of cultural value, and informed consent (Hermes, 1999; Hudson & Taylor-Henley, 2001). Additionally, when conducting research with reservation communities, investigators must go through the tribal institutional review board (IRB) process; an IRB approval from a mainstream institution is not sufficient (Lomawaima, 2000). Although less has been written about working with urban populations, where the benefit of tribal approval of the research is not possible, forming a local advisory committee within the community and seeking institutional support of local organizations is a good idea. Our work reflects these criteria and approaches.

Research context and communities involved. Our 3-way partnership is not two 2-way partnerships with one partner common to both. Although we describe the Menominee and Chicago Indian communities separately, both communities have worked together with AIC members coming to the Menominee reservation and Menominee community members coming to the AIC for collaborative meetings.

Menominee community. The Menominee are the oldest continuous residents of Wisconsin. Historically, their lands covered much of Wisconsin but were reduced, treaty by treaty, until the present 95,000 hectares was reached in 1854. There are 4–5,000 Menominee living on tribal lands. Over 60% of Menominee adults have at least a high school education and 15% have had some college. The present site was forested then and now—there are currently about 88,000 hectares of forest. Sustainable coexistence with nature is a strong value (Hall & Pecore, 1995). Hunting and fishing are important activities and children are familiar with both by age 12.

The Menominee children in our project attend a tribal school. The tribal school serves K-8 and has approximately 400 students in the school. Although exposing children to the Menominee language is an important focus of the tribal school, the vast majority of science instruction and everyday discourse is in English.

Urban Indian population. There are approximately 40,000 Indian people in Cook county, many of whom were relocated to the area during the 1950s and 1960s during the federal relocation era. The Chicago community is a very diverse intertribal community with individuals representing more than 100 tribes across the country. Native American children are scattered across a number of schools in the district and are a minority in every classroom.

The AIC is the oldest urban Indian center in the country and serves as the social and cultural center of the Chicago Indian community. Menominee and other Wisconsin tribes are well represented at the AIC. The Chicago Indian community faces many of the same problems that other inner city communities face, such as high rates of poverty, lack of access to quality health care, poor schooling options, low employment rates, issues surrounding drugs and alcohol, and high rates of violence.

The Design Process: The Early Stages

The project idea was presented to community members as a critical need in the community. There were three primary kinds of issues that were mentioned at the start. The first was the serious need for more Indian people in STEM fields. We did a quick survey of STEM-related positions across several Indian nations and the majority of them were filled with non-Indian people, including on the Menominee reservation. This was framed as fundamentally an issue of sovereignty because it meant that non-Indian people had a powerful influence on the use and strategic direction of natural resources in tribal communities.

The second issue was the achievement statistics at various levels, including advanced degrees all the way down to state standardized tests. Our previous examination of standardized tests found that Menominee children in Wisconsin test better in science in the fourth grade than any other subject but by eighth grade it is their worst subject (Bang, Medin, & Atran, 2007). It is important to note that performance on other subjects stays stable across time, suggesting that there is something unique going on in science. We coupled this framing with cognitive research we had conducted with Indigenous children, Menominee included, in which basic biological concepts and reasoning patterns were examined (e.g., Ross, Medin, Coley, & Atran, 2003, Bang et al., 2007). The general findings from these studies suggest that Native children come to school with advanced understandings of biology, that their reasoning patterns mirror those of practicing scientists, and further that Menominee fishermen tend to organize knowledge and reason along ecological rather than taxonomic lines (Medin, Ross, Cox, & Atran, 2007). We suggested that this was potentially a deeply productive intellectual asset that schools fail to mobilize or recognize.

The last piece of "evidence" that was used to frame the introduction to this project was a brief survey of science classroom materials we conducted in which we looked at the way content was organized. We found that the systems level analyses in general and the coverage of ecosystems was often the last chapter in textbooks and never used as an organizing principle. Most biology textbooks started with a microlevel or what we call a model species level and then expanded (Bang, 2007). Further, the majority of the textbooks had almost no hands-on or experiential components. We suggested that this assumed trajectory of learning did not align with Native students' ways of knowing or experiencing the world (Bang, 2007). Thus we were proposing to design learning environments with an ecological orientation and community-based practices as the foundation, to see whether student engagement and learning was better in such environments. Once the project team was formed, we also engaged in conversation about the previously mentioned historical perspective on teaching and learning in Indian communities and noted that we hoped that this would be a place for us to reclaim, recover, and refine teaching and learning practices in Indigenous communities.

The early stage of our design process consisted of a series of monthly or bimonthly meetings to make sense of the goals of the project and to develop a shared vision for it. These meetings soon evolved into specific decisions about a range of issues such as content focus, activities, assessment, and community involvement. The majority of the work in the first year consisted of making sense of issues of science and science education from a sociohistorical and larger cultural perspective rooted in a particular place and based on participants' experiences.

Community Design in Action: Social policy and community context. In each of our programs there has been a range of community participation. All of the teachers and research assistants in the project have been local community members. Both communities also had elders and community experts lead activities with children. For example, in Chicago we had an elder share creation stories and stories focused on plants with children. At our Menominee site we have had community members who work for the forestry department, fisheries, and water treatment talk with students. In addition, teachers frequently made connections between the specific tasks children and adults were engaged in with broader issues within the community. Teachers used this as an opportunity to stress needs in the community that invited children to think about science as a career path. For example, while students were learning about issues with the Chicago river specifically, teachers made connections to water issues on different reservations (i.e. the Oneida nation is currently exploring creating a pond for drinking water, the Navajo nation is working to clean up toxins in their aquifers; the Great Lakes Indian Fish & Wildlife Commission was discussed as a community-based scientific organization that was developed to protect our resources and sovereignty). Although these various connections were pointed out some of the time, our efforts were not systematic. We intend to systematically include this throughout the intervention and test its impacts.

Exploring and addressing tensions between western modern science and Native science. The design teams have focused on the ways in which various cultural practices and artifacts, including stories, converge or diverge with ideas in school science, and how to structure activities that facilitate students' exploration of both. Often students are left to navigate and make sense of the multiple cultural contexts in which they live with little support or conversation. Although there has been work on making the practices and expectations of schooling explicit to students, generally this work has been engaged from a deficit perspective, one aimed at ushering students into a different way of doing things (Delpit, 1995). This aspect of our curriculum has begun to emerge by identifying key points within lessons and activities where we think the hypothesized discord is often at an implicit or tacit level or in places where we think there are generative intersections between modern western science and traditional practices and knowledge. We see this aligned with what Gutiérrez, Larson, and Kreuter (1995), Gutiérrez, Baquedano-Lopez, and Turner (1997), and Gutiérrez, Baquedano-Lopez, and Tejeda (1999) have called the third space or places in which "alternative and competing discourse and positionings transform conflict and difference into rich zones of collaboration and learning" (see also Van Eijck & Roth, 2007).

For example, when our students engage with the concept of biodiversity, community-based views about all things being connected and having a role to play is a resource to be mobilized that easily aligns with the western science concept. However, within many Native communities rocks, water, and other entities that would be classified as "nonliving natural kinds" are considered to be different living kinds. We are making these sorts of differences explicit to students and embracing and exploring the reasons for the differences in "classifications," thereby creating a third zone. In this project we are exploring the ways in which the third zone may be supporting the shifts in students' understanding of the nature of science more broadly, in relation to traditions of students' community-based practices, histories, and knowledge.

The learning environments. A significant focus of our project was the creation of curricular units by the Chicago and Menominee CBD teams. The curricula were relationally driven, place-based and problem-based, involving locally meaningful interventions focused on ecosystems. They were organized around the global idea that we (humans, other animals, plants) are all related (see Cajete, 1999, 2000; Kawagley, 2000; Chinn, 2007). The curricula included a breadth of content concerning plant and aquatic life through a series of hands-on experiences (e.g,. cutting down invasive buckthorn from forest), guest speakers (e.g., elders and professionals working in relevant fields), and "labs" (e.g., testing pH levels of water samples). At the AIC we used the medicinal garden surrounding the building as an anchor and then branched out to various local neighborhoods to identify and experience urban ecosystems, local forest preserves, and lakefront restoration sites. On the Menominee reservation our focus was on the forest and waters but the program included activities like visiting the Menominee water treatment plant which maintains its own laboratory for water quality testing. Another specific element of the curriculum is the inclusion of culturally based stories that convey some knowledge about nature, primarily stories about plants and animals.

The following is a brief vignette that exemplifies the kind of activities that were designed and implemented. Although there are some particulars to this activity, generally our designers followed a similar structure and logic for all of the activities.

The Chicago program was based on plant ecology and organized around the big idea that everything is related. Each student "recognized their relatives" by engaging in close study with one medicinal plant species that was in the medicinal garden surrounding the AIC. Students "remade a relative" by interacting with the same plant daily in a variety of ways that were integrated into other activities. For example, part of the summer program involved learning about invasive species. One activity was centered around understanding European buckthorn's (an invasive species) impact on local forest ecosystems. We went to a local forest preserve, accompanied by forest preserve staff (practicing scientists) where buckthorn is damaging the health of oak trees (and thus the forest canopy) and ultimately the entire health of the forest ecosystem.

Upon arriving at the forest preserve, students were first introduced to the history of the preserve and Native peoples' relationships with the forest before European contact. Through this history students were introduced to their community responsibilties to the forest and to the respectful protocol for entering into special places. They were also asked to locate their plant relative in the forest. After each student located their plant we gathered together to learn about buckthorn from the plant's perspective (including its history in the area) in order to strategically clear (cut) some of the buckthorn. Students learned appropriate community-based protocols for cutting down these plants, safe and proper use of tools, as well as species identification strategies at various stagies in a plant's life cycle.

During this time we were visited by a doe and fawn walking through the preserve. The elder on our trip interpreted this as the doe and her fawn welcoming us and thanking us for the good work we were doing. Students, teachers, and other community members then cut buckthorn for a couple of hours. During that time there were a series of mini lessons that took place about other local plants, plant indentification, and plant anatomy. We were also fortunate to observe several other animals during the visit including a possum and possum baby sleeping in the trunk of a tree, a snake, mice, and squirrels.

Design principles of culturally and community-based science programming. The design principles developed in our work address the issue of discord at multiple levels including, but not limited to, content, orientations to nature, participation, and practice. Our own work, and that of others, suggests that culturally based science curricula has at minimum the following design characteristics: They (1) use local, place-based instruction, and hands-on experiences (see Schroeder et al., 2007 for a relevant meta-analysis), (2) are inextricably linked with community participation and practices including community values, needs, language, and experiences (Cajete, 1997), (3) are premised on the idea that nature is not an externality, apart from humans, but rather that humans are a part of nature, (4) are motivated and organized around a big idea, in our case the idea that everything is related and has a role to play in the universe (systems level or ecosystems thinking), (5) place science in an interdisciplinary or holistic contextualized and invite the learner to view phenomena from multiple perspectives, and (6) explore and address the relationships and tensions between Native science and western science (e.g. Cajete, 1997), and (7) place science in social policy and community contexts that highlight the need for participation and leadership (e.g., Aikenhead, 2006).

Community-Based Design: A Closer Look

In the following we focus on a few selected segments from a design team meeting on the Menominee reservation in which elders, teachers, and community members were present. The design team was working on a forest ecology unit and discussing what they wanted the learning goals of the unit to be. In analyzing this section our goal is seeing the larger sociohistorical frame that participants are working with and the ways in which this frame functions in shaping the meanings of science and Native peoples' relationship to science. We explore the variations in these meanings and relationships both across individuals as well as across particular individual's utterances. These variations are sites of struggle for meaning, reclamation, transformation, and sovereignty. We use discourse analysis to uncover these variations in the context of teacher and designer meetings.

Before turning to the meeting in question, the reader must know something about the history and relationship of the Menominee nation with their forested lands. The Menominee have managed a sustainable logging operation, including a logging mill, for more then a century (Beck, 2002; Davis, 2000; Grignon et al., 1998). The forest is more than a source of economic values; many Menominee have a deep sense of identity connected to the forest. The forest is a source of game, firewood, medicines, berries, and a site for cultural practices. Some Menominee say that if the forest were gone the Menominee would no longer exist as a people. Hunters often express a sense of awe when they note that their ancestors hunted on the very same ground where they are hunting now. We once asked a Menominee hunter what he thinks about when he is hunting and his answer was, "I pray."

The Menominee relationship with the forest has not been free of the history of America and the majority culture domination of Indigenous people. Since the present boundaries of the reservation were established in 1856, the tribe has struggled with outside interests and the federal government. The so-called "Pine Ring" attempted to steal Menominee timber and to gain control of and clear cut the Menominee reservation. Newman (1967) estimates that about 1 million board feet of timber were stolen from the reservation between 1871 and 1890.

The struggle has been even more protracted and multifaceted (Grignon et al., 1998). In 1871 Secretary of the Interior agreed that the Menominee be allowed to cut and sell logs to mills outside the reservation. Under pressure from the Pine Ring, the government halted the Menominee logging operation in 1878. In 1882 a special act of the US Congress allowed the tribe to cut "dead and down" timber. In 1888 the US Attorney General ordered another halt to logging on grounds that the timber was government property. In 1890 another Congressional act authorized cutting and sale of timber under the supervision of government superintendents. In 1908 a bill authorized the Menominee to build their own mill and to harvest mature trees under a selective cutting system where Forestry Service specialists would mark the trees to be cut. In 1912 agency superintendents began a policy of clear cutting in direct violation of the 1908 act. Selective cutting was reinstituted in 1926. In 1928 the tribe was able to elect an advisory board and the board went to Washington DC to protest the mismanagement of the forest and mill. It took until 1951 for the tribe to win an 8.5 million dollar settlement for the failure of governmental officials to carry out provisions of the 1908 act.

At present, the logging operation is managed by Menominee Tribal Enterprises (MTE). But even now cutting prescriptions are approved by the Bureau of Indian Affairs (BIA).

At one point, the Menominee nation was one of the most economically successful Indian communities in North America. Despite federal oversight and mismanagement, the Menominee logging operation employed hundreds of Menominee people and generated significant revenues. But in the early 1950s the federal government began a policy known as termination in which the sovereign status of targeted nations was removed. The Menominee termination act was signed into law in 1954 and implemented in 1961. In effect, it was an attempt to legislate the tribe out of existence. The idea was that all Menominees would become American citizens instead of wards of the federal government. The tribe would receive no more financial support from the federal government, the land would be divided up, and the reservation would become nothing more than another Wisconsin county.

The termination act immediately crippled the Menominee Nation financially, because the tribe had no tax base to generate revenue. The tribal clinic and hospital soon closed. There was deep ripple effect on all aspects of the tribal community. Overnight Menominee County became a pocket of poverty.

The Menominee logging operation had to focus on efficiency rather than maximizing Menominee employment. These operations were managed by Menominee Enterprises, which, despite its name, included non-Indians on the board of directors and they often were in the position of casting the decisive vote. In 1968 Menominee Enterprises used several smaller reservation lakes to create a man-made lake, Legend Lake, and sold shoreline lots to non-Indians. In this case, from the perspective of most Menominees, the economic gains were far outweighed by the loss of sovereignty over the lands and the decision triggered a storm of protest and ultimately led to the restoration movement that achieved success in 1973 when President Nixon signed the Menominee Restoration Act.

The logging operation is currently operated by MTE which is under control of the Menominee Tribal Legislature (though the constitutional relationship between these two independent entities is sometimes in dispute). MTE has won several awards for its sustainable forestry practices, yet its current cutting practices have not always been well received by the Menominee community. These practices include 40-acre clear cuts and shelterwood cuts which look quite a bit like clear cuts. Many Menominee people, including loggers, are disturbed by these cuts. They do not see the rationale for abandoning selective harvest, they note that the heavier equipment used for such cuts compacts the soil, they worry about the ecological consequences of these practices and they find them aesthetically displeasing. When community members object to MTE's practices they are often met with the counterargument that "our practices are based on forestry science."

This is a crude gloss of a troubled yet resilient history and we hope it will be enough to enable the reader to see the shared historical experience that may be functioning in the unfolding of the conversation. There are places in the utterances in which we will clarify terminology using square brackets and italics. We begin with Justin,[1] a tribal leader, who has been involved with forest policy issues for over a decade.

> **Justin:** There seems at this sort of moment in time, or in the last decade or two, a great anxiety between science and the way traditionally the forest was managed, and how science is somewhat taking a upper hand at the um, anxiety of a lot of tribal members and loggers and stuff.

Justin begins by locating this issue in a particular moment in time, suggesting that the current problems are different from past problems but are not unrelated. He specifically locates this within the last 20 years or so. He casts science and Menominee traditional practices and knowledge in an oppositional binary and suggests that this binary is causing "a great anxiety." The expression "great anxiety" seems to index a historically infused emotion and perspective and it has the affect of nominalizing anxiety. Justin goes on to characterize the anxiety by linking it with issues of power and domination and locating it within the lives of community members. Note that there is no balance or integration of science and traditional management but rather science has the "upper hand."

---

[1] Here and elsewhere we use pseudonyms.

Interestingly, Justin names both "tribal members" and "loggers" as feeling this anxiety. It is also important to note that at this point Justin has not located himself specifically within this relationship—he is narrating it from a relational distance.

Sarah: Are they doing things more scientifically here now, or what, or is that some of the problem between...?

Sarah takes up Justin's construal of "a great anxiety" and science's dominance. She assumes a comparative frame and wants to analyze the difference in more specific detail. She uses the words "more scientifically," pulling out a possible implication of Justin's comment that science is taking the upper hand and implicitly accepting the opposition of science with tradition.

Justin: There aren't many tribal lumber mills *[reference to the Menominee Mill which celebrated its centennial in 2008]* that are a hundred years old. So they don't have a real, the record that we do, and part of the practice, traditions, and oral history that contribute to how they drew up proscriptions *[plans for forest management]*. But, but science is definitely, I think, is creating a lot of anxiety among different tribes *because the people who have the knowledge aren't the people who are making the public policy decisions*, and, and for some reason they can't talk, yeah come together or talk, find a way to talk about it where they're understandable and make sense vs. what they know to have had success in the past.

Justin's response to Sarah's question is multilayered. He wants to complicate Sarah's quantification of scientific practices and appears to read Sarah's comment as suggesting that previous forest management was unscientific. Further, he suggests that the scientists do not have the same record of sustainable forestry that Menominees do, with the implication that Menominees have deeper database of sorts, implying that Menominee knowledge is older and deeper than the scientific knowledge now driving the management of the forest. The exchange also suggests that Justin has multiple frames for thinking about what power is and where it lies within this situation. Justin suggests that Menominee practices and traditions fleshed out or completed a perspective that drove the management of the forest, something that is missing from the current management plans.

There is also a shift from speaking about science as a disembodied entity in his earlier comment to something people do or knowledge that people have. Note also that he backs off from the simple dichotomy of science and tradition to suggest that part of the problem lies with a lack of communication between policy people (e.g., the Tribal Legislature) and people who have the formal knowledge (MTE). Justin notes that the anxiety that is being felt on the Menominee reservation is not something unique. He expands his argument to something that is felt by many tribes and notes that the people in power are not the ones with the appropriate knowledge.

Justin ends his turn by locating the problem in the dialogue between the people involved and their inability to understand one another. Implied in Justin's comment is that this misunderstanding is one based on how scientists are not making sense in comparison to what people know from experience. This last phrase continues the oppositional dichotomy that was originally cast and the comparative frame that Sarah used, but at a different grain size. It has now been located at the conversational level between people. The power dynamic in this comment is multivoiced because it locates accurate knowledge with the people, but also recognizes that the sociopolitical context of power does not have the accurate voice driving it.

Importantly, Justin continues to narrate this issue from a distance. He has not specifically located himself within the world he is narrating. Sarah in the next utterance notes that Justin has cast this issue on a broader level and wants to bring it back to the Menominee community specifically, she asks "what about here?" Several people speak to this question, talking about issues as broad as intellectual property rights and sharing of information to attitudes conveyed in interactions with decision makers that leave people feeling like they do not understand what is going on.

Daniel, a community member and a long-time logger of the Menominee forest, extends the idea presented by Justin by agreeing that the problem is one of communication. He focuses on the way in which content and naming practices are playing out in the anxiety filled dynamic Justin has identified.

Daniel: They're, they're in charge of the forest (MTE). They manage the forest, and sometimes you get the feeling from them that, 'we're managing it, leave us alone'. Don't, you know, 'we're doing it.' And they're doing. . .science and technology, different things, [unknown], and they call it all different names. Now, in the past 10 years when this has all been really comin' to a head, they're callin' it all different names, and most people don't understand what's goin' on.

Daniel pushes further on Justin's point that there is a problem of communication. He appears to be struggling with how the larger frame that science is power is playing out in the day-to-day and moves to discuss this on a more detailed level. At this point in the conversation the original oppositional binary and the sociohistorical lens that have been dominating the conversation seem to fade into the background. The conversation takes on a different focus, one related to day-to-day forestry practices. Specifically, they focus on the different cuts and the rationales for cuts. Daniel places himself within the situation, and then projects the voice of those in power. He also locates the developing tension within a similar time frame as Justin, but goes on to suggest that there is a deliberate obscuring in the naming practices by the people in charge of forest management (MTE) over the past decade and that the naming practices function as a form of domination. Daniel is also critically reading the practice of scientists and the management of the forest but from a different point of view.

Sarah: 'Cause they don't let us know.

Sarah apparently sees herself in Daniel's comment "most people don't understand what's goin'on." She voices anger about the situation, placing her emotionally in the conversation in a different way than either Daniel or Justin have. In this comment, Sarah speaks from a position of lack of agency.

Daniel: Yeah. You know, there's, like we talked before there's seed tree [cuts] and there's shelterwood [cuts]. They're basically the same thing. But, they're for different trees. It can look like the same cut. But they'll tell you that it's, 'you know we didn't do a shelterwood, that's a seed tree." And, there's regeneration cuts and then there's, uh, conversion cuts, for clear cuts. There's a whole bunch of different words that they can use, and, the average person looks at it, and doesn't understand it.

Daniel reiterates his point about scientific language as a tool for domination and expands on his earlier comment, by noting how content and naming are intersecting and contributing to the misunderstanding between people. Daniel articulates specific kinds of practices that vary with particular kinds of trees in the forest as well as the different terminology used for them. Each of the cuts serves a different function, depending upon the tree biology, the age of the particular section of forest, and the overall management plan for the forest. There are a few questions that follow about what exactly the difference is between a seed tree cut and shelter wood cut and the differences in cuts that some of the community members who are present do not understand (even those who have been loggers). This turn in the conversation reinstates a sociohistoric frame and Justin returns the conversation to the sociopolitical level and to Menominee people's general relationship with "science."

Justin: I think one of the problems with our anxiety about this is that we don't have a [unknown] or we don't own the science or contribute to the decision making process. So as a result, we're, we're allowing our resources to be managed and dictated by, um, science and professionals and I think probably every one of our proscriptions are drafted by a non-Menominee at this point and, and, and that, we in the past we, we had a sense of ownership and knowledge that contributed to that decision making and we don't now.

There is a shift in Justin's stance here. Importantly, he now places himself within the situation and gives voice to the anxiety as "ours" in an inclusive sense and "we" in terms of owning the science. Justin suggests here that we, the Menominee people, do not own or contribute to "science" or the associated decision-making processes. Justin also seems to be struggling with another perspective in this utterance, one that does not take on the accepted role of subordination in Sarah's comment. Justin suggests that we (Menominees) are allowing the situation to happen. Although the phrasing has a negative connotation, we read this as Justin's belief in a transformative potential that is within the control of the community. We could read, "we are allowing" as a deep belief in self-determination and sovereignty. He notes that the collective community once had a sense of ownership and knowledge that was valuable and contributed to the decision making but that it is not present now. This shift in Justin's stance shifts the power frame that was previously in place. Now the power and choices, and potentially the criticism, are attributed to community, not to science. Daniel, picking up Justin's reference to the proscriptions being drafted, identifies his own relationship to the situation and seems to push on Justin's collective we.

Daniel: A big problem with the proscriptions up here, I mean from workin' in the woods, bein' closely related or associated with people who still work in the woods, is, you know they feel so much that it's, the forest is being experimented on. This place is being experimented on, and, you know, they do a lot of good things, and uh, I got problems with some of the things I seen that, you know, that did work, that they were doin', it was right scientifically, but culturally, it just looks so bad. I mean the buffer zone [an effort to insure that there are stands of trees between roads and clear cuts so that they are not so visible], is the best thing they did, and that's the best thing you guys did in stoppin' them from going up [to the road]... And the, the areas that are, you know. The people have a say. They don't think so but they do have a say.

Daniel's response is again multi-voiced. He pushes Justin's analysis to a finer level of critique and returns to a content and practice level analysis of the forest management program. He begins to locate himself and his family as people who have been deeply connected to the woods for a long time. He narrates his identity in relation to the argument he is making at a more specific level of detail than previously.

He states that the people who are deeply involved in the forest feel that the forest is being experimented on. Daniel appears to defend some of the decisions that the scientists are making, pushing on the distinct oppositional binary cast that has been operating in the conversation up to this point. He says that some of the things people were doing are correct by scientific standards, but he tempers that with cultural standards. Here Daniel is struggling with the scientific rationale for the clear cut, that he seems to approve of, but he also knows that the appearance of a clear cut sits in deep opposition to cultural values. He refers to the buffer zone, a policy decision to visually keep the clear cut away from community view by leaving a section of the forest intact between the clear cut and easy viewing access.

Daniel also is struggling with Justin's all-encompassing comment that the community no longer feels a sense of ownership nor contributes to the decision making. He says that the buffer zone decision was a good thing that the people contributed to. Daniel continues to push on a collective stance that Justin puts forth when he uses the phrase, "the best thing you guys did," placing himself outside of the group that contributed. (He does not say the best thing *we* did.) It seems in this exchange Justin and Daniel are wrestling with their more specific identities and roles within the community context (Justin has not been a logger nor worked for MTE but Daniel has). It is unclear whether these are tensions with each other or merely a question of different perspectives. Daniel's return to a larger collective framing suggests that this specific identification is secondary. Daniel appears to reify the transformative potential Justin implied at the end of his comment because he also places the power within the community's hands. This agreement that the people have a voice moves the conversation to articulating a goal for the forest unit.

Justin: And instilling that in our kids is I think is one of probably the most important attributes of this unit.

The conception of the unit becomes one about having children understand that larger sociohistorical context and their role within this context in relation to science. Young people should have a sense of sovereignty and voice, in Justin's view. Note, however, that increasing language or knowledge of the scientific process of scientific way of knowing has not been articulated yet.

Daniel: Yeah, and lettin' them know everything, you know, that they have, they're the ones who can be in charge.

Daniel agrees with Justin's comment but again wants to extend it. "lettin' them know everything that they have" could be read as a reference to the knowledge and history they have. Daniel further notes that the current positions are not static, but rather that Menominees "can be in charge" of the forest.

The subtle differences in these two turns have potentially dramatic impacts on the design decisions that could be made and the priorities for learning. Justin's stance could lead to a unit that privileges understanding of history and meanings of sovereignty from a broad frame. Daniel's stance could lead to a unit that engages students in learning the scientific language and being able to challenge practices at the day-to-day level. Of course, one could argue that both points of view enhance and deepen approaches to learning.

In a separate but related meeting the next day Justin becomes more explicit about relationships between science and tradition. He says "We have to take control of science so that our values are reflected in forestry practices." This statement both recognizes the binary opposition and dissolves it. He goes on to say "and we have to teach our children that they need to take ownership of science so that they can control what happens to our forest."

Although this fragment of community discourse shows a progression from a third person to a first person perspective and a shift from viewing science and tradition as a dichotomy to forms of knowledge that can be integrated, the story is not so simple. Thinking in terms of dichotomies such as school and home or science and tradition, reflects well-engrained habits. These themes have been constantly revisited, challenged, and reconstructed throughout our program.

Note also the interweaving of community concerns with the creation of curricula as ownership of science becomes a central theme. From this perspective, community values should and do become an integral part of science instruction. In our program implementations we noted several times when community members told children that learning about the forest was part of their responsibility as Menominees. Community planning meetings also allow community members to work through their own difficult experiences with formal schooling and to take ownership of science instruction. At a community planning meeting about a year later, Daniel made the following side comment to a teacher; "You know when we first started meeting, I came because I care about our kids, but I didn't see how I could do anything useful. Now I can see how I can help you in lots of ways."

Partnership in Community: Some Consequences

The foundation of CBD rests on the comprehensive participation of community members, including teachers, elders, parents, community experts, researchers, and youth in all aspects of the research, including conceptions of the problems, project design and implementation, data collection, analysis, and dissemination. The project uses the design process for learning environments as opportunities for professional learning both for the teachers and designers of the project.

Some results. There is reason to think that our project has been successful. First, there is evidence that children's conceptions of science have changed as a result of their participation in our programs. Most notably we have witnessed a shift from the belief that one only learns science at school to the statement that one can learn science from parents and elders and by exploration. There is also a shift from seeing science as a body of knowledge in the direction of seeing science as a set of practices for learning about the world. We report the details of these results elsewhere (Bang & Medin, in press). Finally, performance in science on standardized tests has improved substantially since our program began. Although we cannot isolate our efforts as instrumental to this improvement, we are nonetheless encouraged by this development.

Perhaps our most surprising results are the shifts in goals for the people working on our project. Our research and design teams have consisted of about fifteen community members at each site, eight part-time research assistants, five junior research assistants (at the AIC), eight teachers, two full-time research assistants and curriculum specialists, one postdoctoral fellow, three graduate students, and four PIs. Elders and other community members have also been willing and able to participate in the design. Of this group all but two are Native American.

CBD has had a clear impact on the adults working on the project. Two graduate students have completed their dissertations. This contribution to the infrastructure of science was anticipated but the following seven were not: (1) Two members of the Chicago design team have been admitted to the Northwestern School of Education and Social Policy PhD program. (2) One of the full-time research assistants has enrolled in a master's program. (3) A research assistant who dropped out of school and later earned her GED began undergraduate study in the Fall of 2007. (4) Another part-time research assistant working toward an Associates degree transferred to a university with the aim of going on to graduate school. (5) One of our Menominee research assistants started college, and another, 10 years after completing her associates of arts degree, returned to college to obtain a teaching degree. A third has recently also returned to college after an extended time away from it and plans to pursue graduate study in biological sciences. (6) Two other RAs in the Chicago community have indicated an interest in applying to graduate school after they finish their bachelor's degrees. Virtually all of these community members say that working on the project was a key factor in their decision-making. These dramatic changes indicate a deep motivation to take ownership of schools and to assert tribal sovereignty.

Discussion

Our previous work examined the hypothesis that there is discord between Native American cultural ways of knowing biology and the cultural ways of knowing in school science and that this discord is at the heart of student disengagement and underachievement. In part, we have learned that a central feature of the discord students experience is the lack of connections across the multiple contexts in which students learn science. This lack of coordination manifests itself across a range of levels, including, but not limited to, content knowledge, practices, values, and relevance to family, community, and society at large. We continue to work with and refine our understandings of what this discord means and what it looks like in teaching and learning practices, and how addressing it pedagogically opens new opportunities to develop effective teaching and learning strategies that build on the variety of resources for learning Native children bring to the classroom.

This chapter describes our initial effort to explore the process that enabled design teams to construct these types of learning environments. These learning environments have evolved to a place where there is a deep integration of traditional Native knowledge and history and western modern scientific knowledge and processes, focused on contemporary problems and issues. A general problem that the project and design teams are only beginning to address is the analysis of classroom level events, the moment to moment interactions, and unfolding of teaching and learning. We see this challenge as historically rooted and amenable to the framework that the unique structure of our design teams provide.

Developing culturally based science curricula is far from straightforward. One of the key aspects of this work has been the evolution of our understanding of what culturally-based science programming means and the ways in which to design and study the programs. "Culture" and "Science" are two concepts that are strongly subject to stereotyping and simplistic definitions. For example, it may be easy for some people to think of science as a body of knowledge and to imagine scientists as (white) men wearing white lab coats and using beakers and test tubes. Similarly, it is easy to think of culture as a set of ideas about *what* people think or customs rather than as affecting *how* people think. If these stereotypes and reductionist approaches remain unchallenged, then it is natural to take some preexisting science curriculum and build in a cultural connection by "adding culture to it." Indeed this is an approach that has been widely advocated and used (Yazzie-Mintz, 2007; Hermes, 1999) but has failed to have the impacts hoped for, perhaps because it has not addressed the core problems of culture in science.

We think that cultural practices and their connections with Native ways of knowing must be the foundation of a community-based science curriculum. There is a strong body of Indigenous scholarship exploring the philosophies and methods of Indigenous ways of knowing (or "Native Science") the natural world and the relationships and tensions with western modern science (i.e., Cajete, 1997; Deloria, 1979; Deloria & Wildcat, 2001; Kawagley, 1995). A key aspect of developing our framework has been to resist placing western modern science and Native science in an oppositional dichotomy because it has the effect of falsely simplifying both ideas of western modern science and Native science (Cajete, 1997; Maryboy, Begay, & Nichol, 2006).

Culture. One of the most salient shifts in our community design teams concerns the ways in which culture is being conceptualized. Initially, many community members tended to think of culture as something of an "add-on," to be put into our lesson plans after the science part was worked out. This might take the form of "historical connections." Now, almost all community members see culture as foundational where science is built around that base. One of our teachers vividly illustrated this point with a picture she drew representing her conception of science education. She drew a large turtle (she is a member of the turtle clan) and added microscopes, test tubes, and the like on its back.

This shift is also evident in other sociocultural approaches to education. An increasingly influential framework that includes the study of within group variation, for example, Nasir and Cobb (2005), Gutiérrez and Rogoff (2003), and Moll and Gonzalez (2004) propose that, although the construct of culture is problematic, people nonetheless "live culturally." From this perspective, a key object of study is the wide repertoire of sense-making practices that people participate in, particularly in everyday contexts. Lee (1993, 1995, 2001) has used this approach for the design of learning environments that leverage knowledge associated with everyday experiences to support subject matter learning (in her case literacy practices). From this framework, cultural practices can also be seen as providing alternative "perspectives" on epistemologies. This understanding of culture implies that there is no cultureless or "neutral" perspective any more than a photograph or painting could be without perspective. In this sense, everything is cultured (Rogoff, 2003), including the ways schools are organized and education is implemented (Warren, Ballenger, Ogonowski, Rosebery, & Hudicourt-Barnes, 2001; Lipka, 1998), layout of museums (Bitgood, 1993; Duensing, 2006), scientific practices, and the practices associated with teaching science in school (Warren & Rosebery, 2004). Sometimes these perspectives are explicit but they are often implicit in practices and symbols.

This framework is highly relevant to both formal and informal science learning contexts. Ballenger and Rosebery (2003) note that educators often hold stereotyped notions of what counts as scientific reasoning and privilege a subset of sense-making practices at the expense of others. For example, scientists regularly use visual and discursive resources whereby they place themselves in physical events and processes to explore the ways in which they may behave (Wolpert & Richards, 1997; Ochs, Gonzalez, & Jacoby, 1996). Yet, these same practices often are not recognized as useful or a part of science in the classroom and this lack of recognition has the effect of marginalizing students' home discourses (Rosebery & Hudicourt-Barnes, 2006). These and other findings undermine the view that professional scientific practices are largely abstract logical derivations disassociated with the forms of experience and practice in the everyday world (Warren et al., 2001). This observation also underlines the opportunity of educators working in and with designed environments (Hudicourt-Barnes, 2004; Cobb, Confrey, diSessa, Lehrer, & Schauble, 2003; Bell, in press) to take better advantage of the (cultural) practices that a diverse set of learners bring to the environment.

A Second Look at Partnerships and Innovations. We believe that our partnerships can serve as a model for other partnerships among research universities and both tribal institutions and other institutions that traditionally have served underrepresented groups. But we also should caution that it is "easier said than done." The four of us did not just run into each other at a coffee shop or a conference and decide to collaborate and, to the extent we have been successful, we must acknowledge coincidence, challenges, and convictions. Medin was able to start work on the Menominee reservation only because an early contact at the College of the Menominee Nation encouraged him to visit elders, instructed him in the proper protocol, and gave him some important introductions. Bang was not only involved with the AIC of Chicago but also a graduate student in the Learning Sciences at

Northwestern University where she meet Medin. Bang also had contacts on the Menominee reservation through friendships, AIC programming, and the fact that NAES had both Chicago and Menominee campuses. Washinawatok was Dean at the Menominee campus of NAES and our first partnership involved the two NAES campuses and Northwestern. Chapman's Uncle, who was on the Board of Directors of NAES, became involved in our project, and saw the potential synergy that Chapman would bring to the project. So connections are important and chance connections are to be appreciated.

This project has not been without its challenges. Washinawatok provided strong initial leadership on our project but had to step into the background temporarily when she became Tribal Chair. NAES ran into a financial crisis and the two campuses went their separate ways—the Menominee campus was ready to close, but then was rescued at the last moment to become a campus of East-West University based in Chicago. East-West University is not a tribal entity and this long distance relationship has not always been smooth. In Chicago our project focus shifted from NAES, Chicago, to the AIC. And none of the institutions mentioned in this paragraph had a previous indirect cost agreement with the federal government or was very experienced with managing federal grants. So there have been challenges.

But convictions thrive and grow on challenges. Throughout the institutional upheavals there has been a strong group of elders and other community members that have offered perspective, prayers, and passion for our project. Northwestern University has also provided technical advice and training in grant management. (One member of Northwestern's grants and contracts office took us aside and revealed to us that he is an enrolled Lakota and that he would do what he could to help us.) In addition, there has been a drove of young people getting involved. At the AIC we have created a cohort of undergraduate and graduate students (reaching 16 at its peak) that are connected to community but come from several different institutions of higher education. This has changed their college experience and the dynamic that Indian students need to leave community to attend and succeed in institutions of higher education or attend tribal colleges. These college students now have the expectation that rigorous research can be done directly in community and they know that they can navigate between multiple contexts. Our project begins to hint at new configurations of training for Native scholars.

Conclusions

Although this chapter appears to be at a different grain size and perspective than the focus of typical innovations in learning science research, we think it is useful to represent this side of innovative work. If learning sciences research is to have significant impact in the world on the learning and achievement of students from nondominant backgrounds, researchers must begin to recognize the real-world dynamics of community-based research. Often research projects are organized and planned around university-based models and expectations that may not be sensitive to sociohistoric community contexts and relationships with science and science education. Hindsight reveals that we have made many false steps, but also that we seem to be moving in the right direction. Our project has not only had positive results in the areas of our initial focus but also it has had ripple affects that we did not foresee.

Acknowledgments This research was supported by a grant from the Christian A. Johnson Endeavor Foundation, NSF ROLE grant 0815222, and NSF REESE grant 08015020.

References

Aikenhead, G. (2006). *Science Education for Everyday Life*. New York, NY: Teachers College Press.

Ballenger, C., & Rosebery, A. S. (2003). *What counts as teacher research? Investigating the scientific and mathematical ideas of children from culturally diverse backgrounds*. Oxford: Blackwell Publishing Ltd.

Bang, M. (2007). The Cultural Context of Learning: Native American Science Education. Doctoral Dissertation, Northwestern University.

Bang, M., & Medin, D. (submitted). Cultural processes in science education: Supporting the navigation of multiple epistemologies. *Science Education*.

Bang, M., Medin, D., & Atran, S. (2007). Cultural mosaics and mental models of nature. *Proceedings of the National Academy of Sciences*, *104*, 13868–13874.

Beck, D. R. M. (2002). *Siege and survival: History of the Menominee Indians, 1634–1856*. Omaha, NE: University of Nebraska Press.

Bell, P. (in press). On the theoretical breadth of design-based research in education. *Educational Psychologist*.

Bitgood, S. (1993). Social influences on the visitor museum experience. *Visitor Behavior*, *8*(3), 4–5.

Cajete, G. A. (1997). Native science. *Natural laws of interdependence*. Santa Fe, NM: Clear Light Publishers.

Cajete, G. A. (1999). *Igniting the sparkle: An indigenous science education model*. Skyand, NC: Kivaki Press.

Cajete, G. A. (2000). Indigenous knowledge: The pueblo metaphor of indigenous education. In M. Battiste (Ed.), *Reclaiming indigenous voice and vision*. Seattle, WA: University of Washington Press.

Chandler, M. J., & Lalonde, C. (1998). Cultural continuity as a hedge against suicide in Canada's first nations. *Transcultural Psychiatry*, *35*, 191–219.

Chinn, P. W. U. (2007). Decolonizing methodologies and indigenous knowledge: The role of culture, place and personal experience in professional development. *Journal of Research in Science Teaching*, *44*, 1247–1268.

Cobb, P., Confrey, J., diSessa, A., Lehrer, R., & Schauble, L. (2003). *Design experiments in educational research. Educational Researcher*, *32*(1), 9–13.

Davis, T. (2000). *Sustaining the forest, the people, and the spirit*. Albany, NY: State University of New York.

Deloria, V. (1979). *The metaphysics of modern existence*. San Francisco, CA: Harper & Row.

Deloria, V., & Wildcat, D. R. (2001). *Power and place. Indian education in America*. Golden, CO: Fulcrum Publishing.

Delpit, L. (1995). *Other people's children: Cultural conflict in the classroom*. New York: New Press.

Demmert, W., & Towner, J. C. (2003). *A review of the research literature on the influences of culturally based education on the academic performance of native American students*. Portland, OR: Northwest Regional Educational Library.

Duensing, S. (2006). Culture matters: Science centers and cultural contexts. In Z. Bekerman, N. Burbules, & D. Silberman-Keller (Eds.), *Learning in places: The informal education reader*. New York: Peter Lang Publisher.

Grignon, D. R., Alegria, R., Dodge, C., Lyons, G., Waukechon, C., Warrington, C., et al. (1998). *Menominee tribal history guide: Commemorating Wisconsin Sesquicentennial 1848–1998*. Keshena, WI: Menominee Indian Tribe of Wisconsin.

Gutiérrez, K. (2006). *Culture matters: Rethinking educational equity*. New York: Carnegie Foundation.

Gutiérrez, K., Baquedano-Lopez, P., & Tejeda, C. (1999). Rethinking diversity: Hybridity and hybrid language practices in the third space. *Mind, Culture, & Activity: An International Journal*, *6*(4), 286–303.

Gutiérrez, K., Baquedano-Lopez, P., & Turner, M. G. (1997). Putting language back into language arts: When the radical middle meets the third space. *Language Arts*, *74*(5), 368–378.

Gutiérrez, K., Larson, J., & Kreuter, B. (1995). Cultural tensions in the scripted classroom: The value of the subjugated perspective. *Urban Education*, *29*(4), 410–442.

Gutiérrez, K. D., & Rogoff, B. (2003). Cultural ways of learning: Individual traits or repertoires of practice. *Educational Researcher*, *32*(5), 19–25.

Guyette, S. (1983). *Community based research: A handbook for native Americans*. Los Angeles: University of California.

Hall, P., & Pecore, M. (1995). *Case study: Menominee tribal enterprises*. Madison, WI: Institute for Environmental Studies and the Lane Tenure Center, University of Wisconsin-Madison.

Hermes, M. (1999). Research methods as a situated response: Toward a first nations' methodology. In L. Parker, D. Deyhle, & S. Villenas (Eds.), *Race is...Race isn't: Critical race theory and qualitative studies in education* (pp. 83–100). Boulder, CO: Westview Press.

Hudicourt-Barnes, J. (2004). Argumentation in Haitian Creole classrooms. *Harvard Educational Review*, *73*(1), 73–93.

Hudson, P., & Taylor-Henley, S. (2001). Beyond the rhetoric: Implementing culturally appropriate research projects in first nations communities. *American Indian Culture and Research Journal*, *25*, 93–105.

Kawagley, O. (1995). *A Yupiaq worldview*. Prospect Heights, IL: Waveland Press.

Kawagley, O. (2000). Identity-creating camps. *Sharing Our Pathways*, *5*(2), 4–5.

Lee, C. D. (1993). *Signifying as a scaffold for literary interpretation*. Urbana, IL: National Council of Teachers of English.

Lee, C. D. (1995). A culturally based cognitive apprenticeship: Teaching African American high school students skills in literary interpretation. *Reading Research Quarterly*, *30*(4), 608–631.

Lee, C. (2001). Is October Brown Chinese? A cultural modeling activity system for underachieving students. *American Educational Research Journal*, *38*(1), 97–141.

Lipka, J. (1998). Expanding curricular and pedagogical possibilities: Yup'ik-based mathematics, science, and literacy. In J. Lipka , G. V. Mohatt, & the Ciulistet Group (Eds.), *Transforming the culture of schools: Yup'ik Eskimo examples*. Mahwah, NJ: Lawrence Erlbaum.

Lomawaima, K. T. (2000). Tribal sovereigns: Reframing research in American Indian education. *Harvard Educational Review*, *70*, 1.

Maryboy, N. C., Begay, D. H., & Nichol, L. (2006). Paradox and transformation. *World Indigenous Nations Higher Education Consortium, 2*.

Medin, D., Ross, N., Cox, D., & Atran, S. (2007). Why folkbiology matters: Resource conflict despite shared goals and knowledge. *Human Ecology*, *35*(3), 315–329.

Mihesuah, D. (1998). *Natives and academics: Researching and writing about American Indians*. Lincoln: University of Nebraska.

Moll, L. C., & González, N. (2004). Engaging life: A funds of knowledge approach to multicultural education. In J. Banks & C. McGee Banks (Eds.), *Handbook of research on multicultural education* (2nd ed., pp. 699–715). New York: Jossey-Bass.
Nasir, N., & Cobb, P. (2005). *Diversity, equity, and access to mathematical ideas*. New York: Teachers College Press.
National Science Foundation (2007) *Women, Minorities, and Persons with Disabilities in Science and Engineering: 2007* (NSF Publication No. 07–315) (NSF 41. Division of Science Resources Statistics, Arlington, VA).
Newman, J. G. (1967). *Menominee forest of Wisconsin: A case history in American forest management*. Unpublished doctoral dissertation, Michigan State University, East Lansing.
Ochs, E., Gonzales, P., & Jacoby, S. (1996). When I come down I'm in the domain state: Grammar and graphic representation in the interpretive activity of physicists. In E. Ochs, E. Schegloff, & S. Thompson (Eds.), *Interaction and grammar* (pp. 328–369). Cambridge: CUP.
Orfield, G., Losen, D., Wald, J., & Swans, C. (2004). *Losing our future: How minority youth are being left behind by the graduation rate crisis*. Cambridge, MA: The Civil Rights Project at Harvard University. Retrieved July 1, 2009 from http://www.urban.org/url.cfm?ID=410936
Pavel, D. M., Curtin, T. R., & Whitener, S. D. (1998). Characteristics of American Indian and Alaska native education: Results from the 1990–1991 and 1993–1994 schools and staffing survey. *Equity and Excellence in Education, 31*, 48–54.
Rogoff, B. (2003). *The cultural nature of human development*. Oxford University Press: New York.
Rosebery, A., & Hudicourt-Barnes, J. (2006). Using diversity as a strength in the science classroom: The benefits of science talk. In R. Douglas (Ed.), *Linking science & literacy in the K-8 classroom* (pp. 305–320). Arlington, VA: NSTA Press.
Ross, N., Medin, D. L., Coley, J. D., & Atran, S. (2003). Cultural and experiential differences in the development of folkbiological induction. *Cognitive Development, 18*, 25–47.
Schroeder, C. M., Scott, T. P., Tolson, H., Huang, T., & Lee, Y. (2007). A Meta-Analysis of National Research: The Effects of Teaching Strategies on Student Achievement in Science. *Journal of Research in Science Teaching, 44*, 1436–1460.
Smith, L. T. (1999). *Decolonising methodologies: Research and Indigenous peoples*. London: Zed Books.
van Eijck, M., & Roth, W. M. (2007). Improving science education for sustainable development. *PLoS Biology, 5*(12), e306. doi:10.1371/journal.pbio.0050306.
Warren, B., Ballenger, C., Ogonowski, M., Rosebery, A. S., & Hudicourt-Barnes, J. (2001). Rethinking diversity in learning science: The logic of everyday sense-making. *Journal of Research in Science Teaching, 38*(5), 529–552.
Warren, B., & Rosebery, A. S. (2004). What do you think Keenan means? Exploring possible meanings of explicitness in the science classroom. *Speaker Series: Center for the Scholarship of Teaching*. College of Education: Michigan State University.
Wolpert, L., & Richards, A. (1997). *Passionate minds: The inner World of scientists*. New York: Oxford University Press.
Yazzie-Mintz, E. (2007). *Voices of students on engagement: A report on the 2006 high school survey of student engagement*. Bloomington, IN: Center for Evaluation and Education Policy.

Chapter 29
New Science of Learning: Exploring the Future of Education

Myint Swe Khine and Issa M. Saleh

Emirates College for Advanced Education, Abu Dhabi, UAE

Introduction

There is a coherent and strong opinion among educators that education in the future needs to offer qualitatively different approach to meet the demand of twenty-first century skills. Many argued that existing pedagogies and practices are unable to address the new paradigms in education. Profound needs to understand the complex processes of learning transformed by the emerging technologies and social interactions are widely debated in the academia as learning is becoming ubiquitous. In the midst of dynamic changes and the confluence of computers, communication, media, and culture, the notion of learning in schools, communities, and social networking environments need to be freshly examined with theoretical lenses from interdisciplinary and transdisciplinary perspectives. The chapters in this book reported by leading educators and researchers from institutions of stellar distinction share their experiences in providing theoretical frameworks and contemporary research in the role of cognition, computers, and collaboration in education. In this concluding chapter the major contributions and salient features are summarized with a view to inform the readers about the new developments in this area.

Cognition and New Science of Learning

The first part of the book focuses on cognition and new science of learning. Weigel, Straughn, and Gardner from Harvard University report the findings from the project that sought to capture changes in adolescent cognition in Chapter 1. Forty experienced teachers observed youth over time to obtain the data and narratives related to new digital media and examine how these tools impact the classroom learning. The educators reported that there is an overall decline in student attention as compared to the preceding generation. The students seem to respond to multimedia materials

M.S. Khine (✉)
Emirates College for Advanced Education, Abu Dhabi, UAE
e-mails: mskhine@ecae.ac.ae; dr.mkhine@gmail.com

M.S. Khine, I.M. Saleh (eds.), *New Science of Learning*,
DOI 10.1007/978-1-4419-5716-0_29, © Springer Science+Business Media, LLC 2010

and prefer visual and graphics presentation over text-based materials. The authors also noted that new digital media grants students new types of power. The educators agree that students today would benefit from developing metacognitive skills and understanding the rules of the online engagement. For educators, they need to understand how new digital media is transforming students, the engagement with information, and people around them.

In Chapter 2, Stahl urges that in the new global world, knowledge creation is done socially and collaboratively. He proposes a new science of group learning and the need for science that will help to realize the potential of computer networking in formation of virtual groups and computer-supported collaborative learning. According to Stahl, the form of group cognition provides foundation for understanding the work of small groups. By using the Virtual Math Teams (VTM) Project as a model for group cognition he describes the design-based research to explore how the learning take place in small groups. The study shows that students in VTM engage in learning process on their own as individual activities but participate in group as community events. He asserts that small groups are the engines of knowledge building and need to be studied extensively. He concludes that the VTM studies provide a model for understanding the small-group learning that is different from individual participation and community practices.

The chapter by John Black from the Columbia University Teacher College deals with embodied/grounded cognition perspective on educational technology. According to Dr. Black, understanding is not just knowing facts and procedures, but also being able to reason with a mental model that is a perceptual simulation of it. He suggests three stages of learning progression, in which technology can play an important role in all stages. Technology permits embodiment and allows students to gain deeper understanding during the learning experience.

Gholson, Coles, and Craig present the features of computerized multimedia environments that support vicarious learning processes. The vicarious learning occurs in classroom settings as well as in distance learning environments in which learners have no opportunities to physically interact. Their study aims to identify features of multimedia environments that support vicarious comprehension/learning processes. It was found that providing multiple perspectives on new information and using personalized presentation style improve comprehension. They also explored how learners engage in clear activities or vivid learning environments. The chapter concludes with the remarks that directly incorporated cognitive activities and overt activities have a role in improving vicarious learning processes. Particularly, such unambiguous learning process can easily be implemented in multimedia environment with the use of readily available off-the-shelf technology.

Eggen, in his chapter, focuses on the characteristics of human memory, the way humans input sensory data into their memory systems, including organizing the information, making sense, and storing information for further use. He examines the cognitive processes involved in moving information from one component of memory system to another and strategies used in storing information efficiently. Further elaboration is made on human working memory and how technological systems can be designed to capitalize the working memory and increasing human motivation.

Eggen makes connections between the principles of cognitive learning theory and the role of metacognition in learning processes and human memory.

Finley, Tullis, and Benjamin review research on the role of the metacognition in self-directed learning with emphasis on metacognitive control in Chapter 6. They draw attention to a recent development in the study of what people understand about their memory and how they use that knowledge to direct their own learning experiences to achieve their goals. The metamemory will be important, apart from the understanding of metacognitive monitoring and metacognitive control. They also present the role of information technology in learning process and memory citing example software such as SuperMemo and Cognitive Tutor programs that can increase the self-regulated learning skills. The authors conclude that learning can be enhanced by improving the understanding of our own cognitive capabilities.

Rueda, Lim, O'Neil, Griffin, Bockman, and Sirotnik present their findings on self-regulatory cognitive and motivational predictors of academic achievement for Latio/a and white college students using Structural Equation Modeling method. They tested a theoretical model of relationships among sociocultural backgrounds and motivational factors which affect achievement. They found the significant ethical differences in terms of specific effects of background characteristics on motivational and/or learning-related factors. They concluded that the findings from this study are important as college campuses experience both increasing ethnic diversity as well as accountability for student learning outcomes.

In Chapter 8, Keith Taber outlines how researchers and teachers can model cognition to make sense of their learning and understanding of subject matters. He notes that cognitive sciences offer useful conceptual tools in advancing the research in learning of science subjects and understanding of science concepts.

Theresa Horstman and Stephen Kerr analyze the design strategies for creating educational experiences in virtual environment. Their chapter focuses on analyzing the comparative design methodologies used in developing video games and e-learning. The purpose of such analysis is to discover design strategies that would enhance the effectiveness of e-learning courses. After comparing instructional design practices, video game design, video game theory, and analysis and notes, it was found that in order to be successful in e-learning course design, some conceptual shift among instructional designers is necessary. Adopting methods used in game design was proposed to support experiential, immersive, and engaging learning.

Computer and New Science of Learning

The chapters in Part II deal with innovative applications of computer software in learning. In Chapter 10, Stein, Dawson, and Fischer from Harvard University present development of the assessment system with the use of the latest methods in computer technology and learning science. It is noted that the DiscoTest is standardized, formative, and grounded in research about learning. In developing the DiscoTest they use Fischer's Dynamic Skill Theory and Dawson's Lectical Assessment System to design a new kind of testing infrastructure. DiscoTest provides students with an opportunity to engage in meaningful action on their knowledge and offer useful feedback. The test system also generates scores and reports to the user. The tests are provided in the form of teasers and students can take the same teaser several times to gain high-level understanding of concepts. This is possible because the test items are constructed to be answerable at different level of sophistication. The chapter offers theoretical background and capabilities of the system that can be used as a new tool in assessment.

Self-regulated learning with MetaTutor: Advancing the science learning with metacognitive tools is presented in Chapter 11 by Azevedo, Witherspoon, Chauncey, and Burkett. The authors note that the complex nature of the learning content, internal, and external conditions and contextual environment requires students to regulate their learning. Self-regulation involves among others, analyzing the learning context, setting and managing learning goals, determining the learning strategies, and assessing the strategies for learning. In an attempt to understand that complex nature of computer-based learning environment, they propose computers as MetaCognitive tools metaphor for enhancing learning. They describe the theoretical and conceptual assumptions of self-regulated learning and explain the use of MetaTutor, a hypermedia tool in teaching students self-regulated learning processes in biology. The study found four major profiles of learners: each group use different navigational strategies.

Reimann and Markauskaite present how E-research might change technology-enhanced learning research in Chapter 12. They begin by drawing attention to the readers that although learning technologies have advanced significantly, little has fundamentally changed in the technologies and practices of doing research about technology-enhanced learning. They discuss the affordances of existing and emerging technologies and possibilities in enhancing the learning research. Four levels of technology that would enhance the research efforts are recognized. The first to consider is grid technology/semantic networks including clouds computing and Web 2.0. The second level deals with the need and possibilities for distributed and integrated learning research approaches and digital environment. The third area covers methodological challenges and emerging approaches such as video analysis and process analysis. Finally, the issue of how to develop trust in research finding is discussed.

Chapter 13 deals with designing higher education courses using open educational resources. Rennie and Mason present their experiences in designing different models of higher education courses and propose a theoretical framework for the democratization of education through collaborative efforts. The core idea behind the Open Educational Resources (OER) is to provide easy access to the course content that begins with overview, teaching materials, digitized articles, and relevant information from the websites and supply with specific guidelines for study. They concluded that the use of OER in course design shows promise to provide wider access to flexible learning globally.

In Chapter 14, Jackson, Dempsey, and McNamara present evolutionary development of an Intelligent Tutoring System. The automated reading strategy tutor involved various stages and each component has its own capabilities. The training programs were designed to improve the students' ability to comprehend text. Each development cycle was evaluated and investigated to reach effectiveness in improving students' comprehension of text.

In Chapter 15, Robertshaw, Walker, Recker, Leary, and Sellers describe the 8-year-long DLConnect research project. The DLConnect project first developed the instructional architect (IA) which allows teachers to find online learning resources and assemble them into learning activities for their students. A teacher technology professional development model has been developed in order to train teachers how to use the IA and online resources. This professional development model has been refined during the course of the project. Three different models were studied and each has its own characteristics. While Model 1 uses authentic problem and it is a design-centered approach, Model 2 deals with problem-based learning and simple to complex approach. The third model also uses problem-based learning, but it is a design-centered approach. Evaluation findings for all models are presented. The authors conclude that future research will involve continued exploration in whether there are substantive changes in how teachers engage in teaching based on participation in the workshop and if changes do exist what happens to student learning as a result of these changing teaching practices.

In the Chapter "A Dialogic Approach to Technology-Enhanced Education for the Global Knowledge Society," the authors argue that a dialogic theoretical framework can offer a solution to the educational challenges that arise from the shift to a knowledge society. The heart of the approach is to use new communications technology to draw learners into dialogues across difference. The chapter discusses the idea of developing collective thinking through a shift in the identities of learners toward greater openness, not only openness to listening to the voices of others but also openness to new possibilities. The chapter looks at evidence from a number of case studies to show the potential of this combination of new technology and dialogic pedagogy.

In Chapter 17, Lei Liu and Cindy E. Hmelo-Silver argue that hypermedia as a vehicle for conveying conceptual representations. Moreover, understanding and metacognitive thinking can be supported by hypermedia (Jacobson & Archididou, 2000). The authors use the work of McManus and Segner (1991) to support their claim that "Hypermedia can support learning about the facts, concepts and principles of a domain." To do the research, the authors use 20 participants from the educational psychology subject pool at a large public university. The two different versions of hypermedia system (F-hypermedia and S-hypermedia) were used to do the study. The authors concluded from the study that learners in the S-hypermedia condition were more likely than those in F-hypermedia to express lack of knowledge. Learners in the F-hypermedia condition were more likely to engage in checking learning progress, checking understanding, and specific-question driven exploration. Students using the F-hypermedia showed gains in understanding structures and behavior in the post-test than in the pre-test. On the other hand, Students using the S-hypermedia showed gains in understanding structures, behavior, and functions.

In Chapter 18, the authors look at the "challenges and opportunities involved in designing, implementing and evaluating psycho-educational intervention programs that use virtual worlds specifically designed for children." The chapter is based on four different case studies in which Zora was used. These are in a diverse group of children in a multicultural summer camp, with incoming freshman at a northeastern university, with transplant patients at Children's Hospital Boston, and with children in a network of after-school programs. The authors in the chapter take in to account eight consideration when designing and implementing programs that use virtual worlds for children's development and education. These are curriculum, mentoring model, diversity, project scale, type of contact with participants, type of assessment and evaluation, access environment, and institutional context of usage. The authors outline within the chapter the importance of knowing the limitations of the programs that use virtual worlds specifically designed for children.

The authors in Chapter 19 look at systems theoretical approach of learning. German sociologist N. Luhmann's theory and the idea of complexity and contingency are used to frame the research. The aim of the chapter is to understand learning and knowledge in this new environment that offers new possibilities for communication, collaboration, interaction, and student-centered authentic learning. Moreover, the authors examine the impact of the new educational environment.

Collaboration and New Science of Learning

The last part of the book covers how collaboration is shaping, how we learn, and what we learn. In Chapter 20, Heather Kanuka looks a text-based Internet communication as tools for strategies to facilitate active and engaged learning. The author introduces the chapter by pointing out the luck of "consistent and reliable body of knowledge indicating that more effective learning is an outcome of the use of Internet communication technologies" (e.g., Bernard et al., 2004). The author also states the literature that reveals "higher levels of thinking and meaningful learning are not being achieved through the use of text-based Internet communication tools" (e.g., Gunawardena, Carabajal, & Lowe, 2001; Kanuka, 2005; Kanuka & Anderson, 1998; Nussbaum, Hartley, Sinatra, Reynolds, & Bendixen, 2002; Garrison, Anderson, & Archer, 2001; Rourke, 2005; Thomas, 2002). The author looks at several instructional methods such as debates, invited guests, reflective deliberation, WebQuests, and nominal group technique—all using text-based Internet group communication tools. The author concludes that WebQuests and debates are the most "effective pedagogical interventions" to move students toward achieving higher levels of learning compared to invited guests, reflective deliberation, and nominal group technique.

In Chapter 21 "Windows into Teaching and Learning Through Social Annotation Practices," the author argues that applications of the HyLighter online social annotation system can benefit both the students and the professor. Applications in this study included collaboratively analyzing documents, creating concept maps, and developing lesson plans. The author grounded her study using Vygotsky's social constructivism, Piaget's cognitive constructivism, and Dede's distributed learning. Some of the benefits are facilitation of comprehension, memory, and transfer as students learn from and with each other and the instructor. The author claims that social annotation practices promote student and teacher metacognition. The results of the study, according to the author, are that social annotation opened windows into learners' own and each other's thinking and learners' structured interaction with the material and created engagement with the material. The author recommends further research on how social annotation experiences affect preservice and in-service teachers' self-efficacy.

Chapter 22 deals with one-to-one technology in classrooms. This equipment according to the authors provide ability for teachers to manage each child, individual group, and whole class learning activities. The authors argue that this technology solves the problem of "management of the technology-enabled classroom, lack of support for collaborative and whole class working, design of lessons that switch easily between activities, and difficulty in re-use of lesson components" in traditional classrooms. SceDer system is used as one-to-one technologies in this chapter. SceDer helps teachers to design lessons and a delivery of the lesson in classrooms. The authors look at response systems such as EduClick, ClassTalk, and Clicker, which have been shown to be effective in supporting children to learn mathematics in classrooms (Roschelle, Rafanan, Estrella, Nussbaum, & Claro, 2009). The result of the study shows that SceDer has "clear potential for orchestrating learning in one-to-one classrooms" and particularly "efficient in modeling interactions to promote collaboration in one-to-one classroom." The authors further agree that a well-structured lesson design is an important component for SceDer to work well.

The focus of the chapter "Designing Online Learning Environment for Professional Development" is how teachers construct professional knowledge using Internet-mediated networks. The chapter is based on online courses that the author has designed and taught to science teachers. The participants in the study are teachers with at least 2 years of experience. The study is grounded in the assumptions about adult learners from Malcolm Knowles' (1980) work which identified key characteristics of adult learners as (1) adult learners are autonomous, self-directed, and strongly goal oriented; (2) adult learners have accumulated a foundation of life experiences and knowledge and have a need to connect learning to this knowledge and experience base; and (3) adult learners are practical and have a strong preference for learning that is most useful to their work. The author concludes that Internet-mediated social networks provide an avenue for connecting geographically dispersed professionals. Moreover, the author argues that the technology has the potential to encourage critical reflection and reconstruction of teachers' repertoires of informal (everyday) knowledge on scientific foundations, along the lines indicated by Vygotsky (1987). Finally, anxieties about change were a potential barrier to change. Anxieties arose because changes in conceptual knowledge entailed changes in how teachers understood their professional roles. The use of internet-mediated social networks afforded teachers' opportunities to draw support from professional peers.

Chapter "Knowledge Building/Knowledge Forum: The formation of Classroom Discourse" is first introduced by looking at a typical classroom discourse. The authors examine the structure of a discourse by referring to the work of Sinclair and Coulthard (1975), Mehan (1979), and Cazden (2001). They point out that typical face-to-face classroom discourse has three turns and is composed of the following moves: teacher initiation (e.g., ask a question) (I), student response (R) and teacher feedback/comment (F), or evaluation (E) of the student's response (IRF/IRE). The study was done using the grids developed by Hmelo-Silver and Barrows (2008) and a classification system developed by Hakkarainen (2003). The results illustrated a level of explanation in online student discourse that is different from the IRE classroom discourse structure (teacher-initiated question–student response–teacher evaluation) from the work of Cazden (2001) and with the IRF structure (initiation–response–feedback) of Sinclair and Coulthard (1975) and Wells (1993).

Chapter 25 examines the question of how digital video tools in the classroom can support meaningful collaboration and critical advanced thinking of students. The authors introduce the chapter by looking at the work of Cassidy, Stanley, and Bartlett (2006) and also Eckrich, Widule, Shrader, and Maver (1994) to point out how digital video technology is used for professional video analyses. The authors argue that when students design a video-based presentation, they go through an intensive cognitive elaboration and critical reflections on the video content. The chapter tries to answer the following questions: "How do students approach video-based design tasks in a real, 'noisy' classroom setting? How do the technical properties of digital video tools influence collaboration?" Moreover, the authors point out that contemporary literacy concept cannot be limited to individual skills of reading and writing static texts, tables, and graphs but must now be extended toward complex visual media (e.g., Stahl, Zahn, & Finke, 2006). The chapter concludes that "a substantial knowledge and (visual) literacy skills acquisition takes place during a collaborative visual design task, even when students spend only a short period of time with the video material" and also "digital video technologies can act as powerful cognitive tools supporting the learning processes during collaborative visual design tasks."

In Chapter 26, the authors refer to Brophy and Good (1986), Tomlinson (1999), DiGiano and Atton (2002), Fischer, Wecker, Schrader, Gerjets, and Hesse (2005), Gravier Fayolle, Noyel, Leleve, and Benmohamed (2006), Dillenbourg and Fischer (2007), and von Inqvald, (2009) to illustrate how the word "orchestration" was used to refer to "the design and real-time management of multiple classroom activities, multiple learning processes and multiple teaching actions." The authors look at the criteria that we use to criticize "teaching methods" and "learning environments" as researchers and teachers. The chapter argues that "educational research requires that we take into account curriculum, assessment, time, energy, space and safety constraints when designing methods and environments." Within the Chapter 14 design factors related to the ideas of "classroom orchestration and learning ecosystems" are illustrated.

In Chapter 27, Jingyan Lu, Ming Lai, and Nancy Law discuses the challenges and opportunities when building Knowledge Building in Society 2.0. They argue that "designing and developing learning environments to support effective knowledge building calls for a thorough understanding of its social, communicative, and cognitive dimensions." They demonstrate how Web 2.0 can support the social, communicative, and cognitive dimensions of knowledge building by pointing out how online learners use technologies such as wiki, blog, social bookmarking, social networking, and tagging. Web 2.0 technologies not only address the educational needs of learners, but their social and psychological needs as well because communities of practice are affectively, cognitively, and socially structured. This chapter addresses the problems we are facing in building knowledge and how emerging Web 2.0 technologies help to support our understanding of the new sciences of learning.

Chapter 28 discusses the ideas of diversity ways of knowing in teaching and learning environments and its impact improving school achievement. Moreover, the chapter also looks at the growing body of work that evolves conceptions and methodologies for studying cultural processes in the learning environments in which children live. Hence, the research in this chapter revolves around developing a research partnership among the American Indian Center of Chicago, Northwestern University, and the Menominee tribe of Wisconsin. To be more specific, the chapter looks at the methodological and conceptual issues associated with these ideas. The long-term plan of the study is to improve science learning and school achievement for Native-American children. The short-term plan is to explore the possibilities that new configurations and approaches to research can expand diversity. The chapter looks at the collaboration issues, problems within the design of research studies, implementation of studies, and data collection and analysis. The chapter concludes by outlining the benefits to community and university partners.

Conclusion

Educators and research centers around the world are working to better understand the new kind of learning, the place of computers, cognition, and collaboration and redefining the role of teaching in enriched, engaged, and robust educational settings. The common goal is to foster deep learning and maximize the potential of next generation students in constructing knowledge, understanding, supporting, and advancing skills in their chosen fields. The chapters in this book critically examine the scientific understanding of future learning and present thought-provoking ideas, innovative approaches, systemic explorations, exemplary and promising efforts, and future-oriented scenarios in framing the new science of learning. To consolidate the theoretical perspectives and advances in applications, researchers have shared their recent findings in this book. It is hoped that the chapters in this book would provide information on trends and the latest developments and will serve as an impetus for future endeavor in understanding learning.

References

Bernard, R. M., Abrami, P. C., Lou, Y., Borokhovski, E., Wade, A., Wozney, L., et al. (2004). How does distance education compare to classroom instruction? A meta-analysis of the empirical literature. *Review of Educational Research, 74*(3), 379–439.

Brophy, J., & Good, T. (1986). Teacher behavior and student achievement. In M. C. Wittrock (Ed.), *Handbook of research on teaching* (3rd ed.). New York: McMillan.

Cassidy, T., Stanley, S., & Bartlett, R. (2006). Reflecting on video feedback as a tool for learning skilled movement. *International Journal of Sports Science & Coaching, The Sport Coach as Learner, 1*, 279–288.

Cazden, C. B. (2001, 1988). *Classroom discourse: The language of teaching and learning* (2nd ed). Portsmouth, NH: Heinemann (original work published 1988).

DiGiano, C., & Patton, C. (2002). Orchestrating handhelds in the classroom with SRI's ClassSync^{TM}. In G. Stahl (Ed.), *Computer support for collaborative learning 2002* (pp. 706–707). Hillsdale, NJ: Lawrence Erlbaum Associates, Inc.

Dillenbourg, P., & Fischer, F. (2007). Basics of computer-supported collaborative learning. *Zeitschrift für Berufs- und Wirtschaftspädagogik, 21*, 111–130.

Eckrich, J., Widule, C. J., Shrader, R. A., & Maver, J. (1994). The effects of video observational training on video and live observational proficiency. *Journal of Teaching in Physical Education, 13*, 216–227.

Fischer, F., Wecker, C., Schrader, J., Gerjets, P. H., & Hesse, F. W. (2005, August). *Use-inspired basic research on the orchestration of cognition, instruction and technology in the classroom.* Paper presented at the SIG Invited Symposium "Instructional design and empirical research: Experiments and/or design experiments" at the 11th Conference of the European Association for Research on Learning and Instruction (EARLI), Nicosia, Cyprus.

Garrison, D. R., Anderson, T., & Walter Archer, W. (2001). Critical thinking, cognitive presence, and computer conferencing in distance education. *The American Journal of Distance Education, 15*(1), 7–23.

Gravier, C., Fayolle, J., Noyel, G., Leleve, A., & Benmohamed, H. (2006), Distance learning: Closing the gap between remote labs and learning management systems, *Proceedings of IEEE First International Conference on E-Learning in Industrial Electronics*, Hammamet, Tunisie, December 18–20, pp. 130–.134.

Gunawardena, C., Carabajal, K., & Lowe, C. A. (2001). Critical analysis of models and methods used to evaluate online learning networks. (ERIC Document Reproduction Service No. ED456159).

Hakkarainen, K. (2003). Progressive inquiry in a computer-supported biology class. *Journal of Research in Science Teaching, 40*(10), 1072–1088.

Hmelo-Silver, C. E., & Barrows, H. S. (2008). Facilitating collaborative knowledge building. *Cognition and Instruction, 26*(1), 48–94.

Jacobson, M. J., & Archodidou, A. (2000). The design of hypermedia tools for learning: Fostering conceptual change and transfer of complex scientific knowledge. *Journal of the Learning Science, 9*, 145–199.

Kanuka, H. (2005). An exploration into facilitating higher levels of learning in a text-based Internet learning environment using diverse instructional strategies. *Journal of Computer Mediated Communication, 10*(3). Retrieved August 5, 2005, from http://jcmc.indiana.edu/vol10/issue3/kanuka.html.

Kanuka, H., & Anderson, T. (1998). On-line social interchange, discord, and knowledge construction. *Journal of Distance Education, 13*(1), 57–74.

Knowles, M. S. (1980). *The modern practice of adult education*. Chicago: Association Press/Follett.

McManus, W., & Segner, R. (1991). *Hypermedia in construction education*. Paper presented at the Associated Schools of Construction conference. Retrieved August 1, 2003, from http://asceditor.unl.edu/archives/1991/McManus91.htm

Mehan, H. (1979). *Learning lessons: Social organization in the classroom*. Cambridge, MA: Harvard University.

Nussbaum, M., Hartley, K., Sinatra, G. M., Reynolds, R. E., & Bendixen, L. D. (2002). *Enhancing the quality of on-line discussions*. New Orleans, LA: Paper presented at the annual meeting of the American Educational Research Association.

Roschelle, J., Rafanan, K., Estrella, G., Nussbaum, M., & Claro, S. (2009). From handheld collaborative tool to effective classroom module: Embedding CSCL in a broader design framework. In *Proceedings of computer supported collaborative learning practices* (pp. 395–403). Rhodes, Greece: ISLS.

Rourke, L. (2005). *Learning through online discussion*. Unpublished doctoral dissertation. University of Alberta, Edmonton Alberta Press.

Sinclair, J., & Coulthard, M. (1975). *Towards an analysis of discourse: The English used by teachers and pupils*. London: Oxford University Press.

Stahl, E., Zahn, C., & Finke, M. (2006). Knowledge acquisition by hypervideo design: An instructional program for university courses. *Journal of Educational Multimedia and Hypermedia, 15*(3), 285–302.

Thomas, M. J. W. (2002). Learning with incoherent structures: The space of online discussion forums. *Journal of Computer Assisted Learning, 18*, 351–366.

Tomlinson, C. A. (1999). The Differentiated Classroom: Responding to the Needs of All Learners, ASCD. http://www.ascd.org

von Inqvald, E. (2009). *Teachers' implementation and orchestration of Cabri: Initial use of a dynamic geometry software package in mathematics teaching*. VDM Verlag, Saarbrücken

Vygotsky, L. S. (1987). Thinking and speech. In R. W. Rieber and A. S. Carton (Eds.), *The collected works of L.S. Vygotsky, Volume 1: Problems of general psychology* (Trans. N. Minick). New York: Plenum.

Wells, G. (1993). Reevaluating the IRF sequence: A proposal for the articulation of theories of activity and discourse for the analysis of teaching and learning in the classroom. *Linguistics in Education, 5*(1), 1–37.

Subject Index

M.S. Khine, I.M. Saleh (eds.), *New Science of Learning*,
DOI 10.1007/978-1-4419-5716-0, © Springer Science+Business Media, LLC 2010

LaVergne, TN USA
19 May 2010
183231LV00003B/6/P

9 781441 957153